Civil Rights in Black and Brown

Civil Rights in Black and Brown

Histories of Resistance and Struggle in Texas

EDITED BY MAX KROCHMAL AND J. TODD MOYE

University of Texas Press ❧ *Austin*

Requests for permission to reproduce material from this work should be sent to:
   Permissions
   University of Texas Press
   P.O. Box 7819
   Austin, TX 78713–7819
   utpress.utexas.edu/rp-form

♾ The paper used in this book meets the minimum requirements of
ANSI/NISO Z39.48–1992 (R1997) (Permanence of Paper).

Library of Congress Cataloging-in-Publication Data

Names: Krochmal, Max, editor. | Moye, J. Todd, editor.
Title: Civil rights in black and brown : histories of resistance and struggle in Texas /
edited by Max Krochmal and J. Todd Moye.
Other titles: Jess and Betty Jo Hay series.
Description: First edition. | Austin : University of Texas Press, 2021. | Series: Jess and
Betty Jo Hay series | Includes bibliographical references and index.
Identifiers: LCCN 2020054619 (print) | LCCN 2020054620 (ebook)
   ISBN 978-1-4773-2378-6 (hardback)
   ISBN 978-1-4773-2379-3 (paperback)
   ISBN 978-1-4773-2380-9 (library ebook)
   ISBN 978-1-4773-2381-6 (non-library ebook)
Subjects: LCSH: Civil rights movements—Texas—History. | Chicano movement—
Texas—History. | Civil rights workers—Texas—Interviews. | African American
political activists—Texas—Interviews. | Mexican American political activists—
Texas—Interviews. | LCGFT: Essays.
Classification: LCC F395.A1 C58 2021 (print) | LCC F395.A1 (ebook) |
DDC 323.09764—dc23
LC record available at https://lccn.loc.gov/2020054619
LC ebook record available at https://lccn.loc.gov/2020054620

doi:10.7560/323786

Contents

List of Illustrations

Foreword

W. MARVIN DULANEY

In 1970, the US Civil Rights Commission issued a fifty-one-page report entitled *Civil Rights in Texas*. The report concluded that despite the passage of four civil rights acts and the Voting Rights Act between 1957 and 1968, very little had changed for African Americans and Mexican Americans in Texas. In short, schools were still segregated; police brutality still victimized African Americans and Mexicans Americans; voting rights for both groups were still circumscribed; and both groups faced employment and wage discrimination throughout the state. Although the report painted a very negative picture of the experience of both groups, much had changed, and the report would have been more positive if the Texas State Advisory Committee on Civil Rights had done more research on the history of race relations and the civil rights movement throughout the state. My contention is not that the report was inaccurate. It just did not address how Mexican Americans and African Americans had progressed in the state as a result of forty to fifty years of agitation for civil and political rights.[1]

The report reflected the dearth of research on the state's civil rights movement that existed in 1970. When I arrived in Texas in 1981 to begin an academic career at Texas Christian University (TCU) and eventually at the University of Texas at Arlington (UTA), the historiography of the civil rights movement in Texas was still in its infancy. A few books and several articles covered the subject, but much of the history still projected the idea that Texas did not need a civil rights movement, because it was "more western than southern." Thus, the state's history was characterized as being more about cowboys, ranching, cattle drives, horses, oil wells, and oil barons. One writer even wrote that Texas was a part of the "Rim South" and therefore not a part of the "Old South," with its history of slavery, racial discrimination, and the oppression of Black and Brown people.[2]

After completing research that connected the integration of the police department in Dallas with the civil rights movement, I wrote one of the first histories of the movement in the city. My essay built on and corrected an interpretation by the journalist Jim Schutze that insisted that Dallas had not had a civil rights movement. Schutze argued that Dallas's African American leadership had practiced the politics of "accommodation" and capitulated to the city's white business leaders, thereby forestalling the progressive activism that characterized the civil rights movement in other parts of the South. My research showed that the civil rights movement in

Dallas had developed in the 1930s and continued into the 1960s. During that time, it was moderately successful in increasing African Americans' access to housing, education, and political power. Dallas's African American leaders had definitely not "accommodated" themselves completely to white power and white supremacy.³

By the time that I published my essay on the movement in Dallas, historians generally had moved beyond the belief that Texas was exceptional and not a part of the South. Several historians had written essays on aspects of the struggle for civil rights in Houston and Austin, and on desegregation in the state's colleges and universities. Indeed, in the late 1980s and the early 1990s, research and scholarship on the civil rights movement in Texas exploded. But most of it, as indicated above, focused on large cities and the period of the 1950s through the 1960s.⁴

Civil Rights in Black and Brown not only addresses the lack of scholarly research on the civil rights movement in Texas that marred the 1970 report, but also expands on existing scholarship and provides a more comprehensive analysis of the movement in the state since 1970. While some studies have examined the civil rights movement in Texas, most of them have not gone beyond the state's major cities to examine the movement statewide.⁵

This volume is the product of two summers of oral history interviews, archival research, and the use of modern technology to analyze data. More specifically, it is the product of a statewide research project entitled the Civil Rights in Black and Brown Oral History Project (CRBB), funded by the National Endowment for the Humanities and the Brown and Summerlee Foundations in partnership with TCU, the University of North Texas (UNT), and UTA.

In 2014, I joined with Professors Max Krochmal of TCU, Todd Moye of UNT, and José Ángel Gutiérrez, professor emeritus of UTA, to form the CRBB. Maggie Rivas Rodriguez of the University of Texas at Austin joined the project in 2016. We felt it was important to tell the story of the civil rights movement across the state, and the successes of people from all walks of life in winning major concessions in employment, housing, education, and political participation for African Americans and Mexican Americans.

Subsequently, we hired graduate students and embarked on a major oral history project that took us throughout Texas to interview Black and Brown participants in the civil rights movement. Texas is a big state, and the project required travel, accommodations, and food for all of us as we carried out this important project. The logistics alone were a major undertaking.

Over two summers, the project conducted 530 oral history interviews with people who had participated in civil rights movements. Many of the interviewees had never told their stories about participating in the movement. And the CRBB project broke new ground by adding the stories of people in smaller communities to the major narratives about the movements in Dallas, Houston, and San Antonio.

Another result of the CRBB project is this volume. It is about "civil rights in small spaces," and it introduces readers to the movement in East Texas, Deep East Texas, West Texas, and South Texas. By documenting the civil rights movement in places such as Prairie View, Lubbock, Pharr, Odessa, Beaumont, El Paso, Corpus Christi, and Lufkin, the book broadens and enhances our understanding of one of our nation's most important movements for social and political justice. It democratizes the civil rights movement, shows its diversity, and provides future generations many models of how to win equal rights and change our nation.

I am also very proud of two important by-products of the CRBB project. First, the oral history interviews are available to everyone. Thanks to Max Krochmal and TCU, anyone with a computer and an internet connection can access topical clips from the interviews for professional and general use, at crbb.tcu.edu. The Portal to Texas History at UNT hosts full, unedited interviews, at texashistory.unt.edu. It is hoped that the interviews will shape scholarship on the movement in Texas and the understanding of it by students, scholars, and laypeople. Finally, I am especially proud of the graduate students who participated in the project, did the fieldwork, and recorded the oral history interviews. Many of them have contributed to this volume, produced dissertations from their research, and developed as outstanding historians as a result, in part, of their participation in the project. I anticipate that they will shape the scholarship on the civil rights movement in Texas for many years to come.

LONE STAR CIVIL RIGHTS:

Histories, Memories, and Legacies

MAX KROCHMAL

On February 6, 1987, a hundred people staged a rally in front of the Montgomery County Courthouse in Conroe, a farming town that was beginning to turn into a distant suburb of Houston, forty miles to the south. The demonstrators demanded the release from death row of Clarence Brandley, an African American school janitor accused of raping and murdering a young white woman who had come to town for a varsity volleyball match. It was neither the first such protest, nor the first incident in which a Black man had been accused and punished for similar alleged crimes. Indeed, an African American man named Joe Winters was lynched in front of a crowd of thousands at the same location sixty-five years earlier, in 1922. Almost two decades after that, in 1941, Bob White, another accused Black man, was shot and killed in the middle of his trial, this time inside the courthouse. And thirty-two years after that, in 1973, Gregory Allen Steele, a Black man detained for disturbing the peace, was shot and killed while in the custody of the Conroe Police Department. The region had thus witnessed generations of racially motivated killings—and years of patient community organizing among ordinary African Americans. In 1990, three years after the rally in Conroe, longtime activists celebrated as Brandley was exonerated and released following a decade behind bars. Progress had come to Montgomery County, however slow: unlike his predecessors, Brandley survived the ordeal.[1]

Nearly five hundred miles to the northwest, outraged residents of West Texas staged a motorized caravan from Odessa to Big Spring, where they marched on another county courthouse to protest a wave of officer-involved killings—this time of Mexican Americans on the High Plains. The rally, held on February 25, 1978, responded to a series of incidents signaling that law enforcement's customary harassment of Mexicanos had become an epidemic. A few months earlier, in November 1977, sheriff's deputies from Glasscock County, outside Midland, arrested Tiburcio Griego Santome on a routine charge of disorderly conduct. They ended up killing him in the squad car. About a month later, a Big Spring policeman shot and killed an unarmed suspect named Juan Galaviz, following a high-speed chase. Exactly one month after that, Ector County sheriff's deputies in Odessa attacked and arrested Larry Ortega Lozano after he drove his pickup truck off the road into a barbed-wire fence on the edge of town. Lozano made it to the county jail badly beaten but alive, but he died in custody ten days later. An inquiry later revealed that he had suffered a plethora of blunt-force injuries after the car wreck and had been denied access to mental health services.

After three deaths in just over two months, the people in West Texas had seen enough. The Odessa Brown Berets, a youth-led Chicano/a movement group housed in an auto repair shop in the barrio, rallied the region's residents, including Mexican American military veterans from the American GI Forum, to demand change. They called for federal and state investigations, justice for the slain, and retribution for the victims' families. They didn't win all their demands, but they ended the culture of impunity surrounding police violence against Mexicanos. As one Brown Beret later recalled, the movement "turned this city around, I mean it just went from A to Z . . . Hispanics started getting some respect, harassment slowed down. There is still a lot of it out there, but it's not like it used to be."[2]

This short summary of lives shattered, memories seared, and movements built fails to convey the depravity of the separate events or the extraordinary courage of the activists who demanded and won better treatment for their communities in the face of terror. Still, the brutality and routine nature of such incidents serve as useful reminders of the stakes involved in examining the tangled past and present of civil rights in Texas. The long Black and Chicano/a liberation struggles were not polite affairs—they were often matters of life and death.

Nonetheless, beyond the gaze of TV cameras and national newspapers, ordinary men and women in the Lone Star State confronted the racial caste systems to which they had been assigned, challenging the tradition of state-sanctioned racial violence. They built not one but two liberation movements, and they did so, often, in conversation with one another. African American, Chicano/a, and white civil rights activists in small towns and huge metropolises across Texas came together to combat Jim Crow and its anti-Mexican cousin, Juan Crow. Often separated by geography and culture, they organized first and foremost within their own racial groups. Yet in the big cities, and sporadically elsewhere, they also created Black-Brown alliances that gave each partner a helping hand in their distinct struggles.

With nothing but their own hands, resources, friends, and communities, and often in the face of violent repression, Black and Chicano/a organizers boldly set out to transform their cities, counties, state, nation, and world. Drawing on powerful collective memories of white-supremacist attacks, quiet resistance, and ceaseless struggle, they were radicals in the original sense of the word: people who sought to get at the roots of a problem—in this case, institutionalized racism. They tended to be expansive in their visions for change, connecting calls for civil rights with demands for economic justice and, at times, gender equality. Their struggles took place at the grassroots, in their own communities, not in the White House or halls of Congress. They began their organizing long before anyone had ever heard of Lyndon B. Johnson, and they continue even now, nearly a half century after the statesman's death.

Texas civil rights activists sought not simply integration or access but also equity, power, and resources. This book taps a new collection of oral history interviews to tell their stories, in their own words, as they have never been told before. In 2015 and 2016, researchers with the Civil Rights in Black and Brown (CRBB) Oral History Project fanned out across Texas to document firsthand accounts of civil rights struggles, broadly defined. Inspired by past efforts such as the "slave narratives" col-

Civil Rights in Black and Brown research sites. Map created by Erin Greb.

lected by the Federal Writers' Project of the 1930s, researchers dug into local sites—large and small, from the Panhandle to the Rio Grande Valley, from El Paso to the Piney Woods of Deep East Texas—and conducted videotaped life-history interviews with over 530 narrators. They uncovered tales of mass movements that had never been documented, of haunting violence long since covered up, of courageous, creative organizing by unsung heroes and heroines that effected sea changes in the daily lives of Black and Chicano/a Texans.[3] This book recovers their lost stories in a first step toward rewriting the history—and future—of civil rights in the Lone Star State.

The Making of Jim Crow and Juan Crow Texas

Structural racism in Texas is as old and venerable as the state itself. Although shrouded in myth, the Lone Star State's origins stemmed from white southern slave-holders' need to extend their cotton empire west. After winning land grants from a distant government in Mexico City, the founding fathers squatted on unceded Indigenous lands and constructed slave labor camps to cultivate and export the white gold. They soon grew concerned about the prospect of the Mexican government abolishing slavery and declared their independence. They experimented with building a slaveholders' republic but faced international isolation and economic ruin. In 1846, their desire for annexation aligned with that of an expansionist US president, and two years later the Anglo-American claim to Texas was solidified by the Treaty of Guadalupe Hidalgo. Ignoring its provisions requiring equal treatment of the former Mexican nationals in their midst, the white Texan leaders gradually rewrote the rules to seize land and power throughout the state. They joined the Confederate revolt to protect slavery, and when that too failed, they crafted a new constitution to limit the reach of Reconstruction. With federal assistance, they shored up the state's western "frontier" and enacted a genocidal campaign to drive the region's Indigenous peoples across the Red River into present-day Oklahoma. With the state's territory secured, the Texas establishment then beat down the threat of organized farmers and a multiracial People's Party in the 1880s and 1890s and set out to create a new world order, dedicated to the proposition of white supremacy.[4]

Beginning around 1900, white Texan elites, led by large-scale commercial farmers who depended on Black and Brown labor, created a pair of novel caste systems that they hoped would last a thousand years: a new age of racial segregation. In East Texas, they joined their southern compatriots in inventing Jim Crow; in South Texas and West Texas, they looked farther west as they devised Juan Crow segregation. The two systems varied tremendously but had several common features, and both were de jure, that is, upheld by law. In 1903, the Terrell Election Laws imposed a poll tax and other restrictions on the franchise, provisions that barred virtually all African Americans and Mexican Americans from political participation. The few Mexicanos who did vote often did so at the behest of their *patrones*, the landlords, contractors, or foremen who paid their poll taxes for them, piled them into a truck, and made them vote the "right" way. In addition, the state legislature passed a series of ordinances that mandated Jim Crow, creating segregated schools and other public services for African Americans.[5]

No such formal laws existed regarding Mexicanos, but the culture of segregation that emerged similarly sidelined them, and was backed by the full force of the state. A 1929 sign distributed to members of the El Paso Restaurant Association said it all, without the need for punctuation: "NO DOGS NEGROS MEXICANS." Like African Americans, Mexican Americans were confined to separate and inferior schools, segregated underresourced neighborhoods, political disfranchisement, and the very bottom of the occupational ladder. Since South Texas farmers were subsidized in different eras by a mix of federal and state agencies, including the US Department of Agriculture, the US Employment Service, and the Immigration and Naturalization Service, it is fair to say that all these aspects of Juan Crow were created and enforced by the state, and that this, too, represented de jure segregation—despite the absence of state and local statues mandating it. State and local governments chose where and how to build and fund schools, where to build roads or provide services such as running water and sewers, who would qualify to vote, and who would have access to paid employment or unemployment relief.[6]

Most critically, the state determined how it would punish Mexicanos who stepped out of line. While African Americans suffered at the hands of lynch mobs under the watchful eyes of county sheriffs, Mexican Americans were likewise victims of extra-legal violence and state-sponsored terror. Recent studies have shown that at least 232 Mexicanos were executed by mob violence in Texas between 1848 and 1928.[7] Perhaps more significantly, land disputes and talk of revolution in South Texas in the 1910s resulted in the Texas Rangers, the state police force, directly attacking and killing upward of 1,000 Mexican American leaders and landholders in a series of assassinations and massacres. The subsequent war along the border proved so fierce that in 1917 the US Army dispatched an occupying force of 110,000 soldiers to restore order—despite the need for manpower in Europe at the height of World War I.[8]

Thus, in both East Texas and South Texas, Jim Crow and Juan Crow crafted and enforced a new social order, rooted in violence, with a simple and straightforward goal: to keep people of color poor, powerless, and working on farms. The systems had the added benefit of keeping poor whites in the same state, albeit at a notch higher thanks to the wages of whiteness and the privileges bestowed by their pale skin. White tenant farmers and sharecroppers lacked meaningful political power, and their schools were likewise closed half the year for the harvest. But no matter how low their status, poor whites enjoyed the psychological benefits of white supremacy, access to slightly better schools and services, the ability to vote without harassment if they could afford the tax, and representation by elected officials and economic elites who looked like them and depended on their support for their continued reign. The spectacle of lynching gave them a clear sense of superiority and protection as well as an indispensable enemy that distracted their eyes from the culpable ruling class.[9] As Texas began to industrialize after the discovery of oil at Spindletop, foreclosures and economic precariousness drove rural whites off the farms and into the cities, where they claimed and later defended the best jobs, best schools, best neighborhoods, and best public services. Jim Crow and Juan Crow became urban.[10]

Modern Texas was built on this foundation. Urbanization accelerated as farmers were pushed out of the countryside by the Depression and pulled to the cities by the industrial boom spurred by World War II. The skyrocketing defense industry depended entirely on federal subsidies and federal agencies—not the ingenuity of entrepreneurs on the free market. Indeed, the storied Houston tycoon Jesse H. Jones used his post as head of the federal Reconstruction Finance Corporation to build the infrastructure, petrochemical, and defense industries of the burgeoning Bayou City—while lining his own pockets. Federal dollars also underwrote the creation of the Texas aviation industry, and brand-new plants outside Dallas and Fort Worth grew to employ a combined one hundred thousand workers at the height of the war. The rebounding economy undergirded new housing developments for a growing middle class.[11]

Yet the benefits of the boom remained segregated. Depression-era federal relief agencies denied aid to many people of color, and wartime employment agencies steered them away from industrial employment. Despite the promise of federal oversight, the privatized defense-contractor jobs in the factories were reserved for white men, building on a tradition as American as apple pie. For more than three centuries, employers designated the best blue-collar jobs as "white jobs," a phrase that also implied the privileging of male breadwinners; less lucrative posts as (white) "women's jobs"; and the lowest-paying, most dangerous, and least desirable jobs as (male) "Black jobs" or "Mexican jobs" or, in earlier periods, as jobs reserved for "white ethnic" or "Oriental" immigrants. Women of color faced the most discrimination in the labor market, the vast majority of them confined to agriculture or domestic service. Most white people viewed such divisions of labor as natural and unremarkable; unconsciously, they perceived their privileged access to them as a right. With the coming of federal labor laws that protected white male industrial workers, brave union men organized themselves and transformed factory work into lucrative, stable jobs. In Texas and elsewhere across the nation, workers in the defense industry created the white middle class. They bought new suburban cottages near the factories and, later, large ranch houses further afield. They had barbecues, bought boats, and sent their kids to the best public school systems up to that point in human history.[12]

Yet here again, institutionalized racism undergirded their comfort and success. The housing market that allowed white workers to accumulate wealth and join the middle class was segregated. In the early twentieth century, private banks developed a system of assessing risk and making loans that was based heavily on race. Loan officers viewed prospective Black and Mexicano homebuyers with suspicion—solely because of their color (or their Spanish surnames). White homeowners formed neighborhood improvement associations with the express purpose of keeping out nonwhite buyers and tenants. They wrote restrictive covenants into their deeds, attempting to bar owners from selling to "undesirables." Realtor associations demanded that their members steer people of color away from white neighborhoods and maintain homogeneity at all costs. Yet the profit motive proved too much. Some agents broke from their trade associations and brought Black and Mexicano buyers to white neighborhoods and banks. If lucky, hopeful purchasers would pay higher than market value for property, because of their race; obtain bank loans with unfavorable terms, because of their race; move in under the cover of darkness, because of their race; and then immediately lose much of their homes' value as soon as their race was discovered. And after all that, their white neighbors often attacked them, throwing rocks or even bombs at their houses, burning crosses on their lawns, forming mobs in the street outside, and so on. Police departments tended to look the other way.

Indeed, governmental intervention made the problem worse. In the 1930s, the US government chartered two new agencies to stabilize the Depression-era housing market. Together, the Home Owners Loan Corporation and the Federal Housing Authority took the racist private-sector housing and lending practices and made them public policy. Agency staffers drew maps to assess risk based primarily on the racial demographics of given neighborhoods. Officials drew literal red lines around Black and Mexicano neighborhoods, and green lines around white sections. They then provided subsidized loans, but only for low-risk (i.e., white) buyers—for the next half century. A decade later, the Servicemen's Readjustment Act, better known as the GI Bill, added still more subsidies for legions of veterans returning from World War II. Although the law was ostensibly color-blind, white veterans benefited disproportionately from it, since many veterans of color were steered away from its core programs. Moreover, the newly cemented residential segregation of every metropolitan area in America greatly curtailed the housing stock available to Black and Mexicano veterans. State and local governments made the problems worse by choosing where to site new freeways and other infrastructure, including schools. Unsurprisingly, school districts often built gleaming new edifices for white students while shunting nonwhites into one-room shacks or dilapidated old buildings. Municipal zoning practices and public housing authorities further discriminated against nonwhites. All these practices represent a forgotten form of de jure Jim Crow and Juan Crow, one that flourished across the American North, West, and South. When discriminatory markets and subsidies failed to maintain segregation, law enforcement policed the boundaries between neighborhoods and schools. The entire system depended on public policy and enforcement, not simply on individual prejudice or the vagaries of the market's "invisible hand."[13]

The Long Liberation Struggles

In Texas and nationwide, activists in the early phases of the long and wide civil rights movements responded by confronting not just the segregation of lunch counters and water fountains but the entire kaleidoscope of institutionalized white supremacy.[14] The state's Black and Chicano/a liberation struggles were long in their duration, expansive in their vision, and, at times, multiracial in their character. In their early years, economic issues—jobs and housing—were front and center, along with political self-determination and educational equity. Activists in El Paso organized the state's first chapter of the National Association for the Advancement of Colored People (NAACP) in 1915, just six years after its founding in New York. It focused squarely on the right to vote.[15] Roughly two decades later, Dallas activists organized the Progressive Voters League in 1936, winning a series of precincts in municipal elections, and the Texas State Conference of NAACP branches in 1937, bringing organizers from across the state together for the first time.[16]

In cities, activists built movements for "civil rights unionism" that confronted Jim Crow racism while also demanding the inclusion of people of color in the emerging New Deal welfare state. In Houston during World War II, Mrs. Lulu B. White organized thousands of Black industrial workers and their neighbors into the nation's second-largest chapter of the NAACP. Ordinary African American workers breathed life into the civil rights struggle while building powerful Black-led unions or fighting for inclusion in the white-led labor movement. They fought for and won equal pay for Black teachers, and they filed complaints detailing workplace discrimination with the wartime Committee on Fair Employment Practice (FEPC).

Most enduringly, Black men and women stood on street corners and outside factory gates, and passed hats around their churches, to raise money for a pair of pathbreaking lawsuits that cut to the heart of Jim Crow. Back in 1923, the State of Texas had passed a law creating the "white primary," a devious mechanism that kept even the few Black citizens who managed to pay their poll taxes from voting in the most important contest of all, the Democratic Party primary. White officials reasoned that the party was a private club and was thus not subject to the provisions of the Fifteenth Amendment, so they barred nonwhites from choosing its nominees. Houston's civil rights unionists recruited a series of plaintiffs and partnered with the national and state NAACP offices to overturn the practice, decades after the El Paso branch had first challenged it in court. Their 1944 victory before the US Supreme Court in *Smith v. Allwright* ended the white primary across the South, amounting to what Mrs. White called "a second emancipation."[17]

The second case centered on segregated schooling and access to the professions. Another member of the Houston NAACP, a lifelong trade unionist and member of the all-Black National Association of Postal Employees, had repeatedly tried to get a promotion at the local post office. But Black men remained confined to janitorial work, no matter their intellects or abilities, so their applications for upgrades went straight into the trash. The worker filed a series of grievances through his union, all to no avail. So he decided to go to law school, sending his top-notch transcripts and application to the University of Texas, where he was summarily denied admission because of his race. His name was Heman Sweatt. Thurgood Marshall of the national NAACP office carried Sweatt's petition all the way to the US Supreme Court, which ruled in 1950 that separate but unequal graduate and professional schools violated the Fourteenth Amendment. *Sweatt v. Painter* became the key precedent for *Brown v. Board of Education*, decided four years later.[18]

In that latter, more famous case, the US Supreme Court unanimously ordered the integration of all public schools, making it clear that the Constitution forbade Jim Crow segregation. Yet the Court made no provisions for the implementation of the ruling. It did not mandate that schools should be integrated that next fall, of 1954, nor did it suggest that districts do so gradually over the next few years. The executive branch likewise did not issue any guidelines. A year later, the Supreme Court finally took up the logistical problem and, in *Brown II*, ruled that districts should desegregate with "all deliberate speed." The phrase is nonsensical—one can't do something quickly and deliberately. The meaning of the ruling, however, was unambiguous. It signaled to southern legislators that they did not need to do anything different, that minimal compliance with *Brown* would go unpunished. Across Dixie, where lawmakers had sorrowfully resigned themselves to obeying the new law of the land, the defenders of white privilege saw an opportunity and built a new movement that they called "massive resistance." Senators and congressmen signed a manifesto promising to resist federal intervention, and local officials experimented with defying the federal courts. Local chambers of commerce and Rotary Clubs often led the way as local elites flocked to join White Citizens' Councils and the reborn, third Ku Klux Klan. The "rednecks" in the mobs attracted the TV cameras, but white elites sanctioned and directed massive resistance at every turn.[19]

The issue came home to Texas in 1956 when the small town of Mansfield, near Fort Worth in Tarrant County, responded to a local NAACP lawsuit with grudging plans to comply with the law. But a white mob turned back the Black students at Mansfield High School, hanging Black effigies above its entrance and terrorizing the plaintiffs into retreat. Appeals to the Constitution and state and federal officials fell on deaf ears. Instead, President Dwight D. Eisenhower conspired with Governor Allan Shivers to let the mob rule the day. Desegregation was delayed for a decade.[20] A year later in Little Rock, the president did end up intervening, but after the cameras left town, the story soured. The courageous nine students who integrated Central High School faced constant bullying and harassment, as did their families. At the start of the following school year, in 1958, state and local officials opted to close the *entire* public school system rather than face the horror of expanded desegregation—including the deep-seated Jim Crow fear of interracial sex. During the subsequent "lost year," officials instead attempted to provide public funding for white parents to take their kids to brand-new "Christian" academies, the newly chartered Little Rock Private School Corporation, and other independent schools. When the public schools reopened in Little Rock and across the South, school districts responded to the growing threat of privatization by offering managed desegregation. "Pairing" plans exchanged handfuls of students from a designated white school with students from a nearby Black school, and "stair-step" plans limited integration to one grade per year, a twelve-year process to delay the inevitable. Forms of token integration postponed meaningful integration for more than fifteen after *Brown*—into the early 1970s.[21]

Mexican Americans fit awkwardly into this Black-white binary. Juan Crow confined Mexicanos in separate and unequal schools in much of rural and small-town South Texas and West Texas (and across the Southwest), but in urban areas the situation proved thornier. In the Rio Grande Valley, strict residential segregation followed the railroad tracks, and local districts built Anglo and Mexican schools accordingly. Agricultural life dictated schooling, with Mexicanos enjoying shorter school years that were cut even shorter for those who migrated with the crops. Anglo counselors placed Mexicano students into industrial and vocational tracks, and Anglo educators taught solely in English. Well-defined barrios and neighborhoods in the cities—the West Side of San Antonio, the Segundo Barrio of Houston, "Little Mexico" in Dallas, and many more—likewise anchored distinct Mexican schools. In both settings, students and their families faced systemic discrimination at the hands of their taxpayer-funded local and state governments. School leaders excluded them from extracurricular activities, including sports and student government, and subjected them to rampant corporal punishment. In cities and the countryside alike, students were beaten for speaking Spanish at school. The fact that Mexican Americans were legally classified as "white" had little meaning in their daily lives.[22]

By the mid-twentieth century, a small band of Mexican American professionals, including a handful who had managed to attend white law schools, began challenging Juan Crow segregation. In 1947, Mexican Americans in rural Orange County, California, challenged the local school district's practice of segregating students based on their perceived national origins or ethnicity. The case, *Mendez v. Westminster*, enjoyed support from the NAACP and the Japanese American Citizens League and made its way to the US Court of Appeals, which ruled against the practice without explicitly addressing whether it violated the Fourteenth Amendment. Still, in California and Texas and across the Southwest, districts continued to separate students based on perceived language ability. The Texas Education Agency sanctioned this approach, which in practice meant that all Spanish-surnamed students were placed in Mexican schools—even if they spoke perfect English or hailed from proud Tejano families with generations of residency in the state. In *Delgado v. Bastrop* (1948), Mexican American attorneys challenged this practice, with support from the American GI Forum, a Mexican American veterans organization, and the League of United Latin American Citizens (LULAC), the nation's first Mexicano civil rights group, founded in Corpus Christi in 1929. The attorneys did not address the Jim Crow segregation of African Americans but merely argued that Mexicanos shunted into Mexican schools for perceived language deficiencies in fact faced discrimination based on their national origin. The courts again ruled in their favor, but segregation continued.[23]

Meanwhile, leaders of LULAC and the American GI Forum filed another lawsuit challenging another central aspect of Juan Crow, namely, the systemic exclusion of Mexicanos from jury service. In many South Texas and West Texas counties, no Spanish surnames appeared in the pools of jurors available to local courts, thereby denying Mexicano defendants their right to a trial by a jury of their peers. The state argued that Mexican Americans, being white, were not entitled to special treatment; their exclusion from jury pools had more to do with their qualifications than their race. Indeed, LULAC and the GI Forum had long defended their constituents' whiteness, fighting efforts to list them as nonwhite on birth certificates, census forms, hospital records, and more. Yet they all knew that their whiteness was a fiction, that systemic discrimination shaped every aspect of their lives. Thus, when a Mexicano man named Pete Hernandez shot and killed another Mexicano in a bar fight in Edna, he was quickly tried and convicted by an all-Anglo jury. The civil rights organizations filed suit and combatted the state's spurious logic with their own legal innovation: Mexican Americans were "other whites" that were treated as "a class apart" because of their ethnicity. Without challenging Jim Crow, or their client's fictive whiteness, the attorneys argued that Hernandez had been denied due process under the Fourteenth Amendment. Indeed, according to oral accounts, they proved their case during a break from the trial, when they were directed to the courthouse basement bathroom, which had a sign reading, "Colored Men and Hombres Aquí." The suit made it to the US Supreme Court, the first time that Mexicanos had appeared before the nation's highest tribunal. Two weeks before *Brown*, the Court ruled in favor of the plaintiffs, making *Hernandez v. Texas* (1954) a watershed in the dismantling of Juan Crow. Jury pools gradually desegregated. In the aftermath of that victory, Mexican American activists successfully challenged the ongoing segregation of schools and other aspects of daily life in countless small towns across Texas, but their game of Whac-a-Mole produced only piecemeal change.[24]

On a larger scale, segregation continued in schools, in the neighborhoods, at work, in politics, and beyond. It wasn't until the late 1960s that school districts in Texas began to take integration seriously. Yet even then, the Houston ISD and other urban districts cynically parlayed the fiction of Mexican Americans as "other whites" to pair Black schools with Mexican schools, achieving integration on paper without inconveniencing any Anglos. Chicano/a activists and parents responded with a series of school strikes and court cases; they demanded—and won—recognition as an identifiable, nonwhite racial minority in *Cisneros v. Corpus Christi ISD* (1970).[25] At the national level, *Swann v. Charlotte-Mecklenburg* (1971) created two-way busing as a federal remedy, and districts across the South integrated relatively peacefully. But *Rodriguez v. San Antonio ISD* (1973) limited the ability of urban schools to demand resources from suburban districts, and *Milliken v. Bradley* (1974) barred the imposition of metropolitan-level busing schemes that would have brought suburban kids to the inner cities, and urban students to the suburbs. America's brief experiment with integrated public schools reached a premature zenith. Another case from activists on the West Side of San Antonio, *Edgewood ISD v. Kirby* (1984–1995), forced the Texas Legislature to create the "Robin Hood" system of limited resource sharing across the state's hundreds of school districts, but the main beneficiaries have been rural white schools, not urban districts. Many school systems in Texas remained under federal court orders, often on a tri-ethnic basis, into the twenty-first century.[26]

A flood of lawsuits had created hairline cracks in the dams of Jim Crow and Juan Crow by the late 1950s, but the rivers remained within their banks and reservoirs. The long Black and Chicano/a liberation struggles took a huge leap forward beginning in 1960. In March of that year, Black college students in Houston staged the city's first sit-ins, at a downtown department store lunch counter, just one month after the Greensboro Four pioneered the tactic in North Carolina. Students in Dallas, Fort Worth, Austin, and San Antonio followed suit, as did their counterparts in the small East Texas town of Marshall. In these Texas sites and across the South, the demonstrators demanded not merely a hamburger but also access to lucrative sales and clerk positions. Their arrests by local law enforcement renewed calls for reforming the segregated criminal justice systems and reactivated older activists who had been organizing since the 1930s. In San Antonio, Mexican American college students joined the movement, forming their own organization and picketing local movie theaters in solidarity with Black activists. Across Texas and the South, the pressure exerted by sit-in demonstrators forever transformed the politics of Jim Crow as protesters spoke with the "new language" of direct action. White elites were forced to confront their Black counterparts on more equal footing and to make concessions that would have been unimaginable just months earlier. By 1963, successive waves of direct-action demonstrations had integrated lunch counters in the cities (but not in Deep East Texas), opened up a few jobs, forced some reforms in police departments, and created countless new political opportunities.[27]

African Americans and Mexican Americans sought to translate the gains in the streets into one of their movements' age-old goals: independent political power. In the late 1950s, grassroots leaders in LULAC and the American GI Forum organized a series of electoral clubs and associations, which chalked up a handful of local victories. In San Antonio, the civil rights attorney Albert Peña went from filing lawsuits and demonstrating in front of segregated schools to knocking on doors and building a powerful political base, block by block. By 1960, he had helped elect Henry B. Gonzalez to the city council and then the Texas Senate, and Peña himself served on the Bexar County Commissioners Court. Later that year, the two politicos and Dr. Héctor P. García, founder of the American GI Forum, cochaired the Texas wing of the Viva Kennedy campaign, the effort to turn out Mexican Americans for presidential candidate John F. Kennedy (and vice presidential candidate Lyndon Johnson). The effort represented a turning point in the creation of what is now called the "Latino vote." In its wake, Peña organized the Political Association of Spanish-Speaking Organizations (PASO), the electoral arm of the state's Mexican American civil rights movement.

For their part, African Americans responded to a 1956 state injunction against the NAACP by forming new organizations or expanding on old ones, and they too flocked to the Kennedy-Johnson campaign. After the sit-ins, Black activists rebuilt local units of the Progressive Voters League and then launched the Texas Council of Voters (TCV), a statewide liberal African American political network. African Americans and Mexican Americans worked together in local politics, most notably in San Antonio, where Peña partnered closely with Black civil rights activists on the city's East Side.

In the early 1960s the Black-Brown alliance of San Antonio grew statewide, as PASO and the TCV formed a partnership with white "independent liberal" Democrats and the white leaders of organized labor in the Texas AFL-CIO. They called the four-legged amalgam simply the "Democratic Coalition." After a series of fits and starts, and countless acrimonious meetings, the coalition agreed to prioritize the struggles for Black and Mexicano civil rights and to achieve them through coordinated action in both electoral politics and direct-action protests. On August 28, 1963, the same day as the March on Washington, coalition activists staged a March on Austin, streaming from segregated East Austin past the Capitol and Governor's Mansion in 102-degree heat. At a culminating rally in a nearby park, the TCV's president, W. J. Durham, formerly lead counsel for the Texas NAACP and second chair to Thurgood Marshall in the landmark cases of the 1940s, addressed the assembled crowd. "They'll never separate the Latin-American and Negroes again in politics," he began. "They'll never separate labor and the Negro again.... We're going to march on the street, pray on the streets, sit in the streets, walk on the streets. We're going to fight at the ballot box and in the courts."

Indeed, the Democratic Coalition sought to wield the power of the burgeoning civil rights movements to produce lasting political change. Together its members represented a considerable challenge to the Texas establishment, the elite, conservative businessmen who had dominated the Democratic Party and, thus, state politics since the end of Reconstruction. African American and Mexican American activists seized the opportunity to find new allies in their long struggles against Jim Crow and Juan Crow. Most importantly, at the activists' urging, the coalition in 1963–1964 invested in Project VOTE, a grassroots voter registration and education effort conducted on a scale never before seen in Texas politics. With financial support from national foundations, Texas liberal Democrats, and organized labor, it hired dozens of Black and Mexicano organizers in every big city and in the small towns of East Texas and South Texas. It trained hundreds of volunteer leaders and more than ten thousand volunteer block walkers, equipping them with "Freedom Kits" for spreading the gospel of liberation through voting. Countless local activists got their start in these grassroots campaigns. One, an aspiring local attorney who had run unsuccessfully for state representative, gained new tools as a campaign coordinator in Houston. Her name was Barbara Jordan. In 1966, she became the first Black woman in the Texas Senate, and in 1972 she ascended to the US Congress, the first southern Black woman in that body.[28]

And yet, much more work remained to be done. Activists seized on Title VII of the Civil Rights Act of 1964 to finally win equal employment opportunity, though the victories took years to achieve and were often bittersweet: African Americans and Mexican Americans won access to lucrative industrial jobs at the exact moment when those jobs were disappearing because of economic restructuring. The redrawing of political districts and voting maps gradually gave African Americans and Mexican Americans entrée into local and state politics, but their influence became limited as people and resources shifted to the suburbs, where white elites resisted change. Local and state law enforcement continued to run roughshod over Black and Mexicano communities. Schools remained segregated, and opportunities for upward mobility limited. Culturally, Texas and the nation remained unapologetically, often unconsciously white.

In this context a new phase of the civil rights movement began: the Black Power and Chicano/a Power eras. While both movements remain shrouded in myths—starting with the iconic images of gun-toting Black Panthers—they had much in common with earlier periods of the long liberation struggles. African Americans and Mexican Americans had long sought self-determination. When liberal reforms failed to produce sweeping change, activists deemphasized integration as a means toward that end. Instead, they talked about building power within their communities, demanding community control of their schools and services, along with community participation in decisions affecting them. They drew inspiration from long-silenced but proud cultures from Africa and Latin America, transforming signs of stigma into traits to be celebrated. Chicanos/as adopted a new term of self-identification that emphasized their indigenous roots and status as a transnational "Third World" people forced to live in "Occupied America." In one refrain, Chicanos/as noted, "We didn't cross the border; the border crossed us." Likewise, African Americans refused the Jim Crow designations of "Colored" and "Negro" and instead declared, "Black is Beautiful." Both groups celebrated ancestral languages and called for culturally relevant curricula and instruction in schools. Both demanded expanded and culturally appropriate social services, led and provided by members of local communities. They jumped on the opportunities presented by the federal War on Poverty and, often finding those lacking, created their own community-controlled institutions as well.

In other words, the styles of the long movements changed, but the substance did not. Black Power and Chicano/a Power extended and made immediate the longtime goals of their communities. And to a surprising extent, pride in one's own culture facilitated rather than impeded cross-cultural alliances with members of other oppressed groups. Nowhere was this truer than in their joint efforts to combat police brutality and to institutionalize change through electoral politics.[29]

And yet here was where the rubber met the road. At the precise moment that Jim Crow and Juan Crow began falling, when the movements "went north" and to the suburbs and began challenging the most secure bastions of white privilege, they hit a wall. Political power remained limited, jobs continued disappearing, and state legislatures across America reduced expenditures on (still segregated) public education at all levels. Between 1964 and 1968, dozens of urban rebellions—often erroneously dubbed "race riots"—demonstrated how little had changed. Indeed, the federal Kerner Commission, which investigated the "urban disorders," concluded that the problems were structural and that without massive restructuring and governmental investment in social programs, the nation would become "two Americas, one white, one black, separate and unequal." Of course, in the Southwest, there was also a Mexican America, one that the activist Albert Peña argued needed a Marshall Plan just as much as did war-ravaged Europe or post-riot cities in the US North. For both African Americans and Mexican Americans, the late 1960s and the 1970s constituted a period of urgently needed but often inadequate reforms, of identifying the structures that sustained institutionalized racism, and, when government failed to respond, of taking matters into their own hands.[30]

In Texas as in much of America, ordinary Black Power and Chicano/a Power activists carried the long liberation movements forward in unexpected ways. In Dallas and San Antonio, Black activists brought home the organizing tradition of the Student Nonviolent Coordinating Committee and other traditional civil rights groups and transformed them into hubs of Black Power community organizing. Houston's Black activists took inspiration from Chicago and California and built the Peoples Party II and other local groups to advance the struggle—but they found themselves on the wrong side of a police riot in which officers opened fire into dormitories at what is now Texas Southern University.[31] In that same year, 1967, a group of five young Chicano/a students at St. Mary's University in San Antonio—*los cinco*—organized the Mexican American Youth Organization (MAYO), which one scholar called the "avant-garde of the Mexican American civil rights movement." Chapters sprung up across the state, based at universities and in the barrios, and they facilitated a wave of student walkouts at more than forty high schools, protests against educational inequity in every corner of Texas. Other barrio youth formed units of the Brown Berets, a paramilitary-style self-defense Chicano/a organization similar to the Black Panthers.

Yet protest was not enough. MAYO soon created a third-party political arm, La Raza Unida Party, which in turn upset the applecart of Mexican American politics across the state.[32] Black Power activists likewise engaged in electoral politics through a panoply of local, community-based organizations. And throughout the 1970s, the two groups fought police brutality, separately and together—while the state responded with a range of surveillance tactics and the War on Crime, a "counterinsurgency" that replaced the provision of social services with the warehousing of bodies and, ultimately, today's system of mass incarceration.[33] Yet at the same time, ordinary African Americans and Mexican Americans continued the long tradition of fighting for change within the system, gradually gaining access to better jobs, winning seats in local and state governments, and "upbuilding" their communities—for their very survival.

Civil Rights in Black and Brown

In 2015, when the Civil Rights in Black and Brown Oral History Project began to conduct fieldwork statewide, our researchers encountered a Texas that was still slogging through the legacies of this history, often without acknowledging the persistent presence of the past. One team of interviewers was surprised to find a caravan of TV news trucks and countless law enforcement vehicles outside Hempstead, in Waller County, home to Prairie View A&M University, the state's first public historically Black college. The day before, Ms. Sandra Bland, a twenty-eight-year-old African American professional from Chicago returning to work at her alma mater, had been declared dead in custody in the county jail. A few days prior, a routine traffic stop turned into a nightmare when a Texas state trooper began barking questions at her, drawing his stun gun, and blaring a spotlight at her while yelling, "Get out of the car! I will light you up. Get out!" State and local officials claimed that Bland's death was a suicide, but their story had so many holes in it that they ultimately settled with her family for nearly $2 million. After the fact, it became clear that officials had withheld Bland's cell phone video of the encounter from scrutiny by her family, her attorneys, and the public. The hashtag #SayHerName offered one memorial to Sandra Bland's lost life, as did a namesake law passed by the Texas Legislature aimed at curbing police misconduct. Yet the final Sandra Bland Act was stripped of most of its meaningful provisions, leading Bland's sister to conclude, "It painfully misses the mark."[34]

This book provides the backstory to this and other horrific moments when race enters the public arena. It seeks to help Texans and Americans of all colors better address the durable structural inequalities of our time by offering a more complete rendering of past grassroots struggles to eradicate institutional racism. It recovers the contours of Jim Crow and Juan Crow in Texas and demonstrates how small bands of activists came together to transform their world. It reveals the creativity and flexibility of the long Black and Chicano/a liberation struggles, highlighting local variants as well as moments when interracial coalitions advanced each group's cause. And it underscores what was at stake for the movements, detailing what exactly their organizers accomplished and how much remains to be done.

Decades after the events, stories of past atrocities and resistance, of movements built and battles fought, remained seared in the minds of African American and Mexican American civil rights activists. Their memories anchor the following chapters, each of which examines a single locale while exploring five common themes: life under segregation, the role of state-sanctioned violence, struggles for equity in public services, political self-determination and agency, and Black-Brown coalition building. The authors draw heavily on CRBB oral history interviews and supplement those voices with information from newspapers, letters, archived interviews, and other primary sources. Reconstructing these case studies proved challenging. In many cases, local papers blacked out coverage of civil rights protests, and the activists were often too busy fighting to maintain written archives documenting their exploits.

Yet the interviews unlocked whole histories that otherwise would have remained inaccessible. At times, narrators recalled never-before-documented movements; in other cases, their tales revealed the deeper meaning of familiar events. In compiling these case studies, our researchers applied the standards of the discipline of history, working to corroborate the richness of each oral testimony with other available oral and written sources. The dearth of traditional written evidence reinforces rather than detracts from the immense value of the interviews we conducted, the sheer pricelessness of collecting and preserving the memories of the people at the center of the civil rights story. Their voices, in turn, point scholars toward new interpretations, allowing us to rewrite the history of the long Black and Chicano/a liberation struggles in Texas and beyond.

Central Themes

While the interviewees' stories varied across time and place, several key themes emerged. First, the Jim Crow and Juan Crow caste systems in Texas were just as ubiquitous and routine as they were elsewhere in the US South and Southwest. Learning the nuances of these systems represented one of the key formative experiences for those who grew up Black or Mexicano and survived the age of segregation in Texas.[35] Second, as indicated above, white-supremacist violence remained one of the most enduring and consequential features of segregation. Black lives simply did not matter. Nor did the lives of Mexicanos. Accordingly, ending the wanton use of violence as a political tool for shoring up the system of white supremacy, along with the state's permissiveness or active involvement in such attacks, emerged as a key battle for both Black and Brown civil rights activists. Put another way, organizers sought to end state-sponsored and state-sanctioned terrorism.[36]

A third critical area centered on the fight for equity in education and other public services. Perhaps counterintuitively, the integration of public schools represented only a single piece of this much larger puzzle. Activists sought to implement *Brown v. Board of Education* in Texas and to extend its application to integrating Chicano/a students, but the objective throughout was substance rather than style. Parents, students, and communities demanded free, high-quality, culturally relevant instruction. African Americans, in particular, took great pride in their neighborhood schools and teachers, and sought to leverage that expertise in new integrated settings. Students struggled to survive the tense reality of integrated hallways, classrooms, buses, athletic teams, and cheerleading squads. But the larger goal centered on outcomes. Black and Chicano/a activists demanded that schools provide students with a positive self-image, with a pluralistic curriculum, and with the opportunities for upward mobility that Jim Crow and Juan Crow had long restricted. They fought for more resources and autonomy within historically Black colleges and universities and for real inclusion in historically white institutions. And as the brief experiment of integration in America faltered, they launched their own forays into self-determination, creating community-controlled schools and Black studies and Mexican American studies programs, each of which represented a new path forward.[37] Similar stories emerged in regard to the provision of the whole spectrum of health and human services. Black and Chicano/a activists always sought equity and inclusion, and they seized the opportunities presented by the War on Poverty to win unprecedented services for their communities. But alongside that approach, they also built their own self-determined health care providers, free breakfast programs, and other basic social services.[38]

Throughout these struggles, Black and Chicano/a liberation fighters learned and relearned lessons from their distant past: in the final analysis, achieving justice depended on having power, and wielding power required political self-determination, a fourth key theme. Mexicanos had enjoyed political autonomy before the Texian conquest, and African Americans had voted and achieved many victories during Reconstruction. Yet both groups remained politically stunted through most of the twentieth century. Struggles for the right to elect independent politicians capable of substantive representation for Black and Mexicano neighborhoods and communities were always part and parcel of the civil rights movements. Across Texas, when activists staged a sit-in, marched to the courthouse, or demanded community control, they also sought to rewrite the political rules and maps of their cities and state. Token inclusion in government wasn't enough, nor was the elevation of handpicked "race leaders" sufficient for creating political power. Black and Chicano/a activists demanded the right to choose their representatives for themselves. Like the struggles against racial violence and for equity in education and public services, the quest for political self-determination remains unfinished.

Across the board, the interviews demonstrate that ordinary African Americans and Mexican Americans were far from passive victims in the face of Jim Crow and Juan Crow. Rather, they constantly resisted the confines of segregation, creatively navigating and overcoming its worst features. They engaged in formal, outward resistance, and in "wearing the mask," that is, feigning submission to domination while secretly undermining it. Black and Brown people fought back; they exerted agency. They were active crafters of their own destinies, despite the structural obstacles that constrained their choices. Black and Chicano/a communities served as sites of strength and power, and activists depended on their neighbors, friends, and social networks to launch a frontal assault on the whole system. The fact that the movements failed to end all racial oppression does not mean that they had no power at all or that individuals' many actions, big and small, had no impact. Rather, the evidence is clear that daily acts of resistance culminated in permanent changes to their communities, state, and nation.[39]

Last, civil rights fights in the Lone Star State depended on dynamic interactions between the Black and Chicano/a liberation struggles. To be sure, each of the movements remained distinct. Yet they emerged simultaneously, in *relation* to each other. Mexicanos long understood that their status as an oppressed group in segregated Texas situated them somewhere between the white overlords and subjugated African Americans. Still, they harbored few illusions about their own whiteness, organizing themselves instead as a targeted racial-ethnic minority. For their part, Black Texans understood that their location in the borderlands made them qualitatively different from their counterparts in the Deep South. The presence of Mexicanos in the same state offered both opportunities for coalition and, more recently, perceived threats of competition. Both Black and Chicanx activists in Texas organized with one eye on Martin Luther King Jr. and the grassroots struggle that had engulfed the rest of the South. Mexicanos/as also looked toward California for inspiration. Yet the physical isolation of Texas meant that both groups built indigenous movements in response to local conditions, situations that often included considerations of the state's unusual diversity.

Geography and demographics shaped the ability of African Americans and Mexicanos/as to form alliances with one another. African Americans clustered in East Texas; Mexicanos/as lived in South Texas and West Texas. In the countryside in the first two-thirds of the twentieth century, there were few individual interactions between members of the two groups, much less joint community organizing. The cities were another story. As early as the 1930s, sporadic Black-Brown activist coalitions emerged in San Antonio and Houston, and organizers in Dallas and Fort Worth joined their ranks in the 1960s. Even smaller cities such as Corpus Christi, along the Gulf Coast, and El Paso, far out west, saw the small numbers of African American residents banding together with local Mexicanos/as.

Perhaps surprisingly, and contrary to established scholarship on Texas, the deepest coalitions emerged beginning in the late 1960s, in the age of Black Power and Chicano/a Power. Cultural and revolutionary nationalists of all colors—and even some white radical allies—joined together in enduring alliances in all the state's major cities and in a loose, statewide network. African Americans from Houston visited Crystal City, the rural epicenter of the Chicano/a movement's Raza Unida Party. In fact, a Black man in San Antonio ran for office on the Raza Unida ticket. Struggles against police brutality featured a "tripartite alliance" of the Brown Berets, former Black Panthers, and self-proclaimed white revolutionaries. These partnerships were the rule, not the exception, at least in this period.

Nonetheless the residential segregation of the state and even of neighborhoods within the cities meant that most of the people interviewed for the project had little or no contact with their counterparts across the color line. For many narrators, "whites" or "Anglos" were viewed as the enemy, though a few proved themselves reliable allies. In contrast, the "Blacks" or "Mexicans" across town generally remained distant abstractions. Members of the two groups simply did not know one another. In some cases, one might see the other as a foil or as a competitor for jobs, housing, or governmental resources. But these perceptions typically depended on a lack of familiarity, not active conflict. Getting to know one another in substantive ways alleviated tension. In any case, one can only hope to understand the Black and Chicano/a liberation struggles by considering them relationally as well as comparatively, and certainly not by using the monoracial frames that scholars typically apply.[40]

Outline of the Book

Civil Rights in Black and Brown is organized geographically and divided into four sections. Each proceeds somewhat chronologically while uncovering new case studies with overlapping common themes. Part I explores the long African American freedom struggle in the small towns and countryside of East Texas. It begins in Waller County, where Sandra Bland met her murderer in 2015. In chapter 1, Moisés Acuña Gurrola argues that the media response to Bland's death ignored a century-long history of violence and an equally protracted tradition of resistance. Chapters 2 and 3 center on the elusive struggles for equity in education. In Chapter 2, Meredith May compares the chaotic desegregation of public schools and higher education in three Deep East Texas towns: Lufkin, Diboll, and Nacogdoches. In Chapter 3, Eladio Bobadilla examines the Golden Triangle region, anchored by Beaumont in Jefferson County, taking his narrators seriously when they repeat the refrain that "something was lost" with the coming of integration. Chapter 4 surveys a century of violence and resistance in Montgomery County. There, as Jasmin C. Howard shows, the regular murders of African Americans around the county courthouse punctuated a long history of white-supremacist violence—and of Black survival, a constant struggle that includes Black-Brown alliances for social justice today.

Part II turns to Chicanx struggles for self-determination in South Texas and West Texas. In chapter 5, Joel Zapata recounts terrifying stories of police brutality on the High Plains and in the Permian Basin in 1978. Chapter 6 looks back to the early days of the Mexican American civil rights movement; James B. Wall details how the rise of Dr. Héctor P. García and the American GI Forum served to overshadow and obscure other activism in Garcia's hometown of Corpus Christi and along the Coastal Bend of South Texas. Chapter 7 zooms in on Pharr, an agricultural town in the Rio

Grande Valley near McAllen. David Robles shows how a police riot there in 1971 became the catalyst for sweeping political reforms in the city and, by extension, in the region as a whole. Likewise, in chapter 8, Vinicio Sinta and Maggie Rivas-Rodriguez explore competing memories of the Uvalde school walkout of 1970, finding that, in this case, the commonplace youth-protest tactic produced a decades-long lawsuit and ended up defining the lives of a generation of Mexican Americans. Sandra I. Enríquez turns in chapter 9 to Far West Texas, exploring an enduring legacy of the Chicano/a movement in El Paso. She tells the dramatic story of how local activists in the isolated city came together to defend their neighborhoods and to construct their own solutions to the unequal provision of social services.

While the first two sections explore the African American and Chicano/a liberation struggles largely in isolation from each other, Part III focuses on urban areas where the two movements were inextricably intertwined. The key themes remained the same, and thanks to the proximity of living together in the cities, activists at times built Black-Brown coalitions. In Chapter 10, Todd Moye sets the stage by examining Tarrant County, home to Fort Worth and the Mansfield desegregation crisis of 1956. Moye demonstrates that white supremacy was rampant and enduring, despite claims by local boosters that their enlightened "Fort Worth way" prevented racial conflict. Next door in Dallas, as Katherine Bynum shows in chapter 11, a vibrant Black-Brown alliance emerged in support of police accountability and political self-determination. In Houston, as Samantha Rodriguez explains in chapter 12, student activists at the city's two major universities came together to demand ethnic studies and community control. In chapter 13, I show how a new generation of Black Power activists in San Antonio pushed beyond old integrationist strategies by joining forces with La Raza Unida Party, rebranding it in English as the "United People's Party." Finally, in chapter 14, Todd Moye demonstrates that Austin's liberal self-image masked deep-seated racial inequality—and a struggle for representation and equity that continues into the twenty-first century.

Part IV takes readers inside the CRBB project. In chapter 15, I narrate the origins of the collaboration and explain its methodology as well as the development of its accompanying website and database. Finally, the appendix presents selected excerpts of transcribed interviews from the CRBB collection. Some of the featured narrators make cameo appearances in the chapters too, but most of the transcripts feature new voices who fill in stories from geographic areas unrepresented in the other chapters. Readers are encouraged to look up the videos of their testimonies and more on the CRBB website. We also invite you to submit feedback, transcribe additional interviews, or contribute lesson plans, your own essays, or related primary sources via our crowdsourcing project. This approach underscores that oral history remains a collaborative endeavor, one that unites scholars, narrators, and entire communities.

The chapters in this book uncover a wide range of liberation struggles that took place in the cells of county jails, neighborhood schoolrooms, university quads, and the corridors of power at city halls. Written by the researchers who conducted the interviews, the chapters detail stories of segregation, violence, resistance, and community organizing for self-determination in big cities and small towns in every corner of the Lone Star State. They provide ample evidence of the strength of the human spirit. Yet they also reveal that the task of dismantling white supremacy in Texas remains unfinished, that the problem is more intractable than commonly assumed. Fortunately, the chapters conclude that the catalyst for change lies not in distant governments but in ordinary folks—in we, the people.

PART I

VIOLENCE AND RESISTANCE:

AFRICAN AMERICANS IN EAST TEXAS

CHAPTER 1

IGNORED NEWS AND FORGOTTEN HISTORY:

The 1963 Prairie View Student Movement

MOISÉS ACUÑA GURROLA

After the acquittal of George Zimmerman in 2013 for the murder of Trayvon Martin in Florida, the public's awareness of the number of police shootings and anti-Black hate crimes in the United States skyrocketed. In response, African American activists ushered in the era of the Black Lives Matter movement. In Texas, most Black Lives Matter protests were solidarity marches, massive public demonstrations aimed at heightening public awareness of police brutality and anti-Black violence. Racial tensions reached a boiling point in Texas in the summer of 2015 after a viral video portrayed a uniformed police officer forcefully pinning a young African American girl to the ground at a pool party in McKinney, an upper-middle-class suburb of Dallas.

Weeks later, in the East Texas town of Prairie View, Sandra Bland, a young African American woman from Chicago, in town to accept a job offer at Prairie View A&M University, was aggressively detained and handcuffed by Texas state trooper Brian Encinia following a minor traffic violation. The story made national news. Bland was charged with assault and battery on a public servant—a felony. After three days of repetitive police violations and neglect, Bland was found dead in her jail cell, and Texas police departments entered the national discourse on police brutality. Until then, as Dr. James Johnson of Waller County, Texas, explained, "Waller [County] has been kept out of the mainstream in many ways."[1]

Texas has a long history of anti-Black violence and police brutality. It has an equally long history of boosters, politicians, and other officials omitting details about the state's tarnished record of human rights violations.[2] At the same time, media coverage and mainstream recognition of influential public protests has been equally absent from the public record.[3] Thus, minimal reporting of oppression and subsequent minimal coverage of direct-action movements fed the assumption that Texas was unique among states in the South. The reality is that in every region of Texas, civil rights activism was as protracted, organized, controversial, and contentious as it was in states such as Mississippi, Alabama, and Tennessee.

On the heels of Sandra Bland's death, left-leaning journalists published numerous exposés of the "racist history" of East Texas. Despite their mostly earnest intentions to contextualize the death of Sandra Bland within the broader history of Waller County, some journalists problematically implied that the county had not witnessed Black resistance to racism, segregation, police brutality, and mob violence over the last century and a half. To contemporary journalists, accounts of the "racist history" of a Texas locale simply list moments that Anglo Texans violently defended their supposed place at the top of the social hierarchy. Journalists presented racism as a given, a natural phenomenon not needing an explanation for its constant reification through daily interactions. They rarely found the need to define racism as a dynamic political force actively maintained by persons who benefit from white supremacy, which at times includes non-Anglos. In some cases, journalists exaggerated Black victimhood and published inaccurate statistics, as if the reality that African Americans had endured was not brutal enough to attract online clicks by liberal readers. Above all, contemporary journalists portrayed African Americans as mostly inactive victims of brutality and extralegal violence.[4]

Written historical sources and oral history interviews recorded with Waller County residents show that although white supremacy indeed shaped the local political structure, African American residents fought back daily. Black residents contested power structures in Waller, even when their own leaders urged them to remain silent, and they organized across geographic lines and, in rare instances, across color barriers with Anglos who viewed segregation as un-Christian and un-American. This chapter demonstrates that resistance occurred whether activist efforts received mainstream media attention or not.

In the many liberal and left-leaning news sites that published pieces on the "racist history" of Waller County, reporters attempted to expose the legacy of racism that undergirded the founding and maintenance of the county's sociopolitical culture. They correctly contextualized the death of Sandra Bland as another unfortunate instance of anti-Black racism in East Texas. The *Huffington Post* published a piece titled, "6 Things You Should Know About the County Where Sandra Bland Died."[5] The *Atlantic* published an article titled "Sandra Bland and the Long History of Racism in Waller County, Texas" subtitled "The Place Where the Young Chicago Woman Was Found Dead in a Jail Cell Has Seen More Than a Century of Racial Violence and Oppression." What the articles overlooked was that when most of the Anglos in Waller were not murdering, lynching, and assaulting Black Americans, they elected anti-Black compatriots to office and promoted—or at least reinforced—the creation and maintenance of a white-supremacist political culture daily through segregation and the strengthening of Jim Crow rule during the twentieth century.[6] Racism has remained a part of daily life in the county, even on days that gruesome physical violence does not occur.

Before the area was named Waller County, Austin County, as it was known, contained several plantations that depended exclusively on slave labor. During the Civil War, the Confederate military constructed camps near Hempstead, Waller County's future county seat, and built a Confederate military hospital in the town, which also served as a major supply and manufacturing center. After the war, northerners, Republicans, and ex-slaves established branches of the Freedmen's Bureau, colleges, organizations such as the radical Republican Loyal League, and churches in the immediate vicinity of Hempstead and throughout East Texas. Through those institutions, Black residents slowly "upbuilt" political power and eventually occupied county and state elected offices during Reconstruction.[7]

Although several Anglos in the Black-majority county of Austin did not oppose

Black political organizing, most Anglos did. They propagated the belief that ex-slaves, under the new system of free labor, were predetermined to live a life of vagrancy and idleness, sustained by their supposedly childlike dependence on the federal government.[8] The *Countryman*, a newspaper in Hempstead, led the distribution of anti-Black propaganda in the area. As early as 1868, the editors promoted the "Conservative in politics, with a firm resolve to do all we can to secure for the Southern people the rights of citizenship, and to frustrate the infernal plans for aggrandizement and power which the Radicals have laid" through their "Radical doctrine of Negro equality." The *Countryman* promised readers that it would work to swiftly defeat "negro voting, negro laziness, negro insolence, and negro and radical rule."[9] Editors assured readers of their righteousness: "Be comforted, be cheerful, be firm for your rights; be united, and you will regain and maintain them ... God is everywhere, and, sooner or later, justice will be done."[10] In short, the publishers and readers believed that African Americans were unworthy of citizenship.

Over the next few years, conservatives contended with Republicans over the formation of new counties and the distribution of political power. After several compromises, Anglo politicians drew new county lines and formed Black-majority Waller County from parts of Austin, Grimes, and Washington Counties in 1873. They designated Hempstead, an Anglo-majority town of 1,612, nicknamed "Six-Shooter Junction," as the county seat.[11] They named the county after Edwin Waller, the first mayor of Austin, a signer of the Texas Declaration of Independence, a member of the Texas secession convention, and a former slave owner whose family property was located near Hempstead. To put their political power beyond the need for compromise, Anglo men had established local chapters of the Ku Klux Klan and the White Man's Party by the late 1880s. Their goals were to rebuild an exclusively white political machine to dominate Waller County.

Black political power steadily dwindled. Terrorism, countywide anti-Black hysteria, and governmental manipulations by white supremacists convinced enough poor Anglos that Black elected officials from the area were "childlike" and thus a "disgrace to Waller County."[12] African Americans and white Republicans who counted on the Black vote were removed from office, and voters were intimidated and violently coerced to forgo political participation. By 1903, white men had seized majority control of local and state government offices through the Democratic Party.[13] They continued to rely on intimidation tactics to prevent Blacks from voting in local elections. In 1923, three years after Anglo women were granted the legal right to vote, African American women and men alike were barred from the polls by the white primary.[14]

From Reconstruction to the middle of the twentieth century, Waller County built its reputation as a "sundown town," or, in this instance, a sundown county.[15] This meant that the county was extralegally governed by a de facto curfew that banned African Americans from occupying public spaces after sundown. The sundown curfew was enforced by mobs of Anglo civilians who took pleasure in violently upholding that convention. Even when Black men held local office, Anglos in certain pockets of Waller County threatened African Americans, including publicly elected officials, if they entered the area, regardless of the time of day.[16] Anti-Black violence swelled, and by 1931 nearly one in seven African American public lynching victims in Texas had resided in Waller or the surrounding counties (Montgomery, Harris, Fort

Bend, Austin, Grimes, and Washington). From 1890 to the 1930s, Waller County reported eight public lynchings (the second-highest total in the state) and twelve victims (the highest total).[17]

Lynching in this regard is defined as an extralegal act of mob violence perpetrated by an "organized, spontaneous, and ephemeral group that disperses quickly" upon reaching its goals of "publicly killing or severely maiming a person or persons suspected of a crime."[18] If one were to factor in the disproportionately large number of Black men unfairly and unconstitutionally sentenced summarily to death by local courts, the subsequent public spectacle of their execution, and the message that the execution was meant to convey to Black residents of the area, the instances of anti-Black lynchings in Waller and its surrounding counties would be much higher.[19]

The uncounted mob assaults against Black Americans exacerbated the culture of violence that Anglos established. In a 1941 interview in Waller County by John Henry Faulk, a formerly enslaved woman named Mrs. Laura Smalley recalled the fear she felt in public in the late nineteenth and early twentieth centuries. She regularly "didn't know whether they [were] going [to] bother me or not, [even if] I hadn't done nothing."[20] The threat of a nonlethal beating loomed, and with such beatings, Anglos sent a message to their victims and to the victims' families, communities, and other social networks. Moreover, Anglo mobs that beat Black persons without killing them could avoid media and law enforcement attention. The common denominator in each method of anti-Black violence was its intent to publicly subordinate an entire class of people and assert white rule by "manifesting it at its most spectacular."[21]

As late as the 1890s and early twentieth century, Black people who campaigned with or supported Republican or Populist candidates faced the highest probability of being subject to racialized violence. Whereas Anglo Republicans or Populists could easily blend in with other Anglos and keep their political affiliations hidden, Black Americans were marked by the color of their skin not merely as political opponents but also as mortal enemies.[22] Harriet Smith, in a 1941 interview with John Henry Faulk in Waller County, detailed the animosity and violent outbursts of poor whites against African Americans. She described the murders of her brother, husband, and brother-in-law by a mob of poor whites who objected to African American political empowerment during their battles against the rise of Jim Crow and white primaries.[23]

Smith explained that on her husband's way home from Cedar Creek, seven miles north of Hempstead, a mob of poor white men led by "Old W.B." caught up with Smith's husband, J. S. Smith, who was closely affiliated with East Texas Republicans. Following a dispute over several issues, including the ownership of a horse, W.B. murdered Smith. W.B. and his gang left Smith's body by the side of the road. News of Smith's murder spread around Hempstead, and eventually most of Hempstead's population knew that W.B. and his gang had committed the murder. Law enforcement made no arrests in connection with the violent crime.

Thirteen months later, W.B. and his gang struck again, this time targeting Harriet Smith's brother and her brother-in-law for their "politicking" in Waller County. As the men worked in a nearby cotton field, W.B. and his goons surrounded the Smiths and talked at them until the Black men completed their work in the field. At sundown, while still under the surveillance of W.B., the Smiths ended their workday and tied up their final bale of cotton. Suddenly, the gang of Anglos drew their weapons and fired at the Black men. W.B. and his gang left the bodies of the murdered men in the field for Harriet Smith to later discover.

Decades later, Harriet Smith's vivid memory of her brother and brother-in-law's murders still upset her. She "could go right to the spot now nearly where he was killed at." The men, including Smith's husband, were deeply involved with the campaigns of the East Texas Republican W. K. Makemson, who had run for a variety of offices, from judge to governor, beginning in the 1890s.[24] In fact, it was W. K. Makemson who delivered the news to Harriet Smith that her husband had been murdered and his body left by the side of the road.[25]

Activism at Prairie View

The memories of anti-Black violence did not vanish when the rate of lynchings declined during the Great Depression. Counties that had significant Black populations, such as Waller and its environs, remained crippled by fear. In Hempstead, the largest town in western Waller County, Jim Crow cemented the social order. In the town of Waller, near the eastern border of the county, the sheriff's office enforced Jim Crow law violently and with state approval.[26] In between those towns, in the unincorporated town of Prairie View, lay Prairie View Normal and Industrial College, established by the state for Black students, who came from every corner of Texas and the United States.[27] By the 1940s, as Jim Crow law suppressed Black voices in Hempstead and Waller, young students from Prairie View fostered an environment of intellectual and political growth as they worked to dismantle apartheid.[28] But before they could take their fight to the county, they needed first to clear the obstacles laid out by longtime faculty members who answered to the Anglo bosses of Waller County.[29]

Some of the leading men of the college and, later, the university subscribed to political ideologies that affected their and their students' political involvement and activist visibility. In the late 1940s through the 1950s, men such as Dr. Edward B. Evans, the eighth president of Prairie View A&M University (PVAMU), adopted avoidance as the preferred method of dealing with white violence. The administration adopted measures that essentially accommodated mob rule in Waller County. To protect students from anti-Black violence, for example, university officials barred them from socializing off campus after dark. Students felt crushed under the rule of university officials, who feared economic reprisals as employees of the openly racist Texas A&M University system, a system that did not integrate its other facilities until 1964, following federal demands.[30]

The 1950s were a critical time for students who sought to break the double-reinforced chains of Jim Crow in Waller County and the nation. With an administration that acquiesced in the demands of Anglo county bosses, students reached a boiling point. Administrators at PVAMU discouraged all forms of confrontation and went as far as dissuading students from applying to white graduate schools, since county Anglos would view Black ambition as disrespectful.[31] Under direct orders from powerful Anglos in Waller County, university officials even prevented students from applying to white-owned businesses for work or internships.[32]

From 1945 through the 1950s, PVAMU students' morale and the hope that their leaders would push back against Jim Crow remained low. Students were fed up with the suppressive policies put in place by the campus administration.[33] For example, Herbert Cross recalled that as a nontraditional student—a military veteran—in 1954, he and his brother were disciplined for consuming alcohol in their dorms. Had they imbibed off campus, however, the adult brothers would have faced stiffer penalties. They found themselves in trouble again later that year for having attended the State Fair Classic football game at the Cotton Bowl in Dallas without their parents' written permission. The Cross brothers had to remind the dean that they were adults who had stopped depending on their parents' care years earlier.[34]

When PVAMU adopted the formal submission of student complaints in 1960, campus administrators learned that students had reached the limit of their tolerance for suppressive policies.[35] The formal complaint system worked to galvanize students, and within a few months students threatened a general strike.

Despite the official, relatively tame method of organizing students, however, one administrator chastised the student body for not having aired their grievances through the "proper channels." The dean of the men's college and director of student life, Dr. T. R. Solomon, downplayed student complaints as "typical students' springtime reactions." But the resentment that students felt toward campus officials was not a generalized opposition to every authority figure on campus; it was focused on the higher echelons of the university administration, namely, Dr. Edward B. Evans, the president of PVAMU since 1946, and Solomon.[36] Complaints from 400 students cited inadequate on-campus living conditions and restrictions seen as unfair and invasive, policies that had been in place for years at that point.[37]

Responding to the threat of student action, Evans claimed ignorance and said that he had "received nothing concerning the protests."[38] Reverting to their tradition of acquiescence, administrators threatened students with expulsion, thus forestalling the campus- and countywide strike. The PVAMU administration's treatment of students, along with Evans's indifference, planted the seeds of a movement that coalesced with the nationwide movements of the early 1960s.[39]

In June 1963, "the defining year of the civil rights movement," just months before Martin Luther King Jr.'s famous speech in Washington, DC, white business owners in Hempstead, the county seat of Waller, reaffirmed publicly their commitment to segregation.[40] Students recognized that moment as their opportunity to jump into the national current of student-led direction actions.[41] They realized that the first obstacle to defeating Jim Crow in Waller was their own overprotective, nonconfrontational school administration.[42] As one Dallas commentator explained, "The attitude of the authorities on PV's campus, as well as suppression of the rights of the students by Hempstead, where most of the money was spent that the state raised for the training of Negro students, finally brought about rebellion by these students."[43]

Students organized with other Waller County residents to counter the administration's power. Some mailed letters to alumni, asking for support. Others cooperated with nonstudents to form the Volunteer Welfare Community Association and then received activist training in Houston.[44] Defiant professors and other campus employees formed the Waller County Civic League in direct opposition to their Jim Crow–supporting superiors at PVAMU.[45] Eventually, Black and Anglo ministers of the Waller Ministerial Alliance, public school educators, defiant faculty members of PVAMU, and other Black professionals who did not fear economic reprisals joined in support of the university students who demanded the desegregation of Waller County. Students formed the group Students for Equality, Liberty and Freedom (SELF), compiled a list of eighteen grievances, and presented them to the administration. One of SELF's demands was the removal of Solomon from his position; in addition, SELF demanded that the administration prioritize women's concerns on campus, take "a pronounced stand . . . regarding the civil rights battle," and allow students the "freedom . . . to take a stand on social issues, including civil rights."[46]

Beginning in September 1963, hundreds of student protesters rallied in Hempstead, to the chagrin of university administrators, and demanded the desegregation of local businesses. The group publicly named university administrators whom students suspected of disapproving of the demonstration, and it threatened to boycott the school itself if they did not stand with the students. Citing "safety concerns," the university chose not to support the students.[47] In fact, during a demonstration in Hempstead, some Black administrators mockingly shopped inside segregated businesses in view of the students. The students eventually retreated and planned a second, more confrontational demonstration.[48]

Organizers knew that the next demonstration needed to have implications that could not be ignored. As the semester proceeded, students kept organizing on campus and beyond. In late October 1963, students announced a strike of the yearly homecoming football game versus Bishop College on November 9.[49] The PVAMU Panthers, who were undefeated that season, had earned a reputation for dominance via repetitive shows of brute force, cunning strategy, and unrestrained speed. Students knew that using the Panthers' spotlight would illuminate the movement on campus.

Eventually, 2,000 of PVAMU's 3,500 students signed on in support of the strike and a continued boycott of Hempstead's businesses. The threat of ongoing disruption of Hempstead businesses was cause for great concern because the "lifeblood" of Hempstead was the town's segregated businesses, which depended heavily on patronage by university students and faculty. On campus, the students' collective power began to shake administrators' long-held assumptions of stability and quiescence. Leading up to the strike, fifty student officers resigned from their positions, which unraveled the organizations that played a major role in promoting the highly publicized rivalry football game.

On the day of the matchup, arguably the biggest football game of the season, only one hundred spectators were in attendance.[50] Most of the spectators consisted of the parents of football players, some Prairie View administrators, and Bishop College football fans. Meanwhile, over 2,000 students congregated in front of the student union building, away from the stadium. Before and during the game, they did not hand out leaflets, chant slogans, or speak to passersby. They merely congregated and listened to the football game over the radio, laughing "at the announcers describing the terrific crowd THAT WASN'T THERE!"[51] At the game, the PVAMU president commented on the movement, holding fast to his decades-old excuse that he cared too much about the safety of his students to do anything about racism in the county:

Nearly empty stands during a student boycott of the homecoming football game at Prairie View A&M University, November 16, 1963. Photo from the *Dallas Express*.

"I have the same ambitions as any other self-respecting Negro—but in my position I have a responsibility to the state and to the parents of the students entrusted to us. Therefore, I can't endorse anything that would endanger their safety."[52]

Following the game, the embarrassing turnout made it clear to Evans that an overwhelming majority of PVAMU students supported the Hempstead boycott. As one newspaper reported, the boycott was "90 percent effective," with only "uneasy-appearing ... adult fans" in the stands, where "a ghost would have felt right at home," since it "assumed the loneliness of a graveyard." He had little choice but to reluctantly support the students. Other administrators, soon realizing the damages that an un-cooperative student body could inflict on their livelihoods, reluctantly supported the movement, too. In the face of such united opposition, Hempstead business owners later announced plans to comply with the Civil Rights Act of 1964 and desegregate their facilities.

Despite this significant event in the history of racial conflict in Waller County, it gained little recognition beyond Waller County and East Texas. Reporters for the mainstream press hardly mentioned the movement, and details of the organizations and key individuals were covered even less. As Dr. James E. Johnson, a former student and retired professor at Prairie View A&M University explained in an interview, minimal coverage of Waller County activism was typical.[53] Amy Boykin, a former student who participated in the Hempstead boycotts, recalled that the news media was mostly absent during the demonstrations.[54] Of the handful of Texas newspapers that mentioned the Hempstead struggle, the most detailed reports came from Black-owned news publications, including the *San Antonio Register*, *Dallas Examiner*, *Dallas Express*, and *Houston Informer*, but their coverage was not comprehensive.

This dearth of publicity has had tremendous consequences. The absence from public memory of this single example of sustained, organized protest in direct opposition to Jim Crow serves to portray the African Americans of Waller County as inactive

Al and Larneatha Bowdre, Prairie View, Texas, July 14, 2015. Photo courtesy CRBB.

victims of racism and inactive beneficiaries of federal policy changes. Stories such as the student strike of the PVAMU-Bishop football game should beckon historians and writers to explore the histories of rural Texas counties that have been left out of the public memory of "civil rights."

Despite the marginal coverage of major events in newspapers, the few interviews conducted in Waller County by the Civil Rights in Black and Brown Oral History Project suggest that enough source material exists to begin the retrieval of stories about public demonstrations surrounding town incorporation, voting rights, and policing across the county, from the last century to the present day.[55] The starting point for historians interested in uncovering the history of rural areas of Texas in the twentieth century must not be only newspapers but also the people who experienced daily life in seemingly forgotten pockets of the state.

CHAPTER 2

"PLUMB CHAOS":

Segregation and Integration in Deep East Texas

MEREDITH MAY

I saw a large crowd in front of the school. And it just kept getting bigger and
bigger ... so when the bell rang for school to take up, I said, "Let me go check this
crowd...." So I went through the front doors and asked the principal [Ed Casburn],
"What is going on with all these white people out here?" And he said, "They won't let
the Blacks get off the buses."

HERBERT CROSS, VICE PRINCIPAL OF LUFKIN HIGH SCHOOL

After hard-fought resistance to integration, the federal courts forced the schools in
Lufkin, Texas, to integrate on August 31, 1970, under a court order that remained
in effect until July 11, 2000. A month earlier, in June 2000, the Lufkin Independent
School District Board of Trustees agreed in a 5–0 vote that the district had met all
the requirements of desegregation and should be released from the ruling. The two
African American members of the board, Willie Mae Burley and Larry Kegler, who
had experienced integration as a teacher and student, respectively, were not present
for the vote. The LISD superintendent, David Sharp, delighted in the change: "Not
having the dark cloud of the court order gives us a fresh start."[1]

The day after Lufkin's schools integrated, under the "dark cloud of the court
order," the local newspaper reported that everything had gone extremely well. Approximately fifty small windows in the Intermediate School were broken that Sunday night, but the school's spokesperson described it as more a "bother" than a major
incident. The principal at Lufkin High School, Ed Casburn, told the *Lufkin Daily
News* that "everything went as smooth as possible under the conditions of the first
day of school" when all-Black Dunbar High and white Lufkin High combined. He
reported amusing anecdotes of about one hundred male students receiving shaves and
haircuts to meet the school's dress code. The Lufkin newspaper of record seemed to
breathe a sigh of relief and move on to other business.[2]

"As smooth as possible" belies the truth of what happened at Lufkin High School
on August 31, 1970, when white parents appeared with guns to prevent Black students from entering the building, but it is the official narrative of integration and the
broader civil rights movement in Lufkin and the surrounding area. Lufkin and neighboring small towns, such as Nacogdoches and Diboll, did not experience the same
publicized mass resistance or organizing that took place in other parts of the South.

As relatively rural areas, they had maintained segregation throughout most of the 1960s. But Lufkin, more than Nacogdoches and Diboll, maintained its resistance to integration longer. As one African American resident in Diboll commented, and several others seconded, "You can go to Lufkin, and it's a lot different in Lufkin than in Diboll. Diboll didn't have any incidents or any problems at all when they integrated . . . but Lufkin had problems. In fact of the business, still have."[3]

While Diboll's integration was not seamless, Lufkin's was tumultuous. Part of the reason had to do with the nature of the cities. Diboll retained its company-town persona during the late 1960s and early 1970s; Nacogdoches, with a growing university, faced pressure from an increasingly liberal and urban student body. Lufkin had neither. All three cities resisted integration, all three had rampant police brutality and violence, but Lufkin had no central leader, like the Temple family in Diboll, or internal pressure, like Stephen F. Austin State College, to encourage at least the perception of a "smooth" integration.[4] As a result, when the Lufkin schools integrated under the impetus of a court order, the stage was set for resistance. Analysis and comparison of general segregation and violence, police brutality, and school integration in Diboll, Nacogdoches, and Lufkin provide an important addition to the broader narrative of the civil rights movement and the importance of place in determining the trajectory of social movements. Moreover, the contradiction between collective memory, particularly a local white collective memory of a "smooth" integration process in Deep East Texas, and the individual stories of those who experienced it speaks to a determination among community leaders to simultaneously move on from segregation and to minimize any reflection on the damage done to the African American citizens before, during, and after integration.

Nacogdoches and Lufkin were some of the first sections of Texas to be settled by white Americans. Nacogdoches, which claims to be the "oldest town in Texas," was a major trade center from the early eighteenth century. Angelina County, where Diboll and Lufkin are located, split from Nacogdoches County in 1846. On the eve of the Civil War, Angelina County had 427 slaves out of a total population of 4,271.[5] In Nacogdoches County, slaves constituted roughly a quarter of the population and slightly more than half the taxable property in the county.[6] The two counties have continued to have substantial African American populations. With the growth of the lumber industry, Angelina County began to catch up to Nacogdoches in population; Lufkin, founded in 1882 as a railroad hub for the burgeoning industrial sector, continued to expand as an industrial leader.[7]

Diboll, a typical sawmill town, sprang from the vision of a Virginia businessman named Thomas Louis Latane Temple, commonly referred to as T. L. L. Temple. After failing at the lumber business in Arkansas, Temple created the Southern Pine Lumber Company in 1893.[8] As the mill began operation, the workers and their families formed an active community.

Diboll and towns like it were among those that the journalist George Creel referred to as the "feudal towns of Texas" in an article of that name for *Harper's Weekly* in 1915.[9] Men like Temple owned all the land in their towns and set the rules. Diboll did not incorporate until 1962; the Temple family owned not only the major source of employment in the town but also most of the houses and other property for more than half of the twentieth century. Following incorporation, the Temple family continued to have a great deal of influence in city governance; the first mayor, Clyde Thompson, was an executive of Southern Pine. It was generally understood that what the Temple family wanted would be what happened in Diboll. Throughout the 1970s and after, the Temple family's influence spread throughout the region and affected perceptions of civil rights and the memory of the movement in the region, further cementing the belief that everything had gone smoothly. Oral histories of people who lived through the period reveal some definite bumps in the "smooth" narrative.

Segregation in the Piney Woods

The Texas NAACP at midcentury described East Texas as "the meanest part of the state."[10] Racism was deeply entrenched in the region's towns and cities. Nacogdoches, Lufkin, and Diboll remained, and remain in the twenty-first century, geographically segregated along racial lines. Diboll's segregation was explicitly designed and enforced by the company, which owned the houses and buildings and set up the "quarters," as both whites and African Americans referred to the African American side of town, across the railroad tracks from the white employees' homes, which were closer to the sawmill and other production facilities.[11] Shops, stores, and other accommodations, including those within the mills and plants, were all strictly segregated along racial lines.

In Nacogdoches, segregation and the development of Black neighborhoods followed a slightly different pattern, owing to the city's longevity. After the Civil War, African Americans in Nacogdoches created a thriving community along Church Street, toward the back of the white commercial district in downtown. By the 1920s, the street boasted barbershops, cafés, a hotel, and two movie theaters. It was also prime real estate. The local newspaper, the *Daily Sentinel*, began calling for the removal of African American residents from northern Nacogdoches and relocating them to an area in a southeastern part of the city. The *Sentinel* argued that this "would keep the white and colored children from having to criss cross each others' trails as they go and return from school." It also facilitated the white takeover of Church Street in 1929. Nacogdoches whites forcibly removed African American residents and businesses from Church Street to the Orton Hill neighborhood, east of town.[12] There, African Americans rebuilt their extensive business neighborhood. In a group interview, the Nacogdoches residents Margie Chumbley, Anita Farr, Thelma Sexton, and Elizabeth Simpson recalled dozens of Black-owned businesses in Nacogdoches in the 1950s and 1960s.[13] One of the most prominent was Arthur Weaver's general store. Weaver used his relative independence as a store owner to lead Nacogdoches's NAACP chapter and to argue for the rights of African Americans, particularly within the criminal justice system. In addition to the businesses, an all-Black school, E. J. Campbell, lay at the heart of the community.[14]

Less is known about a similar removal of African Americans and rearrangement of African American and white neighborhoods that reportedly took place in Lufkin in 1930, probably in response to the better-documented removal in Nacogdoches.[15] Lufkin had a large and vibrant African American community. Herbert Cross moved to Lufkin in 1958 to teach at Dunbar High School after growing up in Mineral Wells,

Texas. On arriving in Lufkin, he was delighted at the size of the Black community: "I had never seen this many Black folks in one place in my life. I called home, and I told my mother and father, 'You've got to see this. I didn't know there was this many Blacks in the world anyway. And I have never seen this many Black people in my life. They're everywhere.'"[16] By the 1950s, African Americans in Lufkin had been mostly confined to the northern part of the city. Gloria Toran, the daughter of the principal of Diboll's all-Black school, remembered that in Lufkin, where she attended high school, segregation was strict: "The relationship between the Blacks and white in a town this size has not been that good. It was white over here and Black over there."[17]

Larry Kegler, who later became one of the first African Americans to integrate the Lufkin school system, grew up on Paul Street in North Lufkin. The area lacked basic city services into the late twentieth century. When Kegler was a child, in the 1950s, Paul Street did not have sewage; African Americans used outhouses and, later, septic systems, even though they lived within the city limits. The street was paved on the white side, and "right when it got to the Black neighborhood, it became dirt." He recalled of Paul Street: "[It] was like the Legend of Sleepy Hollow, the trees growing out on the road, and there were no curbing or anything like that.... But where the pavement started, you could see they were getting city services more than we were."[18]

African Americans in North Lufkin lacked postal service, unlike their white neighbors. Into the 1960s, they had to retrieve their mail from African Americans who worked for the post office. Betell Benham's father, who worked for the Lufkin post office during the 1950s and early 1960s, saved his earnings to fulfill another need in the community. When African American visitors came to Lufkin, they had few places to stay; most were housed by African American families. In response to that need, Benham's father built the Lewis Motel in the 1960s. The reaction from white Lufkinites was not positive, according to Benham: "He got death threats. People would call threatening his life, calling names and stuff." White Lufkin did not want a Black motel, but as Benham recalled, the motel thrived and catered to famous entertainers such as Ike and Tina Turner, who performed at Lufkin's all-Black, very popular Cotton Club.[19] The club, owned by Clementine and Berline Parker, attracted African American talent—B. B. King, Little Richard, Sam Brown, and others— from across the nation.[20]

According to Benham, many white Lufkinites objected to the presence of African Americans in general outside the boundaries of North Lufkin. To get home from school during the late 1950s, Benham and some other students had to cross Timberland Drive (US Business 59), an extremely busy and thriving part of white Lufkin. The owners of the businesses attempted to force Black children to walk behind the stores and not in front, where they could be seen by white customers. The principal at Dunbar at the time vocally opposed this treatment, and when the white business owners would not yield, parents began taking their children to school or finding alternatives rather than see their children disrespected in such a manner.[21]

When Benham's mother, Bettie Kennedy, was interviewed in 2001, she remembered that African Americans could go into downtown Lufkin only on certain days, with a few exceptions. For example, Kennedy's adopted father, Will Engram, was a builder of both white and African American homes.[22] Downtown Lufkin, when African Americans were allowed to do business there, was starkly segregated. Most

African Americans, when asked to remember segregation in Lufkin, vividly described the separate water fountains in Perry Brothers, a department store. Larry Kegler cited Perry Brothers' water fountains as the first time he really felt the impact of Jim Crow; he and other African Americans remembered trying to sneak sips out of the white fountain whenever the salesperson assigned to watch both the fountains and her sales area looked away.[23]

Downtown Lufkin was also the place where Lela Simmons stated that she first felt truly hurt by Jim Crow. Born in 1935, Simmons claimed that she largely ignored the impact of segregation, taking refuge within the African American community and with her family until she was an adult. Once she had her son, she began bringing him with her while she ran errands around town. They went to Trevathan's Drugstore, where her small son asked for a soda. Then, tired from a long day of shopping, he wanted to sit down to drink it. When Simmons explained that he couldn't because "that's not for you," it hurt his feelings. In that moment, Simmons recalled that she really "felt my blackness."[24]

The medical and hospital facilities in Lufkin and Nacogdoches, located near downtown in both cases, were segregated. In Nacogdoches into the 1960s, African Americans could use only the first floor of the hospital and had no privacy; many African American patients received their care in the hallways and never saw the inside of a room.[25] This was also true in Lufkin, where African American physicians were not allowed to treat their patients in the hospital until the early 1960s and had to rely on the two or three white doctors who were willing to care for African American patients.[26] Some doctors' offices in the area maintained segregated waiting rooms for several years after the passage of the Civil Rights Act of 1964. Anita Farr recalled an incident from the late 1960s:

> I took my daddy to a doctor in Nacogdoches, and he had a little chute for the Blacks, and then the Caucasians had a nice big waiting area. So I said, "Is this where you're going, Daddy?" and he said, "Yes, we have to sit on this side. . . ." And I said, "Oh, no, we can't do this." So I got my daddy and took him to another doctor. And when I got home, my mother said, "What did you do? Why didn't you let your daddy have his doctor's appointment?" I said, "Because we should not be sitting over there. We should sit in the waiting area with everyone else." So I got my dad another doctor, and he was fine.[27]

African Americans objected to the segregation in Deep East Texas through everyday forms of resistance, such as Farr refusing to accept segregation for her father and Kegler and others sneaking sips of water from the white water fountain in Perry Brothers, and via resistance inspired by what they saw in other parts of the nation. Farr and others recalled how African Americans in Nacogdoches and Lufkin had to sit in the balcony of the local movie theaters. "And the Caucasian kids would call us all kinds of 'birds in the balcony' and 'n-words in the balcony.' So when they'd do that, we decided we'd fill them up with ice, popcorn, so that before they left, they had wet hair, popcorn, everything."[28] Throwing ice and popcorn on white patrons showed a social, communal spirit of resistance, yet others chose to make spontaneous, individual stands. S'ydney Benemon remembered that a downtown café in Lufkin in the

1960s required African Americans to use the back door, but she and some junior high classmates decided to go in the front door. When the person at the counter shouted for them to leave, and knowing that the police would be called, the students left.[29]

This was not the only burst of individual protest by young African Americans in Lufkin. Frustrated teens expressed their anger at segregation by throwing rocks at white cars at the drive-in theater and at the police when they were called.[30] Some teenagers were perturbed by what they viewed as the apathy of older African Americans. In the early 1960s, Lela Simmons was having her hair cut and arranged by a friend when her friend's teenage son burst in the room: "He and a bunch of boys were going over to sit down, have a sit-down over there at Dairy Queen. And his mother was begging him not to do that, because she didn't want him to go to jail.... He was telling us, 'You all don't care. This is the time that you need to do something about this.' And of course they went up there, and of course they put them in jail."[31]

The teens were taken to jail, their parents were called, and no charges were filed. The experience, though, made an impact on Simmons: "These younger children got up and got something started that the older folk should have taken care of, you know, been involved in. But it took us awhile."[32] Over 150 of Dunbar's students, mostly seniors and some juniors, staged a protest at the Angelina County airport during 1968 when George Wallace flew in to campaign for the presidency.[33] A small fight broke out, and the protest was considered so controversial that Ralph Steen, a local college president, felt compelled to issue a statement: "NO students from Stephen F. Austin State College were in Lufkin to greet or picket Mr. Wallace. Careful studies have been made of pictures taken at the airport and all the students carrying signs have been identified as Lufkin senior and junior high school students. Stephen F. Austin State College is integrated, but has considerably fewer than 150 Negro students."[34]

Most of Lufkin's African Americans, though, did not openly stage protests and demonstrations. As Larry Kegler recalled, "When I grew up, it was the lifestyle. A lot of us didn't make any waves." That changed as the 1960s progressed. After passage of the Civil Rights Act of 1964, African Americans began pushing for more respect and recognition in Lufkin. Kegler described a notable change: "Places that you went to the back door ... now you could go in the front door. I don't know if people really understood how important that was." Teenagers in particular, like Kegler, were excited about asserting their rights: "I know we went bonkers [after passage of the Civil Rights Act]. We went in the front door, we ordered coffee, we walked out and left it, just because we were that arrogant, that type of thing. Some places, sometimes, especially in Lufkin, things went underground, though."[35]

Segregation in Lufkin had been maintained through rigid laws, traditions, and, as in the rest of the South, the ever-present threat of violence. Deep East Texas was the site of multiple incidents of racial violence; as Lela Simmons recalled, violence often happened "undercover."[36] Many whites, though, felt emboldened to attack African Americans, without provocation, in broad daylight. When Betell Benham was a child, she had an established path through the predominantly white part of town that took her past houses designated by her parents and others in the African American community as "friendly." If she happened by a house or people not in that category, she ran the risk of having them "sic dogs on us or throw rocks at us." She shared one particularly painful memory: "We were living in Lufkin Land [a community in northeastern Lufkin], walking on Paul Street to Chestnut. We had to cross Timberland Drive, and we would cross a path of whites on Paul. And I remember these families would chunk [rocks and other objects] at us."[37]

Benham also recalled the presence of the Klan in Lufkin.

My mother had some friends in the '30s who got in altercations. What would they do back then? They'd lynch you . . . I remember my mother's friends saying they had to leave. And they'd go to California, and they'd leave Lufkin. Plus, the Ku Klux Klan was very dominant back in that time. I remember them marching here in Lufkin and burning crosses . . . My mother took us to the home. I think it was the first Black officer—I'm not sure, because I was really young—just to see the remnants of the cross they had burned. It was still smoldering. But I remember seeing the Klan marching with their hoods.[38]

In fact, most people in Diboll blamed Lufkin whenever Klan members came into their town and marched through the African American section, claiming that Lufkin was a particularly strong place for recruitment and organization. The Temple family had taken a firm stand against any Klan presence in Diboll, and since Southern Pine was the chief employer, the threat of unemployment was enough for most, though not all, of white Diboll to stay out of the Klan. No such impediments existed in Lufkin or Nacogdoches.[39]

Lufkin was, as Howard Coleman stated, a "tough little old town." Interviewed in the 1990s, he recalled a particularly galling murder that took place in the 1940s in the Lufkin courthouse and lodged in the collective memory of the African American community.[40] On November 24, 1941, a seventy-year-old African American named Mott Flournoy was murdered by Roy Morehouse, a white man. Flournoy was standing trial for murdering Morehouse's wife, Lucille. In the courtroom, Morehouse grabbed Flournoy from behind and slashed his throat. Morehouse was charged with the murder of Flournoy (and quickly released after forty-four Lufkin citizens signed a $5,000 bond) and put on trial in March 1942. A day later, he was found not guilty by a jury that had deliberated for less than an hour.[41] Many African Americans in Lufkin believed that there was more to the story. The *Pittsburgh Courier* reported that there was doubt of Flournoy's guilt and that he was murdered in order to prevent his appearance on the witness stand, where he might provide "startling" testimony.[42] The African American community demanded a federal investigation into the case, but Morehouse lived out the rest of his life as a respected member of the white community, even after another (white) person later claimed to have been responsible for the murder.[43] For those who came of age in the 1950s and 1960s, the murder lingered as a warning and as an indictment of the area's criminal justice system.

Police Brutality and Criminal "Justice"

Though not an act of police brutality, the murder of Mott Flournoy was part of a broader system of warped criminal justice in Deep East Texas. Throughout the area, local and county law enforcement officials were part of the system that maintained segregation and created an oppressive environment for African American citizens. Notorious figures became well known for their propensity for violence; the inconsistent "enforcement" of rules and laws was used to maintain the traditional system. Police brutality, as in the rest of the nation, was one of the many aspects of the white power structure that African Americans demanded be changed.

In Diboll, before incorporation, Southern Pine hired people to maintain "order." For most of the preincorporation period, the person charged with this task was Jay Boren. Hired, in the eyes of the African American community, "to corral the Blacks," Boren, referred to as the "quarter boss," gained a reputation as a bully who placed himself above the law, in both the white and African American parts of Diboll, for most of the 1940s and 1950s.[44] White and African American residents feared Boren. He took particular pleasure in terrorizing those who lived in the quarters, most of whose residents were afraid to protest their mistreatment. As one African American resident, Cleveland Mark, remembered: "[Boren] had a license to kill you if he wanted to. Jay Boren could do what he wanted to, and nobody ever stopped him, nobody ever said anything to him."[45]

Boren thrived on intimidation. He rode a large white horse and wore a cowboy hat, like some Hollywood version of a sheriff in the Wild West. Rumors spread that he had been a Texas Ranger, but that was never proved. He often tried to pick fights, particularly with young African American men. Jim Ligon recalled that when he was young, Boren and his "deputies" would come to African American baseball games, "look us over," and "try to pick at them to make them do something." He beat up several people with little provocation and shot at least one person to death in Diboll.[46]

Finally, at the end of the 1950s, an African American resident who had been attacked by Boren and his deputies called the Federal Bureau of Investigation about Boren's behavior and the violence in Diboll. In all likelihood, the federal government contacted the Temple family, who did not want to have to deal with any embarrassing publicity and who had several friends in governmental positions, and the company fired Boren. His reign of terror in the quarters came to an end. A few years later, once Diboll incorporated, the town hired professional police officers instead of thugs like Boren.[47] Interestingly, whites in Diboll remembered Boren as heavy-handed, too, but they often cited him as an aberration in an otherwise peaceful community with good race relations. Arthur Temple Jr. justified Boren's zealousness by noting that crime stayed low during his tenure.[48]

Farther down Highway 59, Lufkin also had a law enforcement system tilted against African Americans. Lela Simmons recalled how African Americans, particularly men, would constantly get stopped while driving, without cause.[49] Police maintained the enforcement of physical segregation, discouraging African Americans from being in certain parts of town, particularly after dark. The police almost always sided with whites during a disagreement or conflict with an African American, even if the white person was clearly in the wrong, a typical pattern throughout the South.[50]

Nowhere in Deep East Texas, though, had a worse reputation for police brutality than Nacogdoches. Lufkin was "not as oppressive, at least in a violent kind of way, like they were in Nacogdoches."[51] The police department in Nacogdoches kept African Americans strictly in their place. Into the 1960s, African Americans had to have the lights off inside their homes after midnight. In the African American community in Nacogdoches, as Anita Farr remembered, "strange things happened." Most of those "strange things" happened at the hands of the local law enforcement, particularly people such as Constable Travis Helpinstill and Marion Charles (M. C.) Roebuck, the chief of police, who served on the force from the 1940s into the 1970s.

Helpinstill was responsible for one of the most infamous incidents between law enforcement and the African American community, one that lingered in the collective memory of those who lived in Nacogdoches in much the same way as the Flournoy murder did in Lufkin.[52] A war hero who had served with distinction on Saipan and Iwo Jima, Helpinstill was elected constable in 1946, the youngest one in Texas. Shortly after assuming office, he had the first of a series of run-ins with African Americans. On February 2, 1947, an African American preacher, Willie Lee Mergerson, ran from Helpinstill after the constable "accosted" him. Helpinstill caught up to Mergerson and beat him so severely that he needed a steel plate put in his head. Someone, probably Arthur Weaver, contacted the national NAACP about the attack, and Mergerson filed a civil suit against Helpinstill. Mergerson continued his lawsuit, even after receiving threats and intimidation from both Helpinstill and his father, J. B. Helpinstill. The suit was not successful, and the NAACP did not pursue the case because Mergerson was never officially arrested; nothing could happen unless "the wrongdoer is clothed with the authority of state law." Helpinstill, although wearing his uniform at the time, technically acted as a private citizen during the assault.[53]

Helpinstill continued his assaults on African American citizens, attacking an African American World War II veteran on March 8, 1948. Helpinstill and other law enforcement officers had reportedly been fixated on Turner White ever since he returned from the war. Helpinstill, Roebuck, and other law officers took White from his home late at night, beat him, and then arrested him for public intoxication. The following morning, Helpinstill released White and demanded that he leave town, which he and his wife and children did almost immediately.[54]

Four days later, Helpinstill stopped Ellis Hutson Jr. and his cousin, who were transporting a hog to market. During the questioning, Hutson did not address Helpinstill as "sir." Helpinstill then reportedly attacked Hutson, and Hutson hit him back. Helpinstill and some of his officers then forced Hutson into the car and beat him during the drive to the county jail. He was then assaulted at the jail by both Helpinstill and Roebuck, who threatened to kill him. Helpinstill tried to get Hutson to promise to plead guilty on assault charges and even tried to get Hutson to touch Helpinstill's gun, so that it would bear Hutson's prints. Hutson decided to contest the charges.[55]

Hutson's father, Ellis Hutson Sr., arrived at the courthouse the following morning to post bond for his son after conferring with a white lawyer, Arthur Lowery. Helpinstill arrived shortly afterward, upset at the news that Hutson Jr. was not going to plead guilty; he called Lowery and threatened to kill him for advising the Ellis family. Immediately following that conversation, Helpinstill ordered Hutson Sr. to follow him into a hallway. Moments later, Helpinstill yelled, "You tried to pull a knife on me!" He shot Hutson Sr. three times, killing him. A pocketknife was found by Hutson Sr.'s body after the shooting, but both the Hutson family and Lowery, who had seen Hutson Sr. that morning, swore the knife was not his and was not on him at the time of the confrontation.[56] Hutson Jr. was released, and he and Arthur

Weaver contacted the NAACP, which sent two investigators to Nacogdoches. Under pressure from the NAACP, authorities moved forward with prosecuting Helpinstill for murder. A grand jury indicted him on May 28, 1948, and he resigned as constable. It was the first time a first-degree murder indictment had gone through against a law enforcement official for killing an African American in Texas. The trial took place over three days in June. On June 9, 1948, after deliberating for less than two hours, the jury found Helpinstill not guilty. Edward R. Dudley, assistant special counsel for the NAACP, wrote to one of the investigators into the case: "We do feel, however, that although Helpinstill was not convicted, the mere fact that he was indicted by the Grand Jury and brought to trial is itself a step forward."[57]

For the African Americans of Nacogdoches, though, this was yet another example of law enforcement officials literally getting away with murder. Moreover, although Helpinstill no longer worked in law enforcement, Roebuck, who became chief of police in 1962, and many of the other officials and deputies who had participated in the violence alongside Helpinstill retained their jobs for decades after the murder of Hutson. Roebuck's reputation as a violent man who felt "disdain" for African Americans continued to grow during the 1950s and 1960s.[58] As Margie Chumbley recalled, "Everybody was afraid of Mr. Roebuck."[59] Into the 1950s, oversized suits, similar to the zoot suits of the 1940s, and big hats with feathers remained popular in the African American community, particularly for men planning to go to the Cotton Club in Lufkin. If Roebuck caught an African American man wearing that kind of suit, he would beat him and slice up the leg of the suit. Most men chose to put on their suits at the club or at the bus station in Lufkin, and to change clothes before returning to Nacogdoches.[60]

As the 1960s progressed, Roebuck was particularly concerned about the possibility of Black militancy in Nacogdoches. Stephen F. Austin, which integrated during the mid-1960s, had a growing population of African American students from other cities, along with a faculty and student body more liberal than the rest of the town. African American students began organizing on campus. In the late 1960s, they formed a chapter of the National Black Students Association and, following the 1968 assassination of Martin Luther King Jr., an organization called the King's Men, to address problems on campus and the common experience of African American students. The King's Men did not last very long, but they did organize a successful protest march on December 7, 1968, against a washateria that had maintained segregation; their action forced an extremely reluctant campus administration to go on record supporting their protest.[61] Most members of the King's Men joined the NBSA as it grew.

Although the NBSA was an officially recognized organization on campus, its members felt like second-class citizens. They lacked a designated place to hold their meetings and often had to hold gatherings outside. Students met with the architect of SFA's integration, President Ralph Steen. "We went to talk to Ralph Steen about it," remembered a former SFA student named Helena Abdullah. "He didn't change anything. I guess you could say the benevolent father was kind enough to listen to us, but there were no changes made." As the disparities persisted and more African American students began sharing accounts of discriminatory experiences in the classroom, students became angrier, as Abdullah noted: "When I saw the disparity between how the white kids were treated, and we couldn't even have a meeting room, that really got me to thinking and being upset."[62]

Members of the NBSA at Stephen F. Austin reached out to one of the national-level organizers, Mickey McGuire, to help them. McGuire came to Nacogdoches and spoke to the NBSA and in the classrooms of sympathetic white professors. SFA students and professors decided to stage a march in 1970, demanding better treatment of African American students. Helena Abdullah helped organize it: "We wanted a place to meet. We wanted better things for the students on campus, better treatment of the students on the campus, in the classroom. They used our athletes ... they were putting SFA on the map, but we weren't getting benefits of them using our guys." Organizers got permission from the city, and the march went off without any issues. A second march, larger than the first, attracting around two hundred people, focused more on concerns of the town and similarly had no problems.[63]

By the time of the marches in the spring of 1970, Roebuck had been notified that McGuire was in town. He contacted the FBI and received McGuire's criminal history, which mostly consisted of burglary charges when he was seventeen years old. Roebuck had a white SFA student keep tabs on McGuire and report on his speeches, as well as those who worked with him. After the student told Roebuck about one such speech, the chief of police reportedly stated that he "could put an end to the n---er situation by putting a 30–30 bullet between [McGuire's] eyes."[64] Roebuck was already on edge. African American residents had staged a successful boycott of downtown businesses, demanding that African Americans be employed in the places where they shopped. A few stores hired "token" people to work the cash registers, but most Blacks continued to work in menial positions. The boycott had proved successful by the end of 1969 after lasting for most of the year.[65]

The arrest of an African American SFA student sparked a series of protests and demonstrations, which were organized by McGuire. Cubie Dorsey was arrested on April 24, 1970, for forging a check, and she reportedly did not receive due process or access to a lawyer during her initial interrogation by the police. Weaver and McGuire attempted to see Dorsey but were prevented from talking to her. McGuire and others staged about fifteen small demonstrations to protest Dorsey's treatment. Police did not directly interfere in the demonstrations, but under Roebuck's orders, they took pictures of the protesters, which many felt was supposed to be intimidation.[66]

On May 4, 1970, the shooting at Kent State University occurred, resulting in the deaths of four students at the hands of the Ohio National Guard. Like many others across the nation, Roebuck feared that something similar might happen in Nacogdoches. On May 11, Helena Abdullah, Arthur Weaver, and others (although not McGuire, who was out of town), met to organize a candlelight march. On May 13, 250 protesters lined up to march from Orton Hill to downtown for what was meant to be both a reaction to Kent State and a march for "black and white brotherhood."[67] Roebuck issued orders to stop the demonstration. Detective Smith Parmer arrested McGuire, who had returned to town, at gunpoint; Roebuck blocked the path of the demonstrators, and his officers began attacking them with mace.[68] As Abdullah described the events, some of the younger "hotheads" began to throw rocks and attempted to set fire to a business owned by a prominent racist. The protesters retreated to Orton Hill.

Youth-led protest march in Nacogdoches, 1970. Photo courtesy of the East Texas Research Center, Stephen F. Austin State University, Nacogdoches.

Marchers at a protest march in Nacogdoches, 1970. Photo courtesy of the East Texas Research Center, Stephen F. Austin State University, Nacogdoches.

When Helena Abdullah's mother left for work the next day, protesters were hard at work in her house planning a follow-up march. Abdullah's mother came back home and said, "You guys cannot march, because there were people down there on top of the buildings with rifles, shotguns, and all kinds of guns. They are waiting for you guys to come through." They decided to abandon the march under the threat of violence from their white neighbors.[69] McGuire stayed in jail for about a week but was never brought to trial for any of the offenses he was charged with by Roebuck. He left Nacogdoches a few months later, although he did bring a suit against Roebuck for unwarranted arrest.[70] The case went before William Wayne Justice, who ruled that the arrest of McGuire was nothing more than an attempt "to intimidate, threaten and coerce other blacks from exercising their constitutional rights to free speech and assembly."[71]

Helena Abdullah felt that Roebuck did receive, in a way, punishment for his mistreatment of the African American community. Her mother was a nurse at Memorial Hospital and recounted to her daughter: "Roebuck had a son, and he was about sixteen years old [and] seriously ill in the hospital. He ended up dying in the hospital, and his wife lambasted him [Roebuck] because, she said, "It's all your fault. All these Black people you have hurt and beat up and done other things to is manifested in our son. That's why he's dead." Mother said she was surprised that she would even mention that, because she said it in front of the nurses."[72]

Although there were no more marches or major demonstrations against the oppression in Nacogdoches after Mickey McGuire left, the successful lawsuit and the resistance of African Americans showed that they would tolerate harassment much less than they had in the past.

Integrating the Public Schools

On August 31, 1970, the police in Lufkin were out in full force at Lufkin High School, along with county law enforcement officers. They were not there to harass African Americans. As S'ydney Benemon remembered, "The police department was there to keep the peace," although given the history of police brutality in Deep East Texas, African American students regarded the officers warily.[73] A mob of armed white parents had arrived on the first day of integration. The new African American vice principal, Herbert Cross, had walked through the armed crowd into the high school, where he and the principal debated what to do.[74] Cross remembered the buses taking the African American students home, but Benemon, one of the students on the bus, stated that, although the police were telling students to go in the building, the students decided to walk home while singing "We Shall Overcome." As they walked through Lufkin, they "started picking up a crowd, and we ended up at Jones Park, and still was singing the old Negro hymns that we were taught in our early childhood."[75] Integration was not off to a promising start.

The incident at Lufkin High School came in the middle of a much longer story that included years of separate education, protracted resistance before the federal government took action, and persistent problems following the beginning of integration. The schools in Lufkin and Nacogdoches, which also integrated in 1970 but without an armed mob, were some of the last in the nation to integrate. Students in Deep East Texas in cities such as Diboll—which integrated in 1968—Lufkin, and Nacogdoches had great pride in their community schools, particularly the high schools: H. G. Temple, Dunbar, and E. J. Campbell. They all remembered excellent teachers and administrators who went above and beyond for their students in spite of a lack of resources.[76] In addition to striving to provide a high-quality education for their students, and some of the same experiences as white students enjoyed, teachers and coaches at Dunbar frequently had to make do without extra or equitable pay. African American teachers in Lufkin who drove school buses for extracurricular activities were not compensated, but white teachers who did the same received extra pay. Similarly, African American teachers who volunteered to work during football or basketball games did not receive any recompense; white teachers did. Individual teachers who complained to the superintendent could receive some money, but most of them did not press the issue.[77]

Before integration, schools like Dunbar endured hand-me-downs from white schools and a lack of attention from school district administrators. Every former Dunbar teacher and student vividly remembered being assigned used textbooks and used supplies; Larry Kegler noticed that the biggest difference between Dunbar and Lufkin High was that when he began attending Lufkin, "it was one of the first times that I saw books that didn't have fifteen names in it."[78] White administrators resisted providing any kind of resources to the African American schools; Emma Jones Callager remembered the white superintendent telling her in the 1950s, "I'm sorry, but you [African Americans] just cannot learn science."[79] Into the 1960s, Dunbar had only a biology course, because it lacked the equipment for a chemistry class.[80] Some teachers at Dunbar discovered ways of obtaining the tools that their students needed. Herbert Cross came to Dunbar in 1958 as a business teacher and became frustrated at receiving secondhand typewriters from the white school. The owner of the local typewriter company, a white man named Dexter Satterwhite, and Cross created a plan to get new typewriters for Dunbar. Cross asked Satterwhite to come and service the typewriters throughout the year at a very high rate and service charge. The superintendent called Cross and complained about the astronomically high repair bill the district had received from Satterwhite. Cross explained that with thirty-two students, he needed thirty-two functioning typewriters. Upon his return from summer vacation, Cross had thirty-two new typewriters waiting for him. It was the first time in the history of Dunbar that the school had received brand-new equipment, and it had taken a year of maneuvering and a massive drain on the district's resources to get it. For years, the school district preferred to pay for repairs rather than purchase new items for Black students.[81]

Diboll and Nacogdoches had a similar pattern of segregated schools with similarly underfunded and underdeveloped institutions. They were also extremely proud of their sports programs. Athletics were the beginning point for integrating schools in Diboll. Arthur Temple, the head of the Temple holdings by the 1960s, saw the writing on the wall regarding integration. He placed indirect pressure on the school board to begin moving slowly, and in 1965, Diboll began a program called freedom of choice—students could choose to go to either the white schools or the Black schools. White parents and their children had no interest in going to the Black schools, for reasons that included, in most cases, outright racism as well as the reality that the Black schools were short of resources; and only one African American child chose to attend the white schools that year. If freedom of choice was going to work, more African American students were going to have to be compelled to attend white schools. Making white students go to the Black schools was never part of the conversation. In August 1966, the school board voted to end the athletics program at H. G. Temple after several coaches resigned, fearing that if integration came, they would lose their jobs. Senior boys, not wanting to lose out on sports in their final year of school, integrated the high school and the football team in the 1966–1967 school year. The rest of the high school integrated in 1967–1968, and the entire school system integrated in 1968–1969.

The general portrayal of Diboll's integration is that it went very smoothly, particularly because Temple wanted it to. He had thrown his support behind integration, and those who balked ran the risk of losing their jobs. He gave speeches in support of integration, calling upon, in a presentation to the African American community, a sense of coming together and acknowledging the concerns of Black parents.[82] This was indicative of a broader tendency in Diboll to paint the Temple family in the best light possible, even years after the family ceased to direct the local economy, and overstated their ability to control race relations. The first year of integration at Diboll was tense. Laverne Joshua stated, "The first day [in 1967] we had to go to campus, all the white kids were standing outside the front door jeering" and hurling racial epithets. Clay Joshua, her brother, remembered that the next school year, in 1968, when there was full integration of all the schools, someone had put chains on the door of the junior high, which students broke through while administrators stood by and watched. The siblings recounted multiple stories of fights and a general feeling of tension throughout the first two years of integration.[83] They and other students, teachers, and administrators, though, acknowledged that once the first few years passed, the tension and violence decreased.[84]

Nacogdoches's school system required court intervention. In the fall of 1969, the Supreme Court ordered, in *Alexander v. Holmes County Board of Education*, the desegregation of all remaining segregated school districts, which included Lufkin and Nacogdoches. Like Diboll, both Lufkin and Nacogdoches had freedom-of-choice plans, which, predictably, saw few takers. In 1970, the US Department of Health, Education and Welfare announced that it would end funding for school districts that were dragging their feet on integration. To the shock and dismay of the African American community, the Nacogdoches school board shut down E. J. Campbell School. Diboll and Lufkin had retained the buildings that once housed the formerly all-Black schools, and merged them into the integrated systems, but Nacogdoches did not, causing a deep blow to the African American community that became a long-standing grievance. In the 1990s, alumni were able to purchase the building they loved.[85] Otherwise, integration in Nacogdoches followed a pattern similar to the one seen in Diboll: tension and fights between white and African American teens in the first year, but fewer incidents in the following years. White resistance, where it existed, was small-scale and rarely made waves.

The integration of the local college provided an example. Although the town was still recovering from the riots and confrontations from earlier that year, issues that caused a decades-long rift between the university and the community, the integration of Stephen F. Austin State University had, under the guidance of Ralph Steen, occurred with few incidents, albeit slowly. Steen wanted to expand SFA, and he needed federal funds to do it. Continued segregation or racial conflict threatened that plan.[86]

But as Stacy Cooke, a resident of Diboll, observed, "Lufkin, for whatever reason, you know, resisted."[87] Like Diboll and Nacogdoches, Lufkin experimented with freedom of choice in order to try to stave off court-ordered integration. At the high school, six students participated in freedom of choice in 1966. Larry Kegler's father decided that he would be one of those students. "I spent the whole summer trying to talk him out of it. I'm a junior," Kegler recalled. "This is the time when all the good stuff happens. . . . This was going to be my glory years, and I had to go to Lufkin High School in 1966."[88] In general, despite being the only African American student in almost all his classes, Kegler did not have as many negative experiences as those who came later, mainly for one reason: "Everybody wanted freedom of choice to work; therefore, people made an effort not to rattle the bushes or not to make a big—. Because after integration, Lufkin experienced some difficulties and some serious things happened, but when I went to school over there—there weren't but six of us—and everybody wanted that to work. A lot of the teachers went out of their way to make it work."[89]

Kegler dealt with run-ins with white students by ignoring them or by making light of racist comments that were not aimed at him. One example among many: while he was on the bus with his white football teammates—Kegler was the only African American player—a white student described a part of Texarkana they were passing through as the "n---er quarter." Overwhelmingly outnumbered by his white teammates, Kegler decided to act as if he had not heard the comment.[90]

Betell Benham also went to the white school during freedom of choice, although her experience at the junior high emphasized the pitfalls of the program.

> I decided to go to the white school. My mother said it was OK because we were leaning toward integration. But when I look back on it at this time in my life, I wouldn't have done it. It was such a lonely time in my life. Going to the white junior high school—it was only . . . probably not even ten Blacks in the whole school. And I was usually the only Black in my classes. . . . Nobody wanted to talk to me. I remember going to lunch . . . and I had one Black friend who didn't always have lunch money . . . Sometimes she wouldn't even eat lunch, because people were so mean, and I'd say, "No, please!" because I didn't want to sit by myself at lunch.[91]

The loneliness came from being almost completely ignored by white students and from physical attacks in her PE class. When she was looking the other way, someone, or possibly multiple people, would deliberately hit her in the head with a basketball.[92]

Although white administrators and teachers wanted freedom of choice to work, Lufkin, like Nacogdoches, could not continue its traditional practices. Unlike Nacogdoches, though, Lufkin stalled when the federal government threatened to take over the schools. Into the summer of 1970, Lufkin refused to comply with orders, issued by HEW and enforced by a local federal court, to integrate, instead choosing to continue to submit slightly modified versions of freedom of choice. In August, the school board frantically tried to come up with a plan to satisfy the courts, realizing, perhaps after Nacogdoches got a plan approved by HEW in early August that embraced full integration, that the district was going to have to abandon freedom of choice. On August 17, the new plan was submitted, and HEW approved it. All students would attend Lufkin High School, Dunbar would be used as a junior high for both white and African American students, and elementary students would be divided by a racial ratio. As the *Lufkin Daily News* reported, "few liked it, but even fewer appeared willing to trade it for what appeared to be the alternative" namely, a complete takeover of the schools by the courts.[93] Lufkin schools would remain under the court order and watched by both state and federal agencies to ensure compliance for decades.

Schools opened as planned on August 31, 1970, and white parents came armed and prepared for a confrontation. The Klan staged a march through downtown Lufkin in preparation for the process and as a sign of white resistance.[94] Given the sheer number of white parents who showed up on the first day of school, local businesses either supported the open revolt against integration and let their employees take off from work, or they forgave them after the fact. But in contrast to what happened in Diboll, no one feared being fired from their job for participating in an armed protest and aggression against African American students. Wherever the students went who were not allowed to disembark, whether to home, as Herbert Cross stated, or on a march, as S'ydney Benemon remembered, administrators knew they could not allow the same thing to happen again on the following day. Cross and the other administrators made their plans. They called a meeting of the district administration, representatives of the Justice Department, and the FBI. The federal government declared that if the mob came the next day, everyone would be arrested. No one came the next day. Cross believed that someone in the meeting warned local whites of the probability of arrest. After the second day, Cross and his fellow administrators breathed a sigh of relief: "Well, that's one obstacle we're over."[95]

But it was only the beginning of the problems besetting the integration of Lufkin schools. The first year of integration at Lufkin High School was, according to one member of the faculty, "plumb chaos." The first years of integration saw numerous physical altercations. Cross remembered that the violence was provoked by both white and African American students, depending on numbers: "If a Black went in the restroom and there were two whites, they'd beat up the Black, and vice versa."[96] Betell Benham described the first year as "pretty rough," particularly on the buses, where there was limited supervision:

> I remember one time there was a real bad fight. The [white] students would put rocks in the paper and chunk at us. Can you imagine that? It wasn't a paper fight; it started as a paper fight, but then they were sneaky. They would put the rocks in the paper and hit us with them, the white students ... It was a real bad fight, and I wasn't real good at fighting. And I remember my cousin—her name was Cynthia—she said, "Betell, get back. I'll protect you. I'll fight." So she got to tearing 'em up. It was rough ... and I think that was the last time we rode the bus.[97]

Administrators hoped that the physical assaults could be reduced by removing a few bad apples. Lufkin's school board zeroed in during the first year on a dozen students, half of them Black, half white, who were at the center of the fighting, and expelled them.[98] The fighting continued, though, and other issues further stoked tensions. The merging of extracurricular activities was particularly difficult. During the first year, the administration decided to have two positions of leadership within student council: two presidents, two secretaries, and two of every other office, one held by a white student and the other by a Black one. Other organizations decided that Dunbar's elections for club leaders and extracurricular positions from the previous year would be invalidated, and only those from Lufkin High would count.[99] African American students resented the loss of Dunbar's identity and the idea that they were now expected to be subsumed in Lufkin's. Herbert Cross had to step in:

> And another problem that we had was that the Blacks wouldn't stand up for the school song. We had pep rallies every Friday during first period. Now, you don't even have to come to the pep rally; you can stay at home for first period. But all the Blacks would come and then they would just sit. Wouldn't stand up for some school song ... So the next pep rally, I just went up in the stands, and everybody was sitting down, and I said,

"Hit the door." And I pulled them all out. It was kind of embarrassing that they had to leave. [Cross told them] "You don't have to come to the pep rally, but if you show up, you're standing up for the school song." They were all standing the next pep rallies.[100]

The integration of sports teams proved very difficult. Dunbar High had put the town of Lufkin on the map through its superior athletics program, which had won the state championship shortly before integration. Integrating the two schools' football teams proved much tougher than it had in Diboll or Nacogdoches. Larry Kegler, who had graduated from Lufkin High by 1970, was the only Black player on Lufkin's team for several years. Reflecting on integrating the football team, he noted the improbability of white Lufkin High adopting Black Dunbar's all-stars wholesale: "Trying to put Dunbar's hall-of-fame football team with Lufkin High's football team, that never won anything, was going to be tough. And it was. Because the all-district, all-state players that Dunbar had—and you couldn't take [white] Mr. So-and-So's son out of his starting position . . . it was hard. In my belief, that was the hardest part."[101]

Herbert Cross remembered that when the white coach at Lufkin High demanded that the new Black arrivals play by his system, many of the Black students decided not to play football. The few who did play refused to talk to the white coach and ignored him when he spoke. They communicated only with the African American assistant coach.[102] Many of the former Dunbar athletes felt as though their head coach, Elmer Redd, who had led them to victory, had been forced out by integration, and some of their coaches, such as Betell Benham's stepfather, had been fired as a consequence of integration. Gloria Toran, the first African American counselor in the Lufkin schools, remarked that as a result of the tension and fighting in the football program, "they had to have the law out nearly every day."[103]

Because of Dunbar's superior reputation at sports, the football team's integration story prominently figures in the collective memory of Lufkin's integration, but for African American students, the problems with integration went beyond sports. According to Toran, the problems coalesced around sports, but the African American students were, in general, deeply hurt by the hurried integration process: "So the next year I went as high school counselor. And Black kids? They were just falling apart. I mean it was just so stressful for them, because they were losing their identity, as far as they were concerned. There was a few of them and a whole lot of the other folk. And there were organizations and clubs and things that they were not a part of. It's almost like, 'I don't belong here' . . . Here were students who physically would pass out. They felt that devalued from the integration process."[104]

A Stormy, Stony Road

Integration at Lufkin High School did not go "as smooth as possible," but over time, tensions eased. As S'ydney Benemon remarked, "They had to adapt to us, and we had to adapt to them. We started out rough, but we ended up on the right track. It was a stormy, stony road at first." Phrasing it more bluntly, "They [whites] realized that there was a court order from the federal government, and we weren't going anywhere, and we had to go where they were."[105] For those who experienced integration in Lufkin, some things changed and others stayed very much the same. Larry Kegler went on to serve as one of the first Black city councilmen and, finally, brought city services to his old part of Paul Street. He then served on the school board.[106]

He did not want to leave the city council when he did. He was one of three African Americans serving on the council in the 1980s, and then the city redistricted. Under the new plan, the African American part of town went from three wards to two wards. In Kegler's and others' opinion, this was a concerted effort to reduce African American representation in Lufkin. North Lufkin continues to fight for economic investment and development.[107]

Herbert Cross, the vice principal of Lufkin High during the integration process, continued to work for the school district. He was promoted to principal of a new elementary school, Brookhollow, where he retired in the 1990s. He faced what today would be called "microaggressions" upon his retirement. Instead of receiving the kind of retirement gift that other principals had received (the previous principal got a three-piece luggage set), Cross was given a wooden duck. Cross does not hunt and does not have any affinity for ducks. It was not an inside joke. He has no idea what the duck means, but he keeps it on his coffee table as a reminder of how people can treat others. Something even more demeaning happened several years later:

> They called me and said, "Would you come out and do a little speech and help us celebrate the twenty-fifth anniversary [of Brookhollow]?" So I did; I went out there. And then some more retired teachers, asked them all to come ... After it was all over, they said, "Let's take a picture for the paper." So we took a picture. I had two white women on this side and two white women on this side ... So I said my good-byes and I came on home. The next day, I got the paper ... and I read in there that Brookhollow had its anniversary and these are the people who retired who visited who helped them celebrate. And it was just four white women standing there in the picture. Now can you believe that? This day and time. I'm nowhere in the picture. Four white women standing there, and they listed their names. And I'm not in the picture.[108]

"Not in the picture" is something African Americans continue to organize and fight against in Lufkin, through organizations such as Impact Lufkin. It strives to bring economic opportunity to North Lufkin, which is currently suffering from a loss of most of the major industries and employers, and a growing poverty rate. An African American woman currently serves as the school superintendent, and Lufkin did not suffer the kind of disinvestment in public schools, through the creation of private "academies," that other cities in the South experienced in reaction to integration. Everyone contacted for the Civil Rights in Black and Brown Project, though, acknowledges that Lufkin still has far to go. Cross is not optimistic about Lufkin's willingness to change. Reflecting on the city, he remarked, "This community. We are integrated, but we are not integrated. It's something else. They're just a lot of die-hard people, and they're never going to integrate nothing."[109]

CHAPTER 3

"SOMETHING WAS LOST":

Segregation, Integration, and Black Memory in the Golden Triangle

ELADIO BOBADILLA

[We] get tied into the world as it is now, but you have to know the beginning to get to the end.
WANDA THOMPSON

Over half a century after the Black civil rights movement began, the historiography of the movement in its various forms stands on well-trodden ground. And yet many histories remain undiscovered or untold. In fact, the vast literature of the civil rights era has taught practitioners and students of history what those who lived through the era already know, perhaps too well and too intimately: that the struggles, victories, and experiences of the era varied greatly from place to place, from time to time, and from group to group—and that the struggle for justice has been an ongoing one and hardly a closed chapter. It is probably fair to say that no two people experienced the humiliation of segregation, the pain of discrimination, or the frustrating process of integration in the same way.

Civil rights history has stubbornly refused to be told as a single narrative. Recent histories of the movement, for example, have taken a longer view, seeing it as much broader, more intersectional, and longer lasting than previously acknowledged.[1] Some histories have focused on the unique experiences of women,[2] and others have tried to restore to their rightful place the economic demands that were central—but, at least until recently, largely ignored—components of civil rights struggles.[3] And others have insisted that while civil rights leaders were committed to nonviolence, it was not the only tactic or ideology used during the struggle, since Black groups and individuals routinely emphasized militant, often armed, community and personal self-defense.[4]

It is with caution, therefore, that this chapter aims to look at the civil rights era through the unique lens of East Texas—specifically, the region known as the Golden Triangle, named for the once-abundant reserves of "black gold" that made it, for a time, a prosperous region, at least for some. The area is anchored by three cities: Beaumont, Port Arthur, and Orange.[5]

I argue, based on conversations with a number of people who lived through the civil rights struggle in the region, that segregation in the Golden Triangle was a diverse experience, one that required a number of strategies for survival and advancement, and that those who lived through the transition to nominal integration, despite rejoicing at the dismantling of segregation and hailing the prospect for a new age of Black emancipation and freedom, nevertheless felt in retrospect that "something was lost" in the process. This argument is based on some two dozen oral history interviews with women and men who lived through segregation, experienced discrimination, survived in separation and neglect in the post–World War II years, and who, in one way or another, can speak to the struggle for equality in East Texas and the nation.

While oral history is an imprecise method, it is extremely useful to historians who have the luxury of working on relatively recent history, and who have the privilege of being able to speak with people about their life histories, to hear stories about events that shaped them and the emotions that defined them, all of which might otherwise be lost to a historical record that until relatively recently had hardly prioritized non-elite voices, especially the historically marginalized.[6]

A note of caution is in order any time one embarks on a study such as this one. Oral historians know that memories and oral histories are subjective and imperfect and therefore cannot be relied on to provide objectively correct, purely factual data. And yet they also know that memory is always a story unto itself, always a historical artifact of sorts, with tremendous interpretative, though not always empirical, value. Even when women and men remember past events incorrectly, a historian has the responsibility to interrogate the why of the matter: Why do people remember things a certain way? Who creates collective memory and how is that memory shaped? How do historical traumas shape the way that individuals and communities remember, interpret, and understand their lives and their pasts?

With the limits of memory and these questions in mind, I nevertheless found it remarkable to hear, again and again, as the title of this chapter suggests, that "something was lost" as the rigid laws and norms of segregation broke down and the process of integration began and took its limited, messy course. That exact phrase, "something was lost," was the first of many surprising and thought-provoking pronouncements I encountered while conducting oral history research in the Golden Triangle, even before I had set up the camera for the first interview. This paper asks, then, why so many residents of the area feel that something was lost—what exactly was lost during integration, in the minds of those who recounted a version of this perspective?—and attempts to interpret the significance and meaning of this loss, particularly within the larger story of civil rights in the Golden Triangle.

Background

Today, the Golden Triangle region is a ghost of its former self. No longer the glitzy capital of entertainment it once was, deindustrialization, white flight, and neglect have transformed an area once known to many as "Little New York" into a poor, struggling place where prisons and environmental threats have replaced the glitz and glamour that once adorned it.[7] To a visitor, the crude joke that Billy F. Gibbons, a member of the popular Texas rock band ZZ Top, once made about his home, might make a degree of sense. He once said that the region was called the Golden Triangle "because it sounds much more romantic than 'Petro-Chemical Wasteland.'"[8] During and immediately after World War II, however, the Golden Triangle lived up to its name. On any given night, local clubs might have been headlined by Ray Charles, Joe Turner, T-Bone Walker, Johnny Ace, Clyde McPhatter, and a host of other big names, who performed under the bright lights of segregated but charming venues in a bustling region.[9]

In the Shadow of the Riot

Beneath the golden veneer of the region's most celebrated period, when it "oiled the world," as the biographer of Janis Joplin, another of the region's most celebrated natives, put it, lay a more sinister reality: racial segregation was rigid and discrimination rampant. Texas, like most of the South and much of the country, was a place where Black and white bodies inhabited and inherited vastly different worlds.[10] But separation could never be absolute in a region so critical to the war effort. The oil that lubricated the American war machine brought immense wealth to the region, although not everyone benefited equally. And the very economic surge that made the Golden Triangle trendy and cosmopolitan also created problems. Public officials began to worry a great deal, from the beginning of the boom period at the turn of the twentieth century, about the party culture that oil money carried with it. Gambling and prostitution, in particular, occupied and troubled the minds of public officials.

There were other, bigger problems to come. Increasing racial tension bubbled under the surface of the area's golden appearance. Racial animosity, suspicion, and mistrust were not uncommon, of course, in any segregated society. But rapid growth, combined with efforts to maintain strict segregation, at times proved explosive. One such social explosion, and perhaps the most memorable episode of racial violence and animosity in East Texas to date, was the Beaumont Race Riot of 1943, when, on June 15 and 16, 1943, white and Black residents clashed after a white woman accused a Black man of raping her. The troubles began on the evening of June 15, when rumors of the accusation reached white workers at the Pennsylvania Shipyard, on the banks of the Neches River.[11] By nightfall, more than two thousand angry workers and some additional one thousand bystanders who had joined the workers along the way had reached the city jail, where the alleged rapist was being held. Armed and angry, whites marched through town, beating up Black residents on sight and indiscriminately setting fire to Black homes, destroying Black businesses, and otherwise spreading terror into frightened, confused Black neighborhoods.

Mayor George Gary responded by asking the Texas National Guard for support. Acting governor A. M. Aiken Jr., who was in charge that evening while Governor Coke Stevenson was en route to Washington, granted the request immediately, and also declared martial law in the city. By the time the riot was squelched, two people, one Black and one white, had lost their lives and at least sixty Black residents had been hospitalized, including some who had been shot. In addition, some one hundred Black homes had been ransacked or destroyed. (And although often forgotten, another Black Beaumont resident died months later of injuries sustained during the riot.)[12] Two hundred rioters were arrested, and all except twelve were acquitted of all charges. Most of the rest were turned over to city authorities.[13] An esti-

CHAMBER OF COMMERCE ESTIMATES THE POPULATION AT 58,746

THE BUSIEST CORNER

IN A VERY BUSY CITY

SABINE HOTEL — PROCTER AT WACO STREET — PORT ARTHUR, TEXAS

Postcard of downtown Port Arthur, 1948. Source: Website of Thomas Jefferson High School, Port Arthur, Class of 1962.

mated two thousand Black residents fled Beaumont, panicked and scared—some, as James Burran wrote, with no plans to ever return.[14] Officials slowly but gradually reclaimed order, but the region has remembered this painful episode as an instance of how racial animosity, forced separation, and economic change could prove to be a deadly cocktail.

The Beaumont Race Riot, historians and those who lived through it have claimed, was the result of overlapping factors that together created the perfect conditions for a deadly racial storm. As an area considered a critical part of the "arsenal of democracy," Beaumont and the surrounding region had attracted thousands of people to its roaring wartime industry. In 1940, the city was composed of fewer than 60,000 residents, 32 percent Black, the rest white. By 1943, the city had grown to some 80,000 people, with the racial composition remaining about the same. Shipyards, according to Burran, employed over 8,000 men, and government contracts totaled $100 million, a massive sum highlighting the region's importance to the war effort and the wartime economy. Oil refineries accounted for a great deal of the economic activity.

In the years leading up to the riot, Black and white people "just stayed to themselves," as May Guillory, a lifelong Beaumont resident remembered.[15] But as consumer goods became increasingly scarce, transportation unavailable, and overcrowding a visible, tangible problem, tensions grew quickly and enormously.[16] The final ingredient in this combustible cocktail, the match that lit a seemingly inevitable fire, was the rumor that a Black man—a draft dodger, no less—had raped a white woman.

The race riot was a reminder that national policy had profound local consequences. Still, local laws, customs, and relationships made each local case particular and unique. As in the rest of the country, many white residents in East Texas resented

A mostly vacant downtown Port Arthur, 2016. Photo courtesy CRBB.

Workers at Beaumont's Pennsylvania shipyard in June 1943, the same month as the city's deadly race riot. Photo courtesy of the Library of Congress.

the gradual progress that Black citizens were making. And wartime requirements necessitated more contact than had previously been allowed, which had the potential to build solidarity or create further animosity and resentment. Accusations such as the one that provoked the riot—which, in the end, appeared to be unfounded—ensured that confrontation, rather than solidarity, would prevail. As numerous historians of the South have noted, false rape accusations were one of the most powerful—and common—ways to incite violence against Black men and Black communities, and there is a long, tragic tradition of portraying Black men as violent sexual predators as a tactic for instilling fear and stoking white rage. It worked remarkably well to undermine peace, even if it did not entirely preclude the potential for unity, or at least better interracial relations.[17] As Marilynn S. Johnson has shown, "the spectre of the black rapist" loomed large well into the twentieth century.[18]

"Everyone Knew the Boundaries"

For decades after the riot, it remained a bitter memory for those who lived through it. The reality of segregation, however, and the daily indignities of life under Jim Crow in Texas continued for decades. The war had required a degree of contact between white and Black communities, and had even opened the possibility that wartime changes might inch the region toward integration. But the postwar period saw a return to a hardened state of segregation, to the old "normal," in which Black and white people lived in distinctly different worlds from the moment they were born until their bodies were laid to rest. Mabel Briggs, who made history when she became part of the first integrated nursing class at the well-regarded Hotel Dieu School of Nursing in Beaumont in 1966, remembered vividly the days when everything in Beaumont was "segregated completely."[19] Similarly, Richard Price, a decorated Korean War veteran, mathematics professor at Beaumont's Lamar University, and local civil rights leader, remembered the rare occasions on which he, in the company of his father, would venture into the white areas of town, where they were met with "whites only" signs.[20] In this regard, the experience of Black men and women living in the Triangle region was remarkably similar to that of members of other Black communities across the Jim Crow South.

Boundaries were everywhere. Sometimes they were physical, material, and visible, and at other times symbolic, unspoken, and unseen, but they were always felt and always deeply scarring and emotionally and psychologically consequential. These boundaries were always understood, even when they were not talked about. Price described memories of those boundaries vividly and with remarkable precision. The Black part of town, he explained, was located in the north part of the city, bounded by Washington Boulevard on the west side, by Cardinal Drive on the south, and by the railroad tracks on the east. The boundaries were seldom crossed, except with explicit permission from whites, or by Black workers employed by white families or individuals. Price recalled that everyone "knew the boundaries" from an early age: "Most of our doings were [limited] by those boundaries."[21]

In much the same way, Port Arthur, twenty miles southeast of Beaumont, near Sabine Lake, had strict but unofficially delineated boundaries. The west side of town, where oil refineries and chemical plants dotted the landscape, and where resources were limited, housed African Americans, and the rest of the city was reserved for whites.[22] "There was only one ethnicity on the west side of the railroad tracks," recalled the Port Arthur native and accomplished artist Harvey Johnson, "and that was to segregate us from white kids."[23] As in Beaumont, Black residents from an early age knew, in the words of Hilton Kelley, who grew up in Port Arthur, "where [the boundaries] were, where we could go, and where not to go."[24] At times, keeping within these boundaries could prove to be a matter of life and death. Kelley, a civil and environmental rights activist, recalled a tragic example. A pregnant woman who was headed to St. Mary's Hospital to give birth found herself caught on the west side of the tracks as a long train crossed town. Because she could not get to the hospital, "this woman lost her child."[25] Such incidents are a common theme in the memories of Golden Triangle residents, who spoke of them with sadness and, at times, palpable indignity and anger.

In the city of Orange, too, Black and white residents lived separate lives and generally avoided contact. Orange prided itself on having a history of relatively peaceful, even if not entirely cordial, race relations. The city did not have a significant history of violence. As one author put it, there were "no riots, no killings, no cross burnings" for most of the town's history.[26] But the possibility always loomed large, as when a white-supremacist group burned a cross in a Black part of town in the 1950s, threatening to ignite a "contagion of violence" similar to the kind that had plagued other regions of the South.[27] No serious conflict materialized, likely due in part to the smaller size of the town and the adherence of Black and white communities to strict separation.

As those who grew up in segregated Beaumont, Port Arthur, and Orange remembered, knowledge of racial boundaries became instinctual and second nature from an early age. Some people, especially the young and adventurous, did occasionally dare to cross boundaries, sometimes out of curiosity, sometimes for the youthful rush of transgressing. In some cases, people violated the boundaries for political reasons, as statements of defiance, though this was exceedingly rare and could prove extremely dangerous.

At other times, Black people could and did "pass" for white and had little trouble infiltrating white spaces such as candy shops and movie theaters. Briggs, for example, had such light skin, as she told it, that if she wanted to—and she, a proud rebel, often did—she could attend whites-only facilities and functions unmolested. Not once, she said, was she ever caught. One time, Briggs, a former beauty queen and still a charming and good-natured woman who admitted that she routinely used humor to cope with discrimination, recalled being invited to join the Ku Klux Klan, an invitation at which she, an African American Catholic, could only laugh to herself later.[28]

Despite such absurd episodes, the cruel reality was, as Briggs's experience illustrates, that a person's skin tone could determine their rights, privileges, and treatment in the Jim Crow South. Knowing this, Black parents sometimes encouraged their children to find light-skinned romantic partners, as Briggs's parents did, though she, in her typical rebellious fashion, fell in love with a dark-skinned man of modest means, something that she never regretted but that her parents resented. (Her home is adorned with pictures of her late husband, of whom she speaks with remarkably youthful emotion.)

Violations of legally mandated segregation were rare exceptions to prescribed norms. "Everything was so separate," remembered Price, who as a child was allowed to enter white areas only to deliver newspapers. "We had paper routes in Beaumont, and we threw papers into white communities but were never invited into the home. That relationship was always tangible."[29] Well into the 1970s, everything and everywhere in the Golden Triangle was racially segregated.

Perhaps nowhere was this separation more visible or of larger consequence than in the school systems. It is no coincidence that the *Brown v. Board of Education* ruling of 1954 is often considered to mark the beginning of the civil rights movement or that the ruling proved fundamental to the course of civil rights across the nation. Schools were where one could most clearly see how segregation truly functioned.

One recurring memory among those who attended all-Black schools was being issued secondhand books and supplies. "In our textbooks," Price said, "when we opened them up" to see who had used them previously, "we saw white names."[30] The message to Black children, Price and others claimed, was simple and unambiguous: Black lives and Black minds were worth less than those of white people. The refusal to provide new books or supplies to Black students was a reminder of the truth of Chief Justice Earl Warren's powerful and eloquent opinion in *Brown*: "to separate [children] from others of similar age and qualifications solely based on their race generates a feeling of inferiority as to their status in the community that may affect their hearts and minds in a way unlikely to ever be undone."[31] Indeed, Black children received the message loud and clear, and despite the best efforts of parents to shield and protect their children from the injustice of segregation, the practice of supplying white students with new books and materials while issuing Black students cast-off school supplies, ingrained in many of them the idea that they were, as Harvey Johnson put it, "cultural zeroes."[32]

Out-of-date textbooks and worn-out classroom supplies were just some of the examples of how the premise of "separate but equal" was a lie. "Everything was a kind of hand-me-down of things discarded by the white schools," said Price. That included sports equipment: "In my '48 and '49 school years, we didn't get new jerseys. We got [used] green jerseys. Those were the colors of South Park. Our colors"—those of Hebert High, the Black high school—"were blue and purple." In response to these institutional slights and insults, parents worked to guard their children's self-esteem and to organize to preserve their dignity in whatever ways they could, including dyeing and painting jerseys and helmets the correct colors so that their children could attend school, learn, play, and compete with pride.

Schools were also places where, in the judgment of Black men and women who lived through segregation, white children often learned prejudice for the first time. Because neighborhoods were spatially segregated, young people generally grew up not knowing many people of a different culture or skin color. Black parents often taught their children why this was and what it meant, though they could not always find a satisfactory explanation for why their children had to attend Blacks-only schools. White children, similarly, eventually became aware of their Black peers, but were taught that their separation from them was a marker of racial supremacy. This inculcation of prejudice, said many Black people I spoke with, ensured that white children never fully developed empathy for those different from themselves. And despite forced separation in schools, many white children did grow up around Black people—usually servants and domestics—and developed deep emotional ties to them. But when they went off to school, prejudice was instilled in them.

Brenda Spivey's mother was, for most of her life, a domestic worker in a white household, and she serves as a perfect example of this unfortunate reality. She would have preferred a more lucrative and secure job, but for the most part, she was happy to have the work. Moreover, like millions of other Black domestic workers who, as one activist put it, "raised America," she developed deep and lasting bonds with the white children under her care, who, according to her stories, loved and saw her as a mother figure in return—until, Spivey said, they began school.[33] At first, Spivey said, her mother told her "she didn't have any issues with racial prejudice in the early part of their lives, but as they started going to school," they picked up hurtful epithets and racist beliefs. Suddenly, "one day, one of the children, the daughter," after a minor disagreement, "confronted her and called her a n---er." Her mother, recounted Spivey, herself holding back tears, "was real hurt." For years, she had fed, clothed, bathed, comforted, and cared for the children as if they were her own, and they appeared to care for her as well—until they adopted the prejudice of their community.[34] She quit soon after suffering that humiliation.[35] Considering the substantial hardship that quitting a comparatively good job inflicted on the already-struggling family, the decision to quit rather than endure insults and put-downs was a clear act the historian Robin D. G. Kelley called "everyday acts of resistance."[36]

Others worked to create self-contained communities that taught children to demand respect. The father of Vernon Durden, a lifelong resident of Beaumont and a former oil worker turned civil rights leader, taught him and his siblings, he recounted with pride, to conduct themselves properly but to also expect courtesies from all people they dealt with, whether Black or white.[37] Others were more militant, at least in certain contexts, and at times prepared their children to handle inevitable confrontations and to physically defend themselves if necessary. The elder Price, who was a young father at the time of the Beaumont Race Riot, chose to arm himself for the not so unexpected. Richard Price saw his father arm the family during the riot: "I remember my father—by then I was about ten years old—my father gave one weapon to my oldest brother, a .45 pistol, and he gave a second weapon to my second-oldest brother, and he told the youngest of us . . . to go in the bedroom and get underneath the bed." It was not uncommon for Black women and men, in the Golden Triangle as across the country, to see weapons as tools of resistance and liberation.[38]

The self-defense strategies of parents and families were testaments to the realization that the law, even if it appeared to be changing, could mean very little in reality. As Johnson pointed out with considerable frustration, "Segregation was, you know, the laws are one thing but practices are another thing. A law can't stop a policeman from calling me a n---er." The indignities of discrimination were facts of daily life—and often extended into death. Hilton Kelley recalled, perhaps all too vividly for his comfort, the murder of his mother—at the hands of his stepfather, he suspected, a man whose struggles with mental health and alcoholism were perhaps the result of a cruel system that devalued Black life. After the death of his stepfather, who, Kelley said, hinted but never confessed to the murder, Kelley embarked on a mission to figure out what exactly had transpired on the night of his mother's murder. Kelley, who for decades has waged all-out war against environmental injustice in the Golden Triangle, finally tracked down the police report, kept from public view for many years, only to find monstrous indifference.[39] His mother's case was summarized by a single gut-punching sentence that brought him not relief or justice, and certainly not closure, but more pain. It read simply, according to him, "One n---er killed another n---er."[40] To Kelley, and to thousands of Black residents of the Triangle, such callousness confirmed their belief that the police and local authorities were not there to protect or serve their communities, but to persecute and punish them when not ignoring them.

Understanding the stakes, Black Beaumont residents received with some hope the promise that the Beaumont school district would work to integrate "with all possible efficiency," echoing, no doubt by design, wording in the *Brown II* decision."[41] Indeed, initial developments were promising, especially when the area college, then known as Lamar State College of Technology, in 1956 allowed the enrollment of eleven Black students. The white response was unequivocal and swift. "Some 25 smartly frocked white women" protested against integration at Lamar, led by H. T. Mercer, described in newspapers as "a Vidor housewife."[42] The protests grew larger. On October 2, Mercer, who said she wanted to send her son to "an all-white Lamar," was joined by some 150 picketers carrying signs that read, "Rebels with a Cause" and "Keep Our Education System White." Two Black students had to be escorted out of the college, since authorities feared they would be attacked. Nevertheless, at least one Black student continued to attend classes, despite continued anti-integration pickets.[43]

Within a few years, acts of resistance spread. In April 1960, a group of twenty-two Black residents hoping to replicate the success of the sit-ins in Greensboro, North Carolina, two months prior decided to test the tactic in Beaumont. At approximately ten thirty in the morning, the group entered the local Walgreens Drug Store, located downtown, and sat at the lunch counter. The store manager promptly closed the store, and the protesters left without incident to conduct a sit-in at the White House, a large department store in Beaumont. The police were called, and the Reverend W. D. Simpson of Nederland, a white antisegregation minister, was arrested later that afternoon for leading the protest. Simpson was rebuked by the Beaumont Ministers Association; the Reverend D. L. Landrum told him and the youths that they could "expect no help" from ministers if they continued to violate local segregation ordinances.[44] For years, whenever activists resorted to sit-ins and other forms of direct protest,[45] city officials and local leaders stressed "respect for order" and called for continued patience and moderation.[46]

Labor unions, too, for many years after *Brown* resisted integration. Although in some instances, unions in the Deep South were essential to integration, many unions saw the introduction of Black members as a threat to white supremacy and the gains made by white workers.[47] In the Golden Triangle, this was the case. Ed Savoy, the president of Local 4–243 of the powerful Oil, Chemical and Atomic Workers Union, was unequivocal when he said that he did "not support the leading of nor the implementing of the program of integration of the races in the public schools of Texas."[48]

"Something Was Lost"

So it was with jubilation and hope that Black citizens and their progressive white allies received the civil rights developments that promised to transform the United States, especially the passage of the Civil Rights Act of 1964 and the Voting Rights Act a year later. But even as the law fundamentally transformed social relations and upended generations of segregation and second-class citizenship for Black Americans, the realities of daily life often changed very little, if at all. In fact, even as things seemed to ostensibly be getting better in many parts of the country, progress stalled in East Texas. The implementation of national-level changes that asserted the humanity and equality of Black people made a bad situation arguably worse for many in the Triangle.

In schools, for example, desegregation continued to move slowly—certainly not "with all deliberate speed," as the law dictated (but did not define)—and often in ways that appeared to Black residents to be acts of cruelty that punished them rather than uplifted them.[49] The Black community understood, as Vernon Durden summarized, that "there's always a consequence, and there's always a sacrifice when you have change," but the level of white resistance and the structural barriers that immediately met desegregation efforts surprised even the most pessimistic members of the Black community. Durden summed up the feeling among many Black leaders and community members most plainly when he said, "We didn't do well with the integration of schools."[50]

State officials and local school boards quickly mobilized to prevent quick and deliberate action on desegregation. When, in the years after *Brown*, some school boards in the state began implementing policies to dismantle school segregation and to gradually integrate, the State of Texas stepped in and ordered them to halt the process, claiming that they could not do so "except by a vote of the people" and threatened to withhold funding from districts that violated the state's edicts.[51] Some proposals went as far as to require, as an official state policy, "that all persons and groups advocating integration" register and "stand regular state inspection," or else risk fines of up to $10,000 and five years in prison.[52] Under these threats—and no one considered them empty—even well-intentioned leaders in Golden Triangle school systems backed off their efforts to right the wrongs of their generation. Decades later, schools remained strikingly segregated.

Over the years, under pressure from a "triple squeeze" consisting of the courts, civil rights-minded politicians, and Black people, Golden Triangle officials began to consider taking action on integration.[53] The Beaumont Independent School District sought to implement a "stairstep" plan, and the South Park Independent School District followed suit.[54] Yet in 1964, a decade after *Brown*, the *Texas Observer* noted that "East Texas is still adamant against school integration."[55] And the *Atlanta Daily World* reported, nearly a decade later, in 1973, that "the school system in Beaumont, Texas, has failed to abolish racial segregation in one-third of its schools," probably a somewhat generous assessment.[56] The story was much the same in Port Arthur and Orange.

Black residents and civil rights leaders continued to push for equality, and for racial and economic justice, which as historians have in recent years acknowledged, were deeply intertwined causes.[57] Activists in Jefferson County in 1965 were agitating for "equal opportunity in employment, school desegregation, and hospital and health services."[58] Black residents in East Texas, like their counterparts across the country, found some success in the arena of public accommodations, mostly because doing business without segregation became, in time, "good business."[59] This move seemed to support the contention of scholars such as Adolph Reed, Cedric Johnson, and Walter Benn Michaels that capitalism is not inherently racist but, rather, exceedingly flexible and adaptable to sociopolitical conditions.[60]

Despite some progress in desegregating public spaces and in allowing Black citizens to become consumers, but not necessarily full participants of a fair and just economy, school integration continued to be the most stubborn challenge. District leaders frustrated Black activists and civil rights allies by routinely engaging in tokenism and calling it integration. Moving a few students to another school was often declared to be enough to call schools desegregated.

Even more nefarious, in many regards, was how teachers were reassigned in order to sell the appearance of integration. In conversations about integration with residents who lived through it, a recurring theme is that the best Black teachers were often sent to white schools, and the weakest white teachers—sometimes well-meaning novices—were thrown into ill-equipped Black schools and given limited resources. "All our better teachers," remembered Durden, "and they knew who they were—they took them to the white schools, and they had their not-so-good teachers sent to the Black schools."[61] The Reverend Jerry High, who first told me that "something was lost" in the process of integration, agreed. A local civil rights fixture, a man of great stature—both literally and figuratively—and the deeply charismatic pastor of West Tabernacle Missionary Baptist Church in Beaumont, he similarly remembered that "they took the best teachers from our schools and put them in the white schools and brought the young white teachers over to the Black schools."[62] Some teachers resisted because they refused to be torn from their communities. Durden believed that "some teachers were so good that they stood out, and they just took these good teachers, especially the ones in math." At least one of those math teachers, Durden recalled, "said he'd quit before going to the white schools." But for the most part, the impact of resistance was minimal, since "school board members," in the estimation of Black leaders, simply "didn't care."[63]

Black children, their parents, and their communities were not unaware of these machinations. They understood that they were, as Spivey put it, falling through the institutional cracks, seen only as problems and potential criminals.[64] High called it disheartening: the system set up generations of Black people and communities for failure, since the Black community, despite concerted and continued efforts, could not effectively counter the massive power of the state and local governments, which seemed willing to make every effort to thwart integration.[65]

The promise of integration was that a "rising tide," as Durden put it, would bring racial equality to a new Black generation. Instead, he and others quickly found, the way that "integration" was implemented "just raised the white boats." "Crap," he added, "rolled downhill."[66] Real progress was slow, and only came when Black communities pressured school districts and other systems, often using the legal breakthroughs that had finally, at least on paper, made them equal before the law. Most often, however, Black residents of the Golden Triangle believed that the best way to make a difference was to act on a small scale—to change, for example, the composition of local school boards. But Black citizens found that custom and the law were forces far more powerful than anyone had imagined. Draconian local rules often seemed to supersede national legislation. Well after *Brown* and the Civil Rights Act, up until the 1970s, even the act of applauding during board meetings for Black leaders such as Price, who at the time was the sole Black trustee on the Beaumont school board, could be banned, in an effort to literally silence Black leaders and their supporters.

Worse still, Black leaders were under the ever-present threat of violence if they got too comfortable or became too successful in their activism. As Amilcar Shabazz has written, segregationists continued to freely espouse racist ideology and to directly and indirectly threaten that "attack[s] on segregation would cause white rioting similar to what took place in the city in 1943."[67] No doubt the threat of violence partly explained why Black resistance was not more pronounced in the Golden Triangle. Such were the circumstances that some observers have gone as far as to say that "there was never a civil rights movement" in the Golden Triangle, or in Houston or Dallas for that matter.[68] The journalist Dick J. Reavis argued that "city fathers" met and "decided they didn't want a reputation like Birmingham had gained." The "whole dirty history" of the region, according to Reavis, consisted of city leaders and Black ministers working together "at every juncture" to ensure matters moved "smoothly." Indeed, many others recounted that the process was deliberately slow and always avoided any hint of radicalism.[69] According to Vernice Moore and Hosea Gabriel, who remembered the period of integration vividly, the priority of establishment leaders, white and Black alike, was to ensure that city elders, rather than "hot-headed youngsters," led the change.[70] Perhaps it was no coincidence that the region's most celebrated civil rights triumph was the successful effort of middle-class golf players to integrate a golf club in Beaumont, whereas the city's schools have remained some of the most segregated in the country.[71]

This aversion to radical change, Black people told me, was largely what led to something being "lost." The accommodationist impulses of Black elites, the failures and setbacks suffered by ordinary people, and frustration with a system that refused to change combined to elicit separatist calls from Black leaders such as David Harrison, who declared in 1970 that "desegregation," even if it occurred, would mean "nothing good for black people."[72] Leaders such as the Reverend High insisted that separatism and rage were "counterproductive," but nevertheless understood why frustration often led to such proclamations.[73]

Neither Truly Free nor "Safe within Our Place"

In light of the reactionary and haphazard integration process, then, it should not be surprising that many Black people who grew up in the segregated Golden Triangle seemingly yearn for a return to a time before integration, when there was a sense of community in a self-contained world of pride, relative safety, and self-reliance. As Gethrel Williams, a Beaumont councilwoman explained, many Black people today lament the state of the education system they are forced to entrust their children to, wishing sometimes for the kind of schools they attended before nominal integration when, despite the poor condition of books and facilities, Black students were taught by motivated, caring teachers who were part of the community. "I was as happy as I could be" attending an all-Black school, remembered Williams, "me and my little friends."[74] The fondness with which African Americans remember their teachers is part of a larger pattern that the education historian Hilton Kelly (no relation to the activist Hilton Kelley, cited elsewhere in this chapter) described in *Race, Remembering, and Jim Crow's Teachers*. As Kelly pointed out, taking seriously Black people's overwhelmingly positive assessments and memories of all-Black schools should not be seen as simple nostalgia nor as a condemnation of integration. Instead, it means accepting that something was indeed lost, that "remarkably good" schools, teachers, and relationships suffered under a system of integration that was at best clumsy and, at worst, malicious in its implementation.[75]

When what passed for integration began, Black communities were often shattered. Their self-contained worlds, where, as Harvey Johnson and other members of the Black community believed, "we were safe within 'our place,'" suddenly gave way to a harsher reality.[76] The current awareness and publicity of hate crimes and police violence, in fact, has made this sentiment stronger and more common among Black families, not only in East Texas but also across the country.[77]

In a segregated world, it was possible for Black parents to shelter their children from what was happening around them. They often felt that their best strategy was to shield their children from a world that hated and dehumanized them. To do this, parents and families devised numerous ways of protecting their young. Some chose to avoid talking about segregation and discrimination, hoping perhaps to keep children from internalizing the dehumanization that segregation signified. Harvey Johnson's mother was one such parent. In reflecting on his mother's choice, Johnson concluded:

A definition had already been assigned to me and to families like me across America. We were Negroes. So it's no wonder my momma didn't talk about my Blackness, about my African identity. Like most African mothers, she understood the radioactive nature of racism. She was protecting us, especially her sons, because she knew that if we knew our identity and it became a household conversation, maybe, just maybe, one of us would have the courage to challenge, to contest the myths. But she also knew that by doing that, her sons would be in peril, perhaps even facing an early [death], and she was right.[78]

It may seem shocking to think that African Americans, in East Texas or anywhere else, remember preintegration years fondly or that they would declare that something was lost in gaining equal legal footing. Of course, a closer look at their testimonies reveals that no one is eager to return to "a subordinate or inferior position," as David Harrison wrote in 1970, but rather that they recognize that as carried out, desegregation meant the worst of the past and the worst of the future for Black communities.[79] "Integration took a lot away from us," according to High. "It brought some good things, but it took a lot away."[80] In a country that still treats Black women, men, and children as second-class citizens; that kills and incarcerates them at a proportionally much higher rate than it does whites[81]; and that does little to alleviate their poverty and destitution, many Black folks yearn for a time when they at least lived in self-supporting, autonomous communities, even if they did so separate from whites.[82]

Today, the mentality of many (especially young) Black people is that their only freedom is "the freedom to fail," as High has repeatedly preached to his flock, with considerable concern. This bleak view seems especially realistic when they survey the social and political worlds they inhabit and see that the structural roots of inequality remain in plain sight. Failure to provide adequate resources to poor (usually Black or minority) schools in East Texas, for example, has ensured that pupils there remain far behind their peers, even when they have teachers, Black and white, who care and who want to make a difference. "Many blame the schools for failing," said Aquila Griffin, an activist. "But they never blame the bad policies put in place for schools." Teachers, she said, "can only teach to a certain extent with the resources [they have]. It's the policies put in place that's failing the students."[83]

In another sense, the frustrations that lead Black women and men to seemingly long for a time when they were segregated are due to the troubling reality that integration never happened in any full or real sense. There was only the appearance of it, and sometimes not even that. The Port Arthur Independent School District, for example, was considered legally desegregated only in 2007, when Judge Thad Heartfield, of the Eastern District of Texas, terminated federal jurisdiction over the schools, which began in 1970.[84] To fight the federal order, the district tried to integrate on "freedom of choice" grounds, but without encouraging or helping Black students to attend white schools (or vice versa), and in reality operating as a racially segregated district.[85] Similarly, "the South Park board" in Beaumont, also operating under "freedom of choice," for decades "waged a calculated campaign to ridicule the federal government and fool the people of this district," as Ed Moore, the first Black Jefferson County commissioner, told *Texas Monthly* in 1983.[86]

And it is not just education that remains a problem, though in many ways it remains the most visible. The inability to learn when, as Durden said, "you're in survival mode" is aggravated if you don't have a decent place to live or a healthy environment.[87] Unsurprisingly, perhaps, housing and environmental degradation have been major ongoing issues in the area. In 1993, efforts to integrate public housing in the small Triangle town of Vidor, still considered by many East Texas residents to be the regional home of the Klan, were met with a KKK march through the town and complaints that Black residents "were being forced on the people of Vidor."[88] The enduring power of structural racism, although less obvious than the out-and-proud bigotry of groups like the KKK,[89] has convinced some observers, such as Maddie Sloan, an attorney for low-income families, that "integration will never work in Beaumont."[90]

The effects of racism, structural and quotidian, were made all the worse by a process of economic restructuring that began in the 1970s and affected regions like the Golden Triangle in especially brutal ways. Before then, Black leaders felt real change coming, joined unions, and stood up against the social and economic systems that oppressed them. Despite seeing, as Bill Sam, a steelworker and lifelong union man did, that "tokenism stuff" was as far as companies were willing to go, many like him were determined—and had reason to believe realistically—that "we're gonna change it, we're gonna make it right."[91] But the process of deindustrialization that battered the country beginning in the 1970s affected minorities, especially in regions such as Beaumont and Port Arthur, disproportionately.[92] There, white flight, deindustrialization, and the decline of union jobs contributed to growing desperation. Whereas the Oil, Chemical and Atomic Workers Union (OCAW), in which many Black workers had found refuge (over time and after serious fights for inclusion),[93] was once aggressive and successful in gaining concessions for its workers, Black and white, by the 1980s the industry had changed; not only OCAW's numbers but also its "rate of success in bargaining elections" were "low and dropping."[94] (The union merged into the United Steelworkers of America in 1999.) Automation, the growth of offshore drilling, the relocation of refineries overseas, and the ascendancy of the Republican Party and its antiunion crusade wiped out thousands of jobs.[95] Slow upticks and hopeful moments did not seem to last, and every boom seemingly was followed by an even bigger bust.[96]

In recent years, Golden Triangle residents have been forced to live with the specter of a petrochemical presence that no longer provides the promise of good, well-paying union jobs, but continues to inflict tremendous environmental damage on residents. They live in a sea of toxic chemicals, some 135 of them coming from the chemical plants that dot the region. The dangers posed by these plants, in fact, have been responsible for almost as much population loss and economic trouble as has deindustrialization. As one recent report put it, "people who can afford to live elsewhere tend to leave" the area. Those who cannot, largely an African American population, are left to contend with an environment where millions of pounds of pollution gather in the air every year and threaten their lives and health. They nonetheless continue to attempt to make strides in other areas of social justice, a fight that has proved anything but easy.[97]

The case of East Texas, its history in the civil rights struggle, and its past provide many historical lessons. For one, segregation was rigid but never impenetrable. Black men, women, and children, as well as white allies and others, always imagined alternative possibilities. Many went beyond imagining and acted, in accordance with the principles of justice they had been taught at home and in the community. Even when sheltered, Black people understood segregation and what it meant. In response, they mobilized, in ways big and small—through direct resistance, by running for political office, by writing and creating protest art, and sometimes by putting their bodies on the line. The result was less romantic, and less ideal, than many would have hoped. Integration and legal developments were never carried out fully or with real and lasting justice in mind. When historical developments did yield meaningful change, it was because of federal action from above and social pressure from below.

To call this story a narrative of decline is to deny the progress that has been made. But to ignore what was lost is similarly a betrayal of history. What happened in East Texas, the way that history unfolded there, in many ways paralleled what happened elsewhere. Population loss, white flight, continued discrimination, and ongoing systemic violence make it a typical rather than an exceptional case.[98] But there are also regional specificities. The Golden Triangle had to contend with severe environmental degradation.[99] And to an extent not seen in many other places, resistance from white elites has prolonged the suffering and the struggle of Black residents. It is shocking to think that it was not until the 1990s that some schools in Texas were finally integrated, to imagine that in 1993 the Ku Klux Klan led a march against public housing in Vidor, or to hear that a return to blatant discrimination is becoming the norm once again.[100] But such are the lessons of history, reminders that progress and the past are not linear, that men and women, with the lessons of history in mind, even today find themselves in the middle of a struggle for basic justice.

But a fundamental lesson can be learned from this past. The first step in healing the wounds of historical injustices, as countless activists have argued, is to acknowledge that they exist. Those who offered their testimony about the past did so with the full understanding that their work is hardly done, that the march of justice has taken several detours, and that the search for a more decent future begins with memory. It also means that to uncover a fuller story, we need to look not only where great moments happened, but also where suffering continues. The Golden Triangle may not be a famous region in the history of civil rights, but its citizens suffered, fought, and risked no less than better-known others to transform the country.

CHAPTER 4

TEXAS TIME:
Racial Violence, Place Making, and Remembering as Resistance in Montgomery County

JASMIN C. HOWARD

Well, you know, Montgomery County is considered a very prejudiced town, and with the incident that happened years ago that . . . my mother told me and aunt told me about, and grandmother, about the lynching there on the courthouse square. So, it has a mark on it.
JIMMIE SHAW

The statement that serves as the epigraph to this chapter, made by a longtime Montgomery County resident named Jimmie Shaw, showcases the persistence of memories of racialized violence and trauma in Montgomery County, Texas. The courthouse was routinely the site of racialized violence and trauma in Conroe. It was where Joe Winters was burned and where Bob White and Gregory Steele were shot, thirty-two years apart. Family members and friends have passed down the oral tradition of racialized trauma to younger generations of Black Conroe residents. In areas such as Tamina, a Black freedmen's settlement, and The Woodlands, a master-planned community, geographic boundaries are racialized, too. African American residents of Tamina have combatted threats of annexation from wealthier neighboring communities, as well as the deterioration of substandard infrastructure, while trying to maintain their autonomy. According to longtime Tamina resident Annette Hardin, "The value developers place on our land is vastly different than ours. What they don't understand is that it's not just our property—it's our legacy. The land represents the blood, heart, and soul of our African American heritage."[1] The Woodlands, an economically prosperous locale, has remained overwhelmingly white despite being just north of racially diverse Houston and having been initially promoted as a solution to urban congestion and white flight. (Technically, The Woodlands is just a census-designated place; despite having more than 115,000 residents, it has not incorporated as a city.) In short, the ritual of teaching African Americans their social "place" in Montgomery County was tied to physical places, as is the collective memory of racialized violence.

Montgomery County is on the northern side of Greater Houston, a sprawling metropolitan expanse that also includes The Woodlands, Sugar Land, and many smaller communities. This chapter focuses particularly on the city of Conroe (the county seat), The Woodlands, and Tamina. The county now includes rural and urban, unincorporated and incorporated areas, but it was rural for much of the twentieth

James Leveston standing beside the Tamina welcome sign, 2015. Photo by Gary Coronado / © *Houston Chronicle*. Used with permission.

century. It has received little scholarly attention because of its proximity to Houston, one of the largest and most diverse cities in the United States.

Mainly through the testimony of oral histories, this chapter documents the role of racialized memory in the history of Montgomery County. While this chapter primarily focuses on the experiences of African Americans in the area, population shifts over the last few decades have resulted in Montgomery County having a significant Latino population. The African American population in these areas, historically and contemporarily, has been much lower than it is in Houston. In 1950, African Americans made up approximately 25 percent of the population in Montgomery County. By 1990, they were 13 percent of the population of Conroe and approximately 4 percent of Montgomery County. In Houston, African Americans were approximately 28 percent of the total population in 1990. Similarly, they made up around 17 percent of the population of Conroe and 7 percent of the population of Montgomery County.[2] This chapter explores what the struggle for civil rights looks like when African Americans and other racial minorities make up a small percentage of the total population of a place. It also looks at the ways that civil rights organizing differed and was similar in rural and urban areas of the county. The analysis takes in political engagement and political representation, the roles of law enforcement, school segregation and desegregation, employment opportunities, racial disparities in infrastructure and other elements. Paraphrasing the words of the famed Black poet Lucille Clifton in her poem "why some people be mad at me sometimes," African American residents of Montgomery County had to remember their own memories, which often conflicted with dominant narratives of governmental officials, white residents, and local media.[3]

Conroe

The Case of Clarence Brandley

In August 1980, a white sixteen-year-old student named Cheryl Dee Fergeson was raped and murdered on the campus of Conroe High School, just days before the start of the school year. Fergeson's death was documented in the August 25 issue of the *Houston Chronicle* in an article titled "Few Clues to Bellville Girl's Rape-Slaying at Conroe High." Cheryl Fergeson would have been a junior at Bellville High School in Bellville, a small city west of Houston. She had traveled to Conroe High School that morning for a volleyball tournament; she served as the student trainer for Bellville's volleyball team. Fergeson's nude body was found two and a half hours after she arrived on campus. It was found by a school janitor on a balcony above the stage of the auditorium. According to autopsy reports, Fergeson was strangled after being raped.[4]

Following the killing of Fergeson, school officials in Bellville and Conroe increased campus security, and public officials issued warnings for young girls.[5] Howard Bennett, a Conroe resident who worked as a security guard, stated, "The city's growing, getting a lot more transient-type people moving around. It's not the safe little town anymore, I guess," implying that Conroe was once a safe place.[6] On August 29, 1980, four days before classes were to begin, Clarence Lee Brandley, a twenty-eight-year-old Black janitor at Conroe High School, was arrested and charged with capital murder for the death of Cheryl Fergeson.[7] The arrest occurred after several people had been questioned and several polygraph tests administered.[8] Police had earlier expressed a desire to make an arrest before the start of school in order "to relieve the fears of students and parents."[9] From the time the murder was known, residents of Conroe and the surrounding areas had expressed great interest in finding and bringing the killer to justice, and within a week her alleged murderer was in custody.

Media interest in the murder case expanded beyond the mainstream press. Local Black press outlets such as the *Houston Forward Times* and the *Houston Defender* ran articles about the case. An article titled "In White Girl's Murder: Black Conroe Janitor's Family Says He Is Innocent" showcased the voices of the Brandley family; early articles on the case in the *Houston Chronicle* largely focused on the perspectives of the family and friends of the victim. From the outset, Brandley and members of his family insisted he was innocent and that Conroe police had violated his civil rights by initially denying him the right to speak with a lawyer.

The controversial case polarized Conroe and Houston and ultimately reached national and international audiences. Some Black Conroe residents initially expressed concern that Brandley would not receive a fair trial. According to Mary Tolbert, a retired Montgomery County deputy sheriff, after being told about Fergeson's death by a referee at the volleyball tournament, a Black resident stated, "Lord, Jesus. I hope he wasn't Black." Tolbert also recalled that the Black community in Conroe had a collective concern for Brandley: they were "all kind of scared, and we knew he would get the death penalty."[10] The Reverend J. Don Boney, the leader of the Houston chapter of the National Black United Front and the Coalition to Free Clarence Brandley, along with the defense attorneys for Brandley, charged that local white people had threatened Brandley's supporters and had engaged in one physical attack.[11] The holdout juror from the first case alleged that he received "thousands" of threatening calls.[12] Jimmie Shaw remembered hearing rumors of Brandley's family being harassed. Recalling the time of the case, Shaw stated, "It was a sad moment in history, I tell ya, for Conroe, Texas."[13]

Brandley's first trial, which was monitored by a representative of the NAACP, resulted in a mistrial after the jury deadlocked 11–1 in favor of conviction.[14] The second trial resulted in a conviction, and a sentence of death was delivered on February 25, 1981. Ozell Brandley, Clarence's brother, got Boney to coordinate his Houston-based Coalition to Free Clarence Brandley with the local Free Clarence Brandley movement. Together, their efforts gained international reach and support. On March 20, 1987, Brandley received a stay of execution from Judge Lynn Coker after key witnesses recanted. An appeals court ordered an evidentiary hearing on June 30, 1987, and on October 9, 1987, Judge Perry Pickett ordered a new trial. By then, multiple television specials had covered the Brandley case, including a *60 Minutes* segment, multiple articles in the *New York Times*, and the involvement of international organizations such as Amnesty International. On December 13, 1989, Brandley's murder conviction was set aside by the Texas Court of Criminal Appeals in a 6–3 decision. The US Supreme Court refused to hear the prosecution's appeal on October 1, 1990, a judge officially dismissed the murder charges, and Brandley was freed from the possibility of a retrial on October 8, 1990. During the appeals process, Brandley was at times days or minutes away from being executed. No one else has been charged for the murder and rape of Fergeson, although Brandley's supporters had advocated for charges to be brought against two white former Conroe High School janitors, James Dexter Robinson and Gary Acreman. Brandley never received compensation for his unwarranted incarceration. Following his release, Brandley lived a modest life and became an anti-death-penalty advocate. At the time of Brandley's death, in September 2018, there was renewed interest in the case, which had been reopened earlier in the year after a box of trial evidence was found in the belongings of a former Conroe police chief named Charlie Ray. Brandley and his supporters had hoped that the material would lead to a declaration of innocence, which would allow him to be compensated for his wrongful conviction and incarceration. Still largely unresolved, the case of Clarence Brandley remains controversial and a source of racial tension in Conroe.[15]

Before Brandley became an international cause célèbre, residents of Montgomery and Harris Counties, including his family members, championed his case. Organized support for Brandley over the years included dozens of demonstrations, investigations, advocacy, media mobilization, fund-raising, and court actions. The tactics also included fasting, disrupting the legislature, and placing the injustice perpetrated against Clarence Brandley in the larger context of extrajudicial killings in Conroe. On February 6, 1987, a rally of around one hundred people was held in front of the Montgomery County Courthouse. Boney stated, "Clarence Brandley is so innocent a blind man could see it. There was an all-white jury that convicted an innocent black man. It's the very first time the black community of Conroe stood up on its hind legs and said 'I'm not going to take it anymore.'" Emphasizing the importance of place, supporters of Brandley placed cow manure from inside an aluminum coffin on the

"Liberty and Justice for Clarence Brandley" rally, Conroe, 1987. Photo by Betty Tichich / © *Houston Chronicle*. Used with permission.

courthouse grounds, and Boney said, "This is the kind of racist B.S. we've put up with." Ozell Brandley, Clarence's brother, likewise brought attention to the courthouse, saying, "All the fingers in the world ought to be pointed at this courthouse. We're going to keep coming back here until my brother is free."[16] The next month, the *Houston Chronicle* reported, "Weekly rallies and prayer sessions at Conroe College draw as many as 140 blacks from Conroe and Houston, some of them ministers, one of them a Conroe councilman."[17] At a rally at the SHAPE (Self-Help for African People through Education) Community Center in Houston in 1987, local congressman Mickey Leland stated, "[Brandley] has been perpetrated with the worst kind of injustice that could happen to a young black man," and Congressman John Conyers, of Michigan, presented Brandley's case to the House Subcommittee on Criminal Justice that year.[18] A large rally in Austin in January 1990 drew hundreds of participants, including politicians.[19] Further, the Coalition to Free Clarence Brandley supported other local causes and the international fight against the death penalty.[20] It was hoped that local activism would have a long-lasting impact beyond successfully freeing Clarence Brandley.

Long History of Racialized Violence

The fears of Black Conroe residents concerning Brandley and law enforcement were well founded and deeply connected with the past experiences of the community. On December 23, 1973, eighteen-year-old Gregory Allen Steele was shot and killed while in the custody of the Conroe Police Department. Steele had been detained on a complaint of disturbing the peace at a local tavern and was subsequently shot by Officer Darwin Bryant multiple times in the booking area of the police station. Bryant alleged that Steele had slashed him with a razor and that he had responded in self-defense. Steele was shot in the back through his heart and stomach.[21] According to some Black Conroe community members, Steele was shot for dating the relative of a local white law enforcement officer.[22] In response to the killing, a white-owned store in one of the Black neighborhoods in Conroe was burned down, and additional property damage was attributed to Black Conroe residents.[23] Bryant was indicted on a charge of murder with malice, but was acquitted by a jury in Livingston, Texas, in the summer of 1974.[24] After the acquittal, Steele's parents were awarded $65,000 in damages by a federal jury in 1977 after initially filing a $15 million damage suit in 1975.[25]

Years after the death of Steele, the officer involved, Darwin Bryant, was convicted of multiple crimes, including armed robbery of a bank, and was accused of additional crimes, including buying a baby and murder.[26] The belief that justice was denied in the killing of Steele remains a popular sentiment among Black Conroe community members.[27] Johnella Franklin, a former classmate of Steele, described the aftermath of his death: "Nobody felt comfortable with the police. You never wanted to be stopped by a policeman. You never wanted to be arrested. You couldn't trust that you could come out alive."[28]

Black Conroe residents' distrust of law enforcement and the judicial system has a long-standing history. Dorothy Reece, a longtime Conroe resident and educator, recalls as a child hearing from other children about "the law" picking up and beating up Black members of the community. Reece stated, "Of course, you know, the Black person always got the worst end of it, and that was a fact. We don't want to say those things now, but it was really a fact. And it was a fear—we had a fear of law enforcement even at that time. I think about what's going on now, but as a child I was afraid of policemen because I didn't think that they were meant for our safety, from some of the things I have heard."[29] Toddrick Proctor and Charles Lee stated that "there is no relationship" between the Black community and law enforcement except for a few good relationships with individual officers.[30] Additionally, multiple Conroe residents described trusting only the few African American officers that served in their neighborhoods while they were growing up. One was Ted Morgan in the 1950s, the first African American law enforcement officer to serve in Montgomery County, and another was Spencer White Jr., who served as the first Black deputy constable in Montgomery County. Morgan was hired by Larry Evans Sr., a white police officer who served as chief of the Conroe Police Department beginning in 1964. Evans served in Montgomery County law enforcement agencies intermittently from 1957 until his death, in 1995. A 2017 article in the *Courier of Montgomery County*, published in Conroe, described him as "stern yet caring."[31]

The complex relationship between Evans and the African American community in Conroe is best described through the experiences of Mary Tolbert, the retired deputy sheriff. As a twenty-one-year-old mother, she feared being stopped by Evans specifically: "He was mean. He would beat Blacks and stuff like this. He wasn't to be played with. He wasn't to be messed with. Yeah, all kind of bad things about him. And that really got me when he stopped me, because at that particular time, Black persons couldn't have new cars," except for the Black principal. Initially Evans called

Tolbert "girl" and asked her whether she had stolen the car. But after she told him that she was married to Leon Tolbert Jr., whose family Evans called "good people," Evans allowed her to drive off without a ticket if she promised to get her license. Tolbert and Evans later worked together in the sheriff's department in the 1980s and 1990s. Reflecting on her experiences with him, Tolbert stated, "He turned out to be okay."[32]

In 1984, Mary Tolbert became the first Black woman deputy sheriff in Montgomery County after facing years of discrimination. She had become an officer in the constable's office in the early 1980s after attending Texas A&M University at the suggestion of a deputy sheriff in Montgomery County who served as her sponsor. Three years after completing her education, Tolbert was hired by the sheriff's department. According to Tolbert, both her race and her gender hindered her initial entry into law enforcement.

In addition, Tolbert experienced sustained racial and sexual harassment during her probationary period in Conroe. Following her probationary period, Tolbert was assigned to patrol The Woodlands, which she described as "the fire" because of the discrimination she experienced there from supervisors, colleagues, and residents. Tolbert chose to leave The Woodlands and return to Conroe as a bailiff in the courthouse because the position offered her more scheduling benefits, but she still faced discrimination there.[33] Partly from facing protracted adversity in her career, Tolbert developed a no-nonsense reputation, which also included her resistance to discrimination and her refusal to quit.[34]

Black community members also had collective memories of past racial trauma such as the lynching of Joe Winters in 1922. Lavern Williams, a resident of Tamina, related the Brandley case and the racial climate following it to the lynching of Winters: "As a young girl, my mama told me about a man being burned on the courthouse square. A black man. I can remember going to the courthouse, too, when I was little and seeing there was water fountains for blacks and whites. I never could understand why I couldn't drink from the other one."[35] Dorothy Reece remembered hearing about the "Black man being burned on the courthouse square" from other Black children, despite her parents' attempts to shield her.[36] Many community members remembered Joe Winters's fate, which was documented in the *Crisis*, the magazine of the National Association for the Advancement of Colored People. According to the editors, two pictures, a newspaper clipping, and three letters about the lynching were sent to the magazine. The pictures were captioned "The Burning Body" and "A Larger Crowd Than . . . The Circus." The clipping reads as follows: "The burning of Joe Winters in the public square at Conroe, Texas, drew a larger crowd than the annual visit of the circus. Winters was accused of attacking a 14-year-old white girl. Bloodhounds were used to capture him and he was chased through three counties. Newspapers advertised the event and thousands of persons, including young women and children, watched him chained to a peg in the public square and a match applied to his clothing saturated with gasoline."[37] On May 21, 1922, the *New York Times* published an article titled "Two Negroes Lynched For Attacks on Girls," which describes the lynching of Winters and others that occurred that month. The article notes that six lynchings had been reported in Texas that month and that they all involved crimes against white women and girls.[38]

Another notable extrajudicial killing occurred in Conroe in 1941. Bob White was shot in the head in the Montgomery County Courthouse by W. S. Cochran, the husband of Ruby Cochran, an alleged rape victim, during his third trial for the crime. Following the shooting, the father of Dorothy Reece was told by a white resident that he should "get home" for his protection, and Dorothy was sent to school in Oklahoma by her father the next year.[39] First charged in 1937, Bob White had been convicted twice, but those convictions were overturned by the Texas Court of Criminal Appeals and the US Supreme Court for being the result of unfair trials. White was represented by the NAACP throughout his case, and his trials and killing received national attention largely because of the organization's involvement and the brazen actions of Cochran.[40] At the 32nd Annual Conference of the NAACP, held in Houston on June 18, 1941, a resolution on "Mob Violence and Lynching" directly referred to the killing of White:

> The cold blooded murder of Bob White in the court room of Conroe, Texas, before the very eyes of the judge and court officials, after his two prior convictions had been reversed by the highest courts of the land, and the subsequent acquittal of his murderer after a trial of less than two minutes, shocks the conscience of civilized mankind.
>
> Not only did that shot destroy the life of an innocent, defenseless, black American, but it killed the souls of myriads of impressionable children, and of thousands of adults who condoned it, and proclaimed to the world anew that American democracy, as it affects the Negro, is mythical. We condemn this murder and the violent and atrocious assault upon our judicial system and call upon the people and Governor of the State of Texas, the Department of Justice and the President of the United States to remove this foul blot from the national honor, by bringing the murderer to justice.[41]

Following Cochran's acquittal, which, as the resolution noted, occurred after two minutes of jury deliberation, he received praise and handshakes from the crowd.[42] Although the memory of the shooting has been passed down through oral tradition, physical memorabilia also exists. According to a *Houston Chronicle* article in 2015, the family of the first female sheriff in Montgomery County, Fannie Surratt, still has a "blood-stained oak chair" from the shooting of Bob White.[43]

White mob violence against Black Conroe residents was an imminent threat from the late nineteenth century to the mid-twentieth century. The British journalist Nick Davies published an article titled "The Town that Loved Lynching" in 1989, in which he referred to almost a dozen extrajudicial killings of Black residents in Conroe and Montgomery County by white law enforcement officers and civilians. The victims of the documented lynchings that occurred in Conroe and the surrounding areas, in addition to White, are the following: Bennett (Andy) Jackson, on December 19, 1885; Frank (Andrew) McGehee, May 15, 1887; John Maynard, March 21, 1904; Charles (Charley) Scott, February 28, 1908; James Kinder and Alf Riley, March 17, 1908; Joe Winters, May 20, 1922; Warren Lewis, June 23, 1922; and Tom Payne on February 1, 1927. Davies highlights both the history of state-sanctioned extrajudicial violence in Conroe and Montgomery County and the continued legacy of that violence. According to Davies, the district attorney who presided over Bob White's case, "W. C. 'Cleo' McLain, was later re-elected to his position and still practices law in Conroe [in the late 1980s]." And there was a blood link between the White and

Brandley cases: "The official who wrote White's confession, Ernest Coker, and who claimed not to have seen a mark on his body, later became a district judge. His son, Lynn, was one of the judges who condemned Clarence Brandley."[44] Routinely, the alleged offense of the lynching victim involved an impropriety between a Black man and a white woman. Conroe residents insisted that other African Americans were run out of town because they feared being lynched.[45]

Given the number of lynchings that occurred over decades in Montgomery County and the authorities' refusal to prosecute members of the mob, it seems clear that white people in the county sanctioned white vigilante violence. After the lynching of Thomas Payne, in 1927, the sheriff stated that the "sentiment of the people in and around Conroe is with the mob"; he publicly promised to charge members of the mob "if we can find out who was in the mob."[46] The lynching of Bennett Jackson, in 1885, highlighted the role of governmental officials and the public's approval of racialized violence. Jackson had been accused of severely attacking the wife and children of John Smith in their home. It was reported that Black community members had also advocated for the lynching and burning of Jackson. The lynching was postponed "out of respect to venerable Judge Mortimer," but after it was alleged that he sought to transfer Jackson to Houston for safety concerns, "a large number of the most influential citizens immediately gave notice that Bennett could not leave the jail alive." Mortimer ultimately left for Houston, but Jackson was taken by the mob and killed during a "lynching picnic." According to the *New York Times*, this lynching was "peculiar" because it occurred in broad daylight, without the perpetrators being disguised. Also, the "lynchers comprised all of the leading planters in the county." Davies notes that days earlier, an article in the *Houston Post* announced the planned lynching.[47]

After referring to two lynchings that occurred on the Conroe Courthouse square, Charles Lee, a current Montgomery County resident, indicated that the memories of Montgomery County's racist distant and recent past remain in the forefront of many people's minds: "You always kept that in the back of your mind, what would happen."[48] The fear of racialized violence that the surviving Black residents of Montgomery County have experienced for over a century was a desired outcome of the lynch mobs and those in power. The Black victims of mob violence served as reminders of what would happen if Black residents did not stay in their assigned social and physical place. Local newspapers reported that while facing death, multiple lynching victims gave speeches telling other Black residents to be good so that they could avoid Judge Lynch. For example, while awaiting death in front of a crowd of three hundred people, Warren Lewis warned other Black residents to "stay in their place," according to witnesses, and to "do the right thing."[49] Years earlier, Bennett Jackson had done the same thing. After Jackson confessed, it is alleged that he "warned all present, especially the colored people, against doing wrong."[50]

Black victims of white vigilante violence in Montgomery County served as mouthpieces for racialized social control even after death, thanks to their "speeches," which were printed in local media and passed on by word of mouth. Further, local and national newspapers always framed the lynchings of Black residents as being the result of the actions of Black individuals and the supposed ills of the Black community—not the actions of the mob or law enforcement. The *Galveston Daily News* reported the "quiet" atmosphere of the lynching of Bennett Jackson, during which the "people deplore the necessity of lynch law, but such a cold-blooded deed, done in broad daylight for a few dollars and to a woman and children, was more than they could let pass and wait patiently for the law to take its course." In this popular framing, the reluctant but compelled lynch mob had no choice but to act, and law enforcement, in the person of Sheriff Adair, had no choice but to acquiesce in the killing. According to the papers, even Jackson's confession was obtained by a Black preacher after a reading of a scripture and a prayer, and not necessarily by the mob of almost a thousand that had been advocating for his lynching for days in the very papers that portrayed the actual killing as a somewhat passive act of vigilante violence.

The lynchings and extrajudicial killings discussed so far—of Bennett Jackson, Frank McGehee, J. B. Walker, Charles Scott, James Kinder, Alf Riley, Joe Winters, Warren Lewis, Bob White, Gregory Steele—as well as the death-penalty sentencing of the now-exonerated Clarence Brandley, are connected. Besides resulting from accusations of improprieties committed against white women and girls, most of them took place on government property. That connection with the state speaks to the importance of the relationship between physical spaces and racialized violence in maintaining segregation. Oral histories of Montgomery County residents mention places to avoid, such as the town of Cut and Shoot (about six miles east of Conroe), and being taught to avoid stopping in Conroe because of its status as a "sundown town," that is, a place where Black people could not be out in public after dark.[51] In 2013, a historical marker erected for the Montgomery County Courthouse made no mention of the history of racialized violence associated with the building. Additionally, a 2017 article in the *Courier of Montgomery County* discussed the courthouse as a "centerpiece of downtown Conroe" but failed to mention how the courthouse was a contentious site of historical memory.[52]

Memories, Place, and School Desegregation

The memories of Conroe's Jim Crow past are etched into the memories of its Black residents. In some instances, remnants of that past remain. For some, downtown Conroe is still a place to avoid. Multiple Black residents remember seeing "Colored" etched into the courthouse bathroom door in the 1980s and 1990s. According to Mary Tolbert, "I started working for the Sheriff Department in '84, and I'm telling you, you could still see 'Colored' on that bathroom door."[53] Toddrick Proctor, who grew up in Conroe in the 1980s and 1990s, remembered seeing and using segregated water fountains at the courthouse.[54] Tolbert also recalled multiple instances of cross burnings and racial intimidation in the 1970s and 1980s, specifically in Cut and Shoot.[55] According to the memories of Black Conroe residents, Jim Crow's past was in some cases not even past.

The courthouse and Conroe High School were places where the Ku Klux Klan rallied well into the late 1990s. According to the *Galveston Daily News*, a KKK rally of around two hundred people took place at the Montgomery County Courthouse on February 19, 1993.[56] Proctor remembered that KKK rallies happened in Conroe throughout his childhood, and that the KKK recruited at Conroe High School until the mid-1990s.[57] A particularly tense moment occurred at Conroe High in January 1993. After a white student raised a Confederate flag and made a hand signal at a basketball game on January 19, he was confronted by Black students. The next day, a "racial fight" broke out, and the school sent many students home. On Friday of that same week, KKK pamphlets were found around the school, and there were rumors of more violence. One story held that some students would wear all white in support of the KKK, and at the beginning of the next week, some students were sent home for being in possession of KKK materials. Other students who were sent home stated that they had been falsely associated with KKK. Also, a Black student was sent home for wearing a Malcolm X shirt with the "racial slogan" "By any means necessary."[58]

As of 2016, vendors were still selling Confederate flags on Highway 59 between Cleveland, Texas, and Conroe.[59] And multiple white-supremacist organizations in the area, including the Cleveland-based White Camelia Knights of the Ku Klux Klan and the Conroe-based Texas-Oklahoma Invisible Empire of the Ku Klux Klan, remained active, with rallies, advocacy, and cross burnings, well into the 2000s.[60]

Threats of racialized violence and shows of force were used to bolster racial hierarchies and segregation in Conroe. The imminent threat of racialized violence, and being outnumbered three to one by white people, undoubtedly contributed to the lack of sustained direct action by Black Conroe residents. It was not until the Clarence Brandley case, in the 1980s and 1990s, that Conroe residents witnessed visible Black protest over an extended period. Conroe College served as a "movement center" in support of Black activism and desegregation efforts, as did Texas Southern University, in Houston, on a larger scale. This followed the pattern of historically Black colleges and universities, and their students, taking on integral roles during the civil rights movement.[61] Conroe College, formerly known as Conroe Normal and Industrial College, was founded in 1903. It was a premier institution for African American education. Adults associated with the college collaborated with high school students to carry out direct actions in the mid to late 1960s. And despite having small enrollment numbers in the 1980s, Conroe College served as one of the organizational spaces for the Free Clarence Brandley movement.[62]

Conroe schools were desegregated gradually. Beginning in 1963, the school district operated under a "freedom of choice," or token, system. Annette Gordon-Reed, a Pulitzer Prize–winning historian and the child of a Black educator and entrepreneur in Conroe, desegregated Conroe schools as a first grader in 1963, and in 1977 became one of the first African Americans to graduate from Conroe High School. In multiple interviews, Gordon-Reed has traced her intellectual genealogy to her time as a Conroe elementary student, when she first developed an affinity for history. Reflecting on her expertise and childhood, Gordon-Reed stated, "Growing up in the end of the '60s, early '70s, I never thought much about studying race but it never occurred to me that it wouldn't be a part of what I was reading about or writing about. It was always there. If you grow up in a place where race matters, that weight is on you, on your mind."[63]

In 1971, Judge William Wayne Justice ruled that East Texas schools had to integrate.[64] Before then, a few Black Conroe students and teachers had begun the process of school desegregation. Also, a few white teachers began to teach at the all-Black Booker T. Washington School (k–12). According to Johnella Franklin, the child of

Black educators and one of the first Black students to desegregate Conroe schools, and others, some of the best Black teachers seemingly were the first to be sent to formerly all-white schools. Students who were the first to desegregate Conroe schools experienced harassment from parents, school staff members, and students. Tommy Wilkerson recalls the derogatory message "n---er go home" being written on the front of Conroe High School. Additionally, the early years of desegregation resulted in many fights between Black and white students. As in other locales that desegregated, many Black teachers and administrators were demoted or fired.[65]

Although Booker T. Washington School often had inferior funding and resources, Black Conroe residents remembered it fondly, primarily because of the care and expertise of their Black teachers. Dorothy Reece did note that she was behind in English when she transferred to an Oklahoma school system in 1942, but she ultimately returned to Conroe and became the longtime librarian at Booker T. Washington after earning a master's degree. Reece recalled fighting to remain at Washington following integration. Reece passionately advocated for resources for the library, including some Black history resources, by threatening "to go to the paper." Reece learned that tactic during the 1950s as a college student in Atlanta. Her experience is evidence that Black residents carried out small acts of resistance throughout the time period.[66]

Booker T. Washington School was one of the integral institutions of African American communities in Conroe and the surrounding areas. Because of the school's importance and community orientation, some Black residents did not want to desegregate. In 1960 and 1965, Washington won the state championship in football. Despite being honored by the African American community, the team was not celebrated in white Conroe or Montgomery County. It was not until 2014 that members of the teams and their families were honored by those larger communities with a ceremony and given community-funded championship rings and plaques. After desegregation, African American student-athletes faced bias and discrimination in extracurricular activities; some of the state-championship players did not receive starting positions they felt they had earned. Claims of bias against African American students in extracurricular activities emerged again during the 1990s.[67]

High school students at Booker T. Washington led three notable direct actions before the 1980s. The first, in the mid-1960s, included a march to desegregate downtown Conroe businesses such as Walgreens drugstore. The second was a Booker T. Washington School walkout in 1968 shortly after the assassination of Martin Luther King Jr.[68] The last one occurred when some Black Conroe High School athletes went on strike in an effort to gain Black representation on the cheerleading squad in the early 1970s and shortly after integration.[69] A similar protest took place in 1991 when some varsity football players boycotted spring drills after alleging racial discrimination in the selection process for cheerleaders. The players were kicked off the team, but after the Texas Education Agency ruled that their punishment was too harsh, they returned after a three-game suspension. The players were subjected to reduced playing time during the season, but school officials agreed to implement a new cheerleading selection process. The players faced additional retribution for their boycott, including suspensions, harassment by school officials, and threats. Rumors also spread that the NAACP and Clarence Brandley had encouraged the players to boycott.[70]Decades-long efforts have been made to teach and preserve Black history in Conroe. Carl White recorded the oral histories of some older African Americans and produced a documentary as an act of remembrance that fits into the larger tradition of Black Conroe residents passing down oral history. In addition, White has run for political office, but his efforts and others' have largely been unsuccessful, in part because of the relatively small Black population, the actions of the political establishment, voter turnout, and the lack of single-member districts. Political representation in Conroe remains largely white.[71] Black residents have advocated to preserve historically Black educational institutions such as Conroe College.[72] The Black Alumni Association of Booker T. Washington School, including key advocates such as Calvin Vinson and Alpha Omega Jones, have challenged the multiple attempts to rename and close the school. Additionally, the association has organized reunions, and other programs and given scholarships.[73]

There have also been efforts to name other Conroe ISD schools after Black residents. Residents successfully petitioned for an elementary school to be named after Lucille J. Bradley, a prominent member of the African American community in Conroe and a longtime educator who attended Conroe Industrial and Normal College as a child and taught at Booker T. Washington and other area schools.[74] In 2009, the legacy of the longtime vocational educator Froncell Reece was commemorated with the Froncell Reece Memorial Gateway, and a statue of Annette Gordon-Reed was unveiled in Conroe's Founders Plaza Park in 2019.[75] Conroe residents have organized the annual J-MAC Black History Month Parade, now known as the Leon Tolbert Annual Black History Month Parade, for over sixty years.[76] During the Free Clarence Brandley Movement, Minnie Brandley served as the grand marshal of the parade one year, and participants "wore 'Free Clarence' shirts and chanted 'Conroe, Conroe, have you heard? This is not Johannesburg.'"[77] Last, because of years of organizing by Black residents, Conroe has a Dr. Martin Luther King Jr. Center, street, and park.[78]

Racialized violence in Conroe meant that mourning became a permanent part of both the town's landscape and Black residents' collective memory. One could argue that within an environment where racialized violence is imminent, survival itself is resistance. According to Kidada E. Williams, a scholar of African American testimonies to racial violence, "These victims' and witnesses' subsequent refusal to endure violence silently constitutes an underappreciated form of resistance to white supremacy."[79] The use of remembering as sustained dissent by Conroe's Black residents is most evident in their oral history and public commemoration practices.

Tamina

As previously noted, memory in Montgomery County, Tamina, and The Woodlands is preserved in part through physical spaces. Residents have made efforts to keep the legacies of the formerly all-Black schools alive by forming alumni associations, preserving school names, and advocating for Black residents in Conroe to be honored with schools named after them. Additionally, residents have sought to maintain land ownership and preserve Black communities in order to retain their legacies. This occurrence is exemplified by the efforts of the Tamina community. Tamina was founded as a Black freedmen's settlement in 1871. Although Tamina was once a thriving community with its own schools and businesses, Tamina schools became part of the Conroe Independent School District in the mid-twentieth century and students were bused to the all-Black school, Booker T. Washington. In recent decades, Tamina has fought to gain basic infrastructure such as water lines, sewage treatment, and paved roads. In addition, residents of Tamina are constantly fighting annexation attempts by the much wealthier, predominantly white communities of Shenandoah and The Woodlands, which were founded in the 1970s and 1980s. The contrast between the wealth disparities of The Woodlands, which was started as a master-planned community by an oil businessman, and Tamina is stark and glaring.

Until recently, Tamina was marked by a tattered green sign that stated, "WELCOME TO THE HISTORIC COMMUNITY OF TAMINA ... SETTLED IN 1871." The sign was replaced, but the old and new welcoming signs are representative of the Tamina community. Tamina residents are proud of their history but also cognizant of their dilapidated surroundings. In recent years, Tamina has been spotlighted by the local and national press because of both its historic significance and its infrastructure conditions. In 2016, the photographer Marti Corn published *The Ground on Which I Stand: Tamina, a Freedmen's Town*. The book documents the Tamina community through photographs and oral history. Further, one of the images in the book was displayed in the Smithsonian's National Portrait Gallery.[80]

Tamina residents retell the history of their community with great vigor, and they connect that historical legacy with their present-day efforts to maintain land ownership and revitalize the community. The Reverend Warzell Booty was one of Tamina's most outspoken residents and advocates. According to Booty, Tamina was in fact founded in 1835. He stated that Tamina was once called Little Egypt and was later renamed "Tammany" by a Captain Berry. Two of the main attractions for the early settlers of Tamina were the nearby sawmills and the railroad, which attracted people of different races.[81] In an article in the *Courier of Montgomery County* in 2017, the longtime Tamina resident Rita Wiltz claimed that Tamina was named in honor of Captain James H. Berry's daughter Tamaney, and that the name may be linked with Tammany Hall in New York.[82]

Scholars have documented the relationship between African Americans and land ownership, and for many, after enslavement, land ownership represented a newfound freedom. In *Freedom Colonies: Independent Black Texans in the Time of Jim Crow*, Thad Sitton and James H. Conrad relate the experiences of "independent rural communities of African American landowners (and land squatters) that formed in the South in the years after Emancipation."[83] While the Tamina community is not documented in *Freedom Colonies*, Sitton and Conrad provide the context for understanding Tamina and its historic and present-day residents. According to Sitton and Conrad, the decline of freedom colonies in Texas was associated with multiple causes: the loss of land from sale or foreclosure, departures due to racial violence, job opportunities in urban areas, legal trickery, illegal coercion, the decline or removal of institutions like schools, significant declines in rural populations, the dilapidation of structures, and annexation.[84] According to the oral histories conducted for the present project, Tamina's decline fits this pattern.

Countless residents tell of a vibrant Tamina past. James Leveston has lived in Tamina since the mid-1940s, when he was an infant, and currently serves as the leader of the Old Tamina Water Supply Corporation. Leveston recalled a time when Tamina was much larger and had its own school, the Phillis Wheatley School, which included first through sixth grade. The school had very limited resources and instructors. The Reverend Warzell Booty moved to Tamina in 1966, and before then, his family had visited this area to hunt. Booty also recalled Tamina as a very close-knit community, with churches and entertainment attractions that were largely built by the residents themselves. Because of redevelopment (including the construction of highways), the establishment of new communities such as Shenandoah and Oak Ridge North, and the selling and loss of land, Tamina is dwindling. But the residents still have hope.[85]

Alongside the vibrant history of Tamina have been simultaneous efforts by outsiders to destabilize the community. Current efforts by Tamina community members to obtain a community-wide sewage system and other basic amenities have been hindered by the larger and wealthier communities of Oak Ridge North and Shenandoah. Although Tamina secured two large grants from the US Department of Housing and Urban Development's Community Development Block Grant Program and from the US Department of Agriculture, failure to come to agreement with governmental officials in Oak Ridge North and, later, Shenandoah has meant that Tamina still operates without a sewage system.[86] The main source of conflict stems from Tamina residents wanting to retain community control. Tamina currently operates its own water company, and in talks with Oak Ridge North, officials sought to retain Tamina's water rights.[87] More recent talks with Shenandoah officials stalled because "terms of the USDA loan would prohibit the city from annexing the area until the loan is paid off, which is expected to take 40 years," according to the journalist Marie Leonard.[88] In short, wealthier communities are withholding their resources because they want to retain the option of annexation and do not want to foot the bill if Tamina residents should be unable to keep up with "the needed rates to cover the service." In a letter dated June 18, 2018, Joanne Callahan Ducharme, Montgomery County's community development director, told Tamina leaders, "Many persons in many entities have attempted to assist Tamina with this project in the past. None of these entities has had an obligation to assist you. Those who have withdrawn have done so for a variety of reasons, none of which have anything to do with race, income, or personal animosity toward anyone in Tamina."[89]

The Reverend Booty stated, "Through the blood, sweat, and tears of these people by continuing paying the taxes is the reason why this community is still here. And they left it for us today to carry on that legacy, but like Brother Leveston said, it's hard when you're up against a system that [is] deliberately holding you back. You take two steps forward, and they pull you back three."[90] His statement encapsulated the passion and motivation behind efforts to save Tamina, but also the hindrances to these efforts. Tamina residents such as Rita Wiltz and Shirley Grimes seek to maintain Tamina through community programming and institutions such as the Tamina Community Center and Children's Books on Wheels and through future projects, including community gardens, improved signage, and other amenities.[91]

Tragedies in Tamina over the years have led to renewed interest by outside communities in helping Tamina residents. On May 12, 2017, a fire killed three Tamina children, Terrance "TJ" Mitchell (thirteen), Kaila Mitchell (six), and Kyle Mitchell (five), and injured several of their relatives and community members. Some specu-lated that the lack of fire hydrants, along with other water issues in the commu-nity, could have hindered the rescue attempts, but firefighters insisted there were no water-flow problems. Firefighters used a water source that was a mile away in Shenandoah.[92] After that tragedy, more fire-safety precautions have been taken.

Finally, residents and outside entities have reinvigorated the cause to preserve the Sweet Rest Cemetery, which has been underwater and without a caretaker for years, so that Tamina residents can be laid to rest with their loved ones.[93] Tamina residents are also leading efforts to document their history through historical markers, books, and events. They are truly seeking to maintain their longevity and autonomy while securing the resources and support they need to continue.[94]

The Woodlands

The Woodlands is a master-planned community south of Conroe and north of Hous-ton. The community was founded by the oil tycoon George P. Mitchell in 1974. The community was supposed to be a model solution to the overpopulation and conges-tion of major cities. Mitchell stated, "I'm concerned about the destruction of our cities, the polarization. The flight of the white middle class to suburbia will ruin cities like Boston, Washington and New York."[95] The Woodlands never achieved the racial diversity that Mitchell promised, and instead became a destination for white flight from Houston. In *The Woodlands: The Inside Story of Creating a Better Hometown*, Roger Galatas and Jim Barlow argue that the lack of racial diversity was not the result of a lack of trying. As a stipulation for receiving a HUD loan, The Woodlands had to meet affirmative action goals. Joel Deretchin, a former director of government rela-tions and vice president for residential operations of The Woodlands, stated: "[The] overall objective was that The Woodlands new community should mirror the com-plexion of the metropolitan area in terms of racial diversity. We were required to have programs and show progress in attracting minorities to live here, and we also had to use minority firms in the development of The Woodlands." Their attempts to attract racial minorities included advertising in "minority newspapers," attending meetings of "minority contractor organizations," reaching out to "minority organizations" and social clubs, attending housing fairs in Houston "that we knew would attract mi-norities," and establishing institutions like an African American church.[96] For com-parison purposes, the Black and Latino population of The Woodlands in 2019 was estimated to be 22 percent; in Houston, it was estimated to be around 66 percent.[97]

While The Woodlands was a dream hometown for many, some people experienced stark racism. In 2017, a Black student at The Woodlands High School was sent a Snapchat message that stated, "We should have hung all u n---ers while we had the chance," after she supported the kneeling protest of professional football players and called the other student a racist. The male student who sent the message received some disciplinary actions but was still allowed to attend school, whereas school ad-ministrators suggested that the female student change schools.[98] During the same year, the chairman of The Woodlands' governing board, Gordy Bunch, apologized for stating that The Woodlands would provide a home for Confederate statues removed from other areas a month after Heather Heyer was killed during the Charlottesville protests over the University of Virginia's Confederate statue. Bunch said in a Facebook message, "I do not condone or accept racism, hate groups, neo-Nazis, KKK or any divisive group . . . I'm not looking to celebrate the Confederacy." This disavowal greatly differed from his original, controversial statement: "We don't have a lot of history here in The Woodlands because we're only 42, 43 years old. For all these folks in Dallas, in Austin and San Antonio and other places looking to relocate their history, might I suggest they can take those assets over here."[99]

Conroe resident and retired Montgomery County sheriff's deputy Mary Tolbert gained great insight about race relations in The Woodlands during her tenure in law enforcement. Tolbert faced discrimination and harassment from her coworkers in the sheriff's department and from residents in The Woodlands. Her coworkers pronounced her name wrong, made up calls, and compelled her to redo paperwork. Some residents referred to her in derogatory terms and questioned her authority. Additionally, Tolbert was sexually harassed while on the job. Despite possibly having grounds for multiple lawsuits, Tolbert stated, "I'm trying to pave a way for other Blacks, and I think I did, because they've had other Black females that come after me."[100]

Montgomery County

In 2016, Conroe was the fastest-growing city with a population of 50,000 or more in the United States. According to an article by the Associated Press, "Conroe, Texas, a northern Houston suburb, was the fastest-growing of the 15, seeing a 7.8 percent increase from 2015 to 2016, a growth rate more than 11 times that of the nation."[101] The population of Conroe was estimated to be 84,378 in 2017, a sharp increase from the 2010 census count of 56,207. The Latino population of Conroe and Montgomery County has increased greatly since the mid-2010s. In Conroe, a 2017 estimate showed that Latino residents made up 24.8 percent of the population, and 17.6 percent of the population of Montgomery County.[102] This demographic shift has not gone unnoticed. The Montgomery County library features a Spanish-language section, and the county has seen an increase in Latino-owned businesses.[103]

The Latino population of The Woodlands is also increasing, and was estimated in 2016 to be 15.4 percent of the total.[104] Latino youth make up around 22 percent of the school population. The Woodlands is likewise experiencing a growth in Latino-owned businesses. In a 2015 article in the *Houston Chronicle*, Julie Charros-Batancor, the president of The Woodlands–Gulf Coast chapter of the US-Mexico Chamber of Commerce, is quoted as saying, "We have to Latinize the Woodlands" in order to attract Latino American business leaders.[105]

In response to the changing demographics of The Woodlands and Montgomery County, there have been reports of heightened anti–Mexican American sentiment in the area in recent years. Some of the accusations include schoolchildren chanting, "Build the wall" and saying that Mexican American children should go back to where they came from.[106] Latino residents attribute the open bigotry to demographic changes and to the election of Donald Trump as president. Multiple well-attended Trump rallies and fund-raisers were held in the area, and one of them became violent.[107] Showcasing the change in sentiments, Stephen Miller, senior policy adviser to Trump, told a rally in 2016, "All of you in this state have seen the effect open borders have had on this country . . . How many innocent Americans have died because we haven't secured our border? . . . Are you ready to protect the working men and women of this country?"[108] In response to concerns about racial discrimination in The Woodlands, the board passed a proclamation in support of diversity in 2017.[109]

Maria Banos Jordan has led coalitions to address the needs of the growing Latino community by securing resources while also fostering the growth of Latino leadership in Montgomery County. Jordan has leveraged the power of prominent political and social leaders to help marginalized Latino communities, which include both citizens and noncitizens. She did similar work in Houston for years, but her work in Montgomery County involves more hours of fieldwork to gain the trust of Latino communities, some of which have not been integrated into larger communities. In 2008, Jordan began the work in Montgomery County part-time, not realizing how the rural nature of the area and the recent demographic shifts would change the tactics and time needed to accomplish her goals. Beginning in 2011, she started organizing in Montgomery County full time and continued to build the organizational infrastructure needed to understand the needs of Latino communities in the area. Using a grassroots leadership strategy based on cultural knowledge, Jordan encourages those she reaches to push past their fear and work to secure a better future for their children and, then, the larger communities. In an interview, Jordan also suggested that multiracial collaborations and diversity in thought were needed.[110] She summarized the multiracial experiences of people in Texas and the importance of power and history in a powerful statement: "Texas has always been a multicultural community. Even through the conflict, we have always had to figure out a way to co-exist. And sometimes it's been ugly. Sometimes it has not been just. So the story has not always properly reflected the reality. And that does something when you change the narrative—that does something to future generations."[111]

Lasting Memories

Montgomery County has a "mark on it," according to Jimmie Shaw. She was discussing the history of racialized violence in the area, particularly the lynchings that occurred in downtown Conroe.[112] That mark of racialized violence and discrimination is both a physical and a psychological manifestation. Reflecting on the experiences of African Americans in Conroe, Johnella Franklin stated, "There was always this sense that it was really hard for Blacks to be really prominent in Conroe . . . There was this belief that you shouldn't show off any success." For Franklin, the history of Conroe makes it "really hard for [her] to dream" of a better Conroe, because "there are still two different worlds."[113] Despite experiencing sustained racial violence, people of color in Montgomery County still resist and work toward a better future. The African American population, despite consisting of not more than 10 percent of the total population, fights to ensure that its history is remembered in the commemorative landscape of Montgomery County. People of color in the county continue to resist efforts to push them out, by continuously laying claim to a place that has been openly hostile to nonwhite people. Noting the importance of surviving and acknowledging what they are up against, the Reverend Booty of Tamina stated, "They are holding us down now from an identity, a future survival of self-sufficiency."[114] They fight to always be remembered in this place. Tamina remains. Booker T. Washington School remains. Lucille J. Bradley Elementary remains. The people and their memories remain.

In short, racial memories in Montgomery County are deeply tied to physical spaces. Physical spaces tell of the struggle for civil rights and in many ways remind residents that their efforts for civil rights did not end in the 1970s and have in fact continued. Lacking significant political representation, Black and Brown American residents have had to assert power and agency mainly through other means, including place making and naming, oral history, and business ownership.[115] While racial violence has indeed left a mark on Montgomery County, African Americans and Mexican Americans have also left a mark on it, and that should be remembered.

PART II

SURVIVAL AND SELF-DETERMINATION: CHICANO/A STRUGGLES IN SOUTH AND WEST TEXAS

CHAPTER 5

THE SOUTH-BY-SOUTHWEST BORDERLANDS' CHICANA/O UPRISING:
The Brown Berets, Black and Brown Alliances, and the Fight against Police Brutality in West Texas

JOEL ZAPATA

Since the early twentieth century, ethnic Mexicans have been the primary labor force in West Texas. They largely built the region's rail and road infrastructure while also helping in agriculture and industry. Despite Mexicans' central role, the region's southern-origin Anglo-American population developed a racialized system whereby Mexican people were kept at the lower socioeconomic rungs of society. Mexicans faced segregation at businesses as well as in the workforce, were isolated in neighborhoods with little or no public services, had subpar public schools, and had their votes—when allowed to vote—diluted through at-large electoral systems. Like people of color across the nation, however, Mexican people in West Texas were not ignored by law enforcement. Instead, they suffered constant police brutality.[1]

Even returning soldiers did not have their rights honored. Recounting his experiences after arriving home in Lubbock from eighteen months of combat during World War II, Raymond Flores—who had been wounded in battle—stated that in 1945, "[I] could not drink or eat where a white man did. And I'd just come back from fighting for this country."[2] Evidently, Anglo-Americans developed a rigid Juan Crow system mirroring the Jim Crow system that African Americans endured across the South, including West Texas and beyond. In death, repression did not end. Lubbock's 166-acre public cemetery remained effectively segregated into the late 1980s. In addition to that injustice, community members accused the city officials of recycling graves in the cemetery's "Old Colored" (Black) and "Old Catholic" (Mexican) sections, stacking multiple coffins on one another and thus visibly erasing the location of older grave sites.[3]

This cemetery exemplifies how West Texas is a sociocultural shatter belt between the South and the Southwest. The region's Mexican population and geographic location link it with the latter. Its Anglo-American population, their re-creation of Jim Crow, and the borrowing of that social system to oppress Mexican people link it with the South.[4] Thus, Mexicans in West Texas had to contend with a ruling white population that identified itself and the region as southern. Conscious of their poor social condition, Mexicans began organizing through church groups, labor unions, the League of United Latin American Citizens (LULAC), and the American GI Forum. In the 1960s and 1970s, the children and the grandchildren of these advocates continued to work toward achieving social justice through the more outspoken

Chicana/o movement. Youth led the movement's rise in West Texas. Like other locations, West Texas had a long history of student — and, by extension, parent — organizing. In the 1960s, however, the region's student movement became intertwined with student uprisings that spanned the globe. Indeed, "Mexican American student militancy intensified as more and more of them became convinced that they were part of an international revolution in the making."[5]

Attuned to national as well as global movements, and in reaction to their local circumstances, young Mexicans in West Texas organized to better their circumstances. They formed groups such as the Mexican American Youth Organization (MAYO) in high schools. Taking note of Chicana/o student walkouts in California, New Mexico, and Colorado, students boycotted Abilene schools in 1969. They had six chief demands: permission to speak Spanish on school grounds, representation in student government, recruitment of Chicana/o teachers and counselors, cultural awareness training for Anglo-American teachers, the formation of a bilingual education program, and a reduction of Chicana/o dropout rates.[6] These goals were not particular to Abilene, however. Chicanas/os across the nation wanted the same things. Also in 1969, Texas Tech University students established a chapter of El Movimiento Estudiantil Chicano de Aztlán (MEChA) in Lubbock. In 1971, students established a MEChA chapter at West Texas State University in Canyon. Tech students hosted the first meeting of the organization's state chapters in the fall of 1971. Thus, West Texas students were active in bringing together the far-flung wings of the Chicana/o student movement. Students from across the state appointed Lucas Trujillo, a Tech student and military veteran, as the meeting's chairman. The meeting and the appointment of Trujillo suggest that West Texas students were leaders in the larger Chicana/o student movement, which demanded that universities fully open their doors to Mexican students, faculty members, and administrators, as well as establish Chicana/o studies programs.[7]

In West Texas, instances of police brutality spurred broad sections of the Mexican population to join the Chicana/o movement and thus force social change. The most active years in regard to Chicana/o protests, political participation, and Black and Brown alliances were precisely the years when the most cases of police killings occurred. This unity included the coming together of the region's Mexican population across lines of political ideology to address and end police brutality. More mainstream social justice organizations such as the American GI Forum, the Mexican American Legal Defense and Educational Fund (MALDEF), and LULAC joined Chicana/o activists, especially the Brown Berets, in protests across West Texas.[8] In West Texas, the protests brought profound sociocultural change. As Nick Hernandez, a leader of the Odessa Brown Berets, which participated in the Chicana/o movement throughout the region, noted in 2016, his hometown's anti-police-brutality activism "turned this city around. I mean, it just went from A to Z. . . . Hispanics started getting some respect, harassment slowed down. There is still a lot of it out there, but it's not like it used to be."[9]

The Police Shotgun Shooting of Ernesto Nerios

Shortly after five in the morning on August 14, 1971, Lubbock police officers stopped a car on Broadway Street. Pedro Nerios, twenty-seven, was driving, and his Vietnam veteran brother, Ernesto Nerios, twenty-one, was a passenger. Officers later said that they stopped the brothers because their car matched the description of a vehicle involved in an attempted robbery, at knifepoint, of the Serve-U Food Market a few blocks away. Chicana/o activists, historian Andrés A. Tijerina, and Mexican American community members asserted that officers stopped the brothers for speeding. Indeed, the initial police story changed. Police officials originally told reporters that officers stopped the car for a traffic violation. The officers then heard about the attempted robbery over the radio. Suspecting the brothers, they "sought to arrest them."[10] Whatever the reason for the stop, the officers arrested Pedro. According to the officers, who did not instruct Ernesto to exit the car, Ernesto climbed into the driver's seat and drove off.[11] The police officers followed, firing, by their own account, twelve times at the car. After driving several blocks, Nerios abandoned the car, according to police. He ran on foot, and "police said he refused to halt on officers' commands and after warning shots were fired."[12] In all, officers fired five "warning shots." As Ernesto ran, Officer Jack Mitchell shot him with a shotgun. Officers found Ernesto lying near the city's railroad yard, with a massive shotgun wound. Wayne LeCroy, a Lubbock County justice of the peace, told the *Lubbock Avalanche-Journal* that "Nerios was shot once in the back of the head."[13] Officers never stated that Ernesto threatened them while driving or after exiting the car. Ernesto drove off—they shot at the back of the car. He ran—they shot at his back. Ernesto died in Lubbock Methodist Hospital at about eleven. He was survived by his wife, his five-month-old daughter, and his disabled mother.[14]

Nephtalí De León, a Brown Berets member and writer, proposed a different version:

> Pedro and Ernesto are out for a ride.... Pedro is driving.
>
> Stop at the store! Pedro stops. Ernesto Nerios goes in. Ernesto Nerios comes out. Let's go!
>
> Police stop them for speeding. Police later say that they had also received a report of an attempted robbery. Pedro gets off the car. Police then order Nerios to get off the car or "we'll kill you!" Ernesto is frightened, steps on the gas and he's off. Gunshots pursue him.
>
> The chase. Police at one point are so close to Ernesto's crawling car (according to eyewitness Mr. Lem Hereford) that they get off their own car, kneel on the road, and fire upon the frightened Nerios several more times.
>
> ... Ernesto's car stalls. He jumps out. Several police officers follow afoot. Spotlights. Perfect target. The night is broken—.38 calibers, 12 gauge shotguns, boom through the night.
>
> ... Did you try to rob a store with a knife? This is what officers of the law say ... They do admit that they found no weapon on your person or in your car. We will never know about Ernesto Nerios. You have been tried and executed on the streets.[15]

Pedro Nerios was arraigned before Justice of the Peace Wayne LeCroy on Monday, August 15. LeCroy set Pedro's bond at $5,000, which Pedro could not afford. He remained jailed. Three days after Ernesto's death, on Tuesday, August 17, the same justice of the peace ruled the police shooting a justifiable homicide. That same day,

Mexican American community members and young Chicana/o activists picketed the city's police station from four in the morning to six at night. Chicana/o activists, led by Nephtalí De León, then confronted Lubbock's Citizens Grievance Commission, which had a regularly scheduled meeting in the Lubbock City Hall's council chambers. The meeting became a three-hour "power struggle between Commission Chairman Virgil Johnson and Nephtali De Leon [sic]."[16] De León made an "impassioned plea" for the city to share in the funeral costs with the working-class Nerios family and for an annuity for Ernesto's widow and five-month-old daughter. Pressured by Chicana/o activists, the Citizens Grievance Commission ended the meeting by voting to ask the Lubbock City Council to investigate the shooting. As LeCroy announced his ruling of justifiable homicide and activists confronted the Citizens Grievance Commission, funeral services for Ernesto Nerios were held in Lubbock's Guadalupe Barrio. He was buried in the segregated City of Lubbock Cemetery.[17]

Police Brutality as Everyday Policing over People of Color

Lubbock, like much of the South in regard to African Americans and the Southwest in regard to Mexican Americans, had a long history of police violence against people of color. The Lubbock City Council established the Citizens Grievance Commission in June before the August police killing of Ernesto Nerios. It had done so under pressure from Lubbock's African American community, the local chapter of the National Association for the Advancement of Colored People (NAACP), and other Black organizations.[18] In West Texas, the South and the Southwest, along with the regions' policing systems, coalesced to brutalize Mexican Americans and African Americans. In response, Black and Brown partnerships emerged.

Having launched a civil rights movement aimed at integrating the city's businesses and Texas Tech University during the preceding two decades, African Americans in Lubbock demanded reforms from the city council in the summer of 1971 to end police abuse of their community, which city officials had segregated in East Lubbock. While Mexicans faced confinement in the de facto segregated Guadalupe Barrio in the northern part of the city, Lubbock officials erected an "'iron curtain' . . . in 1923" through an ordinance that restricted Black residents to East Lubbock.[19] Urban renewal led to Interstate 27 being constructed through a section of Lubbock's African American neighborhood, destroying part of the Black community and further separating East Lubbock from the rest of the city. Additionally, East Lubbock and Guadalupe Barrio were separated from the city's white neighborhoods by several sets of railroad tracks.[20]

When the Black community demanded a meeting with the city council in 1971 regarding police brutality, the community was offered a meeting with one council member. Over 150 members of Lubbock's Black community attended the meeting. Soon after, a group of 50 African Americans addressed the issue before the entire council. It responded by setting up the Citizens Grievance Commission, which both African Americans and Mexican Americans would use as their social justice movements coalesced.[21]

Indeed, during the months preceding and following the police shooting of Ernesto Nerios, numerous African Americans and Mexican Americans accused Lubbock police officers of mistreatment. In one case of excessive force, policemen broke the arm of a Mexican American boy attempting to enter his home section of Guadalupe Barrio, which had been condemned after being largely destroyed by a tornado on May 11, 1970.[22] Then, Mexican Americans accused the police of harassing and beating them on October 23 during a dance at the city's South Plains Fair Park Coliseum. In this case, police jailed almost three dozen people, including families: "Husband, wife, children."[23] Such police actions were common. In the continual cycle of marginalization and abuse, one scholar posited that "the killing of Ernesto Nerios is routine."[24] But city officials failed to respond to the abuse beyond creating the Citizens Grievance Commission and directing it to prepare a report regarding citizen complaints.[25]

In keeping with that line of responsiveness, on Thursday, September 9, 1971, the city council denied Nephtalí De León's request to establish an annuity fund for the Nerios family and to help pay for the funeral. The council quickly closed its investigation—after no serious inquiries—into the police shooting. In fact, De León claimed that the council and the Lubbock Police Department had failed to interview two civilian witnesses to the shooting incident, which had extended for several blocks by car and on foot. Further rebuffing demands for an investigation, council members announced, "The case had been turned over to the district attorney for grand jury consideration at the request of the policemen involved."[26] Elected officials seemingly chose to respond to appeals made by the "policemen involved" in killing Ernesto Nerios, but not to those from their ethnic Mexican constituents.

That same Thursday, over 150 youths, most of them Black, marched to the downtown police headquarters from East Lubbock to demand that fifteen-year-old Jeff Carl Carver be prosecuted for shooting sixteen-year-old Willie Ray Collier at the historically Black Dunbar High School, which was undergoing integration, earlier that day. The shooter was white; the victim was Black. Under pressure, County Attorney Tom Purdom agreed to file charges of murder with malice against Carver in juvenile court. But when the marchers dispersed and headed back to East Lubbock, police dogs attacked. A number of protesters broke the "windows to some businesses in the East Lubbock." In what became a riot, a gas station attendant was beaten, "and a policeman suffered minor injuries from rock throwing during" that incident.[27] In response, Mayor Jim Granberry issued a citywide dusk-to-dawn curfew. Two hours into the curfew, someone critically wounded patrolman Russell McKenzie with a small-caliber rifle as he surveilled East Lubbock. Swiftly, "police dogs, armored tanks, and helicopters" belonging to the city and state amassed in East Lubbock.[28] A white state-owned police tank had "a sign hung on the front reading 'McKenzie Raiders.'"[29] Police said more shots were fired at them throughout the night.[30]

On the following Saturday, local leaders of the United Black Coalition and the NAACP met with the city council during an emergency meeting. They "told the council, without biting their tongues, that they were tired of the armored tank, helicopters, and over-reaction of policemen in the East Lubbock community."[31] By the time officials ended the curfew later that day, police had arrested 102 African Americans, 33 Mexican Americans, and 16 Anglo-Americans for violating it. Despite the curfew being citywide, it "had been enforced mainly against" Lubbock's Black popu-

Composite image of the March of Faith in Lubbock, 1971. Courtesy of Nephtalí De León from his *Chicanos: Our Background and Our Pride* (Lubbock: Trucha Publications, 1972).

lation.[32] The Dunbar shooting and the curfew further united the local, regional, and state NAACP organizations, along with Lubbock's Black journalists, Black churches, and young activists, in demanding an end to police abuse.[33]

The law—or those in charge of carrying it out—was also swift in punishing Pedro Nerios. On September 14, one month after his arrest, a Lubbock jury indicted Pedro for assault and attempted robbery. During the closing days of the following month, Pedro pleaded guilty to both charges. He was sentenced to three years in prison.[34] Whether or not the Nerios brothers committed a robbery, it is doubtful that Pedro was able to afford or obtain suitable legal representation.

The Brown Berets and the March of Faith

Speaking of the injustices that people of color faced, Nephtalí De León bluntly stated that the police "kept killing . . . murdering some of our people," adding, "This was Lubbock, Texas. Late Sixties. So . . . [the] Brown Berets cropped up."[35] One of the founders of the Lubbock Brown Berets and the son of one of Lubbock's first Mexican American police officers (who died on the line of duty in 1947, only months after Gilbert's birth), Gilbert Herrera concurred. In his words, the Brown Berets were a "militant group" that "started fighting the police departments" during the 1960s and 1970s when "Mexicanos were being killed by law enforcement all over the country."[36] Like their counterparts in other regions, the Lubbock Brown Berets called for an end to police violence.

Responding to the lack of official action to stop police brutality, Lubbock's Mexican American political activists—"not the least of which was an outspoken Lubbock 'radical,'" Nephtalí De León—began to plan a mass protest during the months following the Ernesto Nerios killing.[37] The organizers included more mainstream and at times conservative Mexican Americans, such as LULAC members, American GI Forum veterans, lay leaders of the Catholic Church–affiliated group De Colores, as well as people with no activist background.[38] The diverse organizers met at the Guadalupe Center in the heart of the city's Mexican barrio. They decided to call the planned protest "La Marcha de Fe" (The March of Faith) because of its religious undertones and their faith in peaceful political action.[39] The diverse organizers presented a united front. According to De León, word of La Marcha de Fe "spread like fire through the barrios." Yet many parents forbade their daughters and sons from attending the protest. Some were scared that it would be met by violence from the police. Others saw public protesting as antisocial or preferred to remain politically unengaged. But "when the parents realized the commitment of the young people to the march," they also decided to join the protest.[40] Their children pushed them to join the Chicana/o movement, even if only for one march.

On November 7, 1971, Brown Berets from Texas and New Mexico, Raza Unida Party members from throughout Texas, Chicana/o youth, elders who refused to identify as Chicana/os, children, and priests and ministers came together to voice their grievances regarding police brutality and other social injustices. The protest began with over five hundred people gathered to listen to jubilant music in Mose Hood Park. An interdenominational religious ceremony followed. During the ceremony, priests and ministers counseled those gathered to protest "with dignity and peace."[41] While the gathering did not include a significant number of African Americans, Lubbock's Black newspaper reported how the Black community's "Brown Brothers came" together to "denounce the Lubbock Police Department for ... brutality."[42]

Following the ceremony, Brown Berets organized the crowd into marching lines. Headed by a banner of La Virgen de Guadalupe and another banner with the words "People's March of Faith," participants marched toward downtown Lubbock. They carried posters with messages such as "Down with Police Brutality," "We Demand Respect," and "We Can No Longer Be Patient." They raised clenched fists, sang, cheered, and cried, "Chicano Power!" on the streets of one of the most conservative cities in the nation. Brown Beret members and male community volunteers walked alongside the marching crowd as lookouts against altercations or other disturbances. Furthermore, protest leaders urged all march participants to ignore racist taunts from Anglo-American bystanders and the heavily armed police officers clad in riot gear who surrounded the protesters. Anglo-American observers who did not taunt the marchers "appeared to be amused, while others had a horrified look on their faces."[43] No such mass protest had ever occurred in Lubbock or anywhere else in West Texas. This was a new experience for people of color and for Anglo-Americans. It was likely that all present thought their city would forever change.

Mexicans in West Texas en masse demanded social justice for the first time; the marchers were jubilant and full of pride. Overcome by the historic moment, "many of the parents and other onlookers who had followed the march because of family members or curiosity were so overcome that they too joined the march."[44] By the time they reached the Lubbock County Courthouse, the march had swelled to 1,500 people.[45] Although she could not be present because of her inability to walk, Mercedes M. Nerios wrote to Nephtalí De León and other protest leaders: "I am very grateful for what you are doing for our Mexican American" people. She prayed "to God and to the Virgin of Guadalupe" that the protesters would succeed "in our hopes."[46]

Three people spoke: Chon García, Mariano García, and Joe Rangel. They read the protesters' grievances and demands from an outline that a thirty-member committee of students, priests, ministers, laborers, homemakers, and business owners had composed. They began as follows: "We are here to challenge and indict a system which has denied the Chicano his basic human and civil rights. Violence and brutality have been inflicted on our people in the name of law and order. We have suffered too long under a political and social system which promises equality for all but which deliberately denies it to us."[47] They called for equal protection under the law, an end to police brutality and abuse, and juries that demonstrated racial equity. The outline also named officers who mistreated Mexican Americans, and demanded their removal from the police force.[48]

In addition, the committee used the protest as an opportunity to demand social justice beyond policing and judicial issues. They called for equitable representation in city government, an end to discriminatory city employment practices, a remedy for Mexican American dropout rates, the establishment of bilingual-bicultural education in Lubbock, and the hiring of Mexican school counselors and teachers.[49] Police brutality sparked mass political action that generated a wide range of demands never before seen in West Texas.

Change was not to come easily, however. Chon García, Mariano García, and Joe Rangel read the grievances and demands under the presence of heavily armed city, county, and state police. Atop the buildings surrounding the final protest site, police officers stood "armed with movie cameras and high power rifles." To Nephtalí De León, "to be surrounded by high powered rifles, deputies, and guns all zeroed in on you tends to make you feel unwanted."[50]

Despite the protest's commitment to nonviolence, police forces carefully filmed the participants and their leaders, intimidating them with the possibility of adverse repercussions such the loss of employment. Further, the protesters knew that police guns could be used for more than intimidation. When protesting police misconduct, Gilbert Herrera, founder of the Lubbock Brown Berets, remembered "police with their rifle scopes aiming at me, ready for me to do anything to blow my brains out." He went on, "I am pretty sure if a firecracker had went off, there were certain members that would have blown my brains out."[51] He could have faced the same fate as Ernesto Nerios.

Notwithstanding the sizable police response, the city's white power structure publicly ignored or downplayed La Marcha de Fe and the consistent police abuse people of color faced. For example, the local newspaper of record, the staunchly conservative *Lubbock Avalanche-Journal*, reported that police were merely present at the march for "controlling traffic" and did not mention that they were wearing riot gear and carrying cameras and large weapons, or that the protest was a reaction to police brutality.[52]

La Marcha de Fe and Community Transformation

Lubbock city officials made no public comment regarding the protest. No official greeted the protesters at the courthouse or addressed the list of demands and grievances. Yet "city council work notes and minutes reveal a genuine state of concern and anxiety behind the closed doors of City Hall."[53] Officials took note of the protest size and its outspokenness; they realized that reforms would be necessary if they wanted to avoid future protests. Likewise, school officials remained silent but began enacting changes.[54]

Hence, the lack of an immediate public response did not mean La Marcha de Fe was fruitless. Likely already concerned about the African American–led protests of September 9 and the following weekend, the Lubbock City Council quietly assigned the Citizens Grievance Commission the task of making recommendations regarding La Marcha de Fe's demands. The commission's suggestions included the appointment of more people of color to city boards and changing the city's inequitable employment practices. After all, the Citizens Grievance Commission "heard about as many complaints about job discrimination, especially on the part of the city, as it" did about police brutality.[55] Nonetheless, the commission's recommendations centered on police relations with the city's Black and Brown populations.[56]

In particular for Mexican people, the Citizens Grievance Commission recommended that the minimum height requirement for police officers be changed to five feet, six inches, which would allow more ethnic Mexicans to be hired. Under the direction of the Texas Civil Service Commission, which had intervened in Lubbock at the insistence of Chicana/o activists, the city council reduced the height requirement to five feet, seven inches. This occurred eight months after La Marcha de Fe. Within a year, Lubbock began to see an increase in Mexican American police officers, firefighters, and teachers as well as city and county employees.[57] Gilbert Herrera concluded that because of "protests of the Lubbock Police Department," the department began to hire more ethnic Mexican officers.[58] La Marcha de Fe and related actions had long-term results.

More broadly, the Citizens Grievance Commission found that the Lubbock Police Department discriminated against African Americans and Mexican Americans. The commission advised "that the police be required to enforce the law equally in all sections of Lubbock, and that whites, blacks, and chicanos be treated equally under the law." The commission also recommended that officers stop harassing interracial couples. Finally, the commission concluded that there was "no place for discrimination, discourtesy, or the excessive use of force on the part of the police or any employee or official of the City of Lubbock."[59]

Black and Brown Unity

La Marcha de Fe and its repercussions benefited both African Americans and Mexican Americans. Lubbock's Black newspaper of record asserted that the Citizens Grievance Commission's "recommendations were made for all of us."[60] Indeed, one of the primary recommendations was that the city create a permanent Human Relations Commission that would be "representative of all the citizens of Lubbock." Less than a year after the recommendation was made, the city council formed a Human Relations Commission made up of five Anglo-Americans, five African Americans, and five Mexican Americans.[61]

Moreover, while Mexican Americans and African Americans had often benefited from each other's activism and supported each other in word, after La Marcha de Fe, they began to actively collaborate. Rose Wilson, the longtime president of the Lubbock NAACP, recognized Gilbert Herrera for helping organize an African American protest against police brutality. Wilson acclaimed Herrera because "he knew how to form a peaceful march." He had learned to do so from La Marcha de Fe.[62] The African American march that Gilbert helped organize occurred after a police officer shot Tommy Lee Davis, a twenty-seven-year-old African American, in his own home. Police claimed that Davis had a gun, an assertion that the Black and Brown communities refuted. To demand an end to police killings, NAACP members, Brown Berets, and others marched from East Lubbock to the federal courthouse in downtown Lubbock.[63]

At other times, Chicana/o and Black newspaper publishers in Lubbock shared stories, typesetters, and materials to ensure that their periodicals reached their communities. They had to aid each other; as Olga Agüero, the publisher of Lubbock's *El Editor*, rhetorically asked, "Do you think the *Avalanche-Journal* would ever welcome us?"[64] Considering that newspaper's negative reporting on people of color and its origins "as a forum" for its founder's "personal campaign to keep blacks out of Lubbock," the answer would have been no.[65] African Americans and Mexican Americans in Lubbock shared many of the social issues facing Black and Latino residents in other parts of the country. Seeing this, Wilson and Herrera, along with others, continued to collaborate in advocating for social justice in their city.[66]

For example, A. Gene Gains, Lubbock's first African American attorney, filed a lawsuit against the city in 1976, arguing that its at-large city council system diluted minority votes. Mexican Americans quickly joined the suit. After a change in the legal team, the case was decided in 1983 in favor of the Black and Brown plaintiffs. In 1984, Lubbock held its first single-member-district elections for city council. T. J. Patterson became the first elected African American council member; Maggie Trejo became the first elected Mexican American council member. During their time on the council, Trejo and Patterson "became a team." Patterson noted, "There were two of us, Maggie and me, and when we voted nay, they couldn't get nothing through . . . We had some muscle with that." This collaboration, Patterson argued, "paid off for the benefit and the welfare of Lubbock."[67]

The Shootings of Tiburcio Griego Santome and Juan Galaviz

Notwithstanding progress in Lubbock, social justice remained incomplete in West Texas. Throughout the 1970s, police shootings and the abuse of ethnic Mexicans in West Texas, the Southwest, and other areas continued. Six years after the shooting of Ernesto Nerios, Glasscock County sheriff's deputies, along with a retired sheriff's deputy from nearby Martin County, arrested Tiburcio Griego Santome, age thirty-seven, for disorderly conduct at a church festival in the small unincorporated community of Saint Lawrence. (Glasscock County is just east of Midland; Martin County is just north of Midland.) Deputies conducted the arrest at about seven thirty on Sunday, November 6, 1977. They placed Santome in the back of Sheriff Royce "Booger" Pruitt's squad car. According to sheriff's deputies, Santome was "kind of acting up, and they couldn't get him cuffed, so they just put him in the back seat"—completely unrestrained.[68]

Sheriff Pruitt began driving Santome to the Glasscock County jail in Garden City. A retired Martin County deputy named G. B. Therwanger sat next to the unrestrained Santome. On the way to the jail, only about fifteen miles from where the arrest occurred, Pruitt and Therwanger claimed that Santome produced a knife "sort of the size of steak knife."[69] Santome slashed Pruitt's head and cut Therwanger's arm. Nevertheless, Therwanger managed to reach for an automatic pistol lying on the front seat or console—also within reach of the unrestrained Santome. Therwanger fired four shots. Pruitt and Therwanger drove the wounded Santome to a clinic in Big Spring, about forty-two miles from Saint Lawrence, although hospitals were available about forty-four miles from Saint Lawrence in Midland. Santome was dead when he arrived at the clinic. Even if he had been alive, it is doubtful the small clinic could have done much for someone shot point-blank four times.[70]

Less than two weeks later, Rick Hamby, the Glasscock County district attorney, decided not to present the results of his investigation of the shooting to a grand jury. Under the direction of Texas attorney general John Hill, the Texas Rangers investigated the statements of those involved in the shooting. On November 12, 1977, the Rangers presented their results to Assistant Attorneys General Ed Idar and Dan Maeso during a closed-door meeting in Midland. Idar stressed that the state investigation "should not be viewed as an infringement of District Attorney Rick Hemby's prerogatives" or "imply that local enforcement is not doing a proper job."[71] Don Richard, the assistant district attorney of Howard County, where Big Spring is located and where Santome's body was being held by authorities, said that the Texas Rangers' visit was "not on the request of his office and we take a negative attitude about them (the agents) coming."[72] Probing by outsiders into the police shooting was not welcomed by all local officials.

State and local authorities filed no charges against Pruitt or Therwanger. Asked by Santome's widow, Maria Santome, West Texas LULAC councils, along with the LULAC state director, began looking into the shooting. Maria voiced concern about the arrest procedure, which had obviously been botched. According to Pruitt and Therwanger's own testimony, Santome had not been handcuffed; a loaded gun was placed within his reach; and he had not been checked for weapons when arrested. In addition, Maria "was neither notified of the death nor was she allowed to view the body until after it was embalmed."[73] Indeed, authorities informed journalists of Santome's death before contacting Maria.[74]

The nearby Abilene LULAC council started a letter-writing campaign to state officials and President Jimmy Carter. Council members voted to request an FBI investigation into the shooting. While LULAC members were protesting the shooting, Camillo Rosales, a local LULAC officer, stated, "Once a person is in jail he should be protected. And Mexican Americans in jail are not protected, they are being assassinated." Rosales added that "equal justice is guaranteed by the constitution but Mexican-Americans are being judged by a double standard of justice." That is, they were being judged and executed without a trial or a jury. While the council was pleased that Attorney General Hill had responded quickly to calls for an investigation, the council president, Eddie Reina, stated that the Texas Rangers were "a very biased group of individuals when investigating another law enforcement agency." Reina declared that the Rangers had "long been associated with a double standard of justice toward Mexican-American people," which made them the wrong agency for an investigation into the police shooting of a Mexican American.[75]

A little over a month after Tiburcio Griego Santome's death, Big Spring police stopped Juan Galaviz, nineteen, for questioning on December 10, 1977. He was suspected of driving a stolen car and of stealing the car owner's wallet. Juan led police on a high-speed chase. At its culmination, police said Juan reached into his pocket. Sergeant Leroy Spires fired his weapon, shooting Juan in the head.[76]

Juan Galaviz's family filed a wrongful-death suit against Spires and the City of Big Spring. Mexican American leaders declared the police shooting unnecessary. Once again, the Rangers investigated. The grand jury, summoned to hear the results of the investigation by the Big Spring police, returned a no bill, meaning that insufficient evidence was presented to sustain the charge. Instead the grand jury— which was majority white—wrote a letter to the Big Spring City Council. Neither the grand jury nor the council disclosed the contents of the letter, but it might have reflected the jury's dissatisfaction with the police investigation. Jury members could not reach a decision from the evidence they were given. Sergeant Spires, citing harassment of him and his family after the shooting, resigned from the city's police force. If true, it was perhaps because some West Texas Mexicans saw that personally confronting Spires and his family was the only way of gaining some justice.[77]

According to the *El Paso Times*, the back-to-back shootings of Tiburcio Griego Santome and Juan Galaviz "made martyrs of" the two. The shootings also brought "an uneasy and unaccustomed tension" to Big Spring. The community was not used to Mexicans claiming their rights or demanding social justice. Francisco Martinez, a local Mexican American leader, thought the shootings were "just the end result of what's been happening around here for years." Big Spring and West Texas "had always operated under a double standard." He felt "almost certain that if they (Santome and Galaviz) had been white they'd still be alive." As in Lubbock after the death of Ernesto Nerios, these "shootings fired the wrath of the Mexican-American community," especially the youth.[78]

The Arrest and Beating of Larry Ortega Lozano

Exactly a month after Juan Galaviz's death, on January 10, 1978, Ector County sheriff's deputies arrested Alberto "Larry" Ortega Lozano, twenty-seven, at around ten twenty at night in Odessa. The deputies were responding to a disturbance call. Someone had driven a 1967 Dodge pickup off the road and into a barbed-wire fence on the edge of the city. Deputies Lee Roy Murphy and Gene Kloss arrived, and according to their accounts, Larry refused to show his identification, attempted to run, slapped the officers, and thus resisted arrest. According to Sheriff Elton Faught, Lozano "whupped their ass."[79] Two more deputies arrived, Dee Johns and Darry Davis. The four handcuffed Lozano—"just how, isn't said."[80] But during the arrest, he suffered injuries severe enough that he had to be taken to Odessa's Medical Center Hospital. Hospital records revealed that his right eye was swollen shut, and he had multiple bruises on his face, with a large swollen laceration on his forehead. Ector County justice of the peace Virgil Lumpee charged Lozano, once he was released from the hospital, with aggravated assault on the sheriff's deputies and set a $5,000 bond for each charge, for a total of $15,000. No investigation was launched into the injuries that Lozano suffered during the arrest.[81]

Lozano wrote a friend to bring some clean clothing for him to the county jail. In the letter, Lozano told a far different story from that of the arresting deputies. He was on his way to a store when he ran off the road. When deputies arrived and asked for his identification, Lozano wrote, an "officer proceeded to flash light whip me." He repeated the accusation: "When I went to produce it [the driver's license] they slogged me with the flashlight." The mug shots taken the day after the arrest, along with X-rays taken at the hospital, revealed evidence of the beating he suffered. The abuse, though, did not end during the arrest. He wrote that the "booking deputies also tried to whip the shit out of me." They "kicked me" and "started beating on me while I had the cuffs on." Lozano did admit in the letter that "when the officers took the cuffs off I started fighting with them."[82] According to the sheriff's office, after the incidents involving Lozano, four deputies required medical attention. Lozano "had torn their uniforms, beaten their faces, and in the end, wounded their pride." Deputies seemingly had negative feelings toward Lozano.[83]

Rocke Flannigan, a prisoner in the jail when Lozano was brought in, later told a journalist that Lozano had gashes on his forehead and bruises, and both eyes were swollen shut, when he arrived.[84] In fact, the booking photo shows an unrecognizable Lozano: face swollen, both eyes shut, an injured forehead.[85] As in the letter to his friend, Lozano told Flannigan that when he reached into his pocket for identification, as instructed, a deputy began to beat him with a flashlight. After deputies handcuffed him, they continued to hit him on the forehead and face. Lozano also told Flannigan that when he was being booked, they again beat him. During the second beating, Lozano told Flannigan that he had resisted "in self-defense."[86]

It must be noted that Lozano had a history of mental illness. He had become volatile, mad at himself, and incoherent while visiting his sister, Margaret, in Austin the previous year. Margaret committed him to the Austin State Hospital for a month. A state mental health caseworker saw Lozano while he was in the Ector County jail, but he was not sent to a mental health facility, despite a regulation that mentally ill persons should not remain in jail for longer than twenty-four hours.[87]

Police Brutality as Everyday Policing in Odessa

Larry Ortega Lozano's narrative of his arrest would not have been atypical in Odessa. Nick Hernandez, an Odessa activist and Brown Beret member, recalled heavy-handed policing against Mexicans by sheriff's deputies as normal practice. As an eleven-year-old in the early 1960s, he remembered that "one of the deputies was talking real bad" to his mother while arresting his teenage brother. Hernandez recalled that he got between the deputy and his mother "and tried to translate for her because" her English was limited. As a result, the deputy grabbed him and said, "You're going too!" Of his early experience with Ector County deputies, Hernandez recounted: "I spent two weeks in the county, eleven years old. In the cell next to my brother . . . and I didn't do anything but try to translate for my mom." For Mexicans in Odessa, Hernandez stated, "that was the way that it was. It was really, really rough." As a child, Hernandez experienced police abuse as a daily way of life, but even then he knew "it just wasn't right."[88]

As a teenager, Hernandez and his friends were pulled over by deputies for minor infractions or for no reason at all. Often, deputies searched them and beat them before hauling them to jail or letting them go. Even if not searched or beaten, "if you were drinking something, they'd pour it all over your cassettes or eight-track tapes." This was especially true if Mexican teenagers ventured to the north side of Odessa, the white part of the city. According to Hernandez, "it was constant harassment" for the simple fact of being Mexican.[89] Lydia Madrigal, the first Mexican American female journalist in Odessa, noted that "if you were a Hispanic and were pulled over, I mean, you would get your hair shaved off, you would get beat up."[90]

Police abuse went beyond the streets. In some West Texas jails, jailers coupled beatings with the shaving of young men's long hair. At the Ector County jail, for example, the local Mexican community knew of a block of padded jail cells that deputies used to punish inmates—whom deputies at times forced to strip naked before

Nick Hernandez, Odessa, Texas, July 8, 2016. Photo courtesy CRBB.

entering the cells. Moreover, the Mexican community suspected that deaths ruled as suicides at the jail were murders.[91]

Because of these abuses, Hernandez helped organize the local Brown Berets with Raul Guerrero in the mid-1970s. The Odessa Brown Berets began meeting with police officials regarding police harassment, "and it started slowing down a little bit." Indeed, Hernandez remembered being pulled over while wearing a beret, signaling his membership. Onlookers came out of their homes, and ladies began shouting at the police. The officer tore up the citation he was filling out and told Nick "to get out of here."[92] Nick declared that the consistent police harassment made Mexican people "more determined that we had to get past all of that" abuse.[93]

Because of his experiences in Odessa, Hernandez was not surprised when he learned that Larry Ortega Lozano died at the jail where he had been imprisoned as an eleven-year-old child. And having already experienced the difference that activism could make, Hernandez continued to lead the call for an end to police brutality.[94]

The Continued Beating and Death of Larry Ortega Lozano

Larry's fellow prisoner Rocke Flannigan told a journalist that he witnessed Ector County deputies harass and beat Larry during the week before his death. The journalist noted that another prisoner corroborated Flannigan's story.[95] In jail, Flannigan observed deputies "trying to get him [Larry] to lose his cool so they could work on him again." Flannigan continued: "They brought Texas Rangers, they brought state police, they brought city police up and pointed him out . . . and say, 'That's Lozano. See what we done to him?' And laugh about it." Flannigan said that deputies repeated that process several times. He concluded, "They brought most of their deputies up to torment him . . . put him on display—like an animal."[96]

Lozano initially lay silently in his cell, unresponsive to deputies' jibes. His closed, swollen eyes drained blood and water. As he healed, Lozano began talking to other prisoners. Eleven days after being arrested and under consistent harassment by deputies, Lozano expressed his fear to a jail official that deputies would beat him again. Sheriff Elton Faught claimed that Lozano became threatening to other prisoners that evening, "but would not say who or how." Other prisoners reported that the strangest thing Larry did that day was to wear his pants in the shower in order to wash them, since he lacked clean clothing.[97]

In the early-morning hours of Sunday, January 22, 1978, deputies moved Larry from a common cellblock to the block of three padded cells known to the Mexican community as a place of punishment. The padded cell where deputies placed Lozano was officially named the East Green Room. According to other prisoners and one jail official, the cell's toilet was clogged and overflowing. Lozano banged on the metal door and window and asked for a mop to clean the muck off the cell floor, but deputies ignored him. The deputy serving breakfast pushed food through the metal slot before Lozano could get to the door, leaving the food to land in the toilet water and muck. At that point, Lozano started banging on the cell door again. Sheriff Faught reported that Lozano banged on the door to create a nuisance. He also claimed that Lozano clogged the cell toilet himself with vinyl padding that he stripped from the cell.[98]

Whatever caused the toilet to clog and overflow, deputies took Lozano to Odessa's Medical Center Hospital that same afternoon so that medical staff could sedate him. A nurse saw Lozano and administered strong sedatives—30 milligrams of Vesprin and 5 milligrams of Cogentin. At the nurse's request, he also gave a urine sample for a drug screening. Lozano remained unsupervised at the hospital for two hours. He was calm throughout that time. The nurse's notes say Lozano was "Talkative & Cooperative" and "walking in room."[99] Deputies returned Larry to the county jail around four twenty in the afternoon. They placed him in another padded cell, the West Green Room.[100]

At about seven, the night jailer, Deputy Jackie Perkins, reported seeing Lozano hitting his head against the shatterproof glass window of the cell door. Perkins stated, "Lozano had gone berserk … [He] ripped out a brass commode ring." Perkins claimed that Lozano smashed the cell door window with his head. If he did shatter the window, it was likely with the brass ring, since the glass was shatterproof. Perkins stated, "I thought he was going to knock the door down." The door, however, was solid metal. Perkins called for help, and Deputy Phil Martin and Sheriff Elton Faught arrived outside the padded cell. More deputies followed, "along with a Texas Highway Patrolman, a game warden and a member of the sheriff's reserve." They sprayed mace through the food slot. Perkins said, "It didn't do any good," but Lozano "finally poked the brass ring partway out the food slot." At that point, Martin grabbed the brass ring away. According to officers, Lozano then grabbed "chunks" of the broken glass with his hands and placed some in his pocket. Jailers unlocked the door and went in. Deputy Randy Tenny led the way. He "put a hammerlock around Lozano's head," and both fell to the ground. Deputy Perkins attempted "to get chunks of glass out of Lozano's hands and chunks of it out from the pockets of his trousers." To that end, deputies "managed to get Lozano's trousers off." None of the officers from multiple police agencies apparently had handcuffs, because they used a "leather belt brought into the cell" to restrain Lozano. The officers then pulled him out of the cell and found he was not breathing. The officers called emergency medical technicians, but they could not revive him. When a doctor arrived from Medical Center Hospital, Lozano was dead. Justice of the Peace Virgil Lumpee, who had charged Lozano and set his bail, pronounced him dead at eight twenty-five, roughly an hour after his actual death.[101]

Sheriff Faught declared that Larry Ortega Lozano's death was a suicide caused by him beating his head against the metal cell door and its window. The Medical Center Hospital's pathologist, Kris Callapalli, concluded that Larry died of a massive cerebral hemorrhage. The autopsy did not note extensive injuries beyond that. Faught asserted that his deputies only used necessary force to subdue Lozano who, Faught argued, was emotionally disturbed.[102] Moreover, officers from multiple agencies involved in Lozano's death stated they did not kick him. They also stated they did not hit him after they dragged him from the padded cell.[103]

But two prisoners near Lozano's cell said both occurred. Vickie June Day, a female prisoner, "saw a deputy kick Lozano in the face" after he was out of the cell. Eddie Montgomery, another prisoner, said he saw Deputy Jackie Perkins "punch Lozano real hard three or four times in the back" outside the cell.[104] Additional witnesses may have agreed with Day and Montgomery, but the *Dallas Times Herald* ran a story alleging that Ector County officials had offered bail bonds and reduced sentences to three witnesses imprisoned in the Ector County jail the night of Lozano's death. In exchange, the officials wanted testimonies corroborating the police narrative.[105]

Immediately after Lozano's death, officials kept reporters away from the jail. When Lydia Madrigal heard of the death on a radio scanner, she and a cameraman headed to the jail. They went in with their camera filming. Madrigal recounted that deputies "almost knocked me down." The deputies told her and the cameraman, "Get out of here!" At that moment, Madrigal wondered, "Why are they keeping this a secret? What's going on?" When I interviewed her, Madrigal said that she realized "something horrible had happened there."[106]

In possession of Lozano's letter recounting the police beatings he had endured, and knowing of police abuse and previous deaths in the Ector County jail, Lozano's family asked for an independent autopsy from El Paso—almost three hundred miles from Odessa. The El Paso County medical examiner, Frederick Bornstein, found ninety-two bruises and wounds on Lozano's body. Bornstein noted "that blunt violence was applied to the body of the deceased repeatedly," with a "variation of the age of the lesions from nearly immediate to about one week." Bornstein also found "especially extensive" lesions to Larry's face and head, along with internal and external hemorrhages throughout his body. Evidence of choking was present; Larry's larynx was damaged enough to "represent a life threatening injury." Bornstein concluded that "the man died from extensive blunt trauma, such as beating, hitting, kicking, as well as possible small wounds with sharp instruments." Hence, he wrote, "I consider the mode of death homicide. The pattern is incompatible with suicide."[107] These results directly contradicted the official police narrative.[108]

Contracted by Ector County, a third pathologist reviewed the paperwork of the two autopsies conducted on Lozano's body. This pathologist, Harris County medical examiner Joseph Jachimczyk, concluded that a "traumatic injury to the neck by compression on the Adam's apple coupled with resistance of the deceased" caused Lozano's death.[109] That is, his larynx was damaged when Deputy Randy Tenny "put a hammerlock around Lozano's head."[110] Jachimczyk, however, asserted that the injury was unintentional, and he at least partly faulted Lozano for the deadly accident. Upon reviewing Jachimczyk's conclusions, both the pathologists who actually examined Larry's body changed their conclusions to agree with his.[111] Such a change was especially notable in regard to Callapalli, who had determined that Lozano died of a self-induced massive cerebral hemorrhage without noting the deadly injury to his larynx. Bornstein's revised conclusion seemed logically *incompatible* with his first assessment, namely, that Lozano's injury "pattern is incompatible with suicide."[112]

The Rise of a Chicana/o Protest Movement

On the Monday after Larry Ortega Lozano died, the Odessa Brown Berets met to decide on their response. Like the rest of the Mexican American community, they knew of police abuse within and outside the county jail. Led by Nick Hernandez, they decided to have a press conference on Tuesday. Nick began calling Brown Beret chapters around Texas, including the Lubbock Brown Berets, who had already initiated a movement against police brutality. This united effort marked the beginning of what Nick asserted was "the biggest thing that ever happened" in Odessa. In his view, "It changed everything.... So many people got involved.... And all the Berets came here to Odessa."[113] Previous generations of Mexicans—along with African Americans—had taught their children to avoid the police and to never "argue with them, because you may not make it out of there," and to accept police abuse "as part of life."[114] Now, the Chicana/o movement, coupled with the late-1970s string of police killings, changed how Mexicans reacted to police brutality.

On Tuesday January 24, 1978, the Brown Berets hosted a press conference that included Lozano family members. The Brown Berets demanded a detailed investigation by the FBI of what happened to Lozano, and tied his death to the nearby shootings of Tiburcio Griego Santome and Juan Galaviz, and to others across the nation, such as the killing of Joe Campos Torres, whom the Houston police beat and threw into a bayou to drown. Lozano's uncle, Joe Lozano, held the letter in which Lozano wrote that the police had beaten him twice. Margaret, Lozano's sister, also expressed hope for an FBI investigation. The Lozano family and the Brown Berets wanted more than a local or state probe, thinking that local and state agencies would be biased in favor of the police and against the victim.[115]

Margaret told reporters that she did not believe Lozano had killed himself. She remembered her brother as "quiet, neat and orderly." Margaret did acknowledge that Lozano had suffered a mental breakdown in her home and that she had taken him to the Austin State Hospital. But, she asserted, "he had never been in trouble with the law before being jailed in Odessa." Lozano had only recently moved to Odessa from Pecos, where he was born and raised, the son of a World War II veteran. Lozano had been a high school athlete and had married his high school sweetheart. They had two children, and he worked the same job for years in Pecos. But after seven years, his marriage ended. He then moved to Odessa for a new job and to make a new home.[116]

Under pressure from the Lozano family and the Brown Berets, on the Wednesday following the press conference, Sheriff Elton Faught asked Texas Ranger Charlie Hodges, based in neighboring Midland, to launch an investigation. That same day, Virgil Lumpee, the justice of the peace who had charged Lozano with aggravated assault and declared him deceased, said he would launch a jury inquest, an uncommon procedure, "because of the violent nature of the man's death."[117]

While investigations commenced, Sheriff Faught took steps to protect himself and other police officials. Under his direction, sheriff's deputies and other officers involved in Lozano's death gathered in an Ector County Courthouse conference room seven days after the incident. One witness told journalists that Faught organized the meeting so that they would "get their stories straight."[118]

The local investigations did not muffle the "fury and frustration that had been building for years" in the Mexican community.[119] Three Mexican men had died at the hands of police officials within a few months of one another in West Texas. The police abuse that Mexicans suffered "was out in the open." Brown Berets and others started directly naming police officers who were abusive. The Lozano family hired Ruben Sandoval, an attorney from San Antonio recommended by the Brown Berets. He had represented Mexican families in previous cases of police killings, including the 1977 sawed-off shotgun killing of Richard Morales by Frank Hayes, the police chief in Castroville, Texas. Hayes became the first police officer that the US Department of Justice prosecuted for civil rights violations, and he received a life sentence from a federal court. Through Sandoval's lobbying, the FBI's El Paso and San Antonio offices joined the Midland office's investigation into Lozano's death. Sandoval's larger goal, though, was to have the Department of Justice intervene, as it had in the Morales case. The lobbying resulted in the department launching an investigation.[120]

As Virgil Lumpee began jury selection for the inquest, members of the American GI Forum, LULAC, the family of Tiburcio Griego Santome, and others joined the Brown Berets and the Lozano family in protests against police brutality. Although police brutality did not unite African Americans and Mexican Americans in Odessa to the degree that it did in Lubbock, policing issues unified Mexican Americans across the political spectrum in Odessa, Big Spring, and the surrounding area. These activists held benefit dinners—each attended by hundreds—to raise thousands of dollars for the Lozano family's legal expenses.[121]

The protests culminated in several Brown Beret chapters, other activists, attorneys, and community members holding a civil rights workshop, motorcade, march, and rally on February 25, 1978. The day of activism began with a morning workshop centered on police brutality in Odessa's St. Joseph Catholic Church. At the workshop, Ruben Sandoval displayed color pictures of the bloodied and bruised body of Larry Ortega Lozano. The workshop also discussed the shootings of Juan Galaviz in Big Spring and Tiburcio Griego Santome in Glasscock County.[122]

When the workshop concluded, a motorcade of 80 vehicles headed south on the pointedly named Dixie Boulevard to Interstate 20. The motorcade grew to 123 vehicles and drove sixty-two miles east to Big Spring. The people in the motorcade gathered with others at Big Spring's Sacred Heart Youth Center. From there, everyone marched to the Howard County Courthouse. There, at least a thousand people gathered under the watch of police snipers sitting atop roofs. Lubbock's Gilbert Herrera spoke, declaring, "This is the year of the Mexican American." Gilbert pressed for federal investigations and prosecutions, citing the federal prosecution of Frank Hayes. When Juan Aruello, a Big Spring Brown Beret, spoke on police brutality and the death of Juan Galaviz, he asked, "Aren't Chicanos human beings?"[123] Other speakers included Juan Galaviz's widow and an Odessa American GI Forum leader named Arturo Leal. They all demanded that police forces be held accountable for their actions, along with fair local media coverage of police killings.[124]

Verdict and Repercussions

The six-member jury inquest called by Justice of the Peace Virgil Lumpee began April 11, 1978. Over forty witnesses testified, including sheriff's deputies, prisoners, and medical examiners. After testimony on the following day, the three men and three women (including a Mexican American woman named Gloria Gomez Juarez) on the jury returned a verdict of accidental death. Ruben Sandoval called the inquest a circus and charged that Ector County officials had harassed and intimidated the El Paso County medical examiner, Frederick Bornstein.[125] Sheriff Elton Faught told a journalist, "I am relieved at the outcome, and feel my department has been cleared of any wrong-doing in the Lozano death. The pressure is off and I hope that it is over."[126]

The pressure was not off, however. On April 13, 1978, the day after the verdict, about three hundred people surrounded the Ector County Courthouse to protest both the verdict and police brutality. Brown Beret members started the protest at eight in the morning; by nine, the protest had grown to include children, students, and elders, along with members of LULAC and the American GI Forum. While most were Mexican American, Anglo-Americans and African Americans were also present. Protesters called the verdict and inquest a "charade." Carolina Rodriguez, an Odessa Brown Berets leader, derided the inquest as a "kangaroo court." The crowd carried signs that read, "Brown People are Human Too" and "Mexican-Americans Not Dogs."[127]

Sandoval, still working with the Odessa Brown Berets, partnered with the state and national LULAC operations to ask the Department of Justice to launch a federal grand jury investigation in Midland or El Paso regarding Lozano's death. For his part, Texas attorney general John Hill opposed a federal investigation. Although fairly progressive for a Texas Democrat in the 1970s, he seemed steeped in the politics of opposition to federal intervention when it came to investigating police-conducted killings. Yet he did not address Lozano's death in state court. Hill insisted that he could not do so under state law. He argued that state law needed to change in order to be aligned more closely with federal law, which would allow his office to handle civil rights violations by law enforcement officers in state district courts.[128]

Another protest occurred on April 29, 1978. A wide range of the Mexican population gathered at St. Joseph Catholic Church for a Mass. From the church, an estimated 2,500 protesters marched down Dixie Boulevard and around the Ector County jail before returning to St. Joseph. Speakers included Larry Ortega Lozano's mother, Consuelo. She declared, "This is a great injustice they have done to my son." The American GI Forum speaker, Carlos Leal, accused the sheriff and county officials of covering up what had really happened to Larry. Together, the speakers demanded a Department of Justice investigation.[129]

US Attorney Jamie C. Boyd, whose district covered much of West Texas, including Ector County, stated that a federal grand jury investigation would "help clarify things and bring out information to satisfy people who still have questions." Boyd announced that he was willing to convene such a grand jury or to assist others in the Department of Justice in doing so.[130] But decisions to prosecute civil rights violations rested with the US attorney general, Griffin B. Bell, on advice from the DOJ's Civil Rights Division. The Civil Rights Division never convened a federal grand jury in Lozano's case, and the DOJ did not instruct Boyd to convene one, either. During the summer of 1979, Attorney General Bell announced that the department's investigation into Lozano's death had "not yield[ed] evidence legally sufficient to prosecute any person under the federal civil rights laws."[131]

That same summer, West Texas police officers killed two more Mexican men. Near a farm-to-market road on June 5, 1978, an unpaid, reserve sheriff's deputy fatally shot Tim Rosales. Rosales, a twenty-five-year-old farmworker from nearby Hale Center, was unarmed. The reserve deputy, Charles Cypert, also from Hale Center, was responding to a drunken-disturbance call and reported that Rosales got out of a car and struggled with him before running toward a farmhouse. There were witnesses to the initial struggle. Cypert caught up to Rosales, and in the ensuing struggle, he shot Rosales in the head. There were no witnesses to the shooting. A Hale County grand jury did not indict Cypert. In the streets of Hale Center and Plainview, Brown Berets, LULAC members, and others protested the killing and nearby the lack of an indictment. Like other killings of Mexican American men and boys by police officers, the Tim Rosales case brought together a broad spectrum of Mexican American social justice organizations.[132]

Although officers were not prosecuted for the killings, subsequent protests and political engagement did bring about change. Lydia Madrigal noted the sequence of events:

> What happened, though, was that we got exposure. . . . For the first time, there was a name . . . There were pictures, and he was all beat up. . . . What happened to Larry Lozano had happened before. . . . But nobody reported it . . . That was probably the most important thing that happened, was the fact that people knew. . . . And as a result, people were paying attention. . . . Let's expose this, and let's make sure that the whole country knows what happened in West Texas. And they did. . . . People began to take pause with those kinds of incidents . . . And we're going to put a stop to it.[133]

A letter to the editor of the Odessa newspaper helps further explain the improvement. Luis M. Menchaca, who signed his letter as "An Angered Citizen" of Odessa, wrote that "CHICANOISM has come to Odessa and from now on we will no longer tolerate injustices to Chicanos! Our time has come and I hope you realize that—Now

OF ALL TIMES!"[134] Mexican people were no longer willing to accept police brutality or second-class citizenship as a way of life.

Police brutality largely spurred West Texas's Chicana/o movement. Moreover, police killings "spawned seeds of unity among the more militant" and mainstream social justice organizations.[135] Indeed, Ruben Bonilla, the state director for LULAC, who went on to become the national LULAC president, asserted that "the bullets of Texas policemen" brought about the political engagement of Mexican Americans—especially the youth—and unity among disparate groups. In communities such as Lubbock, this common fight included African American and Mexican American political unity.[136]

Moreover, far from cities traditionally acknowledged as the epicenters of the Chicana/o movement, West Texas groups expanded the movement's geographic scope. And West Texas's Chicana/o movement shows how local activism could help forge a national social justice movement as consequential as the African American civil rights movement, the women's movement, or a range of student movements. In West Texas and in the entire nation, people continue to live with the impact of the Chicana/o movement.

CHAPTER 6

THE LONG SHADOW OF HÉCTOR P. GARCÍA IN CORPUS CHRISTI

JAMES B. WALL

By a comfortable margin, the statue of the slain Tejano singer Selena Quintanilla-Pérez is the most popular tourist attraction in the bayside town of Corpus Christi, Texas. A few miles away on the campus of Texas A&M–Corpus Christi stands a different statue, one that rarely lures visitors other than the countless university students that brush past it on their way to class. The nine-foot-tall bronze sculpture memorializes Dr. Héctor P. García, the distinguished physician, veteran, and Mexican American civil rights activist. García propelled Corpus Christi to the forefront of the fight for racial justice by forming the American GI Forum, an organization dedicated to improving the lives of Mexican American veterans and dismantling the system of "Juan Crow" segregation in South Texas.

García's reputation as a community leader and civil rights organizer remains largely unassailable, and for good reason. For fifty years, he played a key role in almost every major campaign to rid the Coastal Bend of segregation and discrimination. His rhetoric of personal responsibility, hard work, and patriotism evoked the noble values of the "Greatest Generation." García's message resonated with a wide audience, earning him praise from poor workers, church fathers, city leaders, and even Ronald Reagan, who awarded García the Presidential Medal of Freedom in 1984. His virtuoso skills and tireless work ethic gave rise to the common description of García as "a man who in the space of one week delivers twenty babies, twenty speeches, and twenty thousand votes."[1]

While no one denies the powerful testimony of García's life, a more human version of the man emerged from interviews with longtime Corpus Christi residents. The most candid accounts revealed García as acutely self-aware—an active shaper of his own reputation, constantly striving to safeguard his leadership. His efforts to control local protest campaigns provided activists with a clear spokesman, someone to mediate disputes between Anglos, African Americans, and Mexican Americans. While García helped chip away at the edifice of segregation and white privilege in South Texas, his death left a leadership void in his community. Throughout his life, García solidified his power by challenging those who tried to share it, and as his advancing years diminished his star, he failed to groom a new generation of activists to succeed him. García's fame propelled the Mexican American civil rights movement into prominence in the decades after World War II, but by the end of his life, his celebrity worked as the spotlight in a one-man show. The Corpus Christi journalist

Nick Jimenez, who saw García work up close for decades, summarized what many Corpus Christians felt about the venerable doctor's larger-than-life stature: "Héctor ... was like this huge sun that blocked off any stars. There was nothing but him."[2]

Far from diminishing García's legacy, a more thorough exploration of his life reveals new stories of unheralded activists who worked to reshape South Texas after World War II. Any efforts toward such an understanding must acknowledge the adulation many still feel for the man they knew as "Dr. Héctor." When Danny Noyola, a longtime Corpus Christi educator who grew up idolizing the man, choked back tears while boasting that Dr. Héctor became "not only a mentor, but a friend," he showcased the raw emotional power that Héctor P. García continues to evoke. Going further, Noyola echoed a common refrain about the doctor's legacy. Calling García "our Martin Luther King," Noyola lamented, "He's not a household name throughout the land. He should be." "What that man did," he argued, "is very comparable to Dr. King, less his assassination." While one can argue that this level of veneration matches his tremendous résumé, such idolization can also narrow the prism through which the Mexican American civil rights movement is viewed. As the historian Jacquelyn Dowd Hall argued in her watershed article "The Long Civil Rights Movement and the Political Uses of the Past," fixating on a movement's "bowdlerized heroes" (in her study, Martin Luther King Jr.) "simultaneously elevates and diminishes the movement. It ensures the status of the classical phase as a triumphal moment in a larger American progress narrative, yet it undermines its *gravitas*."[3]

García's refusal to relinquish his status as a civil rights potentate could be explained by the immense work he put in to achieve that position. He came into the world as Héctor Pérez García on January 17, 1914. His family lived in Llera, a modest farming town in the northeastern corner of Mexico. García grew up in a family teeming with ambition. His parents, José and Faustina, were schoolteachers who demanded hard work and discipline from their seven children, who they hoped would one day become doctors. (Six of them indeed went on to become physicians.) The relative comfort provided by his parents' middle-class careers dissolved when the Mexican Revolution arrived at their doorstep in 1918. Forced to flee, José and Faustina took their children and crossed the Rio Grande into Texas, where they settled in Mercedes, a dusty little town built on the pasture of an old ranch just a decade earlier.[4]

Like most immigrants, the move to America required sacrifice. For José and Faustina García, that meant giving up their careers as educators (since their degrees were not accepted by Texas schools) and moving down the social ladder in Mercedes, where Anglos controlled the town and rigidly enforced "Juan Crow" segregation. The town bore physical markers of racial separation: the ubiquitous railroad divided Anglo and Hispanic neighborhoods. It was there, across the tracks, in the half-dozen city blocks known collectively as "El Pueblo Mexicano," that the Garcías carved out a life for themselves. Héctor's father joined his brothers in the grocery business, which provided a comfortable living until the Great Depression destroyed its profit margins. The dissolution of the family business sent Héctor down a much harder path in life, one that would require endless striving and toil to reach the elusive "American Dream."[5]

García welcomed the challenge with a resolute determination that impressed anyone who came into his orbit. This was a man who was going places, although getting there would take him into the boiling-hot South Texas fields to pick cotton during the summers, and down worn-out dirt roads to thumb rides to the nearby community college. After two years at Edinburg Junior College, Héctor arrived in Austin in 1934, where he attended the University of Texas. A lot was riding on his performance there, including his father's life insurance policy, which his parents had sold off to pay for his education. Héctor didn't disappoint. Two years later, he graduated with a zoology degree and a GPA impressive enough to earn him the only spot reserved for Mexican Americans in the incoming class at the University of Texas's medical school, in Galveston (now the University of Texas Medical Branch). He left for the Gulf Coast without bothering to attend his college graduation. It was time to get to work, and after all, he didn't have the money to buy a suit for the ceremony.[6]

García hunkered down in Galveston and threw himself into his studies, though he took some time off to get involved with the local community by spearheading disease-prevention campaigns in some of the city's poorest neighborhoods. In 1940, Héctor followed his brother Antonio by becoming the second García child to don the white coat. When it came time to apply for residency programs, García couldn't find any Texas hospitals willing to take a newly minted Mexican American doctor. The slightly more progressive town of Omaha, Nebraska, became Héctor's home for the next two years while he finished his rounds at Creighton University's St. Joseph Hospital. By the time he finished, in 1942, the world had gone to war. García, who had shown an interest in the service a decade earlier by signing up for the Citizens' Military Training Camp (CMTC), a preenlistment program for eager young men drawn in by a sense of duty and a fifty-dollar paycheck, volunteered for active service. Not yet sixteen, García lied about his age in order to join, showing traces of a burning devotion to military service that would serve as a guiding value throughout his life. He loved the CMTC, and followed it by enlisting in the Army Reserve, where he slowly climbed the ranks. When he arrived at medical school in 1936, he did so as a first lieutenant.[7]

García wanted to help defeat the Nazis to be sure, but he also wanted the pay and status he deserved. He put in for a spot as a medical officer, but what he got instead was a letter telling him to report for basic training. He would not begin as a doctor, but as an infantry officer in the 591st Engineer Boat Regiment. Only after he had served across Europe by teaching soldiers how to make amphibious landings did García finally come across someone who recognized his talents, though it took persistent effort to prove his medical bona fides to the skeptical white officer. From there on out, he served as an army physician, earning the respect of his peers along the way. The war formed the bedrock of García's life. He brought a thick service record back from Italy and used it to fight against racism at home and to defend himself against criticism from suspicious whites. He also brought back the love of his life, Wanda Fusillo, the well-educated, beautiful young daughter of a Naples school superintendent. Her parents adored Héctor, who impressed them with his sharp wit, knowledge of ancient history, and his career prospects. They begged him to stay in Italy after the war, an idea that he refused to consider—he had a "mission" to pursue back home.[8]

That mission took him to Corpus Christi, a secluded yet bustling blue-collar port city on the Texas Gulf Coast. In earlier years, the lush, semitropical bay where the city would later sit had been inhabited by Karankawa tribes, who built a network of settlements among the islands and the mainland. Spanish explorers arrived in 1519 on the Feast of Corpus Christi (Latin, "body of Christ") and named the area in its honor. The land around the bay remained inhabited by Indigenous groups and sparse European settlers, and was fought over for the next three centuries. Modern Corpus Christi was born in 1841 when a two-bit Yankee huckster showed up. Like many Texas immigrants in the nineteenth century, Henry Lawrence Kinney arrived with a neurotic determination to forget his past—particularly his recent role in a failed canal venture in Illinois and an alleged affair with Senator Daniel Webster's daughter—and make a name for himself. Kinney landed near Brownsville, Texas, in 1838 and insisted on calling himself "Colonel," a title he claimed to have earned while fighting against the Seminole in Florida (though no evidence exists to support his story).[9] Kinney surfaced in Corpus Christi a few years later and threw up a small trading post to sell supplies to Mexican soldiers camped nearby. Over the next seventy years, Corpus Christi became a cultural melting pot set to the steady forward march of New South economic progress.[10]

That march turned into a sprint in 1909 when Roy Miller—a twenty-five-year-old political wunderkind soon to become the "boy mayor of Corpus Christi" and eventually a Washington, DC, power broker—convinced local congressman (and future Speaker of the House and vice president) John Nance "Cactus Jack" Garner to designate Corpus Christi a deepwater port. The federal dollars began to flow, bringing huge construction crews to build what would become the nation's sixth-largest port. It opened on September 14, 1926, when two naval destroyers, the USS *Hatfield* and the *John D. Edwards*, steamed into the harbor and dropped anchor underneath streams of bunting while crowds of onlookers celebrated. Corpus Christi had begun a new era of prosperity.[11]

While construction wrapped up on the port, natural gas wells were tapped, oil derricks and refineries pockmarked the landscape, and engineers searched for alkali deposits across the vast fields outside of town. Farther into the countryside, cotton farming boomed, turning the Coastal Bend into the state's leading producer. Corpus Christi harnessed new streams of federal money, innovations in technology, and a feverish economic boosterism to squeeze unheard-of profits from the region's wealth of natural resources. The port acted as an engine, superheating the local economy and propelling the city into the commercial stratosphere. From then on, politicians with an eye on statewide office added Corpus Christi to every campaign tour. International corporations arrived by the dozens, building rows of new plants and refineries. The economic potential seemed limitless. The only thing missing was the people.[12]

That problem proved to be short-lived: four years after the port opened, Corpus Christi's population had jumped 163 percent. Almost immediately, engineers realized that the channel they had just built would need to be expanded. Meanwhile, the people kept coming. From 1930 to 1940, the population doubled again, to 57,000, and the breakneck pace continued. As 1950 approached, the small coastal town that had claimed around 10,000 residents three decades earlier now boasted more than 100,000. The flood of postwar settlers gave the city the manpower needed to feed its revving economic machine. Héctor P. García became part of that transformation, arriving in 1945 with a new wife, a baby on the way, and an eagerness to tap into one of the most vibrant Mexican American communities in America.[13]

The Making of a Hero

Though a remote industrial town, Corpus Christi became central to a growing movement in 1929 when it became home to the League of United Latin American Citizens (LULAC), a small civic-minded group of Hispanic World War I veterans that quickly evolved into the nation's leading voice for Mexican American rights. Those rights, according to LULAC's founders, would come only after Mexican Americans thoroughly assimilated into American culture. That meant speaking English at all times and embracing capitalism, democracy, individualism, hard work, and an unwavering patriotism. LULAC's ethos led the organization down an exclusionary path: only American citizens could become members; the official language of the group was English; the official prayer was "George Washington's Prayer"; the official song was "America, the Beautiful"; and its governing document required members to "be loyal to the Constitution and to the government of the United States."[14]

Despite its narrow membership guidelines, the organization had an eye on the local community, which, by any standard, was suffering. When Héctor P. García arrived in Corpus Christi, he found a segregated city scarred by concentrated poverty and disease. While Roy Miller and the Anglo captains of industry talked shop in the smoke-filled backrooms of local steakhouses, Mexican Americans lived in poor barrios, in shotgun houses without indoor plumbing or running water, crisscrossed by unpaved streets without sidewalks. The decaying neighborhoods percolated with disease. Corpus Christi had more tuberculosis cases than anywhere else in Texas, and Mexican Americans made up the majority of those infected. García hit the ground running, immediately mounting a one-man public health campaign. He began by talking, first to neighborhood groups and then door-to-door through the barrios, blaring his antiseptic gospel through a loudspeaker tied to the top of his car. Before long, he had company—Gilbert Cásares, an army recruiter who had built some name recognition through a local radio station, where he sold listeners on the merits of serving one's country. Together they joined forces to extend their public health campaign to Corpus Christi's poor residents. Soon LULAC came, armed with knowledge on which communities to target and how they were responding.[15]

Through his public-service campaigns of the late 1940s, García began to shape his persona, and his star rose. He soon had his own radio show, which he used to publicize the sorry state of affairs in his adopted hometown. While lobbying for reforms in the city, García began to move his efforts into the fields outside Corpus Christi, where Anglo planters treated Hispanic migrant workers only slightly better than farm animals. They worked long days with few breaks from the blistering Texas sun, lived in tin-roofed wooden shacks called "chicken coops," which heated up like ovens, and slept on dirt floors before waking at dawn to repeat the whole process. The horrors of the *colonias* of rural South Texas haunted García, and for the rest of his life, he ventured into the fields to document, to investigate, and to help.[16]

The problems that García encountered seemed to mushroom, and soon he fixed his gaze on the appalling neglect of Mexican American army veterans. They had no convenient facilities for medical treatment in Corpus Christi. The nearest veterans' hospital was over a hundred miles away, and García's requests to open up more beds at the local navy hospital fell on deaf ears. To fill the gap, he decided to base his practice around his fellow soldiers, setting up his office next door to the Veterans Administration (VA) building, where he treated returning servicemen for three dollars a visit. Through his practice, he became known to Corpus Christi by a new nickname—"Dr. Héctor." He consolidated the community's goodwill for him by bending the rules. He never turned away a patient who couldn't pay, always telling him to bring him the money when he could. Corpus Christians still reminisce about his generosity. Willie Loa, a longtime school board member and community leader, repeated a persistent rumor about García: "He probably died broke." "If you didn't have any money," Loa remembered, "he'd say, 'Go come on in anyway.' He'll take care of you." [17]

García continued his ascent, becoming president of the local LULAC chapter in 1947. He still felt that the organization wasn't doing enough, particularly for veterans. One year later, that discontent was translated into action when García put out the word for every veteran in town to meet at the Lamar Elementary School. On March 26, 1948, seven hundred men answered his call and became charter members of the American GI Forum, a new organization that became synonymous with Héctor P. García and transformed him from a local hero into a national leader. The "Forum," as it was casually known, took root in small towns across South Texas, where García would arrive in his old white Mercury, clutching a letter of introduction from Corpus Christi's Catholic bishop. "Dr. Héctor drove that white Mercury into the ground," his nephew remembered. In no time, he exchanged his sputtering jalopy for a new blue Cadillac that he drove across the country, drumming up support. But all the driving in the world couldn't have brought the exposure that came in early 1949 when García received a phone call that changed his life. [18]

Felix Longoria had been killed by a Japanese sniper's bullet while marching through a dense forest in the Philippines. He was twenty-six years old. His body was deposited in a mass grave during the summer of 1945. Three years later, his widow, Beatrice, received word from the army that Felix's body was coming home to Three Rivers, a rural outpost of a few thousand about an hour's drive from Corpus Christi. She made burial plans with the only funeral home in town, but was turned away when she asked to use its chapel to display the body. "The whites won't like it," said the owner, Tom Kennedy, though he assured her that he had "lots of Latin friends." On the evening of January 7, 1949, García's phone rang—it was Beatrice's sister. After hearing the entire story, he agreed to help. First, he called the funeral home, only to hear Kennedy complain about "Latin people" who "get drunk and lay around all the time." They couldn't use the chapel, Kennedy said, because "we just can't control them." Then he reached out to the *Corpus Christi Caller-Times* and promised an imminent rally by the GI Forum. Next came a shotgun blast of telegrams to the governor, the state attorney general, the State Board of Embalming, the head of the Good Neighbor Commission, a state senator, two congressmen, the secretary of defense, and President Harry S. Truman—all received notes from a man they had never heard of, asking for justice in a town they had never seen. [19]

A longer telegram arrived on the desk of Lyndon Baines Johnson, a shavetail US senator looking for any chance to scrub away the tarnish from his questionable eighty-seven-vote win over Governor Coke Stevenson in the Democratic primary the previous fall. "Landslide Lyndon" had some personal connection with Mexican Americans, having taught English as a young college graduate in the tiny South

Texas town of Cotulla two decades earlier. Johnson pounced, dashing off a quick telegram that surprised even his closest friends. "I have today made arrangements," the note read, "to have Felix Longoria buried with full military honors in Arlington National Cemetery."[20]

The saga catapulted the American GI Forum into the national spotlight and elevated its leader: the tenacious, well-spoken Mexican American doctor with the political chops to get things done. LULAC had been left in the dust, along with Corpus Christi's old elite. García, from the time of the Longoria fight onward, dominated the local scene. His power was based in conventional realpolitik; he embraced the transactional compromises needed to reserve a seat for himself at the table. He knew that real power required the promotion of Héctor P. García as a hero, a leader, a veteran, a patriot, and a moral compass for the Mexican American community. No one would deny his fitness for these roles, but with each accolade, media profile, and successful campaign, his persona and its underlying power grew, leaving very little space for others at the top.

The Rise of the Bonillas

Among those seeking a taste of the spotlight were the Bonillas, a prolific clan every bit as driven as the Garcías. The two families were cut from the same cloth. Both came from immigrant parents who emphasized hard work, self-discipline, and education as the pathways to success. While the García family had made its way in the border town of Mercedes, María and Ruben Bonilla had settled behind the "Pine Curtain" in Calvert, a small East Texas railroad town with a tight-knit community where one could raise a family in peace. It was a place where a Mexican immigrant could open a successful filling station that would become a bedrock of the community, a place with one school building that housed grades k–12, and a place where an ambitious set of children would leave one day to pursue greater opportunities. While the García children took the Hippocratic oath on the way to economic advancement, the Bonillas, all eight of them, became lawyers.[21]

William, the oldest, arrived in Corpus Christi fresh out of law school in June 1953 and opened a practice. It quickly blossomed—within three years he was living on Ocean Drive, a seven-mile stretch of bayside road lined with palm trees and the elegant homes of the city's economic elite. He was soon joined by his younger brothers Reuben and Tony, also newly minted barristers. Politically minded from the start, the brothers immediately began climbing the ranks of LULAC. By the early 1960s, their efforts had paid dividends. In 1964, William became LULAC's national president. The Bonillas became a household name in the organization, establishing an almost Kennedyesque dynasty. In later decades, William was followed as national president by his brothers Reuben (1979–1980) and Tony (1981–1982).[22]

As the Bonillas matured into key political actors, they entered into Héctor García's orbit. Throughout the 1960s, the two sides forged a complicated relationship that fluctuated from friendly to hostile depending on which way the political winds were blowing. They had worked together, along with the rest of Mexican American Texas, to elect a president in 1960 through the Viva Kennedy organization. But that coalition quickly frayed at the seams when the Political Association of Spanish-Speaking Organizations (PASO), a committee formed to cement and expand on the Mexican American political clout earned during the Kennedy election, drew García's ire. The old and new guard tore PASO apart at the group's 1962 convention, when the establishment and liberal camps split over whom to nominate as the next Democratic candidate for governor. García led a pragmatic group willing to hold its nose and accept the LBJ-anointed John Connally, while a faction of Rio Grande Valley activists pushed for the more liberal Don Yarborough. In the end, García and his crew won the day, settling on a compromise candidate, Price Daniel. Furious Yarborough delegates rejected García's olive-branch offer to reunify the party. They painted him as a sellout more interested in winning elections than in supporting politicians who really cared about Mexican Americans. The PASO skirmish turned some younger activists against García, and it became evident that he was human after all, subject to the same jealousies, tensions, and infighting that plagued other social movements.[23]

García returned to Corpus Christi to stew over the convention fight and to throw himself back into GI Forum business. One year later, he was back in the middle of yet another PASO debacle, this one in the small town of Crystal City, a farming community of several thousand about a hundred miles southwest of San Antonio. During the Great Depression, while other towns floundered, Crystal City blossomed into one of the nation's leading spinach producers, inspiring residents in 1937 to erect a statue of the cartoon character Popeye. The town's agricultural renaissance was built on the backs of migrant farm laborers from Mexico, where the 1910 revolution sent thousands northward in search of refuge and economic opportunity.[24]

The movement started by accident when an Anglo farmer, mad about a high property tax bill, sparked a voter registration campaign in the city's Mexican American community. He wanted to scare the mayor, but instead he unleashed a dormant well of resentment that quickly threatened to upend the city's power structure. The registration drive was a smashing success, and Crystal City's Mexican American residents—80 percent of the electorate—ousted the entire city council, replacing them with "Los Cinco," five working-class Hispanic volunteers from the local community. The astounding revolt had come with an assist from the Teamsters Union and PASO, which helped folks pay their poll taxes and get to their precincts. Never before had such a sweeping political transformation been seen at the local level. It sparked waves of elation from Mexican American activists, who saw a chance to finally put the bottom rail on top.[25]

The high soon wore off and gave way to the same factionalism and backbiting that had fractured PASO at the 1962 convention. Once again, Héctor García was in the middle of it. The first signs of tension came from the new city councilmen, who quickly began to resemble the proverbial dog who caught the car. They simply didn't know how to govern, and their attempts soon deteriorated into petty squabbling. Then there was the "race" issue. It should have come as no surprise that García, an erstwhile LULAC-er and founder of the moderate GI Forum, bristled at the more aggressive tone of the Crystal City uprising. Meanwhile, through back channels, he began sniping at the Teamsters, whom he considered a threat to co-opt the movement. His opposition to the union and the movement itself was not out of character. As García's biographer noted: "Héctor had never developed alliances outside the barrio, especially not with any organization that had more resources and members than the Forum." García, sensing challenges from internal and external forces, started a political knife fight at PASO's 1963 convention.[26]

After the opening gavel, García presented a motion to expel the Teamsters. They were unwelcome interlopers, he claimed, and he called on the delegates to preserve the ethnic solidarity and autonomy of the organization. Echoes of support bellowed out from the crowd. One of those voices came from an old acquaintance: William Bonilla. The soon-to-be LULAC president claimed that PASO "should fight its own battle," and denounced the union for its "unlawful tactics." Despite his consolidated forces, Héctor underestimated the opposition. A large chorus of dissent followed as rival PASO leaders thrashed García, painting him as an accommodationist uninterested in true progress. Héctor stormed out of the convention in a rage, opening a rift that would never be bridged.[27]

In the wake of the convention, he threw gasoline on the fire by reaching out to his friend Robert F. Kennedy, recounting a jaundiced tale of an attempted hostile takeover of PASO and casting himself as the martyr. The altercation soured García, who exiled himself from Mexican American political bodies like PASO for the rest of his days. He continued to play the game as a lone wolf, lending support to candidates of his choosing, but never again did he bind himself to a parent organization. If anything, García's messy divorce from PASO highlighted one of his essential characteristics: he was territorial.[28]

Like anyone who senses his heyday passing, García tightened his grip on power, but he couldn't ignore the new generation. Back in Corpus Christi, Tony Bonilla, twenty-two years Héctor's junior, was on the rise. He and his brothers were injecting youthful energy into LULAC and courting attention from the press. "The media never sought out Latinos," Bonilla claimed, "until the young elements took over LULAC." By the 1960s, Héctor P. García had become "kind of like the elder statesman." In their eyes, the venerable doctor now served as the cautious father figure of the local movement, there to step in when things got too hot. "We'd stir the pot," Bonilla remembered, "and Dr. Héctor would call in the feds." The two elements attempted to reach equilibrium, but it was clear there would be growing pains.[29]

As 1966 approached, the Bonillas had jumped several rungs on the political ladder. William, the former LULAC national president, remained ensconced in the Democratic Party, where he positioned himself as a moderate Hispanic loyalist worthy of a post in the Johnson administration (though the nomination never came). Tony also proved himself a true party man, offering spirited endorsements of Democratic governor John Connally ("the most progressive Governor that we have had in the history of our state") and senatorial candidate Waggoner Carr ("a man with fresh ideas, young and vigorous"). Tony provided staunch support in order to fortify his political base. He was a state senator nearing the end of his first term and seeking a second, but he was facing a new and formidable enemy: Héctor P. García.[30]

Tony found himself matched against Al "Peaches" González, a twenty-nine-year-old former boxer and owner of a job placement firm, who was intent on running to Bonilla's left in the Democratic primary. González claimed that Bonilla had forgotten his roots. The time had come to choose between a candidate with his finger on the pulse of the Mexican American community and an unprincipled political opportunist. Things got ugly fast. For reasons still murky to history, García chose to back the upstart challenger, driving a wedge straight through Corpus Christi's fragile Mexican American power structure. Bonilla fired back, portraying himself as "a representative of all people" who would never use his "Spanish name to secure a block vote." González, he claimed, represented a throwback to the divisive ethnic politics of yesteryear, and beyond that, he was a stooge for García and the GI Forum.[31]

The attacks continued. Salvos were fired back and forth at campaign stops, in newspapers, and constantly on the city's Spanish-language radio stations. García, who only three years earlier had denounced cooperation with the Teamsters as an abomination, now enlisted city labor bosses to line up against Bonilla. Sketchy accusations flew from both sides. Bonilla charged the González camp with sending out misleading sample ballots, "spreading malicious gossip," and looking the other way while union men intimidated voters. González claimed Bonilla was in the pocket of special interests, and vowed to bring "honesty, integrity, and dignity" back to the job. All the while, García stood above the fray, but kept his thumb on the scale with an occasional radio spot. In the middle of the heated campaign, he visited Washington, DC, at the invitation of President Johnson, widening his exposure as a national Mexican American spokesman while the two candidates duked it out back home. In the end, García's name recognition, coupled with the resources and manpower provided by the union, gave González a slight edge. When the June runoff finally came, it brought bad news for Bonilla: he lost by two thousand votes.[32]

Armed with years of hindsight, Tony Bonilla diagrammed his errors. "I was cocky," he admitted, "and thought that I could do no wrong, so I made a lot of mistakes along the way." When asked why Corpus Christi's preeminent Mexican American leader had gone out of his way to crusade against him, he pointed to one moment in the spring of 1966. The flash point came on the morning of April 16, when García testified before the Texas Advisory Committee to the US Civil Rights Commission, delivering an unexpectedly bitter polemic against his home state and the white men who governed it. "We are sick and tired of being abused by the power structure," he said. "You people (the Anglos) are the foreigners. This is our state, but you are welcome," he declared, before dropping his incendiary payload: "Texas is not worth fighting for. We fight for our country." Cheers and applause from the largely Hispanic audience punctuated his speech, but the public reception was mixed. Within hours of García's remarks appearing in print, Tony Bonilla, never anticipating the wrath that would follow, issued a rejoinder. In his speech, Bonilla winked at the crowd, promising them that "unlike some people, I'll fight for Texas." Two months later, he was out of a job.[33]

From that point forward, the Bonilla–García relationship was superficially fine. There were no hard feelings, both sides claimed, but tucked inside interviews, news stories, and the gossip in Corpus Christi social circles, the hints of an enduring grudge remained.[34] For an aging Tony Bonilla, the public spat that erupted in 1966 could be partially explained by understanding the nature of García: "I think, quite frankly, it strictly came down to 'Look, I'm the big boy in town and you guys have to go through us.'" For his brother Ruben, García and his supporters crushed a voice of moderation, opting instead for "a shrill, sort of left-winger liberal." "I could understand why he [García] was opposed," Ruben added, "but it was short-sighted be-

Dr. Héctor P. García with Lyndon B. Johnson, 1959. Photo courtesy of the Special
Collections and Archives, Mary and Jeff Bell Library, Texas A&M University–Corpus Christi.

cause we lost a strong voice in the legislature." While his successful unseating of Tony
Bonilla cast aside doubts about his waning influence, a new movement brewed, one
that would test García's fundamental conception of civil rights activism.[35]

As the 1960s drew to a close, Mexican American youths began imbibing the spirit
of the age—antiwar protests, second wave feminism, gay rights, the New Left, Black
Power—all of which were poking holes in the fabric of the New Deal order. Tactics became more aggressive, and activists more demanding, and beneath it all was a
growing realization that perhaps the time for "assimilation" had passed. That awareness crystallized into action in 1966 when César Chávez, famous for his recent success in organizing farm laborers in California, arrived in South Texas to lead a dramatic march to Austin. What followed was a 490-mile trek during which an intrepid
group of South Texas field hands cut a swath through the region's largest cities, signaling the dawn of a new era, one that would invigorate and push a community to
picture themselves as something different: "Chicanos." Organizations formed to har-

ness the exploding energy that followed: the Mexican American Youth Organization (MAYO) in 1967 and the Partido Nacional de La Raza Unida (RUP) in 1970. The latter, known casually as "La Raza," emerged as a challenger to the Democratic Party in the early 1970s. While RUP activists saw their work as a fresh alternative to a stale liberalism that offered meager returns, older Democratic Party loyalists saw an unrealistic pipe dream that threatened to dissolve a once-powerful coalition.

Héctor García was not a fan. "Dr. Héctor did not like the whole idea of Raza," the RUP leader Vincente Molina remembered. "He had his thing, and we thought he was doing okay, but, you know, don't bother us." Although García had shown a willingness to engage in the kind of tough talk that RUP thrived on, he could not accept any group that sought to weaken the Democrats. He turned down an offer to run for governor on the La Raza ticket in 1972 and continued to spurn the organization after that. La Raza confused and divided the Hispanic electorate, and García, still a pragmatist, would not have that. He had worked too hard to build a name for himself, gather a constituency, and accumulate the political capital to give Mexican Americans a voice in government to see that progress jeopardized. The rest of the party agreed. After 1972, Democrats took dead aim at La Raza, blocking federal grants and campaign financing, and throwing any and every bureaucratic hurdle in its way. When La Raza faded from prominence, Democrats danced on its grave. Ruben Bonilla, for one, could not conceal his schadenfreude at the sight of La Raza "in the political cemetery where it belongs."[36]

Looking back, the longtime *Corpus Christi Caller-Times* reporter Nick Jimenez could not help wondering what might have been. "La Raza Unida, in its day, was a game changer," Jimenez claimed, "even more than Dr. Héctor." The promise of La Raza, in his eyes, could be seen in its language: "Dr. Héctor wanted rights for '*my* people,' as he used to say, because they were Americans, because they were veterans. He wanted their American rights. La Raza Unida says, 'We're *Mexican* Americans and we have rights.' They just kind of laid it out there." Despite its promise, La Raza never made significant headway in Corpus Christi. Joe Ortiz, a Corpus Christi resident and GI Forum member, explained the lack of RUP activity by pointing to an oft-repeated fact about García: "Dr. García was the head man here, and to get anything done here you had to go through Dr. García." Though they tried, La Raza leaders could get no support from the doctor, who, in his sixties, was in no mood to leave the party he had called home for so long.[37]

As the 1980s arrived, García received some of the crowning accolades of his life — at a time when his power finally began to recede. He lost, and was unable to regain, control of his beloved organization. In the last few decades of his life, the American GI Forum eroded. Some of its younger members became more militant, adopting the language of the Chicano/a movement. Established leaders left, others became complacent, old chapters folded, and new ones were nowhere to be found. The economic downturns of the 1970s had dried up governmental funding for Forum projects, which forced the organization to reach out for corporate dollars — something Héctor was never comfortable with. Meanwhile, as the Reagan revolution kicked into full gear, the GI Forum moved to the right, cozying up to the popular new president in order to ensure support for its agenda. García worked tirelessly to breathe new life into the dying organization, traveling across the country to bolster chapters even as his own health began to fail. By the late 1980s, a string of heart attacks and a diagnosis of stomach cancer had forced García to abandon his workaholic lifestyle.

The awards came in succession throughout the 1980s. At the start of the decade, García received the Distinguished Service Award from the National Office of Civil Rights, and in 1984 came the most prestigious: the Presidential Medal of Freedom. From the working-class barrios of Mercedes, Texas, to the White House, Héctor P. García took an acknowledged place among the giants of Mexican American history. And yet it still wasn't enough. Even with his deteriorating health and a lifetime of accomplishment behind him, García grasped for power one last time. In 1988, he went to San Antonio, ostensibly to visit his daughter Cecilia. But there was another reason for his trip: the annual GI Forum convention, where he planned to mount a campaign to take back his old post as national commander. He was seventy-four years old and facing a pugnacious cadre of ambitious young Forum members—there were any number of reasons why he shouldn't have run. But as his daughter noted, "His desire to have better control over the organization was overtaking him to the point that he could not be objective about his own needs."[38]

The bid failed, and García reeled from sadness to denial to outrage. "He felt," his daughter noted, "that there were some members who had turned against him." After the convention, he began to pull away from the Forum, and by the end of his life, "he had learned to let it go." For the next eight years, until his death, García spent his time orchestrating the donation of his papers to Corpus Christi State University (now Texas A&M–Corpus Christi) and returning to one of his original passions: working in the *colonias*, where decades of neglect had exacerbated its residents' horrid living conditions. But his health continued to fail, and in 1996 he closed his medical practice. After that, according to his children, he gave up. The work that had animated his life—medicine and the GI Forum—faded into the distance. Speaking to an interviewer in 1996, Ruben Bonilla lamented "the degeneration of . . . [the] American G.I. Forum," which, without its founder in the picture, was "but a hollow organization."[39]

In the last weeks of García's life, a collection of his friends and family members took shifts huddling around his bed, day and night. In June 1996, his statue was unveiled at Texas A&M–Corpus Christi. The bronze sculpture portrayed Dr. Héctor as his ardent supporters saw him: larger than life, nine feet tall, clad in one of his old suits, wearing his GI Forum cap and Presidential Medal of Freedom, a stethoscope peeking out of his pocket, a book clutched in one hand, the other gesturing outward as if he were giving one of the thousands of speeches he delivered throughout his life. One month later, he was gone.

Aftermath

Héctor García's death left a gaping hole in the community, one that remains unfilled. In the winter of his life, it seemed as though his health and that of the organization he led were intertwined. The American GI Forum, already struggling, almost collapsed after García's death. Looking at her father's casket, Cecelia García Akers could not help wondering whether "the American GI Forum, as the organization that we had known and loved, would also be buried with him that day." An internal power struggle ensued after the funeral. "Each chapter had its own idea of what to do," said Joe Ortiz, "and I guess jealousy took over one chapter from another. There was some in-house fighting . . . Now it doesn't even look like we have a chapter of the American GI Forum anymore."

Looking back, it was clear to some members that the Forum's struggles were self-inflicted. Some of the blame, they suggested, had to be placed at the feet of its esteemed leader. Over five decades, García and the GI Forum had become codependent. "I think everyone agrees with this," Nick Jimenez mused. "Dr. Héctor was a great guy and a wonderful leader and one unique person, but the GI Forum is just now getting to the point where they're having other people come up." "Obviously he didn't intend it this way," Jimenez allowed. "He was such a huge persona, it was hard for anyone else in the GI Forum to take anything from that or rise up from that." The organization's fortunes, he argued, were inextricably linked with those of its founder. "When it was LULAC, it was the organization," he concluded, "when it was the GI Forum, it was Dr. Héctor." Or, as García's close friend Tony Canales answered when asked about others in the Forum leadership: "Leadership? He was the leader who ran the show. No one could match him."[40]

One thing most could agree on was that García, who pushed himself hard, also pushed others. "He was a strict man," Joe Ortiz remembered, "very hard to get along with." Ortiz, himself an overworked GI Forum leader, could empathize. "I guess when you're in civil rights, you carry this with you," he admitted, "and you don't mean to be hard on people. Because of all this hatred that's around you, you sort of get tense. I yell at my family without even thinking about it, so I can understand why Dr. García was hard on people." Still others, such as Butch Escobedo, a local politician, lamented that men like Dr. Fred Cervantes, a key witness in the lawsuit that dissolved Corpus Christi's discriminatory at-large voting system, languished in obscurity while García continued to dominate the city's historical memory. "I loved the man," said Escobedo, "but he was a self-promoter." Escobedo bristled at the thought of reading "another article where they're coming down honoring him or naming another sidewalk or street or whatever after him . . . like there's no other leaders in the Hispanic community other than Dr. Héctor." "Instead of honoring Dr. Héctor for another thing," Escobedo suggested that they honor Cervantes, who "did ten times more than Dr. Héctor ever did and never got credit for it."[41]

As for the Bonillas, García's on-again, off-again nemeses, they continued their work with LULAC, an organization that came to share the GI Forum's struggles. In diagnosing LULAC's growing illnesses, Ruben Bonilla looked beyond the group. "It's become a complacent community," he declared. "Young Hispanics don't take up the cause; LULAC doesn't do a vigorous job of recruiting young people into the organization." "I don't say it's an indifference," he allowed. "I think that we all share the responsibility and the blame." To anyone listening to the Bonillas and Garcías of Corpus Christi, it sounded as if the new generation of potential activists had no desire to follow in their parents' footsteps. For Ruben, there appeared to be a "larger malaise" infecting the city. "I could go out and stand on the corner," he claimed, "and try to incite a riot, incite a march, and I probably would be perspiring pretty profusely by eleven o'clock, because there's not going to be anybody that follows." The traditional motivations that lured the baby boomers and their predecessors—group identity, community engagement, a channel for venting frustrations and protesting discrimination—have been displaced by the digital revolution. In the decades before the explosion of the internet, Hispanic residents of South Texas absorbed information from a select group of media, particularly the radio, which in the 1960s and 1970s gave rise to an immensely popular set of media personalities who saturated "the airwaves with Hispanic activism," according to Ruben Bonilla. As the communications pipeline broadened, the narrow clarity of the analogue era receded, dispersing millennials' sense of civic responsibility. For all its benefits, cyberspace atomized Corpus Christi's Mexican American community.[42]

On one hand, contemporary criticisms of García can be written off as the product of lingering jealousies and resentment. In a more measured sense, however, they are testaments to a larger truth that faded in his wake: Corpus Christi was always bigger than Héctor P. García. As the historian Alan Lessoff has argued, there has been a "tendency to emphasize García as a historical figure who lived in Corpus Christi rather than as a manifestation of the place." For every action spearheaded by García, there were dozens, hundreds, even thousands working behind the scenes. In many ways, García served as an effective spokesman for movements he had little part in sparking. The Longoria affair, which thrust him into prominence, would never have occurred without the courageous widow who challenged the racist folkways of Three Rivers, Texas. Had it not been for an intrepid and determined group of families choosing to withstand the pressures of a lengthy trial and the ire of their neighbors, *Cisneros v. Corpus Christi Independent School District* (1970) would not have extended the promises (and frustrations) of *Brown v. Board of Education* (1954) to Mexican Americans. Had it not been for a vigorous set of teenagers (and the Chicano/a movement that inspired them), García wouldn't have taken part in a famous 1972 sit-in to protest continuing de facto segregation. Had it not been for the thousands of Mexican American citizens willing to trade away chunks of their paycheck for the right to vote, the Viva Kennedy coalition that endeared García to a generation of Democratic politicians would have remained stillborn.[43]

For Corpus Christi's Mexican American community, Héctor P. García will remain woven into the city's historical fabric. No one denies his immense contributions. But in the lingering hangover after his death, organizations splintered in the face of a looming power vacuum while the city they called home struggled to retain the hard-earned progress of the García era. If anything, García's legacy demonstrates both the difficulty and necessity of relinquishing power. Throughout the twentieth century, Héctor P. García fought to make life better for Mexican Americans. As Father Time and the rise of a new generation diminished his prominence, though, he tried to hold on to the organization he built rather than anoint its future leaders. The struggles that followed his death testified to the man's towering presence in life, a presence melded from the unique culture of Corpus Christi and the remarkable character of the doctor from Mercedes.

CHAPTER 7

"IT WAS US AGAINST US":
The Pharr Police Riot of 1971 and the People's Uprising against *El Jefe Político*

DAVID ROBLES

Located in the South Texas–Mexico borderland, the city of Pharr is part of a more extensive network of small towns and cities in a region known as the Rio Grande Valley. "The Valley," or "el Valle," as locals call it, is a region with a vibrant history that is often forgotten or glossed over. From the Spanish *entradas* to the social activism and farmworker movements of the 1960s to the 1980s, the Valley has seen its share of historical events that have shaped not only the region's history but also state and national histories. In the last few years, there has been increased interest from historians and local activists in bringing these forgotten events to light.

One such incident, the Pharr riot of February 1971, occurred in the middle of the Chicano/a movement and brought to light the many injustices that ethnic Mexicans experienced in the Valley.[1] Many in the local community refer to it as the "Pharr Police Riot of 1971" or the "Pharr Uprising of 1971." In Pharr, ethnic Mexicans of low economic standing lived in segregated areas away from Anglos and middle- or upper-class Mexican Americans. Separated by the Missouri Pacific railroad line, which was constructed in the early twentieth century and ran east-west across the city, ethnic Mexican communities lacked essential public services such as sewage lines, adequate water pipes, and paved roads. Also, ethnic Mexicans could not participate in local government because city meetings occurred during the middle of the day, when most of these residents were at work, and the city government ignored the people's request to change the meeting hours to the evening. Another serious problem was the beating of ethnic Mexican prisoners in the city jail by police officers of the same ethnic background. Pharr was an oppressive place for poor ethnic Mexicans on the north side of the railroad tracks, and the living inequalities were highly visible. The riot was a manifestation of the people's frustration with their city government. It was the result of months of protests against unfair city politics, community inequality, and police brutality.

The riot presented the ethnic Mexican community with opportunities to question and challenge the Anglo oppression and rule that had been prominent since the city's founding in 1909. This chapter focuses on the election of Pharr's first Mexican American mayor, in the spring of 1972, and his revolutionary approach to campaigning and governing. A. C. Jaime's governing approach differed from that of the previous Anglo administrations; his policies improved the living conditions and quality of life for the ethnic Mexican community in Pharr. He challenged boss politics in

An arrest during the Pharr police riot, 1971. Photo courtesy of the Museum of South Texas History, Edinburg.

South Texas during his campaign and in his first few years as mayor.[2] Besides improving the living conditions of ethnic Mexicans in the city, Jaime and the city commissioners amended policing tactics, dismantled the practice of boss politics, and made city government more transparent and open to the public. These changes affected politics throughout the Valley.

The events that transpired in Pharr before, during, and after the riot did not occur in a vacuum. Ethnic Mexican neighborhoods and communities across the Southwest experienced social unrest from 1965 to the mid-1970s, during the period known as the Chicano/a movement.[3] The historian Ignacio M. García defines the Chicano/a movement as "a political, social, and cultural catharsis" that led to the creation of both militant and nonmilitant organizations that fought for the betterment of ethnic Mexican communities.[4] During this period of social activism, ethnic Mexicans who identified as Chicanos/as, as well as those who didn't, protested against unfair social, economic, and political practices, many of which had been put in place after the US war of aggression against Mexico. From the late nineteenth century to the twentieth, Anglo farmers, investors, businessmen, and land speculators Americanized the region and gained control of local politics and economy. The society that emerged was one of "disparity and inequitableness between Anglos and ethnic Mexicans in which

Police officers and firefighters during the Pharr police riot, 1971. Photo courtesy of the Museum of South Texas History, Edinburg.

both groups existed in the same general space and only interacted when it was necessary."[5] From 1965 to 1975, activists and ethnic Mexican communities in the Valley began their fight for equality by staging agriculture strikes and student walkouts, creating the first Chicano/a college, and protesting against police brutality.

The land that became the site of Pharr came into the possession of John Connally Kelly and Henry N. Pharr in 1909. Initially, Kelly attempted to establish a town on his half of the land, and Pharr planned to use his land for a sugar plantation. But Pharr abandoned the venture after the second crop failed because of alkaline soil and harsh weather.[6] Kelly founded a townsite company that he named after his partner, Pharr, and by 1911 the new town had a hotel, a headquarters for the sugar company, and a school.[7] By 1915, the town of Pharr had expanded significantly with the construction of new buildings, and its population grew to about 600 residents, a mix of Anglo "pioneers" and ethnic Mexicans.[8] The segregation of ethnic Mexicans and Anglos occurred during the town's early years. Using the newly constructed railroad line as a physical color line, developers placed ethnic Mexicans on the north side of the tracks; Anglos and some well-off ethnic Mexicans resided on the south side.

Five decades after Pharr's incorporation, both groups still lived in separate spaces, intermingling only when necessary. By the late 1960s, those living on the north side of the railroad tracks still lacked essential city services, and three-fourths of the people there were "very poor."[9] The area had no city parks, traffic lights, signs, sewer lines, street cleanup, or trash pickup.[10] There was little communication between its residents and Mayor R. S. Bowe, and the substandard conditions were exacerbated by Bowe's unwillingness to spend city funds for improvement projects equitably. Jaime explained how the barrio's infrastructure became dilapidated and dangerous. When the city passed bonds to pave streets, the money would run out right before work was supposed to start on the north side. The same thing happened with water lines: bond money would run out, and those living in the barrios would not get their lines fixed. A two-inch water line served an entire neighborhood, leading to low water pressure when more than one person used the water.[11]

There were no sewer lines north of the tracks, and those living in the area used outhouses. Yet a sewage plant in the area, located on the corner of Hawk Street, degraded their health and living conditions, even though north side residents were not hooked up to it. All the sewage lines from south of the tracks converged there, and then the sewage was transferred to a plant east of town. The atrocious smell from the Hawk Street plant was overwhelming. Jaime recalled that people pleaded with Mayor Bowe to do something because it was just "downright ugly and unsanitary."[12]

The unpaved roads in the barrio were in horrendous condition, with potholes large enough that, as Jaime put it, "you could practically lose a Volkswagen if a Volkswagen went into those potholes."[13] Bowe, despite the people's pleas, did nothing to address any of these issues. According to Jaime, "The barrios never got the attention that they should have, and it was hard because our people, they saw that, they felt that they were being discriminated upon." But many people in the barrios did not want to make trouble about it, because they knew there would be repercussions from those in power if they did.[14]

The mayor's reluctance to help ethnic Mexicans in Pharr was nothing new to them and their families. Anglo domination had been the norm since the city's founding.[15] Even though educated Anglos in Pharr were not enthusiastic about Bowe, they accepted him because there was no one else to "run the show."[16] Mexican Americans were not absent from city government; a few sat on the city commission after World War II.[17] Yet they did not necessarily fight for the interests of the people living north of the railroad tracks.[18] Bowe and his administration's control of city politics was the worst problem for the people living north of the tracks. Many ethnic Mexicans felt powerless, controlled by these "*jefe politicos*," who maintained a rigid social order by using the police, controlling utilities, and making direct threats.[19]

For ten years, Bowe ran unopposed for mayor, but Jaime and other Pharr residents were under the impression that Bowe was not running the show.[20] Always informed of the people's plans, motives, and problems, Joe Pettita, the city's maintenance superintendent and Bowe's right-hand man, was considered the "brains of the operation."[21] If citizens on the north side questioned the city's neglect of the barrio, Pettita would interfere with the working of their meager utilities, raise their rates, or spread negative rumors about people who crossed him.[22]

Fernando Ramirez, a Pharr resident, pointed out that police brutality and much of the harassment that the "Latino community" experienced happened because Mexican Americans started to vote, especially against the established city council.[23] In response, Pettita organized voting parties for low-income families living in north

Pharr, provided tacos and beer, and asked them to vote the "right way."[24] Maria Magallan, a local activist and member of Volunteers in Service to America (VISTA), recalled seeing this happen regularly.[25]

Besides getting votes from those living in the north side of town for Bowe and his commissioners, Pettita controlled who had access to the mayor and who received city permits.[26] Ruben Rosales, the owner of Sepi's Tavern in Pharr at the time, explained that Bowe was "disconnected" from the people and that it was difficult to talk to him person to person without Pettita being present.[27] When Rosales went to get a city permit for his tavern, Bowe asked Pettita, "Joe, what do you think?" as he looked at Rosales, and Pettita responded, "He's all right." Such experiences lend credence to the idea that Bowe was a political figurehead during his ten-year tenure as mayor, and that Pettita controlled city government from behind the scenes.

Fighting Back

Bowe, Pettita, and city commissioners' attitudes and actions contributed to the woes of Mexican Americans living north of the tracks in Pharr in the 1960s. By 1970, some of those people began organizing to fight the injustices they were subjected to.

They had plenty of examples of activism for social justice in the Valley. In the period 1966–1970, farmworkers in Starr County went on strike for better working conditions. In the cities of Edcouch and Elsa, students walked out of their classes to protest education inequality, and demanded reform. The Mexican American Youth Organization (MAYO) and members of VISTA sponsored voting-registration drives in the barrios. Chicano/a activists created the Colegio Jacinto Treviño, the first Chicano/a college in the United States, located in Mercedes. Finally, at the MAYO national conference held in La Lomita Monastery in Mission, participants endorsed the creation of the Raza Unida Party. These are but a few examples of social justice activism that occurred in the Valley during this era. Many of the activists and volunteers from these movements participated in the protests and activism in Pharr.

After years as an activist in his hometown of Kingsville and at Texas A&I University, Efraín Fernández, a member of MAYO, moved to Pharr to work for VISTA, since the group's office was in the city.[28] Fernández, along with the local community leader Maria Magallan and her daughter Oralia, raised hell at city hall to force Bowe and Pettita to address some of the problems affecting the community north of the tracks. After a while, Bowe and Pettita gave in, deciding that it was not worth the trouble to fight.[29] The trio continued to organize and demand changes throughout 1970. Later that year, after receiving reports of police brutality and misconduct by the Pharr police, Fernández decided to investigate the matter.[30] He interviewed some of the victims and decided that immediate action was needed, because the Pharr police officers were doing inexcusable things.[31]

Jesus Ramirez, a close friend of Fernández at the time, explained that Fernández became fixated on allegations of police brutality. Fernández, not easily pushed around, was unafraid of the police, and animosity developed between him and some of the police officers. Fernández protested by holding signs in front of the police station, sometimes alone and sometimes with Magallan and her son. Unsupported by the broader community, these three were the only people objecting to police brutality in Pharr.[32] Fernández explained that the mainly middle-class ethnic Mexicans south of the tracks saw the world from "a very different perspective than that of north side Chicanos."[33] When "Chicanos" from the north side were beaten and "got their ribs broken in the Pharr Jail," many middle-class Mexican Americans, as well as Anglos, believed that they had it coming.[34]

Ruben Rosales remembered that attitudes toward police beatings illustrated a rift between ethnic Mexicans in Pharr. His older brother, Jose Rosales, a lieutenant in the Pharr Police Department, told Ruben that beatings were frequent in the jail cells, but did not say who did them.[35] He was surprised that those beating Mexicanos in the jail were also Mexicanos. Rosales explained, "It was *Mexicano con Mexicano* ... all the policemen, *los mismos*. German Guzman, Carlos Sandoval, Tito Vargas, Mateo Sandoval, Chief Alfredo Ramirez . . . it was us against us!"[36] Besides the beatings, police officers in Pharr commonly used deadly force.

Fernando Ramirez's family home was in the same block as the police station on East Clark Avenue. As a five- or six-year-old in the late 1950s, Ramirez witnessed an egregious example of deadly force while playing in a vacant lot close to the police station. A person in custody escaped from a police officer while en route to the build-ing. Handcuffed, the prisoner jumped out of the police car and ran away. Fernando recalled that the prisoner was shot to death because he could not understand or hear the police officer's commands to stop; the officer used a voice box, a medical device often employed by people with laryngeal cancer. Tearing up, Fernando described how police left the person's lifeless body in the street in order to convey a message to the community. He explained that seeing something like that as a child "changes you" and that incidents such as that one were normal in Pharr at the time: "It was okay. They could do that."[37]

The use of excessive force by law enforcement agencies toward ethnic Mexican communities in the Valley was not new or unheard of. For much of the twentieth century, especially the first two decades, the area was rife with such violence. For Efraín Fernández and Maria Magallan, allegations of police brutality against the ethnic Mexican community in Pharr marked the tipping point in their fight against social, political, and economic inequalities in the city. After a few failed attempts to make Mayor Bowe and Police Chief Alfredo Ramirez address and act on the allega-tions of police brutality, Fernández and Magallan organized a protest for Saturday, February 6, 1971.

The Pharr Riot

On that morning, thirty-two people from the barrio started their demonstration in front of Pharr City Hall. They demanded that the mayor remove Chief Ramirez for not doing anything about police misconduct, and to fire Sergeant Mateo Sandoval and Officer Gilbert Zuniga for police brutality. By the afternoon, all the demonstra-tors had walked to the Pharr jail and were continuing their protests. Efraín Fernán-dez and some others left the demonstration to attend a meeting at the Methodist retreat center in Weslaco, Texas, to discuss Mexican American civil rights issues.

Around three, the crowd grew into the hundreds as patrons from the cantinas near the police station walked to the area and supported the protestors.[38]

Fernando Ramirez recalled that during the protest, more people started to converge on the police station. Even though there were "Hispanics" on the police force, the community believed that they were "manipulated by the white city council" and the mayor.[39] Such manipulation was no secret. A. C. Jaime, who lived in south Pharr during the riot, knew that the police were under the direction of the mayor, and he felt that the mayor's policy was to "keep the Mexicano down."[40] According to Ramirez, people were tired of the harassment and, influenced by César Chávez, Martin Luther King, and the civil rights movement, they finally began asking why: "It was the first time that the community came together as one voice" to challenge the inequalities the ethnic Mexican community faced daily.[41]

Those protesting against police brutality were wedged between the police and cantina patrons. The situation worsened as the cantina patrons heckled police officers, and in the words of Jesus Ramirez, the situation "took a life on its own."[42] Protesters were not able to avoid the chaos that ensued as the crowd became larger, and the reaction of the police became more physical. According to Jesus Ramirez, the growing number of people in the crowd gave the chief an excuse to call the fire department and ask it to spray the protesters with water cannons, since the police seemed to want a fight.

Fernando Ramirez believed that by late evening, police officers had "got[ten] tired" of the gathering as more and more people came together to voice their opposition to police brutality.[43] Jesus Ramirez stated that the spraying of protesters with water was why the "real riot happened."[44] People began throwing rocks at the fire trucks, police officers, and the police chief. The police used pepper spray to disperse the crowd, too, because, according to Fernando Ramirez, "the police did not want to hear them anymore."[45]

Jaime Garza was at the retreat in Weslaco performing with his theatre group, Los Malqueridos, when a man named Rabel Lopez interrupted the performance and said that the Pharr police had shot someone and that they were hurting people. Garza and many of those attending the retreat headed to Pharr to see what was going on. He and Lopez arrived at a scene of utter chaos. Garza recalled that as soon as Lopez parked the car and opened his door, the police grabbed him and yanked him out. Since Garza was on the passenger side, he managed to get out, run the opposite direction, and evade capture. Afterward, a few people who had been in the crowd told Garza that the riot was started by one of the young activists, not the police. In this account, Gabriel Arrendaño threw a rock at the police, sparking the riot. Garza added that Arrendaño, "a big talker," took credit for starting things. The claim that a Chicano youth started the riot by throwing the first rock is significant, since the narrative of the past forty-seven years has placed the blame on the police chief for ordering the fire department to spray protesters with water. Garza's statements not only challenge this narrative but also complicate it.[46]

As the disorder continued, police from surrounding cities such as McAllen and Edinburg, as well as Hidalgo County sheriff's deputies, state troopers, and one Texas Ranger, converged at the city to help the Pharr police. According to Jesus Ramirez, officers threw tear gas canisters into the crowd, and bullets whizzed by people's heads.[47] Protesters did not know where the gunshots came from or whom the intended targets were, since the shooting seemed random. A man from Elsa known as "Grizzly" on account of his long hair and beard picked up tear gas canisters and hurled them back at police.[48]

Jesus Ramirez and his friend Edgar Ruiz arrived from Weslaco. Ramirez described a chaotic scene and saw two people he knew in hand-to-hand combat with police officers. He and Ruiz were arrested, along with many others in the vicinity, as they made their way to the police station.[49] Fernando Ramirez missed the riot, because he was out on a date. He learned about it when he turned on his car radio and heard a local radio station warn people to avoid the area near the police station. The radio broadcast reported that one person had been shot and that police had closed the streets near the station. Wondering what happened, Fernando ended the date early and drove home, only to find that most of the entrances to the barrio were closed off.[50]

Fernando eventually found an opening and headed home. With his car window down, Fernando looked around at the chaos. When he stopped at a corner directly across from the police station, someone put a shotgun to his head. The unseen man demanded to know what he was doing there, and Fernando replied that he was just going home. When asked where he lived, Fernando pointed to his parents' house, across the street. The man said that he would be watching, and if Fernando did not stop at that house, he would shoot him. Once Fernando was inside his house, his parents were happy and relieved that he was home and not involved in the riot. As the riot continued, people ran into nearby taverns and other locations to get away from the tear gas, violence, and police.[51] Jaime Garza was present when a hundred state, county, and city police officers faced off with a group of young people in front of a building filled with *"señoritas, señoras, and viejitas"* (young ladies, women, and little old ladies) playing bingo. Before anything could happen, the ladies from inside the bingo hall rushed outside, got in front of the young adults to protect them, and told the police to leave them alone. Garza stated that the police backed off, and he and the group of young adults "called it a night."[52]

Jesus Ramirez asserted that the Pharr Riot was a police riot because they were the ones who escalated the situation: "It would not have occurred, I don't think, if the various police departments and the various cities did not have that cooperative agreement to help each other. The city governments did not participate in actively understanding what the local agreement was for cooperation. I think that there was some police departments that wanted to have a showdown. That's why it happened. I sincerely believe that. It's a police riot."[53] One of the negative things that Ramirez noticed was that not many in the community came out to support the activists. Instead, only the people from the cantinas helped the protesters, and a few of them ended up arguing with police afterward, which resulted in some rock throwing. Maria Magallan likewise affirmed that the cantina patrons, though not officially part of the protest, helped and supported those demonstrating by bringing them water and food.[54]

In the chaos of that night, one innocent young man who had nothing to do with the protest or the rock throwing was killed in front of the Ramos Hair Styling Center, a local barbershop on the corner of South Cage Boulevard and East Bell Ave-

The Ramos Hair Styling Center, Pharr, 2015. Photo courtesy CRBB.

nue. With his hands in his pockets, the young man lay dead, with an apparent head wound. A local newspaper, the *McAllen Monitor*, identified the victim as Alfonso Loredo Flores. The following day, local media outlets reported that he had been killed by a gunshot to the head. Roughly a month later came confirmation that the shot that the killed Flores had come from a gun belonging to a Hidalgo County sheriff's deputy. Ruben Rosales explained that the bullet fired by the deputy struck the top of the building—some reports say it hit a rain gutter—and ricocheted, striking Flores in the head.[55] A grand jury indicted the deputy, but he was acquitted of all charges later that spring.

Aftermath

After the riot, tensions were high in Pharr. Anglos and ethnic Mexican residents alike were afraid of what might come next, because nothing like the riot or the police killing an innocent man had occurred in Pharr before. Everyone was on edge. Police arrested Efraín Fernández as well as many other people that night. Jaime Garza explained that all the arrests made people afraid to get involved in the movement.[56] Ruben Rosales, the owner of Sepi's Tavern, wanted to reopen his cantina after having kept it closed for a few days because of the riot. He asked the police whether it would be okay to open on a Sunday, and he was allowed to do so on the condition that he close if there was any trouble.[57] Nothing happened.

Group photo of the Pharr Police Department, c. 1970. Photo courtesy of the Pharr Memorial Library.

A day or so later, a customer walked into Rosales's cantina and told him that something odd was going on. Outside, they noticed that there were people on top of the roofs of local businesses on the south side of the railroad tracks.[58] Rosales could not see who they were, but he knew they were Anglos. Rosales retrieved his binoculars from his house, nearby, and saw that the men on top of the businesses were looking in his direction and holding rifles. Rosales, along with a few of his customers, began waving at the men. Carlos Sandoval, a Pharr police officer at the time, claimed there were rumors of an attack on police, which had Mayor Bowe, business owners, citizens, and the police on edge.[59]

Because of the rumors, the mayor asked business owners to be vigilant. One of them, who happened to be a close friend of Rosales, was Gilberto Espinoza, the owner of a local gas station. He informed Rosales that Bowe had contacted and instructed him to go on his roof to protect the gasoline pumps.[60] Bowe was afraid that troublemakers would use the gas to make Molotov cocktails. Following the mayor's instructions, Espinoza and his brother spent a few days and nights patrolling their business, like other business owners south of the railroad tracks. But the rumors of violence against police officers in retribution for Flores's death never amounted to anything. According to the *Pharr Press*, the city was back to normal on February 18, ten days after the riot.[61] But the fight for social justice was intensifying.

Many citizens of Pharr were concerned about the state of their city, and three citizen groups were established, not long after the riot, to address the issues affecting their community. The Concerned Citizens Committee (CCC) and Mujeres Unidas (Women United) were formed in March, and the Pharr Citizens League (PCL) in June. Made up of "barrio-oriented" middle-class Mexican Americans and Anglos, the CCC and the PCL focused their efforts on finding legal means to solve the

Undated photo of a Pharr Police Department officer. Photo courtesy of the Pharr Memorial Library.

city's problems.[62] The members of the CCC and the PCL owned local businesses, had influence in the community, and included community activists such as Efraín Fernández.

Mujeres Unidas comprised adult women from the barrio, and was led by Maria Magallan. Its main goal was to make sure the mayor addressed the problem of police brutality by removing the police chief and the two officers accused of beating residents. To achieve this, the group repeatedly protested in front of city hall and the homes of the mayor and the police chief. For example, when the sheriff deputy who killed Flores received a low bond during his court appearance in April, Magallan and 150 women marched down the streets of Pharr during a heavy rainstorm.[63] Later that month, Mujeres Unidas staged further protests to pressure the mayor to address the issue of police brutality.[64] Unaware of Magallan's resolve, Mayor Bowe did not take her and the all-women group seriously and underestimated their determination. He ridiculed them and the rest of the ethnic Mexicans in Pharr by reminding them that they were "better dressed today than before."[65] He pointedly ignored their demands. For the rest of 1971, Mujeres Unidas continued to protest, and their tenacity yielded results when Mayor Bowe and all the city commissioners resigned in early 1972.

While these groups were being organized, Flores's funeral was held, and a grand jury indicted ten people, including Efraín Fernández and the Hidalgo County deputy sheriff whose bullet killed Flores.[66] Perhaps the most significant event during this period occurred on the one-month anniversary of the riot. MAYO members and Chicano/a activists from all over Texas and the Southwest, as well as locals, participated in a two-mile march from a church in San Juan, Texas, to Flores's tomb in Pharr.[67] Local media estimated that one thousand to two thousand people participated in the march, and activists feared that police would find an excuse to use physical force against the marchers. To deny the police any pretext for action, no one said a word during the procession.[68] Abel Ochoa, who was in Arizona at the time of the riot, flew to the Valley to participate in the march. Those participating in the walk wore a red armband on one arm and a black one on the other. Parade marshals made sure that no one got out of hand, and Ochoa was one of them.[69] Ruben Rosales had been warned not to attend the march, but people told him afterward that it was "humongous."[70] Tensions between the marchers and law enforcement were high, but the event was peaceful.

Days after the march, ten people were indicted on charges related to the riot. Only one person was found guilty. Alonzo López, a schoolteacher from McAllen, was at the scene before and after the riot started. Police Chief Ramirez accused him of throwing rocks. One witness testified that López did not throw stones and was not present when the riot started.[71] López nonetheless received a five-year probated sentence.[72] Fernández was found not guilty in February 1972. During his trial, Jaime Garza and other members of the Colegio Jacinto Treviño followed the trial in the courtroom. Garza recalled that Fernández's attorney, Warren Burnett, did an extraordinary job in representing him and convinced the jury to return with a "not guilty" verdict. He summarized Anglo attitudes in Pharr: whites were not "ready to accept that there was racism," or "that there was police brutality," or that Chicano youth "knew what we were doing." Anglos knew that the Chicano youths were in the right and that they were "on to something," but given the city's history of political, social, and physical reprisals against those who spoke out against injustice, many Chicano youths feared getting involved.[73] After Fernández's acquittal, charges were dropped against all the others who had been indicted.[74]

Jaime for Mayor

The citizens of Pharr came together to address the social and political woes that plagued the city and had led to the riot. After Mayor Bowe and four commissioners resigned in the late spring of 1972, the people of Pharr had the chance to elect someone who would enact change. Since Bowe still had two more years as mayor, a special election took place. The candidates were Joe Pettita, Bowe's right-hand man, and A. C. Jaime, a young certified public accountant with his own business. Jaime and the people who would be part of his administration ran on the "unity ticket," which promoted progress and change. Months before the election, Jaime and his supporters campaigned heavily in the barrios and listened to people who had been ignored for decades. This approach to campaigning was unprecedented not only in Pharr but also in the Valley as a whole.

Jaime disliked politics. He hesitated when a group of twenty people, ethnic Mexicans and Anglos, asked him to be a candidate in the special election.[75] What made

Jaime appealing to these community members was that he was a young educated Mexican American. He did not ignore or turn away from situations that negatively affected low-income families.[76]

One such situation concerned the city's attempt to build a housing project on eight acres of land that, in Jaime's opinion, was not suitable for it. The land, which was directly across the street from his home in south Pharr, was filled with overgrown weeds and decrepit trees, and kids used the area as a place to play, smoke marijuana, and "do things that should not be done."[77] Concerned for the safety of his kids and everyone else living on the block, Jaime asked the mayor to have the owner clean up the lot. To his surprise, Bowe informed him that the city had plans to build an eighty-unit housing project on the land. This did not sit well with Jaime. He realized that the mayor did not care that the acreage was not adequate for the project. His concerns increased when Bowe informed him that the US Department of Housing and Urban Development (HUD) had approved the project, without consulting those living in the vicinity, though a city ordinance required such consultation. Bowe told Jaime the project was going to get built and that they didn't have to inform anyone, since it had already been approved.

Jaime made it clear that he was not against the building of the housing project, but he was opposed to putting eighty housing units on a small piece of land, which would force people to live "like animals."[78] Jaime left the mayor's office infuriated and decided to inform his state senator about the situation. He wrote a letter explaining that building this housing project in the proposed location would produce traffic, safety, and health hazards affecting not only the families moving in but also families already there. The senator agreed with Jaime, and a meeting with HUD was scheduled in the local federal building so that community members could voice their concerns.

Jaime advertised the meeting in the local newspaper, the *McAllen Monitor*, and the regional *Corpus Christi Caller*, and made flyers, which he distributed in his neighborhood.[79] On the day of the meeting, the only people in attendance were the HUD representatives and Jaime. Although Jaime was bewildered that no one from the community had shown up, he presented his case about the hazards the housing project would bring to his neighborhood. Two months later, Jaime and his wife were interrupted during dinner by someone loudly banging on their front door. When Jaime opened the door, a "little man" said that he was looking for him. The man was the owner of the land where the housing project was supposed to be built, and he was angry because Jaime's objections had "cost him the loss of the sale of his property." Jaime offered to buy the land, and he did. Jaime's initiative regarding the housing project caught the attention of many people who were trying to bring change to the city after the riot.

Jaime believed that his belief in hard work, doing things the "right way," and being respectful played a factor in his selection, too.[80] But he still hesitated. Besides not liking politics, he was in the middle of a busy tax season; further, he knew that if he agreed to run for mayor, his family and business would be under scrutiny by Pettita and his supporters. Jaime asked his wife for her opinion, and, as he recalled, she told him, "Honey, whatever you want to do is fine with me. But if you've ever stepped out on me, you better let me know, because it is going to come out." After receiving her blessing, Jaime informed the group in early April 1972 that he would run for mayor.

Many thanked him, but Jaime told them to thank his wife, because she was the reason he decided to do so.

Jaime knew that running a campaign against Pettita, who represented the old guard of boss politics, would not be easy, but he had a chance if he could garner the votes of those alienated from city government. Jaime recounted that his attorney believed that it was a mistake for him to run, because Pettita was going to win the election regardless of what Jaime did. He responded that he would come up with some ideas that might give him an edge over Pettita.[81] First, Jaime obtained the personal information of every eligible voter in Pharr and then made files detailing the demographics of each household on index cards. By doing so, he gained a better understanding of his potential constituents.

Jaime and his supporters met and talked to the people in north Pharr in order to gain their trust and convince them that he was the only candidate able to help them and address their needs. The campaigners began on the outskirts of the barrio and stopped at every single house to talk to the residents. Pettita mocked them and their attempts to gain votes in that part of the city. Jaime explained that Pettita did this because most of the houses they visited were owned by "Mexicanos," who, as undocumented immigrants, "could not vote." That was true, but Pettita forgot that the children of those residents could vote, and they voted for Jaime because their parents advised them to do so.[82] Jaime and Armando Gomez, one of his commissioner candidates, made sure the community knew that they would try to right the wrongs of the previous mayor and commission, and that they appreciated their support, whether or not they could vote.[83] Maria Magallan also helped Jaime break down barriers that he, as an outsider from south Pharr, would encounter, by telling her neighbors that they needed to listen to and vote for him.[84] On Monday and Tuesday nights, Jaime and Magallan organized campaign events in people's backyards, which were attended by forty to fifty neighbors at a time.[85] By using these kinds of grassroots campaigning methods for weeks before the election, Jaime was able to spread his ticket's message to the voters whose support he needed.

Jaime recalled that on Election Day, a hundred of his supporters walked the streets and handed out cards to people, asking them to vote, whether for him or his opponent. At the main polling location, he approached people voting for Pettita to ask them to consider voting for him. As people came to vote, Jaime kept track of them by scratching off their names on the index cards he had made at the beginning of the campaign. During all of this, Pettita sat in the back of his limousine, laughing and insulting Jaime as he attempted to secure last-minute votes.[86] By the end of the night, Jaime and his unity ticket had won the 1972 election, with 52 percent of the vote. It ushered in a new era of social and political change in Pharr.[87]

The reaction of the ethnic Mexican community to the news that Pharr had elected its first Mexican American mayor was positive. Fernando Ramirez remembered that it was "the first time Latinos, *la Raza*, had an impact," and the most important thing was that "Latinos" voted.[88] The votes that Jaime received from the ethnic Mexican community in Pharr were crucial to his victory and to electing a city commission that was a mixture of Anglos and "Hispanics." Jaime recalled that the people sat back and let him and his new administration "do their thing."[89] Since there were so many things to do and problems to address, Jaime did not have the time to bask in feeling proud of being the first Mexican American mayor of Pharr.

Governing

The new administration immediately began working on how to deal with the sewage plant on the north side. For Jaime, the solution was straightforward. Lift stations were installed to pick up sewage from the south side of the tracks and then send it to the sewage plants east of the city, rather than having the waste stew for days while it made its way north.[90] This act significantly improved the lives of residents living near the sewage plant in north Pharr, and made it clear that Jaime and his city administration could get things done.

When asked about the differences he saw between Bowe and Jaime, Rosales explained that the two were like night and day. Laughing and shaking his head, he said that Bowe "was rough," while Jaime was "*mas pacifico*," more peaceful.[91] Unlike their predecessors, Mayor Jaime and his administration were accessible to the citizens of Pharr. They listened to residents, whereas it had been almost impossible for an ordinary citizen to talk to Bowe in person.

Unlike the previous commission, which had never seemed able to find enough money to pave the streets or install sewer lines in north Pharr, Jaime asserted that he and his commission would find a way to get money for the improvements.[92] "That was just things that you *had* to work," he explained as he described how he managed being both a young CPA and a new mayor. Jaime would get up at six, go to city hall, prioritize the day's agenda, and leave instructions for the city manager, who saw to it that tasks got accomplished. Jaime would then go to his accounting office at eight and return to city hall in the evening to address matters with his commission until one or two in the morning. Jaime and his commission worked long and hard, and listened to the people.

For example, Fernando Ramirez recalled when Jaime and the new city government proposed in 1972–1973 to demolish the small police station and put in its place a new garbage dump, since there was vacant land next to the site; the new police station would be built on the south side of town.[93] People from the barrio had strong concerns about the plan. Since many of the community elders could not speak English, they asked their children to speak for them, including Ramirez's mother, who was ill and could not participate as much as she wanted to.

At a city council meeting, twenty-two-year-old Ramirez spoke for his community. He said that "everything was really nice," but he asked the council to think about the noise and pollution generated by garbage trucks.[94] He reminded them that disposable diapers, spoiled food, and other discarded items would eventually fall out of the garbage trucks onto the barrio streets before reaching the dump. To get his point across, Ramirez appealed to the ethnic Mexicans on the city council by reminding them about the riot, the reasons for the protest, and the consequences of the disorder: "You have to remember the riot that was here a couple of years ago. They fought about injustice, and these people here, these old men and women, and their children, they are ready to do the same all over again for justice, because they do not want it here. And you remember that you are on this council because the people elected you to be their representatives."[95]

Fernando's speech must have struck a nerve, because the proposition did not pass. Still, it is important to note that Jaime and the new administration made themselves available to the people to discuss the proposition, listened to the community's concerns, allowed for public discourse, and respected their opposition. Ruben Rosales stressed this significant difference between the old administration and the new one.[96] This openness to barrio residents' concerns defined Jaime and the new commissioners as city leaders.

As mayor, Jaime did not tolerate unwarranted police violence or corrupt city deals. He acted at the first sign of trouble. When Jaime received a complaint that an officer had punched and beaten a person who was handcuffed, for mouthing off and spitting at the officer, he took immediate action.[97] Jaime told the city manager that he would be fired if he did not fire the officer. The city manager did so. Unfortunately, this was not an isolated incident.

Jaime recalled receiving another complaint of a police officer using excessive force on a person who was handcuffed. Again, the city manager fired the officer. Before long, an attorney representing the victim informed Jaime that he needed to appear in court to answer for the officer's actions.[98] The mayor told the attorney that the officer no longer worked for the police department, and that there was therefore no need for him to go to court. The attorney, who could not believe that Jaime had fired the officer that quickly, told him, "You son of a gun, you beat me to it." Understandably, the attorney was surprised because the previous city administration had never done that in reported cases of police brutality. Jaime explained that by firing these police officers, he was making it clear that no one had to tell him how to run the city.[99]

Jaime's unwillingness to tolerate police misconduct almost seemed revolutionary at the time, since police beatings at the city jail were commonplace. At the time, police departments across the nation were under scrutiny for their actions and reactions against urban unrest and mass demonstrations.[100] From 1967 to the early 1970s, calls for setting up internal review systems within police departments, as well as civilian review boards, became commonplace in the United States.[101]

The Pharr Police Department and its officers were behind the times. Chief Ramirez and many of his officers were poorly trained or even untrained; they lacked new technology and equipment; and they were not prepared to handle incidents like the riot. According to Jaime, before the riot, police officers in Pharr did not receive proper training, and if personnel were needed, "they would pick up just about anybody who wanted to be a policeman."[102] Ruben Rosales confirmed that statement and explained that the hiring of untrained police officers caused many problems. In the decades before the riot, a police officer was someone who belonged to a political faction in the city and worked for it.[103] They could put on a badge, carry a gun, and get to work without receiving any training. Rosales recalled that the police department had one officer who "didn't speak a word in English or could even write." He was on the force "on account of politics."

During Jaime's tenure as mayor, however, the police department underwent a radical transformation. It ended up with adequately trained officers, modern equipment, better training, and stable leadership. He made it clear that there would be consequences for anyone who did something out of line. Beatings in the jail ceased, and officers became professionalized. As they grew better at handling interactions with the public, they encountered fewer problems.[104] This transformation of the police department was revolutionary.[105]

Jaime also reformed the city commission. He called its members into his office in the first few weeks after the election and explained that if any of them stepped out of line, he wanted their resignation letter mailed in.[106] They were not to take advantage of any situation, and to conduct themselves professionally. City employees were warned that if they did anything wrong or illegal, mistreated "Mexicanos" in town, or misused their positions, they would be fired. Jaime made it especially clear to police officers that if they abused anyone, handcuffed or not, they would be terminated.[107] Jaime's point was clear: the city would function professionally and ethically, and if anyone did something contrary to the law or city guidelines, he or she would be fired, no questions asked.

As a result of this stance, Jaime had to fire his first city manager for making racist remarks toward a city clerk named Dora Garza. He remembered that Dora called him, crying, and explained that she could not work at city hall anymore, because the city manager had insulted her and the other city clerks.[108] She explained that since city hall employees did not have a place to eat, they asked the city manager whether they could eat their breakfast tacos in the janitor's office. He said that "he did not want the smell of tacos in city hall," and laughed at them. That evening, Jaime met with the city commissioners, informed them of what had happened, and told them that the city manager had to go. They fired him the following day. To avoid any "unnecessary hassles" or problems, they gave him a cake.

Later, Jaime found out that the former city manager, a "young Anglo man," had constantly bad-mouthed him and many ethnic Mexicans in Pharr while working for the city.[109] Jaime recalled that Bill Schupp, who was the city manager of McAllen, while Jaime was in office in Pharr, told him that he tried to talk sense to the man. When he and Schupp read newspaper articles about the progress being made in Pharr, he would laugh and say that he was not going to do what Jaime and the city commissioners wanted. He told Schupp that he was "going to teach them Mexicans how to run a city." According to Jaime, he was not aware that this was going on behind his back—he had enough reason to fire him for insulting the city clerks.

It was crucial for Jaime and his city commission to avoid any whiff of scandal while they were in office, because politicians, law enforcement officials, and communities around the Valley were watching them. Jaime believed that he was sometimes under federal investigation for being the city's first Mexican American mayor.[110] Some of his accounting clients asked him to launder money, or gave him two sets of books to look over, but Jaime always declined to do anything illegal. Jaime knew that some people or organizations were "checking him out," since many high-ranking officials in the region were on the take. In addition to those trying to make him "slip," others were interested in his approach to "running things" in Pharr.

According to Jaime, Antonio Orendain, the leader of the United Farm Workers in Texas, attended every city meeting after Jaime was elected mayor, just to observe the new city commission's agenda.[111] Jaime explained that Orendain would sit on the floor of the room where the meeting was taking place and just listen, not interrupt. Though they did not know each other, both men knew what each other represented; Jaime did not officially meet Orendain until after he left office in the late 1970s. Orendain and other activists gave the new mayor and the city council time to fix many of the troubles in Pharr, and Jaime never had problems with them. To Jaime, that was a sign of respect.

But many activists were worried that Jaime and his administration would not be able to understand, let alone address, the issues affecting ethnic Mexicans in the city. Many Chicano youths at the time viewed city leaders as middle-class businessmen who did not represent the community in north Pharr and were not radical enough to improve things there.[112] After the end of their two-year term (the rest of Bowe's term), Jaime and his administration addressed some of the woes affecting those living north of the tracks. But it was not until his second full term as mayor that he addressed the blight of cantinas and vice and changed Pharr's identity forever.

Jaime explained that from 1975 to 1979, he and his administration gained the attention of the mafia out of San Antonio because they were shutting down places in Pharr where the mafia operated.[113] One of these locations was a theatre on the corner of Business 83 and I Road that showed "ugly movies" (pornographic films), and the people living nearby had had enough. Jaime enlisted the help of his friends to purchase the property. Soon after the purchase, the city closed the theatre and demolished it.[114] The city likewise closed and demolished other buildings that were sites of illegal activity.

Jaime stated that he and his administration also addressed the nuisance caused by cantinas that stayed open until two in the morning and played their *pianolas* (player pianos) at high volume, bothering the people for blocks in every direction.[115] At the time, there were thirty-four cantinas in an eight-block radius. Vice was a significant problem in this part of the city; prostitutes and pimps worked the area, and drugs were brought in.[116] The prostitutes conducted their business in the buildings behind the cantinas. Jaime had a great professional relationship with the Border Patrol chief, and would request that he send the Border Patrol paddy wagon to pick up all the prostitutes and remove them from the area. The women would be back in the area the next day, and he would request the help of Border Patrol to remove them again.[117] To rid the community of these vice problems permanently, Jaime attacked them at their source.

Jaime learned who owned the properties behind the cantinas and formulated a plan to close them down. He convinced many of his friends and clients to buy cantinas or properties used for prostitution and other illegal activities. For example, he asked a friend who lived in that area to purchase a property. The friend said that he could not afford it.[118] Jaime took him to a finance company to get a loan to purchase the property. After buying the property, his friend closed the building and cut off access to it, as requested by Jaime. The purchase of other properties and cantinas soon followed as his other friends and clients bought them and closed them down permanently. This tactic, however, closed only a small percentage of the cantinas. Jaime and his administration then focused on crafting a city ordinance that would restrict these kinds of businesses.

Jaime realized that he was encountering resistance from his city attorney. Every time Jaime asked him to write an ordinance regulating cantinas, the draft was not to Jaime's liking. Under the ordinance that Jaime had in mind, any cantina that was shut down for violating the ordinance could not reopen as a place that sold liquor or beer.[119] Jaime eventually learned that the city attorney owned four cantinas in the troubled area, and so he dismissed him from his position. Soon after, Jaime hired a law firm in McAllen to write the ordinance he wanted. The process of dealing with and regulating the cantinas took time, but it worked.

In addition, the police department began checking local bars for gambling, prostitution, and other illicit activities. Manuel Chavez, who replaced Ramirez as police chief, started the practice of monitoring the bars. Chavez was in Pharr for only about a year, but his successor, Chief Raul Reyna, continued the practice. Officers checked liquor licenses, looked inside cash registers, and fined employees for not having health permits.[120] The constant inspections drove many customers away from the cantinas.

Cantina owners saw Jaime's attempt to regulate taverns as an attack on their livelihoods. He stated that about thirty-four cantina owners went to Hidalgo county judge Guerra to protest the unfair treatment they were receiving in Pharr. The judge informed Jaime of the situation and warned him that these people were threatening to harm him.[121] Jaime was not easily scared, and he told the judge that he would be waiting for them at his office in city hall. According to Jaime, when he arrived at the city hall in the late evening, many *cantineros* were outside, and one whom he presumed to be the leader of the group was being quite loud. Jaime said that he was ready to listen to them. Afraid that Jaime and the city commissioners might pass more ordinances, twenty of the *cantineros* had hired an attorney, Ronald D. Zipp of Edinburg, to represent them. Zipp informed Jaime that the city ordinances and the constant police presence in his clients' bars were damaging their livelihoods.[122] Gloria Reyes, the owner of the Watergate Lounge, told Jaime that every time police officers walked in her bar, customers left.[123] Ruben Rosales, the owner of Sepi's Tavern, spoke to Jaime, Chief Reyna, and Commissioners Newcombe, Escobar, Anderson, and Gomez. Rosales asked Reyna whether the police went to the American Legion hall to check that ordinances were being followed, or whether they asked Anglo waitresses for documentation, as they did to the ethnic Mexican barmaids.[124] As far as he knew, he sold beer just as the American Legion did, so he wondered why his tavern and his workers were treated differently. Jaime listened to their grievances.

After they were finished, Jaime spoke. He informed them that Chief Reyna and his officers were following orders, and if there were any improper police actions, then he would see to it that they were corrected.[125] Jaime said that they had to close their bars at one in the morning instead of two because they were attracting drunks from all over the Valley and causing severe problems in the city.[126] If the owners did not comply with this soon-to-be ordinance, then Jaime would force them to close at midnight. The *cantineros* argued that they had a right to conduct business, which Jaime agreed with, but not at the expense of residents living near their establishments.

When the new ordinance governing hours of operation was passed, the owners ignored it and continued to keep their bars open until two in the morning.[127] Jaime responded swiftly by asking the city commission to revise the ordinance and change the mandatory closing time to midnight. *Cantineros* protested again, but Jaime did not budge. Instead, he warned them that if they persisted in breaking the law, the city would shut them down indefinitely. Eventually, Jaime and the city commissioners closed many of the cantinas located in the targeted area for not complying with city ordinances, or else did not renew their liquor licenses, for committing a variety of infractions. Jaime's actions faced opposition from cantina owners, but he held steady in his efforts to clean up the city.

Even though some people wanted Jaime to fail because of the progress he was making, many more people supported him and the commissioners. As a *cantinero*, Ruben Rosales disagreed with Mayor Jaime regarding the closing hours of the cantinas, but he respected the man. Rosales has continued to have a lot of respect for him because Jaime kept his word and "did everything he said he was going to do."[128] "I give him a lot of credit," explained Rosales, "because the city of Pharr never had a Chicano as mayor," and Jaime improved the quality of life for the community on the north side of the railroad tracks.

The riot in Pharr in 1971 was, in the words of Efraín Fernández, a tragic situation. What started as a peaceful protest against police brutality ended in violence as protesters, cantina patrons, and police officers clashed in the early-evening hours of February 6. For hours, the scene around the police station looked and sounded like a war zone as rocks were hurled toward the police, firefighters sprayed people with pressurized water, law enforcement officers threw tear gas canisters and shot their weapons in the air, and people ran, screamed, and fought with the police. While all this was happening, Alfonso Loredo Flores was killed while watching the chaos unfold. At the time, Flores's death may have been seen as nothing more than an unfortunate or even inconsequential event. But in fact, his death was the catalyst that provided the community of Pharr with an opportunity to create social and political change in the city.

Though significant activism took place in the city after Flores's death, true change was not seen until a year later, when the citizens of Pharr elected the first Mexican American mayor in the city's history. Over the course of almost seven years, A. C. Jaime improved the squalid conditions in north Pharr, ended police brutality and modernized the department, fired corrupt city officials, rooted out prostitution and drug dealing, and closed cantinas that repeatedly violated city ordinances.

The changes made by Jaime and the city commissioners who served under him had a long-standing impact, one still visible on the streets of the old barrio north of the railroad tracks. The Pharr riot and Jaime's campaign, election, and tenure as mayor, two largely unrecognized historical moments in the push for civil rights in Texas, not only affected the political process in the Valley, but also "opened the political doors for other Mexicanos to walk through."[129]

CHAPTER 8

THE 1970 UVALDE SCHOOL WALKOUT

VINICIO SINTA AND MAGGIE RIVAS-RODRIGUEZ

Elvia Perez recalls pedaling her bicycle the two miles from her parents' home in the South Texas town of Uvalde to her piano teacher's house when she was a young girl in the 1960s. She rattled over the bumpy streets near her house on the west side of town, over the railroad tracks, and past the two-story John Nance Garner House, home of the former US vice president. On the east side of town, the roads were paved and smooth, edged by tidy sidewalks, the houses stately.

"I would ... see the ... big giant houses that they lived in," on the east side, Perez recalled as an adult. "And our houses were smaller."[1] Rachel Gonzales-Hanson noticed another striking difference: for many years, her family used an outhouse. "That was very common ... It was years and years before the sewer lines were put in on the west side of town so that everybody had access to indoor plumbing," Gonzales-Hanson said. "Even that kind of basic infrastructure was sorely missing all over the west side. The streets were not kept up. Forget about sidewalks."[2]

Housing was just one signifier of the inequalities in this town of giant, shady live oak trees. For example, Mexican Americans in the area generally were the workers, dependent on paychecks signed by Anglo bosses. They were generally poorer than Anglos and virtually powerless. Few Mexican Americans were in positions of power; it was not until the mid-1960s that the first Mexican American was elected to public office. Many of the Mexican Americans interviewed by the Civil Rights in Black and Brown Oral History Project and the Voces Oral History Center brought up examples of how they were disenfranchised and made to feel second-class, as if their language and their culture were inferior. For example, Rachel Gonzales-Hanson pointed to something left out of her beloved seventh-grade Texas history book: the county and city of Uvalde were named for Juan de Ugalde, a Spanish military commander.[3] "I never heard that Uvalde was named after General Ugalde," she said. "And how did we get from 'Ugalde' to 'You-valdee'?"[4]

In 1970, many of the men of Uvalde worked in the coal or asphalt mines nearby, or on ranches. Some worked as professional sheep shearers, or *trasqueleros*, hired by ranchers in Texas, Colorado, Nebraska, and other states. Gonzales-Hanson's father was one of them, traveling throughout the state and farther north to ply his trade, and sending money to his family in Uvalde. At home during the off-season, he worked three part-time jobs to make ends meet.

"My mom did everything she could to live as frugal and well as she could,"

Gonzales-Hanson recalled. "So she [did] all the cooking, and the baking was always homemade. Everything from scratch ... a lot of my clothes, which were great. People always complimented me on my clothes, and actually they thought they were store-bought, and they weren't."[5]

Throughout their lives, Mexican Americans in Uvalde were reminded of their place. Even after death, they were buried in a separate cemetery—away from the Anglo graves. Perhaps the disparity of wealth was starkest in the schools, where children were socialized to understand the place of their Mexican culture: speak Spanish on school grounds and risk feeling the sting of "swats" to your calves or bottom with a heavy paddle; eat the bean tacos your mom packed for your lunch and endure the taunts of other kids.

In the 1960s and 1970s, unrest swept the country: antiwar demonstrations, the civil rights movement, women's liberation. Protests, and police action against protesters, were broadcast on the three major television networks nightly. Marchers in Selma, Alabama—seeking simply the right to vote—were met with police violence. Many Mexican Americans watched knowingly, recognizing that they faced many of the same conditions as African Americans in the Deep South.[6]

Tensions simmered in Uvalde. Some of the more restive people there had been chafing against discrimination for years, unable to get much traction in their efforts to change things. Many were afraid to speak up, fearful of losing their jobs. In neighboring Crystal City, about half an hour south, Mexican American activists had already staked their claim, and they became a model of how a community might rise up.[7]

On the morning of April 14, 1970, Mexican American students in Uvalde staged a walkout. In the following days, an ad hoc organization of Mexican American parents pressed their demands on the school board; Anglo parents countered by creating an organization and making their own demands, mocking the Mexican American parents. If the Mexican American students and their families believed their call for change would be heeded, they were sadly disappointed. The all-Anglo school board was unyielding. The notorious Texas Rangers descended, sometimes literally by helicopter, as a show of force, an attempt to intimidate the uprising and demonstrate support for the school administration, for the status quo.

The 1970 walkout defined that generation of Uvalde's Mexican Americans. Half a century later, one woman complained that the walkout had ruined her senior year; some men said that it led to them getting drafted and being shipped to Vietnam; and many said that they continue to believe their actions were justified, even if personally painful. This chapter examines the experiences of the men and women who participated in, or were affected by, the walkout. The event that sparked the student boycott was the flash point; the problems in Uvalde were of long standing. The student action was one of the few weapons in a limited arsenal against a system that had held more than half its population in a subservient position for too long.

The walkout wasn't the only manifestation of the racial problems at the schools. The heavy involvement of Mexican American parents—many of them the product of the segregated schooling system that students protested against—resulted in the involvement of allies and later launched a lawsuit that took decades to resolve. Uvalde would never be the same.

The Roots of the Walkout

If you ask the men and women who took part in or supported the Uvalde walkout in 1970 what started it, you will likely hear that it was because George—or Josué—Garza's contract at Robb Elementary School was not renewed that spring. But all acknowledge that Garza's contract was only the catalyst; the roots of the trouble went far deeper. Many had grown up under the conditions that held Mexican Americans in subservient roles, with little political power or control over their circumstances. At different times in their lives, Mexican Americans in Uvalde became aware of the inequalities and determined to improve conditions in their communities. One of those was Abelardo Castillo, whose awakening came right after he graduated from high school in 1964 and took a job at a funeral home.

"The first day that I started working there ... I was assigned to work a funeral for a ... white lady who belonged to the First Baptist Church," Castillo said. "I rolled the casket in with my boss and I started looking around and I saw all these people and the cars they were driving, the way they were dressed, you know the church inside and I started thinking—I'll never forget this—I started thinking, 'What's the difference between us and them? Why are they different?' And that's what really inspired me to do other things and look into those differences."[8]

Castillo concluded that the differences revolved around education and inherited money. "There wasn't new money [in Uvalde], and so it was very evident that these wealthy ranchers—mostly ranchers—there in Uvalde, were leaving a lot of property and a lot of money to their kids ... [I thought:] 'We're really living slavery again, but it's a new, modern type of slavery: they hire us and they pay us just enough money to survive. The old type of slavery, of course it's outlawed, but they still maintain this,'" he recalled.[9]

The local Anglo ranchers, attorneys, and business owners, including Dolph Briscoe, who served as Texas governor from 1973 to 1979, formed a powerful ruling elite. They wielded an outsized influence, many of those interviewed said.

One of the most dramatic examples of the power they wielded concerned the case of José "Joe" Uriegas, a high school football star quarterback who was either forced out of, or felt pressed to leave, town in the 1950s. The youngest of eleven children, the son of a custodian at the local school, Uriegas was bright and driven. He decided in elementary school that he needed to attend a school that had more Anglos, recognizing that he would need to compete with them. Through a series of interventions by a kindly principal named Sam Houston Foster who tutored him, and, later, a junior high football coach, Uriegas excelled, making his mark in athletics.[10]

His close friend Elías Menendez recalled that "Joe was very fast and he worked out every day, even outside of the school ... He worked all year long. Even before practice started, he would be out there, working ... throwing passes and so forth. So he was probably the best quarterback at that time in our home district group, which included Eagle Pass, Del Rio, Hondo, Carrizo Springs and South San [Antonio] and a couple of others," Menendez said. "There was no quarterback as good as him."[11]

Uriegas said that his family doctor urged him to leave town because Anglos didn't like seeing "a Mexican in charge," that is, as quarterback.[12] "Evidently, he [the physician] and several other people were talking about that," Uriegas said.[13] Menendez saw it differently: Uriegas sat on the sidelines while the son of a prominent attorney played quarterback. For Uriegas to play quarterback, he would need to move—and Del Rio, where his old junior high coach, Walter Levermann, was coaching high school track, about eighty miles to the west, was a good option. "He [Uriegas] knew he didn't have a chance there [in Uvalde], even though he was a much better player," Menendez said.[14] Uriegas said that Levermann helped arrange for Uriegas and his parents to move to Del Rio, where they lived in the San José housing project. "They gave me a job taking meal tickets [at the school cafeteria] . . . So I got a free meal, a place to stay. And I moved to Del Rio," Uriegas said.[15] He was a high school sophomore.

Although Uriegas's parents moved with him to Del Rio, a few months later they returned to Uvalde.[16] Uriegas said that his mother's health—she had recurring nosebleeds from broken capillaries—pushed them to return to Uvalde.[17] Uriegas was ineligible to play football during his first year at Del Rio, but he ran track for Levermann. In his junior year, he joined the football team, and with him as quarterback, the Del Rio High School Panthers beat the Uvalde Coyotes twice. He sometimes dined with the Levermann family, and came to have strong friendships with his football teammates and their families. Uriegas graduated from Del Rio High School in 1958.

The outspoken and recalcitrant Gilbert Torres was among the Mexican Americans who found ways to avoid becoming dependent on their wealthier Anglo neighbors. Born on the nearby Pulliam Ranch in 1936, Torres was discouraged by his counselor at Uvalde High School from attending college and instead was steered into vocational school. He learned furniture upholstery and refinishing in San Antonio and later opened his own shop in Uvalde. His business provided for his family. And Torres had a supplemental income: he had joined the Texas National Guard as a teenager, and later enlisted in the army reserves. He served a combined forty-two years in the guard and the reserves. That extra income afforded him a measure of independence, he told an interviewer in 1998. Torres was elected to the Uvalde County Commission in 1976, unbeholden to the Anglo establishment.[18]

The reality that the Mexican American community in Uvalde was by and large dependent on the wealthier, Anglo establishment emerged repeatedly in interviews. Eleazar Lugo, who was a student council leader at Uvalde High School, participated in the walkout, but later was hired by the telephone company, one of the few employers not controlled by local power brokers. Employment opportunities that offered a measure of independence were slim: small businesses, the rare state job, the phone company. "I've known people that work at a job for fifteen years and never got a raise," he said. "I mean, because . . . where are you gonna go? You need a job—you gonna stay there and work."[19]

Many school-age Mexican American students were disadvantaged because they were migrant farmworkers: they left for the fields in the spring, before the end of the semester, and returned after classes had started in the fall. Lugo was one of them. He recalled being classified as a slow learner until junior high, when it became evident that he was bright. "I was president of student council; in high school I was in the student council, I was president of the French Club . . . I was an A and B student . . . but I never cracked a book . . . I retained everything that they taught," Lugo said.[20]

The Role of Language

Many of the Mexican American children had familial ties to Mexico, which was as close as Ciudad Acuña, across the border from Del Rio. Some were born there— or else one or both parents were from there, as was the case for José Aguilera. The use of the Spanish language, then, was a powerful cultural signifier—and perhaps why it created a battlefield. It was common to be beaten for speaking Spanish: boys were told to lift up their pant legs and were then swatted on the calves with wooden paddles, which had holes drilled in them to deliver a stronger sting.

But there was another way to inflict pain, perhaps leaving a more lasting impression. Aguilera recalled that during recess in elementary school, he said a few words in Spanish. His teacher called to him and grabbed him by the ear. "And she drew, on the wall, on the building, a circle there and she told me to put my nose in that circle and she put it right at the height that I had to stand on my tippy toe to put my nose in that circle there, as punishment because I was speaking Spanish," Aguilera said. He remained there for the rest of the period. "I didn't understand why they were doing it."[21]

Today, Uvalde is 82 percent Hispanic and 16 percent non-Hispanic white.[22] In March 1970, the student population of Uvalde public schools was majority Mexican

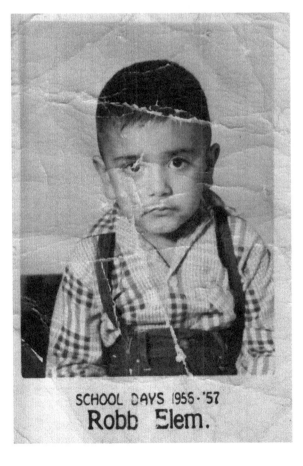

José Aguilera, 1956–1957 school year. As punishment for speaking Spanish on the school grounds, Aguilera had to stand with his nose in a chalk circle on a brick wall on the playground. Photo courtesy of the Voces Oral History Center, University of Texas at Austin.

Table 8.1. Mexican American student population in Uvalde schools as of March 2, 1970

School	Mex. Am. students	Total students	% Mex. Am.
Anthon	441	455	96.9
Benson	205	368	55.7
Dalton	132	566	23.3
Robb	536	601	89.1
Jr. High	321	572	56.1
High School	460	908	50.6
Special Education	84	102	82.3
Total	1,377	3,572	61.0

Source: Statement of José V. Uriegas and Jesús J. Rubio, Jr. before the United States Senate Subcommittee on Equal Educational Opportunity, August 19, 1970, Washington, DC.

American: 61 percent. But there were only 17 Mexican Americans out of 185 teachers, and no Mexican American administrators, according to figures presented in an August 1970 hearing before the US Senate Subcommittee on Equal Educational Opportunity. At the time, the district had one junior high and one high school; but in the four elementary schools, segregation was evident. Mexican Americans made up 97 percent of the students at Anthon Elementary and 89 percent at Robb Elementary. Benson Elementary was more evenly divided, with Mexican Americans making up 56 percent; at Dalton, it was 23 percent.[23]

Not all Mexican Americans felt discrimination. Olga Charles, the daughter of a sheep shearer, recalled her childhood on South Park Street as idyllic. She was surrounded by family and playmates, all Mexican American. "It was a great neighborhood. It was a great life," she said. "My life existed around that four-block area. I would go to school at Robb which was in the four-block area. And I would come home on Fridays. I would meet my mother downtown as she came from Williamson-Dickie, paid our bills, picked up a sandwich and went home. So, I lived in that area the entire time . . . Growing up, I lived very, very sheltered . . . I stayed in my little four-block area, played with my friends, became very close," Charles recalled. "They were my family."[24]

In 1970, when she was a senior in high school, Charles heard about the unrest in Crystal City. The Mexican American community there was protesting discrimination, including exclusion from the city swimming pool, except on Mondays, right before it was cleaned. Charles assumed that there was no such discrimination in Uvalde. "I don't even think at that time we had a pool," she said. "So, you know, that was nothing that really bothered me, because I didn't understand."[25] So when her friends said they would be picketing in Crystal City, Charles demurred. "I couldn't care less what was going on in Crystal City," she said. "And I'd go home and my father says, 'You know what, we've never had that problem. We're not gonna get involved.' Okay,

Olga Charles, Uvalde, 2016. Charles, who was a senior at Uvalde High School in 1970, said she never felt discrimination. Photo by Eli Reed, courtesy of the Voces Oral History Center, University of Texas at Austin.

so we didn't get involved." But others, including Sergio Porras, another high school senior, took notice. "It was in the news that, you know, the actual walkout [in Crystal City] and why they did it," Porras said. "And that's when I think it was a consensus here: 'Hey, they can do it, we can do it.' And that's how it happened."[26]

The Case of George Garza

Josué "George" Garza, the son of an itinerant protestant preacher, was born in San Antonio in 1938. After moving around small Texas towns, he graduated from Uvalde High School in 1958. After earning a degree at Texas A&I University, in Kingsville, he worked for a crop duster before getting hired in Uvalde as a teacher. Garza was part of the Mexican American middle class; his father was a Mexican Assembly of God minister who had also owned several small businesses. Garza himself was an entrepreneur; he and his brother learned early to become salesmen: selling oranges, and sometimes homemade tortillas, door-to-door.

"When my grandmother came from Mexico, she would make corn tortillas by hand. And we'd sell tortillas. And I would say, 'Look, they are special—made by hand by my grandmother. She's from Mexico, she really knows.' And I began to develop salesmanship skills."[27]

George Garza, Uvalde, 2016. The decision by the principal of Robb Elementary not to renew George Garza's teaching contract precipitated the 1970 school walkout in Uvalde. Courtesy of the Voces Oral History Center, University of Texas at Austin.

He wasn't the only Mexican American teacher in Uvalde. "There were three types of . . . Mexican American teachers: the nonconformist, the conformist, and then the superconformist," Garza said. "Now, there were some of us that were . . . in between conformist and nonconformist. "There was a rule that if you got caught speaking Spanish, you [would] get two licks. A superconformist teacher, Hispanic teacher, Mexican American [would say]: 'Hey, come here, you're talking Spanish, bend over.' Pow pow pow! That's a superconformist. The conformist was the guy that [said], 'Hey, come here, don't speak Spanish, because they're gonna give you two licks.' The nonconformist [said], 'Speak Spanish, man.'"[28]

Garza sometimes surprised the students. One day when he was on cafeteria duty, he noticed a little girl eating a taco. "But she had to cover it with a napkin. And I was walking around and kind of chatting with the kids. 'Hey, *mija*, what are you eating?' 'It's a taco.' 'Why do you cover it?' 'No, because they make fun of me,'" he recalled. "I said, 'I eat tacos all the time.'" The little girl offered him an extra taco, and Garza very publicly ate it in the cafeteria.[29]

Garza's principal, E. P. Shannon, chastised him, saying, "It's not good for you to be doing that," because the cafeteria had a menu and the children were supposed to be encouraged to eat the cafeteria food. "Well, the kids . . . every once in a while they'd bring me some tacos," Garza said. He enjoyed his taco gifts with steaming coffee from a thermos.[30]

Garza became popular as an advocate for non-English-speaking parents. "Because of their lack of English . . . I would go with them to the principal, or tell the principal. And that was acting like an assistant principal in a way, and he didn't mind it at first," Garza said.

Despite Garza's rapport with students and parents, his contract wasn't renewed. Two events led up to his termination. The first came out of his desire to further his education. In the summer of 1969, a few days after the end of the school year, one of his friends started taking graduate-level classes at Southwest Texas State University, in San Marcos.[31] His friend suggested Garza join him, and the two took six hours of graduate work towards certification to become school principals. When the school started up again that fall, Principal Shannon was noticeably distant. "We had been coffee-drinking buddies—during my break, I'd drink coffee with him in his office," Garza recalled. But that fall, when Garza approached him for coffee, the principal responded that he had already drunk his coffee. Finally, when Garza confronted the principal about the problem, the principal called Garza a "double-crosser," accusing him of trying to take his job.[32]

"Why did you take graduate classes and not tell me?" the principal asked. Garza answered that he didn't think he needed the other man's permission. "And then I explained to him, 'It was after you were gone and everybody was gone that I decided to go with my best friend and take some classes over here.'" Shannon insisted that Garza and "that Raza group from Crystal City" wanted the principal's job. Garza tried to assure him that although he did aspire to be a principal, it would be elsewhere, not at Robb Elementary.

The second event was when Garza ran for Uvalde county judge later that year. Shannon took notice. "Less than a week later, after I filed for county judge, I received a letter from my principal advising me that my contract for the 1970–71 school year was not being renewed. And I quote him. He said, 'I hired a teacher, not a politician,'" Garza recalled.[33] Garza lost that election; but he did manage to bring out the Hispanic vote—1,600 people voted for him. Garza received no support from the school superintendent, who washed his hands of the matter. The school board tabled a final decision repeatedly. It was time to boycott classes.

What Started Changing

Developments in the 1960s and 1970s gave people in Uvalde a new lens through which to view their world. Neighboring Crystal City's uprising in the early 1960s was a victory for Mexican Americans. Then, in the late 1960s, Crystal City had a second uprising, which unnerved the Anglo mainstream—and inspired Mexican Americans in other small Texas towns.

At the time, a few older Mexican Americans wanted change. One of them was the charismatic José Uriegas, whom one person described as "the "Henry Cisneros of Uvalde."[34] After graduating from Del Rio High School, he earned a college degree from St. Mary's University in San Antonio and then worked in San Antonio for a time before returning to his hometown to buy and run a small grocery store, Uriegas Grocery and Market, and teach special education in the public school. Uriegas was elected to the city council in 1966—at the age of twenty-six. But before completing his term, he set his sights higher and ran an unsuccessful campaign for state representative. After that, Uriegas moved to Austin and began working with federal anti-poverty programs. But all the while, he kept up with Uvalde, maintaining his store and counseling residents there and in other South Texas towns about strategies. His methods included finding hard-working women to help get out the vote—it was the women who could be relied on. Later, he learned to form alliances where possible. In fact, he and Dolph Briscoe worked on economic development projects in South Texas, channeling them through the Rural Mexican American Coalition, about 140 representatives from throughout Texas. "That's a crazy thing—[I went] from being a hell-raiser to joining with a conservative guy and he joined a hell-raiser to do some good projects ... for Mexicanos," Uriegas said.[35]

A few years after Uriegas' electoral victory, Abelardo Castillo and a like-minded friend, Gabriel Tafolla, decided that Tafolla should run for city council. Tafolla had a degree from Texas A&I and was teaching school in Uvalde. "So, we went and he filed and then when the ballots were printed, his name was not on the ballot. We went and argued, 'What happened here?' And the mayor said, 'Well, we didn't feel that you were qualified,'" Castillo recalled.[36]

The city attorney had determined that only Uvalde property owners were eligible to run for office, so Tafolla's name was left off the ballot.[37] Outraged, Castillo and Tafolla reached out to a San Antonio lawyer named Pat Maloney, who had developed a reputation for helping Mexican Americans. Maloney sued the city and took the case to the state's Fourth Court of Appeals. Maloney won, but it was too late. "The ballots had already been printed and the election was going to be real soon," Castillo said. "But you know we did win the case—thanks to Mr. Maloney."[38]

There were predecessors to the Uvalde school walkout, the biggest being the "blowouts" in Los Angeles in the spring of 1968, in which about 10,000 students at five high schools left their classrooms to picket and make demands. That fall in Edcouch-Elsa, in South Texas, 192 students walked out.[39] A brief walkout had prompted the local school board to pass a rule banning student protests or demonstrations at the school: "Any student who participates in a demonstration or walk-out not previously approved by the office of the principal, shall be expelled from school for the remainder of the semester and no credit may be earned during that semester."[40] The student complaints in Edcouch-Elsa were similar to those voiced in Uvalde: students being punished from speaking Spanish on school grounds, Mexican American students being steered into vocational careers, unequal treatment of Mexican American and Anglo students.[41]

Chicano/a Activism

The late 1960s were times of consciousness-raising. By 1967, Mexican American or Chicano/a youth groups had formed throughout the Southwest, and young people flocked to them. In Texas the leading group was the Mexican American Youth Organization, or MAYO.[42] In Uvalde, young activists began holding MAYO meetings in a two-story building. Alfredo Santos recalled that it was Amaro Cardona and Rogelio Muñoz, as well as Gabriel Tafolla, who led the meetings. Discussions revolved around fundamental questions: "Why are the roads on this side of town in good shape? And the roads over here in not-so-good shape? And how come there's Mexi-

Alfredo Santos, one of the students who participated in the 1970 school walkout in Uvalde. Photo courtesy of Alfredo Santos.

can Americans aren't chosen for 'Who's Who' or, you know, all the different school things, and the Anglos are?" Santos recalled. "That's what started triggering a lot of questions in my mind. And then . . . I . . . realized that these are all good questions, and they deserve good answers. So my *concientización* started to develop, my consciousness, and I started asking more questions."[43]

Soon, the MAYO group began regular picketing of the Uvalde County Jail to protest police brutality. There were cases of Mexican American men who, after being taken into custody and while in transit to jail, had "strange things" happen to them, resulting in broken bones and bruises, Santos said. "There was a lot of police brutality." MAYO members who were still in high school also began "Chicano Day," sporting Mexican-style vests or serapes on Fridays. "And we would take tacos to school. Because back then tacos were taboo—tacos in public, in Uvalde back then," Santos recalled.[44]

In late 1969 and early 1970, Santos was among the Uvalde students who supported the school walkout in Crystal City. The school board there quickly acquiesced in the Mexican American students' demands. Then came the decision by E. P. Shannon not to renew George Garza's contract at Robb Elementary School. The school board was set to vote on the principal's decision in February, but tabled the vote twice. Finally, in April, it came up again.

Rachel Gonzales-Hanson was in seventh grade at the time. "My aunts and I had talked to my mom about it and had explained the situation. And my mom said, 'Yes, we know, we'll go, we'll go to support,'" Gonzales-Hanson recalled. "The school board meetings were held at the central office downtown. And the room was not huge. It was a regular size, kind of a meeting room. And there was nowhere to fit everybody that showed up. So people were packed in that room. And I mean, packed—much to the dismay of the school board . . . They were packed into the hallway and packed into the lobby area, if I remember right, and then outside. There was a huge outpouring of support for Mr. Garza to get his contract renewed. And it was not done. The school board said no."[45]

Alfredo Santos was there, too. "And that's when everybody came outside and gathered around Mr. Garza," Santos said. "He gave an update of what was happening and what the next steps might be. And that's when his attorney, Jesse Gamez, said,

'Well, if I lived here in Uvalde, I wouldn't let them treat me like this.' And Gilbert Torres said, 'Well, I'm not going to send my children to school tomorrow—until this matter of George Garza's contract is cleared up one way or the other.' And then someone yelled, 'Walkout!'"[46]

Santos recalled that a group of about fifty people showed up at Gabriel Tafolla's house. "Surprisingly there was a lot of sign-making material there and fifty people there by the time I got there," Santos recalled. The group began making signs and preparing for the walkout.

The Walkout

When Juan Alonzo showed up to school on Tuesday, April 14, he found an intense energy. "I was taking Spanish 4. Mr. Sherman was a teacher. And I can remember going in there, and it felt like . . . I don't know, like the air was charged with electricity," Alonzo said. "Everywhere you went, all you could see was like lightning bolts and the crackling and sizzling of electrical things. And then we walked out and things return to normal, it wasn't doing that anymore," he recalled. "As we were walking out—there was no air condition, so all the windows were open," he said. "And you [could] see all the students that weren't walking out and the teacher, sitting in the windows looking at us as we left the school and got in our cars and drove off. And we're going down the street . . . heading south . . . We could see all the kids, the junior high kids are walking down the street, heading in that direction. It was just amazing, the response to this."[47]

One of the people inside that building was his classmate Olga Charles. "I remember them getting up and leaving. And the Anglo kids are going like . . . 'Hey, why are y'all walking out? What's going on?' I guess I was embarrassed that they got up and left . . . And they [school administrators] announced: 'Everybody will go ahead and go about their business, follow your schedule.' . . . And we did. So, it's lunchtime, and they're walking, they're picketing, and you're standing there watching your friends picket . . . I couldn't understand why they walked out. Because they kept saying, 'Well, you know, *no quieren los Mexicanos* [they don't like Mexicans], you know, they treat us badly.' . . . I never had that problem, that was never an issue for me. But I understood that they were getting out trying to make a point that they were doing this for all of the Hispanics. But I couldn't understand it, because in Uvalde, I never felt that . . . we were being treated badly."[48]

Interviewed in 2016, Charles said the protesters "felt in their heart that there was a lot of discrimination and they were trying to make a point." She added, "They had good in their heart . . . They believed in it with all their heart because they believed that that was going on. I myself never felt that I was discriminated against, so that was why it was so hard."[49]

José Uriegas arrived in Uvalde from his Austin home on the morning of the walkout. He parked in front of his store, catty-corner from where the protesters were standing. As he got out, he was promptly arrested for leading a parade without a license. As the protesters watched what was happening, two more men were arrested, including Gilbert Torres. The other two men were released quickly, but Uriegas was

Student picketers, Uvalde, April 1970. Photo courtesy of the Voces Oral History Center, University of Texas at Austin.

taken to the county courthouse for formal charges. It was decided to release him on personal recognizance, but Uriegas refused to sign the release form. Finally, everyone left, leaving Uriegas alone. Later, he sued the city. "We beat them," he said. "They did not file the proper notice for that ordinance, because they were used to doing shit like that."[50]

Alfredo Santos used his 1954 Chevy panel truck to ferry students to freedom schools (see below) and take lunches to students, and he picketed in the afternoons at whichever school had been selected. There were meetings at night. "I was not a leader in any shape or form," Santos said later. "I was a follower."[51] Santos said that the MAYO members, some of whom were jeans-wearing troublemakers, took a backseat to clean-cut students such as Elvia Perez, Oscar Castro, and Lee Lugo, many of whom came out of the Catholic Youth Organization (CYO). "They lent a legitimacy to the walkout," he said. "They were more photogenic, more acceptable. Like the Rosa Parks thing, right?"[52]

Within days, members of VISTA (Volunteers in Service to America) arrived in Uvalde to organize "freedom schools." High school students and volunteers taught the younger children. The parish priest lent the freedom schools a church building that was no longer in use. Rachel Gonzales-Hanson recalled the lessons of the freedom schools. "It certainly taught me that I did not know an inch of what my culture was really about," she said. "Aurelio 'Hershey' Montemayor from Del Rio came. And I remember him very vividly as a very, very animated and very motivational speaker, presenter, and he did some great lessons about, about the history of Hispanics . . . 'Let's make the Mexican Americans and the Mexicans . . . be proud in our culture and to be proud of who we were, but to strive for the American Dream, you know, because that's why we were here, right?' That's what our parents had wanted for us, right? And we should want the same thing and then want that for our children in the future."[53]

Gonzales-Hanson said she couldn't recall the names of other outside speakers, but acknowledged their importance: "They were very instrumental in helping us sort of keep focused and not be out just running rampant, because obviously we wanted to avoid the impression that we just wanted . . . to be off and we didn't know what the hell we were doing, right? So that was the point of keeping it structured, and it served a good purpose."[54]

George Garza also participated in the protests, but identified the leaders of the effort as José Uriegas, Gilberto Torres, and Gabriel Tafolla. Their efforts garnered attention from other activists. "We had Dr. Hector Garcia from Corpus Christi, the GI Forum founder," Garza said. "He counseled with us. He said, 'Look, you can march all you want to, you can have your signs. . . . The police have to protect you. But the minute one of you breaks a window [or] starts a fire, you no longer have rights,' he said. 'It's gotta be peaceful,' that's what César Chávez would counsel. Your rights will stop when other people's rights start.' And that's what we followed here."[55]

The Role of the Texas Rangers

The walkout forced some of the students to see their town in a new light. Elvia Perez, the product of Catholic schools, a straight-A student, walked out, believing the demands were reasonable. But when she showed up for a school board meeting, she encountered an alarming hostility.

> It was a shocker . . . that we were seen as radicals and . . . and agitators, and I remember [thinking], "Gosh, that's not who I am. I was awarded the Citizenship Award last year as a junior. The Optimist Club recognized me as a good citizen. And all of a sudden I'm a radical and an agitator?" And I remembered that we were walking into that building . . . where the school board met—and looking up the barrel of a Texas Ranger's rifle. They were on the roof with guns pointed down at us. That was harsh. That was hard. I thought, "Gosh, this is America. We have the right of citizens to speak up and to speak out." . . . I just, I didn't understand that. That's . . . the one thing that I remember very, very clearly . . . and it was painful.[56]

The display of firearms continued during the walkout and became emblematic of the powerful opposition to the action. Roberto Morales, son of the firebrand Genoveva Morales, was a sixth grader who walked out. He recalled attending the freedom school classes for a few hours and then picketing. "I remember they brought in the Texas Rangers and Highway Patrol, and they're up on top of the junior high—it was a two-story building—and they would be up on top with rifles, you know, pointing at us," Morales said.[57]

Rachel Gonzales-Hanson, too, recalled the guns overhead. "It's like, 'Okay, how much do you think we can do? We're just marching.' We were marching quietly. . . . Especially if it was during school hours, we were quiet. If it was, you know, a little

Elvia Perez, Uvalde, 2016. A possible valedictorian in 1970, Perez found herself staring up at the barrels of rifles trained at protesters during the Uvalde school walkout. Photo courtesy of the Voces Oral History Center, University of Texas at Austin.

after school was getting out, then we did some chants." One day, when the protesters marched around the jail, somebody turned on the sprinkler system. "So we were all getting wet," she recalled.

> And then somebody opened the door and threw out a bar of soap. The saddest part was that it was a Hispanic female that worked for the county jail. Now, did she do it on her own, or did she get coerced into doing it? I have no idea. But that was very insulting, degrading . . . At that point, I didn't give her the benefit of the doubt. At that point. I was mad at her for being Hispanic. Obviously, now as an adult, I can think, "You don't know why she did it. She may have been coerced." Because there was in the community, there was this sort of undercurrent of, if you're Hispanic and you worked for a white-owned business or white-run business, you know, you did what they [Anglos] wanted, even in voting . . . or you will lose your job. If you want to keep a job, you got to do this . . . So again, looking back, I don't know if she was coerced or if she did it on her own.[58]

Uriegas, never one to be intimated, confronted the famous Texas Ranger Alfred Y. Allee as law enforcement encircled the marching students and television cameras from San Antonio stations recorded the encounter. "I asked him—I said, 'Captain Allee,' being cynical as shit . . . I said, 'What happens?' and he says, 'What do you mean, "What happens?"'" Uriegas recalled. "'Well, you're always saying "One riot—one Ranger." 'You've got fifty Rangers here with all these children. They're children. They're children—what's the problem?'"[59] Uriegas said Allee, in frustration, knocked down a cameraman from KENS-TV.

Some of the students eventually went back to complete the semester before the boycott was called off. Juan Alonzo, who was a senior, was pressured into it: his father worked at a cattle ranch west of town, El Mirasol. "The owner of the ranch, Mr. C. A. McDaniel, who's a great guy, and we always really seemed to think that he was a very, very caring person—and he was," Alonzo recalled in a telephone interview. "But he was on the board of directors of the Uvalde First State Bank."[60] Alonzo's understanding was that McDaniel met with other bank board members every morning for coffee, and they were pressuring him to bring his employees in line.

Then came the threat. "Finally [McDaniel] called my dad in and said, 'You know, I'm really sorry. You're either gonna have to have Juan not stay here at the ranch or I'm gonna have to fire you.'" The older Alonzo started getting ready to move, and when his son asked about it, he explained McDaniel's ultimatum. When the younger Alonzo learned of this, he returned to school and managed to take his finals. He walked across the stage, and the very next Monday he left for summer school at Texas A&M University, never to return to live in Uvalde. "So I think, as opposed to some of the other kids that have stayed in town and tried to continue the effort, I just kind of bailed and left. And I've gotta tell you, I was really very angry when I left," he said.[61] At the time of his interview, Alonzo was living in Missouri.

In the end, the school board refused to acquiesce in any of the Mexican American parents' demands as the school year drew to a close. Those students who had missed the final five weeks of school would be required to repeat the year, since school officials had documented in their records that they had not completed the required work for promotion.[62] Parents of boycotting students, who by then had organized into the Mexican American Parents Association, or MAPA, tried to salvage the academic year by meeting with the school board to request the creation of a summer program that would allow boycotting students to make up for the lost school work.[63] Those negotiations fell through after the board announced that any summer coursework would be subject to tuition fees.[64]

Elvia Perez, who had taught the younger children at the freedom schools, noted that one of the "very unfortunate and sad consequences was that a lot of kids lost a year of school."[65]

The walkout created other rifts, outside the schools. Eleazar Lugo, who had been on the student council, noticed that the more prominent Mexican Americans in town didn't support the walkout. "They had their jobs—they had their views on it—but they weren't gonna support and . . . come out and actually be in the . . . public eye," Lugo said.[66] Abelardo Castillo likewise noted that many of Uvalde's Mexican American population remained aloof. "There was the old-timers, the ones that really . . . to put it bluntly, the ones that bow down to the Anglos, you know. The one thing that we heard the most was, 'Yeah, guys. We need this and we need that, but you're going about it the wrong way . . . you're going about it the wrong way,'" Castillo recalled. "'Oh, what is your way? Why haven't you done it?' So, they were very quick to criticize—not so much to our face, but behind our backs," Castillo said.[67] Students like Rachel Gonzales-Hanson, who returned to school and repeated seventh grade, found their schoolwork "rather boring." But she was able to use her newfound knowledge from the freedom schools to demand her rights a few years later. "We felt a little bit of pushback from the teachers. You know, I remember having Miss Sutherland as a teacher, before the walkout. And actually, she was one of my favorite teachers. I learned a lot from her, she made it fun. And she sort of took me under her wing."[68]

But things changed. "Well, then I also had her afterwards in high school," Gonzales-Hanson said, "and I remember we were having a test and I turned in my test.

> I was done. I was sitting in the back by myself. I sat in the back [by] myself because I talked lot—can you tell? And then there was another student that had turned [in] his test after that, and he sort of came to the back and sat next to me ... and we were talking in Spanish, right? I remember this ... little teacher, older teacher got so upset, and she banged her hand on the desk. I swear the desk jumped, you know, really hard. And she goes, "Stop speaking Spanish!" She just yelled. And ... I was startled because ... okay, this is like one of my favorite teachers. What is she doing? Why is she so upset? And, me, smart aleck that I am, said, "Excuse me, but the Guadalupe Hidalgo Treaty says I have the right to speak Spanish." And she goes, "Well, you might be cheating." "I've turned my test in; he's turned his test in. We're not talking to anybody else. And we're not talking about the test."
>
> And at that point, she said, "We're going to the office." And so she took me to the office to go see the vice principal, who at the time happened to be Mike Mirelez, another favorite of the students. Mr. Mirelez was a wonderful person ... and he knows my family, of course. When Mirelez hears the teacher's explanation, he says simply: "You don't want me to call her father, you really don't. You should just let her sit here for the end of the class and I'll send her [to] the next class." And she made some comment or something."[69]

Mexican American Parents Step Up

As the 1969–70 school year waned and the walkout came to an end, some student protesters saw their lives gradually return to the rhythms of a typical summer. Then came the new school year and questions of how to deal with the aftermath of the boycotts. Some students, such as José Aguilera and Rachel Gonzales-Hanson, repeated the previous grade; others left school to go into the service or take on other duties. But for parents, especially those who got deeply involved in supporting the protests, the struggle to reform education for Mexican Americans in Uvalde was just beginning.

"They kept on working at it after we were done," said Aguilera, in reference to a group that included women such as Genoveva Morales, Frances Ybarra, Anita Cano, Manuela Flores, and Olga Rodriquez. These mothers of Mexican American student activists took up the mantle of education equity—and by extension, of broader civil rights—at great personal risk during the following decade and beyond.[70]

Mexican American parents in these years were not just surrogates for their school-age children. Many of them had grown up attending segregated schools, or had memories of the "Mexican school" that concentrated Mexican American children in one place during the Great Depression. Those who attended that segregated campus, such as Chris Reyes Mendeke, recalled being neglected by teachers and feeling that any activities that provided joy or entertainment were off-limits. Mexican American children of the era were essentially left to their own devices.[71]

Parents were involved from the beginning of the walkout, making signs, providing food to protesters and—of course—marching along with the youth. But as direct action encountered the firm resistance of local school authorities, parents—primarily mothers—assumed a central role in representing Uvalde Mexican Americans before the school board, in the broader public sphere, in governmental institutions, and in the courts.

Starting at the height of the walkout in April 1970, a core group of parents wrote often to the local media and to state and federal authorities. Olga Rodriquez, who worked at the telephone company and whose toddler was years away from attending Uvalde schools, was highly involved from the start. She frequently sent pointed letters to the editor of the local newspaper, the *Uvalde Leader-News*. While she remembered that initially her letters were published with mistakes—in order, she believed, to make her "look ignorant"—she also remembered having a rapport with Harry Hornby, owner of the publication—at least to an extent.

> Because of my previous letters to the editor, I had a good relationship with Mr. Hornby, the owner of the paper, and sometimes he would call me at the telephone company and say, "Hey, how did you like the headline I gave your letter?" We would talk and I would say, "You know, it would really be nice if you would let me have a column in Spanish and let me inform . . ." And he would say, "Okay, I can't do that. My parents, my father would turn over in his grave if I did that."[72]

Some of the most deeply involved parents eventually came together under a unified voice. In early May 1970, a group of parents announced the formation of MAPA, and in a statement to the *Leader-News* outlined their purpose: "To prevent any similar situations in the future that would result in a school walkout and to help anyone of our people that is abused, or that has a just claim against the school system."[73] The statement, reproduced by the newspaper in its entirety, traced the origins of the walkout to earlier efforts and decried what they described as a lack of interest by the principal of Robb Elementary, E. P. Shannon, and by the school board in the firing of Garza. Frances Ybarra was the first president. Olga Rodriquez, the first secretary of the organization, took on the duty of dealing with the media.Once MAPA was constituted and established an identity, parents had a unified voice for dealing with the school board and with external organizations, including state and federal authorities.

In addition to the early efforts to establish summer classes to prevent boycotting students from failing the school year, MAPA members started to involve federal education and civil rights authorities in the struggle for educational equity in Uvalde. A story from the Associated Press quoted Manuela Flores, speaking on behalf of Mexican American parents, saying that the organization had reached out to the Dallas and Washington offices of the US Department of Health, Education and Welfare (HEW), the Texas Education Association, and the two US senators from Texas. Flores also announced that the group would soon host representatives from HEW

Olga Rodriquez, Uvalde, 1977. Rodriquez was the mother of a toddler in 1970, but she took up the cause and became a spokeswoman for the protesters in Uvalde. She began her newspaper, *El Uvalde Times*, in 1977; it closed in 1980. She wrote a column for the paper titled "Esto Lo Tengo Que Decir" (This I Must Say). Photo courtesy of the Voces Oral History Center, University of Texas at Austin.

and the US Civil Rights Commission, who would be visiting the city to gather information on problems with local schooling.[74]

Undisclosed at the time, however, was that one other Washington official slated to visit Uvalde was the Minnesota senator and future vice president Walter Mondale, an insistent supporter of civil rights. As the incoming chair of the Senate Subcommittee on Equal Educational Opportunity, Mondale was directly involved in issues pertaining to educational inequalities. In this capacity, Mondale spent part of the year conducting a series of information-gathering visits to sites of unrest related to school discrimination. He also led a series of Senate hearings on the issue.[75]

In what became one of the most notable publicity coups for the cause of Mexican American students in Uvalde, MAPA hosted Mondale, Texas state senator Joe Bernal, and Richard Avena, a staffer for the US Commission on Civil Rights, for a meeting. As part of a short tour of Texas and Alabama, Mondale met with MAPA members for about five hours at the home of Frances Ybarra on July 16.[76]

The Minnesota senator followed his visit with a statement in which he expressed outrage at the inequities observed in the region, as well as the lack of cooperation by local authorities. Notably, he called attention to the reprisals faced by protesters and their families: "At least in communities I visited, discrimination and repression of minority groups is severe and blatantly open. This ranged from police brutality to insults, to economic sanctions such as firing of parents of black and Chicano/a (Mexican-American) students who are protesting discrimination, etc."[77]

Federal inquiries into the situation in Uvalde intensified during the summer. In late July, representatives of HEW moved ahead with a "last chance" series of meetings to settle school-desegregation disputes burning through the state. In the span of two days, HEW met in Austin with officials from thirty-eight Texas districts. Uvalde school board members declined the invitation, with the explanation that not having received written notice from Washington, they had not been "ordered" to participate.[78]

At the end of the summer, the tables were turned, and Uvalde was represented in Washington DC. In a hearing before Mondale's Subcommittee on Equal Educational Opportunity on August 19, José Uriegas, then a member of the Texas State Advisory Committee on Civil Rights, and Jesús Rubio, from the Mexican American Development Group, provided a detailed briefing on Texas walkouts. Uriegas and Rubio emphasized regional trends and the interconnections among the school protests led by Mexican Americans across Texas. They then presented specific data from Uvalde, pointed out issues of underrepresentation and mistreatment, and provided recommendations to ameliorate the problem.[79] Local news coverage of the hearing emphasized a claim by Uriegas and Rubio that all male protesters over eighteen had been reclassified by the local Selective Service review board, which was managed by Ruth Webb.[80]

This series of meetings and hearings involving federal stakeholders hinted at a national push for educational equity. Barely a week after the hearings in Washington, and shortly after a MAPA meeting at which leaders warned of a shift to firmer intentions and "more demands," Genoveva Morales initiated what became a long and protracted legal fight to reshape Uvalde schools.[81]

The Lawsuit

In the last week of August 1970, as Uvalde schools reopened for the new school year with little fanfare, two suits filed in federal courts targeted schools in the Uvalde Independent School District. In the first, a class-action lawsuit on behalf of Mexican American students in Uvalde, Genoveva Morales sued E. P. Shannon, the principal of Robb Elementary, and UISD leaders for what the suit alleged was a lack of "due process" in addressing inequity issues pointed out by activists and student boycotters in the previous months. The following day, a suit with George Garza as plaintiff demanded his reinstatement as teacher, plus damages.[82] In both cases, the Mexican American plaintiffs were represented by the San Antonio attorneys Pat Maloney and Jesse Gamez, joined by Mario Obledo from the fledgling Mexican American Legal Defense and Educational Fund (MALDEF). The legal aid organization, incorporated in San Antonio only two years before the Uvalde walkout, had built a track record of winning education-discrimination cases, starting with a favorable settlement between Edcouch-Elsa school authorities and Mexican American activists in 1968.[83]

As in Edcouch-Elsa, the Uvalde suit, known as *Morales v. Shannon*, attacked what the plaintiffs' attorneys described as a violation of due process in the school board's refusal to have a productive meeting with student activists and their parents. The suit specifically accused the UISD of violating the Fourteenth Amendment and the Civil Rights Act of 1964 by denying student protesters and their parents a fair forum in which to present their demands. *Morales* also sought relief in multiple areas pertaining to enrollment, curriculum, and school management. It accused the district of segregating Mexican American students into Robb and Anthon elementary schools, of neglecting the need for bilingual and bicultural programs, and of failing to hire a sufficient number of Mexican American teachers and administrators. In addition, the plaintiffs sought to limit reprisals against Mexican American students.[84]

In October, both camps shuffled their leadership. Al Dishman, president of the UISD school board, resigned at the start of the month, citing health concerns, and was appointed to his seat by Gilbert Riojas.[85] A couple of weeks later, MAPA held a meeting at the American Legion Hall to vote on a new slate of officers, and Genoveva Morales replaced Frances Ybarra as president.[86]

In the spring of 1971, as another school year came to an end and shortly before the first anniversary of the walkout, a final attempt was made to foster a dialogue outside the courts. In letters to the editor of the *Uvalde Leader-News*, Genoveva Morales requested that MAPA be included in an April 1971 school board meeting in order to discuss their demands. The newspaper ran Morales's repeated requests, together with a response by Superintendent R. E. Byrom, declining them. Byrom wrote that with the two overlapping lawsuits underway, it would not be appropriate to discuss matters pertaining to the walkout or to Mexican American students outside the legal process.[87] That did not stop members of MAPA from attending the board meeting on April 12, 1971, and asking to be placed on the agenda—without success.[88] Two days later, seventy-seven Mexican American students skipped school to commemorate the first anniversary of the walkout. Others wore black armbands to school.[89]

Legal Battles

Both of the Uvalde school lawsuits—*Morales v. Shannon* and George Garza's suit to get his job back—were filed in the US District Court for the Western District of

Texas and placed on the docket of Judge John H. Wood Jr., a conservative judge appointed by President Nixon. From the start, Wood, who had been confirmed by the Senate mere months before the initial conferences, showed skepticism toward the complaints.[90] At the initial meetings to schedule hearings for the *Morales* and *Garza* cases, Wood stated that these complaints appeared to be strictly a "local matter" and remarked that he could not think of anything "more democratic than a school district" where elected officials made all the decisions.[91] Olga Rodriquez remembered hearing Wood give this opinion in one of the hearings conducted over the five years that the case was litigated: "He asked the question . . . He says, 'I don't think this case is a matter for the courts to decide. I think it's a matter for the local community to decide. Why don't you do what Crystal City did and elect your own school board members?' So he was not a very friendly voice."[92]

Months later, Wood's initial skepticism on the merit of the Uvalde lawsuits turned out to be a faithful preview of his initial ruling. Following a motion by the UISD, Wood swiftly dismissed *Morales v. Shannon* in open court on June 1, stating that the complaints by the Mexican American activists would be disruptive to the workings of a public school system in which decision makers were elected democratically. Local newspaper coverage of this decision emphasized his remark that the school district had "never segregated Mexican American students."[93]

The response of Mexican parents was immediate. MAPA, through the pen of Genoveva Morales, announced that an appeal of Wood's decision to the Fifth Circuit of the US Court of Appeals was already in the works. In a notice for the next MAPA meeting submitted to the *Leader-News*, Morales rebuked the newspaper for what she called lopsided coverage: "Uvalde has been misinformed by both the local radio station and the local newspaper," wrote Morales. She said that the radio station and the *Leader-News*, "the only two sources of public information, chose to 'glorify' the school board by only stating portions of Judge Wood's comment and by not having the courtesy to contact the president of MAPA for a comment so that it could appear at the same time the dismissal of the case was released."[94]

Long before any appeal by MAPA activists reached the Fifth Circuit, the case hit the first of several delays. In the end, the case lasted the better part of the decade. School-discrimination suits were being heard by federal courts through the country, leading to decisions that created new precedents regarding the federal courts' authority over local education matters and on the standards of evidence needed to show discrimination. Most notably, the Supreme Court decision in *Swann v. Charlotte-Mecklenburg Board of Education*, in April 1971, boosted the authority of federal courts to mandate desegregation policies such as busing.[95] Noting that the Fifth Circuit had just reversed a ruling by a district court in El Paso based on the *Swann* precedent, Judge Wood stayed his final judgment on *Morales* in late June, reserving his decision on the outcome of the El Paso case.[96]

In the interim, George Garza and his attorneys were unsuccessful in regaining his job or winning the requested damages. *Garza v. Shannon* went to trial before Judge Wood on July 26, 1971, in San Antonio.[97] Wood remanded the case to the Uvalde school board, ruling that Garza should get an opportunity to "confront" Shannon in the context of a board hearing, which would satisfy the demand for due process.[98] The board hearing, held on September 10, resulted in the board deciding not to rehire Garza by a vote of 2-1, with four board members—defendants in the lawsuit—abstaining.[99] Following the chain of command of the Texas education system, Garza appealed the decision to the Texas state education commissioner, J. W. Edgar, which led to one more hearing, this time in Austin. MAPA members accompanied Garza for moral support.[100] Edgar reaffirmed the Uvalde board's vote in early 1972.[101] A final attempt to appeal Edgar's decision to the Texas Board of Education was defeated in a unanimous vote. This series of defeats left Garza with the original suit in Wood's court as a final recourse.[102]

A Matter of Persistence

More than two years after the initial filing, the two Uvalde school-discrimination cases were slated for oral testimony in San Antonio in November 1972.[103] In the space of two days, Genoveva Morales and four witnesses testified before Judge Wood. The witnesses included a mix of local allies of MAPA, including George Garza, and, as experts, the bilingual education scholar José Cardenas and James Littlejohn, an HEW official. The Uvalde ISD, for its part, called on a series of administrators, including a number of newly minted Mexican American ones.

Garza, involved in both lawsuits as a plaintiff and as a witness, remembered that the plaintiffs' attorneys were prepared for a negative decision from Judge Wood; their sights were set on higher courts. "We knew we're going to lose," said Garza. "In fact, Pat Maloney Sr., in an exchange with the judge, said, 'Judge, I can anticipate a negative ruling. But I'm just getting ready to appeal it to the Fifth Court.'"[104]

In early 1973, Judge Wood announced a new delay in his verdict in *Morales v. Shannon* as he waited for the Supreme Court decision in *Keyes v. School District No. 1, Denver*, another school-discrimination case that could bring clarity to what he deemed "conflicting" decisions from the Supreme Court in *Swann* and from the Fifth Circuit in *Cisneros v. Corpus Christi Independent School District* and *U.S. v. Texas Education Association and Austin Independent School District*.[105] While Wood delayed his judgment to wait on the resolution of *Keyes*, his initial Memorandum Opinion rejected the plaintiffs' arguments, finding no discriminatory intent by the Uvalde Consolidated Independent School District (now UCISD) in any of the complaints regarding school segregation, bilingual and bicultural curricula, or faculty hiring.[106] This position remained unchanged when Wood made a ruling against Morales in August 1973.

As promised, Morales's attorneys appealed the case to the Fifth Circuit Court of Appeals, based in New Orleans. This time, an army of MALDEF staff attorneys helped litigate the case: Jesse Gamez and general counsel Mario Obledo, Vilma Martinez, Drucilla Ramey, and Sanford J. Rosen.[107] After hearing oral arguments in December 1974, the Fifth Circuit reversed the district court ruling on segregation—ordering Wood to mandate a desegregation plan—and remanded all the other issues back to the district court for further deliberation. Those issues included bilingual education and the hiring of Mexican American teachers and staff members. In an opinion written by Judge Griffin Bell and filed on July 23, 1975, the circuit court found that the neighborhood-based school-assignment system favored by the

UCISD consistently "froze" Mexican American students into two of four elementary schools; further, he cited the earlier existence of a "Mexican school" and patterns in the construction and location of new schools as indicative of discriminatory intent.[108] In covering the reversal, the local newspaper reported that "the general feeling" of the school board was that whatever the plan, it had to be implemented "as quickly as possible" and "as equitably as possible." Alternatively, the newspaper reported, "the ruling could be appealed."[109]

The school district set out to do both. Wood's court directed the district to draft a desegregation plan within sixty days, postponing a hearing on the rest of Morales's complaints over Mexican American curriculum and staffing to a future date.[110] The board complied with the order, but also voted to appeal the Fifth Circuit ruling to the US Supreme Court. The plan filed by the district, based on "common pairing"— assigning all district students from each grade to one Uvalde school—was presented to Wood on November 7, 1975. The following month, the Supreme Court dismissed the appeal by the UCISD. The segregation part of the lawsuit was over.[111]

The rest of the lawsuit was resolved swiftly. Judge Wood ruled that the "graded" or pairing plan from the UCISD was constitutional on April 27, 1976, and signed a decree on June 28 ordering the district to enact the plan at the start of the next school year.[112] The plan filed by the district also incorporated a proposal for a bilingual-bicultural curriculum. This addition preempted further hearings in that realm, leading Morales's attorneys to drop that part of the complaint.[113] Following a final hearing before Judge Wood on December 16, 1976,[114] the plaintiffs were awarded $8,000 in fees, out of the $20,000 requested.[115]

This allocation of attorneys' fees by Judge Wood closed the chapter on courtroom battles. But the lawsuit's conclusion also ushered in decades of legal oversight. Wood's decree regarding desegregation went far beyond student allocation; it also enacted specific orders related to classroom seating, the hiring of staff, transportation, construction, consolidation, and site selection "in a manner which will prevent a re-occurrence of a dual school structure."[116] Furthermore, the decree gave the court jurisdiction over the case until the court could determine that a segregated system could never recur. It also compelled the district to submit annual reports every April 15.

In practice, these stipulations gave the plaintiffs, led by Genoveva Morales, a degree of oversight over issues pertaining to Mexican American students in the Uvalde CISD. In spite of multiple attempts by the district to end this arrangement, the case remained open and under court oversight until a final settlement in 2008. It took nine more years for the district and MALDEF to dismiss the lawsuit, after both parties agreed that Uvalde schools had finally complied with the terms of the settlement.[117]

Roberto Morales, one of Genoveva Morales's eleven children, remembered a regular parade of school officials visiting his mother to try to persuade her to end the lawsuit. "Every time they hired a new superintendent, the board members would [tell him], 'This is your first job: go speak with Ms. Morales and ask her if she can lift the lawsuit,'" said Morales. "And my mom would have a meeting with them and everything. And she would tell them, 'It's not as pretty as they painted it.'"[118]

What Was Accomplished

If you ask the men and women who participated in the Uvalde school walkout what was accomplished, the answers are likely to fall into three broad categories: those who believe it signaled an increase in the political power of Uvalde's Mexican Americans; those who believe nothing was accomplished; and those who believe that it was a character-defining experience for all involved, especially the young people. "I try to see what ... we accomplished as far as our personal lives with a walkout—and I don't see it," said Eleazar Lugo. "I don't see any strides gained by doing it, other than the fact that we did, you know, show force in backing Mr. Garza."[119]

George Garza said that the walkout created community leaders. For instance, Gilberto Torres, who supported the walkout, ran for the Uvalde County Commission five years later. Torres said his role in the protest served him well: "That first campaign, I didn't really spend that much money. The filing fee was, I think, $300. And I went house to house just taking a little card saying, 'Vote for Gilbert Torres.' And of course, the school walkout had promoted me in the community quite a lot—that I was a man of my word, that I was a man that would not sell out. So I didn't spend that much money, but I had five opponents on that first election."[120]

Elvia Perez said the walkout was painful. "I was one of the top kids in the class and the rumor was that I was going to be the valedictorian," she said. "And so I gave it up. For the greater good, I think."[121]

The activism in Uvalde continued for some time. José Uriegas won a seat on the city council in 1966 and served for one term. Rachel Gonzales-Hanson became active in the Raza Unida Party (RUP) and even helped bring the RUP gubernatorial candidate Ramsey Muñiz to town. "It didn't endure too long, certainly not as long as we had hoped it would, for a lot of different reasons," she said. "I think part of it, unfortunately, may have been that there started to be, in my recollection[,] ... a split between leadership on which way should we take it or what should we do next. One [faction] wanted to continue ... as radical as we were ... and the other one wanted to work through the system," she said. "I feel that you still probably needed both. Because that radical part still needed to happen to enable the part of working through the system. Because it wasn't going to happen otherwise. Looking back, if perhaps the solution would have been to try to go through it with those two prongs, a two-pronged approach, perhaps that that would have been the solution."[122]

Roberto Morales pointed to the many Mexican American teachers and school administrators—and Anglos who are supportive of greater inclusion and equality—as a win.[123] Sergio Porras considered the question carefully. The changes did not come overnight, he concluded. Yes, Uvalde changed to some degree, he thought. But there was another change in how the students perceived themselves, even in April and May 1970. Porras recalled thinking: "I contributed to the change here that, you know, we're going to stop this discrimination. We're going to make some changes here. And then, thankfully, we did."[124]

Olga Rodriquez continued trying to give a voice to Mexican American concerns in Uvalde's local media outlets. For a while, she had a radio program, but that was cancelled. In the fall of 1977, she left her job at the telephone company, and with her final paycheck, she started a community newspaper.

George Garza couldn't immediately get a job in Uvalde. Instead, he commuted daily to Crystal City and then attended graduate school in California before returning to Uvalde. He later became involved in local politics again, serving as a trustee of the school district from 1981 to 1986. He won a mayoral election in 1996. He lost the next one, but then was reelected and served until 2008.[125]

José Aguilera maintained that despite having to repeat his junior year because of the walkout, it was worth it in the long run. "My view of all this: politically, we lost. I mean, I don't think we gained anything politically—not at that moment," he said. But personally, Aguilera said, the walkout gave him a chance to use his constitutional rights to stand up, to "express" himself. "And naturally, that defined me as an American ... Even to this ... moment, you know, after I served [in] the navy ... I see the American flag rise, and golly, I get a lump in my throat ... It helped me define who I was. And that's what I'm proud of."[126]

CHAPTER 9

"A TOTALITY OF OUR WELL-BEING":
The Creation and Evolution of Centro de Salud Familiar La Fe in South El Paso

In September 1992, the dreams of a number of Mexican American mothers became a reality when Salvador Balcorta became the chief executive officer of Centro de Salud Familiar La Fe in South El Paso.[1] Founded by neighborhood women in 1967, La Fe Clinic launched a movement to address health disparities and the social and economic conditions in the border neighborhood. From the clinic's inception, the founding mothers believed that having a director who understood the struggles of the Southside and the history of the clinic was crucial for the survival and evolution of La Fe. Balcorta was the perfect candidate. Raised in El Segundo Barrio, he played a role in the growth of the clinic from its humble beginnings in a Southside tenement to a multimillion-dollar institution. Balcorta recalled, "I started at La Fe when I was involved in the Mexican American Youth Association. I got my first full-time job here at La Fe when I was eighteen [as] a youth outreach worker at the clinic."[2] During his tenure, Balcorta has kept the vision of the founding mothers alive—an institution that holistically addresses the needs of South El Paso while uplifting its Mexican American community.

For over fifty years, La Fe has served the working-class Mexican American border community of South El Paso. Although El Segundo Barrio was one of the oldest neighborhoods in the Southwest, it was at the political, economic, and social margins of the United States. Spatial segregation, disinvestment, and disenfranchisement in local politics troubled the community for over a century.[3] Born out of a tragedy, necessity, and grassroots activism by the Chicana/o movement, the clinic is today one of the most respected social justice institutions on the US-Mexico borderlands. The success of La Fe is reflected in its more than twenty health and social service sites that it operates, as well as in its recognition as one of the largest federally qualified health centers in Texas.[4] The clinic's numerous accolades and community standing, however, were achieved only through an immense fight and commitment from South El Paso residents.

This chapter traces the evolution of La Fe clinic from its beginnings, in 1967, to the present day. It reveals the labor of Mexican American mothers, community leaders, and activists in tackling racism and discrimination in public health by bringing accessible, high-quality health care to the community of South El Paso. Through their vision of a community-controlled neighborhood clinic, the founders of La Fe created an institution that uplifted their families and their community. The history of

La Fe clinic is a case study in self-determination and an important episode of institution building during the long Chicana/o movement.

In addition, this chapter looks at public health within the larger context of Chicana/o historiography. As the historian Felipe Hinojosa notes, scholarship on Mexican Americans and public health mostly focuses on experiences at the turn of the twentieth century.[5] He argues that because of this emphasis, "we know little about how the fight for public health resources after World War II gave rise to a Mexican American generation whose struggle later carried over into the political terrain of the Chicano generation."[6] By contrast, this chapter examines the grassroots efforts of working-class mothers and activists tackling public health discrimination in South El Paso beyond the social movements of the 1960s and 1970s. These struggles coincided with War on Poverty programs and the energy of the Chicana/o movement. As a result, the founders of La Fe emphasized access to health care as an important tenet of the local Chicana/o movement. They believed that in addressing health disparities in South El Paso, they could also improve the socioeconomic conditions of the Mexican American community.

The history of La Fe mimics that of several grassroots health-care initiatives that occurred roughly simultaneously across the country. But similar radical efforts such as the Brown Berets' Barrio Free Clinic in Los Angeles, the Black Panthers free health clinics, and health initiatives led by the Young Lords in Chicago and New York did not become institutionalized. Grassroots endeavors such as Operation Life in Las Vegas succumbed to cuts in federal funding during the Ronald Reagan and George H. W. Bush administrations.[7] The story of La Fe demonstrates that it was possible to beat the odds. Although the clinic faced much turmoil because of conflicts over community control, mismanagement, and bureaucratization, its founding philosophy—to serve South El Paso's Mexican American community—remains at the heart of its activities.

La Fe grew out of women's community mobilization, and in the early years of the clinic, the voices of influential community leaders such as Enedina "Nina" Cordero and Amelia "Amy" Castillo were prevalent in newspaper articles and other sources. But as La Fe expanded and became institutionalized, the experiences of the founding women were relegated to the past.[8] Thus, the story of La Fe told here comes through the voices of men such as Salvador Balcorta, activists, and residents of El Segundo Barrio.

"People Did Not See Solutions to Their Problems"

El Paso's location along the US-Mexico border contributed to the continuous racialization and marginalization of its ethnic Mexican population. The city emerged as a vital railroad hub in the 1880s, becoming an important industrial and transportation center. The region's economic growth at the turn of the twentieth century created the need for an exploitable labor force. The city served as an important port of entry for thousands of Mexicanos fleeing the turmoil of the Mexican Revolution, but also attracted many to stay for employment opportunities. Newcomers found jobs in manufacturing, construction, smelting, agriculture, and the service sector. As the historian Mario T. García noted, El Paso's economy "became dependent on the Mexican *obreros* [workers]."[9] This dependency relegated ethnic Mexicans to low-skill and low-wage occupations that kept them at the bottom of the city's economic ladder for much of the twentieth century.[10]

Although people of Mexican heritage historically made up the majority of the population, their numbers did not necessarily translate into political power or representation. In 1970, when La Fe was in its early stages, El Paso's population totaled 322,269 people, with about 58 percent (184,627) being of Mexican descent.[11] Ethnic Mexicans, particularly those belonging to the working class, formed an invisible majority within the city. The historian Oscar J. Martínez observed that "Chicanos were effectively excluded from the system for decades." Between 1881 and 1951, no person of Mexican origin was elected to serve on the city council.[12] A political breakthrough came in 1957 when Raymond Telles was elected El Paso's first Mexican American mayor. Although Telles's victory brought hope to the ethnic Mexican community, city politics remained unchanged until the 1960s and 1970s.[13]

White power brokers maintained the status quo. Like many other cities and municipalities, El Paso restricted voting through measures such as poll taxes and at-large voting districts. These practices continued until the poll tax for city and state elections was ruled unconstitutional in 1966 and the city created single-member districts in 1977. Also, El Paso was informally governed by political machines throughout the twentieth century. Groups of elite white business owners, bankers, lawyers, and professionals formed coalitions such as the Democratic Ring and, later, the Kingmakers, which put the interests of industry over the needs of ethnic Mexican residents.[14] Fermin Dorado, who later became El Paso's city engineer, recalled that, politically, "Mexicanos had no chance because it was the same clique—everybody mostly from the Westside, the affluent side of town—that got elected because they ran as a team."[15] The political obstacles erected by the white elites in El Paso inculcated what the activist Antonio Marin called a "political apathy" within the community. Marin explained that Mexican Americans, especially those residing in the Southside, did not trust the political system because "people [did] not see solutions to [their] problems."[16] Apathy, coupled with voter suppression, fostered distrust for city government, leaving the ethnic Mexican population to take matters into its own hands.

Economic inequities and political disenfranchisement segregated Mexican Americans in substandard living conditions in South El Paso. As immigrants arrived in El Segundo Barrio to fill jobs in the city's booming industries, power brokers built tenements to house them. The *presidios*, or prisons, as ethnic Mexicans called the structures, were two- or three-story brick buildings that housed multiple two-room units. The structures lacked proper ventilation, plumbing, or heating, and relied on shared outdoor restrooms. Some of the worst tenements were *los Seis Infiernos*, or the Six Hells, a complex of six buildings in half a city block that housed about eight hundred people. Salvador Balcorta recalled that residents cleverly called them *los Siete Infiernos*, since "the seventh hell was having to live there."[17] Housing conditions worsened in the latter half of the twentieth century as South El Paso became home to around twenty-five thousand ethnic Mexicans. In a 1970 visit to the city, Patrick Moynihan, President Richard Nixon's urban advisor, told the *El Paso Times* that "housing in the Southside rank[ed] with the worst in the nation."[18]

South El Paso was plagued by problems caused by poverty and overcrowding. According to census data from 1970, households there averaged $4,800 in yearly income, in comparison to $9,000 for white families and $6,500 for Mexican American families outside the barrio.[19] The Southside had the city's lowest levels of education, highest percentage of unemployment, and highest percentage of alcoholism.[20] These social ills contributed to severe health problems. South El Paso had high levels of infant mortality, tuberculosis, dental problems, mental illness, and drug addiction. Homero Galicia, a VISTA Minority Mobilization Program activist and an early organizer of La Fe, recalled that in the years before the clinic was established, "South El Paso had the highest TB rate in the country, the highest infant mortality, the highest [rates] in all these health issues."[21] The multiple, interrelated problems that Mexican Americans faced in El Segundo Barrio kept them tied to a never-ending cycle of poverty.

For ethnic Mexicans, especially those living along the US-Mexico border, obtaining medical services has always been a concern. Despite the Southside's alarming problems, local, state, and federal governments did not prioritize the residents' health care. Historically, the Southside lacked health clinics. According to Galicia, five small doctor's offices in the barrio served close to twenty thousand people.[22] Thomason General Hospital, the county hospital, was located about four miles away from the Southside. Although the hospital was relatively nearby, barrio residents often relied on public transportation, which was not suitable for emergencies, and the hospital's ambulances seldom made it to El Segundo. Most importantly, Thomason lacked bilingual and culturally competent services and frequently refused to treat Mexican Americans because of their inability to pay. When nurses and doctors did treat South El Pasoans, patients had to wait long hours before being helped, which led community residents to distrust the hospital. Many Southsiders, like Galicia's grandmother, refused to go to Thomason. He recalled, "I remember my grandmother when we took her to the hospital, she said, 'No, don't take me to the hospital. People go there to die.'"[23] The community's inability to pay for doctor visits, the absence of clinics in the barrio, and mistreatment at Thomason forced South El Pasoans to rely on home remedies, visit Ciudad Juárez for medical care, or forgo medical attention altogether.[24]

When the idea to start a neighborhood clinic first arose, South El Paso was a hotbed of national and local Chicana/o movement activities. In fact, El Paso became the cradle of the movement. The city hosted President Lyndon B. Johnson's Inter-Agency Committee on Mexican American Affairs in 1968 and the first Raza Unida Party National Convention in 1972. When the United Farm Workers union needed support for its boycotts, the local Mexican American community picketed labor agencies that hired strikebreakers. The student and labor movements also had a strong presence in the city. El Pasoans challenged racism in local schools and at the University of Texas at El Paso (UTEP) through organizations such as the Mexican American Youth Association (MAYA) and the Movimiento Estudiantil Chicano de Aztlán (MEChA).[25] Similarly, Mexican American women protested working conditions at the Farah Manufacturing Company, launching a two-year strike for the right to unionize and a national boycott of Farah slacks.[26] This local activist fervor motivated Southsiders to challenge long-standing inequality in El Paso.

The arrival of the War on Poverty and other social welfare programs in the border-lands likewise fueled the activist sentiment of El Segundo Barrio residents. The city's Community Action Agency, Project BRAVO (Building Resources and Vocational Opportunities), and programs such as the Juvenile Delinquency Project, the Mexican American Committee on Honor and Service (MACHOS), and Volunteers in Service to America (VISTA), provided barrio residents a platform for politicization. VISTA brought in white volunteers from the East Coast who were unfamiliar with the conditions facing poor Mexican Americans. To recruit people familiar with struggles in barrios, Gonzalo Barrientos from Austin and José Uriegas from Uvalde suggested using local volunteers. As a result, VISTA founded the Minority Mobilization Project (MMP).[27] El Paso had its own VISTA-MMP, led by Homero Galicia. The program recruited barrio residents who became integral community organizers. Felipe Peralta, who was involved in the clinic's early efforts, became an MMP trainer. Peralta recalled that he trained volunteers in a variety of ways: "We used Saul Alinsky's *Rules for Radicals*, we had [courses] on the history of Mexicanos ... We bombarded them with ideas of what they could do if they worked together. We would teach them their rights. We would explain the role of the city council, who were their representatives, the role of the El Paso School District, [and] how they can make some changes. We would just get them ready."[28]

As expected, the VISTA-MMP and other War on Poverty programs trained youth to become activists. These activities mobilized parents, too—in particular, mothers such as Enedina "Nina" Cordero. Cordero became involved in housing activism where she learned "that the government could do so much to help our condition."[29] These experiences prompted her involvement in South El Paso.

While local War on Poverty efforts seemed promising at first, their shortcomings soon became apparent. Amelia "Amy" Castillo, a social worker during the early years of La Fe, shared with the *El Paso Herald-Post* that "there was so much anticipation that the government would be moving into El Paso with anti-poverty programs in 1965–1966."[30] Yet those efforts were unable to cope with the numerous problems of the barrio. By the end of the 1960s, Project BRAVO had lost federal funding and cut back on its programs. Although War on Poverty efforts organized the community, Chicana/o leaders believed that it had done "little to help the woes of the Chicano."[31] Despite the shortcomings of these federal programs, participation in them, VISTA-MMP in particular, gave the Mexican Americans of El Segundo Barrio the tools to voice their needs.

The energy of the Chicana/o movement, the shortcomings of the War on Poverty, and a series of deadly tragedies gave rise to a number of robust grassroots movements in El Segundo Barrio in the late 1960s. Through self-determination, Southside activists tackled the most desperate conditions in the barrio. As Carmen Felix, a barrio leader pressing for better housing, declared, "What we're trying to do is let the people run things ... If we depend on the city and the agencies, everybody's got an excuse. Everybody throws it on somebody else, and nobody does anything."[32] The creation of La Fe clinic and the movement for accessible and affordable health care became what the *El Paso Times* deemed in the mid-1970s a "notable success" in community control.[33]

Barrio Mothers Start a Movement

Tragedy sparked the creation of La Fe. The story's specifics have been lost to memory, but activists such as Salvador Balcorta and Guillermo Glenn recalled that the incident became the catalyst for establishing the clinic. One afternoon in 1967, a five-year-old girl carrying an empty glass bottle tripped, fell, and cut her wrists. A few witnesses noticed that her injuries were very serious and called an ambulance to transport the girl to Thomason General Hospital. The ambulance did not arrive at the scene quickly, and the young girl died en route to the hospital.[34] Balcorta reflected that although activism and conversations around health issues were already taking place in El Segundo Barrio, this accident "sparked a big movement within the area to get a clinic."[35]

As the community mourned the loss of the little girl, Southside activist groups such as MACHOS and the Ochoa Parents Association—parent groups mostly involved in housing—argued that if there had been a medical facility or small clinic in the barrio, the death could have been prevented. Tired of the multiple medical-service barriers in the area, members of these organizations, under the leadership of Nina Cordero, conceived the idea of a barrio clinic.[36] Through this effort, barrio women focused on health concerns in the Southside while addressing other social ills tied to poverty.

Although newspaper articles and personal memories downplay the role of Mexican American women in the creation of La Fe, Balcorta emphasized the labor of the founding mothers:

> I say the women are the founders because I think founders are the ones with the visions. I think founders are the people with the ideas. I think founders are the people that create the movement. It's not the person that writes the grant. Because a lot of times that happens—you get the guy or the woman [who wrote] the grant, and all of the sudden they become the founders. They were told by somebody to write that grant ... That's why we depict the history as mostly single mothers that were the founders [of La Fe].[37]

Nina Cordero, the mothers, and VISTA-MMP organizers such as Homero Galicia worked to start the clinic. They recruited Dr. Raymond Gardea, who was raised in El Segundo Barrio and understood the health problems of the area. Gardea provided his services as a volunteer and lent medical equipment and supplies for the clinic.[38] The women enlisted two volunteer nurses, identified basic funding sources, and secured a space for the clinic. Galicia recalled searching for a suitable location: "At that time, the director of the City[-County] Health Department was Dr. Manuel Hornedo. [He] owned a tenement in *los Seis Infiernos*, the southernmost tenement. So we went to him and asked him if we were able to rent a room. We rented a two-room apartment from him, we paid for it, and Dr. Gardea helped us with that. And [that's how] we started the clinic."[39]

As the clinic approached its opening day, barrio mothers wanted to name it after an important community leader. In the 1950s, a Jesuit priest named Harold Rahm worked to better the conditions of South El Paso and improve the lives of its Mexican

Salvador Balcorta, El Paso, July 23, 2015. Photo courtesy CRBB.

American population. During his twelve years in the Southside, Father Rahm delivered breakfast daily to the elderly and founded Our Lady's Youth Center, an outreach and recreation center. As Father Rahm became heavily involved in the community, he also planted activist seeds in El Segundo. In turn, the Catholic diocese transferred him to Brazil to prevent him from further agitating Mexican Americans.[40] Balcorta recalled that the mothers believed Father Rahm "had done a lot for them," and they named the clinic in his honor.[41]

The Father Rahm Clinic opened its doors in April 1968.[42] Perhaps the mothers and volunteer staff members underestimated the community's initial commitment to the success of the clinic. Galicia recalled, "[On] the first night of the clinic, a man from one of the tenements [came]. He walked up with a box of gauze and a bottle of alcohol, and he said, '*Aquí, para la clínica*' ('here, for the clinic')."[43] Before long, the clinic's mission of "providing medical services, transportation and informing the residents of the Southside of services available" spread throughout the barrio.[44] As the months passed, South El Pasoans lined up outside the small clinic every Wednesday night to get free medical attention, or simply stopped by to donate money and supplies.

The founders and staff quickly realized that the clinic did not have the capacity to address the medical needs of the barrio. Joe Olvera, a writer for the *El Paso Times*, recalled, "It soon became evident that if residents were to be adequately served, a permanent funding source would have to be found."[45] The women engaged in an arduous campaign to raise funds. In 1969, Cordero, with the help of MACHOS and VISTA-MMP, organized a fund-raising dance at the Sacred Heart Church Gym. An article in the *El Paso Herald-Post* encouraged El Pasoans to attend the dance, because "the urgency is now to raise money for better facilities, equipment and medicine, or donations of these requirements."[46] The following year, the women obtained $5,000 from the El Paso Urban Coalition, "to provide medication and initiate steps towards the

Homero Galicia, El Paso, July 21, 2015. Photo courtesy CRBB.

formation of a pharmaceutical co-operative for the 'medically indigent' in South El Paso."[47] Although the Father Rahm Clinic continued to be operated by volunteers and with grassroots support, the founders and the clinic's staff identified sources of funding necessary to keep the effort afloat.

In 1970, the founding mothers took measures to upgrade the clinic. First, it was moved into a building at 419 South Virginia and became incorporated as the Father Rahm Health Services Center, Inc., a 501(c)(3) nonprofit. In June of that year, the clinic was awarded a $72,000 federal grant from the US Department of Health, Education and Welfare (HEW). The grant established an experimental information, referral, and personal assistance program (I&R) for the underserved Mexican American population.[48] Through the I&R services, clinic staff and volunteers went out to the streets of South El Paso to educate barrio residents and provided "as thorough an evaluation as possible regarding medical and social problems." They also helped families "reach the appropriate source that le[d] towards [the] resolution of their problems."[49] The I&R program marked an important transition for the clinic, since it prompted its bureaucratization.

The Professionals and Social Workers Arrive

With the I&R services in place, the founding mothers aspired to professionalize the clinic. According to Balcorta, "social workers and professionals came in, [including] Pete Duarte, Manuel De La Rosa, Ralph Aguirre, Joy Martin, [and] Amy Castillo, to name a few."[50] This group wrote numerous grants to ensure the survival of the clinic. Dr. Raymond Gardea continued to volunteer at the clinic, and he enlisted the help of others such as Dr. Raul Rivera and Dr. Pablo Ayub. The founding mothers urged the professionals to keep the Father Rahm Clinic a community-controlled institution. To represent the voices of the barrio, the clinic established a board of directors drawn mostly from Southside residents. Pete Duarte, who later became the executive director of the clinic, served as one of the first board members.[51]

The clinic became a vehicle for training the next generation of health professionals. With a $28,580 grant from the National Urban Coalition, the mothers hired "personnel to conduct training and employment of local Mexican-American youths interested in the health care and medical fields."[52] In 1973, El Paso Community College obtained a University Year for Action grant, a program from the Nixon administration that encouraged college students to volunteer while obtaining college credit and receiving a stipend. In El Paso, the UYA placed ten volunteers at the Father Rahm Clinic to serve as youth outreach workers, one of them being Salvador Balcorta.[53] He recalled that his responsibilities were "registration and enrollment and a lot of information and referral" for families.[54] Through this endeavor, the mothers and professionals provided barrio youth with important professional experience and a small stipend in hopes of breaking the cycle of poverty.

Despite receiving federal funds, the clinic still operated at a grassroots level. At the South Virginia location, the clinic moved into a shared space in the I&R services office. Cordero and the staff realized that the location was too small for operations. In 1971, the Lydia Patterson Institute, a United Methodist school in the barrio, gave the mothers the use of a building for four to five years.[55] Southsiders enthusiastically donated funds, materials, and labor to transform the Fourth Street building into a functioning clinic. The new facility had three examining rooms, a co-op pharmacy, X-ray capabilities, and a multipurpose room.[56] As the clinic grew in size and operations, Nina Cordero reiterated one of its founding principles: "Not a cent would be charged to those who cannot pay for services. Father Rahm Clinic is of the poor, for the poor, by the poor."[57]

As demand grew for medical care in South El Paso, professionals at Father Rahm looked for funding sources that would allow them to expand it from a neighborhood clinic into one offering comprehensive health care. Grant writers hoped to "lessen the historical inequities by developing a Comprehensive Health Care System which will incorporate community residents, businessmen and public and private health professionals in a venture designed to create a non-profit community-controlled health delivery system."[58] The countless applications brought in a few small grants. In December 1971, the Father Rahm Clinic obtained $18,000 from the Commission on Religion and Race of the United States Methodist Church to fund a pharmacy co-operative in the barrio. Besides bringing affordable prescription medicine to patients, the co-op would train barrio residents interested in the field.[59] The clinic also won a grant from the Zales Foundation to train licensed vocational nurses interested in social work.[60]

Establishing a health center in South El Paso came one step closer to reality when HEW awarded the Father Rahm Clinic a $300,000 developmental grant in 1972. The award allowed the clinic's staff to survey South El Paso's health problems, identify solutions, and conceptualize plans for an outpatient clinic in the barrio. In addition, the clinic would develop prepaid medical plans for the community.[61] With this grant, the founding mothers and the board of directors hired Guillermo Glenn, a public health organizer who had set up several community clinics in the

Rio Grande Valley. His job was to implement the provisions of the HEW grant and transform the Father Rahm Clinic into a proper and permanent health center. When recalling memories of his first days at the clinic, Glenn observed, "La Fe was a very basic community project. The community [who had developed the clinic] were very much in charge."[62] Glenn's leadership ushered a period of tremendous growth for La Fe.

Glenn worked alongside Father Rahm Clinic stakeholders to develop a plan for a comprehensive health center. The envisioned outpatient clinic would be open eight hours a day, five days a week, and provide "medical care, dental care, optometry, physical therapy, mental health, [and] alcoholic treatment." Additionally, the center would provide a space for "a Seniors Citizens Center, Social Services, [and] Family Planning."[63] The clinic would be staffed by bilingual professionals culturally sensitive to the conditions of low-income Mexican Americans. Manuel De La Rosa, a member of the board, told the *El Paso Times*, "One of the hopes of the clinic is to develop a health service delivery system that will relate to the needs of South El Paso."[64]

The HEW grant helped the Father Rahm Clinic gain local and statewide recognition. News reached Texas Republican senator John Tower, who found the clinic's efforts commendable. In a statement released to the *San Antonio Express*, Senator Tower stated, "What truly inspires me about these people is that they alone conceived and formed this clinic working without large amounts of money or technical assistance."[65]

But as the clinic's profile grew, local opposition came to light. Guillermo Glenn remembered, "It was pretty difficult. The medical community here was very much against the clinic getting going."[66] Many believed that the outpatient facility was unnecessary, given the barrio's proximity to Thomason General Hospital. Those opposed to the clinic noted that Thomason already followed HEW guidelines in providing medical services to the poor. Others, such as El Paso county commissioner Clyde Anderson, objected because the clinic would serve only El Segundo Barrio and not "every public housing unit in the county."[67] Further criticism landed on the use of federal money to fund the clinic. Detractors feared that once the funds expired, the burden of sustaining the clinic would fall on local taxpayers. Despite the opposition, the Father Rahm Clinic gained the support of the executive committee of the West Texas Council of Governments, the Health Planning Advisory Committee of the Council of Governments, and the El Paso County Medical Society.[68]

The clinic also faced obstacles set by the State of Texas. Neftali Ruelas, who succeeded Guillermo Glenn as director, stated, "Texas law works against the whole for the benefit of the few and as a result, while the rest of the country was obtaining Federal funds for health programs, Texas blocked them." Whatever federal funds came into the state were what Ruelas called "a drop in a vast sea of need."[69] In addition, laws made it difficult for clinics like Father Rahm even to exist. For example, in 1971 the founding mothers applied for an HEW grant to fund the pharmacy co-op. Lamar A. Byers, HEW's acting regional program director for community health service, informed Amy Castillo that the proposal would be "confronted with many problems," starting with the fact that the pharmacy would need to be licensed.[70] Father Rahm faced an even larger obstacle in building the outpatient clinic. Under the Texas Medical Practice Act, any corporation practicing medicine—including nonprofit corporations—had to be completely controlled by doctors.[71] Although the clinic had been under the control of the community, the limitations established by the Texas law confronted the founding mothers and the staff with important decisions regarding the future of the project.

To build the health center and qualify for an HEW operational grant, the founding mothers had to relinquish control of the clinic to the medical professionals. Under the stipulations of the Texas Medical Practice Act, the Father Rahm Clinic as it was then constituted could not directly hire physicians. Dr. Gardea and other doctors had volunteered their services. But since the clinic expected to grow, it needed a licensed medical facility to hire and provide physicians.[72] Guillermo Glenn recalled, "We couldn't get any doctors. I started working with this Methodist minister, Joel Martinez, to try to get the doctors at Newark Hospital. Joel and I were able to convince Dr. [Kenneth] Kurita to be the first doctor for the clinic."[73] Established in the 1930s as part of the settlement house movement, Newark Methodist Hospital served as a maternity ward and well-baby facility in South El Paso.[74] Over the years, many Mexican Americans were born at Newark, and it became an important institution in the community.[75] The hospital's long-standing history in the barrio and the role of the Methodist Church in the initial success of the clinic created a bond of trust between the church and the founders of Father Rahm. As a result, the mothers and board of directors began negotiations with Newark Methodist to hire doctors to work at the envisioned outpatient clinic. By negotiating with Newark doctors, the founders professionalized the project while maintaining control of the clinic.

The Father Rahm Clinic's first major internal conflict happened in the midst of its expansion, marking what Salvador Balcorta called "the first revolution of La Fe."[76] In the early days of the clinic, the founding mothers articulated the need for reproductive health care.[77] In September 1971, Thomason General Hospital subcontracted the Father Rahm Clinic to begin a community-wide program for family planning services. This HEW-funded effort provided women a wide range of services, including birth control, pre- and postnatal care, obstetrics and gynecology, and family-planning counseling.[78] In 1973, however, the Catholic diocese, in keeping with the faith's teachings, sent the clinic's leadership a letter opposing its focus on reproductive health. Felipe Peralta recalled the diocese insisting that the clinic "[could] not have the name Father Rahm and be providing family planning services."[79] This brought on an internal conflict regarding the name of the clinic. Balcorta explained that the younger generation of mothers refused to change the name because the clinic was not affiliated with the Catholic Church. The elderly founding mothers and religiously conservative supporters of the clinic argued that they needed to change the name because, in Balcorta's words, "the bishop is asking us to remove it."[80] To avoid exacerbating tensions in the community and with the Catholic Church, the founding mothers and the board decided to take action. "We had a contest to rename the clinic, and La Fe was the name that was selected," recalled Balcorta.[81] According to the *El Paso Herald-Post*, "La Fe was chosen because of 'the faith' many individuals had in their efforts to establish the center."[82] Since then the clinic officially became Centro de Salud Familiar La Fe (Faith Family Health Center).

Despite the renaming, La Fe continued to be successful. In January 1974, the board of directors announced that HEW had awarded the clinic a $700,000 operational grant. These funds transformed the clinic's size and services. La Fe's first federally funded health center began operations at 608 St. Vrain in a vacant building owned by the Church of Latter-Day Saints.[83] Members of the community volunteered their labor to renovate the building. The new outpatient clinic was inaugurated in 1975. The facility had a reception room, examining rooms, a nurse's station, a laboratory, a medical records room, a social worker's office, a limited pharmacy, and a children's playroom.[84]

The new clinic revolutionized La Fe's services. At the old building, the staff provided services for 35–40 people daily; the new clinic saw an average of 100 patients a day. Clients could receive services from four general doctors, three pediatricians, registered and vocational nurses, lab technicians, gynecologists, and social workers.[85] The number of families covered by the prepaid medical plan grew. In 1974, the clinic enrolled 100 people in plans; a year later, that figure was 7,500.[86] Patients were excited about La Fe's growth. Salvador Dominguez and his wife, both enrolled in the prepaid plan, told the *El Paso Times*, "We're very pleased with the services they provide here. They treat you very well. It would be very difficult for us to see a private doctor; the center is very good." Another patient, Maria de Jesus Escobedo, stated, "If this clinic were ever to close, I'd be one of the first to cooperate any way to keep it open."[87] Staff members and grant writers understood the need to keep the clinic afloat on a stream of outside funding. In response to the successful expansion, HEW verbally agreed to award La Fe a $750,000 continuing grant so that it could maintain operations. Neftali Ruelas, the executive director, told local newspapers that with the outpatient clinic, La Fe could extend its comprehensive health care services to include dental and mental health treatment, and the Women, Infants and Children Program.[88]

In less than a decade, the founding mothers, grant writers, and professionals had achieved the bold dream of establishing a community-controlled health center in South El Paso. But La Fe's success produced a false sense of security for its future. Guillermo Glenn stepped down as the clinic's director in 1974. In his recollection, "I felt the clinic had gotten going. We had done all the work to break the ice with the medical society, and we had all the agreements to get started. So I resigned. We had a good board for the clinic, so I didn't feel bad in leaving."[89] Founders, supporters, and professionals associated with the clinic's early history moved on from the project, too. In newspaper accounts and other sources, the voices of women such as Nina Cordero and Amelia Castillo were replaced by those of the professionals. Raymond Gardea resigned as the clinic's medical director in 1975 because of philosophical differences regarding the type of medical care provided at the clinic. He wanted to deliver comprehensive rather than crisis care for patients.[90] The professionalization of La Fe diminished the voices of the founding mothers and their philosophies in the daily operation of the clinic.

"The Second Revolution of La Fe"

The year 1977 marked a tumultuous period for La Fe. In March of that year, Ramon Salas, chairman of the clinic's board of directors, and Roberto Lerma, its treasurer, planned to significantly cut La Fe's expenses, claiming that the physicians were "costing too much money."[91] In an effort to hire cost-effective doctors, Salas and Lerma secretly approached the Texas Tech University School of Medicine (which was affiliated with Thomason General Hospital) about partnership options that could supply the clinic with interns inexpensively.[92] When it came time to renew the clinic's physician contracts, the board voted to not rehire Dr. Alberto Chavira. At the time, he and executive director Don Garcia advocated paying doctors an hourly wage rather than six dollars per patient encounter. The "collectivist principles" introduced by Dr. Chavira led to him being labeled an "activist type."[93] Following his dismissal, the board of directors also fired Garcia and two nurses, Roberta Watson and Martha Apodaca. This led Southsiders to believe that the ousting of staff members had been politically motivated.[94] Salas and Lermas's clandestine visit and the alleged wrongful terminations exposed financial mismanagement at the clinic and abuses of power by the board. These incidents sparked what Salvador Balcorta called the "Second Revolution of La Fe."[95]

Southsiders were outraged that Salas and Lerma had made critical decisions without the knowledge of the rest of the board. Abel Aguilera, a former board member, wrote to the *El Paso Herald-Post*: "Bringing interns from Thomason to 'La Fe' does not provide the services of practicing private doctors for the people of South El Paso. The argument for dismissing private doctors is to save money. Money is not a problem."[96] When Salas and Lerma attempted to enter La Fe on March 23, they were greeted by angry protesters. According to the *El Paso Herald-Post*, 75–100 people showed up to contest the potential affiliation with Texas Tech. The newspaper reported that "several protesters with canes closed off the gate entrance [w]aving their sticks, while others, shouting at the two and waving clenched fists, began throwing dirt."[97]

The clinic's internal turmoil had started several years earlier. When Guillermo Glenn left in 1974, the clinic went through a number of directors in rapid succession. Glenn believed that his successor, Neftali Ruelas, was a good choice: "Mr. Ruelas had showed me all these proposals he had written. I thought he was on top of the whole situation. The board seemed to be happy with him."[98] Ruelas was terminated in 1975 when the board voted to end his contract because of unsatisfactory evaluations.[99] Former board member Abel Aguilera wrote in the *El Paso Herald-Post*: "La Fe is in hot water because there are so many internal problems which the present board of directors has created. Since 1974, there have been five executive directors at the Center. One of the reasons that the executive directors did not last was because the board as a whole did not like the way the directors administered the center."[100] The constant changes in leadership caused the board to assume a larger responsibility managing the clinic, but without proper accountability to the Mexican American community.

A story published in the *El Paso Journal* exposed the severity of La Fe's problems. The piece identified several concerns, including wrongful termination of personnel, misuse of HEW grant money, the commissioning of expensive computerized studies and reports, and conflicts of interest stemming from the sale of health insurance policies to patients. Salvador Balcorta recalled details of the last problem: "[There were] fiduciary issues [because] the board was involved in selling the health insurance to the organization [and] involved in doing the billing. *Muchas chuequerias* [lots of crookery]."[101] Roberto Lerma, the board's treasurer and an insurance agent, earned commissions totaling $5,000 a month in premiums on a policy he sold to La Fe.[102] In addition, board members mismanaged federal grants that funded operations at La Fe. Dr. Pablo Ayub, one of the clinic's physicians, admitted that the board spent over half of a $750,000 HEW grant on expenses unrelated to medical costs.[103] The alarming reports led to disputes over the control of the clinic as South El Pasoans demanded that Salas and Lerma resign from the board.

On April 14, 1977, the founding mothers, Chicano/a activist groups, and barrio residents occupied the clinic. According to Balcorta, the community, especially the mothers of La Fe, asked the city and HEW officials to intervene. He recalled that people were "asking the government to come and check it out. *Y nadie venia* [nobody came]." While Balcorta was not involved in these demonstrations, he witnessed the community rallying for the organization: "The community came in and forcefully took over the clinic with guns and rifles."[104] The local Chicana/o newspaper *El Mestizo* reported that more than one hundred people took possession of the clinic and its administrative building.[105] According to Salvador Avila, then a member of the UTEP MEChA chapter, the mothers of La Fe called on the organization to provide support. Avila recalled, "It was the elderly ladies who called and said, 'This man [Salas] is messing with the clinic, and no one is stopping him.'"[106] Fernando Chacón, another MEChA member, used his position as UTEP student government president to publicize the troubles at La Fe.[107] Soon, the founding mothers enlisted the support of several Chicana/o organizations and activists from South El Paso and outside it.

Community activists and allies formed a coalition called Los Amigos de La Fe (Friends of La Fe). Cecilia Vega and Daniel Solis, Southside community activists and spokespeople for the group, published a list of demands in the *El Paso Herald-Post*. Los Amigos de La Fe wanted the following:

1. The present board of directors to resign.
2. A new board, composed of at least 51 per cent of members of the Southside community, as required by law, be appointed.
3. A complete investigation of the present board of directors by the Department of Health, Education and Welfare.
4. That [fired] staffers of the La Fe Clinic, Dr. Alberto Chavira, Director Don Garcia, and nurses, Martha Apodaca and Roberta Watson, be rehired.[108]

Los Amigos de La Fe also circulated newsletters across El Paso, informing the community about the situation at the clinic, the goals of the coalition, and the planned demonstrations to take control of the institution. The coalition simply "wanted to return La Fe Clinic to normalcy."[109]

During the takeover, the *Herald-Post* reported that "protesters blocked access to both buildings [clinic and administration], allowing only emergency clinical service to be performed."[110] Los Amigos de La Fe held twenty-four-hour vigils and even organized a Catholic Mass in one of the buildings. During the demonstrations, from 40 to 300 protesters showed up in support of reforming La Fe. The Chicano activist Daniel Solis told the *El Paso Herald-Post* that he was disappointed "that no city or civic leaders have come to discuss the problem with the people," adding, "We've asked them for help. But so far no officials, no councilmen have come."[111]

Although the demonstrations were peaceful, conflicts at La Fe quickly escalated. On April 19, the board demanded that the El Paso Police Department evict the protesters from the clinic and the administrative building.[112] *El Mestizo* reported that the EPPD broke doors and windows, and used dogs in its "invasion" of the building. At the end of the night, nine people, including the former La Fe social worker Felipe Peralta, were arrested. He recalled:

> I got a call around 10:30 [saying,] "Felipe you better get over here because I think the cops are going to come in and arrest everybody. If you're here, maybe we can get the people out." There were a group of about twenty, and about eight or nine of them were elderly citizens. [The cops] told me, "We're going to give you an hour to try to talk to those people and get them out of there." I think within five minutes, the cops come in breaking the windows and doors and [shouting,] "Everybody get out of here!" And I said, "Wait, wait, wait. We are just here . . ." [And they said,] "Oh, and he is the leader." And they [took] us all to jail.[113]

The dispute intensified in the summer, when the board issued restraining orders against the volunteer staff and some of the more vocal activists.[114] The tensions worsened when Los Amigos de La Fe claimed its members had been harassed by Salas, Lerma, and the EPPD. *El Mestizo* reported that since the April takeover, "People of the barrio had been arrested, slandered, and threatened by the courts, the police, the sell-out media, and the opportunist group who does not want to leave the clinic."[115] The future of La Fe remained uncertain in the months after the takeover.

Amid the conflict, patients, residents of El Segundo Barrio, and Los Amigos de La Fe wrote numerous letters to HEW, begging it to launch an investigation. Louis Hines, the regional program consultant for HEW, came to La Fe in June. During the three-day visit, Hines met with clinic staff members, Southsiders, and the board of directors to learn about the clinic's internal problems.[116] More than 200 South El Paso residents voiced their concerns during a community hearing with HEW officials. Nina Cordero attended the meeting and denounced the recent actions by the board of directors. The founding mother also criticized the board members, who, in her opinion, had abandoned La Fe's philosophy of serving the Mexican American community. Cordero told the investigators that "The [HEW] money is provided for the people of the community not for the people of the board who have forgotten where they come from."[117]

A week after the visit, Dr. Floyd A. Norman, the regional administrator for HEW, gave the board of directors an ultimatum: resolve the clinic's problems or lose funding.[118] HEW officials identified "several objectionable actions by the board," including the misuse of travel funds, questionable payments to certain businesses, and conflicts of interest.[119] The organization accused the board of escalating the tensions with the community of South El Paso. In the letter, Norman stated, "No evidence is seen of improved communication or initiatives taken toward better relationships (with the community). In fact, it is believed that rigidity of positions and dogmatic decisions have contributed to the loss of confidence which the community displays toward the board of directors." Norman also ordered the immediate resignation of Ramon Salas and Roberto Lerma from the board, the reinstatement of fired staff, and a new board election within forty-five days to ensure that La Fe patients made up over half of the board.[120]

As the forty-five-day deadline approached, Los Amigos de La Fe took matters in hand. On August 6, the group held elections that ousted members of the old board. According to Daniel Solis, about 69 percent of the clinic's eligible voters cast ballots. The new board, which was formally installed on August 11, reappointed Don Garcia as the director of La Fe and rehired wrongfully terminated staff members.[121] In the aftermath, a local MEChA publication noted, "The strength and courage of the people is such a strong force that victory was inevitable. The old board of directors 'mafia,' after trying every dirty trick, opted for accepting their defeat."[122]

The six-month protest to save La Fe demonstrated that Mexican Americans still felt ownership of the clinic. This sense of possession was reflected in the hundreds of people who protested and occupied La Fe's buildings, the countless letters written to HEW, petitions, meetings, and the resiliency of activists and community members, even when they faced harassment and arrests. When threatened, Southsiders actively defended the founding mission of the clinic by asserting that La Fe belonged to the people of the barrio.

"Se Comenzó a Calmar Todo" (Everything Began to Calm Down)

La Fe found stability in the 1980s. Salvador Balcorta recalled, "In 1980, the community selected Pete Duarte to come in. *Y ahí se comenzó a calmar todo* (and from there, everything began to calm down).[123] Duarte, a native of California, had spent time in the Dominican Republic working with the Peace Corps. He arrived in El Paso in 1968 with the hope of organizing South El Paso around health issues. Duarte recalled, "The Chicanos here wouldn't accept me because I was an outsider. They didn't trust me at all."[124] When the movement to start La Fe began, Duarte joined forces with the founding mothers, becoming one of the original incorporators. His work in the early stages of the clinic helped him "gain the *confianza* (trust) of the leaders of South El Paso."[125] After his initial involvement with the Father Rahm Clinic, he was hired at UTEP, where he worked as a sociology professor and served as the director of Upward Bound (a college-prep program for disadvantaged students), a position he held until chosen director of La Fe.

Taking the reins of a community clinic close to extinction was no easy task. In the aftermath of the 1977 protests, La Fe faced a financial crisis. The clinic had overspent the $750,000 HEW grant, and no new funding was in sight. In March 1980, HEW granted the clinic a six-month provisionary period in which to resolve its financial problems, or else La Fe would be forced to close.[126] Duarte and the board immediately faced difficult decisions about how to wipe out the deficit and save the clinic. They cut funding by 35 percent, laid off a third of the clinic's staff, and slightly increased the price for medical services. Within Duarte's first six months as executive director, the clinic was removed from probationary status. Subsequently, La Fe increased both its operational budget by several million dollars, and its staff and services. For the remainder of the decade, the clinic thrived financially through federal funds, state monies, and donations from the community. Neither the City of El Paso nor El Paso County contributed to the maintenance of the clinic.[127]

With its growth, La Fe bolstered its image beyond South El Paso and played a major role in local health promotion and outreach. The clinic implemented programs on diabetes health and dental education for all ages. La Fe also spearheaded grassroots self-help initiatives such as programs for summer youth employment and senior citizen housing.[128] In 1992, the clinic partnered with the El Paso Public Library to distribute information on health literacy at library branches and at the clinic.[129] Duarte and the clinic's staff also collaborated in important local HIV-AIDS prevention and education efforts through the Chicano AIDS Coalition.[130]

Although the founding women had long been disconnected from La Fe's operations, they witnessed the recognition and praise that the clinic received. La Fe became a model for clinics operating under the US Public Health Service, and was chosen by the Kellogg Foundation as an exemplary model for grassroots community-based clinics for South Africa—a project that Pete Duarte helped develop.[131] Most importantly, La Fe became accredited through the Joint Commission on Accreditation of Healthcare Organizations (JCAHO), a recognition essential for hospitals but not required of small neighborhood clinics. La Fe became one of two clinics in Texas to obtain JCAHO accreditation, and one of four in the nation. An opinion piece in the *El Paso Times* stated, "What this accreditation tells them [La Fe patients] is that while the neighborhoods around the clinic may be the third poorest in terms of income in the United States, the health care at La Fe is superior by any standard."[132]

Despite the growth of La Fe, the clinic's staff, leadership, and board of directors embraced its grassroots beginnings and community-centered mission to become a vehicle for social justice. In an interview with the *El Paso Times*, Duarte stated that he believed in "involving people in the solution of their own problems," and that La Fe contributed to "the democratization of the politically powerless."[133] For twelve years, Duarte and his team advocated for health care reform, championed community-based organizations, and became vocal supporters for health care services for communities along the US-Mexico border. In 1990, Duarte testified before Congress to urge the government to prioritize access to quality and affordable health care for Mexican Americans, migrant farmworkers, and other underserved groups.[134]

At a time when the Reagan administration was cutting funding for welfare programs, La Fe came out better than other community health clinics born from the Chicana/o movement, the civil rights movement, and the War on Poverty. While La Fe became bureaucratic and perhaps impersonal in the eyes of many, the clinic's staff "[kept] in mind our need to remain true to the most essential of our principles. And that is that the clinic must serve south El Paso, first, last and always."[135] Pete Duarte stepped down as director in 1992 to become the chief executive officer of Thomason General Hospital—a feat the mothers of La Fe never imagined. As the clinic moved into the 1990s, its grassroots beginnings were long gone. Its evolution, however, fulfilled the founding mothers' vision of uplifting the Mexican American community.

A Dream Fulfilled

The founding mothers' dream came full circle in August 1992. With Duarte's departure, the community elected Salvador Balcorta, a son of El Segundo Barrio and a Chicano activist, to direct La Fe. When interviewed by Latino USA, Balcorta stated, "Some of the elders always wanted somebody from their own barrio to lead the organization."[136] Balcorta fit the bill—his youth activism and work in La Fe had led him to a career in social work. As the chief of community health services for the El Paso City-County Health Department, he gained ample experience in working on problems affecting Mexican Americans in the Southside.[137] Marlo Santana, a newly elected board member at the time, told the *El Paso Times* that he supported Balcorta "because he represents a new type of leader—one who's been active in the community and who hasn't forgotten the struggle."[138] Balcorta recalled that upon his appointment, one of the founding mothers, Maria de la Luz Zubia, told him, "You're the first one of the barrio that we selected to direct [La Fe]. We will be watching you closer than the others. But I also want you to remember that we will always be praying for you. God will look over you."[139] Since becoming director, Balcorta has endeavored not only to continue bringing quality health care to South El Paso, but also to meet the needs and expectations of the Mexican American community.[140]

Balcorta's involvement in the early stages of La Fe as a youth outreach worker cultivated in him an awareness of the clinic's community-centered philosophy. His experiences around the founding mothers and early activists like Nina Cordero shaped his vision for the clinic and its future. When he reflected on his involvement in the creation of La Fe, Balcorta recalled, "I spent a lot of time with Nina when I was a young kid. I used to drive her around [and] take her to places. I learned a lot from that lady, a lot. I was there with her, hearing the stuff she believed in [and] the stuff she was dreaming of."[141]

Under Balcorta's twenty-nine-year tenure at La Fe, the clinic has expanded its services while maintaining its reputation as a successful model for community-controlled institutions. In 1992, the clinic employed 70 permanent employees and had an operational budget of $3 million. Today, La Fe has over 450 employees, a $26 million budget, and twenty-two medical and social service sites in the barrio and across El Paso in areas with high populations of working-class Mexican Americans and Latinx groups.[142] When Balcorta arrived at the clinic, he thought, "We got to start our own engine in producing our own money so that we ourselves can run our organization." Today that transition is complete: only 25 percent of the clinic's budget comes from the federal government—the rest comes from insurance and patient payments, and smaller sums from private fund-raising and grants. Balcorta and the board of directors maintain a very strict accounting system. He recalled, "When I came in, I told the staff that stayed with me, we're going to do a different type of accounting. We're going to run with 75 percent of the income," reserving the remainder for contingencies.[143] Together, these budgetary measures ensure that La Fe is self-sufficient and that its future will be determined by the community, as the founders envisioned, and not by outside funding sources.

Balcorta transformed La Fe's mission into a holistic approach toward community well-being. For example, he recognized the continued need for better housing

The mural *La Salud de la Comunidad* by Jesus "Cimi" Alvarado, currently on display at the Centro de Salud Familiar La Fe. In English, the banner reads, "Community health is faith." © Centro de Salud Familiar La Fe, courtesy of Centro de Salud Familiar La Fe, Inc.

in El Segundo Barrio. Consequently, the organization began building, purchasing, and renovating housing units there. One result was Magoffin Park Villas, a mixed-income housing development owned by La Fe.[144] The organization is also engaged in cultural celebration and preservation in El Segundo Barrio. In 2003, La Fe inaugurated the Culture and Technology Center (CTC), which celebrates Mexican Americans' heritage through cultural programming, including dance, music, and arts and crafts. The center houses a state-of-the-art recording studio, an auditorium, a graphic arts center, a computer lab, and an educational kitchen. The CTC offers nutrition classes, GED courses, and English and citizenship classes. This "family campus learning environment" provides educational and technical opportunities to strengthen the Southside community.[145]

One of Balcorta's most ambitious efforts was the establishment of La Fe Preparatory, a charter school in South El Paso. The idea for the school came from the need for a high school in the barrio, particularly to address high dropout and pushout rates among Mexican American youth.[146] La Fe Preparatory, which opened its doors in 2007, has a mission and philosophy parallel to those of the clinic. Balcorta believes that the "students may be little children, but at their tender age, they are already beginning to understand that their community needs to unite and demand their rights to a good education, a dignified home, to fair wages in a safe workplace, and to a quality, affordable health care."[147] The school emphasizes dual-language instruction; offers an arts, culture, and technology curriculum; and has heavy parental involvement. La Fe Preparatory serves about three hundred students in prekindergarten through the eighth grade, mainly from El Segundo Barrio.[148]

For the most part, the South El Paso community has positively received Balcorta's expanded mission for La Fe. When asked about the growth and success of the clinic, he stated, "We have people here from all ages that are constantly super proud. They love these buildings. The elderly come in and say, 'Look at what became of our dream.'"[149] Nevertheless, some have criticized Balcorta's leadership. Felipe Peralta, who was involved in La Fe's early stages, has been a vocal critic of Balcorta. Peralta believes the resources of the clinic have not been used to the fullest: "[Balcorta] has got such a stronghold there in the community ... and he's done some good work, I'm not going to deny it. But yet he's isolated [from barrio issues]. That platform could have been used so we could bring other groups together." Others consider La Fe a "giant octopus" due to its varied ongoing projects in South El Paso.[150] But Balcorta does not let the criticism affect him or his vision for the community of El Segundo Barrio. As he recalled, "Sometimes with all the criticism and all the naysayers, all you need to do is look around and say, 'I've contributed a little piece to this giant phenomenon called El Movimiento Chicano.'"[151]

The Legacy of La Fe Clinic

While most of the Mexican American mothers who founded the Father Rahm Clinic, including Nina Cordero, have passed away, their spirits, visions, and dreams live on through La Fe's work. Salvador Balcorta reflected that when he gets caught up in the day-to-day tasks of the clinic, he remembers something important. Before cutting the ribbon at a new building's dedication, one of the mothers told him to hold on. Librada Chavez, one of the founders, approached him and said, "All of us are born dreamers. Some of us go on and achieve our dreams; most of us don't. But then there are people like you who dream in such a way where your dreams become all of our dreams. Through your dreams, our dreams get fulfilled."[152] Since his first day, Balcorta has acknowledged the importance of keeping the visions of women such as Librada Chavez, Nina Cordero, Amy Castillo, and the rest of the founders present in the activities of La Fe.

Although written records, local newspapers, and reports lauding the institution acknowledge the involvement and work of professionals such as Dr. Raymond Gardea, Pete Duarte, and Salvador Balcorta in the successes of La Fe Clinic, these sources often ignore the labor of Mexican American mothers. The women were not professional health care providers, nor did they have experience in writing grants. But they sparked South El Paso's movement to start a health clinic, and are the reason why La Fe continues to operate today.

For over fifty years, La Fe has exemplified the ideology of self-determination and has become a symbol of the long Chicana/o movement's victories. The efforts of the founding mothers mirrored those of other underrepresented groups across the country during the social movements of the 1960s and 1970s. Although the odds of surviving were stacked against La Fe, the clinic continues to serve its community. What makes La Fe unique is the Mexican American community's investment in the institution. At times of crisis, the founding mothers, activist groups, and residents of El Segundo Barrio fought to defend the clinic. Despite La Fe's eventual bureaucratization, Pete Duarte and, especially, Salvador Balcorta maintained the founding mothers' core philosophy rooted in the needs of the community: "*la totalidad de nuestro bienestar*" (a totality of our well-being) for the people of South El Paso.

PART III

COALITIONS AND CONTROL:
BLACK AND BROWN LIBERATION
STRUGGLES IN METROPOLITAN TEXAS

CHAPTER 10

CONTESTING WHITE SUPREMACY IN TARRANT COUNTY

J. TODD MOYE

At the end of World War II, Tarrant County, like the rest of Texas, was white men's country. Still mostly rural, the county urbanized and diversified rapidly through the second half of the twentieth century and into the twenty-first, driven by the Dallas–Fort Worth Metroplex economic engine, but its social order remained rooted in the plantation-era South. One of Fort Worth's civic champions, Amon Carter Sr., advertised the county seat as the place "Where the West Begins," but when it came to race relations, Tarrant County was "Where the South Continues."[1] (The county's second-largest city, Arlington, was named for Robert E. Lee's slave plantation. From 1951 to 1971, sports teams at Arlington State College—now the University of Texas at Arlington—were known as the Rebels. The school band played "Dixie" at their games, and for most of that time, a Confederate flag flew over the campus.[2]) What Randolph B. Campbell, the dean of Texas historians, had to say about the problems with white Texans' collective Civil War memory holds true for Tarrant County's collective memory of the civil rights era. "So long as Texas is not seen as a southern state," he wrote, "its [white] people do not have to face the great moral evil of slavery and the bitter heritage of black-white relations that followed the defeat of the Confederacy in 1865."[3] One could add "brown" to that formulation. Since World War II, Black, Brown, and allied Anglo residents of Tarrant County have fought—sometimes on parallel tracks, sometimes in coalition—using a variety of tactics, to dismantle the vestiges of white supremacy and make the county something more like a multiracial democracy.

For most of the twentieth century, Jim Crow and, to varying degrees, Juan Crow dictated which institutions and public spaces Anglos could exclude African Americans and Mexican Americans from, and whites had unchecked political power in the county. White supremacy took many forms, but the result was always the same: plain injustice. As Bob Ray Sanders, an African American who grew up in Fort Worth in the 1950s and 1960s, explained, "Many of the things that my parents and grandparents paid taxes for, I couldn't use."[4]

African Americans and Mexican Americans began to test the boundaries of the white-supremacist sociopolitical order as soon as cracks began to show in the edifices of segregation at the national level in the mid-1950s. Anglos struck back to defend white supremacy with an intensity and consistency that has seldom been acknowledged.

Mexican Americans and African Americans in Tarrant County worked hard for the integration of public institutions, especially schools, and for political power. Mexican American students were not formally segregated from white students in Tarrant County schools throughout the twentieth century, but residential segregation generally confined them to substandard neighborhood schools with few whites, and a disproportionate number of Mexican American students were tracked into vocational education programs. Political power proved elusive during this period, and the lack of it made it difficult for families to contest the system. A Mexican American was elected to the Fort Worth City Council for the first time in 1977, and to the Fort Worth Board of Education for the first time the following year. In 2000, Mexican Americans made up roughly 30 percent of Fort Worth's population, and more than 40 percent of Fort Worth Independent School District students, but accounted for only two members of the school board (out of nine), and held none of the eight city council seats. African Americans fought intense, decades-long battles over access to good schools and had slightly more success in the fight for political power.[5]

"The Fort Worth Way"

By the latter half of the twentieth century, the local political order had coalesced around what people in power proudly called "the Fort Worth Way," a system in which white elites, with occasional cooperation from well-to-do African Americans and Mexican Americans, managed political and social change peacefully. That system extended more or less throughout the county. Fort Worth Way solutions tended to result in good public relations and a positive business environment, but they severely limited the range of opinions that city fathers considered when making decisions that affected the entire city. They therefore tended to minimize social change.

As Kelly Allen Gray, a Fort Worth City Council member, put it in 2020, "It's not a secret that in Fort Worth, how we dealt with the end of Jim Crow laws was that we simply just took down the signs and then went on as if racism never existed." The inability of the Fort Worth Way to deal forthrightly with the structures and institutions of racism, rather than just its trappings, continued to limit democracy and uphold racial hierarchies well into the twenty-first century.[6]

Describing the system for the journalist Katie Sherrod in 1995, a Black professional in Fort Worth said, "The power brokers have evolved a process that is impressive, a process that has the appearance of participation, and even more so, the *appearance* of some personal stake in the outcome, but it's illusory. . . . My assessment is that the powers-that-be . . . write the script for the city." The anonymous businessman was right: the Fort Worth Way denied real power to the vast majority of its citizens. African Americans nonetheless at times found ways to work against and within this system to advance their interests. Despite a few exceptions, they did not generally work in coalition with Mexican Americans between 1950 and 2000, but Black-Brown coalition building has been more common in the twenty-first century.[7]

The Fort Worth Way has long affected how Tarrant County residents remember their local civil rights history. No less an authority than Sanders, a longtime reporter and columnist for the *Fort Worth Star-Telegram*, insisted, "In spite of the Jim Crow laws and the unequal treatment that accompanied them, Fort Worth was regarded as having a benevolent brand of racism, generally leaving the black community alone with little of the harassment or abject violence demonstrated in other cities. There were incidents in the first half of the twentieth century, including a lynching in 1921, which were ugly indeed. But, for the most part, whites and blacks got along as each kept their place."[8] This is as good an example of the Fort Worth Way version of the city's racial history as any. Like other nostalgic views, it overlooks a great deal of contradicting evidence that shows that Blacks organized against the Jim Crow social order in Tarrant County, and that whites fought again and again to uphold it, sometimes in corporate conference rooms and sometimes in mobs.

A Fort Worth historian illustrates another form of the myth when he claims, "Despite the strict segregation line and the blatant bigotry of the white majority, Fort Worth managed to maintain remarkably harmonious relations between Blacks and whites over the years. There were never any mass demonstrations and no armed clashes such as some other Southern cities experienced." Most of these assertions are easily disproved, not least by the same historian, who documents multiple instances of bombings and other forms of mob violence against Black homeowners who dared cross the color line.[9]

Comparing civil rights movements in his hometown to those in its larger neighbor to the east, the longtime community organizer Estrus Tucker said, "Dallas is in-your-face, very confrontational.... Fort Worth has taken pride in being conciliatory and noncombative."[10] Another longtime Fort Worth resident, Marilyn Jean Johnson believed that while the Fort Worth Way tended to cut down on outright aggression, it ultimately discouraged African Americans from fighting for their rights as citizens. In contrast to the violence that whites unleashed against integration campaigns in the Deep South, Johnson thought that "Fort Worth was very subtle about their situation." But that also meant that African Americans in Fort Worth were, in her judgment, "complacent": "They missed out on a whole lot, and I don't know whether it was due to the leadership in Fort Worth or whether it was due to just the complacency of the people."[11]

It is true that mass demonstrations along the lines of those that rocked southern communities like Nashville and Birmingham were rare in Tarrant County—mainly because of the violence and harassment that local whites and state actors employed to defend Jim Crow. It is equally true that local people launched school-desegregation suits, picketed downtown Fort Worth cafeterias and department stores to force integration, and occasionally engaged in more radical forms of protest, just as people did in other southern communities. Local civil rights groups have been active in the city for a long time. Tarrant County's racial history is not better than that of famous civil rights hot spots throughout the Deep South, and it is not worse. It is depressingly similar.[12]

Indeed, for much of the city's history, the Fort Worth Way entailed actively maintaining a profoundly unjust and unequal social order. In this sense, Fort Worth was as southern as Atlanta or New Orleans. City codes and traditions segregated public places, state statutes segregated public schools and hospitals, and white mobs did their best over and over again to keep their neighborhoods lily white. The Ku Klux Klan dominated Tarrant County in the 1920s, as it did much of Texas. The Klan's state headquarters were in Fort Worth, and the local klavern claimed to have 6,000 members. That number is almost surely an exaggeration, but the klavern's ranks did include prominent ministers, elected officials, police officers, lawyers, doctors, bankers, and teachers. It proudly used violence to force community members to abide by the Klan's standards of public behavior.[13] Before, during, and after the Klan's heyday, whites consistently used similar means to police the color line. Mobs destroyed Black-owned businesses in 1911 and 1913, and attacked Blacks who bought homes in previously all-white neighborhoods in 1925, 1926, 1939, 1940, 1953, and 1956—and those were just the instances that attracted the attention of newsmen. There were surely others.[14]

Juan Crow

Whites in Tarrant County proved willing to use violence to uphold white supremacy, and they have certainly used the law to maintain power, but the unwritten rules of Jim Crow and Juan Crow that dictated the ways Black, Brown, and Anglo citizens interacted were in some ways just as pernicious. Fort Worth did not have strict Juan Crow laws on the books, but a set of unwritten rules, developed over time. They determined which spaces Mexican Americans could and could not occupy, how Mexican Americans could and could not interact with their Anglo counterparts, and which jobs were and were not available to Mexican Americans. For instance, according to one historian of the Mexican American experience in the city, "There did appear to be an unwritten understanding as to the limits or boundaries within which [Mexican American–owned] businesses could be set up and operated. These widely understood geographic limitations dictated that Hispanic businesses remain within the confine of the barrios" before the 1970s.[15]

There have been Mexican Americans in Fort Worth nearly since its founding, but before the 1980s they made up a small minority of the city's total population. The 1880 US census was the first to find Mexican Americans in the area—fourteen laborers and agricultural workers, all men. Mexican migration to Tarrant was light before the Mexican Revolution of 1910–1920, and a great many, perhaps most, of those who came to the area for work intended to return to Mexico once they had saved some money.[16] The revolution proved to be a significant push factor, and hundreds of thousands of Mexicans crossed the border into Texas for good during the decade. Good jobs for unskilled laborers in Fort Worth provided a pull: industrialists sought out and hired recent immigrants from Mexico at the time of the revolution, because organized labor was in the midst of a push to unionize the city's stockyards and steel mill.[17]

Roughly five thousand Mexican Americans lived in Fort Worth in 1930, nearly all of them in La Diecisiete, La Corte, the North Side, El TP, and the South Side barrios. During the Depression, more than two thousand of them left Texas, either by choice or under threat of deportation after out-of-work Anglos decided that perhaps they were willing, after all, to do the dirty jobs at reduced wages that the industrialists had hired the Mexicans to do.[18] Those who remained still tended to work for the meatpackers, railroads, and steel mill that their enclaves abutted. They founded businesses, nourished church communities, educated their children as best they could, and built lives in the barrios. Fort Worth's brand of Juan Crow provided much more "separate" than "equal," and life in the barrio was tougher than it was in the larger community. Mexican Americans had worse schools, less sanitary living conditions, less access to health care, and less access to high-paying jobs than their Anglo counterparts throughout the twentieth century.

The strictures that Juan Crow put in place were no less powerful for being unwritten. Mexican Americans had precious few opportunities to break out of the barrios, and when they did, their Anglo neighbors reacted much as they did when African Americans moved into previously all-white communities. When Salvador and María Gonzalez bought a house in a previously all-Anglo North Side neighborhood in 1947, nearly all the other houses on their street hit the market.[19] The city's newspaper of record did not cover such struggles. As with their Black neighbors, residents of the barrios never saw their accomplishments heralded in the *Star-Telegram*. With very few exceptions, the only Black and Brown residents of Tarrant County whose names appeared in the newspaper were accused of crimes.[20]

Juan Crow rules changed over time. Compared with Jim Crow rules, they were often more permeable and subject to the whims of store owners, bus drivers, and other Anglos who had day-to-day opportunities to lord their privilege over Mexican Americans. Louis Zapata stated flatly that in the downtown Fort Worth of his youth, "there were restaurants and bars [that] wouldn't serve Mexicans"; but by 1977, conditions had changed to such a degree that he won a seat on the city council. In the 1930s and 1940s, Mexican Americans who attended movies at the Isis Theater on the North Side—the neighborhood that is home to the Fort Worth Stockyards and whose Mexican American population grew steadily throughout the century—had to sit in the balcony with Blacks, though whites did make exceptions for elite Mexican Americans like the star North Side High School football player Raúl Manriquez, who was allowed to sit with his white teammates. By the 1950s, all Mexican Americans could sit where they wished in the theater.[21]

One of Raúl Durán's memories points out how permeable Juan Crow's dividing lines were, even as Jim Crow's remained rigid. Durán, who grew up on the North Side in the late 1950s and 1960s, remembered being allowed to sit on the back seat of public buses, in the designated "Blacks Only" section, simply because he liked the long bench seat, even though his family preferred the "Whites Only" section. In contrast, Mae Cora Peterson, the leader of the Colored Branch of the Fort Worth YWCA and later an educator, recalled being kicked off a city bus in the 1940s with a companion when the white woman insisted on sitting with her in the Colored section.[22] Durán also remembered the anti-Mexican slurs he occasionally heard from Anglo parents at the Marine Creek playground on the North Side. While he noticed the Jim Crow accommodations at downtown Fort Worth department stores and cafeterias and felt that his family members were allowed to shop and try on clothes like white customers, he did not feel as though they were quite treated as equals.[23]

Eva Sandoval Bonilla, a fourth-generation Fort Worth native, described what it was like for children to have to find their place in a segregated society when it wasn't quite clear where they fit. She recalled a birthday trip in the late 1950s with her grandmother to Leonard Brothers Department Store, the venerable downtown

Fort Worth institution, where she was to choose a present. Bonilla remembered that it was her first time on a city bus and her first trip downtown. When they arrived at the store, Bonilla needed to use the restroom, so she asked her grandmother for directions. Her grandmother had lived in Fort Worth all her life, but she spoke only Spanish and had a hard time explaining the segregated facilities. Eight-year-old Eva had to figure it out for herself. Faced with two clearly marked women's rooms to choose from, she applied elementary school logic to the illogical situation: "I have to be 'colored,'" she decided, because "I tan [in the summer] . . . My sister never tans; neither does my brother. They must be white." She tried the bathroom marked "Colored" first, but the women there told her, "Honey, you don't belong here." She tried the "White" bathroom next, but the women in there made her feel unwelcome, too. She used that facility anyway, scooted out under the glare of the white ladies, and rushed off to find her grandmother.[24]

Jim Crow

Jim Crow took multiple forms, but its purpose was always to exclude African Americans from public spaces and from power, and to assert white supremacy. For most of the twentieth century, Fort Worth whites enjoyed public parks and swimming pools and the Forest Park Zoo 364 days a year, but Blacks could use the facilities only on Juneteenth. The courthouse downtown had separate water fountains and restrooms. Some privately owned lunch counters and restaurants provided separate accommodations for Blacks and whites, but most facilities and all the city's hotels served one race or the other exclusively. Tarrant County's John Peter Smith Hospital provided care to Black citizens, but only in the basement.[25]

Marilyn Jean Johnson, an African American, was born and raised in Champaign, Illinois, and attended college in Missouri. She did not live in a place with "Colored Only" signs over water fountains until she married a Fort Worth native and moved to town with him in 1952. "You were treated as a minority at any of the stores downtown," she said. "You'd notice a difference of the treatment of the people. In certain stores you—well, you'd prefer not to go in because they treated you that way." She found it very difficult to adjust: "I didn't know where I was supposed to go and where I wasn't," and when she rode the bus from her all-Black neighborhood, Como, down Camp Bowie Boulevard past the all-white neighborhood of Ridglea Hills, "they were looking at me awfully funny because I wouldn't get up and walk to the back." For a time, Como and Ridglea Hills were divided by the "Ridglea Wall," a barbed-wire-topped fence that served as an all-too-physical symbol of the divide between the two neighborhoods.[26]

Other African Americans remembered the Jim Crow era with something like nostalgia. Calling Fort Worth "a special place," the community activist Eddie Griffin said, "We were not fazed so much by segregation, because whatever the white community had, we had. They had their downtown; we had our downtown. . . . We had a pretty vibrant community" on the South Side, with multiple movie houses, restaurants, nightclubs, and other businesses, he said. "The fact that we were segregated pretty much localized our businesses, so you had the circulation of money within a very small community."[27] Blacks in Tarrant County during Jim Crow did have their own community institutions, and they did find ways to support one another. But they did not participate in society or the local economy equally with whites, and nostalgia for the period depends in part on forgetting the resistance to Jim Crow that took place.

Essie B. Sturgess provided a test of the Fort Worth Way in 1951 when she refused to abide by a city statute that segregated the races on buses and sat in a section designated "Whites Only." Sturgess was arrested, but rather than try her for a violation of section 4–6, chapter 10 of the city code, "the city quietly dismissed the charge to avoid an embarrassing public spectacle and possible racial conflict." By doing so, the city also denied Tarrant County Blacks an event to rally around in the way that African Americans in Montgomery, Alabama, united around the arrest of Rosa Parks in a nearly identical situation a short time later. By such methods, the Fort Worth Way stymied mass organization and mass demonstrations.[28]

Desegregating Tarrant Schools

Sturgess's head-on challenge to Jim Crow was not unheard of, but it was rare. Until 1954, African Americans in Tarrant County, like those throughout the South, tended to focus their efforts on achieving what has been called "separate but *truly* equal"—access to public accommodations, especially high-quality schools, even if they maintained racial segregation. They asked for better school facilities, more new books and buses, and equal pay for African American teachers. After Thurgood Marshall and his stable of attorneys from the NAACP's Legal Defense Fund convinced the US Supreme Court to strike down Jim Crow in public education in *Brown v. Board of Education*, however, African Americans had the backing of federal courts if they wanted to try to integrate schools.

But integration was long in coming, in Tarrant County as much as anyplace else in Texas. T. M. Moody, a sharecropper, pastor, and NAACP leader in Mansfield, a town of roughly 1,500 residents (approximately 350 of whom were Black, and no more than a small handful of whom were Mexican American) southeast of Fort Worth, was one of the many Black Texans who reacted to *Brown* not by calling for immediate integration but by attempting to leverage the threat of legal action into gaining separate-but-closer-to-equal schools for African American students in his town.

Mansfield was a perfectly common southern farming community. Social life for people of both races revolved around the church. For African Americans, many of whom sharecropped for white cotton farmers, that meant Bible study on Wednesday nights and hours-long Sunday services. Most worshiped at Bethlehem Baptist Church, still a thriving institution that memorializes the town's civil rights history.[29] On Saturdays, Blacks from miles around congregated in town on a corner of Broad Street to share news and swap tall tales.[30] Whites could patronize the drive-in restaurant near downtown, but Blacks could not.[31] Mansfield had one movie theater, the Farr Best. It was completely segregated: whites watched Randolph Scott cowboy movies from seats on the main floor, and Black patrons sat on a bench in the "crow's nest" upstairs.[32] Black consumers who wanted to shop in downtown stores had to enter through a back door and could not try on items they wished to purchase; they had to buy them and hope they would fit. Even the town cemetery was segregated: African Americans rested in eternal slumber on one side of a chain-link fence, and whites on the other.[33]

Moody was highly respected among both Blacks and whites, and he had served for some time as an unofficial adviser to the local school board, which provided facilities for Black students through the eighth grade. African Americans were banned from Mansfield High School, so those who wanted to continue their education had to catch a Continental Trailways bus to Fort Worth every morning and pay the fare themselves. After an hourlong ride, the bus dropped them off in downtown Fort Worth, and they had to walk roughly twenty blocks from there to I. M. Terrell High School. They walked back to the station to catch the bus each afternoon, which made it difficult for them to participate in extracurricular activities, and for much of the year they arrived back home in Mansfield after dark at the end of twelve-hour days.[34]

Floyd Moody, a cousin of T. M. Moody, was one of the students who had to ride the bus to Fort Worth to continue his studies. He grew up on the west side of Mansfield in a sharecropper's shack without indoor plumbing, running water, or electricity; it was heated by a wood-burning stove. Hauling water and chopping wood took up much of his free time; he did his homework beside a kerosene lamp.[35] Moody and his fellow students from Mansfield were hardly alone in having to go to such lengths to earn high school diplomas. I. M. Terrell was the only high school in Tarrant County available to African Americans. Students from the communities of Hurst, Euless, Arlington, and Grapevine, even from as far away as Weatherford in Parker County, thirty miles to the west, were without access to schools in their towns and had to travel to Fort Worth to attend high school.[36]

In 1955, T. M. Moody initiated what became the first significant test of the post-*Brown* order in Tarrant County. It is unclear whether he did so based on his own reading of the local situation or in response to the NAACP national office's directive that local chapters throughout the country petition local school boards to comply fully with the *Brown* rulings, or whether it was some combination of the two. He asked the Mansfield school board to provide a bus for the students who had to pay their way to Terrell, and to make safety improvements to the Mansfield Colored School, whose outdated buildings—they lacked electricity and running water—sat alongside busy West Broad Street. Moody also asked for new schoolbooks for the Colored School, some help for the two teachers (a former student remembered one of the two teachers lamenting, "'Lord, why did you give me this education and make me Black?' I've heard him say that so many times. He would say, 'I can't use it. They won't allow me to use it.'"), and a flagpole. The citizens whom Moody represented wanted to fly the American flag outside their school.[37]

Moody's actions hardly constituted a full-on assault on the segregated social order. The school board might have been expected to grant the commonsense requests, but Moody likely misjudged the balance of power that had developed in the wake of *Brown*. The decision may have emboldened local African Americans to believe that the federal courts would support their efforts to soften, or even dismantle, Jim Crow, but it also encouraged whites to unite in defense of total segregation. Mansfield whites organized a chapter of the Citizens' Councils, the prosegregation network that had sprouted in the Mississippi Delta the previous year and spread like kudzu throughout the South. (This organization should not be confused with the group of Dallas business leaders who used the same name.) It was popularly known as "the white-collar Klan" because its members engaged in mostly nonviolent campaigns to terrorize their Black neighbors from trying to register to vote or send their children to "white" schools. In October 1955, 125 white Mansfield residents attended a town hall meeting sponsored by the chapter. In unison, they condemned the idea of school integration and pledged to do everything in their power to stop it.[38]

In this atmosphere, the school board was less willing to cooperate with T. M. Moody and denied his requests. According to one source, members of the school board also threatened to lynch him.[39] It should be emphasized that none of Moody's requests to this point asked for or hinted at desegregation. At a conference of NAACP state branches in Dallas, Moody met Clifford Davis, a young Arkansas-born attorney who was developing expertise in desegregation cases and had recently settled in Fort Worth to set up a practice. Davis rejected separate-but-closer-to-equal arguments; he was a proven and unabashed integrationist. In a 2015 interview, he described a scenario showing how separate-but-equal schools would still have allowed for rampant discrimination against African Americans after graduation:

> Here I'm from the Black school with a degree in biology, compared with a white kid who went to the white school with a degree in biology. [Under Jim Crow] they can always claim a difference in the training, in the quality. But if we went to the same school, got our degree in biology from the same department, they've got a problem trying to explain why they think one is better than the other, more qualified than the other.... So you eliminate that argument, make that argument untenable. Let's drink out of the same cup so we know we've got the same tea.[40]

Working with the Dallas attorney U. Simpson Tate and with Robert Carter and Thurgood Marshall of the NAACP Legal Defense Fund, Davis filed suit in federal court in Fort Worth on behalf of the students against the school board and Superintendent R. L. Huffman that October. Nathaniel Jackson's name fell first alphabetically among the three plaintiffs whose families agreed to take the risk of adding their name to the suit (Floyd Moody and his cousin Charles Moody were the others), and the school board president was O. C. Rawdon, so the suit was called *Nathaniel Jackson, a minor, et al. v. O. C. Rawdon, et al.*, or *Jackson v. Rawdon*.

Jackson v. Rawdon was not the first case of its kind in the state. In fact, as it was going to trial, the Texas Supreme Court ruled in *McKinney v. Blankenship* that Big Spring ISD's desegregation plan should proceed because *Brown* had rendered the state's school segregation statutes unconstitutional, and similar suits were working their way through the state and federal court in other parts of Texas. School systems in Amarillo, Austin, Corpus Christi, El Paso, San Antonio, and San Marcos were already moving toward some form of school desegregation. US district judge Joe E. Estes initially ruled that the members of the Mansfield school board had acted in good faith and that the district was moving toward desegregation in keeping with the US Supreme Court's May 1955 *Brown II* directive — "with all deliberate speed."[41]

Davis appealed to the Fifth Circuit Court of Appeals, and in June 1956 the court reversed Estes's decision. Writing for the court, Chief Judge Hutchison ruled, "[The] plaintiffs have the right to admission to, and to attend, the Mansfield High School on the same basis as members of the white race [and] that the refusal of the defendants to admit plaintiffs thereto on account of their race or color is unlawful."[42]

It was a clear victory for the plaintiffs and the cause of integration, but the principal of Mansfield High School and the school board refused to abide by the court's decision. Worse, Governor Allan Shivers announced that he would not act to enforce it. Effigies made to look like African Americans hanging from nooses appeared throughout town as the beginning of the school year approached. Townspeople burned crosses. A mob assembled at the high school on the day that students were to enroll, worried that the plaintiffs in the suit might be among them. T. M. Moody and Clifford Davis concluded, however, that it would not be safe to bring the students onto campus, so they never tried to enroll. The decision was prudent. The mob swelled—estimates put it at 200–500 people, the higher figure representing nearly half the town's white population—and engaged in violence. The mob roughed up an Episcopal priest, a Tarrant County assistant district attorney, and several newsmen, and demagogues, including former governor Pappy O'Daniel and a man who claimed to be the second coming of Jesus Christ, kept it riled up. Tarrant County sheriff deputies retreated from the melee, but Shivers sent two Texas Rangers—not to disperse the mob but to make sure the Black students really did stay away from campus. President Dwight Eisenhower, a Shivers ally, declined to intervene in any way.[43]

Backed by the state, the mob succeeded in keeping Mansfield High School all-white, as it would remain until the 1965–1966 school year. The US Supreme Court's 1955 *Brown II* decision left it up to local districts and states to decide how best to implement desegregation, which placed the onus on local people like T. M. Moody and local lawyers like Clifford Davis to bring about practical school integration. It took district-by-district challenges, federal judges who were willing to accept the *Brown* precedent and rule that it should be implemented swiftly, and state and local authorities who were brave enough to enforce court decisions, whether or not their communities agreed with them. The white mob in Mansfield zeroed in on the weak spot in that scenario and provided a blueprint for other white southerners who were committed to massive resistance to integration. In other words, Tarrant County was every bit the proving ground for segregationist massive resistance that places like the Mississippi Delta, Little Rock, and Birmingham were. We should think of it in the same terms.[44]

Floyd Moody had agreed to be a plaintiff in the suit only reluctantly, and it was his life that would have been on the line had Davis pushed the matter on the grounds of Mansfield High School. He was conflicted. Moody had made many friends at Terrell High School. He liked many of his teachers and felt supported by the administration. He also knew how unwanted he would be at Mansfield High School. But he understood from his conversations with T. M. Moody, his father, and Clifford Davis that extremely important principles were at stake, so he agreed to fight to desegregate Mansfield High School—only to see the elected officials who were sworn to uphold the Constitution decide that his rights did not count for much. He was not conscious at the time of all the high-level machinations surrounding his case, but reflecting on

Tarrant County sheriff Harlon O. Wright, displaying an effigy from the Mansfield High School anti-integration protest, 1956. Photo courtesy of the Fort Worth Star-Telegram Collection, Special Collections, University of Texas at Arlington Libraries.

it later, he said, "What really bothered me was that President Eisenhower didn't do anything about it." He knew then that "nobody was coming to help us out," and he was not the only one who came to that conclusion. The Mansfield crisis crushed any possibility of local organizing.[45]

Looking back from 2015, Davis viewed the glass as half full. He said, "The importance of it was that we did get a federal court in Texas saying, 'You must integrate,' even though we did not get immediate follow-up results." But he acknowledged,

"We did have a bad precedent because the mob's gathering [proved that it] could discourage integration."[46] In fact, the reaction to the Mansfield crisis was devastating for the NAACP state conference and for African Americans throughout Texas.

Faced with the prospect of fighting NAACP-sponsored desegregation cases throughout the state, Governor Shivers and Attorney General John Ben Shepperd brought the power of the state crashing down upon the NAACP and the lawyers, including Davis, who had brought the suits. The state legislature had already embarked on a "Kill the NAACP" initiative led by Representative Joe Pool, from a district just east of Mansfield.[47] The state charged the lawyers and the NAACP itself with barratry (persistent pursuit of groundless litigation) and tax fraud. That fall, a state trooper, a Texas Ranger, and a deputy sheriff showed up in Davis's modest downtown Fort Worth office to serve a civil subpoena against Davis and search for *Jackson*-related papers. As he noted, that meant the state sent more lawmen to raid his law office than it had sent to control the mob in Mansfield.[48]

Shepperd obtained an injunction in October 1956 that prohibited the NAACP from operating in the state and kept the organization tied up in court for a year. In addition to harming the lawyers' ability to make a living, the gambit drained the NAACP state conference of resources and prevented it from capitalizing on the victory in *Jackson v. Rawdon*, thereby ensuring that Texas schools would remain segregated by race.[49] With the NAACP in crisis, African Americans' best mechanism for community organizing disappeared. A few local chapters throughout the state weathered the storm only because they coupled huge membership numbers with dynamic, creative leadership. Dallas provided one of the best examples: Juanita Craft, who had done much to build the organization as an employee of the state conference, concentrated her efforts on the Dallas branch's youth council and turned it into a direct-action dynamo. But Fort Worth's chapter fizzled, and Mansfield's died on the vine.[50]

Desegregating Fort Worth Neighborhoods

While whites were rioting in Mansfield, Lloyd Austin, a Black World War II veteran, purchased and moved into a house at 209 North Judkins Street in the Riverside neighborhood of Fort Worth. Lawrence Peters, an African American, had moved into a house on an adjacent block, and whites had bombed his car in 1954. The Peters family nonetheless stayed, and other African Americans bought homes on his block, but Austin's white neighbors decided that they could not tolerate his family's presence.[51]

Hundreds of white men, women, and children—some from the neighborhood but many others from outside it—gathered at Riverside Elementary School on Sunday September 2, 1956, where E. G. Brown, the leader of a Riverside neighborhood group, urged a show of force. Brown had surely been emboldened by the scene in Mansfield. He claimed not to want violence, but he encouraged the attendees to march outside Austin's home on the attractive, tree-lined street. Others encouraged more aggressive behavior. Members of the local Citizens' Council passed out literature. George Seaman, a former member of the Fort Worth City Council, advocated

White mob at the home of Lloyd Austin, Fort Worth, 1956. Photo courtesy of the Fort Worth Star-Telegram Collection, Special Collections, University of Texas at Arlington Libraries.

a tried-and-true Citizens' Council tactic when he urged the crowd to ratchet up economic pressure on the family: if they could get Austin and his wife fired from their jobs, the Austins would default on their mortgage and have to leave the neighborhood. Jack Lamont, a white resident of the nearby Diamond Hill neighborhood, and others made signs with violent messages. Others called for whites to hang Negroes like Austin who stepped over the Jim Crow line.[52]

Chanting "N---er get out!" the crowd from the elementary school marched to 209 North Judkins and gathered on the sidewalk in front of the house. A friend of Austin's made a show of walking from the home to a nearby car, retrieving two rifles from the trunk, and returning to the house. A white woman from the neighborhood, full of liquid courage, banged on his door and goaded the crowd: "One n---er man and all of y'all, and y'all can't make him move?" The police arrived and spoke to Brown, who offered to purchase the home, and Austin, who said he had no plans to sell or leave. According to Austin, he informed the police that he had guns in the house and knew how to use them. The police told him that he could not shoot anyone on the sidewalk, but if anyone came into the yard, he could do whatever he had a legal right to do in order protect his home and property.[53]

At some point in the evening a few dozen teenage boys from Polytechnic High School arrived. They hung an effigy of a Black man from a tree in Austin's front yard and began throwing rocks and Coke bottles at the house. When they broke several

White youths with racist signs at the protest near Lloyd Austin's home, Fort Worth, 1956. Photo courtesy of the Fort Worth Star-Telegram Collection, Special Collections, University of Texas at Arlington Libraries.

upstairs windows, Austin fired back with his rifle. No one was injured, but the blast damaged a car parked in front of the house. The police returned and finally dispersed the crowd. Fort Worth television station WBAP provided a riveting account of the conflict on its evening newscast, then segued into a story on the Mansfield school board's successful petition for a stay to the federal court order compelling the deseg-regation of the high school. The sight of the dramatic images of the effigy on North Judkins, followed closely by shots of the effigies on the Mansfield High building and atop its flagpole, which were still there when the WBAP news crew filmed on Sun-day, suggested that whites in Fort Worth had been taking notes from the mob in Mansfield. Chief of Police Cato Hightower made a show of force over the next week, blockading North Judkins Street and posting as many as ten policemen at a time on either end of the block to prevent the crowd from re-forming, and the neighborhood returned to an uneasy peace.[54]

The Continuing Fight for Integrated Schools

The Fort Worth NAACP chapter formed an education committee at the beginning of the 1955 school year and asked the school board and Superintendent Joe P. Moore to draw up plans for district-wide desegregation. Moore met with the committee to consider the request, but he and the board would agree to nothing more than further study. The committee members were persistent, however. They remained engaged with the school board and systematically encouraged African American parents to attempt to enroll their children in "schools of their choice" in hopes of chipping away at Jim Crow.[55]

As noted earlier, Black students in the 1950s traveled from as far away as Weatherford, Grapevine, Mansfield, and parts in between to attend I. M. Terrell High School. But the Fort Worth ISD embarked on a building boom as the *Brown* case worked its way through the federal courts. Just as the US Supreme Court found separate-but-equal school systems unconstitutional, district leaders increased the number of segregated high schools to which African Americans had access, in hope of maintaining the fiction that they were providing equal educational opportunities. By 1960, African Americans could attend the brand-new Como High School in western Fort Worth, Paul Lawrence Dunbar High School to the east, and Milton L. Kirkpatrick High School in North Fort Worth, in addition to I. M. Terrell.[56]

The communities around Como, Dunbar, and Kirkpatrick quickly became intensely proud of them, but it bears repeating that the separate schools were never equal. In comparison with their white counterparts, the Fort Worth ISD consistently spent less per pupil on instruction at Black schools, less on transportation to those schools, less on the maintenance of the school buildings, and less on the salaries of Black teachers and school administrators. Black families supported their schools as best they could, but they also continued to challenge segregation: throughout the late 1950s, Black parents attempted to enroll their children in "white" schools that were closer to their homes than the "Black" ones they were forced to attend. One such parent was Technical Sergeant Weirleis Flax Sr., an airman at Carswell Air Force Base in Northwest Fort Worth. Flax's children had attended integrated service-provided schools at other bases where he had served, but Carswell did not provide one. When Flax tried to enroll his daughter at the school nearest the base, he was informed that Fort Worth ISD regulations prevented Blacks from attending school with whites, so she would have to go to Como Elementary, which was twice as far from their home. Along with another African American parent, Herbert Teal, and with Clifford Davis as their attorney, he filed a class-action suit (styled *Flax v. Potts*) in 1962 on behalf of all the African American families in the school district.[57]

A series of federal courts found the Fort Worth ISD's segregation regulations unconstitutional, but the school district delayed full implementation for over a decade, and the district remained under court supervision until 1992. *Flax* and the other federal court decisions that followed from *Brown* provided a mixed blessing (at best) for Black and Brown families in Tarrant County. Just as the threat of federal action after *Brown* had encouraged the Fort Worth school board to open more schools for African Americans on terms that were advantageous to whites, the implementation of desegregation orders likewise proceeded on white terms.[58]

Remarkably, in the early 1970s the district complied with the letter, though not the spirit, of the courts' desegregation orders by closing three of the four African American high schools, leaving only Dunbar on the East Side. It was especially difficult for African Americans to swallow the decision to close the venerable I. M. Terrell. African American students were dispersed to integrate previously all-white schools, but very few whites ever attended Dunbar. African American teachers and administrators either went to work with white colleagues who tended not to want them around, teaching white students who tended not to respect them, or lost their jobs.[59]

All the burdens of desegregation fell on African Americans. Estrus Tucker was born in 1954, two months before the US Supreme Court announced its original *Brown* decision, but he did not attend an integrated school until Como High School closed after his junior year and he transferred to Western Hills High School as a senior. Tucker and his classmates had a relationship with Como that was "woven into our identity, who we saw ourselves as." Learning that Como would close just weeks before the beginning of the 1972 school year "felt like being orphaned," he said. He had followed the *Flax* case and the ways that Fort Worth officials delayed integration and then implemented it by destroying cherished Black institutions. "As a student, as a seventeen-year-old, it felt disrespectful. It felt like they definitely could [not] care less about the quality of our education, let alone our overall well-being," he said. There were no public hearings on the plan to close Como, Kirkpatrick, and Terrell, so Black families like his had no chance to weigh in on the decision, much less oppose it. "It was clear that they would rather close those schools than bring equity with resources and bus white students into Black communities. That didn't seem to be an option for them," Tucker concluded.[60]

Tucker had been active in the National Honor Society at Como, but while he found white teachers and classmates at Western Hills were eager to invite students like him to join the football, basketball, and track teams, he was never even informed of National Honor Society meetings at his new school. The entire experience, he said, taught him a lot about "the quality and the integrity of the district and our local leaders."[61]

While Fort Worth ISD was dragging its feet and desegregating its schools in a way designed to inconvenience white families minimally and African American families maximally, it also had to contend with a new wave of Mexican American activism. Rufino Mendoza Sr. chaired the Mexican American Educational Advisory Council (MAEAC), a group of World War II–generation and Chicano/a-generation advocates who pressed the school district throughout the 1970s to hire more Mexican Americans, offer more bilingual instruction, and demonstrate more respect for their community and their children's needs. In 1971 the federal judge who oversaw the implementation of the ruling that desegregated Fort Worth's schools allowed MAEAC to join as plaintiff in the ongoing *Flax v. Potts* litigation. He empowered a Citizens Advisory Committee, chosen by the members of the school board, the original parties to the suit, and MAEAC, to hold public hearings and come up with a triethnic integration plan. The judge approved that plan, one of the most democratically arrived at policies of its kind in Fort Worth's history, in 1983.[62]Desegregation proceeded similarly in Mansfield, which finally agreed to desegregate only after President Lyndon Johnson signed the 1964 Civil Rights Act into law. As was almost always the case throughout the United States, African American students, teachers, and administrators bore the brunt of the difficult desegregation process. Brenda Norwood, a senior who transferred against her wishes from I. M. Terrell to Mansfield High School for the 1965–1966 school year, said, "Knowing that we weren't wanted here, it was terrible." The teachers at Mansfield High let it be known that they were "not very pleased," and the white students told their new classmates "they did not want us in the school."[63] The school board closed the all-Black Willie Brown School and laid off all the teachers rather than have them teach white children.

"I graduated in spite of it," Norwood said. She was working at the cafeteria at the University of Texas at Arlington, among other odd jobs, in the late 1960s when a school official visited her home and recruited her to work for the Mansfield ISD as a special education aide. Flattered, she agreed to give it a try. Norwood found that she loved the work—so much so that for much of the 1970s, while working as an aide and supporting a family, she commuted to Texas Woman's University in Denton at night to work on the degree that would allow her to become a science teacher. In the midst of this, she learned that she had been hired as a token. "The reason why he really wanted me to come [was] because there was no Blacks in the school system at all," she said. "Not one Black teacher. . . . Mansfield would have lost their federal money if they had not had any Black [employees] in the school system, [so] he came out and asked me and I went. But I found out later why."[64] Norwood made tremendous sacrifices to become a teacher and enter the middle class. Unfortunately, that route was closed to other African Americans, even those with proven experience from the segregation era.

African American Political Organizing

In addition to the school-desegregation battles, Clifford Davis fought to help Black home buyers desegregate previously all-white neighborhoods and to create single-member districts for the Fort Worth City Council and school board. Breaking into the political structure had long been a priority for Black activists, but it was all but impossible for them to win at-large elections in the majority-white city. (Not completely impossible: Dr. Edward Guinn won an at-large seat on the city council in 1967. He was succeeded in 1971 by Leonard Briscoe, an African American real estate developer with friends in the white business establishment, but their victories were exceptions to the general rule.) In addition to democratizing local government, they believed that direct representation would ensure better city services and provide access to municipal jobs.

Improved city services in Black areas had long been a goal of Black activists. George D. Flemmings, president of the local NAACP branch, announced in 1952 the group's intention to "seek a bigger share of the city services and facilities." He said, "The City Council has refused to provide us a fair share of street improvements, garbage service and other facilities and has refused to appoint Negro policemen."[65] The campaign for single-member districts, which Mexican Americans joined and which Davis and others fought in the courts, the state legislature, and—in the true Fort Worth Way—smoke-filled backrooms, finally came to fruition in 1977 with an agreement with the city. Davis and his allies made sure to maximize Black representation by splitting the major centers of the African American population into separate districts. Mexican Americans were not as fortunate: though they have traditionally made up significant pockets of population throughout the city, Mexican

American candidates have been able to win only one seat on the city council, the one representing the North Side, and have fared little better in school board elections.[66]

Fort Worth also had its share of Black radicals during the civil rights era. The United Front, a group of roughly college-age Blacks who had been influenced by Malcolm X and the Black Panthers, was especially active in the late 1960s and early 1970s and may have been the most colorful and consequential of the radical organizations. "There were eight or nine of them [in the organization], but like the Black Panthers, they made [whites] think there were thousands of them," Bob Ray Sanders said. "This city was scared. It was really scared."[67]

Roy C. Brooks, the son of the Black activist physician Marion J. "Doc" Brooks and a longtime public servant himself, remembered, "It was an activist organization of young people whose goal was to get equal rights. One of the things that they pushed for was integration of the newsrooms at the *Star-Telegram* and the various TV and radio outlets, and jobs at the City of Fort Worth. Back during that time, a Black man couldn't even [get hired to] drive a garbage truck . . . They were much more confrontational, but not particularly violent. They would get in the cops' faces, and not back down."[68] Marjorie Crenshaw, a Fort Worth teacher, agreed. "Now they [the United Front] were belligerent, but they were a little bit younger, that's the reason they were like that. And they would speak out, and boy, the white folks didn't like them at all, because that was trouble," she said. "It's a funny thing: it's like how people feel about Malcolm X. They were more of that Malcolm X type, and whatever they thought came out. . . . I don't think the powers that be liked them too well because they spoke truth and would try to do things to resist." According to Crenshaw, African Americans preferred other forms of activism and ignored the group: "They were ostracized; there was no support, even though they were trying."[69]

"Doc" Brooks engaged in all sorts of political activism, from voter registration to more radical pursuits, including mentoring the United Front. Vivian Wells, a Fort Worth Realtor and political activist who also worked as Clifford Davis's secretary during the 1950s, said of Brooks, "He was *the* leader in the Black community. Marion J. Brooks was the most respected leader in the Black community . . . and he was a part of everything. He'd close his office and go downtown and picket." Brooks could afford to take on leadership of various campaigns because he did not depend on whites for an income.[70]

Mexican American Political Organizing

Mexican Americans have been politically active in appreciable numbers in Fort Worth at least since the immediate post–World War II era. They founded a chapter of the American GI Forum in 1948, and the League of United Latin American Citizens (LULAC), the Raza Unida Party, the Political Association of Spanish-Speaking Organizations (PASO), the Brown Berets, and the Mexican American Youth Organization (MAYO) all had active chapters in the city.

Community advocates of the World War II generation, including Sam Garcia, Gilbert Garcia, Jesse Sandoval, and Rufino Mendoza Sr., worked for Mexican American civil rights and greater educational and employment opportunities, and encouraged greater civic participation among Mexican Americans in Fort Worth. Garcia in particular planted seeds in the early 1960s that would flower later; working with the veteran African American organizer Erma LeRoy, he barnstormed the entire state of Texas to help local activists set up poll tax and voter registration drives. He and fellow World War II veterans had some success in Fort Worth in the 1960s and 1970s, as did activists of the Chicana/o generation, who tended to emphasize Chicano/a identity as a means to power. But throughout most of this period there were not enough raw numbers of Hispanic voters to mount major threats to the existing local political order.[71]

More than any other grassroots political activist, Pauline Gasca-Valenciano personified the long struggle for Chicano/a rights in Fort Worth and the many forms it has taken. Over a long career as a community organizer, she joined or supported just about every Mexican American civil rights or political organization in the area, including LULAC, the GI Forum, Viva Kennedy clubs, PASO, the Incorporated Mexican-American Government Employees labor union, and the United Farm Workers union. She helped organize lettuce and grape boycotts in Fort Worth and fasted alongside César Chávez, fought to desegregate public parks and schools, forced the city to devote more resources to Brown neighborhoods, and registered Mexican American voters and agitated for single-member districts. Widowed at a young age with four children to care for, she worked full time and devoted nearly as many hours in the week to political causes. Gasca-Valenciano refused to be bullied, and pushed back against acts of machismo she encountered in Chicano/a political organizations. She demanded that she be taken seriously, no matter her gender.[72] "I have the balls you lack," she told men whom she deemed too timid to follow her lead.[73]

Gasca-Valenciano decided she could be most effective by working from within the Democratic Party, and she did everything in her power to will into being a culture of civic and political engagement among Tarrant County Chicanos/as. Her father had followed politics and included her in conversations from a young age, and her fifth-grade teacher took her to see President Harry Truman when he visited Fort Worth. From then on, whenever a national politician made a trip to North Texas, she made a point of attending the speeches or rallies so that she could draw her own conclusions about the candidate and his ideas and determine for herself whether he might be worthy of her community's support.[74] She called the Viva Kennedy clubs that formed around JFK's 1960 campaign her "wake-up call," and she actively campaigned in 2016 for Hillary Clinton.[75]

When Mexican Americans finally had the numbers to influence local politics, they stepped into a sociopolitical milieu that Anglos and African Americans had created. There was little they could do to change the rules of that game, but their increasing numbers pointed toward eventual electoral success and political power. In 2000, 16.3 percent of Fort Worth's population was foreign born, and more than a quarter of residents spoke a language other than English at home.[76] In 2016, the US Census Bureau estimated that nearly 30 percent of the county's population identified as Hispanic and that Anglos, for the first time, were not a majority.[77]

Many Blacks who had sacrificed over generations to win basic respect for their rights as citizens and at least minimal political representation did not respond well to the political aspirations of Mexican Americans who arrived in the county after the

Eva Bonilla and Lee Saldívar at the Raza Unida Party District 12 office, Fort Worth, 1974. Photo courtesy of the Fort Worth Star-Telegram Collection, Special Collections, University of Texas at Arlington Libraries.

major civil rights battles of the 1960s had been won. (Clifford Davis arguably had a harder time with this than anyone.)[78] Politics is often a zero-sum game, particularly for minority groups that find themselves pitted against one another in competition for dwindling resources within a system created to serve the needs of white supremacy. It was certainly treated as a zero-sum game during the most recent rounds of redistricting, when Blacks held fast to city district maps that gave them comfortable control of two city council seats and at least that many seats on the school board, whereas Mexican Americans fought for rezoning that would allow them more representation. Yet across this period there have also been instances of successful Black-Brown coalition building.[79]

In 1955, the NAACP state conference of branches urged local chapters to seek opportunities to work with Mexican Americans and Anglos to desegregate Texas schools. That year they launched door-knocking campaigns to find potential African American, Mexican American, and Anglo supporters and potential plaintiffs in desegregation lawsuits, and they encouraged youth councils to welcome Mexican American and Anglo members.[80] Unfortunately, these goals tended to go unrealized in Tarrant County and throughout the state, but African American and Mexican American activists did collaborate locally when the national political winds shifted and gave them the idea that large-scale change was possible.

Working hand in hand in the late 1960s in Fort Worth's Community Action Agency with African American activists such as Viola Pitts and "Doc" Brooks on War on Poverty programs, Gasca-Valenciano said, "I was exposed to the best of the best" community organizers.[81] Using community block grants, she and her African American colleagues were able to bring multipurpose community centers to several Black and Brown neighborhoods. "We really supported one another," she said.[82] The city's Neighborhood Advisory Councils, with which Gasca-Valenciano worked in the 1970s and 1980s, had the effect of democratizing power and decentralizing decision making in Fort Worth, at least up to a point.[83]

Recent demographic changes—namely, the growth of the Mexican American population, which some African American communities have experienced as a "takeover," and contemporaneous white flight from within the Fort Worth city limits—have provided challenges, but also opportunities, for multiethnic coalition building. According to Estrus Tucker, the student who desegregated Western Hills High School and became a community organizer, over the past few decades Black-Brown coalitions have been "hopeful but struggling" among "people who have the capacity and the competency to see the intersection of our issues and to be able to frame them in a way that it's not [solely] Black or Brown." In particular, ethnic tensions can be subsumed by economic ones: "Far more than the racial politics of Black and Brown, it has to do with class and economic interests and equity."[84]

The Polytechnic Heights ("Poly") neighborhood of East Fort Worth provides a good example. Tucker was a leading organizer for Liberation Community, a compassionate inner-city ministry project in Poly in the 1980s. He learned that the ethnic diversity within the neighborhood made coalition building seem much more organic. "Our model for civic engagement and organizing was grassroots, from the ground up, and on the ground was Black, Brown, and white residents," he said. "It made sense that we had to cultivate an appreciation for respect and cooperation across racial lines," because that was the neighborhood residents' lived reality. "There's something about being neighbors," he continued. "When you live in the same area, that's a beautiful framework—better than politics. It's more of a foundation. In politics, the political season comes, then there's relational trust already established. It's not just with a political agenda."[85]

African Americans had desegregated Poly neighborhoods in the 1960s, and Tucker estimated that Poly's total population had become evenly divided among Anglos, African Americans, and Mexican Americans by the 1980s. By the late 1990s, the area's Hispanic population had roughly doubled, and by 2005 he reckoned that Poly was 75 percent Hispanic, 15 percent African American, and 10 percent Anglo. The district continued to be represented by African Americans on the city council and the school board, which caused heartburn for Mexican Americans who longed for more representation. The coalition-organizing Liberation Community at least provided productive spaces for community members to discuss, even if not resolve, those tensions.[86]

The North Side offered additional opportunities for coalition, as well as for conflict, simply because it has long had a large number of both Mexican American and African American residents. The stockyards and meatpacking plants drew wave after wave of immigrants. A visitor to the area at the turn of the twentieth century could have heard workers and their families speaking Russian, Czech, German, Greek, Ukrainian, Spanish, Polish, or one of a half dozen other languages. The Black population there was large enough by the 1950s to support an all-Black high school, Kirkpatrick, but those numbers began to dwindle after the meatpackers closed in 1971. As in other Fort Worth neighborhoods, African Americans and Mexican Americans there have worked together as members of labor unions, PTAs, and other nongovernmental organizations, but city elections have tended to pit the groups against each other.[87]

Tucker thought that the best model for coalition building could be found in the experiences of the African American and Hispanic Chambers of Commerce. As president and CEO of the Black chamber in the 1990s, he found a kindred spirit in David Navarette, his counterpart at the Hispanic chamber. "We connected in a way. We saw common interests, we both were trying to continue a tradition of economic development with equity, to get a fair share of the pie from the City of Fort Worth," he said. "We collaborated a lot with the Fort Worth chamber and the City of Fort Worth for contractor opportunities. We found value in having our own meetings, just the two of us, just wanting to see how a greater collaboration between the two chambers, what kind of impact that would have. That cultivated some seeds that are still [growing] today." Tucker conceded that "getting the two chambers to become a Black-Brown coalition was difficult from an economic development perspective, but they are doing a lot of things that are well aligned, that are bearing fruit in the ways that city-contractor and vending opportunities are working now."

Time will tell, but at this writing an emerging coalition between groups concerned with the overpolicing of both Black and Brown communities provides reason for hope. Cooperation among Black Lives Matter activists and United Fort Worth, an organization formed in 2017 to encourage the City of Fort Worth to join a lawsuit against SB 4, the state law that gives local police officers the right to request proof of immigration status from anyone they detain, effectively turning them into ICE agents, could bear more fruit.[88]

The 2010 US Census found that more than half of Tarrant County residents were Anglo. It will be the last to do so. A 2016 update estimated that the figure had fallen to 47.9 percent; the trend suggests that it will be closer to 40 percent in the 2020 census. Non-Hispanic whites will no longer be able to dominate Tarrant County and Fort Worth city politics through sheer numerical advantage, but the systems they created to support their social and political interests will not change as quickly as the county's demographics have. Indeed, more than fifty years after the civil rights revolution of the 1960s, important aspects of the systems still reflect Jim Crow and Juan Crow power relationships. Mexican Americans, African Americans, and Anglo allies will have to find creative ways to replace these systems with truly multiethnic, multiracial democratic institutions that are worthy of Tarrant County's people. Fortunately, they can look for inspiration to a handful of past movements that were able to overcome ethnic divisions and effect change.[89]

CHAPTER 11

CIVIL RIGHTS IN THE "CITY OF HATE":
Black and Brown Organizing against
Police Brutality in Dallas

KATHERINE BYNUM

In the early-morning hours of July 23, 1973, Dallas police officer Roy Arnold saw three Mexican American youths running away from a filling station located in the Little Mexico barrio, just north of downtown.[1] Suspecting a burglary, Arnold called for backup and met Officer Darrell Cain at the home of twelve-year-old Santos Rodríguez and his thirteen-year-old brother David, who, according to the officers, were known to cause trouble in the neighborhood. Without a warrant, Cain and Arnold barged into their home and wrestled the two sleeping youngsters from their beds, ordering them into the front and backseats of the police car. Cain drove the youngsters to the scene of the alleged crime and demanded that the young boys confess their involvement. According to Cain, he opened the chamber of his gun, took the bullets out, and closed it. He put the gun up to Santos's forehead and told him to tell the truth. "Who was the other boy?" Cain demanded to know. "Who was with you?" Santos denied any involvement, and Cain pulled the trigger. The gun clicked and a startled Santos froze, paralyzed by fear. "Tell the truth, hombre," Arnold said. "Or this time he's going to shoot you." Cain pulled the trigger again; the gun fired and the car filled with smoke. As the haze began to subside, David saw the blood flowing from Santos's head.[2]

The death of Santos Rodríguez caused outrage in the city's Mexican American and African American communities. To protest the shooting, several hundred Black and Brown activists gathered on July 28, 1973, at Kennedy Memorial Plaza, where the protesters marched peacefully on Main Street toward Dallas City Hall. "It was a family event," stated René Martínez, one of the organizers of the march. "A lot of women and children and people that I knew [were in attendance]."[3] About an hour later, a substantially younger crowd joined the demonstration, and the enthusiastic protesters grew more agitated and vocal because of the large police presence on the sidelines.[4] "Kill the pigs! Kill the pigs!" wailed a woman toward the Dallas Police Department (DPD). She climbed on top of a squad car and repeated her chants. "The police killed my son! Kill the pigs!" The crowd suddenly erupted in anger. Men and women hurled bottles at officers and knocked over a police motorcycle, causing it to burst into flames. Some kicked out windows of department stores, looted jewelry and shoes from the Neiman-Marcus department store, and overturned street newspaper racks.[5] Though Dallas had managed to avoid the kinds of urban uprisings that cities

Protesters carrying the Mexican flag at the March of Justice for Santos Rodríguez, 1973. Photo courtesy of Andy Hanson Photographs and Papers, DeGolyer Library, Southern Methodist University, Dallas.

like Chicago, Detroit, and Newark experienced in the previous decade, the city did not escape the destructive outburst on that hot summer day.

Cain was arrested and charged with murder with malice. During his trial, he admitted to pointing the .357 Magnum at Santos's head, but claimed the shooting was accidental.[6] His defense attorneys portrayed Cain as an all-American boy who used poor judgment when interrogating the Rodríguez brothers. Those who knew him, however, said that Cain had earned a reputation as a brute on his beat. In April 1970, more than three years before Santos's death, Cain shot and killed eighteen-year-old Michael Morehead, an African American resident of East Dallas, who had fled police with his older brother after stealing food from a local restaurant. Cain opened fire as the brothers ran away, hitting Morehead in the back. Witnesses claimed that Cain continued to shoot Morehead as he lay wounded on the ground, pleading for his life. The Dallas Police Department, the FBI, and the Greater Dallas Community Relations Commission investigated the circumstances surrounding Morehead's death, but ultimately Cain and his partner, Jeffrey Kirksey, were no-billed on murder charges by the grand jury.[7] For the murder of Santos Rodríguez, however, Cain was found guilty. He was sentenced to five years in prison.[8]

The reaction to Santos's death reveals the frustration of Black and Brown activists who refused to silently bear the abuses of the Dallas Police Department. Charges of police misconduct and brutality occurred unabated throughout the twentieth cen-

Young protester with a sign linking the murders of Michael Morehead and Santos Rodríguez with Dallas police officer Darrell Cain, 1973. Photo courtesy of the Fort Worth Star-Telegram Collection, Special Collections, University of Texas at Arlington Libraries.

tury in the city's communities of color. Countless Mexican American and African American residents reported abuses against local law enforcement, but each violation resulted in little to no change within the Dallas Police Department. The outburst downtown in 1973 was the tipping point in relations between people of color and the DPD and city government, both of which refused to hold officers accountable and did little to investigate misconduct thoroughly. Conflicts between the police force and the city's Black and Brown residents escalated so much that the Associated Press declared Dallas the number one city for police shootings in the nation in 1987. According to the report, the department's officers killed people at a rate of 1.03 per 100,000 residents, which came to a staggering total, since Dallas was the ninth-largest city in the United States.[9]

The uprising in downtown Dallas in 1973 tells only one facet of a much larger story. Underneath the anger and hostility that exploded downtown on July 28 lay a rich and dynamic history of Black and Brown civil rights organizing. The Black and Brown freedom struggles, which had largely run along parallel lines for decades, intersected in the 1970s on the shared issue of police brutality. After a series of police shootings of Mexican Americans and African Americans in the city, the two populations and their white allies joined forces and rallied against the DPD, targeting the discriminatory policies that allowed such abuses to continue. They formed what newspapers called a "triumvirate alliance," in which the Black Panther Party, the Brown Berets, and the Bois d'Arc Patriots, a white working-class organization, marched in the streets and demonstrated in the chambers of city hall, challenging the forces of class and racial antagonism. As the years wore on, however, and as many of the direct-action protests failed to provide substantive results, many Black and Brown activists worked to restructure the political system, which had excluded communities of color and white working-class residents for decades. Ending police misconduct by establishing a police review board with investigative and subpoena powers remained a central goal for the women and men who entered the political system at the municipal level.

The Black Freedom Struggle in Dallas

At the turn of the twentieth century, African Americans were targeted by a series of discriminatory laws designed to keep them in a permanent state of second-class citizenship. In 1903, the Texas Legislature passed the Terrell Election Laws, which imposed poll taxes, literacy tests, and other mechanisms of disfranchisement to prevent most African Americans from voting. Later, state officials enacted the white primary, effectively barring African Americans from voting in all primary elections — the only elections that mattered in a single-party state like Texas — because of the color of their skin.[10] The City of Dallas likewise passed several discriminatory ordinances. In 1907, Dallas revised its charter and established segregation of the races in all aspects of city life, including public schools, housing, and recreation.[11] Because of such policies, African Americans in Dallas lacked access to adequate housing, jobs, and schools.

White Dallasites used terror and violence to keep African Americans in their purported place. In 1910, a white lynch mob murdered Allen Brooks, an African American man accused of assaulting a white girl, and hanged him from a telephone pole downtown on Akard and Main Streets.[12] Little distinguished vigilantism from formal law enforcement during the 1920s, when the reinvigorated Ku Klux Klan made Texas a stronghold for its political message.[13] The Dallas Klan chapter grew rapidly, enacting revenge upon African Americans who crossed the color line. On April 1, 1921, Klansmen abducted Alexander Johnson, a Black bellhop, took him to the Trinity River bottom, and beat him before burning "KKK" on his forehead with acid. They accused Johnson of sexual involvement with white women—one of the worst offenses, in the Klan's eyes, for African Americans to commit. Despite a *Dallas Times-Herald* reporter witnessing the entire scene, law enforcement made no arrests—unsurprisingly, since the Dallas County sheriff, deputy sheriff, chief of police, and nearly all of Dallas's police officers were Klansmen. The collaboration between white vigilantism and formal law enforcement greatly strengthened the forces of white supremacy.

Despite such segregation, disfranchisement, and terrorism, African Americans developed numerous civil rights organizations to combat the injustices of Jim Crow. In 1926, Black middle-class businessmen formed the Negro Chamber of Commerce. Though largely ineffectual in its first few years, the chamber received a boost when it hired A. Maceo Smith as executive secretary in 1932. Under Smith's leadership, the Negro Chamber worked to improve Black residents' living standards, which were generally substandard. African American neighborhoods in Dallas lacked paved streets, decent housing, access to good jobs, electoral participation in municipal elections, and an unbiased police force. Though these issues existed well before the 1930s, the Great Depression exacerbated their poor living conditions.[14]

Smith was also instrumental in the development of the Progressive Voters League (PVL), a Black voting organization created in 1936 to challenge the Citizens Charter Association (CCA). A civic-business organization run by Dallas's elite, the CCA had dominated city elections since its founding in 1930, when it amended the city charter to require all elections to be nonpartisan and conducted at-large—which all but eliminated the influence of Black and Brown communities in local elections. Nonetheless, the PVL established an African American voting bloc, convincing more than seven thousand African Americans to register to vote. The bloc influenced the outcome of the 1937 municipal election by forcing white civic associations to bargain with a unified Black electorate.[15] The PVL's influence, however, was short-lived. By 1939, city elections had swung back in favor of the CCA after it aligned itself with the Dallas Citizens Council (DCC), an organization formed in 1937 by R. L. Thornton, a former Klan member and president of the Dallas Chamber of Commerce who became Dallas's mayor in 1953.[16] Together, the CCA and the DCC solidified corporate control over the Dallas political arena, dominating local elections for decades.

Smith also helped rejuvenate the Dallas chapter of the National Association for the Advancement of Colored People (NAACP). Organized in 1918, the chapter had lain dormant for years after being intimidated out of existence when the Klan-dominated police department demanded an officer be present at any organizational meeting.[17] Smith, Juanita Craft, and George F. Porter reorganized the Dallas NAACP chapter in 1936 and affiliated it with the Texas State Conference of

Branches, which helped overturn the white primary in the 1944 US Supreme Court decision in *Smith v. Allwright* and aided in the desegregation case against the University of Texas Law School in the Court's *Sweatt v. Painter* decision in 1950.[18] The NAACP's local legal counsel integrated grand and petit juries, raised Black teachers' salaries to the level of whites', and organized the NAACP Youth Council under the direction of Craft, who led many of the desegregation campaigns in the 1950s and 1960s. In 1955, following the Supreme Court's *Brown v. Board of Education* decision, the Dallas NAACP filed a lawsuit against the Dallas Independent School District, officially beginning the school-desegregation process. The same year, Craft and the Youth Council engaged in nonviolent direct-action campaigns, including protests at the Melba Movie Theater downtown, which refused to sell tickets to Black customers, and the State Fair of Texas, for its segregated "Negro Achievement Day," the only day African Americans could attend.[19]

The direct-action protests led by the local NAACP threatened the Dallas establishment. In the 1950s, city leaders became increasingly preoccupied with the city's image as hundreds of thousands of transplants moved to the burgeoning metropolis. As capital flooded into the city, civic leaders played on the city's mythical origin story—that Dallas had no reason to exist except for the hard work and bootstrap mentality of white professionals. They called the philosophy the "Dallas way," a civic mystique that had existed for decades in the local lexicon but reemerged with a vengeance in the postwar era.[20] Racial violence threatened to tarnish Dallas's reputation. Between 1950 and 1951, the city was rocked by racially motivated house bombings as white residents unleashed a campaign of terrorism against Black home buyers for moving into all-white neighborhoods in South Dallas. More than a dozen bombings shook the city, and white city leaders and the Dallas Police Department often blamed Black home buyers for causing the violence.[21] The picketing and protesting led by the NAACP in the mid-1950s, white leaders reasoned, could incite more white reactionary violence, crippling future business endeavors. Fearing bad publicity, Mayor R. L. Thornton (who was also president of the Dallas Citizens Council) arranged several meetings with Craft and George Allen, a Black businessman, to discuss plans to desegregate. In one meeting, Allen threatened a Black boycott of the downtown city bus system. Following the Montgomery bus boycott in 1955, Mayor Thornton decided to end segregation policies on city buses immediately.[22]

Desegregating city buses was an easy concession for white civic leaders. The threatened boycott had the potential of not only crippling the entire public transit system but also bringing unwanted negative publicity. The NAACP's continued efforts to desegregate public schools, on the other hand, led white local and state politicians to pursue a permanent injunction against the organization. As the historian Marvin Dulaney has shown, the Dallas NAACP's lawsuit against the school board in 1955 precipitated action by white Texans to fight the Supreme Court's order in *Brown* to desegregate public schools.[23] In 1956, Texas attorney general John Ben Shepperd opened an official investigation into the Texas State Conference and filed a temporary restraining order prohibiting the NAACP from "doing business in the state." Shepperd then filed a lawsuit charging the NAACP with inspiring racial unrest, failing to pay state taxes, and illegally initiating litigation.[24] In *State of Texas v. The National Association for the Advancement of Colored People et al.*, state district judge

Otis T. Dunagan, in Tyler, placed the Texas NAACP under a permanent injunction in the state, barring the organization from operating in Texas altogether. The injunction effectively ended desegregation efforts across the city, and the organization took more than three years to recover.[25]

By 1960, the Citizens Charter Association and the Dallas Citizens Council were back in control of city politics and had managed to neutralize Black organizing in the process. But as the sit-in movement made its way across the South in early 1960, the DCC grew nervous and decided to preempt similar demonstrations. In March, DCC leaders called together a group of seven African American civic leaders and seven white leaders. Together, they formed the Council of 14, and the biracial group worked behind closed doors to negotiate how to manage the desegregation of restaurants, downtown department stores, movie theaters, and schools.[26]

Despite the managed desegregation plan, the committee could not prevent all African Americans from nonviolently protesting. On April 30, two ministers, one Black and one white, entered S. H. Kress and H. L. Green stores and asked to be served. Though the two were served without incident, the stores continued their policy of racial segregation and refused to serve Black customers at their lunch counters going forward.[27] Following the failed sit-in, other activists in Dallas organized more desegregation campaigns. In December 1960, the Reverend Earl Allen, who later formed the Dallas chapter of the Congress of Racial Equality (CORE), demonstrated at the Greyhound bus station and later at the University Drug Store outside Southern Methodist University.[28] Throughout 1962 and 1963, the Reverend H. Rhett James of the Dallas NAACP organized a series of boycotts against downtown businesses. He later joined forces with Clarence Broadnax, who helped organize a twenty-eight-day sit-in at the Piccadilly diner downtown, with Juanita Craft and the Reverend Allen. The largest demonstration occurred in March 1965 to protest the murder of the Reverend James Reeb, a white Unitarian minister who supported the civil rights movement in Selma, Alabama, and was killed there, and to encourage the passage of a national voting rights act.[29] Ultimately, the direct-action protests and the Council of 14 helped desegregate some aspects of city life, including lunch counters, swimming pools, and parks.

The majority of Dallas, however, remained segregated. White flight accelerated throughout the 1950s as Black residents continued to buy homes in South Dallas neighborhoods. Despite a court order in 1961 to desegregate the Dallas ISD, only eight district schools had admitted Black students by the end of 1962. The limited effects of the Civil Rights Act and the Voting Rights Act, along with the slow pace of managed desegregation, inspired several organizations outside the purview of the Committee of 14 to continue protesting. In 1967, a Dallas native named Ernest McMillan organized a local chapter of the Student Nonviolent Coordinating Committee (SNCC). By that time, the organization had moved toward Black Power philosophy—encouraging African Americans to control their own communities both politically and economically.[30] In 1968, SNCC (pronounced "snick") organized a boycott against the OK Supermarket, a local chain of grocery stores, in an effort to buy out white-owned businesses in South Dallas. As part of the boycott, McMillan and his fellow SNCC member Matthew Johnson led a "bottle smashing raid" in which twenty to thirty Black protesters filed into the supermarket and began breaking bottles of milk and throwing produce on the floor. The protest caused more than $200 in damage. McMillan and Johnson were promptly arrested and later sentenced to ten years in prison.[31]

SNCC's activism also led Dallas officials to use police harassment to disperse their activities. Fahim Minkah (formerly Fred Bell) and Charles Beasley organized the Kaka Tayari ("brother's ready" in Swahili), a police watch service that followed law enforcement officers in Black neighborhoods and took pictures when they made arrests. Despite their efforts, several members fell victim to harassment by law enforcement.[32] Members were arrested throughout 1968 and 1969, including Fahim Minkah, who was sentenced to six years in the federal penitentiary in Leavenworth, Kansas, for a bank robbery he did not commit. Minkah appealed his conviction and was released in October 1970 after spending more than two years in jail.[33] Police harassment forced other members into exile or jail. By 1969, the organization faced dissolution.

The remaining members of SNCC managed to stay afloat. In June 1969, they joined with Black college students at El Centro Community College to form a Dallas chapter of the National Committee to Combat Fascism (NCCF), an offshoot of the Black Panther Party. The Dallas NCCF adopted the Panthers' Ten Point Program, organizing free pest-control services and a free breakfast program for children.[34] After Michael Morehead's death in 1970, they joined forces with the Reverend Peter Johnson of the Southern Christian Leadership Conference (SCLC), who led a two-hour March Against Repression in downtown Dallas on May 24, 1970. A few months later, the NCCF and the SCLC organized a boycott of Safeway grocery stores as part of the SCLC's broader Operation Breadbasket.[35] Like SNCC, the Dallas NCCF chapter endured intense police harassment. Police manipulated tensions within the organization, and members formed opposing groups after suspecting that Curtis Gaines, the leader of the Dallas NCCF, was a police informant.[36] Law enforcement managed to splinter these Black Power groups.

The Black freedom struggle in Dallas spanned several decades and addressed the myriad issues of Jim Crow discrimination. Black activists applied a range of tactics—organizing as unified voting blocs, legal action, negotiation, protests, boycotts, and picket lines—to break the stronghold of white corporate control of city politics. But the structurally racist policies embedded in local government via the at-large election system and police harassment prevented African American activists from fully realizing their goals. By 1970, Black activists had begun adjusting their organizing strategies, allying themselves with another politically active racial group that also had routinely challenged the status quo. Black activists' alliance with Mexican American and Chicana/o activists signified a crucial turning point in the city's multiracial liberation struggle.

Dallas's Long Chicano/a Movement

Mexicanas/os across the American Southwest endured Juan Crow discrimination, which forced residents into certain jobs, forced them to live in segregated neighborhoods, and limited their access to political power, all of which made them vulnerable to state-sanctioned violence. Relatively few Mexicanas/os called Dallas home before 1900. The majority of ethnic Mexicans arrived in North Texas after the turn of the twentieth century. Beginning in 1910, the Mexican Revolution led to violence, starvation, and a lack of employment opportunities, providing the impetus for thousands to migrate to the Lone Star State; a small portion of them settled in Dallas.[37] As the Mexican population in Dallas grew, most of them resided in a small neighborhood (and former red-light district) known as Little Mexico or La Colonia north of downtown. Over time, as more Mexicanas/os settled in the area, the district became overcrowded, and more Mexicans were pushed into unincorporated West Dallas.[38]

Most Mexicans received menial wages and endured poor living conditions. Housing in the barrios was generally substandard. Some lived in houses made of scrap wood and tarpaper. Railroad workers often inhabited boxcars near the tracks on the fringe of Little Mexico. Tiny shotgun houses with small front porches lined the unpaved streets. Homes in both Little Mexico and West Dallas had few amenities or none. Few houses had hot water, nearly three-quarters of the residents lived without gas heating or indoor plumbing, and roughly 60 percent lived without electricity.[39] The congested and unsanitary living conditions exposed residents to a plethora of diseases. Exceptionally high rates of tuberculosis, typhus, and pellagra affected more people in Little Mexico than in anywhere else in the city. Between 1934 and 1936, for example, Little Mexico had the highest death rate in Dallas from tuberculosis, accounting for nearly 3.2 percent of deaths, although the Mexican American population of Dallas was around 2.3 percent. They also experienced high infant mortality rates—as high as 35 percent, compared with 9 percent for white residents.[40]

Mexican Americans were also subjected to segregation and discrimination in public accommodations. Mexicanos/as often saw "No Negroes, Mexicans or Dogs" signs outside restaurants. Francisco "Pancho" Medrano remembered that when he and his family traveled downtown to buy a hamburger, they were not allowed to sit inside the restaurant—forced instead to eat their meal on the hot pavement.[41] Some movie theaters, such as the Hippodrome Theater downtown, permitted Mexicans to attend only one day a week, while others, including the Majestic, forced Black and Brown patrons to sit upstairs in the balcony—what many called the "buzzards' roost" or the "peanut gallery."[42] Public transportation on the city's downtown trolley cars and, later, buses was also segregated—forcing many Mexican Americans to sit in the back. Discrimination affected Mexican residents in their own neighborhoods, particularly regarding the use of public parks. Pike Park, established in 1913 in the heart of Little Mexico, prohibited Mexican children from accessing its facilities, including the swimming pool.[43]

Despite such treatment, Mexican Americans engaged in extensive campaigns for social justice. According to the historian Mario T. García, the political climate of the Great Depression, World War II, and the Cold War helped generate a new wave of Mexican American community leaders. This "Mexican-American Generation," as García calls it, established numerous civil rights organizations. In 1929, Mexican Americans living in Corpus Christi, Texas, organized the League of United Latin American Citizens (LULAC), one of the most important civil rights organizations for Mexican Americans at that time.[44] Military service also fueled Mexican American activism. In 1948, Héctor P. García of Corpus Christi established the American GI Forum, a civil rights organization that pursued social-welfare benefits and rights for returning veterans. The GI Forum gained national attention when it protested a funeral home in Three Rivers, Texas, after the owner refused to bury Felix Longoria, a decorated Mexican American war hero.[45] Both the GI Forum and LULAC teamed up many times throughout the 1940s and 1950s, including to litigate the school-desegregation case *Delgado v. Bastrop ISD* (1948). In 1954, the United States Supreme Court ruled in favor of LULAC in *Hernandez v. Texas*. Essentially, the case protected Mexican Americans as a group under the Fourteenth Amendment.[46]

García characterizes this ascendancy of Mexican Americans in the political realm as part of a generational movement—namely, that first-generation Mexican Americans developed a hybrid identity in which they not only maintained ties to their traditional ethnic culture but also assimilated into Anglo-American society.[47] The prominent Martínez family best represents this model in Dallas. Miguel "Mike" Martínez, the patriarch, moved to Dallas from Mexico during the Mexican Revolution and began working in the service industry as a dishwasher and later as a waiter before starting El Fenix, a Tex-Mex restaurant, with his wife, Faustina. The Martínez family built the restaurant from the ground up, catering to the tastes of the barrio's ethnic Mexicans.[48] Over the decades, the eating establishment became popular with Anglo residents too. As their white clientele grew, the Martínez family implemented strict segregation policies—serving Mexican Americans away from white patrons and refusing service to African Americans entirely.[49] Adhering to segregation inspired by white-supremacist norms afforded the Martínez family the ability to assimilate into the dominant, Anglo society, and that acceptance opened the door for them to acquire political and economic power in Dallas. In 1969, for example, the Citizens Charter Association supported Anita Martínez, a mother and housewife who married into the Martínez family, in the city council elections.[50]

Few Mexicanas/os could reach such a position. The majority belonged to the working class, and the intersections of their identities did not allow them to benefit from whiteness as middle-class Mexican Americans did. Instead, they drew on their experiences as both working class and Brown. Francisco "Pancho" Medrano forged such a movement. He began his activism during World War II when he landed a job at an aircraft plant in Grand Prairie, where he organized the local chapter of the UAW and recruited African Americans and Mexican Americans for the union. Because of that activism, Pancho committed himself to the quest for social justice. He organized the local chapter of the American GI Forum, became a member of the NAACP, and joined Black students in the sit-ins at downtown Dallas department stores. He collected poll taxes for the Progressive Voters League and organized Mexicans into the first local Viva Kennedy club and the Political Association for Spanish-Speaking Organizations.[51]

Medrano also directly challenged middle-class Mexican Americans who benefited from whiteness. In 1964, Medrano helped organize a multiracial coalition of white, Black, and Brown activists to stage a sit-in at an El Fenix restaurant. Mike Martínez, the manager and owner of the restaurant, came over to the group, informed the protesters that he had called police, and asked them to leave or face arrest.

When Medrano and the others refused to vacate, Martínez abruptly closed the restaurant for the day.[52] Indeed, Martínez refused to integrate even after the Committee of 14 pushed several downtown eating establishments to remove their discriminatory signs.

Dallas's labor movement, though small compared with its counterparts in other parts of the state, influenced the development of Mexican American and Chicana/o organizations. Many activists turned their attention to the dire conditions in West Dallas, segregated schooling, the dearth of Mexican American teachers and principals, and the lack of bilingual education. Frances Rizo and her husband, Robert Arredondo, organized the Mexican American Political Association (MAPA), a neighborhood organization that originally focused on the poor living conditions of Mexican residents in West Dallas. Born in 1947, Rizo dropped out of school and married eighteen-year-old Arredondo, who worked at a local manufacturing plant. As a strong unionist, Arredondo helped organize a chapter of the United Brotherhood of Carpenters and Joiners of America at his company, but had difficulty organizing the female workers without causing trouble with their husbands. As a result, Arredondo often brought Rizo to speak to the wives and convince them to join the local council.[53]

As Arredondo reached higher positions in his local, Rizo accompanied her husband to meetings of the American Federation of Labor–Congress of Industrial Organizations (AFL-CIO) in Dallas. There, she learned valuable organizing techniques and participated in numerous political campaigns. She applied those tactics directly to neighborhood politics, especially when she joined the PTA after her oldest son enrolled in Gabe P. Allen Elementary. "They didn't like seeing me there," she recalled of the white mothers, who often dominated the organization and refused to conduct meetings at night for working parents, or in Spanish for non-English-speaking families. That attitude inspired her to rally her neighbors and family together and have them join the parent-teacher group. "I got my *comadres*, my mother, my aunt, my friends . . . to join the PTA," she remembered. Because of those new memberships, Rizo soon after was elected president. "Those white ladies hated me even more so because not only did I get elected, but so did my *comadres*, who were also elected vice president, secretary, [and so on]," Rizo recalled. As president of the PTA, Rizo worked to establish bilingual education and later helped develop a pilot program with Dallas superintendent Nolan Estes. The following year, Rizo became vice president of a Mexican American advisory committee to the superintendent and went to Washington, DC, to negotiate a federal grant to fund the program at all Dallas ISD schools.[54]

Another group of organizers with labor connections was the Dallas Brown Berets. Inspired by the development of Brown Beret chapters across the Southwest, Pancho Medrano pitched the idea to his sons, Robert and Ricardo.[55] The Medrano brothers had frequently participated in political organizing as youngsters. Both children joined the NAACP Youth Council under Juanita Craft and protested the State Fair of Texas for its Negro Achievement Day. In their mid to late twenties, they continued their political endeavors. Robert became the first in his family to attend college, enrolling at the University of Texas at Arlington. There, he joined Ernest McMillan of SNCC (and later the Black Panther Party) in protesting the Confederate theme on campus. In 1968, Robert landed a job with the local War on Poverty initiative, in which he applied the organizing techniques he had learned from the Black Panther Party to the West Dallas Community Center, where he eventually became director.

Ricardo likewise involved himself in the local politics of the Mexican American community. In 1964, he purchased a grocery store in Little Mexico called Kiko's, which he and his mother, Esperanza, helped run. At the store, Ricardo, Pancho, and Esperanza registered people to vote, offered informal day care services, and allowed Mexican American organizations to use the space for meetings.[56] Kiko's also hosted meetings of the local chapter of the Brown Berets once it was formally organized, in 1968 or 1969, with Ricardo serving as the group's first prime minister.[57]

The Dallas chapter abstained from violent direct action, instead favoring civil disobedience. "We already knew the theory of nonviolence from Martin Luther King and Mahatma Gandhi," Robert indicated. Initially, the Berets used themselves as "radicals" in the Dallas political arena. But their goals were no less radical than those that other Mexican American middle-class leaders or organizations had fought for, such as renaming public schools after Mexican American figures, serving culturally Mexican food in schools, and hiring more Mexican American teachers and principals across the district. But instead of using negotiation and compromise, as many middle-class Mexican American activists had, the Brown Berets engaged confrontationally with the establishment, often leading picket lines and protesting directly to the city council.[58]

Their outspokenness drew attention from the entire Dallas community. One woman approached Juan Pérez, a Beret member from West Dallas, and told him the Brown Berets had done little to help the community and that they were "nothing but drunks, marijuana smokers, and criminals who were used by the Medranos to attack political opponents."[59] In addition, police frequently harassed members of the organization, monitored their activities, and attempted to entrap them. In one incident, Ricardo became suspicious when a group of reporters approached him about doing a story on the Brown Berets. When he invited them to the clubhouse for a meeting that evening, one reporter asked him to make sure all the members were present and for "everyone to bring their guns."[60] Ricardo seemed perplexed by the request. "We knew [and] we feared that we could get hurt easily based on things we've heard that happened—getting apprehended and getting in a squad car and never being heard from again," Robert said. To combat the harassment, the Brown Berets took extra precautions when staging their protests—holding them in the daytime instead of at night and asking for help from the local news media.[61]

Juan Crow discrimination led a cadre of Mexican American and Chicana/o activists to challenge the existing power structure. Though some gained influence by acquiescing in whiteness politics, others used their identities as Brown and working class to push for change. Labor activism also provided a strong foundation upon which Black and Brown residents could organize together. They experienced some success in their attempt to desegregate El Fenix in 1964. Additionally, Robert Medrano's cross-racial student activism led to his position with the War on Poverty. The issue of police violence further fused the two groups.

Policing Black and Brown

Discrimination in law enforcement was evident for both African Americans and Mexican Americans in Dallas and across Texas. Complaints ranged from police indifference — in that officers failed to arrest drug users, thieves, vandals, and domestic abusers — to outright hostility. According to the Texas Advisory Committee to the US Commission on Civil Rights in 1970, African Americans and Mexican Americans in Texas reported that police officers often verbally abused them or used excessive use of force when making arrests. Others reported that officers harassed residents, employing "stop and frisk" tactics in the streets.[62] And many complained that Mexican Americans and African Americans were underrepresented in the police ranks. In 1971, for example, the Dallas Police Department employed 23 Mexican American officers — only 1.3 percent of the entire 1,788 officers on the police force — and 35 African Americans, accounting for about 2 percent of all officers.[63]

Police violence against Black and Brown residents was not a new problem. Over the decades, African Americans and Mexican Americans reported innumerable beatings, shootings, sexual assaults, unlawful entries, and random disappearances of loved ones.[64] As the Black and Brown freedom struggles unfolded and intersected — in brief instances of organizing in the labor movement and the War on Poverty — the question of how to address police violence united Black and Brown activists, prompting them to form broad-scale coalitions in their shared struggle for police accountability.

The catalyst for the coalition was the death of three sheriff's deputies in early 1971. Late on the evening of February 15, four deputies were investigating a potential home invasion in West Dallas. Two Mexican American residents managed to disarm and kidnap the officers. After driving them to the Trinity River bottom, the men shot and killed three deputies when they tried to escape. Deputy A. D. McCurley managed to flee. He identified the perpetrators as René Guzmán and Leonardo López, two well-known offenders who often supported their drug habits by stealing.[65] Within hours of the shooting, the Dallas County Sheriff Department and the Dallas Police Department launched an expansive manhunt for the two suspects. In the process, police terrorized members of the Mexican American community, arbitrarily pulling over motorists for *looking* Mexican. "I saw where, justifiably or not, we were screened," former Dallas LULAC president Richard Menchaca recalled.[66] "Every tip they got, they wouldn't go and knock on the door, they'd go kick doors in," Frances Rizo recalled. "They would pull shot guns in front of kids' faces and elderly people. They would knock over furniture like they were looking for drugs."[67]

A few days after the murders, the police department received a tip on the whereabouts of Guzmán and López, whom investigators presumed were hiding in an East Dallas apartment complex. Early on the morning of February 18, plainclothes police officers stormed into the apartment of Tomás and Berta Rodríguez (unrelated to Santos Rodríguez), a married couple with eight children. Fearing a burglary, the startled Tomás grabbed his revolver and shot toward the intruders. The police returned fire, wounding Tomás in the chest and a pregnant Berta in the leg. After an extensive search of the Rodríguez home, the officers realized that they had mistakenly kicked down the wrong door. About thirty minutes after the police raid, officers located the two fugitives in the adjacent apartment. Guzmán admitted to the killings and informed officers that he and López had stayed in Dallas to be close to their heroin supplier. Meanwhile, Dallas police transported Tomás and Berta to Parkland Hospital, held the couple under arrest, and eventually charged Tomás with attempted murder.[68] Law enforcement denied any wrongdoing, even after Guzmán confessed to the killings. To cover their mistake, law enforcement officials crafted a far-fetched story that supposedly linked the Rodríguez family to Guzmán and López, stating that Tomás was their drug supplier.[69]

The assaults on the Rodríguezes outraged Mexican Americans and African Americans throughout the city. Days after the Rodríguez raid, Fahim Minkah of the Black Panther Party approached the city council as an unregistered speaker and told the council members that the deaths of the sheriff's deputies was "poetic justice." Minkah continued, "It was the same river bottom where traditionally police took blacks, Mexicans, and poor whites and beat them up. Often times they didn't even arrest us, just beat [us] up and let us go. Or sometimes beat us up and then take us to jail." He then stated that Black, Brown, and poor white residents would "work together to resolve this issue of police abuse of citizens."[70]

In March 1971, Minkah attended a rally organized by MAPA and the Brown Berets at which nearly 150 protesters condemned the raid on the Rodríguez home. At the protest, the Berets and the Panthers met Charlie Young, a white working-class activist from East Dallas. Young had moved to Dallas in 1970 to work for the local PBS affiliate on a show called *Newsroom*, a news program reporting on the social and political culture of Dallas. At the time, Young was living in an old fourplex in East Dallas, a white working-class community. He noticed the dwelling was infested with roaches and rodents. When he and other tenants complained to the landlady, she refused to take any action. In protest, Young took his .22 pistol, loaded it with bird shot, and started shooting the roaches and rodents and sweeping their remains into the communal hallway. The landlady and other tenants didn't find the protest amusing, and he was forced to vacate. But he noticed that wherever he lived as a tenant, the dwelling was infested with vermin. To make money, he began offering low-cost pest-control services, and his conversations with other frustrated tenants led him to organize the Bois d'Arc Patriots, a tenants' rights organization, in early 1971.[71]

Young decided to attend the Rodríguez rally because of his dissatisfaction with city politics and the Dallas Police Department. About a month before the Rodríguez raid, a Dallas police officer killed Jerry Ray Taylor, a twenty-two-year-old white man, after he suspected Taylor of burglarizing a car. At the rally, Young met Pancho and told him of Taylor's untimely death. As a result, Pancho invited Young to speak on the police abuse of poor whites to the crowd of Black and Brown protesters. "From there," Young recalled, "people just started meeting each other."[72]

The Brown Berets, the Bois d'Arc Patriots, and the Black Panther Party formed what Dallas newspapers called the "Triumvirate Alliance." They staged large-scale demonstrations in the streets of downtown Dallas throughout the 1970s. In late 1972, the activists stormed the streets after Dallas police officers shot and killed three unarmed Black men within the span of two weeks. They marched after Santos Rodríguez was murdered in 1973. Along with three hundred other activists, they gathered in downtown Dallas, where the protest turned violent.[73] In 1975, the triad organized a march to protest the recent deaths of African American men in South Dallas as well as rising unemployment rates, which disproportionately affected Black, Brown, and poor white residents throughout the city.[74] Three years later, activists from the three groups reunited after Santos's death to protest the failure of the US Department of Justice to bring federal charges against Officer Cain, whom many believed had violated Santos's civil rights. The following year, on November 3, 1979, the three groups helped organize a counterdemonstration to a Ku Klux Klan march celebrating the group's revitalization from the 1920s.[75]

Still, the murder of Santos Rodríguez hit the Mexican American community especially hard. "It hit me so hard. It was like it had happened to one of my sons," Rizo stated. At the time of his murder, Santos and his brother David lived with their grandfather; their mother, Bessie Rodríguez, had been sent to prison for murdering sixty-two-year-old Leonard Brown.[76] "People would say, 'Well, what do you expect from a kid that like, from the streets. His mother is in prison,'" Rizo said with disgust. "Those are not people you want to trust." In her grief, Rizo, married with four young children, decided to investigate Santos's circumstances and family life. What she discovered resonated with her: "She was in prison because she had killed her abusive ex-police, white, common-law husband. Because he was beating her up." According to Rizo, neighbors called the police on the couple several times, and law enforcement knew that Brown routinely abused Bessie. "It just so happened that that last time, she managed to get the gun away from him and shoot him. And she emptied the gun into him," Rizo confirmed. As a victim of domestic violence, Rizo understood the difficult circumstances that Bessie experienced. "He was a very abusive husband," Rizo remembered of her own husband. "Very jealous. Very possessive. And the longer we were married, the more abusive he got."[77] Rizo and Arredondo divorced in 1975, and much of her activism after their marriage directly related to domestic violence. She served on several committees and task forces whose work eventually led to the establishment of Family Place, the city's first battered women's shelter, which opened in 1980.[78]

The violence toward the Rodríguez family and Santos Rodríguez, as well as to his mother, Bessie, reveals the multifaceted relationship between Mexican Americans and the police. The Dallas Police Department sometimes acted overzealously in the barrios—unjustly targeting and racially profiling Mexicans, allowing the actions of a few to be ascribed to the entire Mexican community. Or as one Chicano activist stated, "For the mistakes of some, the masses suffered the consequences. When a Mexican does something wrong, all Mexicans do something wrong."[79] On the other hand, in the case of Bessie Rodríguez, a Mexican American woman, police disregarded the abuse that she suffered at the hands of her white ex-police-officer husband and refused to intervene, despite knowing that Brown had repeatedly assaulted her in their relationship. Domestic violence was largely seen as a private, family matter, and police indifference to the abuse endured by victims thwarted efforts by women, especially women of color, to receive the necessary protection by law enforcement. Their only source of legal protection was from an entity they severely distrusted. Facing a dual system of injustice because of their gender and their skin color, Black and Brown women were often silenced on matters of family violence.

The direct-action protests unveiled the anger and frustration of civil rights activists and of the Dallas Black and Brown communities more generally. Their public display of anger and their connections with the news media allowed activists to raise public consciousness on the issue. But raising hell in the streets could not solve the inequities within city government. The cadre of Black and Brown activists in the 1960s and 1970s who engaged in direct-action protests therefore inserted themselves in the political system. Their efforts tell a much larger story of how political power became a tool in the fight against police misconduct.

Though the Citizens Charter Association and the Dallas Citizens Council had controlled city politics for decades, the city developed an image problem in the 1950s and into the 1960s when it became the bedrock of the rising, ultraconservative wing of the Republican Party. Figures such as US Representatives Bruce Alger and Joe Pool, along with the John Birch Society, among others, espoused fearful, paranoid conspiracy theories about alleged communists working in the government. Over time, defectors from the traditionally Democratic state joined the Republican Party, and their influence in the political arena altered Dallas's image through a series of scandals. In one case, an unhinged Republican woman spat on Lady Bird Johnson as she left a campaign visit in 1960, an incident that Richard Nixon was convinced cost him the presidential election that year. And during a speech in Dallas in 1963, UN ambassador Adlai Stevenson was struck on the head by a sign-wielding female protester. Those incidents, and especially the 1963 assassination of President John F. Kennedy, branded the city of Dallas as the "City of Hate"—alluding to the idea that ultraconservative organizing cultivated a general tolerance of bigotry and violence that ultimately led Lee Harvey Oswald to pull the trigger.[80]

Following the assassination, the city worked to restore its image. In 1964, white city leaders launched Goals for Dallas, a series of civic and social programs designed to ensure that Dallas's recently tainted image would not have long-lasting effects. This pursuit also involved diversifying the body politic. The city council remained lily white until 1967, when Mayor Erik Jonsson appointed a Black businessman named C. A. Galloway to fill the remaining three months of another council member's term.[81] Two years later, the city council further diversified after the Citizens Charter Association supported two candidates of color—Anita Martínez and George Allen, a Black businessman and member of the Committee of 14, for the city council. Both won easily in their elections in April 1969.[82] The CCA engaged in what the political scientist Benjamin Márquez calls "descriptive representation" campaigns—handpicking and selecting certain persons of color to run in an effort to appear democratic and fair.[83]

Black community activist Al Lipscomb challenged the "descriptive representation" policies of the CCA. Born in 1925, the native Dallasite graduated from Booker T. Washington High School. He joined the army air force during World War II, in which he served in Squadron C, the "colored squadron." In 1947, he was honorably discharged and returned home to Dallas, where he worked as a waiter in many of the city's finer restaurants.[84] His interest in community activism inspired him to seek employment with the War on Poverty initiative. In 1966, he was hired by that program, which led him to form close relationships with the Medrano family. Two years later, the Greater Dallas Council of Churches recruited him for Block Partnership, a community organization that matched predominantly Black and impoverished neighborhood blocks with church or civic groups from more affluent parts of town. He developed friendships with SNCC and, later, NCCF activists before organizing Grassroots, Inc., with Curtis Gaines.[85] Around that time, Lipscomb formed the South Dallas Information Center (SDIC) at the home of the Black activist Elsie Faye Heggins. The SDIC became a valuable resource for African Americans who needed information about their political and legal rights regarding zoning, evictions, domestic violence, and police brutality.

Lipscomb's frustration with the limited political power available to people of color inspired him and a cadre of others to try to dethrone the dominance of the Citizens Charter Association and to restructure the entire political system in Dallas. In January 1971, Lipscomb announced his intention to run for mayor—the first African American in the city to campaign for the position. He ended the race a distant third, losing to the white city council member Wes Wise, an independent who also defeated Avery Mays, the CCA-backed candidate.[86] Even though Mays lost the election, the CCA managed to reelect nearly all its other candidates, including Anita Martínez and George Allen.[87] Despite the inclusive measures of the CCA, Lipscomb and other activists, including Heggins, the Reverend Peter Johnson of the SCLC, and Pancho Medrano, filed suit against the City of Dallas, challenging the constitutionality of the at-large system.[88] The plaintiffs argued that at-large elections and the persistence of segregation prevented people of color from getting elected to city positions. In 1974, US district judge Eldon Mahon ruled in favor of Lipscomb and ordered the city to devise a new, "constitutionally acceptable plan." The city presented a combination plan consisting of eight single-member districts and three at-large positions, commonly known as the 8–3 plan. Judge Mahon deemed the plan acceptable, and it went into effect in 1975.[89]

The ruling in *Lipscomb v. Wise* hardly resulted in a more democratic election process in Dallas. Proponents argued that the 8–3 plan, which imposed residency requirements on candidates for the eight single-member districts, provided Black and Brown candidates the ability to run and win in the precincts in which they lived. The 1975 election of the former NAACP Youth Council director Juanita Craft to the city council, who replaced George Allen after his appointment as a justice of the peace, supported their contention. But the election did little more than exchange one Black representative for another. Furthermore, the plan reduced the number of racial-minority council members by keeping place 9, which covered most of West Dallas, an at-large district without residency requirements. Pedro Aguirre, a Mexican American architect who won place 9 in 1973 and replaced Anita Martínez, ran for reelection to retain his position after the 8–3 plan went into effect. He lost to Garry Weber, a white council member who was deemed ineligible to refile in place 4, the spot he had held previously, because of the new residency requirements.[90] Not only did the combination plan fail to address the routine exclusion of Black and Brown candidates, but it also actively worked against Mexican Americans in West Dallas by keeping place 9 an at-large seat.

Still, Black and Brown activists found other ways to ascend politically. In 1980,

Albert "Al" Lipscomb, Dallas, c. 1970. Photo courtesy of the Herbert J. Croner Papers, 1963–1984, Dolph Briscoe Center for American History, University of Texas at Austin.

Elsie Faye Heggins, who ran a tight campaign against Juanita Craft in 1975, and a Black real estate agent named Fred Blair won seats on the city council. The former Brown Beret and labor organizer Ricardo Medrano formed an alliance with LGBTQ residents, helping him secure his position in place 2, representing the Oak Lawn neighborhood, a "gayborhood."[91] Medrano, Heggins, and Blair secured their positions without the political backing of the CCA or the Dallas Citizens Council, the first council members of color to do so.[92]

Their ascension came at an important time in the struggle against police brutality. In 1979, Dallas police killed nine people and wounded seventeen. In the first four months of 1980, police shot nineteen people, killing six.[93] The alarming escalation of police violence inspired Councilman Blair to push for the formation of a police review board with investigative and subpoena powers. Activists had advocated the creation of such a board for years, but council members in previous decades had ignored or rebuffed the recommendations. Medrano seconded Blair's motion, arguing that "anything less than a citizen review board is non-negotiable." The board was ultimately rejected by an 8–3 margin in which Medrano, Heggins, and Blair, the only three members of color on the council, voted yes.[94]

Activists over the decades had grown impatient with the Dallas City Council, which had the authority to launch investigations into the operations of the police force when incidents of alleged misconduct occurred. Diane Ragsdale, a seasoned activist, engaged in such a battle against the city. "At some point in time, you want to move from direct action to progressive public policy," she stated.[95] Ragsdale worked extensively as a community organizer and became an effective woman in the local political arena. She was born in 1952 in Dallas, where her activism began as a young child. At the age of nine, she and her older sister Charlotte joined the NAACP Youth Council under Juanita Craft and sold memberships to the Maria Morgan YWCA chapter. While she was in high school, Lipscomb recruited her and Charlotte to volunteer for the South Dallas Information Center. Shortly after graduating, she joined the Dallas chapter of SCLC, participating in Operation Breadbasket and anti-police-brutality marches. Ragsdale was also active during her college years, both in Dallas and in Denton, forty miles north. While attending Texas Woman's University, she formed the campus NAACP chapter and staged a sit-in with two hundred others on the lawn of university president John Guinn's estate, in protest of frequent abuses toward Black students on campus.[96] On weekends, she returned home to Dallas and sold copies of the Black Panther newspaper in front of H. L. Green's department store downtown.[97]

In the late 1970s, she joined the Black Women's United Front. "We were antisexism, anti-imperialism, anticapitalism, anti-economic-exploitation," she recalled with a laugh. "Those [are the] things that tend to oppress."[98] As a child of the movement, Ragsdale developed a political voice that echoed the militancy of Black Power politics but sustained her relatability to the larger Black community. Her ambition to alter the status quo and her determination to fight for the disfranchised were crucial in her rise to politics in the 1980s.

Her determination to put in place a police review board gave rise to her political career. In June 1980, Ragsdale and the former Black Panther Party members Fahim Minkah and Marvin Crenshaw formed the Citizens United for a Review Board and attempted to collect enough signatures to put on the ballot a city charter amendment that would create a citizens' police review board with investigative and subpoena powers.[99] The petition failed to garner enough signatures largely because of actions by the Dallas Police Department and the Dallas Police Association, the department's union. DPA president Dick Hickman placed half-page advertisements in both the *Dallas Morning News* and the *Dallas Times Herald* that encouraged voters to oppose the amendment. Hickman argued that the city council was not hearing from the "law-abiding, tax-paying citizens" and that the council had seen only the "vocal radicals" on the issue.[100] He told *Texas Monthly* that police confrontations with "minorities" were regrettable but also inevitable. "Thirty-five per cent of our citizens are minorities," he began, "but 65 per cent of the felonies are committed by them. They are more exposed to being killed."[101]

The DPA became a formidable opponent to the creation of any kind of police review board with investigative powers. It appealed to the white majority by using crime statistics to assign responsibility for individual actions to the entire Black and Brown population, and recounted their ideas of crime and race to the local officials and the general public. "I tell you what," began a former police officer to the city council, "if I was out late at night, I'd much rather have a policeman come up to me than some of these people who are proposing a citizen review board."[102] Police offi-

The activist and future politician Diane Ragsdale at a congressional field hearing on police violence, Dallas, 1987. Photo courtesy of the *Dallas Morning News*.

cers drew upon centuries-old notions that inextricably linked race and crime, justifying their use of force as ethical and fair, given the high levels of crime in Black and Brown neighborhoods.

The defeat of the proposal for a police review board ended the multiracial coalition's strength in the political arena. As a compromise, the city council approved a police advisory committee, later renamed the Dallas Citizens / Police Relations Board. An independent nine-member organization, the board could make recommendations to the Dallas chief of police and the grand jury regarding police brutality, but it could not "interfere with an investigation by the police department" or conduct an independent investigation of its own. The advisory board had little influence on police department policy, and most African American and Mexican American activists resented its creation, calling it "a joke."[103] Its development, however, inspired the Dallas Police Association to limit the influence of the council members who proposed the review board. When Ricardo Medrano ran for a second term on the city council, in 1983, he lost to twenty-seven-year-old Paul Fielding, a white candidate who received support and backing from the DPA.[104]

To complicate the problem of inadequate minority representation on the city council, Heggins and Blair resigned their terms to run for county commissioner in 1984, a position that the Black activist John Wiley Price secured. In special elections, Al Lipscomb and Diane Ragsdale were elected in April 1984 to replace Heggins and Blair.[105] As the council members of color, they were forced to make adjustments in their strategies against police violence.

And that violence continued unabated. Between 1980 and 1985, Dallas police shot and killed thirty-five African Americans, twelve Mexican Americans, and twelve

Anglo Americans. The years 1983 and 1986 both tied for the record number of police shootings in Dallas—twenty-nine—since the department began keeping count, in 1973. The shooting death of Etta Collins, a seventy-year-old South Dallas resident, by Officer Mark E. Kraus was particularly egregious. Collins had called police about a burglary at the duplex next door. Kraus claimed that Collins refused to stop pointing a revolver at officers responding to her call, but some neighbors disputed Kraus's statement, alleging that Collins was shot while still inside her home.[106]

As a result of the shooting, Ragsdale and Lipscomb joined forces with Marvin Crenshaw and the local activist Roy Williams, and invited Congressman John Conyers of Michigan, a member of the House Subcommittee on Criminal Justice, to visit Dallas. After much urging, Conyers agreed to hold a congressional hearing in the city.[107] The all-day hearing on May 8, 1987, included testimonies and recommendations from Black and Brown activists, elected officials, and members of the Dallas Police Department. Ragsdale and Lipscomb both charged the department and the Dallas Police Association with racism, arguing that police officers perceived all African Americans as criminals and used those stereotypes to "justify the unacceptable number of blacks being shot by white police officers." They both argued for more Black and Brown officers on the force, especially in supervisory positions. They also advocated for more hours of training that focused on "preservation of life" and a system of checks and balances that would help identify problem officers before they killed someone.[108]

As elected officials, Ragsdale and Lipscomb largely stood alone in their accusations against the Dallas Police Department. Other officials from the city government, including Councilmen John Evans and Craig Holcomb, Mayor Annette Strauss, and City Manager Richard Knight recognized the need to "improve communication and understanding between the police department and our minority citizens," but also commended the Dallas Police Department for its seriousness in "protecting and serving all our citizens." The only elected official to side with Ragsdale and Lipscomb was the white city council member Lori Palmer, who testified that officers needed more sensitivity training in the field and that more Black and Brown officers should be hired for the force.[109]

Testifying police officers denied any wrongdoing. They pointed to officers' high levels of education—more than 40 percent held a bachelor's degree—as a sign of their success. "The Dallas Police Department is truly one of the best educated in the nation," stated Captain John Chappelle.[110] Others defended their policing practices by arguing that the department has been "unjustly criticized by the public and officials for slight and sometimes accidental errors." Captain Rick Stone pointed to the heroism of Officer J. D. Tippit in his apprehension of Lee Harvey Oswald forty-five minutes after the assassination of President John F. Kennedy as one of the triumphs of the DPD—a patriotic deflection from the issue of police brutality.[111] Dallas chief of police Marlin Price grew frustrated at the accusations leveled against his department and even more so with the witnesses' recommendations. In his supplementary statement given to the hearing panel, Price argued along the same lines as former DPA president Dan Hickman. "It is evident," Price wrote, "from the data on who is committing violent crime, who is being arrested for violent crimes, who is being arrested for offenses involving weapons, and our response times in minority areas, that the reason police are using deadly force against minorities more often than whites is because we encounter minorities more often in violent situations."[112]

The denials and deflections of the Dallas Police Department signified officers' indifference to the problem of police misconduct. Police continued to blame entire communities and populations for individual acts and subscribed to racist notions to back their claims and their justifications for abuse. Ten days after the hearing, for example, two Dallas police officers fatally shot eighty-one-year-old David Horton, an African American resident of South Dallas. Officers claimed that Horton fired his rifle at police, but nearby residents stated that Horton, a Crime Watch volunteer, was trying to protect cars in the parking lot when police approached him. Regardless of the circumstances, Horton's death set off a chain reaction among local officials. Dallas county commissioner John Wiley Price stated the Horton shooting "made a mockery" of the hearing and requested an investigation from the Civil Rights Division of the US Justice Department. Diane Ragsdale said the shooting showed the need for better training of police officers. "The fact is that these officers threw themselves into a position that forced a deadly conflict instead of a peaceful resolution," Ragsdale stated.[113]

Two weeks after the shooting, on May 30, 1987, Ragsdale, Lipscomb, and Price organized a demonstration that they called the March for Human Dignity. Several hundred people gathered at the home of David Horton in South Dallas before marching toward Dallas City Hall to protest his death and the increase in police abuse against Black and Brown residents. On the steps of city hall, Ragsdale urged the crowd to attend the upcoming city council meeting to support the need for police reform. "The mayor, the City Council, and the city manager have lost total control with respect to the issue of police abuse," Ragsdale stated. "We cannot continue to dialogue and dialogue and dialogue and die and die and die."[114]

Horton's death, following closely on the congressional hearing on police brutality, embarrassed many of Dallas's city officials into action. Police chief Billy Prince created the Office of Minority Affairs within the police department, which sought to improve police-community relations and work with investigators in the Internal Affairs Division to resolve complaints between officers and residents of color. Mayor Annette Strauss created an advisory committee on crime, to which she appointed Black leaders to form a subcommittee and submit recommendations to the Dallas City Council and the Dallas Police Department.[115] The committee submitted a recommendation to create a Citizens Police Review Board, which the city council approved in November 1987. But the majority-white council voted against granting it unlimited investigative and subpoena powers. Instead, the board could request subpoena power through a majority vote, and a two-thirds majority was needed to initiate an investigation.[116] Despite those limitations, after more than a decade of protests, picketing, and political activism, Black and Brown residents finally had a review board with the potential of holding officers accountable in cases of police brutality.

The Black and Brown civil rights movements, which had run along parallel lines for some time, intersected in the 1970s and 1980s in new ways that brought about a vibrant and potent cross-racial collaboration. Though Mexican Americans and African Americans had worked together previously in the labor movement and the War on Poverty, their mutual concern about police violence provided a new energy to the overall movement. The deaths of Michael Morehead, Jimmy Ray Taylor, and Santos Rodríguez, and the assault on the Rodríguez family, were watershed moments for Black, Brown, and white residents of Dallas. Suddenly, they found themselves among other activists whose living and employment conditions were not dissimilar to theirs. The fact that all three had experience with police brutality provided them with the necessary ammunition to take to the streets, demanding that the city government provide better opportunities for working-class people and to stop police-related assaults and killings.

Their entrance into city politics signified a crucial turning point in the drive to end police brutality. As police violence continued to escalate throughout the 1970s and 1980s, Black and Brown activists fought to win important seats in the municipal government, in order to push for the creation of a police review board. Despite the white-dominated city council, the Dallas Police Department, and the Dallas Police Association banding together to stop them, Black and Brown activists finally prevailed, after an inexplicable police shooting soon after a locally conducted congressional hearing. After nearly two decades of multiracial organizing, Black and Brown activists managed to transform city politics in an effort to end police brutality.

CHAPTER 12

SELF-DETERMINED EDUCATIONAL SPACES:
Forging Race and Gender Power in Houston

SAMANTHA M. RODRIGUEZ

In commemoration of its fortieth anniversary, the University of Houston Center for Mexican American Studies (UH CMAS) hosted a panel of Tejana/o student activists who in 1972 had made the program possible: Jaime De La Isla, Mario Garza, María Jiménez, Elliot Navarro, and Cynthia Perez. Former members of the University of Houston Mexican American Youth Organization (UH MAYO), each panelist took turns discussing the sociopolitical conditions that informed their struggle for Chicana/o studies, and the numerous obstacles that students faced in launching a viable ethnic studies program. Throughout the nation, the fight for Chicana/o studies was a part of a larger movement for ethnic-based teaching and research centers, including African American studies.[1] María Jiménez not only located the fight for Chicana/o studies within the broader struggle for racial liberation, as many others had, but also underscored the barriers that Tejanas faced in addressing gender equality within the Chicana/o movement. She vividly recalled that "one of the areas where [she remembered] feeling personal discrimination was always on the gender issue."[2] Jiménez's pursuit of race and gender freedom was not always well received. There were Tejano activists who verbally attacked her at the time for bringing up Tejana feminism in multiple spaces. Echoing Jiménez's *testimonio* (testimony) regarding the Chicana/o movement, Cynthia Perez maintained that Tejanas organized to ensure that women's rights were central to the struggle for Tejana/o educational self-determination.

During the protests of the 1960s and 1970s, Tejanas/os in Houston battled for self-determined educational spaces both at the university and in the community.[3] Their struggle for ethnic studies became part of the larger quest for race and gender power. For UH MAYO, Chicana/o studies was the conduit for the self-awareness and community research necessary to reverse structural anti-Mexican practices dating back to the early nineteenth century. Students who engaged in this education battle came of age while witnessing the virulent racism of the segregated South. Indeed, leaders of the ethnic studies movement were driven by the desire for racial justice as well as energized by the push for African American studies, as they identified with the tactics deployed in the Black Power movement. While racial liberation loomed large in discussions concerning the formation of UH CMAS, Tejanas intervened in the campaign to underscore their plight as female students claiming their own gender liberation. That is, Tejanas ensured that ethnic studies would be a site for gaining the mental tools critical to dismantling entrenched sexism in addition to racism.

Scholars of the Chicana/o movement have documented the struggle for ethnic studies since the 1980s. But few works have focused on Texas and, particularly, on the ways that segregated southern environments like Houston produced antiracist and antisexist activism that fundamentally shaped educational self-determination.[4] Indeed, the scholar-activist Maylei Blackwell asserted that Chicano/a narratives often erroneously portray feminism as occurring outside the Chicana/o movement rather than within it.[5] Since Houston Tejanas were central to the creation of UH CMAS, it is critical to illuminate their roles and demands. Additionally, the fight for UH CMAS developed in relation to the struggle for African American studies. That is, Tejana/o students not only supported their Black peers but also learned tactics that proved useful for their own ethnic studies campaign. Tejana/o and African American students recognized that both communities had experienced decades of racial oppression, state-sponsored violence, and the lack of culturally relevant education. A relational examination of self-determined Black and Brown educational spaces can broaden our understanding of ethnic studies and collective race, gender, and class formations in the South.[6]

Drawing on the Civil Rights in Black and Brown Interview Database, newspapers, collections, and radio programs, this chapter traces the ways in which racial and gender liberation were central to the ethnic studies movement in the Juan Crow and Jim Crow South. After witnessing decades of anti-Mexican violence and the inability of accommodationist tactics to fundamentally transform their communities, UH Tejanas/os in the 1960s and 1970s charted a new, self-determined educational path inspired by the United Farm Workers (UFW) and connected with the national Chicana/o studies struggle. Tejanas championed gender empowerment through female leadership, student services, and Chicana studies. Tejana/o race and gender militancy at the University of Houston culminated in the establishment of a sustainable, culturally relevant education center.

State-Sanctioned Violence and the
Mexican American Youth Organization

The push for self-determined educational spaces was rooted in ethnic Mexican fights for equality dating from the early nineteenth century.[7] In 1836, after fourteen years of Anglo settlement in Texas, many Tejano elites joined the cause for Texas independence, with the goal of securing their economic and political positions. In the years following independence, however, these elites steadily lost their economic and political power and became subject to anti-Mexican violence. In the 1840s, the *Houston Telegraph and Texas Register* described Tejanas/os as backward and degenerate.[8] Fearing that ethnic Mexicans would act upon calls for *reconquista* (reconquering) that appeared in Mexican newspapers in the 1850s, Anglos advocated for the blanket removal of Tejanas/os by way of social exclusion and lynchings.[9] From 1848 to 1928, the Texas Rangers policed Tejanas/os, and 232 Tejano men were subject to Anglo mob violence.[10] According to the historian Arnoldo De Leon, Anglos described ethnic Mexicans as "greasers": an ugly, thieving, inferior class suitable only to work as field hands. In the 1870s and 1880s, this promotion of the "greaser" racial slur encouraged the Texas Rangers to carry "out a campaign of terrorizing the Mexicans of the Rio Grande Valley (and Mexico) at every opportunity on the premise that the more fear they created, the easier would be their work of subduing the Mexican."[11]

In the second decade of the twentieth century, Tejanas/os experienced further racial marginalization as the Mexican Revolution (1910–1920) destabilized the border and sparked migration to Texas. Anti-Mexican violence could turn deadly when Anglo ranches were raided. For example, in 1918, in response to an attack on an Anglo homestead, the Texas Rangers, members of the US Cavalry, and local ranchers descended on Porvenir, a village in Presidio County where 140 refugees, including women, children, and men, resided. Although the posse found no arms or stolen items, fifteen ethnic Mexican men and boys were executed for suspected banditry. For the historian Miguel A. Levario, the Porvenir massacre "exposed the extent of the Ranger violence against Mexicans as well as the sense of impunity with which they acted."[12]

Accompanying the decades of terror was the flagrant denial of citizenship rights and access to a decent education for ethnic Mexicans. While the Treaty of Guadalupe Hidalgo (1848) allowed ethnic Mexicans to enjoy the fruits of citizenship if they remained in the United States, they nonetheless experienced second-class treatment. Indeed, ethnic Mexicans endured generations of segregation that, among other deleterious effects, kept their education levels low. Racist conceptions of Tejanas/os emboldened Anglos to oppose moves to promote educational equality.[13]

The violent, racist landscape of the borderlands, particularly in the early twentieth century, prompted Tejanas/os to deploy accommodationist tactics. In 1929, the Tejano middle class worked with World War I veterans to launch the League of United Latin American Citizens (LULAC). To gain social and political equality, this integrationist organization embraced Americanization, sought access to white privilege, and stood against undocumented migration.[14] For LULAC, the courts were the battlefields where the educational situation of ethnic Mexicans could be improved. The historian Guadalupe San Miguel noted that the organization's litigation strategy rested on "a treatment of Mexican Americans as part of the Caucasian or white race in order to achieve social equality."[15]

During the protests of the 1960s and 1970s, however, Tejanas/os openly rejected LULAC's legal and accommodationist strategies. The Texas Chicana/o movement emerged at a time when Tejana/o youth were still enduring the depredations of entrenched Juan Crow policies despite LULAC's integrationist campaigns. Houston Tejanas/os were largely segregated in the ethnic enclaves of the Segundo Barrio (second ward), Magnolia Park, Denver Harbor, and the near Northside, where families lived below the poverty line, police brutality was rampant, and speaking Spanish in schools was forbidden. This oppressive environment, found in barrios across the state, left lasting impressions on future Tejana/o activists, particularly regarding language. A member of UH MAYO, Daniel Bustamante recalled being placed in a Mexican elementary school in Mathis, Texas (northeast of Corpus Christi). On the first day, in a classroom of students who did not know English, the teacher wielded a stick and commenced "hitting all kids who were speaking Spanish and telling them not to speak Spanish."[16] Thanks to his family's connections with officials of the Mathis Independent School District (MISD), Bustamante was soon transferred to an integrated, Anglo school. He continued to experience mistreatment, however, since his first-grade teacher was "the former superintendent" of Mathis ISD, which he described as the most racist school district in Texas.[17] In the 1950s, when Bustamante was attending elementary school, Tejanas/os regularly encountered signs that read "No dogs, no Negros, and no Mexicans" and "We serve whites only, no Spanish or Mexicans," reminding them of their marginalized place in society.[18]

Stark marginalization shaped Tejana/o activism in the 1960s and 1970s. Instead of integrationist approaches, Tejanas/os opted for the militant rhetoric and direct-action tactics of the Black Power movement. Informed by the tactics and principles of the Student Non-violent Coordinating Committee (SNCC) and the Black Panther Party, José Ángel Gutiérrez, Willie Velásquez, Ignacio Pérez, Juan Patlan, and Mario Compeán formed MAYO in San Antonio in 1967. Dismissing the value of whiteness, members of MAYO embraced their indigenous heritage and rich Mexican history, asserting a bold, uncompromising identity. The organization meticulously studied SNCC and the Black Panther Party and adopted their confrontational methods, including fiery speeches, marches, and rallies, to advance their quest for self-determination.[19]

While the founders of MAYO were men, Tejanos were not the only ones dedicated to racial liberation. Childhood experiences with entrenched racism and segregation in the Juan Crow South fueled Tejana participation in educational self-determination. As both a migrant and an ethnic Mexican, María Jiménez faced terrifying language barriers at Franklin Elementary School in Houston in 1957. She "was told not to speak Spanish or [she] would be expelled," and consequently, she lived "in the fear of being expelled." She "could not even ask where's the restroom" or say, "I need some water," since "those were all offenses for expulsion back then."[20] Moreover, Jiménez could play only at the designated "Mexican park" in her neighborhood and was forbidden from going to "Mason Park, which was only a mile and a half away," because Houston parks were segregated.[21] Beyond language discrimination and physical confinement, Houston Tejanas experienced racial paternalism. Louise Villejo recalled that as she was growing up, she "was always the little Mexican girl," and this Anglo perception of ethnic Mexicans translated into low expectations.[22] In school, Villejo was told that she "would be a great beautician" and was "put in a certain level of classes," which were too easy for her. Although she was transferred to higher-level classes once she complained to the principal, Villejo understood that as a Tejana, there were "no expectations, no support on how to go college or what that would entail." Racial oppression and exclusion defined Tejanas' lives in the 1950s and 1960s and set them on a path toward forging a culturally relevant education.

For Tejanas, MAYO was the principal Chicana/o movement organization for channeling their social justice work and developing their racial and gender consciousness. While *mujeres* (women) were initially relegated to secretarial and housekeeping duties rather than leadership positions in MAYO chapters throughout the state, Tejanas soon asserted their voice in the decision-making process. Jiménez's keen awareness and organizational prowess placed her in a respected leadership role in Houston.

Arturo Eureste recalled that male activists "wouldn't disrespect María," and that if they ever did, "the women would eat [them] up alive," since UH MAYO had many strong, educated Tejanas, including Louise Villejo and Inés Hernández Tovar. As Tejanas advocated for ethnic studies, on the grounds that it was central to the fight for racial justice, they simultaneously called for gender liberation.

Ethnic Studies: Transforming the Ivory Tower

A principal focus of MAYO in the 1960s was the creation of culturally relevant institutions of higher education that would direct energy toward solving community problems. Throughout the nation, Chicana/o activists mobilized to establish self-determined schools that would meet their needs. In 1969, Chicana/o students, faculty members, and staffers gathered at the University of California, Santa Barbara, for a higher education conference called by the Chicana/o Coordinating Council on Higher Education, which had been formed two months earlier at the National Chicana/o Youth Liberation meeting in Denver, Colorado. Over one hundred primarily Chicana/o student delegates, from twenty-nine campuses across California, labored for three days to develop a national plan of action that would facilitate the growth of a Chicana/o discipline. The fruit of this collective effort was *El Plan de Santa Bárbara: A Chicano Plan for Higher Education*—a comprehensive blueprint for establishing Chicana/o self-determination at all levels in academia, sustaining student activism, generating recruitment and support programs, developing Chicana/o studies curricula, and initiating "community cultural and social action centers."[23] An instrumental template for the ethnic studies movement, *El Plan de Santa Bárbara* guided MAYO's efforts for educational self-determination across Texas.[24]

Beyond *El Plan de Santa Bárbara*, the United Farm Workers campaign in Texas shaped the struggle for ethnic studies. Arturo Eureste, Daniel Bustamante, María Jiménez, Cynthia Pérez, and other Tejanas/os undertook grassroots activism and witnessed anti-Mexican violence while advocating for farmworkers' rights. Steering the UFW fight for collective bargaining, Delores Huerta and César Chávez sought unionization in South Texas. Tejana/o students at the University of Houston eagerly joined this movement, since many of them had family ties to farmworkers or were from the Rio Grande Valley, where ethnic Mexican poverty and racial subjugation dominated the social and political landscape. Accordingly, UH MAYO supported UFW grape and lettuce boycotts. Pérez remembered "working very hard to support the lettuce boycott," going so far as visiting "the offices of the cafeteria administration" weekly and getting "the lettuce off [the UH] campus."[25] Some Tejana/o students arrived at the university already engaged in the farmworkers' struggle. Bustamante began supporting the grape and lettuce boycotts while attending Del Mar College in Corpus Christi in the late 1960s. Once at UH, he "tried to do everything [he] could to support the farmworker support committee."[26] Bustamante asserted that the UFW campaign in Houston "provided opportunities to work in diverse communities," and that "it wasn't just Chicanas/os," but rather "Chicanas/os, Blacks, Jews, whites, students, and families."

In addition to gaining grassroots and cross-racial organizing experience, Tejana/o activists witnessed the violent, repressive tactics of the Texas Rangers during the 1967 La Casita farm strike for better farmworker wages in Starr County. While conducting mass arrests, the Texas Rangers shoved, abused, and beat picketers.[27] The

Rangers swung shotgun butts at the heads and necks of two ethnic Mexican strikers and kicked them when they fell to the ground, provoking outrage across the state.[28] Encounters with excessive force in the farmworker movement ignited Tejana/o engagement in other direct actions.

The cultural and political elements of the UFW campaign informed Tejana/o involvement in racial justice battles. In part through the UFW campaign, Tejanas/os developed a self-determination philosophy and solidified their racial identity. The UFW deployed ethnic Mexican symbols and slogans in their boycotts and marches, including Mexican flags, the black eagle on the UFW's red flag, the Virgin of Guadalupe, "Si Se Puede" (Yes, we can do it), and "Viva La Raza" (Long live the people). These cultural symbols, along with campus talks by Chávez and Huerta, fueled the Chicana/o movement.[29] Tejana/o student participation in the UFW struggle emboldened UH MAYO to push for university courses that would not only speak to ethnic Mexican cultural experiences but also address labor campaigns and other battles for social justice.[30]

The Tejana/o struggle for self-determined ethnic studies coincided with the broad African American revolution on university campuses. In the mid-1960s, African American students at both historically white universities and colleges and historically Black colleges and universities were subject to predominantly white male professors and Eurocentric courses. Against the backdrop of the Black Power movement and urban uprisings, African American students disrupted Eurocentric fields of study in their quest for community and culturally relevant courses. The African American student movement also transformed academic environments by increasing the number of students of color and diversifying faculties.[31] This national Black educational movement shaped local battles at universities and campuses across Texas.

In the late 1960s, African American students at UH grappled with a hostile campus environment. According to Black student activists, the few African American students were subject to "overt and covert acts of individual and institutional racism."[32] Black protest at UH centered on the creation of an ethnic studies curricula, the admission and retention of African American students, fair housing, and ending discriminatory practices on campus. This African American student movement built on decades of struggle, advancing what the historian Ibram X. Kendi described as the "Long Black Student Movement."[33]

After emerging in the mid-1960s as an antisegregation organization, the Committee for Better Race Relations (COBRR) at UH became a more militant group as the Black Power movement gained political traction across the nation. Michelle Barnes recalled that COBRR was known for being "diplomatic" in ensuring that African American "voices were heard and were responded to in the most positive way possible."[34] After hearing Stokely Carmichael and Bobby Seale call for Black Power and decry "brainwashing education" on campuses, however, COBRR changed its name to Afro-Americans for Black Liberation (AABL) and leveled charges against UH for "imitating the racist society at large" and maintaining "White Anglo-Saxon Protestant" institutions.[35] The shift from COBRR to the AABL occurred in tandem with the student movement at Texas Southern University.[36] The student leader and AABL member Omowali Luthuli-Allen remembered that it was only natural "to link with the brothers and sisters at Texas Southern," since TSU and UH students

Omowali Luthuli-Allen, Houston, June 17, 2016. Photo courtesy CRBB.

had similar grievances.[37] Luthuli-Allen added that "Texas Southern students were back and forth to our campus," and UH students "were back and forth to their campus."[38] The AABL, in particular, resisted white supremacy in higher education by exerting "control over [the] physical, economic, social, spiritual, and physical aspects of [members'] lives" and being "prepared educationally to meet the needs of [their] community."[39] This quest for self-determination fueled the campaign for African American studies (AAS). Luthuli-Allen noted that the AABL drew on the ideas of Marcus Garvey, who asserted that "a race without knowledge of its past is like a tree without roots; [the tree] cannot survive."[40] In its quest to make African American studies a reality, the AABL conducted sit-ins in the president's office at UH and held informational sessions, press conferences, marches, and rallies.

Tejana/o students in UH MAYO not only supported African American students' push for an African American studies program, but also learned critical tactics from them. On March 7, 1969, UH MAYO participated in the AABL's march to President Hoffman's office, where they submitted ten demands focused on the empowerment of African American students.[41] In addition to calling for the creation of an African American studies program, the ten points called for African American administrative and faculty representation, student recruitment and retention, adequate housing, the creation of a Black Student Union, credit hours for community work in the ghetto, and a "committee to alleviate the racist practices in instruction and grading."[42]

In the years following, UH MAYO delivered its own ethnic studies proposal. It reflected the AABL's demands, calling for Mexican American faculty hiring and student resources.[43] At UH—one of the first universities in Texas to offer Mexican American studies courses—Black and Brown activists collaborated to advance ethnic studies as well as student rights initiatives. According to Luthuli-Allen, to "bring [various] movements to fruition," it was critical to "build coalitions and allies."[44] Accordingly, the AABL worked with "Chicano students [and the] Mexican American

Youth Organization."[45] Both the AABL and UH MAYO believed that culturally relevant programs were critical to transforming their second-class status as students of color and members of oppressed communities.

Tejana Leadership and Gender Empowerment at UH

The self-determined education movement at UH was also a site for Tejana leadership and gender empowerment. Tejanas in UH MAYO played a critical role in the fight for a Mexican American studies program, and while doing so, they sought to transform the white patriarchal institution of higher education. That is, Tejanas were dedicated to shaping Mexican American studies, addressing the particular needs of female students, and generating Chicana studies. When UH administrators delayed the creation of a Mexican American studies program, stating that Tejana/o students were "going to have to wait" until African American studies was fully established, Cynthia Perez, María Jiménez, Inés Hernández Tovar, and others marshaled resources to ensure that Mexican American studies became a reality.[46] They promoted university policies that facilitated the growth of Tejana students and integrated the voices of ethnic Mexican women in Mexican American studies coursework.

To bring the Mexican American studies program to fruition, Tejanas labored alongside their Tejano brothers and sympathetic faculty members to pressure the administration, lobby the state legislature for funding, conduct sessions on admissions and financial aid, and participate in Black and Brown student recruitment and retention projects.[47] As a keen strategist and coalition builder who possessed the gift of gab, Jiménez shepherded many of these endeavors. According to Jiménez, "[UH MAYO] took over the president's office constantly. Basically, whatever issue we had, we would mobilize people and we would fill the office and we wouldn't leave until our issues were addressed and until they came and talked to us."[48] In 1971, Jiménez became the first female and Tejana/o Student Government Association president at UH.[49] She received broad support from African Americans, Anglo radicals, women, and international students. Seeking to meet the needs of working-class students, Jiménez fought for the establishment of night information centers and for student control of service fees.[50] Moreover, she used her position to allocate university funds for community programs in Houston barrios and ghettos. Jiménez recalled that UH MAYO and other organizations, including African American student organizations, realized early on that "the value of being a part of a student association was the resources for the projects [they] had," and that they learned "how to maneuver resources."[51] Through student government, money was allocated for a food co-op in the Northside, "a joint [project] between UH MAYO and Barrio MAYO" that served about "200 family members"; in addition, resources "went towards a tutoring program in Third Ward," a historically African American neighborhood.[52] In addressing Tejana student issues, Jiménez advocated for day care, free contraceptives, and a female gynecologist at the student health center. She believed that the small "number of Chicanas in colleges [was] detrimental to La Causa," since the advancement and development of "future generations [were] in the hands of Chicanas."[53] Jiménez confidently fought for gender equality in higher education because she understood that

María Jiménez, Houston, June 13, 2016. Photo courtesy CRBB.

"the history of the Mexican people included the fight for women's equality."[54] Committed to broad educational self-determination, Jiménez and other Tejanas labored for women's educational opportunities while intervening in academia.

In the early 1970s, UH MAYO students worked with sympathetic faculty members to ensure that the Mexican American studies program contributed "to the discovery, application, and transmittal of knowledge with special emphasis on [solving] the distinct social problems of the Mexican American community."[55] Jiménez recalled that "the issue of the denial of our Mexican heritage and who we were, our place in history, and our contributions to US society was part of the Chicano Movement; as an extension, we wanted to ensure other generations were not deprived of what we had been deprived."[56] Beyond documenting the ethnic Mexican experience, UH MAYO envisioned a center geared toward interdisciplinary social justice research and instruction. In proposals for the Mexican American studies program, students and faculty members outlined courses such as "The Barrio," "Socio-Economics of Discrimination," and "Comparative Studies in Racism."[57] Such classes would introduce Tejana/o students to interlocking systems of oppression and instill in them the value of community engagement. More importantly, Mexican American studies courses would foster a resilient racial identity that refuted the idea that ethnic Mexicans were inferior or backward.

Tejanas extended the research and instruction goals of Mexican American studies by serving as the first professors. While students and faculty members succeeded in establishing the UH Center for Mexican American Studies in 1972, they faced resistance from the administration in the hiring of full-time ethnic Mexican professors in political science, anthropology, and history.[58] As Jiménez recalled, there "was a constant tension" regarding "the hiring of Mexican [American] faculty," since the administration claimed that the center "would have fourteen, and actually even a woman who married a Mexican was counted. There was actually no one."[59] Inés

Hernández Tovar, a doctoral student in English and UH MAYO member, fulfilled the demand for instructors who had personal knowledge of ethnic Mexican experiences and cultural values by submitting a proposal for a Chicana/o literature class. Stanley Schatt, the director of lower-division studies in the English Department, responded to her request by accusing Hernández Tovar of not going through the proper channels for course approval. He further stated that he was surprised that she held a master's degree in English, "with a thesis directed by one of our most outstanding scholars and teachers," yet still had "problems understanding basic English."[60] UH MAYO drafted an open letter to President Hoffman to address this "prejudice and bigotry," insisting that Schatt "be reprimanded seriously for his action, and that, at the very least, he be removed from the position of responsibility which he holds."[61] Hernández Tovar personally challenged Schatt's contention that she did not understand the proper procedure and reported him to the chair of the department. These efforts resulted in Hernández Tovar getting her course approved and Schatt no longer overseeing lower-division studies in the English Department.[62] With the support of fellow UH MAYO activists, Hernández Tovar faced down anti-Mexican racism and fulfilled her mission to teach Mexican American studies courses.

As one of the first UH CMAS instructors, Hernández Tovar focused on the writings of ethnic Mexican women in her Chicana/o literature class and laid the groundwork for the later emergence of Chicana studies. Alongside the writings of Tomás Rivera and Octavio I. Romero, Hernández Tovar's course focused on the works of the Tejana writer Estela Portillo-Trambley. Portillo-Trambley's themes shaped the trajectory of Chicana literature. She drew on her experiences of growing up in El Paso and wrote about Chicana characters who challenged their assigned roles while pursuing independent lives.[63] In addition, Hernández Tovar incorporated literary concepts "that allowed [students] to see [themselves] and what [they] were doing and the creative and critical process that [they] were engaged in by studying the literature … seeing [themselves] in the literature.[64] Her introspective and creative frameworks critically shaped how her female students, who included emerging activists, approached their gender interventions. UH MAYO member Louise Villejo remembered that Hernández Tovar's class was an entrée to doing both community work and women's work. Given the choice of doing a paper or performing *teatro* (theatre), Villejo opted to employ her kinesthetic skills. Inspired by the experience, she and other *mujeres* "would make up plays and go to parks or we would go to events and put on *teatro*."[65] For Villejo, *teatros* "crystallized and verbalized what [an issue] was all about in an entertaining way, so that other people [who] might not know so much about the issue would be drawn in." Tejana *teatros* in Houston centered on "female empowerment and Chicanas being involved in the *movimiento* (movement)." Accordingly, Villejo and fellow Tejanas formed Mujeres Unidas (Women United) at UH to host conferences, panels, and workshops highlighting ethnic Mexican women's issues.[66]

In 1975, Hernández Tovar advanced Chicana studies by teaching "La Chicana in America" at the University of Texas at Austin. In this American studies and Mexican American studies course, Hernández Tovar addressed the "Chicana and the often narrow role that she has had in the Mexican-American culture, where men were considered leaders in movements" and "women were thought of only as workers in the movements."[67] She highlighted sexism within the *movimiento*, traced the genealogy of Chicana feminism, and assigned students the task of documenting Tejana resistance through interviews. Hernández Tovar also required her students to keep a journal to chronicle their burgeoning awareness of Chicana issues. Through the deconstruction of stereotypes, the recording of Tejana activism, and reflections on gender oppression, her students gained an understanding of women's issues. Hernández Tovar perceived her interventions in academia as creative acts rooted in race and gender empowerment, linked with the struggle on campus and in the community.

Sustaining the University of Houston Center for Mexican American Studies and Memorializing Tejana/o Student Activism

Because of the leadership role of Tejanas and the effective pressure that Brown and Black students put on the UH administration, the CMAS was formally established in 1972. But this self-determined educational center faced hurdles in cementing its place at the university. The first director, Guadalupe Quintanilla, faced funding and other challenges head-on and, with the help of Tejana/o students, created a sustainable program. Serving on the front lines of the ethnic studies battle, UH MAYO memorialized the race and gender power they had acquired through their fight for culturally relevant education.

While some UH MAYO members believed that Quintanilla was a bit conservative, Tejana/o students nonetheless supported her position as the CMAS director, since she had proved to be a "dedicated person with an insatiable appetite and a sincere interest in the betterment of the Chicanos."[68] For UH MAYO, it was imperative that the head of the CMAS be an ethnic Mexican who personally understood the Chicana/o experience and exhibited a commitment to students. Despite student support, Quintanilla had to fight to secure her directorship. She recalled "sitting with Dr. [Philip] Hoffman, who was the [UH] president at the time, and he told [her], 'Well, we just want you to do it interim while we look for somebody [else].'"[69] Quintanilla refused the offer, stating, "If you give [the directorship] to me as permanent, I'll take it, but it is permanent."[70] Quintanilla not only served on the faculty-student program committee that facilitated the birth of the CMAS, but also designed ethnic studies courses, bolstered Tejana/o student success, and listened to student feedback on what the ethnic studies program should embody.[71]

When Quintanilla became director, UH MAYO had already laid the groundwork for the center by writing proposals, increasing the Tejana/o student population, creating new courses, and pressuring the university to hire Chicana/o faculty. But the program still faced obstacles. Quintanilla had to ensure that the University Council approved the courses for the program. To gain that approval, she had to defend the intellectual viability of Chicana/o studies and lobby department heads so that a cross-section of instructors could teach the core Mexican American studies classes.[72] To incentivize the hiring of Chicana/o faculty members, Quintanilla worked out a plan with the administration whereby "if a department hired a Mexican American professor, the department would pay half and the administration would pay [the other] half."[73] She also advocated for the hiring of scholars Michael A. Olivas and Tatcho Mindiola, since she wanted to "retain students [through] role models and professors who would care about the Hispanic students and understand them better." Another major hurdle for the CMAS was to secure sufficient funding. Refusing to wait for the administration to locate program funds, Quintanilla labored with UH MAYO to successfully lobby the Texas Legislature for money. A leader in this campaign, Jiménez recalled that UH MAYO "went to Austin multiple times to get funded" and "to ensure that Mexican American studies continued," adding that funding was "a number one priority" in sustaining the program.[74] The campaign proved success-ful—UH CMAS acquired a line item in the state budget. According to Jiménez, UH MAYO's success was in part due to studying "proposals from other places where they had established [Mexican American studies]," since their movement was connected "with the Chicano movement nationally."[75]

Once UH CMAS was on a sustainable trajectory, UH MAYO procured university funding to create a mural in the University Center's Cougar Den that would cap-ture the Tejana/o student quest for race and gender power. The Cougar Den was the main location where Brown and Black students gathered and strategized. In 1973, UH MAYO painted a mural that depicts, on one side, revolutionary ethnic Mexican figures, such as Emiliano Zapata and Miguel Hidalgo, who represented Chicana/o history. The other side of the mural, labeled "*Raza* rising up," included portraits of José Ángel Gutiérrez, Reies Lopez Tijerina, and Rodolfo "Corky" Gonzales. As the UH MAYO member Edward Castillo recalled, in the middle there was a "*calavera* (skull) with a flag suit, showing that he was manipulating [Tejanas/os]."[76] Castillo furthered stated that if Tejanas/os continued "going through him, it was going to be [their] death."

As the mural was being painted, María Jiménez noticed that only men were represented. Refusing to accept this depiction of ethnic Mexican history and the Chicana/o movement, she advocated for the inclusion of Sor Juana Inés de la Cruz, a prominent Mexican feminist writer, and Alicia Escalante, a Chicana activist who fought for welfare rights. It was fitting that Jiménez, who was central to the fight for ethnic studies and Tejana empowerment, demanded that the mural reflect the struggle for both gender and racial liberation. Moreover, Sor Juana was heralded for being a forthright philosopher who championed the educational rights of women in colonial Mexico. Jiménez, more than three hundred years later, pursued ethnic studies while seeking Tejana educational self-determination.

For Tejanas/os in the protest era, racial liberation was paramount. It was the way that the ethnic Mexican community would realize the rights that had been denied to them throughout the nineteenth and twentieth centuries. Convinced that self-determined educational spaces were key to individual and collective racial empowerment, UH MAYO directed the fight for the University of Houston Center for Mexican Ameri-can Studies. Beyond culturally relevant courses, UH MAYO demanded the hiring of Chicana/o faculty members, better conditions on campus, and Tejana/o student re-cruitment and retention. Against the backdrop of the Chicana/o movement and the Black Power movement, UH MAYO fought a potent ethnic studies struggle. Indeed, UH MAYO not only built on the labor of Chicana/o students nationally, but also relationally defined their ethnic studies movement according to the confrontational methods and values of their counterparts in Afro-Americans for Black Liberation.

In Houston, Brown and Black students united to leverage their collective strength in transforming the ivory tower. This unity was critical in a segregated city where students of color were marginalized.[77] At UH, Tejanas carved out culturally relevant spaces and fought to have policies and courses that empowered them as female students of color. Through their leadership in UH MAYO, Tejanas challenged racism and sexism. For Tejanas, it was not enough to address structural racism. As Louise Villejo noted, Tejanas in the protest era "were looking at the broader landscape of what was happening around the nation and really not seeing [themselves] reflected in that broader landscape."[78] As a woman who experienced racial discrimination in her formative years, she was committed to claiming gender liberation within the Chicana/o movement.

CHAPTER 13

FROM POLICE BRUTALITY TO THE "UNITED PEOPLES PARTY":
San Antonio's Hybrid SNCC Chapter, the Chicano/a Movement, and Political Change

MAX KROCHMAL

There are people here who do not know about San Antonio, because they came here from other places. They don't realize the struggle that went on here. And just because it was not a bloody struggle, they think there was no struggle. Those jobs that they are getting the benefit of now, they are here because somebody said, "Hell no! Ain't going to do that no more."

But it's good—as long as they teach their kids what really happened, you know? That's what is so good about what you are doing now, because it will teach the kids what really happened and how it happened and why it happened. There are going to be those that say it happened because of Black rage, [but] that is not why I did it. I did not do anything out of rage. I did it because it was time to educate ourselves and do something about it if you want to change it. And it was time for a change, and if not me, who? That's what we did. Just a like-minded group of guys got together and started doing stuff.

CLAUDIS MINOR, SAN ANTONIO SNCC

Unlike San Antonio's Black liberation struggle, the city's Chicano/a movement has come to occupy a nearly mythic status in Texas political culture. Whispers of it are today deployed as badges of courage, proof of street cred, or evidence of the city's ostensibly postracial present and future. It was on the Westside of San Antonio that the iconic organizer José Ángel Gutiérrez joined with four of his comrades at St. Mary's University to found the Mexican American Youth Organization (MAYO), the "avant-garde" of the *movimiento* in Texas and the progenitor of La Raza Unida Party, the movement's national electoral wing. One of Gutiérrez's first collaborators, Willie Velásquez, is today remembered as a pioneer in the mass mobilization of Mexican American voters across the US Southwest. Another MAYO member, Ernesto Cortés, developed a new model of faith-based community organizing that brought much-needed municipal services to the city's barrios and then spread across the nation.[1]

Taken together, a series of "second-generation organizations" inspired by the Chicano/a movement succeeded in transforming San Antonio from an exemplar of Anglo domination into a vibrant (though still imperfect) multiracial democracy.[2] Pundits point to 1981, when movement veterans helped elect the nation's first Mexican American big-city mayor, Henry Cisneros. Likewise, in the twenty-first century, the twin politicians Julián and Joaquín Castro can trace their dedication to public service back to their hardscrabble upbringing in the Juan Crow barrio and, critically, to their mother Rosie's example as a forgotten leader in the Chicano/a liberation struggle. Only in San Antonio, the former mayor turned housing secretary Julián told audiences on the 2020 presidential campaign trail, could his tale of upward mobility even be possible.

To be sure, the new San Antonio owes much to the heralded Chicano/a organizers of the 1960s and 1970s, and the tales of their past activism merit remembering and celebration. Yet their counterparts and coconspirators in the city's Black liberation movement have been all but forgotten, as Claudis Minor later reflected, along with the larger span of San Antonio's African American history. Although they have been erased from civic lore, Black San Antonians did, in fact, wage their own, decades-long struggle against Jim Crow in pursuit of power, resources, and self-determination. They forged their own civil-rights-organizing tradition, and they did so in intimate conversation with Mexican American and Chicano/a activists across town. Collaboration across racial lines had emerged as a potent weapon for Black and Brown organizers in the Alamo City as far back as the 1930s. That cooperation remained evident in the "classical phase" of the postwar civil rights movement and continued during the heyday of the Chicano/a movement and beyond.[3]

Beginning in the late 1960s, a new cohort of Black Power activists launched a new phase of struggle against structural racism in San Antonio. They formed a late-stage chapter of the Student Nonviolent Coordinating Committee (SNCC; pronounced "snick"), the "shock troops" of the civil rights movement, which led the grassroots struggle from Maryland to Mississippi beginning in 1960. Yet SNCC in San Antonio was something new, apart, and different. The San Antonio chapter was born out of frustration with unending police brutality and durable racial inequality, and its leaders called for a mixture of equity and self-determination for the city's Black communities. They deployed confrontational tactics and militant rhetoric but also pounded the pavement and provided direct social services in their long-neglected Eastside neighborhoods. They connected with Black Power activists from across the state and the nation while always adapting to local needs. They forged enduring alliances across generational and racial lines, building close ties with older African American activists, white radicals, and Chicano/a members of the Brown Berets and the Raza Unida Party. SNCC activists also played a key role in the multiracial San Antonio Committee to Free Angela Davis, the Black Power philosopher whose political imprisonment spurred a successful international campaign for her release.

Across the board, San Antonio's SNCC chapter provoked both reaction and substantive change. One demonstration ended in a violent confrontation, a mini-rebellion that was followed by police reprisals—a forgotten tale that calls into question the city's official narratives of peaceful integration and harmonious race relations.[4] Yet at the same time, Black Power activists' community organizing translated into the electoral arena as they joined with Chicano/a activists to help dethrone the representatives of the city's Anglo elites—the self-proclaimed "Good Government League" (GGL)—and to usher in a new political regime.[5]

In the late 1960s, San Antonio's race relations resembled what one scholar termed a "leaking caste system." For decades, a multiracial coalition of African American,

Mexican American, and white labor and liberal activists had waged a series of campaigns against Jim Crow and Juan Crow. Earlier in the decade, students and elders staged sit-ins at local lunch counters and stand-ins at movie theaters, always demanding good jobs and neighborhood improvements in addition to immediate, complete integration. The city's white economic and political elites responded with a piecemeal program of "voluntary" desegregation but refrained from passing local ordinances against discrimination. The War on Poverty offered new opportunities to Black and Brown activists, but leaders in San Antonio—like their counterparts across the nation—chafed against federal calls for "maximum feasible participation" by the poor and instead sought to redirect antipoverty funds to policing, especially of juveniles. As the historian David Montejano showed, young people and activists nonetheless took advantage of the new structures to build an oppositional movement culture, ironically succeeding in ending gang warfare (for a time) via militant activism rather than the tidy provisioning of social services. Still, the city remained a tinderbox. The GGL dominated local politics, allowing white elites to handpick all but a handful of Black and Mexican American local officials. Such token representation failed to produce equitable outcomes, and formal equality under federal law did little to overcome more than a century of structural racism. Youthful and older activists who sought independent political power and economic justice—in a word, self-determination—chafed against the persistence of unequal policing, limited opportunities, and the neglect of their neighborhoods by city hall.

Appropriately, the city fathers decided to throw a party. Led by Congressman Henry B. Gonzalez, an "old school" liberal who had championed civil rights throughout his career but had grown increasingly out of touch, San Antonio succeeded in its bid to host the 1968 World's Fair. Dubbed "Hemisfair '68," the exposition aimed to showcase the city's romanticized Spanish and Mexican past and to deepen the city's connections with Latin America in the midst of the Cold War. Boosters promoted the city's tranquil race relations and productive workforce while conveniently ignoring the abject poverty of San Antonio's barrios and the formerly segregated Eastside. The performance of prosperity in a sea of suffering produced great anxiety for local officials, who waited with bated breath, hoping against hope that wild-eyed radicals would not disrupt the proceedings. Indeed, unattributed threats claimed that protests would take place at the fair's opening on April 6, 1968, two days after the assassination in Memphis of Dr. Martin Luther King Jr. triggered rebellions in more than a hundred cities across the country.

San Antonio remained quiet for the moment, but several weeks later a "'massive disturbance' by milling youths" disrupted the annual King's River Parade, part of the city's annual "Fiesta," a tradition with a Spanish name that celebrated the US conquest and, for much of its history, included the crowning of separate Anglo and Mexican royal courts. The "melee" was "'racial in nature,'" according to city police, but the "'several hundred' persons who were involved in scuffles and fistfights" were easily and swiftly subdued by the department's forceful crowd control. One observer, a seventeen-year-old Black male, was shot in the leg and hospitalized. Mayor Walter McAllister, the septuagenarian who had headed the GGL ticket since 1961, declared himself "gravely concerned" about the fracas and then apologized to bystanders caught in the crossfire. Still, he and other city leaders remained upbeat. They declared the Hemisfair a success and congratulated themselves on the city's progressive vision—conveniently overlooking its dark underbelly and apparently believing their own spin.[6]

Reality hit hard and fast on May 8, 1968, when six San Antonio police officers brutalized Bobby Joe Phillips, a twenty-eight-year-old African American construction worker and resident of the Eastside, resulting in his death. Like most cases of police brutality in the era before viral videos, the exact facts of the encounter remain disputed, yet the incident's impact on the community was clear. As the San Antonio SNCC organizer Carlos Richardson later recalled, "[Phillips] had gotten hold of some bad drugs or some bad alcohol and was acting a fool, going around to several bars and stuff, causing trouble. On the corner of New Braunfels [Avenue between Dakota and Nevada Streets] . . . the police caught up with him. They all gathered around, and they said he had a knife."[7] Fearing that he would attack, police reported, a "sergeant crept up behind Phillips and struck him on the head with the barrel of his service revolver."[8] It did not end there. Five other cops joined in, beating Phillips with blackjacks and nightsticks before taking him to a hospital in a paddy wagon, not an ambulance. In Richardson's recollection:

> They literally beat him to death with their sticks. He was still alive, but in the process of beating him to the point when he could not resist anymore, they had broken his neck. He was still breathing, but he was in bad enough shape that they had to send him to the hospital. When they put him in the hospital—well, when they took him to get his X-ray, he was beaten about the face, the head, and the back, and the chest. They laid him on the table to take an X-ray of his head, and when the fellow took his head to lay it to the side, they snapped his spinal cord and killed him. The medical examiner deemed it a homicide.

Local officials immediately declared the use of force necessary, sparking a hasty protest march of around one hundred Black youth and calls from older activists for a full investigation. Yet, predictably, the civil service commission cleared the officers of wrongdoing, and a grand jury confirmed those findings and no-billed them. Still, the beating struck a chord in San Antonio's Black communities, haunting activists and city officials for years to come. "That was totally unnecessary—there were too many police for him to have to be murdered in that manner," Richardson added. "It affected me. . . . But it charged the atmosphere here."[9]

San Antonio's SNCC chapter was born out of this moment. Soon afterward, the youthful Carlos Richardson began organizing his peers. Born in Jefferson Davis Hospital in Sugar Land, Texas, in 1947, Richardson experienced life under Jim Crow in the Lone Star State. Although his father's air force career offered some reprieve, Richardson recalled being shunted to the back of the school bus when it left a base in Abilene, Texas; the bus dropped off the white students at their schools before depositing him and other Black students at Woodson Elementary School, ten miles across town. "We were just kids," Richardson remembered. "We'd have our faces planted up against the windows, waving good-bye to our friends as we descended into hell. It was awful."[10] Over time, the family developed a home base in segregated San Antonio, in a small Black enclave in the predominantly Latino Westside. Schools there were slowly integrating, but guidance counselors pushed Black students, like Richardson, to pursue trades or the military rather than higher education. Seeking to avoid the war in Vietnam—what classmates called the "great cull" for Black people—Richardson attended the two-year San Antonio College briefly while working as an electrician's helper, gaining experience in television and radio repair. He then transferred to the University of Texas at Austin and got a job at an early tech start-up, Texas Instruments.[11]

But the civil rights movement pulled him away from school and work alike. On campus, he met members of Students for a Democratic Society (SDS), and in all-Black East Austin, he began hanging out at the Victory Grill. The scene there proved electric, transformative. "It was sort of a focal point for Black culture there in Austin. I was walking around there in a daze, and I had never seen Black people with this kind of attitude. There was Malcolm X playing on the loudspeaker. I was just in my medium. That is where I wanted to be," Richardson recalls. "I ended up asking people, you know, 'Where do you get involved with the civil rights movement here?' And I was directed to [Larry] Jackson. He was an interesting person. . . . He had a great deal of political education. I determined there that I was going to get as much out of it as possible." Jackson was the head of the SNCC chapter in Austin, a relatively new group that sought to build a united front for Black liberation in the city. For his part, Richardson met activists from around town, and he was hooked. He started turning over his wages to the movement, supporting other organizers despite getting fired from his job at TI, and he armed himself with a pair of .22-caliber revolvers for protection against the city's lawless police force. When the San Antonio police killed Bobby Joe Phillips, Richardson asked Jackson for permission to return home to organize a new chapter of SNCC. Jackson signed off, gave Richardson the title "field organizer," introduced him to a white UT law student to help him stay out of trouble, and dispatched them to the Alamo City.[12]

The SNCC organization that Carlos Richardson carried to San Antonio from Austin was not the heroic, sanctified SNCC of civil rights lore. Founded in 1960, the better-known SNCC grew out of the unprecedented wave of student-led lunch counter sit-ins that rocked the South early that year. Many of its early leaders and ideas came from the Nashville Student Movement, where future congressman John Lewis and his collaborators developed a deep philosophical commitment to both nonviolence and integration. Black and white students joined SNCC in hope of building a beloved community; they courageously endured countless beatings, threats, and murders at the hands of white-supremacist terrorists. In 1964, SNCC appealed to the conscience of the nation through its well-publicized Summer Project and Mississippi Freedom Democratic Party campaign, but those efforts led to disillusionment when white America—from President Lyndon B. Johnson on down—refused to go beyond granting African Americans formal rights. In 1966, SNCC activists began calling for "Black Power," coining an oft-misunderstood phrase that resonated powerfully in Black communities nationwide. A new group of SNCC leaders forged new ties with the Black Panther Party and other self-professed radical activists in the United States and abroad. They rejected nonviolence in favor of armed self-defense and advocated community control instead of integration. Still, many scholars maintain that the shift in rhetoric proved more dramatic than the change in substance. Indeed, for many Black activists, the movement had always centered on winning the ability for Black people to decide their own fate—and to enjoy freedom from ongoing white-supremacist violence, policing, and exploitation. In many ways, Black Power represented a continuation of the civil rights movement, not a radical departure. In any case, by the time of the Phillips murder, the national SNCC organization had all but collapsed, leaving the struggle for liberation in new hands.[13]

Progress often arrives late to Texas, where SNCC emerged only *after* the organization's public shift to Black Power in 1966. Local activists, often veterans of SNCC campaigns in the Deep South, had organized chapters of SNCC or "Friends of SNCC" in Dallas and Houston by 1967. The former group pushed Arlington State College, between Fort Worth and Dallas, to abandon its rebel mascot and Confederate iconography, and the latter led a broad push for equity on Houston's college campuses and for its Black neighborhoods. In May 1967, after Houston police opened fire on a dormitory at Texas Southern University with hundreds of rounds of ammunition, authorities charged five Black students affiliated with SNCC with murdering an officer. (Later investigations concluded that he had been killed by friendly fire, with a police-issued firearm.) The next year, Lee Otis Johnson, a SNCC organizer in Houston, was handed a decades-long prison sentence after being entrapped by a plainclothes detective whom he handed a marijuana cigarette. Several key Dallas organizers found themselves imprisoned by the end of the decade. In each case, SNCC adherents and allies statewide rallied in defense of their comrades, but the message from the powers that be was clear: protesting ongoing structural racism could easily beget police beatings, mass shootings, and even political imprisonment.[14]

Undaunted, Carlos Richardson dove headlong into the Austin movement and then brought it home to San Antonio, as planned. Like his counterparts in other Texas cities and nationwide, he began recruiting at college campuses. At San Antonio College, he found Mario Marcel Salas and other student leaders hanging out at the Methodist Student Center. As Salas later recalled:

> That was a gathering place of African American students there. They had different activities, people coming in to speak, etc. He [Richardson] went over there one day; I did not know him from Adam. He told me this story, he told me, "I asked around, 'Do you think anyone here that is going to SAC that you know of might be interested in the Black Power movement? Interested in liberation theory?'" and all of that. And for some reason, and I think I know why, but for some reason he said three or four students pointed at me, who was sitting over in a chair. So he came over there, he organized me, I became a member of SNCC.[15]

The story repeated itself at St. Phillip's College, a historically Black institution on the city's Eastside. There, Richardson approached Claudis Minor Jr., a complete stranger. Richardson told him about his plans to start a new SNCC chapter and asked whether Minor was interested. "And so we talked. We talked," Minor later recalled. "That started it there. We started talking. Because I trusted no one. Nobody, man. You know? And so, I said, 'How did you find me? You don't know me.' And to this day, I do not know how Carlos got in touch with me, but we started talking and I go, 'Yeah, I'm in. I'm in.' That is what we did. That is how I ended up being the minister of defense for SNCC in San Antonio."[16]

Mario Marcel Salas, 1975. Photo courtesy of the Mario Marcel Salas Papers, University of Texas at San Antonio, in partnership with the Portal to Texas History.

However he found them, Richardson succeeded in identifying some willing and ready recruits. He taught his new disciples about SNCC's work in Austin and beyond and gave them leadership positions in the fledgling local chapter, which they formally launched in November 1968. Together they formed a critical mass of activists. They opened a storefront office just around the corner from the site of Bobby Joe Phillips's murder, in the Denver Heights section at the heart of the Eastside, and got to work.

Much of the new chapter's early activities remained unglamorous. Organizers focused on the daily work of selling movement newspapers downtown and building a network of supporters on the city's many college campuses. Salas recalled that the new SNCC of the Black Power era melded organizing traditions from across the country. "SNCC in those days was interesting. It was a hybrid organization," he remembered. "It became at least half Black Panther and half SNCC. Even the garb was such, so that members of SNCC would wear denim blue jeans like they would wear in the South, [like] sharecroppers would wear them in the South, but with a black beret with a 'Free Huey Newton' button on the top of the beret. SNCC members actually sold SNCC newspapers and Black Panther Party newspapers in San Antonio on the corner of East Houston and Alamo Street every Saturday."[17]

During the week, many SNCC organizers attended classes or hung out on campuses talking to other Black youth. As the Third World Liberation Front strike roiled San Francisco State College and the Black student movement spread across America, SNCC activists in San Antonio provided leadership and technical expertise to help organize the first Black student unions (BSUs) in the city. First came San Antonio College, which Salas and other activists attended, and then they organized unions at St. Phillip's (a Black college) and two smaller religious white universities, Incarnate Word and Our Lady of the Lake. Black students at the historically white and Latinx St. Mary's University on the Westside organized independently of SNCC, but they later joined the successful SNCC-led effort to build a coalition of BSUs from all area institutions. Like their counterparts elsewhere, San Antonio's BSUs became launch sites for propelling the liberation struggle both on and off campus. Such activity may appear mundane or obvious in the twenty-first century, but the BSUs represented something new and radical in 1968. SNCC supported this work, recruiting new organizers and building an expanded base of rank-and-file supporters for the long haul.[18]

The San Antonio SNCC chapter mirrored other elements of the Black Panther Party for Self-Defense, generally known as the Black Panther Party, the Oakland-based vanguard of the Black Power movement, which had chapters across the United States. Ideologically, SNCC activists in San Antonio embraced revolutionary nationalism—a linking of the racial justice, anticapitalist, and decolonizing struggles that allowed for interracial and Third World coalitions—but eschewed narrower versions of cultural nationalism. On a practical level, around the same time that the Oakland Black Panthers set up their Free Breakfast for School Children Program in late 1968, San Antonio SNCC started collecting donations and distributing free food to kids on the Eastside, first at Antioch Baptist Church and later, after the pastor there asked them to leave, at Mt. Zion First Baptist Church. They later added free lunch and academic tutoring services, and later still a summer "Liberation School" and a free clinic for testing for sickle-cell anemia. San Antonio SNCC organizers corresponded with national Black Panther Party leaders and inquired about receiving a dual charter as a local party unit. Internal strife in the national party delayed formal recognition of the Alamo City chapter, but Black Panther Party alumni granted it official status posthumously, in the 1990s.[19]

Clearly, the leaders of San Antonio SNCC approached their work pragmatically, despite their radical ideological orientation. They borrowed from the older SNCC's organizing tradition, meeting Black youth at their schools and in their neighborhoods and creating new programs to respond to the basic needs in their communities. As a classic Mississippi freedom song put it, they would "do what the people say do." Yet that philosophy meant that they never strayed far from their origins in the fight against police brutality, an arena that soon led them into a direct confrontation with the city's ruling elites.

"SNCC 'Coming to S.A.'" ran the headline in the *San Antonio Express*, part of an ominous warning published midway through the paper's "Family" style section on January 21, 1969. This first newspaper account of the new chapter noted that approximately thirty people, including "young Negroes wearing black berets," attended an organizational meeting, from which reporters were barred. The article warned of ties between the new San Antonio group and other radicals in Austin and statewide, including SDS members, dissident lawyers, and former GIs. Many readers would have been familiar with the subtext: by late 1968, local newspapers had reported on the TSU "riot" in Houston, on a series of shootouts outside SNCC's national office in Washington, DC, and on the criminal convictions of SNCC members in Dallas. And a month before the SNCC meeting in San Antonio, in December 1968, the US Commission on Civil Rights held widely publicized hearings in San Antonio, at which Black and Brown residents testified for days on the city's racism, including their smoldering outrage over the police killing of Bobby Joe Phillips. The city's carefully crafted image of racial harmony appeared more vulnerable than ever.[20]

Still, even the alarmist local dailies remained unprepared for what came next. On December 29, San Antonio police killed Eloy Vidal, a seventeen-year-old Mexican American, shooting him in the back as he fled the scene of a burglary. Dozens of mostly Mexicano/a activists appeared at a subsequent city council meeting, leading to a fiery exchange between Councilman Pete Torres, a Mexican American independent, and Black and Brown councilmen aligned with the establishment GGL. For their part, the activists demanded action. Mrs. Rene McCalebb, the president of the Cassiano Resident Association, a tenants' group based in a Westside housing project, spoke up on behalf of its 2,984 "fed up" Mexican American, Anglo, and Black members. "If there is not something done about this issue, the Vidal case; we saw the Bobby Joe Phillips case go down," she said. "Now it can be someone else's son that this same thing happened to. We are not going to just stand ... with no kind of results being done of it." If police killings continued, she concluded, there would be a "terrible crisis" that might include an uprising or rioting.[21]

SNCC's Carlos Richardson appeared before the council the following month, on February 20, adding fuel to the flames in militant Black Power style. Richardson noted that the city had a "bad reputation of being down on people" and that the government did not reflect its diverse population. "We have some Latin American Uncle Toms on the City Council and one Negro [Uncle Tom] and if the council really represented San Antonio, then the mayor would be a Latin-American," he said. Richardson pointed to other disparities, including the glaring gaps between the city's historically white San Antonio College and its historically Black school, St. Phillip's. "Citing a list of SNCC demands for the Eastside, Richardson said they included drainage improvements, traffic lights for some school areas and better police understanding of Eastside problems," according to a newspaper report. He called for the hiring of Black policemen and then concluded with a bang: the meeting minutes read that he "referred to the [white] Police Officers as being no more than wild dogs running around with a license to kill people." Mayor Walter McAllister responded that Richardson was "out of order and the City Council doesn't want to listen to you." Richardson later recalled, "He got up and he said, 'I do not believe that.' And he got up and left the room. Everybody was sitting there, [asking,] 'What?' They did not know what to do. This was the boss [of San Antonio]."[22]

Richardson's incendiary comments earned him a spot on the front page of the *San Antonio Light* and, to his surprise, a surprising new ally. He later recalled:

> When I left that meeting at city council, I met a fellow and several other fellows. They came up to me in the street, [and they] had been sitting in there, apparently waiting for me to come in and say what I said. One named Willie Velásquez. It turned out that he, here in San Antonio, had the same program and had taken the same route as Stokely Carmichael in SNCC had taken. The man was a genius. He had studied the civil rights movement. He had started the [Southwest] Voter Registration [Project]. It was a mirror image of what was going on in SNCC. He was interested in working with us. He stated that much. So we talked and figured out some way we could work together.[23]

Few scholars or present-day San Antonians would liken Velásquez to Carmichael, but Richardson's comparison is revealing. Before he became known as a nationalist or even uttered the words "Black Power," Carmichael had distinguished himself as a SNCC field secretary in the Deep South and as one of the greatest proponents of the proposed Black Belt Project, an ambitious voter registration and mobilization effort in majority-Black counties across Dixie. It was during a related pilot program in Lowndes County, Alabama, that Carmichael and local people first used the black panther as a symbol of their movement. Velásquez had studied the Black freedom movement in the South during the early days of founding MAYO and had been in close contact with leaders of the Georgia-based Voter Education Project. By 1969, even as Carmichael was turning away from electoral politics, Velásquez drew on Carmichael's and SNCC's earlier southeastern example to launch a new broad-based registration drive among Mexicanos across the Southwest. At the same time, Richardson's likening of the confrontational militant Carmichael with the subdued pragmatist Velásquez suggests that there remained a vast gulf between how activists in the two struggles understood and, at times, *mis*understood each other.[24]

Nevertheless this chance meeting on the floor of a repressive city council chamber led to many more interactions across the color line as San Antonio SNCC grew ever more bound to the rising Chicano/a movement across town. The latter struggle snowballed rapidly in 1969. On March 30, some three thousand MAYO activists and allies from across Texas descended on the small border town of Del Rio, 150 miles west of San Antonio, to protest cuts to the VISTA Minority Mobilization program, an antipoverty effort that MAYO members had creatively hijacked to get governmental funding for their organizing efforts. Independent politicians from the Alamo City joined the massive demonstration that day, Palm Sunday, which included a mock funeral procession for a slain rabbit named "Justice" and the nailing to the county courthouse door of the movement's manifesto and demands.[25]

Meanwhile back in San Antonio in early April, Mario Compeán, a cofounder of MAYO, finished third in a crowded race against Mayor McAllister, sweeping the city's barrios and declaring himself the "mayor of the Westside." Scarcely more than a week later, on April 10, MAYO members called a press conference at which José Ángel Gutiérrez, another of the group's founders, called for "eliminating the gringo," by which he meant ending institutionalized white supremacy. Yet "if worst came to worst," he admitted when pressed, Mexicanos would turn to "killing the gringo" in self-defense. Finally, as Mrs. McCalebb had done a few months earlier, he warned that riots or other violence could occur in the absence of real change. Congressman Henry B. Gonzalez, already a fierce critic of MAYO, denounced the movement's members as communists associated with Castro's Cuba and then issued a stern warning: unspecified Chicano/a "militants" planned to disrupt Fiesta's sacred King's River Parade, where they would "hurl objects—as well as epithets—at the participants." All sides seemed to agree that the city's social fabric was coming apart, and that violence was inevitable and imminent.[26]

Such dire predictions proved only partially true. At the parade on Monday, April 21, SNCC organized a march against police brutality, citing both the attacks on Black youth at the previous year's parade and the killing of Bobby Joe Phillips. The demonstration started off small: thirty to forty SNCC members and allies assembled at the Victoria Courts housing project just south of Hemisfair Park and then proceeded into downtown. "People were chanting, 'Remember Bobby Joe Phillips,' 'End police brutality,' 'Stop police brutality,'" Mario Salas later recalled.[27] By the time they reached Houston Street, they had been joined by as many as a thousand demonstrators, a multiracial group that police characterized as predominantly Black (along with "several white hippies") but that activists remember as majority Mexican American. SNCC's minister of defense, Claudis Minor, added that the police had been trying to sow discord between SNCC and the Brown Berets, a politicized group of Chicano/a street youth. "They wanted us fighting all the time. There was a plan to just get us to just—all-out war between each other," Minor remembered. But instead,

> We met with them and told them what our ideas were, and we went to their territory, over on Guadalupe Street, and met in their offices and said okay. So that night at the River Parade, they came from the Westside, we came from the Eastside, and police were all over the place, and they knew there was going to be this big fight that they had been trying to get going. Division between the two groups. We met right there by the Texas Theater, man, on St. Mary's and Houston Street. We just came together and everybody held their breath when we started hugging and laughing and backslapping each other. And that is it, it was all over. The fight did not happen, what they planned. So it backfired on them.[28]

SNCC's Carlos Richardson affirmed the presence of Chicano/a militants at the march, but cautioned that their counterparts failed to attract a large crowd, as promised:

We had made a pact with a group of Latinos to have a demonstration at the River Parade.... No signs or anything—it was going to be impromptu because we did not like the way that the city allowed you to have a demonstration. They were determined to really make it into something. It was a clandestine operation; it was just going to pop up. Well, they were not able to pull off their part of it.... There were some— the Latinos, they had long hair, you could tell they were, they were ready to go. But they were not able to inspire the people down on the river to come up on to Houston Street.[29]

Still, Richardson and other Black and Chicano/a activists joined the procession, chanting "Beep-beep-bang-bang-Ungawa, Black Power!" Hundreds more joined them before being met by a line of police officers. The march descended into chaos as some demonstrators clashed with police while others began breaking windows. Rumors spread that SNCC members had already been arrested. The head of the police department's Community Relations Bureau pleaded for calm from demon-strators and cops alike, offering the megaphone from a police cruiser to "a group of youths." SNCC's Salas then jumped onto the roof of one patrol car, stomped on it, and demanded the release of his arrested brethren. Remarkably, a full-scale riot did not ensue. Organizers turned the march around, and the police stood down. In the end, nine were arrested, and none were beaten beyond a few shoves. A few protesters looted stores on their way home while others followed the SNCC leaders back to their office at Iowa and Pine streets on the Eastside.[30]

It appeared that the city fathers had contained the unrest for the moment—the police had shown restraint, earning praise from many of their frequent critics, and SNCC had declared a temporary "truce." Yet the peace lasted less than twenty-four hours; the following evening, a group of vengeful officers retaliated against SNCC with a new wave of violence. Members of the Dallas SNCC chapter had driven down to San Antonio that Tuesday to offer their support after hearing about the skirmishes at the parade. As the group strategized that evening, police officers cruised by the building housing the SNCC office and looked on with growing alarm as a few activ-ists carried firearms inside. The slow-rolling cop cars stoked the simmering tensions. SNCC members, joined by the company of the Langston Hughes Afro-American Theater, housed downstairs, yelled at the passing policemen, calling them "pigs" and "numerous names ... [and] cursing and threatening the officers." The patrol unit called for backup, and some fifteen officers carrying "sawed-off shotguns, rifles, and billy clubs" soon stormed into the growing crowd of about twenty-five Black youths outside. The *San Antonio Light* reported one SNCC member's description of what happened next: "We all screamed 'pigs' and one of the pigs said to us, 'Are you talk-ing to us?'" Then police grabbed several members of the theater group and struck one of them, Oncy Whittier, on the head. "Blood flowed everywhere," the witness said, and the police looked enraged, "like mad dogs.... Other brothers were brutally beaten." Four SNCC members and one ally were arrested after the altercation. Their ranks included San Antonio chapter founder Carlos Richardson, who had also been charged with stealing guns from a pawnshop the night before.[31]

The next day a group of Black and Brown community leaders rallied to their de-fense at a fiery meeting at city hall. Convened and moderated by the independent councilman Pete Torres, the gathering brought together the city manager, the chief of police, and the head of the local Community Relations Commission—all white—along with a delegation of "about 20" African Americans that included Whittier and other young members of the theater group. Two older, veteran activists who attended summarized the mood. The Reverend Claude W. Black Jr., the pastor of Mt. Zion First Baptist Church and a leader of civil rights demonstrations throughout the decade, said, "Bobby Joe Phillips was killed and we talked. Our children were beaten last year and we talked. We're getting tired of talking. If we're not going to do anything, let's break this up. I'll go to my prayer room and pray that black boys won't die." G. J. Sutton, an undertaker and organizer who had been active since the 1930s, added, "The city manager should say, 'treat blacks like you treat whites.'" Instead, he noted, "The [same] mayor says 'law and order' and 'shoot to kill.' This is a racist community, in a climate like this, you won't get anything done." Activists noted the disparities in policing the different sections of town, pointing out that a predominantly white community theater on the Anglo Northside would never be subjected to similar treatment. In contrast, police responses to alleged crime in Black communities were swift and forceful, they noted, and officers acted with impunity. "Our experience is that police have been exonerated an hour after a murder," Sutton added. Instead, city officials should "call the dogs off," he said. "We want this racist mayor to stop inflaming the community."[32]

SNCC leaders offered an even more militant critique that same day at a press conference at the Methodist Student Center at San Antonio College. After denying (somewhat unbelievably) that SNCC had had anything to do with the violence at the King's River Parade, organizers threatened retaliation if the police continued to attack their members. "You don't harass people in the Student Non-violent Coordinating Committee because they are non-violent up to a point," Carlos Richardson said, "up to the point where they are harassed." The group announced that it was planning a mass meeting for the following evening, Thursday, at the Reverend Black's church, and activists suggested that "plans for a disturbance Saturday have already been made." They remained vague on the details of any future protests, but they were clear in justifying their motive and purpose. Claudis Minor added, "Anytime a policeman can come to the black community and take a man just for being a black man, it's time to change the police department and the city. . . . It's up to the city how it's going to be changed. . . . [San Antonio] can be a beautiful city. But it can also be ashes. We will not be beat again. We've asked the man (police) to get off our back. Next time we're going to get him off ourselves." Minor also noted that SNCC members had the right to protect themselves, including with firearms, pointing again to the disparities in how their activities were policed. "If a black man has a rifle, it's a revolution," he said. "If a white man has a rifle, he's going hunting." When asked about connections between SNCC and the SDS or MAYO, the activists refused to comment. Instead, they shared plans to organize another SNCC chapter in nearby San Marcos and continued to emphasize their own strength and desire to double down on their militant efforts.[33]

The threatened next "disturbance" never took place, but the week's events clearly had an enduring impact. Mario Salas later wrote, "This was one of the few times recorded in San Antonio's history that a group of armed Black men stood up to police brutality and stood their ground in the face of overwhelming odds."[34] More generally, SNCC members had announced their presence to city leaders and the local press corps. They had forged an alliance on the streets with the Brown Berets and won the public support of older activists such as the Reverend Black, G. J. Sutton, and Councilman Pete Torres—all veterans of a previous generation of militant Black-Brown alliances in the city. Together they had kept the memory of Bobby Joe Phillips alive and made it clear that law enforcement could no longer act with impunity.

At the same time, SNCC leaders paid a price for their advocacy. Local police continued to monitor their activities, and before long, the Federal Bureau of Investigation began surveilling SNCC members. Confrontations with the police led to the publication of activists' names and addresses in the newspapers, at times leading to retaliation. As SNCC member T. C. Calvert later recalled, "The FBI and J. Edgar Hoover considered these guys communists, considered them leftists, and considered them a threat to the internal security of the United States. That is why I know I am on file, because, you know, they used to come and visit my mother and my father and say, 'Your son is hanging around these groups.' You know what my mother told them? 'These boys come over here all the time and they're good kids. I think you need to go and investigate somebody else.'"[35] Carlos Richardson similarly added that he sought to protect the young people who participated in SNCC activities:

> They are going to be attacked first, but then their families are going to be attacked, too. It happened to the Whittiers—Dr. Whittier, one of the two Black doctors here in town. His son went to jail with us. He was a bleeder. He got hit on his head, and he was a bloody mess by the time I was going off. I was very upset, you know. They eventually busted his father. He—I do not know if he went to jail, but they put him out of business as a doctor.[36]

Richardson ended up pleading guilty to burglary in connection with stealing guns from the pawnshop the night of the King's River Parade. He got off easy: the judge sentenced him to three years' probation following his plea.[37]

Others were not so lucky. Across Texas and the nation, Black Power activists faced imprisonment or worse for their militancy. Claudis Minor recalled that his duties as minister of defense carried especially heavy weight:

> My job was to keep my people from getting hurt so that they can live longer, man, because, truly, we could have died. Live long enough to teach the kids, teach the community, what we want, what we are doing, and what we are all about. And that is what we did. And a lot of people did not join us because you *could* die doing that, man. You could get your head blown off really easily, or you could just disappear, and it happened. There is many cases of guys just disappearing, or you end up getting some crazy thirty-year sentence for half a joint somewhere that gets planted on you. It happened to [SNCC member] Lee Otis Johnson in [Houston].[38]

Despite the high stakes and the very real risk of retaliation, San Antonio's SNCC members redoubled their efforts, rallying in support of Lee Otis Johnson and organizing the new chapter in nearby San Marcos.[39] They dug deep, recruiting and politicizing Black youth on the Eastside by fighting for equity in schools while continuing to protest police brutality and poor conditions in the Bexar County jail.[40] Their efforts soon garnered more attention as they worked together with Chicano/a and white radicals to transform the political landscape of the Alamo City.

Fortunately for the activists in San Antonio SNCC, that landscape was already shifting beneath their feet. On July 6, 1970, Mayor McAllister appeared on NBC's nationally televised evening news program, *The Huntley-Brinkley Report*, to respond to charges of racial discrimination put forward by the city's Chicano/a movement activists. In the interview, the mayor began:

> You have to bear in mind that there is a special temperament, a difference of temperament between the Anglos and our Americans of Mexican descent. Our citizens of Mexican descent are very fine people; they are very fine people. They are home loving. They love beauty, they love flowers, they love music, they love dancing. Perhaps they're not quite as, let's say, as ambitiously motivated as the Anglos are to get ahead financially, but they manage to get a lot out of life.

McAllister's statement seethed with paternalism and racist assumptions, belittling his constituents under the guise of false praise and essentialist cultural appreciation. He then added that he did not object to Mexican Americans being "discontented with [their] condition," since such unease exemplified the "mentality" he believed they lacked as well as the "motivation" required for improving their status. At the same time, McAllister flatly contended that the alleged racial discrimination did not exist, especially when it came to law enforcement. "I will defend the police department of the City of San Antonio and say to you that, in my judgment, there is no harassment of any particular ethnic group," he said. "And that, of course, I want to say, again, is a common communist cry. That's the first thing they'll holler wherever they are: 'Police brutality, police brutality.'" McAllister thus blamed the victims of police violence and trotted out the red herring that any discontent stemmed from foreign ideologies, not domestic inequality. He concluded with a prescription: "And it's just too bad they don't crack them over the head more frequently than they do."[41]

McAllister's incendiary comments led to an immediate outcry. Activists flooded the next city council meeting, on July 9. Councilman Pete Torres moved to censure the mayor, but could not muster a majority vote from the GGL-dominated council. Local units of the often-staid LULAC and the American GI Forum likewise denounced the mayor's remarks. The weekend following the interview, two thousand Chicano/a activists at a statewide Raza Unida conference in Austin passed a resolution calling for a boycott and pickets at a savings and loan firm owned by the mayor, the San Antonio Savings Association (SASA). A few days later, "an ad hoc committee of La Raza Unida" in the Alamo City launched the boycott and set up a subcommittee to help Mexican American depositors transfer their accounts elsewhere. On July 27, a group of approximately 35 activists began picketing the SASA's downtown headquarters, and that evening, "some 250 persons attended a rally at Main Plaza to garner support for [the] boycott." Bexar county commissioner Albert Peña, the longtime leader of the city's liberal Mexican American faction, also announced his support for the cause.[42]

Despite its promising start, the campaign made little headway until late August, when younger Chicano/a activists took charge. A meeting at Mario's Restaurant on August 20 brought the mayor and thirty boycott committee members together, but exploded after McAllister refused to apologize for his remarks. Instead, he issued a public statement claiming that his comments had been taken out of context. Activists broke the stalemate after the August 29 Chicano Moratorium march against the Vietnam War in East Los Angeles, a peaceful demonstration that erupted when local sheriff's deputies beat protesters, fired tear gas into the crowd, and killed Ruben Salazar, a preeminent Chicano journalist. San Antonio activists who had traveled to Los Angeles returned home ready to renew the local struggle, as did countless others who had watched the faraway police riot on TV. Soon a group of Chicana activists led by Rosie Castro took charge of the SASA boycott committee's operations, organizing a new wave of militant pickets outside the bank and demanding that the mayor not only apologize but also take steps to end systemic employment discrimination at SASA and the city alike.[43]

The SASA boycott reached a climax on September 9 and 10, when San Antonio police arrested twenty-nine demonstrators for disorderly conduct on the picket line during a day of action dubbed "Business and Professional Men's Day." Among the arrested were Castro, Commissioner Peña, the Eastside activist G. J. Sutton, and the restaurateur Mario Cantú, who had hosted the failed parley weeks before. The following day, as protesters again flooded the city council chambers, San Antonio police joined bank security staff in attacking a number of Chicanas on the picket line, including one who was pregnant, "bang[ing] people against the walls and sidewalks" before arresting ten of them. In response, the boycott committee presented the mayor and council with a revised list of demands, including the granting of subpoena power to the Community Relations Commission and the removal of the chief of police. In the end, McAllister issued a mealymouthed nonapology, maintaining that his televised comments "were not intended . . . to be derogatory or insulting to any citizen" and "were no insult as they came from [his] lips." Accordingly, the council's GGL majority continued to back the mayor, blaming the firebrands Torres and Peña for the entire conflict and stonewalling all attempts at reform, including activists' calls to strengthen community oversight of the police department.[44]

Yet the controversy surrounding the mayor's interview and the SASA boycott reenergized the city's Chicano/a movement—and deepened its alliance with Black Power activists across town. Indeed, for the leaders of San Antonio's SNCC chapter, McAllister's comments and the Chicano/a movement's response signaled a new chapter in the city's racial formations and, by extension, in its political history. Carlos Richardson later recalled:

> When I was in high school, there would be terrible fights between the Latinos and the
> Blacks after football games. It was stupid. But it was divide and conquer. "The rulers
> here" had fermented this anxiety and this atmosphere of competition, and it was awful.
> It was barbaric. . . . At any rate, we had a Latino population that was going along with

the program because they had the title: "We are white." ... They were confused. The race thing was really getting in the way of them making any progress.[45]

Richardson added that Latinos had previously disagreed about their place in the US racial hierarchy. There were some "Latinos who were nationalists that said, 'We are Chicanos, we are Latinos, we are the people—*la raza*,'" he noted. "And [other Latino] people were saying, 'We are white people just like these other people. Sit down. Everything is going to be okay. They love us!'" In Richardson's view, McAllister's comments and the protests that followed clarified the situation and transformed this debate:

> [Latinos] had gone through all this trouble. They thought, "We made it now. There are going to be no miscegenation laws forced upon us," or anything. "We are white." And the mayor says, "That's bullshit! You are still Mexicans. You are poor because you are just not as good as white people." ... That is where this [whiteness] defense evaporated. And everybody—not *everybody*, because there are still some holders-on—everybody said, "Hey, this man had to tell it to us. We are Latinos." It made a great difference because now there isn't this Black population against *everybody*. We are all in this together.[46]

In a singsong tone, Richardson paraphrased McAllister—"'Well, they do not have the spirit and the willingness to work that the Anglos do here.'" He then concluded: "There it was. It began a change in the landscape of San Antonio with those few words."[47]

Richardson undoubtedly overstated and oversimplified the impact of McAllister's interview on Latinos' internal self-identification. Indeed, Richardson's memory likely reflected his own growing awareness of Mexican American living conditions and Chicano/a activist struggles, rather than a singular shift in the racial identities of the city's barrio residents. Historians point to not one but many factors that explain the gradual shift in Mexican Americans' individual and collective positioning, from the selective and uneven adoption of whiteness as an uplift strategy after World War II toward a near-wholesale embrace of Brownness during the Chicano/a movement in the late 1960s. While scholars continue to debate the degree to which Mexicanos ever embraced whiteness internally, even proponents of the thesis that Mexican American leaders aligned themselves with whiteness (and in opposition to Blackness) caution that working-class and poor Mexicanos rarely if ever benefited from their official classification as whites. Yet it is indisputable that some Mexican American leaders did adopt whiteness as a political strategy, and this tactic had, at times, represented an obstacle to coalition building with African Americans. For Richardson and other SNCC leaders who were still learning about their counterparts across town, though, the SASA controversy of 1970 seemed to tip the balance from whiteness to Brownness, opening new avenues for collaboration. Critically, the vocal minority of Mexican American leaders who self-identified as "white" ceased to be an impediment for Black Power organizers. Instead, Richardson now reinterpreted the city's racial formations as "We are all in this together."[48]

The growing militancy of a distinctively Brown movement culture drove home another conclusion: that Black Power organizers and their allies shared a common enemy with activists in the Chicano/a movement: McAllister's Good Government League. These battle lines were not new, but they now stood in sharp relief. The same city police had been beating and killing members of both communities since time immemorial; now they attacked protesters from both groups while the same politicians refused them redress. Both groups of activists encountered opposition in their own communities; the GGL-aligned African American and Mexican American leaders stood behind the mayor and, by extension, the city's economic elites. A Black-Brown coalition brought together the city's radical and liberal community organizers, while businessmen and conservatives formed their own multiracial alliance in support of the status quo. A pair of campaigns over the next eighteen months cemented the ties between the activists and made their work more visible than ever.

On December 27, 1970, a diverse group of activists came together to form the San Antonio Committee to Free Angela Davis (SACTFAD). Davis had gained notoriety after being fired from a faculty position at UCLA for her heterodox politics, which included support for the Communist Party, the Black Panthers, and prisoners' rights. After a breakout attempt at a court hearing resulted in the death of a superior court judge, California authorities charged Davis as an accomplice to murder, kidnapping, and conspiracy. She had not been present during the incident, but the guns used in the killing were registered in her name. Davis fled, appearing on the FBI's most-wanted list before being captured several months later. By the end of 1970, she was being held in jail without bond for a crime in which she did not participate. Civil rights and civil liberties activists nationwide rallied behind her, pledging funds for her defense and signing petitions demanding that she be released on bail.[49]

SACTFAD was thus part of a nationwide push to "Free Angela." The local SNCC chapter was at its center, with Carlos Richardson serving as the committee's chairman and Mario Salas as its secretary, yet its composition was broader, and its impact extensive. The group's first newsletter, seemingly written by Salas, outlines the group's purpose: "To make the need to free Angela Davis a live proposition in San Antonio. . . . This young lady is being railroaded, made a scapegoat, because she is black, female, and a Communist, in order to intimidate people in our country who are fighting for the rights of black people, for peace, for the labor movement." Within weeks, the activists had written a petition and made plans to circulate it on the streets, at shopping centers, through churches, and by setting up tables at other public events. They planned to meet weekly at the headquarters of the American Friends Service Committee (AFSC), a social action project of the Quakers, located across the street from the Hemisfair grounds. They asked others to join their efforts and to sponsor the campaign and hatched plans for a mass rally in the spring.[50]

Although it seems to have begun as a SNCC project, SACTFAD drew on the city's nascent multiracial activist coalition for its membership and its appeal. Twelve names topped the petition forms that the committee circulated publicly, a list that represented a who's who of the city's veteran Black and Brown organizers. On the top line were John Inman, an African American communist, and G. J. Sutton, the Eastside's leading civil rights and political organizer. The Reverend Black occupied

FREE ANGELA DAVIS
Rally & Dance

Sunday, May 23, 1971   8:00 p.m.   La Villita Assembly Building
                                                    San Antonio

DONATION 99¢   SPEAKERS: DAVID POINDEXTER
MUSIC BY:
  Langston Hugh's - AFRO Americane Theater   Rev. C.W. Black - San Antonio
  LIFE & DEATH
  others . . .   Franklin "Tortillas" Garcia - S.A.
FOR INFORMATION —
924-8711   924-1541   223-3371

Flyer for the Free Angela Davis Rally & Dance, San Antonio, 1971. Photo courtesy of the
Mario Marcel Salas Papers (private collection), Portal to Texas History.

the second line, along with the activist publisher Eugene Coleman. Next was county
commissioner Albert A. Peña Jr., followed by the union organizers Franklin "Tortillas" Garcia and Erby Rendon, the activist Marty Martinez, and Rosie Castro, the
SASA boycott leader who was now a candidate for city council on the Committee for
Barrio Betterment ticket. John Stanford, a white communist warhorse, served as the
group's treasurer, and Tom Flowers of the AFSC provided crucial support.[51]

An early newsletter listed many of these luminaries, noting, "It is espacially [sic] important that there is broad based local support in San Antonio for this freedom campaign." Similarly, the committee's rationale for defending Davis spoke directly to the connections between the Black and Chicano/a liberation struggles, and their encounters with police brutality and political imprisonment. The newsletter noted that Davis was

> a symbol of the oppression which is faced by many other people in this country, resulting from our economic and political system. In the Rio Grande Valley, Chicano migrant farm workers face the same poverty that their brothers in California faced, prevented from bettering their lot by the conditions of their employment and by an "impartial" legal system which works against organizing a union. At Pharr, Texas, Texas Rangers have callously shot at and terrorized Chicanos, and have incurred no penalties for doing so. Here in San Antonio a Black teenager is convicted of felonious assault on a policeman despite the fact that his arms were handcuffed behind his back at the time he was supposed to have committed the assault.

The newsletter added that the group had collected over five hundred signatures in less than six weeks, and it called for residents to sign up for a bus trip to California to join a vigil outside the jail where Davis was being held. "Success in freeing Angela Davis will help the cause of all political prisoners," the newsletter concluded before inviting readers to the next weekly meeting.[52]

SACTFAD members continued their daily petition gathering and weekly meetings, building up to a mass rally at the city's historic La Villita Assembly Hall downtown. They had tried to secure Angela Davis's mother as a keynote speaker but ended up with David Poindexter, a Black activist who had just been acquitted of "knowingly harboring" the fugitive Davis and was now embarking on a national speaking tour on her behalf. They sold tickets "at Union Halls, head shops, and on the street" for a ninety-nine-cent donation. As Salas put it in another newsletter, "SACTFAD members had to overcome three major obstacles posed by the city power structure." First, the local press had seemingly imposed a news blackout on the group's activities, providing zero coverage of the committee, petition drive, or rally until the day of the event. Second, the city refused to grant them a license to sell beer, forcing the activists to give it away instead, which ate into the group's eventual donation to Davis's bail fund. Last and "most crucial was the last minute refusal to make sheriff's deputies available to guard the meeting." Although the county-owned venue required security services, the sheriff refused, on ideological grounds, to send his troops, and the county executive refrained from intervening. As a result, G. J. Sutton "loosed a blast in Commissioners Court," and the local ACLU office worked through a litany of federal and state judges to convince the city police department to send its officers. Ironically, a protest campaign against overpolicing and political imprisonment nearly foundered because of a lack of police protection.[53]

These bumps did not derail the event. A "standing room only crowd" of as many as 1,500 people jammed La Villita on May 23, 1971, to hear Poindexter speak and call for Davis's release. "He spoke out for freedom of all political prisoners, making it clear that this freedom rested with the audience and other people like them," the SACTFAD newsletter reported. "Poindexter carried a message from Angela, asking that black, brown, red, white and poor people form a coalition to make this country a better place in which to live. This message, we felt, had special relevance here in San Antonio, with . . . an absolute majority of its people brown and black." In addition to Poindexter, the "leading San Antonio churchman Rev. C. W. Black spoke with great power and eloquence," as did the veteran civil rights activist Franklin "Tortillas" Garcia of the Amalgamated Meat Cutters union, who added that "he had never worked so hard for a meeting as he had for this one . . . because he felt that Angela Davis was being persecuted rather than prosecuted."[54]

Following the rally, SACTFAD continued to collect petition signatures and planned to show films on Davis's life "in housing projects and [the] barrio . . . [produced] by roving projection crews." Mario Salas pounded the pavement, dropping off petitions at churches, funeral homes, union headquarters, pool halls, street corners, and everywhere in between. For a while, he received some support from the Southern Conference Educational Fund, the white-led civil liberties group based in Louisville that had stood at the vanguard of southern radicalism since the 1930s. Salas remained in near-daily contact with Franklin Garcia, Albert Peña, and other Mexican American and Chicano/a allies across town, and they aided the campaign until it disappeared from the historical record. Six weeks after the rally, in early July 1971, Salas and other SACTFAD members joined Chicanos/as in picketing the City Produce Terminal in support of the United Farm Workers' grape boycott. Two months later, SNCC's Carlos Richardson penned a powerful letter to the editor, protesting the "murder" of George Jackson, Davis's close friend and comrade, in prison in California. In the end, SACTFAD's multiracial coalition gathered as many as thirty thousand signatures demanding Davis's release from jail, which she secured in late February 1972. Soon thereafter, she faced trial and was acquitted on all charges.[55]

San Antonio's radical Black-Brown coalition had gelled as never before. SNCC, the key activist cadre in the city's Black Power movement, had forged close ties with their Chicano/a and Mexican American counterparts and overcame state repression to stage one of the largest "Free Angela" rallies in the country. The campaign tied them even more closely to national and international activist networks while also extending their local struggle against what we now call the "carceral state" and the local power structure that upheld it. The brief fight on behalf of Davis represented a crucial moment of deepening solidarity among San Antonio's nonwhite majority population. Its success led SNCC and Chicano/a movement organizers to flex their muscles together in a new arena: electoral politics.

To be sure, San Antonio's SNCC activists had confronted the city's power structure, including its elected officials, from the group's beginning, and they had forged partnerships with militant political activists such as G. J. Sutton and the Reverend Black. But unlike their counterparts in the Chicano/a movement across town, they had refrained from fielding or endorsing candidates. By 1972, SNCC organizers had changed their minds, accepting politics as a "necessary evil." Yet they engaged the electoral field in an unusual manner: by throwing their lot in with the Chicano/a-led Partido de La Raza Unida, the "United Peoples Party" (or, alternatively, the "Party of the United Race," Raza Unida Party, or RUP).[56] As the African American journalist Ken Bunting explained that year in a mainstream newspaper special titled "Black

San Antonio," "SNCC is entering the political arena, ... openly challenging conventional practices." The chief novelty, Bunting noted, was SNCC's desire to forge an unusual alliance with the RUP. "It's going to be hard to change the generally hostile attitude the two minorities have toward political cooperation," SNCC's Mario Salas told Bunting, drawing a subtle distinction between electoral collaboration and joint demonstrations or ad hoc campaigns such as SACTFAD. The reporter added, "Peculiarly, local blacks are generally weary of any type of political coalition with Mexican-Americans, a larger minority with much greater political power." Both assertions — by the activist and the reporter alike — overlooked the decades of multiracial coalition building in which Sutton, Black, and other older militant activists had allied with firebrand Mexicanos led by Albert Peña, a collaboration that represented a familiar and still-vibrant model for the youthful organizers. Nonetheless, it remained true that any new electoral partnership among the young radicals was anything but natural. Indeed, rank-and-file voters would need more than a little persuasion to join such an effort, while established Black leaders could be counted upon to reject it. "None of the traditional political brokers of the East Side has been consulted," Bunting noted ominously, in exceeding deference to the existing power brokers. "Success or failure of the coalition may rest on their reaction."[57]

For the activists of the RUP and SNCC, however, the calculation proved different. In their view, with the exceptions of Peña, Councilman Pete Torres, and a few lesser officeholders, none of the Black and Brown politicians or self-appointed race leaders had delivered for their struggling communities. Both the established Democratic Party and the rising Republican Party had spurned them, and the Black and Brown councilmen aligned with the Good Government League had long thwarted progress in local policy making. As a result, both groups of younger militants determined that the traditional Black and Brown elites were no longer needed. A radical, independent, coordinated, multiracial third party represented the best — indeed, the only — path forward. Thus, at their first meeting on January 25, 1972, SNCC leaders Salas and Calvert joined with RUP representatives to quickly forge an "informal agreement" to work together, with details to be determined later. Myriad tensions remained, but both groups saw collaboration across racial lines as a necessary step in winning their own fights for liberation.

SNCC's alliance with the RUP came at a critical juncture in the insurgent political party's history. La Raza Unida had emerged organically out of MAYO, the youth-led "avant-garde of the Chicano movement" in Texas. On the ground, two streams fed its growth: the Committee for Barrio Betterment, which fielded slates of candidates for municipal offices in San Antonio in 1969 and again in 1971, and the RUP proper, which was born in Crystal City in 1970 and quickly expanded across South Texas. After winning county-level races in the countryside, the party held its first state convention in San Antonio in October 1971. Delegates decided to expand further by fielding candidates for statewide posts. After flirting with a number of possible gubernatorial candidates, including two prominent African American activists, the RUP selected Ramsey Muñiz, a young lawyer with movie-star looks and widespread name recognition thanks to his standout football career at Baylor University. Soon after, party leaders recruited candidates for the remaining state executive positions and as many legislative races as they could muster. In San Antonio, a recent court decision had broken up the massive Texas House District 57 into eleven new single-member voting districts. The new maps meant that Democratic candidates of color and white Republicans had unprecedented opportunities to win their way to Austin based on focused campaigns in new, smaller, more homogeneous districts. Both statewide and locally, the RUP hoped to win where it could while organizing protest votes or serving as a spoiler in places where the deck was stacked against it. Either way, the party hoped that its direct engagement in electoral politics would force the establishment to take the Chicano/a movement more seriously than ever before.[58]

On February 9, just two weeks after the initial meeting between the RUP and San Antonio's SNCC chapter, the party announced its Black and Brown slate of candidates. It fielded members in six of the eleven newly established districts, including Mario Salas in 57-C and another African American, James Roy Alexander, in 57-E. George Velásquez, the brother of MAYO cofounder and SNCC friend Willie Velásquez, ran in 57-I. After some initial shuffling, Albert Peña III, the son of the firebrand county commissioner, filed in 57-J. Further down the ballot, SNCC's Carlos Richardson sought a post on the junior college district board, and T. C. Calvert served as a precinct committeeman. Salas became the party's chairman on the Eastside, and George Velásquez took its reins on the Westside. In its slate and officers, then, the Raza Unida Party in San Antonio reflected the previous three years of Black-Brown coalition building in the streets. Now the activists in both groups sought to carry their overlapping social movements from the streets to the ballot box.[59]

A closer look at the San Antonio party's appeals to Black voters reveals the coalition's depth as well as the ways in which the concerns of Black activists substantively expanded the platform of the predominantly Chicano RUP. The "United Peoples Party is an alternative for Blacks," one rare campaign letter that survives in the archives begins. "Black people throughout Texas have taken the brunt of Police Brutality. . . . What have the Republicans and Democrats done to alleviate such things? . . . The Democrats take it for granted that the Black vote will always be there . . . but no Blacks are ever consulted on a mass level, or involved in policy making." RUP represented an alternative to the two-party system, the letter added, because it "knows of the problems that confront Black people every day." It also had a proven record of success, having already captured control of local governments in South Texas. RUP "has seen a dream come true in Crystal City. We can see our dream come true by helping the Party."[60] The letter called on readers to sign petitions to place the RUP on the ballot statewide; only those who did not vote in the two major party primaries were eligible, and more than 22,000 signatures were needed to qualify. Put another way, the RUP rested its entire future on expanding the electorate to new potential voters who had given up on traditional politics. In present-day terms, they sought to mobilize low-propensity Black and Brown voters for a political revolution.

The back of the letter contains a list of frequently asked questions, offering answers that likewise reveal the profound implications of the intimate connections being forged between SNCC and RUP organizers in San Antonio. After assuring voters that the RUP was indeed a real political party, with plans for long-term growth, it addressed the question of the Black-Brown coalition head-on, in a remarkable imaginary exchange:

Question: Is United Peoples only for Chicanos?

Answer: United Peoples has a Chicano base for organizing purposes. Past party work has been in South Texas which is overwhelmingly Chicano. *The issues [are] self-determination for people to change those things which control their lives*: Schools, courts, employment [and] government issues. These issues [are] shared by all those presently denied. Chicano, Black, Women, the poor. United Peoples IS a way—a party organized for these people and all those who wish for change on these issues.

Question: Why keep the name Raza Unida if it is for everybody?

Answer: First, the history given above shows that we have a Chicano base. The name is Spanish, the United People, [but] has meaning for all. Also, we feel the name says from the beginning that we intend to be different. Acceptance of a different language is symbolic of acceptance of all people no matter how different they are....

Question: From where does the money from the party come?

Answer: What money?[61]

For Salas and SNCC, the advantages of joining such a coalition were obvious. Their embrace of the Chicano/a-led party, their admiration of its past successes, their desire to apply the same theory of self-determination to their own community, their celebration of bilingualism—the United Peoples Party in San Antonio challenged the orthodoxies of their time in ways that forced contemporaries to rethink the nexus of race, class, and power in their city and state. It likewise provided a model for political empowerment today. "Our goal is a new form of governing so that all voices of the electorate can feel they belong—*equal but different*," the letter concluded. "Raza Unida is a way of life—a commitment to a principle that all people have the right and the responsibility to have a voice over the issues that run their lives—self determination for dignity and change. We feel our first victory is in ourselves."[62]

Between May and November 1972, SNCC and the RUP built a vibrant movement culture centered on Black-Brown collaboration, contributing to the party's national and international impact. Salas and the RUP candidate for US Senate, Ricardo Flores Amaya, penned a letter to Le Duc Tho, the head of the North Vietnamese delegation to a Paris summit aimed at ending the war. The duo pledged the party's support of "peace loving people" in Southeast Asia and proposed a direct negotiation for the release of Black and Chicano prisoners of war. On the home front, SNCC and the RUP reprised the SACTFAD strategy by sponsoring a musical "Show & Dance" at San Antonio's Convention Center Banquet Hall, selling $1.50 tickets to raise funds for the party. A flyer for the event features the Chicano/a movement's Aztec eagle on one corner opposite the Black Power fist on another. In August, they celebrated as the Reverend Ralph Abernathy and Coretta Scott King surprised observers by going to Dallas to offer the Southern Christian Leadership Conference's endorsement of Ramsey Muñiz, the party's gubernatorial candidate and standard-bearer.[63]

Their long-shot campaigns fell short at the ballot box in November, but as the above account suggests, they achieved their first victory: believing in themselves and in one another, and in their collective right to have a voice. In the end, Salas served as a spoiler, helping deliver House District 57-C to a Republican newcomer. Albert Peña III performed best among the legislative candidates, losing by a seven-to-four ratio. Still, "Amid rousing shouts of 'Viva La Raza Unida' at the party's headquarters," Peña told supporters, "We have accomplished what we set out to do, and we have only just begun."[64]

In its final years, San Antonio SNCC continued to build new programs that linked its community's needs with the struggle for political representation, fairness in the criminal justice system, and international human rights. Like the similar efforts of its Black Panther counterparts nationwide, SNCC's local Free Breakfast for School Children program became a template for state- and school-district-run provisions for poor kids that persists today. Beginning in 1972, SNCC secured funding from the United Methodist Church to establish a legal defense fund and legal aid services on the Eastside. The group also pioneered programs to raise awareness and offer treatment for sickle-cell anemia, a disease that disproportionately strikes African Americans. SNCC continued to fight against discrimination at local colleges and secondary schools, and to confront instances of police brutality. In 1973, Mario Salas, writing as the SNCC state coordinator, began working to support the struggle against apartheid in South Africa and in solidarity with other anticolonial liberation movements on the continent. The chapter continued to function until 1976, making it the last local unit of SNCC in the United States.[65]

By that point, both the Black Power and Chicano/a movements had splintered in a thousand directions, victims of extreme state repression, countless personality clashes and ideological schisms, unanswered questions of intersectionality, and the weight of their own considerable success. Across the United States, a bipartisan "counterinsurgency" strategy extended the War on Crime, normalizing acts of police brutality, launching a new wave of surveillance and political imprisonment, and recasting militant liberation movements as simply beyond the pale. This changing environment led many activists to turn inward, both to self-reflect and to call out their former comrades.[66]

For thirty years after the decline of San Antonio SNCC, Salas grappled with its history and meaning, producing an impressive series of drafts of essays and other iterative manuscripts, all of which ultimately informed his 2004 master's thesis. In one piece, he expressed deep regret about working with the Raza Unida Party, a group he labeled "reactionary nationalist" and "petty bourgeois." In another, Salas critically examined San Antonio SNCC's own failures, a long and wide-ranging list that included its small membership base, unexamined male chauvinism, vulgar romanticizing of the "lumpen" proletariat, and fundamental misunderstandings of race and racism. Salas's corpus of writings clearly merits additional research. At the same time, his observations should be evaluated in the specific context of their creation and alongside other available written and oral evidence. With the benefit of hindsight and some critical distance, Salas eventually grew proud of his work in SNCC as well as the chapter's collaboration with Chicano/a movement groups. Yet his earlier critiques underscore the emotional and physical toll that SNCC's efforts exacted on its organizers as well as the rarity and precariousness of coalition building across the color line.[67]

Even as they engaged in introspection and combatted the conservative shift in American politics in the late 1970s, many activists found new ways to carry the struggle forward. In 1978, two years after the dissolution of San Antonio SNCC, chapter alumni founded Organizations United for Eastside Development (OUED) following the murder by private security guards of another Black man, Webb Eugene Boyd. The group helped secure the conviction of Boyd's killers and waged ongoing fights against police brutality and for improved public services in the city's Black neighborhoods. Significantly, the OUED also maintained close partnerships with Chicano/a and Mexican American activists across town. Among other feats, they worked together to convince the Texas Legislature to establish the Dr. Martin Luther King, Jr., holiday, and founded one of the nation's largest and most diverse annual MLK Day marches.[68] Former SNCC members continued to hone their craft as each new organization begat another. The OUED morphed into a series of "community empowerment centers," community-based development groups, and neighborhood alliances on the Eastside. T. C. Calvert recalled that he and other SNCC members grew more pragmatic over time, developing a new praxis. "The basics of organizing is that you do not do for people what people cannot do for themselves," Calvert recalled.

It has always been about what the people want. So what we would do is we would ask the citizens, "Ms. Martinez, can you tell us what your top three issues are that we can get you to come to a meeting on?" And so she would say, "Well, Mr. Calvert, when it rains it floods. At night there are shootings here, and I do not have any sidewalks that are code compliant." So that is where the transition took place. I became a Saul Alinsky-style organizer.... What we found out [was] that most neighborhoods across the United States of America all have the same issues. They all have problems with housing. They all have problems with bank redlining. They all have problems with crime. They all have problems with street and drainage problems.... We organized the people on what they wanted in their neighborhoods. You would not like if I came into your neighborhood and I told you what is good for you. That is a mistake a lot of political people make. It is that top-down thing. Well, I do not organize like that. And I still do not do that today.[69]

San Antonio SNCC's legacy includes the creation of countless organizations, a long list of accomplishments big and small, and the transformation of dozens of ordinary people into lifelong activists. Perhaps most importantly, what Claudis Minor called a small "like-minded group of guys" helped end the Good Government League's decades-long domination of local politics, transforming the race relations of the city in the process. "I would make the argument SNCC destroyed [Mayor Walter] McAllister, or at the very least set in motion to destroy his racial setup of city politics," Mario Salas reflected. "Later, MALDEF [the Mexican American Legal Defense and Educational Fund] and the NAACP put the legal touches, the final touches on that," and many other groups contributed to the change. "SNCC did not do it by itself," Salas cautioned. "It was also done, like I said, with the help of the Mexican American community [and] progressive whites as well." While many groups deserve credit, the story of SNCC, long since forgotten, is worth remembering alongside those of the RUP, the Brown Berets, MALDEF, and the pantheon of Black and Chicano/a civil rights heroes nationwide. We were "just as militant as the original SNCC'ers in our fight against McAllister," Salas added, "because ... we took segregation head-on and were threatened with death."[70] The San Antonio chapter's founder, Carlos Richardson, added,

> McAllister was a boss. He chose who was going to be on the [city] council. If there was a Black person, he was going to choose who that person was, and they were going to cooperate with whatever he wanted them to do. . . . What we wanted was more representation. . . . We wanted the police to treat us like human beings. No more being beaten to death in the street. No more being stopped for no reason. . . . Respect our lives. We are human beings.[71]

The transformation of electoral politics in the city took some time but proved profound. Badly bruised from the controversy surrounding his television interview, McAllister left office quietly in 1971. In 1972, the SNCC ally G. J. Sutton easily won a seat representing District 57-E in the Texas House of Representatives. (RUP's candidate withdrew from the race before Election Day.) The following year, the desperate leaders of the crumbling GGL selected another SNCC ally, the Reverend Black, to join its slate, despite having fought him bitterly since his first candidacy for office a decade earlier. Two years after Black took office, in 1975, the GGL lost its majority on the city council; two years after that, the GGL was defunct and San Antonio held its first elections with new single-member districts that finally offered the city's communities of color the opportunity for meaningful self-determination. Four years after, in 1981, a multiracial coalition backed Henry Cisneros as he became the city's first Mexican American mayor in the twentieth century. And in 1999, SNCC's own Mario Salas won a seat on the city council representing the Eastside's District 2. Finally, in 2001, Julián Castro, the son of the SNCC collaborator and Chicana activist Rosie Castro, began his extraordinary political career, starting with a seat on a thoroughly transformed city council.[72]

From its founding in late 1968 through the RUP campaign of 1972 and beyond, the San Antonio chapter of SNCC made an indelible mark on the city's political scene and social movement landscape. Born out of calls for justice for the slain Bobby Joe Phillips, SNCC built alliances with the Brown Berets, La Raza Unida, and older Black activists in order to call out the lingering inequities baked into the Alamo City's "leaking caste system." They spoke truth to power at city hall and carried radical third-party politics from the Westside barrios to the all-Black Eastside. They waged a big-tent campaign to free a distant political prisoner who symbolized the state's routine repression of activists who confronted institutional racism. They helped start a "riot," endured attacks from a vengeful police force, and kept on fighting. In a quite literal sense, they translated the Chicano/a movement for Black audiences, forging surprising ties of solidarity while also deepening and extending Raza Unida's conception of self-determination. Their experiences belied San Antonio's carefully crafted image of a peaceful "Fiesta City" and demonstrated that African Americans contributed in critical ways to the city's transformation into a more egalitarian — though still imperfect — multiracial democracy.

CHAPTER 14

"YOU EITHER SUPPORT DEMOCRACY OR YOU DON'T":
Structural Racism, Segregation, and the Struggle to Bring Single-Member Districts to Austin

J. TODD MOYE

Austin is a political paradox. Texas's shining city on a hill for the Left, it had thriving chapters of radical organizations such as Students for a Democratic Society (SDS) and the Brown Berets in the 1960s; it fostered a progressive political culture that sent liberal lions such as Wilhelmina Delco, Gonzalo Barrientos, and Kirk Watson across town to the state legislature in later decades. Its residents have long supported vibrant neighborhood associations and grassroots activist groups such as People Organized in Defense of Earth and Her Resources and the Save Our Springs Alliance. They have sustained vibrant local chapters of national organizations such as the NAACP, MALDEF, and United Farm Workers of America, among other civil rights, Black Power, Chicano/a, and organized labor groups. Yet the Democratic Party stronghold also embraced racial segregation through the inertia of impersonal social forces and the conscious choices of white voters, and maintained an exceptionally undemocratic voting system long after other cities had abandoned theirs. Larry Jackson, a longtime Austinite with experience in the Student Nonviolent Coordinating Committee, the antiwar movement, and Black Power organizations, put it bluntly in a 2016 CRBB interview: "Austin is a very racist city, always has been and always will be. And it's more racist now than it was in the 1960s."[1]

Austin's at-large voting system was among the highest-profile institutions under-girding that racism, and by the time it was replaced, it was certainly the most anachronistic. The voting system made it prohibitively difficult for African American and Mexican American candidates to win elections for city council and the mayor's office until 2014. David Van Os, a longtime Austin attorney who worked on two lawsuits and several other grassroots efforts challenging the at-large system over five decades, argued, "In a democracy, the right to vote is *everything*," and the at-large system diluted that right. Van Os, who is white, began to develop his devotion to radical democracy as a member of UT's SDS chapter. He pinpointed the problem of Austin's white liberal ruling class having allowed the at-large system to last as long as it did: "Democracy is democracy, and you either support maximum egalitarian democracy or you don't." The same white liberal Austinites who detested the majority-Republican state legislature's redistricting efforts following the 2000 and 2010 censuses managed to live with a voting arrangement in their city that severely curtailed the political power of minority voters, in part because Republicans were among those minorities. They identified as liberals without behaving as Democrats, and they sacrificed the rights and interests of their Mexican American and African American fellow citizens.[2]

The Voting Rights Act (VRA), enacted in 1965 and subsequently renewed and expanded on five occasions (one of which, the 1972 version, covered Texas for the first time), remade the political order in Texas and other southern states over the first five decades of its existence. It allowed hundreds of thousands of African Americans and, later, Spanish speakers who had been disenfranchised to register to vote. Just as significantly, during periods when the US Department of Justice (DOJ) enforced its underlying "one man, one vote" ethos to the fullest extent possible, it used the VRA to alter voting systems, which made possible a significant democratization of southern politics on the local level. In states that had to get DOJ preapproval before altering their voting procedures, the department and the federal courts forced cities and towns to move from at-large systems to single-member districts, and kept white elites from gerrymandering districts to benefit themselves. By the early 1980s, the political science literature had come to firm conclusions: "The effect of changing to districts is unequivocally toward greater equity.... The representational effect of changing from at-large to district elections is striking."[3] Incredibly, a half century after the VRA began remaking American politics, Austin was the largest city in the country without single-member districts.

The at-large system recognized minority voters' right to cast a ballot, but it denied minority candidates an equal opportunity to run competitive races for city offices. With few African American and Mexican American officeholders, Austin became a vastly unequal place—by some measures of economic inequality, more segregated and unequal in 2015 than it had been in 1965.[4] Denied an equitable share of political power, African Americans and Mexican Americans in Austin were unable to stop the forces of racial segregation throughout most of the twentieth century, and they were unable to protect their interests when desegregation—in the form of gentrification—took hold in the twenty-first.

Because it has been inextricably intertwined with Austin's other major injustices—namely, residential segregation and the inequities that flowed from it—the fight to replace the at-large system with single-member districts became arguably the most important focus of Black and Brown civil rights organizing. It was also one of the most successful campaigns in which Black and Brown communities in Austin worked in coalition, the culmination of decades of organizing. Its story is still unfolding.

Segregating Austin

Like many other political stories in Texas, this one begins during Reconstruction, when formerly enslaved Texans elected dozens of African Americans to state offices and hundreds more to local posts. After white Democrats "redeemed" the state by force in the 1870s, they began denying African Americans and their political allies the right to vote. When and where they could not, they imposed other limits in the form of literacy tests, property qualifications, and poll taxes. They gerrymandered districts in some cases and imposed at-large systems in others in order to dilute minority votes. For a time, they successfully defined the Democratic Party of Texas as a private organization that could set its own membership rules, which allowed them to bar Black and Brown voters from participating in the party primaries, at a time when the Democratic Party was the only game in town. African Americans had been effectively disfranchised by the early twentieth century; Mexican Americans voted in large numbers in some parts of the state, but nearly always under the watchful eyes of Anglo patrons.

Civil rights groups in Texas fought for the franchise throughout the first two-thirds of the century, and they won some notable victories. The US Supreme Court sided with the NAACP Legal Defense Fund in 1944, ruling in *Smith v. Allwright* that in prohibiting minorities from voting in its primaries, the Texas Democratic Party violated the Fourteenth Amendment. But that was far from the end of the story. Following the decision, according to the legal historian J. Morgan Kousser, "when southern Blacks threatened to vote in large numbers for the first time since the turn of the twentieth century, white Democrats reverted to such reliable means as racial gerrymandering, at-large elections, and felon disfranchisement, as well as employing variations of other subterfuges," in addition to the tried and true methods of violence and terror.[5] Democrats expanded the discretionary powers of registration and election officials "to enable them to increase informal discrimination that was difficult to document in court." Austin leaders and voters may not have set out to disenfranchise or dilute the political power of racial and ethnic minorities, but whatever intentions they had in maintaining the at-large system for as long as they did in the post-VRA era, the system they consistently voted to maintain produced that outcome.

Despite its cherished, self-identified progressive character, Austin has a troubled racial history that was formed by both individual acts of white supremacy and wide-ranging policies and structures that exacerbated racial segregation and institutional racism. African Americans founded several freedom colonies within the city limits following emancipation. They were scattered throughout the city, which posed problems for elected officials during the age of Jim Crow: it would be prohibitively expensive to provide those neighborhoods with separate accommodations that even approached equal status. Either African Americans and Mexican Americans would have to be concentrated in one area, or whites would have to accommodate residential integration. The city contracted with Koch and Fowler, a city-planning firm in Dallas, to create a new master plan for Austin in 1928, and it recommended building facilities for African Americans and Mexican Americans in East Austin only. Koch and Fowler frankly admitted that it was attempting to find a way to segregate the Black and Brown populations by using means that the US Supreme Court would find constitutional. In the midst of the discussions that surrounded the city plan, the *Austin American-Statesman* thundered, "This is white man's country" in an editorial, lest any readers miss the point of the plan.[6]

The mayor and all-white city council adopted the master plan (critics later called it the "Yes, Master" plan) unanimously, and soon thereafter the Austin school board closed "Negro" schools in West Austin and built E. H. Anderson High School in East Austin. Before the plan passed there were still remnants of freedom colonies in Wheatsville and Clarksville on the western side of East Avenue—what is now Interstate Highway 35—but after adopting the plan, the city no longer provided amenities to serve them. By 1930, when Mexican Americans made up roughly 10 percent of the city's population, Austin had developed a "tri-ethnic pattern of segregation."[7] According to the 1940 US Census, 75 percent of the city's Black population lived in two East Austin census tracts, and the Mexican American population was almost as concentrated on that side of the city. Clarksville (just east of present-day MoPac freeway and just south of Enfield Road) held on as a small, self-sustaining African American community for longer than most, but its residents lived without city sewer service until 1979.[8] "Although Latino segregation was not mandated in the plan," the historian Andrew Busch found, "similar forces coalesced to push the vast majority of Austin's Mexican American population into the neighborhood just south of the African American one" in East Austin.[9]

African Americans and Mexican Americans could not be completely excluded from the life of the city during Jim Crow. They crossed East Avenue to visit the downtown shopping and entertainment districts, but they were segregated there too. They had to sit apart from whites in the Ritz and other public theaters on Sixth Street and Congress Avenue, and they were prohibited from trying on clothes before buying them in downtown shops. Susana Almanza grew up on East 10th Street in the 1950s and 1960s, which at that time was a dividing line between African Americans and Mexican Americans. "I had a very unique upbringing, because I grew up in that era where, you know, Blacks and Mexicanos were really looked down on," she said. "Us because we spoke a second language. The Blacks because of the color of their skin. We faced a lot of indignities."[10]

The logic of enforced separation held that Black and Brown communities would be better off not having to compete with white communities for housing and public accommodations, that they could better develop on their own terms in their own neighborhoods. But "separate but equal" was a lie. Once they had been confined to East Austin, Black and Brown citizens had to fight for minimal, much less equal, police and fire protection, access to health care, and access to public libraries, among other basic amenities, and their housing stock was rated as far below average for the city. By the early 1950s, white liberal city boosters had come to consider East Austin an embarrassment. Writing from their point of view, the sociologist Anthony M. Orum asked, "How can you show yourself off to the world, be a first-class place to live, be the dream of Northerners who wish to come South, if you have poor people?" Even as the legal structures that provided scaffolding for Jim Crow began to fall away in the postwar Sun Belt, it became increasingly necessary, those boosters felt, to separate the fate of East Austin from the rest of the city, and "segregation became more rigid because it became more linked to economic growth."[11]

The city's political structure under at-large voting created these conditions. There was little that Black and Brown East Austinites could do to defend their interests through the political process. They occupied the worst of both political worlds: together they made up a minority of the city's population, so even with sustained voter registration and political-organizing campaigns, it was nearly impossible for them to win city council seats, much less the mayoralty, in citywide elections. They were concentrated into an area of town where segregation might have had the backhanded effect of making one or more districts winnable in a single-member system, but Austin clung to the at-large system.

Arthur DeWitty displaying a poll tax receipt, Austin, 1955. Photo courtesy the Texas AFL-CIO Executive Board Office Records, Special Collections, University of Texas at Arlington Libraries.

Austin voters reaffirmed the at-large system in a 1953 revision to the city charter, after a surprisingly strong showing from Arthur DeWitty, the head of the local NAACP branch, in the 1951 city council elections. (DeWitty finished a close sixth in a citywide race for five seats.) Under the new system, a candidate for city council would run for one of five places, and whoever won the most votes for each place would hold office. It would be even more difficult for African Americans and Mexican Americans to win elections in the new at-large system. That did not stop them from trying, however.

Whites saw the writing on the wall. In the late 1960s, they entered into a "gentlemen's agreement" to allow one of the city's five council seats to go to an African American acceptable to representatives of the white business community, which financed campaigns. The city's Mexican American population grew enough in the 1950s and 1960s that after the council was expanded to seven seats in the late 1960s, white elites entered into a similar agreement to allow Mexican Americans a seat. The agreements were never written down, much less formalized in the city charter; they amounted to "an unenforceable but largely accommodated tradition."[12] David Van Os believed that the agreements resulted from white Austin leaders' canny belief that by cracking the door open for "acceptable" minority candidates, they could forestall voting-rights lawsuits that might have blown the doors wide open for everyone and challenged the status quo. "Chicano and Black access to the system was slotted into two places on the city council, and [the fact that] these were two places that were granted by the largesse of the white community was not real democracy," he said. He also emphasized that the parties to the pacts were white businessmen in particular, who agreed not to fund white candidates who ran against "acceptable" minority candidates. They were not bargains among African Americans, Mexican Americans, and the larger white community.[13]

Charles Urdy, who held the seat reserved for African Americans from 1981 to 1994, thought the arrangement benefited the community as a whole: "It's to our benefit to elect one that the African Americans are supporting, so that's sort of what folks looked for, to see what your support was in your respective minority community. So, as long as you maintained that support, to me it was sort of a vested interest in the rest of the community to support that. They didn't have anything to lose." Urdy also believed that the gentlemen's agreements incentivized African Americans and Mexican Americans to work together, at least in some ways. "There was a lot of interaction, politically, between those two communities," he said. "The greatest support I received in terms of percentage was in the African American community and the second was the Hispanic community. If I had an African American opponent that was credible, I might get a higher percentage of support in the Hispanic community than in the African American community."[14]

Although the agreements reserved places in the deliberative body for Black and Brown representatives, they hardly democratized city politics. African Americans and Mexican Americans who welcomed the gentlemen's agreements as half-a-loaf measures that improved on previous arrangements quickly learned that having one seat reserved for them meant having *no more than one seat* reserved for them. The agreements were holdovers from the era of Jim Crow and Juan Crow. As Van Os put it, "Chicano and Black access to the system was slotted into two places on the city council. And that these were two places that were granted by the largesse of the white community was not real democracy."[15]

Other developments in the 1960s gave the lie to Austin's progressive reputation. Interstate 35 was completed in 1962, atop the footprint of East Avenue, the longtime dividing line between white West Austin and Black and Brown East Austin. According to Busch, it "reinscribed a physical and mental landscape of segregation

on central Austin in a much more brutal and impassable form," and some Austinites took to calling it "Interracial 35."[16] Throughout the period, African Americans
fought a running battle for improved housing stock and greater investment in East
Austin, alongside their demand for equal political representation, and they found
white allies few and far between. In fact, according to Busch, "while most narratives
portray a slow improvement of race relations after the contentious battles fought over
civil rights in the late 1950s and early 1960s, in Austin racial tension appears to have
increased during this period." Disagreements over political representation, public
school desegregation, and, especially, open housing were as intense in Austin as they
were in Little Rock, Atlanta, or any other southern city. Despite its "relative tolerance and a lack of racial violence endemic to many cities," Busch noted, "Austin was
one of the most segregated in the South through the 1960s."[17]

The open housing issue exploded in 1967–1968 when the city council created the
Austin Human Rights Commission and charged it with creating a fair housing ordinance that would forbid discrimination against prospective renters, leasers, or buyers
of residential property, on the basis of race, color, religion, or national origin. The
council, which had a core of three liberal members, accepted the commission's recommended ordinance (which was the result of painstaking work and organizing),
publicized it widely, and enacted it. Then all hell broke loose.[18]

Local Realtors denounced the ordinance as "forced public housing" (it was of
course no such thing) and "just another government attempt to restrict and control
your individual freedom and to tamper with the most basic human right, private
ownership of property." (The latter assertion may seem absurd to some, but it evinced
the Realtors' talent for framing an issue of plain racial justice in nonracial terms—
and it hit a nerve with a huge majority of Austin's white voters.) The Austin Board
of Realtors launched a petition drive for a referendum on the ordinance. Within ten
days, 27,000 Austin residents had signed it—around 10 percent of the city's total
population. When the referendum appeared on the ballot, Austin voters crushed the
fair housing ordinance, and when the three liberal council members came up for reelection in 1969, the voters replaced them, too.[19]

The support for residential segregation among Austin Anglos was overwhelming, but it ran up against a more powerful force—the need to satisfy corporations as
Austin took part in the Sun Belt boom—and almost immediately proved difficult to
enforce. When corporations such as IBM began transferring employees to Austin
in large numbers in the late 1960s and early 1970s, they demanded guarantees from
city government that their employees of all races could purchase housing wherever
they chose.[20] Those guarantees hardly provided the same level of protection for all of
Austin's residents as the open housing ordinance had, but they did create cracks in
the wall. Burl Handcox, one of the African American IBM employees (his job title
was equal employment opportunity coordinator) who purchased a house outside East
Austin, became the first African American to serve on Austin's city council, winning
election in 1971.[21]

In any case, investment in the Black and Brown eastern half of Austin continued
to lag, and residents who did not have the backing of multinational corporations were
denied a tool to break out of their restricted area. By 1977, 51 percent of the housing
stock in the predominantly African American northern section of East Austin (east

of IH-35 and north of Seventh Street) was rated substandard. The city rated as substandard 53 percent and 65 percent of the housing stock of two Latino neighborhoods south of Seventh Street and east of IH-35.[22]

The city's postwar economic boom brought billions of dollars of new investment to Austin and created hundreds of thousands of new jobs that led to impressive increases in per capita and per family income, but it did not create a rising tide that lifted all boats. "For minority residents segregated on the city's Eastside ... the city's economic boom only exacerbated conditions of inequality that they had endured for decades," Busch found.[23] Austin's economy grew faster than almost any other American city's during the 1980s, but in 1990 more than half the residents of central East Austin lived in poverty. Economic expansion and population growth continued into the twenty-first century, but also continued to reinforce decades-old inequalities, as Busch pointed out: "African Americans['] and Latinos['] household income in 2010 was roughly half of Anglo income, the same percentage as in 1970. Despite its relatively robust economy, Austin's [citywide] poverty rate in 2010 was more than 18 percent, almost 4 percent higher than the national average."[24]

The Brown Berets and Black Power Groups

As segregation hardened and economic inequality worsened in the 1960s and 1970s, some Black and Brown Austinites rejected the fight for change through the political process and pursued radical alternatives. There was always a ready supply of leftists on the University of Texas campus, but most African American and Mexican American activists learned about community organizing and radical challenges to capitalism and the electoral system in the school of hard knocks. Gilbert Rivera explained the problems inherent in working with white radicals from the university: "We were very angry, and that anger translated into a lot of militant organizing. We wanted to confront the system, we wanted to let people know exactly what was going on, and we wanted to do it *now*." White students who had read Leninist and Maoist theory tended to come in and critique their strategies and tactics, saying, "Well, this the way Mao does it." According to Rivera, "If we didn't do it the way Mao said it or Lenin said it," the students claimed that "we weren't real revolutionaries." But Rivera told the Anglo radicals, "'We don't *care*. This is the way we're doing it. We need to do what we need to do, and we know how to do it, and we're going to be successful at it.' But they wanted us to follow them."[25]

Rivera's involvement developed over time. After graduating from high school, he met UT students who had joined the Mexican American Youth Organization (MAYO), started reading books they suggested, and began to think more critically about US history and his place in it. Rivera continued to study Marxist and revolutionary theory, but he arrived at his brand of activism through experience: "How do I ... become a Brown Beret and become politically involved? *Life*, brother. ... You experience it every day. You experience it through racism, you experience it through sexism. You experience it through your dad being treated like he's a nobody, your mom being treated like she's a nobody, and you're treated like you're nothing. ... To me that's the most beautiful thing about being an organizer, about being an activist:

you learn it through osmosis." The part of the East Austin barrio where he grew up in the 1950s had no water service, no paved streets, and no electricity. That government-imposed deprivation spurred him on: "That's how you become politically involved, because you *see*. What I saw was the suffering of my parents."[26] A beating at the hands and nightsticks of Austin police officers and then being brought up on trumped-up charges that included destruction of public property (he bled on a police car) turned him into a militant. He had been reading Brown Beret literature from California, and when he got out of jail, he was determined to start a chapter in Austin. "I tell people I was beaten into militancy," he said.[27]

"Little by little we became pretty big here in Austin," Rivera said. Austin police were the Brown Berets' most efficient, even if unintentional, recruiters: when members of the community heard that the Berets would help family members who had suffered brutality at the hands of the APD, they contacted Rivera. He and his comrades formed an alliance with Larry Jackson and Black Power groups like the Black Panther Party. They began saying to each other, in Rivera's recollection, "Look, what they're doing to us, they're doing to you. We need to come together and form a stronger alliance among ourselves." Rivera thought, "That was very, very good, because we began to realize that it wasn't just us and it wasn't just them. It was people of color [together] and poor people [together].... You begin to become more politically conscious and begin to think of it as a class struggle. It's an issue of class, not of Black or white, even though we were targeted [because of our race and ethnicity]. It's basically the poor versus the wealthy."[28]

According to Rivera, the Panthers were more established and better organized in Austin, so the Brown Berets began to emulate their programs, with Jackson's blessing. They opened El Centro Chicano, which offered literacy programs, child care, afterschool programs and free meals to local children. Parents followed children to El Centro, and pretty soon they became involved, too. "Before you knew it, you began to develop this core group of people that was 150 percent behind you," Rivera recalled. "You could not do wrong [in their eyes], because they knew that you were helping your community. They would always say, 'I support the Brown Berets because you are defending us.' We were not afraid to stand up to the police, we were not afraid to stand up to oppression."[29]

Jackson ran a host of organizations that embraced Black Power ideology, and various collaborators emphasize his role with one or another of them. Some sources suggest that an organization called the United Community Front, which Jackson also ran, was more influential than the Black Panther Party in Austin, although it too seems to have followed the Panther playbook. "Black Panthers" seems to have become a generic term that people used to describe a range of Black Power groups that may or not have been part of the BPP. In any case, Jackson, who also served as state chairman of SNCC during its Black Power phase, embraced Black Power ideology, which in his mind involved organizing the Black community in coalition with other like-minded minorities. "Black Power means me going out here and finding a group of Blacks out there on the street or at the church or elsewhere and talking about improving our condition as a people," he said. "Then after we come together ... we formulate something with the Hispanics, and we need to do *this* with the [white] liberals, and we need to do *this* with women's groups. It's about us finding where the merger helps bring about real Black Power, because what we have done [by that point] is we have integrated ourselves into a system of fairness. That's different from Black Supremacy."[30]

Roen Salinas found other ways to pursue the interests of his East Austin neighborhood. Salinas was born in East Austin in 1965 to politically minded Chicano/a artist-activist parents, and he continued that work as the leader of Ballet Folklórico Aztlán de Tejas. "Austin has always segregated communities of color, so it's got a racist history," he said.[31] Salinas captured the essence of East Austin's dilemma. Segregated into the part of town with the fewest amenities, East Austinites bloomed where they were planted. Growing up in a nearly all-Mexican cultural environment and physical space had its advantages. "We would always have to go to other spaces to work, but there was this idea of always coming back home, to know your *familia*, to know your neighbors, to understand your culture," he said. "The barrio works in a couple of ways, in that it insulates from the oppressiveness of societal institutions. It's this gorgeous, delicious cultural space, which I find the most attractive facet of the barrio. The flip side of that is that the mainstream has a way of containing those" who live there.[32] "For me there's something so rich about barrio space that gives meaning to me, gives meaning to my body, gives meaning to the choreographies that my body can create," Salinas said. "The barrio is a place where you see your culture, you hear your culture, you smell your culture." He remembered East Austin buildings awash in colorful murals of *nuestra gente*: "All of our spaces were painted. It goes back to that idea of having a place of belonging, of home."

Gentrification

The breakdown of legally enforced segregation provided new opportunities for African Americans and Mexican Americans who had previously been forced to live in East Austin, but it also opened that half of the city up to gentrification at a time when the city was undergoing massive economic change. In the 1980s Gilbert Rivera and other East Austin activists created the Chicano Economic Development Corporation to encourage the development of their neighborhoods in ways that benefited the residents, not developers and high-income tech workers.[33] They emphasized the need for affordable housing and spaces for cultural events, but they were outflanked by developers who had more sway over the city government. White builders came into the community, bought and razed single-family homes, and converted the properties into multistory condominium or mixed-use complexes. Most residents did not have the necessary training or skills to enter Austin's high-tech workforce, but a few did, and they got out of East Austin. Many others were pushed out by high property taxes or, in some cases, cashed out their equity one step ahead of the bulldozer. They moved to Pflugerville, Round Rock, and other suburbs whose populations boomed and diversified as a result. Those who wanted to hold onto their modest homes in East Austin found even that difficult to do as the new developments sent property values, and property taxes, soaring.

Gilbert Rivera purchased his East Austin home for $39,000 in 1983. Developers bought neighboring residences over the ensuing decades and built McMansions, apartment or condominium buildings, and commercial properties. By 2016, Rivera's home was being taxed at an appraised value ten times the amount he had paid for it, and property taxes ate up half his annual retiree's income. "My Social Security [benefits] don't go up, but my taxes do because there's another condominium going up, there's another McMansion going up, there's another bar going up."[34]

Just as worrying from Salinas's perspective, as investment began to pour into East Austin and gentrification intensified at the turn of the twenty-first century, the barrio's distinctiveness was sometimes literally whitewashed. As soon as East Austin properties changed hands, he said, "The very first thing that happens, on day one: they get white paint and paint it all over. So all of a sudden you see this ... [literal] whitewashing that comes in to erase us, to erase our histories, our legacies.... Gentrification has been traumatic for our community."[35] When Salinas noticed new owners whitewashing nearby properties, he hired *muralistas* to cover the Folklórico Aztlán de Tejas building's walls "as a statement of resistance to protest what's happening in our barrios and to defy the unbridled capitalism that's cannibalizing our communities." He responded to the twenty-first-century problem of East Austin's gentrification with a civil rights–Black Power–Chicano/a mind-set. "We're in it for the long haul," he said. "At the end of the day, it's about our identities and our communities ... and we're all in it together."[36]

Environmental Racism

The gentrification of East Austin played out against the backdrop of a different kind of development: the creation of a grassroots, Black and Brown environmental justice movement in East Austin. Decades of underinvestment and inequitable zoning practices had kept East Austin property values low and made it an attractive place for waste-producing manufacturers. The thriving, predominantly white environmental movement that had begun to gain power in Austin in the 1980s showed little concern for the city's east side and its Black and Brown residents. "While Westside environmental groups focused on preserving open space and quality of life by mitigating development, Eastsiders faced far more extreme environmental threats and suffered a higher percentage of pollution-related illnesses and daily inconveniences," Andrew Busch found.[37]

Mexican American activists like Susana Almanza began organizing around issues of environmental racism and justice in East Austin in the early 1990s. With Sylvia Herrera, Gilbert Rivera, and a handful of others, she founded PODER (People Organized in Defense of Earth and Her Resources) and began to investigate the processes that resulted in the City of Austin building infrastructure in southeastern Austin for Sematech, a high-tech semiconductor chip manufacturing consortium that received tens of millions of dollars in local and state tax abatements, at a time when many East Austin neighborhoods still lacked sidewalks. PODER feared that Sematech and other high-tech manufacturing firms that were moving into East Austin would pollute their neighborhoods and harm their neighbors, and organized proactively with the manufacturers to keep that from happening.[38]

PODER next took on the issue of large fuel-storage facilities, known as "tank

Susana Almanza, Austin, Texas, June 8, 2016. Photo courtesy CRBB.

farms," that had been built in residential areas of East Austin. Some of the tanks were adjacent to homes, and five schools were located within a one-mile radius of the complex. Three pipelines to the storage facilities went directly under people's houses, and residents could feel the vibrations when fuel was being pumped into the tanks. The pipes and tanks would sometimes leak, and vapors would escape if hoses weren't working correctly. Air tests revealed that benzene, a carcinogenic component of gasoline, was present in East Austin's air at 720 times the allowable rate. As a result, "a lot of people" in the surrounding neighborhoods "had a lot of different cancers, and a lot of people died," Almanza said. PODER got the City of Austin to do a land-use study, which revealed that 95 percent of the land zoned for industrial use in the city was in East Austin. Almanza added, "We were being poisoned. We were really being poisoned by all these plants across the street from schools, around the corner from our homes. But they didn't exist in West Austin; they only existed in East Austin."[39]

PODER worked closely with Mexican American and African American neighborhood associations and called for public hearings that focused local and national attention on the multinational oil companies that stored gasoline at the tank farm. The corporations had nearly unlimited resources, but PODER had savvy organizers and a community that was primed to be organized. They staged the "Toxic Tour," which led local elected officials, state representatives, county commissioners, city council members, and other community leaders through East Austin. The smell of gasoline permeated the community during the tour, and organizers discussed many ways that the chemicals affected the community. Kids, they said, regularly suffered seemingly unprovoked medical problems or illnesses such as nosebleeds or colds. The conditions would clear up if the children went away for the summer, and would return when they came back home. Trees were constantly dying. Gas and oil spots regularly appeared on the ground; when children played outside and fell into one of the spots, they would break out in sores where their skin had touched the slick.[40]

Using educational meetings, phone trees, and other organizing techniques that Almanza and others in PODER had learned as members of the Brown Berets and other radical groups in the 1960s and afterward, they had Black and Brown neighborhood groups marching in lockstep. PODER forced the city and county to begin investigating the environmental effects of the tank farm, which encouraged the oil companies to begin pulling out of East Austin. The tank farm was closed in 1992, but the process of fully decommissioning it took more than twenty years to complete. Ironically, once the tank farm ceased operations, neighboring property values skyrocketed, which priced out many of the residents who had had to live with its emissions for decades and who had forced its removal.[41]

Environmental activists won some important victories in Austin in the 1980s and 1990s, but East Austinites did not share equally in those gains. For example, PODER tried to convince white-led environmental groups that Oak Springs, on the East Side, deserved the same protections that the Save Our Springs Alliance had won for Barton Springs, but they were unable to do so. When the City of Austin began to offer residential recycling on a large scale, Herrera, Almanza, and others in the PODER orbit cheered the news until they realized that the city would build only one recycling facility for the entire area, and that it would be placed in East Austin. That would amount to "an open-air mini-landfill full of newspapers and glass and so forth," Herrera said. "We're not against recycling, but think about it. Where is it going to? What does it look like? They're crushing glass in the middle of the night, waking up the residents. There are newspapers flying out of the facility because it's not even an enclosed facility. It's flying out into the neighborhood and trashing the neighborhood."[42]

When Austin created a new Smart Growth Initiative in 1998, it designated most of West Austin for environmental protection and most of East Austin for development. City leaders wanted "people from the suburbs to move into the development zone, as if people don't already live there," Herrera pointed out. "So where do they go?" She drew a connection with the past: "To me, that's just another continuation of that master plan where there's disregard, total disregard, for people and their history and their connection to the community in East Austin."[43]

Politics Not as Usual

African Americans and Mexican Americans chipped away at the political status quo in the late 1960s and 1970s. Wilhelmina Delco won election to the Austin school board, the first African American to do so, in 1968, and soon moved on to a seat in the Texas House of Representatives. Burl Handcox won election to the city council in 1971, the first African American in over a century. Richard Moya won a seat on the Travis County Commissioners Court in 1970, making him the first Hispanic elected to office in Travis County's history. John Treviño, who managed Moya's campaign, followed him onto the Austin City Council in 1975. By then, Gus Garcia had been elected to the school board, and Gonzalo Barrientos to the Texas House, where he and Delco represented adjacent East Austin districts.[44]

Single-member-district proponents challenged the at-large system just as Black and Brown candidates began winning citywide elections. They had two avenues available to them: convince Austinites to change the system voluntarily by voting to revise the city charter, or use the provisions of the VRA to convince a federal judge to force the change by court order. Their first petition drive, in 1971, failed to gain enough support, but their second, in 1973, forced the city council to put a single-member plan up for a vote that year. That vote failed, as did the next five attempts—some of which proposed a purely single-member system and some of which proposed a hybrid system of single-member and at-large seats. Six times between 1973 and 2002, East Austin precincts voted in favor of single-member or hybrid-district voting systems, but each time their votes were overwhelmed by no votes from Central and West Austin.[45]

Each election had at least one, and sometimes more than one, complicating factor. Over the years, single-member or hybrid proposals that might have passed on their own were tied to campaign-finance or term-limit proposals that voters hated. But Van Os believed that Austin voters kept choosing the at-large system for more deep-seated reasons: "Many white liberals in Austin believed that the at-large system was working for liberals, mostly on environmental issues," he said.[46] By the 1980s, business-minded Anglo liberals had gained the upper hand under the at-large system, and white environmentalists were the best-organized interest group in the city. Why should they do anything to upset the status quo? While Van Os might have agreed with environmentalists and Anglo liberals on many issues, he said, "That was not real democracy." He had bought a house as a young white civil rights attorney in the one part of town where he could afford to purchase, East Austin, so the issue was personal for him. When he bought the house, nearby streets were unpaved, and there was not a single fire station on that side of IH-35.[47]

African Americans and Mexican Americans in Austin agreed on the need for single-district representation and fought in tandem to achieve it over four decades. Having failed at the ballot box, the NAACP Legal Defense Fund and MALDEF joined forces in 1976 to sue the city, but that effort died on the vine. They tried again in 1984. In *Overton vs. City of Austin*, Van Os represented the NAACP and three African American plaintiffs; his cocounsel, José Garza, represented MALDEF and three Mexican American plaintiffs. Van Os said that MALDEF was generous with its resources and easy to work with.[48] With Garza, he set out to prove that Austin had revised its at-large system in 1953 for racially discriminatory reasons. "And I'm convinced that it was. The documentary record proves it," he said.[49] Attorneys for the City of Austin convinced federal judge James Nowlin otherwise, and he ruled in favor of the city and the at-large voting system. More than thirty years later, Van Os was still unable to explain the decision. His team proved, he said, that the "nondiscriminatory appearance" of the at-large system "was a hollow façade, and that it was enacted for racially discriminatory purposes . . . it was unconstitutional." Cities throughout Texas and all over the United States moved to single-member districts in the 1970s, but the at-large system remained in place in Austin for another thirty years.[50]

The last city council elected at-large under the gentlemen's agreements testified to the system's antidemocratic and inequitable nature: it had one African American and one Mexican American, and five Anglos—at a time when Anglos had ceased to be a majority of the city's population. In addition, the at-large system and gentlemen's agreements cultivated a feeling in voters that business interests controlled city politics to such an extent that it didn't matter what the voters did. Whereas close to 60 percent of eligible voters participated in the 1971 city council election, by 2011 intense voter disenchantment had set in, and fewer than 8 percent of voters bothered going to the polls.[51]

The 2012 effort to reform the city's electoral system brought together a diverse coalition representing myriad interests in favor of a "10-1" plan (ten single-member districts and a mayor elected at-large). The coalition included Van Os, Barrientos, NAACP chapter president Nelson Linder, and Travis County Republican Party vice chair Roger Borgelt, among many others. "This is the most diverse coalition I've seen for any city election, and I've been involved in city politics since 1969," Peck Young, an Austin Community College political science professor and political consultant, said. "This was a grass-roots, citizen-driven effort from the beginning." The coalition, which called itself Austinites for Geographic Representation, knocked on hundreds of doors and raised enough money to outspend the opposition. Austin voters approved Proposition 3, the single-member plan, in a landslide, but much hard work remained. The proposition mandated the creation of the Independent Citizens Redistricting Commission to draw the map dividing Austin's voters into ten districts. It soon hosted the first of fourteen public meetings that took place over a year's time.[52]

Much had changed since the onset of the gentlemen's agreements and the original court challenges to the at-large system. Austin's Mexican American population had soared to an estimated 35 percent of the total according to the 2010 census, and while it was still concentrated in East Austin, it was no longer confined to the barrio. The African American population had decreased just as precipitously, to less than 8 percent of the total by 2010, just slightly higher than Austin's Asian American population. Cheaper home prices in the suburbs combined with rising property values east of IH-35 to both pull and push African Americans outside the city limits. The redistricting commission was determined to create at least one African American "opportunity" seat—one representing a district with a critical mass of Black voters and likely to be filled by a Black representative—but after multiple attempts, the best it could do was to draw lines around a constituency that was 28 percent Black for District 1 in northeastern Austin. The commission created three Mexican American opportunity districts. When Austin voters went to the polls in 2014 to vote for the first time under the new system, they elected one African American and three Mexican Americans to office as part of an almost entirely new council slate. The new members included Delia Garza, the first female Mexican American member in the history of the city council, and Gregorio Casar, a young progressive who operated very much in the Chicano/a community organizing tradition.[53]

Austin's equity problems developed over decades as a result of several forces, so the move to single-member districts will not solve those problems overnight or by itself. Opinions about its efficacy, even among African Americans and Mexican Americans, remain divided. It sacrifices what Larry Jackson considered the most important benefit of the gentlemen's agreement within the at-large system: "I think Austin was a better system when the person elected was accountable to everybody," he said. Elected officials who represent an entire city are in theory more likely to consider the needs of the people of a city as a whole than are those who represent slices of it. But Jackson also described a problem with those who sought to benefit from the gentlemen's agreement: "See, racism isn't necessarily manufactured totally by racists. There are Black people in this town who exploit racism, Hispanics also, because while they are interested in getting something personal, the racists' method may be the process to reward them. It punishes everybody else." In any case, he believed it was easier under the at-large system for Black Power–oriented African Americans to build coalitions with Mexican Americans and Anglo progressives to further their interests.[54]

Despite Jackson's reservations, it is reasonable to hope that the new voting system will produce more equitable outcomes than the old one did. After all, the leaders whom Austinites elected under the city's at-large voting system created and maintained a profoundly segregated city that alienated the vast majority of its voters. Public opinion polling from 2015 found that Austin voters expected that the new 10–1 system "would improve representativeness and responsiveness of city government; that the new structure would help close socioeconomic, racial and political divides; and that there is a need for urgent action by city leaders to be sure this moment does not pass us by."[55]

Voter participation under the new system's first few elections provided grounds for optimism, in part because when voters chose the 10–1 plan in 2012, they also chose to move city elections from May to November to coincide with state and national elections. In the November 2014 election, in which Austinites chose a new mayor and new city council members under 10–1 for the first time, they voted in much larger numbers than they had in decades; more than 40 percent of eligible voters cast ballots. More than 15 percent returned to the polls to vote in the runoff to settle the mayoral and eight council races. In 2018 more than 60 percent of eligible Austin voters participated in the general election, and more than 11 percent—significantly more than voted in citywide elections under the old system—returned to vote in the December 2018 runoffs for three council districts.[56]

David Van Os said, "You either support democracy or you don't. I support democracy all the way. I think it's good for the political health of the whole body politic that everybody's viewpoint be represented on the governing body."[57] Time will tell whether the single-member system produces more equitable outcomes, but it has already produced a more diverse and representative city government and a more vibrant political culture that come closer to being worthy of the city's progressive reputation.

PART IV

INSIDE THE CIVIL RIGHTS IN BLACK AND BROWN ORAL HISTORY PROJECT

CHAPTER 15

RECOVERING, INTERPRETING, AND DISSEMINATING THE HIDDEN HISTORIES OF CIVIL RIGHTS IN TEXAS

MAX KROCHMAL

The long African American and Mexican American liberation struggles spanned the vast geographic bounds of Texas, put forward expansive visions for social and economic justice, and permanently transformed the state's race relations, political configurations, and educational systems. Few if any traditions or institutions remained untouched. Yet a full or even a preliminary accounting of grassroots civil rights battles in the Lone Star State has remained elusive—until now. Indeed, this history likely would have remained lost, confined in the heads of ordinary activists and beyond the reach of present-day readers had it not been for the establishment of the Civil Rights in Black and Brown (CRBB) Oral History Project. With support from a National Endowment for the Humanities Collaborative Research Grant and private foundations, an interdisciplinary and interinstitutional team of scholars and graduate students worked to recover these forgotten, interlaced tales by collecting over 530 new, videotaped life-history interviews with activists at twenty sites throughout Texas.

These interviews form the basis of this book, a collaborative effort that, for the first time, seeks to reconstruct the history of the overlapping African American and Chicanx liberation movements across the Lone Star State, from its metropolises to the understudied small towns of East Texas and the border cities on the Rio Grande. While most research on American race relations has used a binary analytical lens— examining either "Black versus white" or "Anglo versus Mexican"—our project used a multiracial perspective to draw new insights into the Black and Chicano/a struggles as well as the intersections between the two movements. No previous studies linked urban and small-town activists together on a scale as big and diverse as Texas. By drawing on our hundreds of new interviews as well as related archival research, and by defining "civil rights" expansively, this book digs into these movements more deeply than ever before. The chapters in this volume move beyond the most visible places, organizations, and leaders to engage with several key areas of inquiry: life under segregation, the role of state-sanctioned violence, struggles for equity in public services, political self-determination and agency, and Black-Brown coalition building.

The interviews also form the basis for the project's digital humanities website (crbb. tcu.edu), a free, user-friendly, and public-facing resource featuring a database of over 7,800 video clips, each of which is catalogued with detailed metadata. Oral history interviews are typically catalogued as though they are books, with vague Library of Congress subject headings that force researchers to wade through hundreds of pages of transcripts or hours of streaming content in order to find specific people, places, themes, and events. In contrast, our site features short segments that are indexed using narrow subject terms and tags that enable users to easily search for detailed information across the entire collection. The CRBB website also features thematic multimedia essays, visual aids, and other exhibits designed to help users understand the larger meaning of the interviews. Students, teachers, journalists, and others can pair the tales told in these pages with the readily available primary sources online.

This chapter outlines the project's technical end: its scholarly contributions, origins, and quotidian activities as well as the methodologies that we deployed in conducting, cataloguing, interpreting, and sharing our 530 interviews. In addition to detailing the project's place in the historiography, the chapter shows how and why the questions we asked could be answered only via collaboration. It contends that the story of Texas, a state both broadly representative and unique, matters on a national scale. Last, it explores why and how we sought to make the interviews more accessible than those from previous oral history projects, creating a new "people's history" beyond these pages by providing a new documentary source base for the historians and activists of the future.

Scholarly and National Significance

Covering the period from the twilight of the Jim Crow and Juan Crow eras until today, the CRBB project illuminates in unprecedented ways the lived experiences of Black, Brown, and white activists on the ground as well as their interactions across the color line. Previous scholarship has surveyed different pieces of this story, but few works have placed the African American and Mexican American freedom movements into a single, relational narrative frame, and none have sufficiently integrated the voices of grassroots organizers. Moreover, while the role of "local people" has received renewed attention in the rich literature on Black civil rights, the relationships between African American, Mexican American, and white activists remain poorly understood.[1] At the same time, the scholarly literature on both the "Mexican American generation" of postwar activists and on the Chicano/a movement of the 1960s and 1970s is just beginning to include community studies and research on the grassroots organizers of those struggles. For their part, African Americans remain all but absent except as distant foils in most Chicano/a historiography.[2]

Research on labor and working-class history tends to assume that Black and Brown civil rights activists abandoned the fight for economic justice in the face of Cold War repression, leaving the movements of the 1960s in the hands of respectable middle-class leaders who emphasized race alone and prioritized access to public accommodations rather than economic justice or real political power.[3] New scholarship on the War on Poverty demonstrates that civil rights activists made it their own, seizing the opportunity to use federal resources to organize their communities, combat economic inequality, and build political power. Poor African Americans and Mexican Americans, led by women, challenged the established leadership of their neighborhoods and forged new alliances with youth activists that gave rise to the Black Power and Chicano/a Power phases of the long movements.[4] These stories are typically told in isolation, with few links tying the local people of the sit-ins or the countryside to the antipoverty activists and cultural-nationalist movements, or linking grassroots activism and formal political power in the late twentieth century and into the twenty-first. In Texas, popular memory largely forgets that civil rights struggles ever occurred, let alone that they were organized by local people in all these spheres, at times operating across the color line.[5]

Much of the problem stems from the lack of sources. Manuscript records tend to focus on the immediate activities of their authors, and newspaper reports on civil rights activism remain sporadic. In the age of Jim Crow and Juan Crow, segregation required the physical separation of racial groups into separate neighborhoods, social organizations, and schools. Meanwhile, traditions, custom, and language led whites, African Americans, and Mexican Americans into distinct churches, political formations, and subcultures. Geographically, African Americans clustered in East Texas, while Mexican Americans predominated in South Texas and far West Texas. (Their distribution mirrored in microcosm the nation's larger Black and Brown population trends.) As a result, the few surviving written records provide details on these separate worlds, but they rarely speak to one another across racial lines.[6]

Civil Rights in Black and Brown aims to rectify this omission by drawing upon our new, vast, representative base of oral sources. The life-history interviews produced by the project allow the present collaborators and future researchers to recover events and actors absent from the written record and also to better scrutinize their meaning. As the Italian oral historian Alessandro Portelli has noted, the fact that interviews are not strictly factual is not a liability but an asset: the way that narrators tell their stories and the values they ascribe to historical events are themselves useful guides with which historians can improve their analyses of fragmentary written evidence.[7] Our extensive field research in every corner of Texas allows us to bring in the voices of a wide range of African American, Mexican American, and white civil rights, labor, neighborhood, religious, educational, fraternal, political, and other activists. Placing the African American and Mexican American civil rights movements in a single frame allows for comparative and relational inquiry, deepening both the Texas and the national historiographies of those struggles while also interrogating the nature of Black-Brown relations in the period.

Historical research on the latter subject first emerged during the explosion of "whiteness studies" in the mid-1990s. The historian Neil Foley fired the first, controversial shot in 1997, contending that Mexican American civil rights activists in Texas after World War II made a "Faustian pact" in which they saw themselves as white and attempted to prove their whiteness in order to achieve legal equality. In suggesting that they were "other whites" treated unjustly as a "class apart," Foley added, Mexican Americans at times positioned themselves as hostile to the Black freedom struggle and even to African Americans generally. Legal scholars have since responded that the attorneys used the "class apart" strategy only as an instrumental tool within the state's Jim Crow courtrooms, and the historian Carlos Blanton forcefully challenged Foley's depiction of the era's activists as fundamentally anti-Black.[8]

Still, Foley's introduction of whiteness studies to Chicano/a historiography led to a new wave of interest in the history of Black-Brown relations in the post–World War

II period. Among those who have recovered moments of collaboration are Shanna Bernstein and Laura Pulido. Both examined the history of Los Angeles and discovered deep ties between African American and Mexican American civil rights activists, and each scholar explained the sympathetic roles played by Jews and Asian Americans, respectively.[9] Similarly, Lauren Araiza found myriad areas of cross-fertilization between the United Farm Workers and five major Black civil rights organizations. John D. Márquez uncovered unexpected coalitions and hybridity in cultural forms among working-class Latinos/as and African Americans in Baytown, Texas, an industrial suburb of Houston.[10] Likewise, Gaye Theresa Johnson, Luis Alvarez and Daniel Widener have pioneered efforts in cultural history to better understand the mutually beneficial borrowing and sharing of popular art forms across racial lines in Southern California.[11]

In contrast, scholars led by the California sociologist and attorney Nicolás Vaca have emphasized the numerous instances of conflict between Mexican Americans and African Americans, differences originating in labor markets, discrimination by the state, and struggles for political representation. In his 2004 book, *The Presumed Alliance*, Vaca charges scholars and activists with wearing "rose-colored lenses" when invoking moments of Black-Brown solidarity during the civil rights era.[12] Brian Behnken and Michael Phillips likewise work in that vein, using a broad array of archival sources while expanding on Foley's whiteness framework. Each has concluded that disagreement dominated Black-Brown relations, and Behnken added that mutual distrust and competition over resources and power doomed any possibility of a multiracial freedom struggle in Texas. Robert Bauman, William Clayson, and others reached similar conclusions in their studies of Black-Brown conflict during the War on Poverty.[13]

The newest scholarship has moved beyond the poles of cooperation and conflict toward examining what Mark Brilliant called "the wide space between." Brilliant's study of California showed that Japanese American, African American, and Mexican American legal and political strategies developed along different trajectories and that the separate struggles only occasionally overlapped. Although cooperation occurred, the African American movement became the lens through which allies and observers understood all civil rights struggles, obscuring the particularities of the other groups' movements and blurring the multiple color lines at play.[14] Likewise, Gordon Mantler concluded that during the Poor People's Campaign of 1968, African Americans, Mexican Americans, American Indians, and whites each developed distinct "social constructions of poverty" that led to frequent intergroup tension.

Still, there were fleeting moments of multiracial coalition.[15] My own *Blue Texas* dissects the long process of experimental, trial-and-error coalition building among Black, Brown, and white labor, community, and political organizers in Texas. I concluded that distinctions of class, ideology, political tactics, and strategy at times mattered more than did simple ties of race or ethnicity.[16] In a similar vein, Sonia Song-Ha Lee and Frederick Douglass Opie have recovered Black-Brown coalitions in New York City across the twentieth century, in postwar organized labor, in the Black Power and Brown Power movements, and in formal politics.[17] Other works on grassroots and legal struggles surrounding school desegregation and political representation have extended the map to Denver, Philadelphia, and Camden, New Jersey.[18] Finally, Allyson Brantley's book on the decades-long Coors boycott provides new insights into the meanings of coalition building while tying civil rights struggles to aspects of organized labor, consumption, and LGBT histories.[19]

While scholarship on the modern civil rights struggles reveals many types of intergroup relations, recent research on the Black Power and Brown Power movements of the late 1960s and 1970s has demonstrated that the two struggles frequently overlapped, interconnecting in routine but productive ways. In many cases, the individual activists and organizers who led these struggles cut their teeth in War on Poverty programs or the "classical," liberalism-oriented movements of the early 1960s. As a result, many of their ostensibly nationalist organizations remained committed in practice to reformist agendas—expanding social services and winning electoral power, for example—despite a newly aggressive language that emphasized self-determination over integration. Both continuity and change are apparent. Still, scholars consider the rise of self-styled Black Power, Chicano/a Power, and similar organizations a new phase in what activists increasingly referred to as domestic Third World "national liberation" struggles.[20]

Perhaps counterintuitively, most scholars agree that the rise of nationalisms and, later, "identity politics" fueled rather than hindered the growth of Black-Brown alliances. A heightened sense of racial difference did not preclude cooperation, since many Black and Mexican American (and other nonwhite) activists recognized either the pragmatic need to combine forces and build power against a common oppressor or the more theoretical, internationalist vision of solidarity with oppressed peoples of color not just in the United States but across the globe. Class politics, and especially the revolutionary forms of nationalism espoused by groups like the Black Panther Party, further facilitated collaboration across racial lines.

A decade of scholarship has uncovered and complicated this tale. Jeffrey Ogbar's seminal study contends that the Black Power movement helped engender multiple shades of ethnic nationalism that at times coalesced into "Rainbow Radicalism."[21] Other scholars agree with this telos, giving the Black Panthers sole credit for interethnic forays such as the "Original Rainbow Coalition," led by Fred Hampton in Chicago.[22] George Mariscal has correctly countered that the Chicano/a Movement drew on a decades-long organizing tradition among Mexican Americans, and its radical "Brown Power" phase did not merely parrot or mimic the politics of its Black counterpart.[23] Likewise, the geographer Laura Pulido's study of the Third World Left in Los Angeles in the 1970s demonstrated the multidirectional cross-fertilization of Black, Chicano/a, and Asian American radical activists, with the groups borrowing from one another while also collaborating in common cause.[24] A pair of excellent, unpublished dissertations on the radical Black, Chicano/a, Asian American, and American Indian movements of the San Francisco Bay Area show that radical ethnic nationalism did not emerge solely out of the Black freedom movement, but that each group had a distinct, ethnically specific genealogy. Still, their similarities, including their commitments to radical internationalism, decolonization, and revolutionary class struggle in the United States facilitated multidirectional cross-fertilization and collaboration between the movements.[25] Critically, the historian Jason Ferreira centered the "profound political and personal ties that existed *between activists of color*" who were "rooted *within* a particular community, yet simultaneously *opened outwards* to embrace the struggles of others."[26]

Together, these works have reconnected the African American and Mexican American liberation struggles and deepened the study of each, forging a new historical subfield on Black-Brown civil rights. Yet each text remains fragmentary, offering portraits of a relatively small number of actors over a short period in a specific place. Although all of them incorporated oral sources, none, unlike our collaborative project, drew on hundreds of interviews. Most limited their analyses to the most visible organizations and leaders and only began to cover the full story of grassroots activism across the decades of the long movements, the spatial range (from urban to rural), and the intersections of class, gender, sexuality, and political power. Only close examinations of individual activists and their relationships with one another can shed light on these deeper questions. A large corpus of oral sources is simply invaluable. Finally, few of the extant works have adequately extended their analyses of life and activity on the ground beyond a single community study.

The Lone Star State, despite its size and diversity, offers an ideal case study for a systematic, large-scale, multiracial history of civil rights. The state's particularly diverse demographics and the longtime presence of African Americans, Mexican Americans, and whites give it historical depth and make it representative of larger trends across the United States. Likewise, its location in the borderlands of the American South and Southwest (along with Mexico), combined with its long history of racial conflict and resistance, helps make the Lone Star State a microcosm of the regions it abuts. Although Texas was neither Mississippi nor California, one can learn much about the surrounding regions by using it as a case study. The state's rapid population and economic growth since World War II and its major, growing cities at the center of the Sunbelt reflect broader trends in US political economy in the past half century, for example, as defense spending and migration shifted resources and people southwest. Texas also holds significance because of its outsize influence on American politics and culture.

At the same time, Texas exhibits some exceptional qualities that make it a revealing laboratory. While studies of California and New York detail Black-Latinx relations in comparatively open and politically liberal contexts, the Texas story shines light on Black-Brown civil rights in the heart of conservative America. Only in Texas did Mexican Americans and African Americans come into contact and, at times, collaborate under the weight of the formal, legal Jim Crow structure of the South. Moreover, only in a large diverse state like Texas can one observe rural and urban versions of both the African American and Mexican American civil rights struggles within the same political unit—a fact that helped both movements identify a common enemy and find ground for concerted action. The backwoods of East Texas were not unlike the Mississippi Delta, but there was no similar region in California or New York. Nor were there Mexican Americans in such large numbers and across time elsewhere in the South, including in Florida.[27] On the other hand, Texas did not exhibit extensive Asian American or Native American civil rights activism in the postwar period, differentiating it from its coastal counterparts. More research and archival collecting will be needed before these histories can be brought into conversation with the African American and Mexican American tales.[28] Texas sits at the crossroads of unique and broadly representative. The future of Black-Brown and multicultural relations in America has much to learn from the lived history of the Lone Star State, and only a collaborative oral history project could uncover it.

History of the Project and Research Methodology

Collecting this history represented an urgent task. Each month, it seemed, legendary civil rights organizers across the South and Southwest were passing away, and in some cases their stories were being lost with them. The problem was especially acute in regard to grassroots activists, in contrast to the few organizational leaders who produced the fragmentary written records that survived the test of time and were preserved in archives. Indeed, many of the local people who served as the community organizers of the Black and Brown civil rights movements produced few documents, and those that did rarely had offices or secretaries to maintain their files. Many others doubted that their story would be of interest to the keepers of history, and yet others mistrusted preservation efforts. In short, the stories remained in the participants' minds. Only oral history could add them to the record.

Soon after arriving at Texas Christian University in 2011, I began planning an undergraduate research course centered on conducting oral history with local civil rights activists. I quickly learned that other scholars in the Dallas–Fort Worth area had begun doing similar work, so I reached out to them for guidance and advice. I taught my course in the spring of 2013, helping my students conduct some of the first interviews that would become part of the CRBB collection. By the end of the year, I had formed a close working relationship with colleagues at two nearby universities, and we began looking for funding sources for an ambitious, statewide oral history project. We prepared a proposal to the National Endowment for the Humanities that proved unsuccessful, but other sources of support for our work allowed us to get the project off the ground. The dean of the TCU Library offered us substantial staff time and brought together librarians, archivists, and digital-systems personnel from multiple institutions in order to hash out processes for data management, workflow, and archival preservation. TCU's AddRan College of Liberal Arts promised to purchase equipment and provide office space and a graduate student assistant for the project. The University of North Texas Oral History Program, led by this volume's coeditor, Todd Moye, and the UNT Library's Portal to Texas History agreed to collaborate, and the Department of History at the University of Texas, Arlington, offered additional support.

Most importantly, with help from TCU's Office of Advancement, we presented a series of grant proposals to private foundations in early 2014. The Brown Foundation, Inc., of Houston responded with a charitable grant of $100,000, and the Summerlee Foundation of Dallas followed suit with an additional $40,000. Using these funds and in-kind contributions, we created a first draft of the website (crbb.tcu.edu), hired student workers, purchased new video cameras and audio equipment, uploaded clips

Pauline Valenciano Gasca (1936–2018) being interviewed by Sandra Enríquez at her home in Fort Worth, Texas, June 10, 2015. Photo courtesy CRBB.

from our separate existing oral history projects to the CRBB online database, and began planning for our first phase of field research.

We started by generating a list of community organizations and individual "gate-keepers" who could help us gain entrée into the African American and Mexican American communities at each of our planned field sites. Potential partners included local branches of the National Association for the Advancement of Colored People, the League of United Latin American Citizens, the race-based "constituency groups" of the American Federation of Labor–Congress of Industrial Organizations, Democratic Party clubs, local historical and cultural societies, colleges and universities, and countless immigrant, civil rights, and labor organizations as well as individual community leaders. We began calling some of these gatekeepers to discuss the project, but in the end, we were not able to develop deep relationships with them before diving into the field.

Instead, as the summer of 2015 approached, we hurried to recruit, hire, and train four graduate student research assistants (RAs), the individuals who would conduct the bulk of the interviews. We advertised the positions nationally via online job boards and screened the candidates in Skype interviews. We aimed to hire a diverse staff of men and women that include a large percentage of African Americans and Mexican Americans, preferably bilingual. We ended up hiring four Mexican Americans, three of them bilingual, two men and two women. After selecting them, we sent each RA a packet of information that included required readings on oral history methodology, African American history, and Mexican American history, as well as online training modules on the protection of human subjects.

At the beginning of the summer, the RAs came to TCU for an intensive hands-on training workshop led by faculty collaborators and library staff members. After two days of seminar discussions in the classroom, we spent one week engaged in on-the-job training, helping the RAs practice their community outreach and interviewing skills in Dallas and Fort Worth. Throughout this dry run, we coached them on the methods of interviewing and helped them practice using the equipment, the online database software, and archival processing. They also worked the phones, contacting many of the gatekeepers that we had identified at our high-priority remote field sites: East Texas (centered on Tyler and Marshall), the Brazos River Valley (Bryan-College Station to Prairie View), and along the US-Mexico border (from the Lower Rio Grande Valley to Laredo and El Paso).

Following the training, the RAs paired off and fanned out across the state, working in pairs for a total of six weeks of full-time field research. At each stop, they began by contacting the gatekeepers, who often had stories of their own to share and, in most cases, provided us with lists of people to contact in their communities. Based on these initial lists, each team then identified additional interviewees via the "reputational" method, that is, by asking the initial interviewees to suggest others and to put us in contact with still more people. We prioritized interviewing people whom the initial narrators mentioned most frequently, to ensure that the most significant actors were included. We did not advertise openly in newspapers or other public outlets, preferring instead to follow the vestiges of the social movement networks of the past. This method was not without its limitations: despite making some telephone calls before we arrived, some researchers ended up "parachuting in" to relatively unknown communities in which we were not deeply enmeshed. (By contrast, two of the RAs were natives of their field sites and, indeed, were writing dissertations on them.) Regardless, our use of community gatekeepers allowed us to gain access and trust by drawing on the reputations and relationships of our partners. Gatekeepers generously opened their hearts and their address books to us. In some cases, we were able to provide small stipends for their help, but more often they participated simply because they wanted to make sure that the disappearing history of civil rights struggles in Texas was preserved. Some gatekeepers provided physical spaces for interviews; others shared newspaper clippings or archival files. All of them put their time, energy, and names on the line for the CRBB project. We can't thank them enough for their tremendous contributions.

For our part, the four faculty collaborators supervised the teams and visited each team for two weeks during the fieldwork period. We sat in on some interviews, providing coaching to help the RAs improve their methods, and assisted with logistics and other snags that arose along the way. We helped the graduate students establish contact with local gatekeepers and surveyed local libraries and historical associations for additional sources that might be used for a future book. Last, we joined the RAs in conducting a handful of the interviews and debriefed each exchange with them, coaching them to improve their interviewing techniques.

Our previous experience with numerous oral history projects in California, Texas, Mississippi, and the Carolinas suggested that fieldwork would unfold unevenly, but not wholly unpredictably. As expected, the first few days or even a week in the field tended to move slowly as contacts were established, relationships were built, and rapport was created. After some initial frustration, the researchers began to schedule and conduct interviews, and eventually they established a rhythm. The final days or weeks of field research, in contrast, were often characterized by a flurry of apparent dead

James Wall (*center*) and Moisés Acuña Gurrola interviewing Victor Treviño, a retired member of the United Steelworkers and former school board member of the West Oso Independent School District, in Corpus Christi. Photo courtesy CRBB.

ends turning into leads that suddenly bore fruit as would-be narrators began returning calls, community partners redoubled their efforts to ensure that the researchers got what they needed before returning home, and up to four interviews got squeezed into a single day.

Overall, we expected that each team would conduct an average of two interviews per weekday, or a total of fifty over the course of the summer. In the routine, middle weeks of fieldwork, this translated to one interview in the morning and one in the afternoon, but the exact numbers varied according to the ebb and flow noted above. In some cases, the RAs returned to a particularly interesting narrator for a second, follow-up interview. Much of the work occurred on nights and weekends, and everyone needed to be on call in order to pursue all possible leads. In the end, we met our numerical goal with ease, collecting 116 interviews in the summer of 2015. More importantly, the content of many interviews was outstanding, opening unprecedented windows on the hidden histories recorded in this volume.

We had hoped that the RAs could begin processing the interviews while still in the field, backing up the full video files on an external hard drive, writing a short synopsis of each interview, and—as time and internet access permitted—creating video clips and applying metadata for our online database. In reality, the students lacked the time and energy, as well as reliable internet service, to get very much of this done. Instead, at the end of the summer, the RAs returned to TCU to do the first bits of processing and preserving the data—making sure the files were transferred and backed up, organizing all the consent and copyright release forms, verifying the narrators' addresses and other contact information—before handing it off to

The CRBB research assistants discussing oral history methodology with Todd Moye (*front, right*) during the project's summer training seminar at Texas Christian University, Fort Worth, June 2, 2016. Photo courtesy CRBB.

the professional archivists at the TCU Library. They, in turn, shared the videos with the Portal to Texas History, where the full, unedited interviews are now archived in perpetuity.

This basic process repeated itself the following year. We resubmitted our application to the NEH and won a Collaborative Research Grant for $200,000, half of which was designated as matching funds to be released in conjunction with the third-party gifts we had already received. We had originally asked for more money, so we needed to tweak our work plan and compress the remainder of our planned field-work into the summer of 2016. We again issued a national call for RAs, and we hired a diverse team of graduate researchers from across Texas and the nation, including students from Duke University, the University of Michigan, Ohio State University, and the University of Georgia. We again struggled to develop close ties with gate-keepers before summer arrived; there were simply too many sites and not enough time to visit with or even call all of them. Yet in other ways, we had learned from our mistakes. Half the graduate students we hired hailed from or were writing disserta-tions on our target research sites. Instead of bringing the RAs to TCU for an entire week of training, we assembled for only two days as a large group on campus before going to the field sites for the on-the-job coaching. For example, I traveled with one team to Beaumont, in southeastern Texas, before joining another, more experienced group in Houston. I helped each group identify and contact community gatekeep-ers, build relationships, and conduct their first interviews. Thereafter we held regu-lar conference calls, which allowed me to help them process their days and fine-tune their work. After four weeks in the field, we held a two-day retreat at the University of Texas at Austin, hosted by our collaborator Maggie Rivas-Rodríguez of the Voces

The CRBB team, Texas Christian University Commons, Fort Worth, June 3, 2016. *Front row, from left*: Katherine Bynum, Maggie Rivas-Rodriguez, Sandra I. Enríquez, Samantha Rodríguez, Max Krochmal; *second row*: Karen Wisely, Meredith May, Jasmin Howard, Eladio Bobadilla, Steve Arionus, Danielle Grevious, Moisés Acuña Gurrola; *third row*: W. Marvin Dulaney, Vinicio Sinta, Joel Zapata, James B. Wall, and J. Todd Moye. Photo courtesy CRBB.

Oral History Center. We decompressed over hours of often-painful seminar-style conversations, discussing our progress to date, addressing challenges and obstacles, and making adjustments for the remaining month in the field. The RAs then traveled to new field sites to begin the process anew, with assistance from the faculty collaborators.

Finally, at the end of the summer, the RAs reconvened on the TCU campus, where we held two days of meetings to debrief their experiences, catalogue their interview data, and identify and prioritize the highest-quality interviews for inclusion on the website. Taken together, the six teams had conducted 420 additional interviews. Again, the quality of the exchanges was extremely high, revealing never-before-documented stories of civil rights struggles—some of which appear for the first time in this book. Significantly, the midsummer retreat and late-summer meetings allowed us to identify common themes across the collection, to debate key turning points, to draft a common time line for the book, and to begin interpreting the overarching story that connects the community studies into a cohesive whole. As a result, each chapter in this volume centers on a single locale, but all are based on and speak to the larger, statewide histories of Black and Chicanx liberation. We agreed that each researcher would begin drafting a chapter on a designated place, adding relevant newspaper and archival sources to the rich oral evidence. Over the next two years, we workshopped the essays through an internal peer-review process to make sure that all the chapters followed similar formats and spoke to the overall history of the overlapping movements across Texas.

Creating People's History: Coding the Data, Making the Website, and Beyond

In addition to recovering the disappearing voices of Black, Brown, and white civil rights activists in Texas, the CRBB project aims to make the interviews widely available to the general public. This goal is not novel. Indeed, one of the central tenets of oral history research over the past half century stems from its origins in the milieu of New Left activism and contemporary calls to democratize the historic record by documenting and preserving "people's history." Southern historians and dissidents going back to the New Deal's WPA sought to create a biracial source base that could correct the distortions of often-partisan written texts, accounts that, at times, were penned by the perpetrators of interracial political violence.[29] Likewise, in the Southwest, oral history represented a way out of the methodological traps created by conquest and the erasure of Mexican American, indigenous, and working-class voices.[30] The new labor historians turned to oral history to understand the rank-and-file members of unions and ordinary workers who were not being well-served by their unions.[31] The newest generations of professional social movement historians have followed suit, routinely collecting oral history interviews as important sources for their books but often giving little thought to the preservation and dissemination of their primary sources.

Ironically, despite these democratic impulses, most oral history interviews are not readily accessible to the "people's history" enthusiasts that the method's practitioners seek to serve. Instead, they get lost in historians' file cabinets, at worst, or buried in a university or public library archive, at best. There, in climate-controlled special-collections warehouses, they languish, indexed in a subject guide or maybe given a single entry in the library catalogue, but rarely seeing the light of day. This was especially true in the days of analogue tapes and paper transcripts, but surprisingly, the digital revolution has only partially reversed this trend. A scholar with ample time and creative searching techniques might be able to track down any given interview, but the insights buried in oral histories often remain lost to the general public.

The CRBB project disrupts this tragic tale—by design. From the outset, we planned not only to collect the interviews but also to share them, in new ways. Our approach grew out of my frustration during my dissertation research, more than a decade ago, which coincided with the rise of widespread digitization. I visited numerous archives housing rich collections of oral sources, but locating individual interviews that matched my topic proved to be a chore. Most libraries catalogue oral histories as though they were books, assigning each one an author (the interviewer or perhaps both participants), a title (typically a variation of "Oral history interview with" the narrator's name), and other metadata, including a date, time, and place as well as Library of Congress (LOC) subject headings and call numbers. One repository I visited classified all the interviews from a decades-long oral history project under the same LOC call number, since all focused on the same broad subject matter, and then tacked on at the end of the string a nonstandard "OH no." followed by a sequential number. Fortunately, each interview "book" appeared separately in the library's digital catalogue, and the LOC subject headings varied. Instead of simply

Paul Jones, a local leader of the NAACP, being interviewed by Danielle Grevious and Eladio Bobadilla, Beaumont, Texas, June 7, 2016. Photo courtesy CRBB.

listing the broadest topic (e.g., "African Americans—Civil rights—Texas"), the card in the virtual catalogue might also include subject headings such as the narrator's name, place of activism, organizational affiliations, and so on. Such information at times helped me determine which interviews to request from the locked stacks, but the metadata told me precious little about the specific contents of the interview. Did this narrator participate in a sit-in? What type of work did she perform? Was she a union member? Was she focused on civil rights in education, politics, or something else? Or was the subject a he, and a social-gospel minister at that? For years, the only way to answer these questions was to find the interview in hard-to-access brick-and-mortar archives and then pore through endless pages of paper transcripts. One might have the luxury of finding an appended index, but those were rare, and the index terms were often limited to proper nouns. Tracking down the interviews, traveling to the archive, reading page after page of transcripts—this was not the stuff of accessible people's history.

The coming of cheap digital technology carried great promise but ultimately failed to deliver a silver bullet. Libraries began to digitize transcripts, but archivists' worries about privacy and copyright often kept them off public websites, and one still had to submit to screening by library professionals. Those worries persist, but they have become less controlling, and today anyone can find an oral history transcript with a simple Google search. After downloading a PDF or a Word document, users can search within the document—using the Control-plus-F keystroke—and easily find any word uttered during the interview. That represented a huge step forward, but what if neither the interviewer nor the narrator said the word that the people's historian was seeking? Many of our narrators participated in direct action demonstrations, for example, but few used that phrase. Some participated in sit-ins, but that word can appear with or without a hyphen, depending on the typist. CTRL-F was progress, but much good information could still slip through the cracks.

Moreover, as the oral historian Michael Frisch and others have demonstrated, a transcript is never an entirely faithful or even complete record of an interview encounter. Much is lost in translation between the original exchange and its being represented as typed characters on a page. The spoken word—the sound of interviews—has intrinsic value; it is far more powerful to listen to a person's choked-up, unsteady words or deep-belly laughter than it is to read in a transcript "[shaking voice]" or "[laughs]." The narrator's emotion and affect lie beyond the power of transcription.[32] Portelli provides another great example, dissecting a moment when an African American narrator in Kentucky shared that her descendants were "s-s-s-slaves." The transcript reflects her stutter, and he is careful to explain its full meaning. Still, her own, unmediated voice is lost.[33] These problems were compounded when oral historians began to record interviews on video. How much of a person's facial expressions, gesticulations, and body language is left out of the transcript?

The rise of the internet allowed for the streaming of interviews, an easy alternative to the flatness of transcripts. Interviews could be made available with ease, yet locating the correct sources and finding information within the streaming content remained obstacles to realizing the dream of oral history as people's history. As I continued with my dissertation research, libraries started posting full, unedited streams of interviews, first with audio only and later with video as well. This represented another giant leap forward, since researchers no longer had to visit an archive in person to cue up an analogue audiotape or find an old, scratched-up reel-to-reel player or VCR. At times, the streaming players were accompanied by digitized transcripts; in other cases, the raw audiovisual file displayed on its own. In either case, problems of accessibility remained. If a user took the time to read an entire transcript to find whatever they were looking for, they still had to search through the multimedia file, clicking to fast-forward and reverse and then waiting for buffering, before finding the corresponding moment in the digital media. The advent of the Oral History Metadata Synchronizer (OHMS) tied the transcript to the virtual tape, making it easy to search for a keyword in the transcript and then jump to the correct place in the player.[34] But what about "sit-in" spelled "sitin"? Or that direct action that was called something else? Or that very influential person who inspired the narrator tremendously but whose name she just couldn't recall? (Or the countless interviews that never had the good fortune of being transcribed?) Finding the right interviews and the key moments within them remained as difficult as ever, since the new streaming content continued to be classified with the same LOC system designed for books. Indeed, the barriers to access remain so great that rich interviews can still be lost forever in an archival vault, gathering dust until some archivist selects them for online publication or a lucky researcher stumbles on them via the clunky subject headings of the library catalogue.

At the dawn of the CRBB project, I had identified these questions but still had few answers. I had experimented in my undergraduate courses with shooting video and with asking students to create micro-websites displaying their findings via interpretive multimedia essays weaving together text and short clips from the interviews.

It was indeed possible to log or transcribe and then thematically code the relatively small sets of interviews that they collected for a semester-long project, but how could such fine-grained interpretive work be accomplished on a larger scale? I knew we couldn't afford to invest time or money in costly, cumbersome transcription services. We needed to develop a better way to help not just researchers but also laypeople—people's historians—find the interviews that we were recording, locate the specific content that they sought within each source, and be able to look for the same narrow subject matter across multiple interviews throughout the collection. Journalists, teachers, students, activists, and other general users don't have the time or, often, the interest to watch every interview about "African Americans—Civil rights—Texas," no matter how easy it is to stream a single file online, nor can they feasibly search for keywords across endless transcripts. Of course, researchers need access to multiple primary sources that speak to one another, that is, diverse perspectives on the same narrowly defined subject. We needed to create a method that would enable average consumers of oral histories to find mentions of a particular march or demonstration—or a specific school or person or company or occupational group—in their hometowns. It needed to be fast and easy in order to be useful.

After bouncing these issues off my students and collaborators, I took a wish list to the staff at the TCU Library. The digital services librarian assigned to the project, Jacob Brown, is an expert in information technology, library science, and digital humanities, with advanced degrees in each field. We told him that we wanted to build the CRBB project around a website on which we would post video clips, not full interviews; to be able to code each segment with detailed subject terms and other metadata; and to assemble what amounted to a database for a large volume of qualitative sources. The key shift we hoped to undertake would be to abandon the old LOC classification system in favor of a new one in which the units were smaller. Each clip would run up to five minutes in length, we surmised, and the themes would be very specific. Instead of the standard LOC heading, we developed a hierarchical tree of subjects, such as "Student Activism › Sit-ins › Student Demands for Jobs" and "White Resistance to Civil Rights › Extrajudicial Violence › Ku Klux Klan (KKK)." The librarians and archivists told me that this was called a "controlled vocabulary" and that we simply needed to generate a list of terms before beginning the coding. I also wanted to create a system of tags or categories for more specific information and, ideally, to be able to allow many end users to add these tags. The TCU archivist Mary Saffell determined that these would be best for proper nouns such as "Texas Farm Workers Union (TFWU)" or "Lincoln High School." Yet another field in the database would allow us to input geographic information for each clip.

Last, I wanted the site to be smart. One of my students, a business and engineering major who was fulfilling his last general-education requirement in the humanities, told me that the features we all use to shop on Amazon and other e-commerce sites were not all that difficult to replicate. It would be easy, he said, for the site to provide auto-suggestions that would pop up automatically as users entered text into the query fields. Search-refinement tools could allow users to drill down to the results that interested them most, and individual clips could be accompanied by a list of similar clips with related subjects, titles, tags, or other metadata. Users could even gain the ability to view "recommended" clips with similar content, somewhat in the way that Amazon's engine suggests items that "Customers also viewed" based on users' unique browsing histories. I was dumbfounded. Why not? Amazingly, Jacob took my wish list and made it a reality, combining several open-source library applications into a custom-built, user-friendly software package that would be accessible to anyone with just a few clicks of the mouse. Of course, the CRBB research team stood to benefit: as we wrote the chapters of this book, we had the unprecedented ability to search our customized database to find narrow subject information, filtered by location or other tags, and then to immediately watch the corresponding interview clips. On the website, the general public can chart customized courses through the vast collection as well.

Now, any user—people's historians from all walks of life—can easily identify patterns in the vast interview data, seamlessly move from one interview clip to the next, and readily compile information for synthesis and comparison. No previous oral history project has allowed researchers to search in this manner and on this scale. Although some access issues persisted, we successfully launched a bold experiment that has already made our narrators' stories more accessible and usable than ever before.

To be sure, the creation and coding of interview clips require labor-intensive processing, but the work is less time-consuming and more rewarding than traditional transcription. Using our controlled vocabulary of subject terms, a trained graduate student spends roughly five hours processing each 1.5-hour interview, a procedure that includes converting the raw video file to a compressed form, dividing it into clips, watching the clips, assigning titles, adding the relevant metadata (subjects from the controlled vocabulary, tags, locations, etc.), and uploading the compressed clip and metadata file to our online database. Some of the five hours is lost to computing—the work could be done faster with better hardware and a faster network. Undergraduate work-study students require roughly twice as much time, along with enhanced supervision, a pair of trade-offs that ultimately proved inefficient except for the most extraordinary students. Both the CRBB project manager and TCU Library archivists completed quality-control checks on newly uploaded data and via random audits of the collection. They have standardized tags, reclassified miscategorized subjects, and made other corrections, and we continued to update the records as we used the sources to write this book. This represents a substantial investment of time, but overall it proved much faster and cheaper than transcription—and infinitely more useful. The site displays more than 7,800 clips from 467 interviewees. Students, journalists, teachers, nonprofit organizations, community groups, and researchers from across the state and nation visit the site, and we recently added a series of crowd-sourcing features that will allow users to share the essays, articles, lesson plans, documentaries, and other products derived from the collection.

Other concerns remain. The site is not compliant with the Americans with Disabilities Act, a growing ethical concern for those who care about equity and a pressing legal concern for many universities and public libraries. Captions are unavailable, since the majority of our interviews lack transcripts. Likewise, the interviews are not translated from English to Spanish or vice versa. Accessibility for monolingual users is diminished as a result. Translation would require transcription. We looked into using a Google API (application programming interface) to create automated transcripts similar to those found on YouTube videos, but the cost was excessive, and more importantly, the transcripts were so error filled that the resulting text would have required an extraordinary amount of editing in order to be useful, and we lacked the labor and the funding for such a massive task.

In addition, the database privileges our subject terms far beyond all other tags, including those generated by ordinary users. The search results are doubtless distorted by the list of subject terms that we generated at the outset, despite our adding new terms as student assistants identified the need for them while processing the data. More importantly, we researchers created the subject headings—not the narrators themselves—nor do they derive from the raw words contained in the interviews (as text mining would allow). The subject headings thus reflect our scholarly biases and language. Additionally, there are regional and ethnic variations surrounding the phrases and terms that narrators (and researchers) used to describe their actions and the meaning of those acts. Something seen as a major transgression in one context might be unexceptional in another. Last, transcribing the entire collection would allow for the application of other automated digital-humanities techniques centered on the written word, but our research design and budget prioritized working with video sources. Emerging voice-recognition technology may make mass transcription and text mapping possible, but it would require another round of resource-intensive processing and analysis.

Nonetheless, we hope that the inclusion of user-created tags and crowdsourcing features will mitigate these limitations over time. As more narrators and community members log in to the site, they can add their own tags to the database and attach narrative comments to individual clips. (We recently added a discussion board for each page; users can log in and post using their Google or Facebook credentials.) The website remains a work in progress and will continue to evolve, though the long-term sustainability of anything on the internet remains an open question. We are currently working on a series of digital exhibits and resources that will include short multimedia essays, minidocumentaries, and podcasts launched to coincide with the publication of this book.[35]

Above all, we encourage other researchers, educators, and activists to pick up where we left off. The database of interview clips on our website can be used for a nearly infinite range of scholarly projects, in disciplines such as anthropology, folklore, literary studies, political science, and many more. Researchers could interrogate the form of our testimonies, the interviewees' narrative techniques, or the silences created throughout the interview exchange. Historians can mine our oral sources and compare them with written archives, writing new accounts of specific aspects of the long and wide liberation struggles. Oral historians across fields can imagine their own new, big and bold projects or fill in the gaps left by the CRBB project. Digital-humanities researchers and media and communications scholars can turn the videos into text and analyze them in new ways, or develop new technologies for analyzing the moving image. We invite readers to use our archive to expand the history of civil rights struggles in Texas to new locales, to deepen it in well-trodden places, to identify new areas of inquiry, and to challenge the interpretations and narratives set out in this book.

The vast expanse of the collection, the ease of using the free online database—these combine to make the CRBB collection a potential tool for an unimaginably broad set of applications. To date, we have received innumerable inquiries about the project from journalists investigating local histories and the backstories of national figures, k–12 educators creating lesson plans, teachers providing training on culturally relevant curriculum and pedagogies, and advocates, policy makers, and grassroots activists seeking to use our history to redress past wrongs and forge new futures. One urban planner called after discovering a clip with a story about unequal public services; foundation officers and public administrators have asked about using oral history as a basis for truth and reconciliation; groups of alumni of long-shuttered Black and "Mexican" schools have asked for help in recording and writing their own collective histories. The interest in our interviews has far outstripped our capacity to assist with all these endeavors, but we remain gratified that the stories we collected and shared have inspired such a wide array of creative initiatives by such a diverse set of professional and lay researchers. We challenge all of you to join us in adding to the CRBB website, interpreting the interviews, and making this people's history matter in the world today.

Appendix: Selected Interview Transcripts

Living with and Challenging Jim Crow

Sandra Burrell / Segregation in Liberty, Texas

Interviewed by Meredith May and Jasmin Howard
Liberty, Texas, July 29, 2016
https://crbb.tcu.edu/clips/3728/segregation-in-liberty-tx

May: What was the first experience you had with Jim Crow or discrimination, or the one that made the biggest impact on you?

Burrell: My grandparents lived in Louisiana, and we went to my grandparents' for holidays and we stopped to get a hamburger. At times we had sandwiches, but we didn't this particular time, and it was a place we had never stopped before. My dad went to the wrong entrance to be waited on. He went to the side for the white [customers] instead of the Blacks, and he was mortified. He was so embarrassed, and they waited on him anyway, you know, they didn't make a big deal out of it, but they did tell him that he had gone to the wrong counter or entrance, and he was so embarrassed, and his embarrassment just affected the whole family. We were on the road traveling, we were just stopping to get a bite to eat, just like any other family would, so it was just—it didn't sit well with us. It made us feel bad.

May: And we have heard in other places in this area there were often either sites that you couldn't go to after certain hours or whole places that African Americans were discouraged from going to. Do remember hearing about these kinds of places or anything like that?

Burrell: We rarely went to the movies, but when we did, we had to go and sit in the balcony. And I remember the white customers who were sitting [in seats] on the floor always turning around and looking up to see who was in the balcony, and we were always looking down from the balcony. We had great seats—I didn't understand why we had to go sit in the balcony, but we had a terrific view. But we didn't go to the movies very much. My dad explained to us when we went to the courthouse—we went for some reason—that we couldn't drink out of the water fountains. He would always explain to us how things were, and since he was a truck driver, he was restricted from going to a lot of places, and he traveled to a lot of different cities, so he made it a point to explain to us that you can't drink out of the same water fountains, and talked about segregation. Our parents talked to us about the impending integration, so we were informed about these things.

And not all the kids were, because a friend of mine that I've talked to recently told me that she didn't realize about the difference—yes, she went to a Black school, yes, she went to a Black college, but that was just the way it was. She didn't digest the fact that she should have been able to go to the same school anyone went to. That never occurred to her, and I couldn't understand why. Why didn't she think about these things? But she said her parents never talked about it, and our parents did talk to us.

May: So your father did talk to you a lot about these things. Did he ever talk about what it was like navigating the system as a truck driver, someone who had to travel?

Burrell: He didn't necessarily talk to us about that. One thing that he talked to us about that was interesting is: My dad's father was Mexican, and he could go in the drugstore and he could buy candy, but his Black friends could not. So they would pool their money, and his Black friends would sit on the curb outside the store, and my dad would go in the drugstore and buy candy, and then he'd come out and split it with his friends. I thought that was interesting that he could go in, but he was born in 1931, so when he was a child, that was all right at that time in Liberty. Now later on, things did change, and of course you had to have medicine, so you had to go to the drugstore, but he didn't talk so much about those kinds of things.

Barbara Cooper / Jim Crow in Bryan, Texas

Interviewed by Katherine Bynum and Moisés Acuña Gurrola
Bryan, Texas, July 17, 2015
https://crbb.tcu.edu/clips/527/jim-crow-in-bryan-texas

Cooper: Jim Crow: I think a lot of it was basically how your parents felt about it. We knew that establishments—we talked about this a lot of times, the fact that if our church had a meeting, hotels were not available. So what people did was to open up their homes, and they would provide housing for people that were attending those meetings there, you know, in their homes. They would provide meals for them there.

Jim Crow is still well and alive. It's just hidden, and people still don't really realize that we are all human beings with the same feelings, that it takes hard work to make it. I think that probably a lot of the fact is that when people look, they think about Jesus the Christ, they look at him as being a certain color. And so that color that has been put into their heads or into their minds, they feel like it gives them the upper [hand], that "This is for us, you know, it's not for you." But whenever we come to the realization that God created us all in his image, and it's just a difference. He wanted us to be different, but he wanted us to love, and so until we get to that point where we realize that as human beings there's nothing different about us, we might not be as prosperous or whatever as the next fellow. But whatever we have, we have to learn to be grateful for that and not to really look down on anyone else because he doesn't have.

In the last few Sundays' lessons, it has been teaching us about how we should help those who are not doing as well, those who do not have—not to just step down on them and think it's okay to do that. So we really have to do better, and it's a mind-set for people. That's what Jim Crow was, a mind-set for people.

John Crear / Historic Relations with the Police in Houston

Interviewed by Sandra Enríquez and Samantha Rodriguez
Houston, Texas, June 6, 2016
https://crbb.tcu.edu/clips/3515/historic-relations-with-the-police-in-houston

Rodriguez: Before the recording started, we spoke a little bit about other incidents with the police in Houston's history. Can you speak a little bit about the incidents that happened way back in the early 1900s?

Crear: Yes, well, Camp Logan—Fourth Ward's not there anymore, but Fourth Ward was always a Black community in Houston.

Rodriguez: Can you talk a little bit about Fourth Ward?

Crear: Fourth Ward was always a Black community in Houston. Jack Yates, who the [high] school is named after, that's where they all lived. It was called Freedman's Town. It was established by ex-slaves, and they had an army camp there, I guess around the time of World War I, that was for Blacks. Black soldiers. It was Camp Logan.

What happened was, well, a sergeant [*sic*; Corporal Charles Baltimore] had gotten assaulted by the [Houston] police and beat up real bad, and a rumor spread that he was dead. So a group of the soldiers, Black soldiers, they marched on downtown. It was a bloody mess. I mean, several policemen were killed, and some soldiers were killed. But then I think they executed maybe about fifteen soldiers after that. But that was—you know, the history of the Black community and the police in Houston goes *way* back.[1]

I remember as a kid, growing up in Fifth Ward. I mean, the police walked around with dogs, and they sicced a dog on a person in a minute. This Black policeman [Edward Thomas] that just passed a little over a year ago, he was the first Black policeman. He had to catch the bus when he arrested somebody. He had to put them on the bus to take them downtown [to the jail].

You know, the South is for so-called separate-but-equal stuff, but with us—just like with Carl [Hampton], that was innocent. But like I was saying, the mayor got on TV with the police chief saying within a year all members of People's Party II and the Black Panther Party were going to be dead, in jail, or cease to be revolutionaries. And they meant it. They tried. I mean, there was harassment. Right before I got here in 1971, they raided our [People's Party II] office, they took James to jail. James wasn't even there. He came up just to see what was going on, and they took him to jail. We were constantly harassed.

I remember, I must've went to jail at least thirteen times, just behind bullcrap. What they would do, they would pull us over, and they would give us a bogus ticket, but they wouldn't let us sign the ticket until they got us downtown. So then we're downtown, and he said, "You gotta pay bail to get out." You know, it was just a form of harassment when they drained our funds—plus, they're trying to break your morale.

But I remember one particular incident in Fourth Ward. We used to just sit there counting them going by, just trying to pace them. So we left, we got in the car, we see them, they're about two blocks down, and so we say, "Let's go." And we pull around the corner, and here they come. And they got to the car with shotguns, you know, got us out of the car, one by one. "Y'all got any weapons?" "No! We don't have no weapons." So people start coming out of their houses. They tried to intimidate the people: "Y'all need to get back." People said, "Nah, we're not going nowhere!"

So they took us downtown. When we got downtown, the press was there waiting: the Black press, the *Chronicle*, the *Post*. It shocked the hell out of them, because the people called. So they took us upstairs to CID, Central Intelligence Division, and they apologized. They said, well, the police didn't know who you all were, and everything. And no, that was a bunch of crap. You see, the people called. That's why we say, "Power to the people," like with the programs, because they came out, and the people weren't going nowhere. They were trying to intimidate them.

I mean, they tried to harass us, break our spirit, break us financially—not just in Houston but nationwide. We were public enemy number one to them, and they brought everything they had: FBI, CIA, you name it. They used—and local police were like their lapdogs to do all their little dirty work. Yes. Like I said, many of us, like myself, doing this, I'm sixty-four [now]. When I'm nineteen, twenty, twenty-one, and forward, I didn't expect to live, because that's what we said. Like, Huey P. Newton wrote a book called *To Die for the People*, and that's what we expected, because they were definitely trying.

Living with and Challenging Juan Crow

Mario Cruz / Discrimination and Jim Crow as a Kid

Interviewed by Steve Arionus and Vinicio Sinta
Uvalde, Texas, July 13, 2016

Arionus: What about public spaces in the town itself? Do you recall instances where if you were out in the downtown area, did Mexican Americans or Mexicans have to go to the backdoor to eat, or—?

Cruz: Oh, sure, there are instances that I remember very vividly. Everybody's dream was to be able to go to the El Lasso Theater, which was in the Anglo part of town, downtown on Getty Street, on a Saturday to see the matinee and the cartoons. Everybody's dream, you'd look for it on a Saturday, was to go to a place, a café that was adjacent to the theater, and buy a bag of what we called tostadas—it's today what you guys are calling Fritos—but you would get a big bag of tostadas with a drink—that was a nickel, if at all—and you would sit there and watch the flicks and cartoons, and everybody had a good time. But you know when you went to the Hangar VII [Grill], you were automatically, depending who was on duty—not everybody was that way—but depending on who was on duty, who the waitresses were, the minute you walk in the door, someone says, "Nah, nah, nah what do you need? To the back. To the kitchen. They'll take care of you." So we'd go out the front door, and we did as we were told, and we'd go out to the back. And there was a gentleman that worked there, who was the cook, and was Black, and we would tell him what we needed, and he would get them for us; the drinks we would get at the theater. But yes, that was nothing uncommon.

In fact, I remember as a child there were certain places that you just didn't go into to be served a bite to eat of any sort, because it was a standing informational piece that Mexicanos were not welcome in those places. There was a place called the Elite, it was on Main Street, it was owned by a Greek family, but they did not allow any Mexicanos in there. And I remember the discussions of some of the Mexicanos and young people, young men that had come back from the service. And they attempted to go in to be served, and they were summarily ordered out—and they were in full uniforms, from what I understand—summarily ordered out of the café and told to get out. But it's something that, you know, you just did, it was just part of life. You knew your place, so to speak.

I remember working in a hotel here, which is where I got my experience washing dishes when I was maybe about thirteen or fourteen, and my job was a dishwasher. And I was a good dishwasher, I mean, I think I did a good job. The fact remains that the chef, who was German, Charlie Walker, instructed anybody and everybody that when you went into the dining room, your job was just to go to retrieve the trays that had all the dirty dishes in it, and you kind of blended into the wall and you didn't acknowledge anybody, didn't speak to anybody, and back into the kitchen you went. Which is very interesting. I mean, some of these people I grew up knowing who they were by name, not association but by name. But yes, those were his instructions: you just walked in and walked out. You didn't speak to anybody, you didn't do anything, you did your job, and that was it. And if you did anything other than what you were instructed to do, you're going to have a little discussion about what we're supposed to be doing.

It's interesting. It carried forth, because years later I started working in health care. I used to take care of a rancher in Uvalde who had a neurological procedure and was left paralyzed. Since I worked in a hospital and knew about bathing patients and exercising and assisting them, they hired me. And I needed the extra money—wasn't much money, but let me tell you, forty-five cents was forty-five cents. I would take him to the Kincaid [Hotel], that was the place to go, all the ranchers, all the bigwigs in Uvalde would go to the Kincaid. And so I remember many times taking the gentleman to the Kincaid, and was just told sit here, stand against the wall, and again, you don't say anything. You couldn't help but hear some of the insults that sometimes these people threw out: "Goddamn Mexicans, blah, blah." All this and all that, and it's very hard to take, you know. I just had a sense of anger that I wanted to go up there and just whack them on the side. But what was I going to do as a thirteen-year-old? So you just stood there and just internalized it to some degree, much to my dismay and disappointment, but you just took it in and you hurt and that's what you grew up with.

So eating at places in Uvalde, the theater, the Lasso, I remember very vividly. The building is still standing, it's an art gallery now, but nonetheless when you went to the Lasso there was always a rope. The theater had kind of sloping down to the screen, and so in the front seats there was about maybe about ten or fifteen rows of seats. It was always a rope across the back of those seats. And guess what? We knew that Mexicanos didn't sit beyond the rope. You sat behind the rope. And if it filled up and there was no room downstairs, you wound up in the back. That's where you were told to go.

Lupe Mendez / The Silent Minority in Galveston

Interviewed by Sandra I. Enríquez and Samantha Rodriguez
Galveston, Texas, July 06, 2016
https://crbb.tcu.edu/clips/5956/the-silent-minority-in-galveston

Rodriguez: What was the Latino presence, growing up on the island?

Mendez: There's a phrasing that we grew up with called "the silent minority." It's this almost getting into, like, a counterculture, if that makes any sense. If you were to speak to my folks today—I'm still fascinated. I'm actually thinking of interviewing them and trying to figure out a way to write a book about the history of Latinidad in Galveston County. It's a very quiet, hushed thing that being in it, you know it exists, but outside of it you don't know that it's a thing, right? To hear my parents talk about it there was always a cantina, Gloria's or La Ruby's or something—that was where men went to. But I can't find a one of those damn bars now to find to make a dent. I can tell you all the white bars, and I don't know any Black bars, so it's one of those things that you think about culturally. There used to be, apparently, a Spanish-language, Spanish-film movie house called El Rey, on the island. I can't tell you where the hell it was. My parents, if they argue it with one another, they'll probably figure out the address, but I didn't even know it existed. We did have one church that was all Spanish-speaking, a mission, Reina de La Paz. It was my church as a kid, and every Brown kid that I knew that spoke Spanish all went to church there. Every *quinceañera* girl that I knew always had their stuff there.

Every *baile* [dance] was either at the Galveston Convention Center, which is torn down now, or the El Mina Shrine Temple, which has also been torn down. But that's a part of that cultural growing up, right? Every *quince*, every *bola* [ball], every whatever, those were the two spots that that you went. There was another spot—it's still there—there's a bingo hall just as you get off of 45 and it turns into Broadway. On the back half there's like a Home Depot, Target thing on the left side. If you go straight down that street further down, there's this old bingo hall. I don't even know if they still use it, but I remember being a little girl, and that bingo hall was El Salón Para Baile, and bands would play there when I was a kid.

So that element, it was there, but growing up it was a very different—like, almost like, you do this at home, and then what you show to the world is something different. I'd go to school, and I couldn't—I don't even know how I would describe what I grew up knowing to the white kids I went to school with, because it just seemed like two different worlds for me.

Narciso Alemán / Consciousness Formation

Interviewed by David Robles and Sandra I. Enríquez
Weslaco, Texas, June 29, 2015
https://crbb.tcu.edu/clips/460/consciousness-formation

Alemán: Greg Montoya became the first state representative for this area to go to Austin. He had a significant impact for us. I had him [as a teacher] when I was in sixth grade. I also had Mrs. Carrizales when I was in sixth grade, and it was in sixth grade that a lot of the distinction between us and the rest of the school system became apparent to us. At least we could begin to verbalize what that tenuous, inexplicable distancing between Anglo teachers and us was. Our generation was prohibited from speaking Spanish in school. The belief, of course—to the extent that can be given at least acknowledgment, if not credit—is that they believe that if we continued to speak Spanish, we would never learn English. They were not adherent to any kind of bilingual education. They thought you speak English or Spanish, but they prohibited [children] from speaking Spanish and giving them the benefit of the doubt, because they thought it would be better for us. But it is that kind of paternalism, that kind of colonial attitude, that then gave way to the conditions and situations now in this country and really throughout the world. But for us it was a microcosm in the school district.

And so the resistance for us was to speak Spanish. A group of us standing anywhere, when there was a teacher coming, somebody would always say, "If you think you're so bad, why don't you speak to me in Spanish, [loud enough] so the teacher can hear you." Because if they would hear us, they would spank us. And so it was an act of defiance. At the same time there was—it was an adolescent manifestation of some kind of rebellion or resistance, but for us we grew up that way.

But Mrs. Carrizales and Mr. Montoya taught us pride, you know, what we were and who we were and why. It was a sense of pride instead of just a breakdown and a denial of who we were, and so to that extent, they planted some of the seeds that Francisco Briones was talking about on Sunday: some of those seeds that once planted, begin to eventually grow and bear fruit. And so that's how I grew up. Also, Mrs. Carrizales and Mr. Montoya taught us academic excellence: "You need to excel academically if you're going to get ahead. You need to be a straight-A student, you need to be an excellent student," not only in Spanish, and not only your social sciences, which is where Mr. Montoya taught, but also in English. And so groups of us learned English, and some learned it better than the gringos, and we could speak and write better than they could. But it was that motivation to excel that drove us.

Diana Abrego / Reasons for Joining the Brown Berets

Interviewed by Steve Arionus and Vinicio Sinta
Del Rio, Texas, July 19, 2016
https://crbb.tcu.edu/clips/2906/abrego-s-reason-to-join-the-brown-berets

Abrego: To me, the Brown Berets—what it meant to me—maybe when I was younger it had a different meaning, and my heart was set on what I wanted to see and bring to the group. I knew that I wanted to see better education for our Brown children because we lived in a *frontera* and kids were treated differently, especially if you were poor. You knew who those people were, and you knew they were never going to have the same opportunities. If they were going to arrest Mexicanos, Chicanos, you knew they were going to cause harm to them. They would right away accuse them. If it had been an Anglo, I guarantee you they were going to treat them different really quick. And the same thing was in school, whatever you did, so of course we knew those things.

My mother was a maid for a very wealthy family here in Del Rio, a very prominent, wealthy family. My mom used to wash for them, took care of their children, make tortillas, food, clean their house every day of the week. She would walk to their home and work for them. My mother would take two of us, either my older sister, my middle sister, or me. She would take one or two of us, and the rest would stay home. My mother worked hard raising that family's children, their daughters, their children. And then they accused my mom of stealing some really expensive [jewelry], what they called a tennis bracelet and a ring that was very, very high priced. She had been working for them for five years. My lord, why would she have decided then to steal? They came and arrested my mother and took her from the house. All of us crying, all of us torn. "*Que se estaban llevando nuestra madrecita?*" [That they were taking our mom away?] I mean, can you imagine what that—imagine if they took your mother out of your house and the police were saying, "You're arrested for theft." "*Porque te robaste esta señora que esta buscando.* [Because you stole, this lady is accusing you.]"

I was like, "How dare you?!" My mother, who takes care of your children, who feeds you and washed your clothes, cleans your restroom. Well, let me tell you, a year and a half went by, maybe two, and they found the bracelet and the ring. That lady came to the house and kneeled in front of my mother, and I just remember my mom cried at the door. She wanted to go and say she accepted the apology, but we didn't, me and my brother. We were mad. We told her, "Don't you dare humiliate yourself like that, Mom. *Tu tienes más dignidad, Madre. No te vayas a humillar con esta señora* [You have more dignity, Mom. Do not humiliate yourself before this woman]. Yes, we're suffering, we're struggling, *pero* she accused you of theft after she reported you to the police, and they arrested you, Mother. And you're going to tell her, 'Okay, and I accept your apology'? I said, 'No, Mom, you can't do that. What are you showing us?'"

I remember feeling so angry inside. I was so angry. I thought, this is not right and this is not fair. How easy it was for her to just come and do that to my *madre*. And my poor mother, that walked every day to their house, every day ironing their clothes—she would get my sister and I to iron clothes. Cleaning their restrooms. And I just thought no, and I said, "Mom, no more, Ma. You don't need to. *Tu no eres una animal. Tu eres una humana con corazón.* [You're not an animal. You are a human being with a heart.]"

Ordinary Women, Extraordinary Activism

Barbara Lange / Activism in Houston

Interviewed by Meredith May and Jasmin Howard
Liberty, Texas, July 28, 2016
https://crbb.tcu.edu/clips/3845/activism-in-houston

May: So after the Shamrock Hotel, what else did you participate in as far as activism in the civil rights movement?
Lange: I went to work for Neighborhood Centers, as I said, a United Way agency, and I was the very first Black person that ever worked there.
May: How did that feel?
Lange: It felt like—well, I guess I'm kind of naive in a whole bunch of ways. I was in a sandwich generation, or the reverse of an Oreo, all of my life, and I was never afraid to put my foot in the water. So when I went to work for Neighborhood Centers, the funniest things would happen. It was a settlement house, a huge settlement house, and we had a *huge* front porch, and I was told things like "Now, Barbara, don't let those Black kids sit on that porch. You know they're out hanging out, and we're in an Italian neighborhood, and we don't want the neighborhood to come and confront us." I said, "This is an Italian neighborhood. I'm sure they all Catholic. I'm Catholic. We will deal with this on my terms." I never restricted those kids from sitting on the front porch, and that may seem like a minor, minor thing, but the idea that someone could come up to me, a Black woman, and say, "Don't let those Black kids sit on the porch because we don't want to mess up the neighborhood, the neighborhood don't want those kids in here," and just a series of things.

I remember all of the foundations and everything used to buy tickets [to various things] and send them to our organization so we could give them to the Italian kids, and the staff would be invited as well. There was another staff person about my age on the payroll with the agency, and she was in charge of giving out the tickets, and they gave her tickets to a theater, a show, and she gave me two tickets, one for me and one for Tom. And the poor thing came back crying later on. She said, "I wasn't supposed to give you those. I didn't know that they don't let Black people go to the theater." And I said, "Well, this Black person is going to the theatre." We did, and they didn't turn us around or anything like that, but I don't think they'd ever seen any Black people in that theater before, which is now the Alley Theatre. It was a little, small, small theater in the Montrose area, and that must have been in like 1965 or something like that.

After that time, I was on the community relations [committee] for police and community, and we met for about five years, and the policemen would come over to the Neighborhood

Centers. And we would talk about situations and issues—I'm finding that history does repeat itself, because lots of things that I see happening now. I took great pride in having been exposed to [Saul Alinsky]—to me he was not a communist or any of those other things that he's being accused of. He put the University of Chicago on the map and taught Obama how to be an organizer. And so we did a lot of the organizing that we had been taught to do. As a graduate student at Texas Southern, I was involved and doing some of the things that you're doing now.

Guadalupe Quintanilla / Community Activism and Addressing Racism in the Houston Police Department

Interviewed by Sandra Enríquez and Samantha Rodriguez
Houston, Texas, June 30, 2016
https://crbb.tcu.edu/clips/5883/community-activism-and-addressing-racism-in-the
-houston-police-department

Quintanilla: When I moved to Houston, I became extremely active in the community. The reason I did is because I have two boys. And the first thing I heard was that there was a lot of racism in the police department, and that a lot of the youngsters, the Hispanic youngsters, were stopped by the police. The students asked, "Why did you stop me?" They would handcuff them and take them, because they were calling it resisting arrest. This was the reputation the police department had. I was very frightened. What would happen with my boys? As a matter of fact, it was very real.

Herman Short was the police chief at the time, and he had the reputation of being really very difficult with minority people. Once I got to the university, I was introduced to Eddie Corral. Eddie became the first Mexican American fire chief in the history of Houston. And Eddie helped me a lot, because Eddie introduced me to the leadership in Houston. There was only one woman who was extremely active at the time, Olga Gallegos. Olga was very active. Her daughter is an attorney now. Olga was very, very active. The people of my generation, the women, there is only one alive, Dorothy Karam; the rest of them are dead. But I made it my business to know the leaders of the community because I was afraid of the police for my children.

I made it my business to understand, and especially to know attorneys. So I got to know David Lopez and Judge Hernandez, who was the first Mexican American judge in the history of Houston. I met all the leadership through Eddie. ¿Si? And that's how I knew about Leonel [Castillo] and about David. I had talked to David about what do I do to protect my children? He said to me, "Mira, I'll give you some cards, and if they get stopped for anything, tell them not to say anything but 'Yes, sir, yes, sir, yes, sir' and call me." So that gave me the idea.

What we did is, I talked to different [Mexican American] attorneys in the city. There were about five at the time, and we got cards from them. And then we went to the schools, and through the counselors we got permission to talk to the students, and then we put them together and we told them, "If you get stopped by the police this is what you do. You just say 'Yes, sir, yes, sir, yes, sir.' Do not ask questions. Do not anything. You have the right to one phone call. Carry this in your wallet." And we gave them cards from the attorneys. That was the first thing we did. They had cards.

Diana Montejano / Becoming Heavily Involved in Student Activism, the Brown Berets, and Gender in the Brown Berets

Interviewed by Steve Arionus and Vinicio Sinta
San Antonio, Texas, June 29, 2016
https://crbb.tcu.edu/clips/4218/becoming-heavily-involved-in-student-activism
https://crbb.tcu.edu/clips/4219/the-brown-berets
https://crbb.tcu.edu/clips/4221/gender-in-the-brown-berets

Arionus: You were just about to tell us how you got involved with the Chicano activist movement.

Montejano: At that time, I was involved with Rosie Castro. They were asking for volunteers. I was right there at the Crystal City boycott. Same thing, same principle as Edgewood and Lanier [High Schools, sites of the first school walkouts], and these guys really went on strike. These guys were asking, because they did not want the kids to lose touch with school—because we were education majors—they asked for volunteers to go and spend the Christmas break, the month we were off, in Crystal City. We went, and José Ángel [Gutiérrez] was there. I met Luz [Gutiérrez]. We worked with the kids in this big old community center. I will never forget that. I think the girls had a house to themselves. Some of the people had two houses, one for the guys and one for the girls. And we would go and teach these kids in this big community hall. And we would play with them, read to them, help them with their writing. We did that for a whole month.

That is when they were organizing the Raza Unida Party. Actually, Rosie became a Raza Unida candidate. That's how I started getting involved and going to all the functions and meetings and all this. I started going to this place right there on Barkley and Castroville. I want to say it was a barbershop, it used to be a barbershop—I don't know what it was, but they would lend us this place. Somebody lived upstairs. They would lend us this place, and all the leaders would come and meet there, and they called it Barrios Unidos. It was Juan Patlan, he was the original head of the Mexican American Unity Council. They had MANO there, the Mexican American Neighborhood Organization. They had MAYO there, and they had Teatro. That was with George Velásquez. Then they had this little-known [person] starting the Brown Berets.

I used to go volunteer there because Rosie told me they need volunteers. We used to go there supposedly like secretaries and do filing and typing, and do whatever it was that these men wanted. That is how I started going to these different functions and volunteering for fund-raisers and things like this. I also went to a lot of the protests, you know. As a citizen, protesting—not belonging to any one group just yet, just going as an individual protesting for the rights.

What attracted me to the Brown Berets is—I don't know. I went to the Deiz y Seis de Septiembre celebration, and they had a booth there, and they were all there dressed like *soldados* [soldiers]. Something to me about the discipline they had at that time attracted me. But then I was dismayed that they did not have any women. They did not have any women in the Brown Berets, and that was where I met my compadre Jerry Arispe. I baptized his daughter. Actually, I just talked to him not that long ago. It was his birthday. I started hanging around with them, with Jerry. I met some of the other Berets, and I actually became a—I guess you want to call it "lover" or "girlfriend" to one of them. I am not going to say his name. That was pretty hot and heavy for a while, but it really had nothing to do with my commitment to La Raza.

Finally, I approached Juan Guarjado, and we talked about the possibilities of opening up a women's chapter. But my job was not done, because he said, "You need to bring some women that are truly committed." They were like soldiers. That is what they were, and he explained to me what it was, and I was, like, all militant. It was like I was going to join the Chicano version of the Weather Underground Movement, you know. We were going to blow up things. Really. Go back to Malcolm X: "By any means necessary." So, I was like that already. My mind was there. I honestly had a hard time around women that wanted to go that route, but I did. Two of them were from Del Rio, my hometown. One of them was a former roommate, Silvia Hernandez, and Lettie Gallegos. They came. They wanted to be Brown Berets. Lettie actually made the Army her career.

   ...

Montejano: It was just a handful of women.

Arionus: Why do you think it was so difficult to recruit Chicanas?

Montejano: First of all, I do not think they were ready to be *soldadas*. Number one, I mean, pick up a rifle. We would have been labeled terrorists today if we would actually have carried out our plans the way we had kind of set them up. I know we were [on] the FBI radar. We were

[on] the police department's radar for sure. I knew that that was part of it. And the other part was that we still had to struggle with this "*Yo el hombre, tú la mujer*. [I'm the man, you're the woman.] You are going to do what I say." And that was even—that was hard for me. You can ask my big brother about that, because he says—my mother says she raised all these men, but the aggressive one in that family was me. I was the *peleonera* [aggressive one]. I said, "I had to grow up competing with you guys, so of course I have to go the extra distance."

I was ready and very committed to the changes that were supposed to come about by any means necessary. We *marchamos*. We protested. I never got arrested for protesting, though. It just seemed by *la gracia de dios* [the grace of God] that we never did. One of the positive things that I think came out of that was—ah, his name is Ralphie and he was running for sheriff, but I cannot remember his last name—Ralph Lopez. He was a sergeant with the police department. He knew Juan, and he started coming around the [Brown Berets] headquarters. We were all antipolice, man. Our main thing was the police were beating up on these Chicanos for nothing. Just beating them up, killing them, shooting them, harassing them. The young people, that was one of the things that we did: we used to tail the police when they were on their beats. Not too many policemen liked that, but we did it....

That was the first step into creating the community relations office with the police department. Prior to that, I don't think they had one. So in a big way, they were instrumental. The Brown Berets were also instrumental in creating the so-called "truce"—or war councils, they would call them. We would sit down and have these "peace talks" with these different gangs. I don't remember sitting in on any of those. Were they successful? I'm not sure. I can't tell, because I saw a lot of conflict within the Berets' different barrios. So, they had that kind of uneasy truce that was very precarious....

Arionus: Can you tell me how as a woman, as a Chicana, you were treated differently than other Brown Berets?

Montejano: Well, I wasn't treated differently by *some* of the members. There were some expectations, like I said, from even some of the Westside Berets, because there were some that believed the women should be at home making supper and raising kids and putting up with everybody's shit, you know. Those were just, like, basically individual attitudes. Overall, generally, among the Westside Berets—because that is my initial experience—I was not around long enough to tell you about the south side, but pretty much they accepted me.

I went through the training, and I had to deal with those attitudes sometimes. But mostly I went through the training. I learned how to dismantle rifles and put them together, to load them and unload them. We went through self-defense training. We had our prime minister of self-defense, and I still talk to him. He is a minister, by the way. He preaches. So, anyway, we went through the whole—it was like military training, man! It was the whole thing. I was pretty physically fit at that time. It was just incredible. We were expected to march alongside them. There were several incidents. My compadre can probably tell you about that. We were in the Valley and had several confrontations. We came this close to actually having it out with law enforcement.

Arionus: Can you tell us about one of those instances?

Montejano: Yeah. I can't tell you the particulars because I don't remember too much. All I remember is, I was loading and passing out rifles, loading and passing out rifles. It was the *whole* block. We had the whole block [armed]. I was going to get it, in other words, because I was in the van passing these things out. We had the whole van loaded with rifles. I remember coming back, we got stopped at the immigration checkpoint. And they opened the van, and we're sitting there [laughing], and the guy just closes the van and says, "Go on." He didn't even ask, "Are you United States citizens?" He didn't do anything, just like, "Get going." It was so funny, coming back. But when we were there, I actually thought, "We are going to shoot it out here." And that was my job, to load up those rifles and keep them coming. So I loaded them all. I knew how to do it, they taught me how to do it. We were doing it in record time, *vamanos*.

Arionus: What were some of the protests you did in San Antonio with the Berets?

Montejano: We protested Mayor [Walter] McAllister and his savings and loan about that fiasco, his comments about "You give them beer, mariachis, and tamales and they'll vote for you." That protest. We protested police brutality. That was our number one focus, police brutality. We joined with the César Chávez *marcha* and went to Austin, with that *marcha* over there. Have you talked to Jorge Velásquez? Where we raised the Mexican flag over the Capitol of Texas. And I will never forget that, because you know how they have their little basement or whatever? All the police in Austin were there in their riot gear, and we were looking at them because that was one of the things. We were supposed to be the protectors of the marchers, and so we passed on the word that those guys are over there were just waiting, just waiting. I will never forget, and I don't know who has the pictures—because I know that people took pictures of us raising the Mexican flag over the Capitol building. That was so awesome, just something else. But they didn't say anything. Mainly, it was the *marchas* for the farmworkers, for equal rights, the equal pay, education, more educational opportunities, and of course the police brutality. And at that time, I'm sure you read about they killed that thirteen-year-old boy [Santos Rodríguez] in Dallas. Yeah, they shot him under the house. That was one of our [issues], and a lot of the kids on the west side were getting beat up by the police.

Ofelia de los Santos / Hidalgo County Women's Political Caucus

Interviewed by Sandra I. Enríquez and David Robles
Edinburg, Texas, June 26, 2015
https://crbb.tcu.edu/clips/385/hidalgo-county-women-s-political-caucus

De los Santos: I met some women that said, "Why don't we form a Mexican American—or a Women's Political Caucus?" We couldn't be "Mexican American," because we had a lot of Anglo women that were at the university. And one of them was the wife of the editor of the *Monitor* at the time, Barbara King, and we became good friends. And so we women decided to form this organization.

Well, it created a big problem with our husbands because our husbands were Mexican Americans, Chicanos, la Raza. And so we were "joining a white woman's movement," to quote my husband. I remember telling him, "But it's not just a white woman's movement, because Mexican American women are also getting oppressed by the husbands, the boyfriends, the men." And he's like, "No, you don't know what you're talking about." And this is an educated person, but uneducated in the political activism of women. But we women went ahead with it, and we started the organization, and we got very involved.

Enríquez: What was the name of the organization? Do you remember?

De los Santos: It was Hidalgo County Women's Political Caucus.

Enríquez: And what year was this formed?

De los Santos: That would have been the 1980s—

Enríquez: How did you get involved on campus, as a group, and in the community?

De los Santos: In the community, we would meet in McAllen, and women would come from the different organizations that we were members of. In La Jolla, it was a very political town run by "Big Leo"—we called him "Big Leo," Billy Leo's father. Mr. Leo was a very smart man, smart enough to understand and not be threatened by women's political activism. He gave us our initial kind of, like, blessing, and so the men couldn't do too much about it. The husbands weren't too happy about it, but I took nine women from La Jolla with me to the first meeting of the formation of the Women's Political Caucus.

One of them was Maria Luisa Garcia ... She's related to me. She's a lot older and had been involved in politics a lot longer than I had. But she became one of my first women mentors, and she understood what we younger women were talking about in terms of wanting our own place within male organizations, albeit Chicano, Mexican American, whatever. We were tired of being the ones that fixed the rice and the beans for the *pachanga* [party], and not being the president or the vice president or in any important position, the negotiators with the powers that be. The UFW helped us quite a bit because the United Farm Workers were led down here by Rebecca Flores Harrington. She was a member of our caucus. She was a very strong woman leader. And of course if you know the story of César Chávez, you know that Dolores Huerta was his right hand. Dolores Huerta became another model for us. Another model for me became Martha Cotera from Austin. She's a dear friend. I love her to death. We just went up to see her a few weeks ago, and all her writings influenced me quite a bit. My husband worked with her husband, and so he had nothing to say when I showed him her writings and said, "Look, Martha writes about the Chicana feminists. There is such a thing." And then he just kind of, hmm, there wasn't much he could argue after that.

I think that educated men eventually get over that machismo, that *machista* syndrome, with women like me that learn to speak up and, in a loving way, take them to places where they don't want to go, which is to recognize their own ways of oppressing others. I think it behooves all of us that when we get to a place where we're in positions of control or authority, that we not become like the people that we have replaced. Some say that it's human nature to just do that, that it's an automatic thing that the position changes the person, but I really believe that one can fight against that, but not alone.

You've got to have a strong faith. You've got to have a belief in something other than yourself in order to do that, to control those desires within us that say, "I want to be famous. I want to have power. I want to be number one." Because that's what this country teaches, that you have to be number one and you can pull yourself up by your bootstraps. But if you look at anybody that's successful, you realize that that's a myth. Everyone has someone that that they lean on to get to where they're going, and successful people rarely get there by themselves.

Marilyn Clark / Ruth Jefferson and the Welfare Rights Organization in Dallas

Interviewed by Katherine Bynum
Dallas, Texas, July 26, 2017
https://crbb.tcu.edu/clips/7534/ruth-jefferson-and-the-welfare-rights-organization-in
-dallas

Clark: About Ruth Jefferson? Oh yes, we don't have hardly any information on Ruth ... But this is what I know ... I didn't really do enough with them, because they were fierce! They weren't making phone calls in the kind of stuff I did, you know. They were serious mothers who were on welfare raising children, talked a lot of noise. They were into ideology; I read books and they got after it. So I kind of stood in awe of them and just kind of hung around on the fringes in terms of real work—of which I did hardly any.

But Ruth, as I understand it, came up in a West Dallas housing project. And I don't remember how she got involved, if it was through her boyfriend Kwesi who was involved with SNCC ... I don't know how she got involved. Stuff was in the air—unlike now. People ask, "Why don't poor people rise up?" But there's nothing. It was like lightning out here. On every corner it was blasting, people are moving, things are happening during this. It appeals to your imagination, this possibility of getting this going. But yes, she was very compassionate. Fearless. She's the kind of person could knock you out. I mean, just physically knock you out.

Ed Harris used to tell the story ... because he was intimately involved with welfare rights, I mean, because they raised hell. I mean, when we tried to raise money, [we asked], "Will you please give us a dollar?" They'd go to businesses and stick 'em up. "Where are you doing this work?" You know, "I need some money, we need to be fed, we got children, this is what we're doing for you, because of this kind of crime is going on in the community against Black people, and I need to come in here and get some milk and some diapers, blah blah blah, if you ain't got cash." That's what they did.

Now, I'm from the farm. I couldn't possibly say that. But they were able to do it, and Ruth was very much part of that straightforward, direct-action kind of mobilizing, and at the same time she was the most humane, sweet, wonderful, encompassing, loving, compassionate kind of person. But when she meant business—Ed would tell us about when Kwesi, her boyfriend, her man, got arrested. And she went down to the jail and told, I guess, Bill Decker, who was the sheriff then, "Let Kwesi out of here ... and then I'm going to kick your motherfucking ass." I mean, you know, just that direct—"Here, I got the bail money." Boom, and he got out, the way he tells the story. But the mere fact of how does that happen when you envision how the jail works, how that kind of system works. But obviously, it was a lot more open and direct. But that for me is how I remember Ruth being portrayed and how I experienced her.

Guillermo Glenn/ La Mujer Obrera and NAFTA and Workers' Committees

Interviewed by Sandra Enríquez and David Robles
El Paso, Texas, July 16, 2015
https://crbb.tcu.edu/clips/2449/la-mujer-obrera
https://crbb.tcu.edu/clips/2451/nafta-and-workers-committees

Enríquez: I wanted to ask you if you could share with us what La Mujer Obrera is and a little bit of its history and what your role has been within the organization?

Glenn: La Mujer Obrera was formed by some of the Farah workers back in 1981 and '82. Their charter for nonprofit was in 1981. And their leadership was primarily women. They worked on providing information to [garment workers] when there was still factories here, in 1981. They were basically working on education, taking on problems that the garment workers had. I know that they did some [work that] concentrated on women's health. And that's how they got the name, although we started out as Centro del Obrero de Fronteriza. But since they concentrated on women's health—for instance, they got permission in some of the factories to go in and test for the brown lung and do other health screenings. And so, that's how they got involved. And so the women started talking about La Mujer Obrera in those factories, and that's how—this is from my point of view—how they got the name La Mujer Obrera. But that was in the early stages. When I got here—it had to be about 1987, something like that— they were primarily doing a lot of education work. Then they moved to this barrio where a lot of the factories were, and they had worker committees in thirty factories.

Enríquez: What were some of the factories?

Glenn: Action West, and the Farah, and La Union—I forget some of their names—and one of the Levi [Strauss] factories. And then there was a lot of sweatshops, and they changed their names. And that's when they started protesting from these committees, because the changes that were occurring in the garment industry, *este*, was when some of them started to leave already.... You get this development of a lot of smaller factories and, essentially, sweatshops. And the Mujer got a lot of complaints that a lot of these shops were not paying the workers. You know, they were not paying their overtime, they owed them hours and everything. And that's when they were able to get the Department of Labor to come down.... But this is when some of the women chained themselves to one of the machines until the owner would pay the workers....

Enríquez: So what happens when NAFTA is instituted? And how does that change the organization?

Glenn: Well, where the Mujer had thirty committees, now it dwindled down to practically none. They just had an assembly of workers. But before NAFTA, every Wednesday, they at least had a committee from the different factories. They would gather, and they had a little co-op, and they would share—like, the *mujer* would buy frijoles, rice, sugar, milk, and then every Wednesday they would divide it, and the workers would pay at reduced cost. And they had this whole education thing going on in all these factories. They reached a lot more workers.

After NAFTA, when they started closing down all the factories, well, all the work went to Mexico, practically. Not just to Mexico, but at that time the association became more active. The Border Workers [Association], that's when we were protesting for—we lost the battle to keep the factories here. Because the Mujer met with the city officials, government officials, saying, "How can we develop part of the industry here? What niche? We have all of these experienced workers." It takes ten years to train a good garment worker, you know. But there was no money to develop—what could the workers do? What kind of niche could they go into? What kind of clothing could they do to preserve their skills? Because you have close to thirty thousand workers, and the majority being women who didn't have a GED, who could not speak English, whose professional skill was sewing, right, and they were out. That means not only did they lose their independence, especially the women, but they lost health insurance, they lost the pension, the IRA, whatever they had with the company.

So it was a brutal kind of change that NAFTA brought about to the organization. The alternative to not having a job was "How are we going to retrain you?" And you can go on unemployment, but if the majority of the women workers and men workers did not speak English, there was no bilingual training. So that's what La Mujer and the Border Association started working on. You've got to change the training. And we even sued. The Border Workers Association sued the Labor Department, the Texas Workforce Commission, and the local here. And the lawsuit went on for a quite a while. Saying that they were discriminating against the workers, because their NAFTA training programs were built around a national *onda*, perspective, and they did not take into consideration that in order for a woman to learn English, get a GED, and then get training, she couldn't do that in nine months, which is what the unemployment was, right? Because the training was tied—if you couldn't get unemployment, how could you get the training? You couldn't afford it. So that's why we went, we filed the lawsuit, and we didn't win; we had to settle because it went on so long, and what were the workers going to do?

So we settled for changes in the law, and they promised to send in $6 million for a new program. But that was a drop in the bucket, we thought. We had lost, right? We settled, but we didn't win what we wanted. We wanted bilingual training for the workers, and we still don't have it in El Paso. There was a lot of money poured into El Paso, and the Mujer Obrera fought to have a training program. They went to Washington and submitted a proposal for $75 million, not necessarily to go to the organization, but to set up a bilingual training program to hire and train the teachers at the community college, *donde sea* [wherever], so the workers can get the training. They were not successful, because the unions were against it.

Lorena Andrade / La Mujer Obrera

Interviewed by Sandra Enríquez and David Robles
El Paso, Texas, July 17, 2015
https://crbb.tcu.edu/clips/3276/la-mujer-obrera-2

Enríquez: How did you first become engaged in the history of your community, or of Chicano history?

Andrade: In Minnesota. When I went to the University of Minnesota, I think that's where, at that time. Now when you go to Minneapolis, there's a lot of Mexicans and all of that, but that's not how it was before. So there was only a few of us Mexican women that were studying at that time, so that was one of the first things we did. We started looking for each other and doing that.

Enríquez: How did creating that community of Chicana women help you become—or shape you as an individual?

Andrade: Well, for me it was important because it was the *compañeros* [comrades] in the 1970s. They fought to give us, to leave for us, a Raza Student Cultural Center. So it was supposed to be a place for Chicanos to gather and to have support, to support each other and to have some computers. Before, not everyone had computers like now, so it was important for us to have those things and for us to organize events. But what had happened was, by the time I showed up in the early nineties, then it was dominated by rich Latin American men. *¿Verdad?* [Right?] And so when, as women, we decided to get to know each other and unite, one of the first things we did was organize to push them out of our Raza Student Cultural Center and make it a safer place for women and for Chicanas. Because they would tell us, like for me, for example, they would say, "People like you in my country are my servants." *¿Verdad?* So it was also class. It was gender, obviously, because women were not, did not, feel comfortable walking into the center, because of the way the men—like, sometimes they would stand in a line and critique the women as they walked in. I would hear things like that about the center.

I started taking some Chicana studies classes with Dennis Valdez, he was our professor, and Guillermo Rojas was our other professor. And we only had two, and *este*, it was a small department. But I started learning about the history, and I read *Occupied America* [by Rudolfo Acuña], you know, and that was really important for us to be able to say, "Hey, there is something wrong here. And why didn't anyone ever tell us about, you know, all the horrible things that happened to our people? Or why did I grow up just accepting the conditions that were in my neighborhood?" *¿Verdad?* So it was that in combination with "Where is my safe place at this university?" and it being controlled by these men. And so that also gave us something to organize around. Like, do we need a place for women so that we can help each other through the university? It also helped us organize against something, like for something, defining who we were, and against something. *¿Verdad?* That brought us together....

Enríquez: What did you do after you graduated college?

Andrade: After I graduated from the university, I came to [El Paso to work with] La Mujer Obrera. I went to Los Angeles for a little bit, but then I was able to come here and volunteer at La Mujer Obrera. And that's when I started having like a paying job here. It was in February of 1998.

Enríquez: How did you learn about La Mujer Obrera, and what convinced you that this was your calling?

Andrade: I liked the fact that it was women organizing for labor. That was interesting for me. When I was [first] here at La Mujer Obrera, there was the time before, when we had the social enterprises. It was when the women were getting laid off from the factories. So we could be in a meeting like we are now, talking. And then, just, one hundred workers would walk in the door because they had just received notice that they were being laid off. Because before, the factories wouldn't give you notice. It would just be like, "That was your last shift." Or the door wouldn't open. And that's how you would know it was gone. *¿Verdad?* So it was around that time that they were getting laid off just like that, without notice. That's when I started. And so that's very romantic to me. *¿Verdad?* Because that's what you want to do— protest, and do that kind of organizing. And that's what I had studied in Chicano studies. I took it very seriously. Like, if I studied Chicano studies, that means you're going to struggle for your people. This seemed like a good place, and it was woman centered—well, other than Guillermo.

Enríquez: Can you tell us about the history of La Mujer Obrera? And I know you have been a part of it since 1998, and I know there is a longer history of it before, but—

Andrade: My interpretation?

Enríquez: Yes, your interpretation of what La Mujer Obrera has stood for in the community and what it is.

Andrade: La Mujer Obrera started in 1981. And the way I interpret it is that it was women who had participated in the Chicana movement, like Cecilia Rodriguez and, I think, a couple of women who had participated in the Farah strike. And that we understood that maybe the voice of women was not as strong as it should be, maybe, in the Chicano movement and in the Farah strike. Because the women in the Farah strike started their own women's organization within the union because their voice was not being acknowledged, and the union was making decisions without informing the workers. This is how I interpret it. And so that is why they decided they should begin La Mujer Obrera.

Also because our vision had to be community based, not just fighting for a contract. I mean, fighting for our rights, and to get paid in the factories, and our rights within the factories, but also education, nutrition, health, political liberty, peace, housing. And it was just a broader—as women, we felt that we needed to have a broader vision about the struggle to improve our community, and that it was about our rights in the factory, but it was also more than that. *¿Verdad?* And so we did a lot of popular education, learning what our place is in the economy, and in history. And learning to have a critique of the economic system was very important to us because we are workers, so that focus was important, and it helped us when we were analyzing what was happening in El Paso. It helped us to see far in the long term.

For example, we knew that the garment industry was going to leave, and we knew it had started to downsize, and we understood that it was going to create things like sweatshops. So we were ready when the battle in the sweatshops occurred in the very early 1990s, late 1980s, early 1990s. I think that that was a very important *etapa*, a stage for La Mujer Obrera, because when the women weren't getting paid, we would go and say, "We're going to have to shut it down" or "We have to take over the garments and pay ourselves," or, you know, negotiate with the garment boss. Things like that. After a while, the women were calling us and saying, "We took over the garments. Come and back us up." So I think that it was important that women were able to take those actions, understanding that it was an organization that was there, that was going to be there for them. *¿Verdad?*

Also, here we have taken big actions. Like, we're here on the border, and it seems like we are very separated from the national [institutions]. *¿Verdad?* And nobody really seemed to care whether women were being paid for working or not. So one of the actions that Cecilia and the other women took was to chain themselves to the machines, in one of the sweatshops, and that always brings us—if we take actions like that, it brings national attention.

Enríquez: When was this?

Andrade: The chaining themselves to the machines? I think it was in—I want to say 1991. It's back then, in a newspaper article. And then when NAFTA—at that time they were already starting to talk about the North American Free Trade Agreement, a trade agreement that was coming between Mexico and Canada. And again, the women at La Mujer Obrera and the Farmworkers Center were saying, "This is going to be horrible for us. We're going to lose our jobs." You know? Just like the *compas* [partners in Mexico] were getting ready to say that this was a death sentence for the native people of Mexico. So we were seeing that, but it was very difficult for us to convince others, whether it was unions or environmental groups or others. There was some coalitions, but nobody really believed us, or they did believe us, but who are we to have an analysis of the economy? *¿Verdad?* We were just a bunch of workers. *Este*, but we were right. And when NAFTA came, we lost more than thirty-five thousand jobs, and that's when we lost the garment industry in El Paso.

Enríquez: Aside from the obviously losing thirty-five thousand jobs, which is a huge chunk of the workforce here in El Paso, what were some of the economic and social consequences of NAFTA from what you understand, even now?

Andrade: Well, the economy, when it's changing to a new phase, as, *como los decian* [as they said], "*un nuevo etapa de economia*" [a new economic phase], or they would say, "progress." *¿Verdad?* Like, "progress" is not a good word for us, because it usually means we have to [laughs ruefully]—we're the consequences of whatever they define as progress. *¿Verdad?* So for example, when I tell you we were fighting the sweatshops? There were factories that didn't pay the workers very much, or they didn't pay them at all, but we also had the Levis and the Farahs that paid you $10, $11, $12 an hour. *¿Verdad?* We're talking forty years ago, or thirty years ago. I don't know how far back NAFTA was. *Este*, forty years ago, for our population right now, that is a really good-paying job. Like, if I had $10 an hour, I'd feel like I was middle class, you know? *Este*, because we don't have those jobs where you can get an hourly minimum wage, but it doesn't guarantee you the forty hours. *¿Verdad?*

Entonces, anyways, so when we lost the garment industry, it wasn't that we were just losing jobs that didn't pay us. The women were losing their jobs, and they were already buying their homes. You know, they had mortgages. They had moved out of the barrio and bought these homes. You know, sending their kids to the university. They were living a different life than they had here, so I don't want to romanticize the time in the factory, but they were also very good-paying jobs. They were very difficult jobs, and they were getting hurt, but they were stable, and they were very good-paying jobs. *¿Verdad?*

And so, as women, being two-thirds of the women that lost their jobs, they were the head of household, and that's your economic independence, right there. *¿Verdad?* And those jobs, they didn't plan for those jobs coming back. NAFTA promised that they would bring them back jobs that paid the same, or more than the jobs we had. *¿Verdad?* But that never happened. NAFTA and the economy, they just, they just—there is just this entire population that is just left over. Like when they do their calculations, we are not even in their calculations. There are just entire populations that are no longer necessary. *¿Verdad?*

Just like Segundo: in this barrio, if you see Segundo, the housing, it was structured for men who were going to live by themselves and go out to the farms and work. And they were going to be laborers, and in our community, you can see it was designed around serving the needs of the factories. *Entonces*, when the big farms don't need us anymore, and the factories don't need us anymore, *¿para que quieres barrio?* [What do you want the neighborhood for?] Why? Our community, our neighborhoods aren't necessary anymore. That's why there's no investment in this neighborhood unless we fight for it. Because then, what is the point of having our neighborhood anymore? We're just kind of left out, so that's kind of the implications.

And then we lost our economic independence. Now you have to work two hours here, taking care of an elderly person, and then you get on a bus, and then there is another two hours. All of a sudden they were asking for a GED and English [proficiency]. We never had to do that. And we don't need it. Practically, you don't need it here. But that was kind of the thing they were putting so women couldn't—we were not having access. Some of the people were telling us, "The women you're working with are too old. They only have ten years of productivity left. We have to invest in the young people." *¿Verdad? Este*, so we were too Mexican, and we don't assimilate enough, you know? We were too Mexican. We don't speak English. We were too old. *¿Verdad?* Everything was just an excuse to keep us out of the economics. I mean, there is no place for us, and there was no reason to bother with us, so....

That's why in La Mujer Obrera, we always had to battle about "What does progress mean in our community? What does the community mean for the women workers of El Paso, or for this community?" *¿Verdad?* And you know, when they talk progress, it usually means that we are the ones who have to suffer the consequences so that others can benefit. Just like the factories benefited from our labor, we created the wealth, and now there's a whole part of the city who are living off the wealth we created while our communities are abandoned. *¿Verdad?* And the women themselves are abandoned. *Y nosotros en La Mujer Obrera* [And we in La Mujer Obrera], we have to be able to continue to struggle against the economics that are being imposed. And still try to be creative and try to build something different from it in the wake of the destruction that NAFTA caused.

The Fight for Educational Equity

Betell Benham / Integration in Lufkin

Interviewed by Jasmin Howard and Meredith May
Lufkin, Texas, June 27, 2016
https://crbb.tcu.edu/clips/2359/intergration-in-lufkin

Benham: High school. I think it was still freedom of choice, and then they integrated. And the year they integrated, that was a pretty rough time. A lot of hatred came up. That year they had two valedictorians of the graduating class, two salutatorians, everything was combined. Cheerleaders, all combined. Drill team, whatever. There were a lot of fights. I can remember I was living in Lufkin, going to high school, and we had school buses at that time going to the high school, but it was rough riding on the school bus, and usually there were a lot of fights. School buses were integrated, but then we didn't always have a seat, so you'd get on the bus, and a lot of times we had to stand up. They didn't have two buses going to our neighborhood.

So I remember one time it was a real bad fight. Students would put rocks in the paper and chunk them at us. Can you imagine that? It was like a—it wasn't a paper fight. They started doing a paper fight. They were sneaky. They would put the rocks in the paper and hit us with them. The white students—have you heard of that story? [Laughs] So I remember it was a real bad fight, and I wasn't real good at fighting, and I remember my cousin told me—her name is Cynthia, and she said, "Betell, get back. I'll protect you. I'll fight." So she got to tearing them up! [Laughs] It was rough, but she was like, "Betell, you get back because you know you can't fight." I think that was the last time we rode the bus. I don't remember riding anymore after that, the real bad fight. I don't remember riding anymore.

Howard: So your parents were always responsive to y'all's protection in terms of school and stuff like that. So if you didn't ride the bus . . .

Benham: They would take us to school, and they would leave real early. They would take us to school. Then I started driving. I got my driver's license my junior year, so I could take my mother to work and go on to high school.

Howard: So what other indelible experiences were there during integration in Lufkin?

Benham: The white parents came to school—I don't know all the details—they came to school with guns. They let school out early that day, and I remember my mother came to school with one of her friends, another white teacher, to see if I was okay. And I think I had driven the car to school that day. I can't remember the details, but I was okay, and I made it home some kind of way. And I remember some of the Black students protesting, marching through downtown.

Howard: What was the response of the administration or the police to the white people coming with guns?

Benham: I can't remember how they resolved it.

Howard: The next couple days, it was pretty much back to normal? Remember, earlier you were talking about how good Dunbar was in athletics. How did it affect that—?

Benham: The Black athletes had to go to Lufkin High School and become a part of the Lufkin High School football team, so that was not always good. I remember some disputes, fights, or whatever that took place. I can't remember all the details, but it was kind of rough.

Howard: And for you, how did your experience change when integration happened? Because you had been going to integrated schools, but you were one of the few Black students. How did your experience change when you were one of more than a few Black students?

Benham: It was a little better because there were more African American students there at the time, but then they didn't know me, since I didn't go to school with them. I went to another elementary school, so they had to get to know me. It was still kind of like a lonely existence, making new friends within the Black church. If I went to church with them, they knew me.

Howard: How important was the Black church to the Lufkin community?

Benham: Oh, my, it was everything. That's where you went to learn about more about your religion and Vacation Bible School. It was a real pillar of the community. They had events for the neighborhood, so the church was where you met—it was a gathering place for everybody.

Armando Treviño / Mobilizing Students

Interviewed by Sandra I. Enríquez, David Robles, and Max Krochmal
Laredo, Texas, July 7, 2015
https://crbb.tcu.edu/clips/1948/mobilizing-students

Enríquez: Were there already students mobilizing at the junior college in Uvalde and were they creating organizations?

Treviño: There was a guy that I met who was a rabble-rouser. His name was Rogelio Muñoz. As a matter of fact, later on he became an attorney, and I believe he also became a district attorney there in Uvalde County. And there was another guy from Uvalde by the name of Joaquin Rodriguez, who also became an attorney and who was an activist—as activists go at that time. None of us were radicals per se, but we spoke our minds.

Enríquez: Was there a MAYO chapter at the junior college or any other organizations?

Treviño: No. God forbid. [Laughs]

Krochmal: Can we back up quickly to Crystal City, to the high school? Were you involved with any of the student organizing there?

Treviño: Yes. I graduated from high school. And then the following year there was the contest for [high school] cheerleaders, and at that point in time Crystal City had four cheerleaders, three Anglos and one Mexican or Mexican American or Latin or whatever it is that they called themselves. And if this person got selected when she was a freshman, she would be the cheerleader for four years. After I left school, unbeknownst to me, that was a young lady by the name of Diana Palacios. She was a beautiful little girl, beautiful little body that was nothing wrong with that you could see. And she did a perfect performance, and everybody was saying, "Congratulations, you got it," but the one that had been there was Diana Perez, who was in the same grade level as Diana Palacios, so she didn't win; it was the other one.

I used to commute to Uvalde in a bus that was provided by the college because Zavala, Frio, and Uvalde [Counties] are the tax base for the college. On one of these days when I got home there were cars all over the street, the yard was full of people, and I said, "What is going on?" And it was the students were angry because of what had happened, and they remembered that I at least was vocal if nothing else. So they came and said, "What do we do if this happened and this happened and this happened?" I said, "The only thing that we can do is [demonstrate] unity. We can get a petition and see what we want to do." This was toward the end of the year. So, "what do we do?"

We made a petition and we talked to some people. What made this different was that the people that got involved were the smart kids, not the dummies, not the rabble-rousers, not the troublemakers. So there were four individuals who got together, and we wrote a petition. One of them was Blanca Treviño, who is my sister, who is now a doctor. The other one was Lydia Serna, who I believe lives in Wisconsin and has a master's and is a principal or something. I don't remember the others. So they wrote a petition, and they wanted such *outrageous* things as to select the most beautiful girl that was the most beautiful, whether it was Mexican American or Anglo, it didn't matter. That the students select the most popular, the most likely to succeed, all those things.

The school district said, "How could they do this?" So apparently they went to the principal, and it was about two weeks before school was out. So the principal said, "Why don't we do this? Let's have four Mexican cheerleaders and four Anglo cheerleaders. Let's have a most beautiful Mexican and a most beautiful Anglo. And all down the line." And Lydia and Blanca said, "That doesn't sound right. What do we do?" Two weeks left, so it ended, and as far as everyone was concerned, that was a great victory, but not the ones that had any inkling of what was right. They said, "It's not a victory. It's a piece of steak to shut us up." But that's what the people wanted, and that's what we got.

Daniel Acevedo / Weslaco walkout

Interviewed by Sandra I. Enríquez and David Robles
Weslaco, Texas, June 29, 2016
https://crbb.tcu.edu/clips/457/activism-as-a-young-student
https://crbb.tcu.edu/clips/493/acevedo-chicano-roles-in-school-setting

Acevedo: There's a lot of injustices here. We already knew about the walkout in Edcouch-Elsa. So we went out there to the walkout and said, "They're not isolated. They're not by themselves. We're here also, we have the same problems right here. Real bad [problems]."

We had a similar situation, but we decided to go at it in a different way. We walked out, but we also had instructors, teachers, for the children. Even the elementary school kids walked out. The parents decided to do that. They took out their children, everybody, all of the children, from the schools. We had instructors to teach them.

Enríquez: When was this?

Acevedo: March 10, 1970. They came in and they were instructed. We found businesspeople [to teach classes] and the church, St. Joan of Arc, who would allow us to go ahead and use their classrooms or their facilities, and they taught the children. Being that I was in high school, we didn't have that much instruction, but the elementary school children [did].

There was concern, like, "Okay, why are you all doing this?" So Narciso and us—Jorge,

Oscar, and myself—got together and we came out with a grievance list: we needed more Mexican American or maybe Chicano teachers, Chicano instructors, Chicano educators, everything—coaches, administration. [There were] no principals, no assistant principals that were Mexicans, or very few. So we said, "What's the deal?" We needed to get it all together.

Of all the grievances that we put on there, there were thirty-one grievances, we did it with a different approach. We got together with Bob Sanchez, an attorney from McAllen with the Mexican American Legal Defense Fund, and once we got all the grievances done, we sent it to the US Commission on Civil Rights and the TEA [Texas Education Agency]. They got it, and within three weeks they came down to the school. And they decided to go ahead and instruct them that they had thirty days to come up with a prospectus in regard to all the grievances that we had, and sure enough it worked. This is the perfect way to approach it instead of going, "*Huelga! Huelga! Huelga!*" [Strike! Strike! Strike!] They said, "You have thirty days to fix the school." So one of the approaches that we did was a single-grade campus [for the entire school district]. The Mexicanos were usually on the north side [of Weslaco], and the gringos on the south side, and then everybody had to go to the same campus, and it worked. It was something that had never been done. So we did it correctly.

Enríquez: Why do you think that the Weslaco walkout and your fight is not as known as the Edcouch-Elsa one?

Acevedo: Because Edcouch-Elsa was the first one and it continued on. But Weslaco, all I can say is it was a success because the US Commission on Civil Rights and the TEA told them, "You're wrong and you have to correct it." And that was thanks to the Mexican American Legal Defense Fund and the other attorneys that we had.

Enríquez: I'm really interested in the Mexican American Legal Defense Fund's involvement in this. What made you think, "We're going to take it through the legal way" as a student, and did Weslaco High School have a MAYO [chapter] already?

Acevedo: See, the thing is that when we got together, we were involved with MAYO, Mexican American Youth Organization, and we had a person, Narciso Aleman, and Narciso was very sharp and into it. And he said, "We've got to do it this way. Let's try to do it this way." And then we would have a caucus, okay, and say, "Where do we approach it from here?" And he had contacts like Reid Bella, Juan Gutierrez, Raul Yzaguirre, of the Mexican American Legal Defense Fund. Those were people that we got introduced to because of Narciso. So that was probably one of the reasons that we conglomerated everything together, to make sure that this did not fail. But yes, it's not as famous as the Edcouch-Elsa walkout.

Susana Almanza / Cross-Racial Student Protests

Interviewed by Steve Arionus and Vinicio Silva
Austin, Texas, June 8, 2016
https://crbb.tcu.edu/clips/6263/cross-racial-student-protests-part-one

Almanza: It took us a couple of years before we got organized, and what happened then was we were caught up in that movement, that walkout movement, the Chicano walkout movement. So what happened was in our senior year [at Austin High School], we said we're going to organize and we're going to do a walkout.

Arionus: What years?

Almanza: That was 1970 and 1971. So we say we're going to do the walkout, and we used the phone trees because they had a directory. So we broke that out with the student committees. We started calling everybody and saying, "Look, this is what we want: we want them to drop the grade point average because you can't get in [to advanced courses]. We want it to be mandatory for people of color to be on the student council." Those things were really important to us. What happened was, we said, "When the second bell rings, we're going to walk out of the school." Well, somebody told, so they locked the doors so we couldn't get out of the school building, and neither could the media get in. So we went to plan B, and we headed to the auditorium. So we all went to the auditorium and we demanded to speak to the principal and said we wanted the superintendent there in that meeting. We began the negotiations with them about the inequality and the injustices that were happening.

Arionus: How many students were there?

Almanza: We must have had over one hundred students there in that auditorium. We got a lot—in that senior year we were able to change the grade point average [requirement], we were able to demand that at least one Mexican and one Black get on as cheerleaders. It was a lot of changes that happened. We weren't going to benefit from it, but the other students coming up would benefit from it.

The other thing that we did that same year was: there was this African American guy, Tyrone Johnson, and he really was a basketball player. He was, like, the tallest guy in the school—not only the tallest, but the best basketball player, and by himself he could win the game, you know, because that's how good he was. When it was time for the student council elections, of course we couldn't get on the ballot, so we told Tyrone, "Look, can we do a write-in? Can we do you as a write-in on the student government, as the president?" and he said, "Yes." And so again we got the directory, we broke it up, we started calling people. But then we also called some whites that we knew would support Tyrone Johnson. Because the whites were like, "Wow, he's a star!"

So after the write-in vote and after the voting was tallied, they come on the speaker and they say, "Well, we don't know how this happened, but there was a write-in vote, and Tyrone Johnson got so many votes"—. He didn't win, but it was enough to shock everybody that we had done it, that we had gotten him on and it had gotten noticed and he had gotten all of these votes. It was enough that when we did do the walkout, that people were aware that the student government was not being fair in their elections and stuff and how we were never able to get on the student council.

So those were some of the things we organized. We did the lettuce boycott for César Chávez at the school. We'd tell people not to eat at the school. We told schools they needed to buy union lettuce in support of the [United] Farm Workers.

Elayne Hunt / Residential Segregation and Discrimination in Odessa

Interviewed by Karen Wisely, Joel Zapata, and Todd Moye
Odessa, Texas, July 15, 2016
https://crbb.tcu.edu/clips/3547/race-relations-at-school-and-in-their-neighborhood
https://crbb.tcu.edu/clips/3548/housing-discrimination
https://crbb.tcu.edu/clips/3549/education-integration-and-white-flight
https://crbb.tcu.edu/clips/3550/white-resistance-and-housing
https://crbb.tcu.edu/clips/3572/a-new-neighborhood
https://crbb.tcu.edu/clips/3575/school-integration-and-their-children

Hunt: In 1964, right after President Johnson signed the Civil Rights Act, we began looking for a home. We did that for two years because we knew that that law included [protections against racial discrimination in] housing [sic].[2] We had tried to have a room added onto our home after the second child arrived so that each one of them could have a room for themselves. Daryl was growing. He was four years older than his baby brother, but they were sharing a bedroom together. They had twin beds, and they were sharing the room. But Daryl was growing, so in 1966—I mean, we'd looked for a couple of years, and the Realtors began to talk about this Black couple that's looking outside of the redlined area that they're supposed to be living in, they're looking for a home. Of course, in Odessa, being the small town that it is, it became knowledgeable by all that this couple was looking for a home.

Right after that, the school district had to present [a desegregation plan], because in that law you could no longer have segregated schools. So the school district had to present to the federal government their plan for integration. Well, they presented that plan in 1966, and because of the friendship that had developed—now, I'm going back to the owners of the [music store] that sold instruments [to my husband, Walter, the band director of an all-Black school], because of the relationship that had developed between my husband and the trust level that had developed as well. We had often been invited to their home, because they had two children as well.

[Out of all the school band directors in Odessa] we were the only Black couple in the city. Once a year we would have a picnic for all of the band directors and their families, and we would always go with our children. Sometimes the children were not invited, but the couples were there, so we got to know all of the band directors and their wives in the city of Odessa, because that's just the way it was. We all became friends.

But we still had to go back to that redline place before dark. When [the band directors] traveled [together], they could get out and go into a restaurant to have lunch on the way. But they would have to bring Walter's out to the car. And they didn't like it, that didn't set too well with them. So after a while when they traveled, they would send someone in to get sandwiches and they would all eat sandwiches [together] along the way. Again, I go back to how important it is to talk to each other. Once you talk, and once you develop this relationship, you begin to see what's different. Because this skin is white, not white, but light skinned, and this one is dark brown, various shades of brown, what's the difference? We are all human beings. We all need to eat. We are all working for the same thing. Why do they have to live over there, separated from us, when we are friends?

So we continued to look for houses, and we thought we were able to purchase one. But the school district knew that just because Johnson had signed that law, the Realtors were really not going to sell property to an African American couple in the same area in which they lived, where the bankers lived, where the mortgage owners lived. They were just not going to do that, for whatever reason they thought was the difference [between us]. Because we were equally as educated as any one of them, even though we were not able to go to their schools. But they didn't know what we were learning in ours, either.

So one day we were talking, and we mentioned that we thought we had purchased a home. And we had given a down payment on a Sunday afternoon and asked the Realtor if he would hold the check until Monday afternoon to give my husband an opportunity to transfer the little money we had saved to put down on a new place, could transfer it from our savings to our checking account so that he could get the check [to clear]. And he promised us that he would. The next day after work, I got a phone call, and it's the Realtor. He needed to come by and talk with my husband and me, and I told him that I was very sorry but my husband worked late, but I would receive him. So he came by, and he was very apologetic that he had sold us the house that Sunday afternoon. When he did that, he did not realize that someone else had sold it earlier. That's what he shared with me. So he sat there with our check and he began to tear it into small pieces and he laid the pieces on our cocktail table.

I was furious because, you know, why are you tearing up my check? All you need to do is give it back to me and I can put it with the others so when we look at what our expenses were this month, we know that we can take this $500 and do something else with it, you know? I was furious. I said thank you, and he left. But something said to me, "Put this check back together and see what you get." So I get tape and I put it back together. And there I saw, on the back of it, he had run it through the bank early the next morning, and it had in big letters "Insufficient funds." Okay? Now, he obviously didn't wait. He did not do what my husband asked him to do. And that was when we found out that our backs were against a brick wall. The school district knew that when they wrote the integration plan, that they wrote it in such a way that they would have the backing of the Realtors, they would have the backing of the bankers, they would have the backing of the mortgage owners, and they would have the backing of the vast part of the community. So they were in a good place.

After that incident, my husband and I decided that we're just going to stop, delay it for a while until we can come up with something else to do. Because obviously, no one—there were so many experiences that we had that I don't have time to share. Like [sellers] were afraid for the neighbors to know they were showing the houses to a minority family. They would hide in the shrubbery. They would do all kinds of interesting things that you would think would not happen, but they did. Or they would park down the street and walk up there [and watch us], but those things happened. We just decided we would just stop [looking for a new house].

Nineteen sixty-six: I suppose that was the same year that they made [the all-Black] Blackshear—it had been Blackshear Junior-Senior High School—they made it a junior high school only and sent the seniors to Ector [High School]. Okay, that was satisfying the federal government because they were integrating. But what was so interesting is that the Blacks were going to be bussed, but they were going farther away from the Anglo students than they were in the beginning. And the Anglo people who had lived in that area and were sending their children to Ector were moving like you would not believe. Okay? And they were selling their homes to Blacks. Now you tell me, you know, we're intelligent people here, how did they know to do that? Without having been forewarned? Even before the letter came to us that this was going to happen to Blackshear and our children would be going there? So they were getting the Anglo parents ready to get out if you wanted to or stay if you wanted. So, not having talked, again, they began to move and began to sell their homes to Blacks.

In January 1968—January 19, it was a Saturday, it was 1:00 in the afternoon, this was after my husband came home a couple of weeks prior, grinning from ear to ear and asking me if I would like to buy our best friend's home. Now, this was in the newest addition for Anglo families in Odessa, Texas. There was nowhere else. I mean, the homes were beautiful. There was nowhere else for them to move. So they had to stay there. But the owner of the music store said [to my husband], "My wife and I have talked and we would sell our house to you and Elayne." Well, we didn't have any money. [Laughs]

But to show you the way God works when he steps in—now remember, we stepped out because of the torn-up check. But the moment we stepped out, God stepped in. And I am a firm believer of that today. Because it did not matter what kind of money we had. We could pay them any kind of way we wanted to pay them as long as we could pay the monthly mortgage. That's all they were doing, giving that house to us because they can buy them another one tomorrow, simply because of the color of their skin. So we took them up on it, and we just prayed, "Okay, God, this is a blessing from you, and I know this is a blessing from you. Some kind of way you are going to make it work."

So we decided that we would do this, and on that Saturday afternoon, January the 19th at 1:00 in the afternoon, we met in their attorney's office to seal the deal. Now, it was cold, I never will forget, it was wet, but as I write in the book, with the quiet stroke of a pen, Odessa housing was changed forever.[3] ... When word got around, oh, I heard so many things about a house that I didn't know I had bought, because it wasn't anything like people were saying. Once they heard that a Black couple had bought this house, of course, there were people— first they went to the superintendent and they were asking for our jobs, because they knew that if we didn't have jobs, we couldn't afford the payment. Well, the superintendent knew he could not fire us, because we had impeccable reviews of our work. So he had to let them know. And he could not fire us for another reason, because it would have been against federal regulations. So he settled the people down and let them know that he had no reason to fire this family simply because they were looking for a better place to live and they wanted education for their children.

Once we got that done, one afternoon the minister of First Baptist Church here in Odessa and several of his deacons came by to welcome us to the community. And as Dr. Roscoe would say at my husband's eulogy, he said, "You know, we went by to visit with Walter and Elayne, and we just, we're going to spend fifteen minutes so we can welcome them to the community, and we ended up spending over an hour and asking them if they would please consider becoming members of our church because we, too, needed to integrate our congregation."

We had been active in our church, in our community, and it was a very hard thing to do, but Walter had said to me, "You know, Elayne, this is God's work. And if he has used us to this point, if he is asking us to do something else, I think we should follow what is happening here, because not only will we expand the neighborhood, we will expand the city. Because people come to First Baptist Church from every direction, and we will be a part of that congregation." My husband sang in the choir. He was part of a quintet of men, and they made the most beautiful music that anyone—every time they were scheduled to sing, everybody was ready to hear these five men. And they sang their hearts out together for as long as my husband was well enough to do so. So when I say that we made Odessa a different place than it was before—

Now, along the way—when we first tried to move into our house, we were met by two men in a pickup truck. They jumped. They heard that we were at the house. It was late on a Sunday evening, and Walter had said to me, "Now, Elayne, if you hear me yell, you need to come, because I'm being confronted." I was inside, trying to determine where we were going to place the furniture, and I just happened to step out on the patio, and someone had warned all of the men in that area that we were there. And the men had all come down to the house directly behind us, and they were all standing in the backyard looking over [the fence]. It shocked me so, because I just happened to step out onto the patio to see what size the backyard was, because I had no clue.

So the moment I went back inside, I heard my husband, and, oh God, I was—fear came over me like I had never felt before. But we had made plans to take care of ourselves in case of a crisis. And I was the one who had to implement that plan. I thought, "Oh God, please, please, please, you brought me here for a reason." So I walked out through the front, and there stood two men who had jumped out of a pickup truck, left the motor running, the doors hanging open, and there was this long rifle hanging in the back window of the truck. And they had approached my husband and told him all of the things you've probably heard people say: "We don't want you in the neighborhood," "You're not going to enjoy living here," da, da, da, da, da.

My husband was saying, "But this is our home. We are going to live here. And as long as my family is happy, we'll all be happy together." So I walked out, and I heard this conversation, and I stood right by my husband. I stood side by side that evening, and I had my hand in my handbag, and I know the men saw it, and I was praying, "Please, please God, hold my hand," and the men began to back away. Because we were not there for any reason but to improve our lives, get the better quality of education for our children, and to give our oldest son this opportunity, because the best school for that was in that area.[4]

Everything was just falling in line for success for this family. We found a larger home, so my two sons had their own separate rooms, and as soon as we moved in, they put signs up on the door: "Daryl, you don't come in to my room," "Kevin, I dare you," [laughs]—you know, all of the things that children do. They were just so happy to have [their own] rooms, and we were happy for them.

But then the strangest thing would happen. My principal came to my classroom to tell me, "Mrs. Hunt, just because you and your husband have found another, larger home, it does not mean that you can't continue to bring your children to work with you every morning" [at a still all-Black school]." And I said, "Excuse me?" And he repeated it. And I said, "But, you know, we've read the new integration plan. And your words written on this plan say that children who live in the community must go to school within the community in which they live." I said, "As we're members of the faculty of the school district, we certainly do not want to be the first ones to break your rules, so we've already made plans for our kids. They will be going to the school in the community in which we now live." So that forced them to open up the school district to follow the integration plan that had been approved by federal government. Now, we paid for that. We paid big time. They had to integrate.

Political Self-Determination

Arturo Eureste / Redistricting and Voting

Interviewed by Sandra I. Enríquez and Samantha Rodriguez
Houston, Texas, June 8, 2016

https://crbb.tcu.edu/clips/4052/redistricting-and-voting

Eureste: I got really involved in an effort to redistrict. Willie Velasquez and I were very good friends. I was someone, because of my Raza Unida roots, that he would call me a lot and get advice about how to deal with things. When I was eighteen, I got Willie to fund a voter registration drive in Richmond, Texas. I couldn't break into the Ben Reyes and Leonel Castillo Democrat apparatus here, but over there, there was nothing. We met a lady named Dora Olivo and her husband, Victor Olivo, and they formed the LULAC group, and they got funding to do voter registration by Southwest Voter [Registration Education Project]. So I was involved with Southwest Voter a lot, and we got involved while I was at AMA—Mr. Cano let me get involved in the redistricting [effort], and back then there was no computers, so we did redistricting on a little calculator. [Mimics tapping]

I'll never forget it: we were cutting a district where we could win and trying to get a second district, and I found that the demographer for the school district had missed a bunch of census tracts. So, of course, we made the front page, right? I forget the guy's [last] name, but it said, "Joe is chagrined." I had to look up that word, "chagrined." What does that mean? I chagrined the man, whatever that meant. [Laughs] So it was fun, and we got a lot of good redistricting work in.

The next time, in the 1990s, I was very involved in redistricting again. We got ourselves a new city council position, and another school board position, and potential city council positions and state representative positions. We said, "Hey, I think we're going to be going in this direction." But we have grown a lot quicker than we anticipated. We still don't vote.

Enríquez: What were the areas that were targeted in the redistricting?

Eureste: The Latino areas. We were still kind of locked in, landlocked a little bit, but we had kind of taken over the Gulfgate area, and we were moving out further north in the north side to Irvington and Cavalcade and all those areas out there. So there were new precincts now that we could—we had enough population, and we could manipulate the lines.

Enríquez: What was the reaction from the establishment?

Eureste: They hated us. Mexicans with calculators? We had a computer, and we had Willie helping us out, but even Willie didn't have the programs. He sent one person to help us, but, literally, we would be all sitting around a table. [Mimics tapping on a calculator] The school district had a computer, but they were "chagrined."

Enríquez: How did the redistricting benefit the community?

Eureste: It gave us votes. Or threats of votes. In 1990 we created a district where we felt a Latino could win in Congress, but Gene Green just—you know, nobody could take him on.[5] Everybody tried, but he was just a damn good campaigner. And that district is seventy-some percent Hispanic right now, and he sailed away with the nomination from Adrian Garcia here recently. There's just something about that district. There's a way to win it, but you have to really sit down and create an opportunity. But creating opportunity was enough, because then Gene Green has to be responsive to us. So that's good, because it's the guy that's elected there now, and you better pay attention and not make enemies and make friends. So if we don't do that kind of work, then we're going to get parlayed off into little pieces of stuff. And that hasn't happened yet here in Houston. We've kept it from happening. But our Latino population is so expanded all over the place. It's a lot of immigrant communities, so there's more need to be registering the children and the young people again.

Frances Rizo / Recent Dallas Redistricting

Interviewed by Marvin Dulaney, Katherine Bynum, and Moisés Acuña Gurrola
Dallas, Texas, June 10, 2015
https://crbb.tcu.edu/clips/1166/recent-dallas-redistricting

Dulaney: In 1990—as you know, we got to fourteen [city council districts in Dallas]—you were quoted in the paper, talking about how great that was, because there should be possibly two or three Hispanic—

Rizo: [Hispanic-majority] districts were possible.

Dulaney: Well, as you know, three years ago, we went through redistricting again, and I think that I read that you were one of the ones that was pissed off that they were still going to give five seats, or five districts, to African Americans, or was it six districts to African Americans? Compared to the five for Hispanics. I think that was you. No?

Rizo: I don't remember what the numbers were specifically, but the controversy was about the redistricting lines and that Hispanics or Latinos were still being classed as second-class citizens, like we didn't count, and that was the basis for the statement. You know, reporters and editors print things that may or may not be in context—very rarely are they in context—and they usually print them to be controversial or to sell more newspapers and to create divide-and-conquer games, because they're part of the establishment. They are *owned* by the establishment, but redistricting is always an issue.

We're living with it now, and even though we've gone before the court for the last two times we've had redistricting, even though the census numbers *show* that we should have better, more equal representation, you're never going to get the exact numbers in each district, no matter what geography you're talking about. But you can be fair. You know, as long as we have to go to court, they keep getting away with it. Look at the state legislature, look at the congressional districts. Let me give you a parallel and then come back to the city council—in any decade that you want. [Laughs]

[US] Congressional District 33 was created to make it possible for "a Hispanic" to get elected, and now they talk about it being possible for "an African American or Hispanic" to get elected. Bullshit. It was supposed to be [created] to allow Hispanics to elect a Hispanic member of Congress, because of the increase of Hispanic population in the state of Texas, and North Texas deserved one of those, which we got. Well, what happens? You wind up creating a district line, and not only does it go from Dallas County to Tarrant County and all through the suburbs, but you make it so that the Black state rep and the Chicano have to run against each other. It was a divide-and-conquer setup from redistricting, and these things don't happen from one year to the next. These things are planned out, and there's the game plan.

Because when the Republicans write the district lines—and of course, they say when the Democrats are in charge, they do the same thing. Well, I'm sorry, and I'm not saying the Democrats don't. It's just that we have to keep fixing the mess that the Republicans make. All they want is to stay in power. No one gives up power; it has to be taken.

Nothing, no political lines, no configuration of a representative government has been accomplished without having to go to court in Dallas, Texas. We've always had to go to court. You have to get *ordered* to do it, and that's because of the Voting Rights Act, and what are the Republicans doing with the Voting Rights Act?

Dulaney: Trying to destroy it.

Bynum: Piece by piece.

Rizo: Because Latinos are the largest minority group, they don't want Latinos in power. As long as they keep the division between African Americans and Latinos, even though together we're the majority, they're still in control. They make all the institutions, they make all the money, but if they keep playing these games and we keep letting them get away with it, we're never going to get anywhere. If we don't speak up—we have a saying in Spanish, "*El que no habla, Dios no lo oye.*" If you don't speak up, God doesn't hear. Okay? Which means if you want to do something, *you* have to do something. I learned that in the Girl Scouts, and I taught it to all of my Girl Scouts. We have a little song and a little ditty, and a little thing in the Girl Scout law, but basically it comes down to "If it's to be, it's up to me." You don't sit on the sidelines; you organize.

Domingo Garcia forever and ever has said, "Don't get mad, get organized!" It's there. The knowledge is there, and we have to keep fighting. The Republicans aren't going to be able to stay in power for very long. We've got too many numbers and we're getting smarter and we're getting more education. It was really, really hard when I was in my twenties and thirties, trying to get people to register to vote, but now that we've gotten more kids into college and in professional positions and more lawyers and doctors, et cetera et cetera, it's still a hard job, but now we have the numbers to go along with it, and people are understanding. They're not doubting it so much.

David T. Lopez / Houston's Political Climate and KKK Presence

Interviewed by Sandra I. Enríquez and Samantha Rodriguez
Houston, Texas, June 27, 2016
https://crbb.tcu.edu/clips/4676/houston-political-climate-and-kkk-presence

Lopez: When I was on the school board, we had a school board area and offices with the restrooms and all. And we had a break [during a board meeting], and I decided I wanted to go back over there to the public restroom. And as I then turn to go out, there were three pretty beefy guys with vests that said "KKK." This was right through the desegregation stuff, and I mean there was nobody else there. And I guess Providence sometimes helps, because I said, [in a good-ol'-boy voice] "How are you boys doing?" And it was so unexpected that they reared back, and I just walked out *very* quickly, but those were tough times. I mean, those were tough times.

Rodriguez: You don't really hear too much talk about that, how Houston was when you were [on the board], and the climate here—

Lopez: The climate in Houston was pretty rough. When you have guys with KKK regalia on at a school board meeting, that just shows you.

Rodriguez: Wow, this was the early 1970s, and you would have folks coming to the school board meeting like that, openly just—

Lopez: Yes!

Enríquez: Openly?

Lopez: They were there, three of them with their KKK stuff. I guess you've got to realize that although we know some of those people react to violence, that they are primarily bullies, and then that if you don't show the fear or concern, they are not likely to bother you too much.

Rainbow Coalitions

Ben Reyes / Black and Brown Military Experiences

Interviewed by Sandra I. Enríquez and Samantha Rodriguez
Houston, Texas, July 14, 2016
https://crbb.tcu.edu/clips/5697/black-and-brown-military-experiences

Reyes: Where we moved into Denver Harbor, there was a little corner for where the Mexicans were at. And if you crossed Wallisville [Road], it was a little Black neighborhood, and we didn't know it was there until somebody told me they had a great ice cream right on the other side of Wallisville. There was this store back there, best ice cream around, and we didn't even know that a whole community of Black people lived, like, right from here to two or three houses down behind us. We just had to cross the street. A lot of stuff like that.

I guess a lot of that contributed to the whole idea of bringing people together, because we were all suffering the same way. I mean, they had the same problems we had, and when we went to Vietnam, it was—when you get out and do the shittiest work in Vietnam and look around, most of us were minorities. They were either Black or Hispanic. We were in Khe Sanh, one of the worst places marines can be, and I walked around the perimeter of Khe Sanh and I ran into a guy that graduated from my high school. I ran into a guy that was a cousin of mine on the other side. I mean, we were there, but not just there. We were in the front.

And the Mexicans—because we were—here's our size disparity. A lot of us were short guys. They made great tunnel rats, and we were good at that, and those guys that did that stuff were in hell. They were just—you know, they would just crawl down the hole. We always knew that when the guy got down the hole, we going to hear a .45 go—poof!—go off, because they would put a snake down in these holes. And then the guys would go through the tunnels and mark them, and we would we would take the tunnels out. We learned when we came back from Vietnam, there was so much bitterness toward us by the—you know, we were "baby killers" and all that other stuff. And we were Mexicans and Blacks. We said, "Goddamn, what were we going to do? Not go?" No, we were going to do our share, go do our deal.

James Aaron / Activism in Houston

Interviewed by Sandra I. Enríquez and Samantha Rodriguez
Houston, Texas, June 6, 2016
https://crbb.tcu.edu/clips/2502/activism-in-houston

Rodriguez: In the late 1960s, you get involved with the People's Party II. Y'all were dealing with many issues in the community, one of which was police brutality. You were dealing with other issues like housing and whatnot. What programs did *you* engage in? What were you involved in?

Aaron: Well, we initially started selling a newspaper, and we had a free clothing program. That was one of the first programs we started here in Houston in our office. We got some clothes and started giving them away to the community. We had what we called political education classes. We'd have political education classes and invite the whole community to come to them, you know. That was our initial programs. Selling the paper, giving away clothes, and political education classes.

Rodriguez: What papers were you selling?

Aaron: We were selling the *Black Panther* newspaper—no, no, no. When we first started off, before we started selling the *Black Panther* newspapers, we started selling *Space City!* newspapers. Do you know anything about *Space City!* newspapers?

Enríquez: Can you tell us about *Space City!*, please?

Aaron: The *Space City!* paper was started by some whites in the movement. Liberal whites, whatever you want to call them.[6] They called themselves revolutionaries. They used to have an office right out here in Third Ward. We used to relate to them. Communicate with them. We used to work with them on certain things, and they had a newspaper. We had to have some kind of way of getting some money. They allowed us to sell their newspaper, and we'd keep some of the proceeds. We sold *Space City!* newspapers, and then we eventually got hooked up with the *Black Panther* newspaper, and we started selling that paper instead of *Space City!*.

Enríquez: Were you able to write some of the stories in the *Space City!*?

Aaron: Oh, yes, yes. They'd carry articles, speeches of Carl [Hampton]. He would have his speeches in the paper. We worked—we got along very well together. That's one reason we sold the paper, because they would have pictures of Carl in there. Articles, things like that. So we were putting out our word by putting out their newspaper.

Enríquez: Do you know when it was first started, the *Space City!* paper?

Aaron: I don't remember when it was first started, but it was going on before the party, before the People's Party. It was going on before us, but I don't remember when it got started.

Rodriguez: You said it was white activists in the city. What organizations were these white activists involved in?

Aaron: Outside of *Space City!*, they had the John Brown Revolutionary League, and we had a coalition over there. They had MAYO, Mexican American Youth Organization. Those two groups we worked very closely with. We had what we called the Rainbow Coalition, and all of us were involved in the *Space City!* newspaper. We were all very close. Yes.

Eloy Padilla / Boycott at UT Austin

Interviewed by Sandra I. Enríquez and David Robles
Del Rio, Texas, July 19, 2016

https://crbb.tcu.edu/clips/5239/boycott-at-ut-austin

Padilla: This is what occurred. Let me give you a little bit of background on it. Don Weedon was a former Longhorns football player, alumni, and he had several businesses around the UT campus, a Conoco service station and some nightclubs. This young man who was a band student, one of the first Black band students at UT, was employed by Don Weedon at his nightclub, playing [trumpet] in the band.

That evening on TV there was a heavyweight boxing match between Joe Frazier and Jerry Quarry. Jerry Quarry was considered the last Great White Hope of the whites to take back the heavyweight championship after Muhammad Ali had given it up, or they stripped him of the title. So they did a tournament to see who was going to take over Ali's title. So Frazier was taking on Quarry, and Joe Frazier beat the you-know-what out of Jerry Quarry.

Don Weedon got so upset, and the first Black person he saw was one of his employees, the trumpet player. He picked up a barstool to hit him over the head and knocked him out. He had to be taken to the hospital at Brackenridge, and the young man was hidden in the hospital for at least a week before he was identified, because he was like in a semi-coma. And so naturally the Blacks on campus were furious, and they were furious because [Weedon] was never arrested, he was never charged. Because of the outcry that the students at the UT campus made, they finally charged [Weedon] with simple assault. He sent his attorney to the court, paid a $25 fine for simple assault, and that's it.

So people started saying, "No, that's not enough." So they said, "Well, let's boycott his business," and the nearest one was his Conoco service station. And so the Mexican American Student Organization supported them. There was SNCC, the Student Nonviolent Coordinating Committee, SDS, the Students [for a] Democratic Society, and other Black groups. For a few days they were picketing, marching around the station, and this one day that I went, I was in my economics class. In fact, we were going over [the concept of a] boycott as an economic tool to change society, and the professor made a face and said, "Hey, why are we sitting here in a classroom talking about theory when we can see it in action? Let's go." So he took the whole class. *Vamos*, we walked from campus up there, and I was across the street with my class and my friend David Montejano, always getting me in trouble, and Joe Limón—no, I don't remember if Joe Limón was there—and the rest of the MASO group was there.

They said, "Come on over, Eloy." So I walked across, picked up a picket sign, and started marching with the rest of the group. And then the Blacks said, "We're going to sit down in front of the cars and stop traffic and get arrested." They knew they're going to be arrested as soon as they sat down. As long as you were walking, they were not going to arrest you. They would just let you do that. It was packed. Across the street, it was some fraternity guys screaming and yelling insults, and it was big. It was a big deal back then. So then the Blacks sat down, and they arrested them, and then some of the white SDS students sat down, and then some of the girls sat down. And so the Mexicanos said, "We can't be left behind." And there were only about five of us, so we took a seat, and they took us to jail.

So I spent a couple of hours up there at the Travis County Courthouse in the drunk tank. The irony was that when we were going in there—we never were handcuffed—"Just get in the car and let's go"—the police officers that took us were telling us, "You're dumb. You ought to just take Don Weedon out to the alleyway and beat the crap out of him." We were laughing about that, but we were also chastised by some of the Black elderly people inside the jail. Oh, they chewed us out, saying, "What are you boys doing here? Don't do that, stay in school, you have to get your education, that's how you do it." I remember that so clearly. The guys, you know, were alcoholics. They were sleeping off what they had drunk the night before, and they really got after us. But we were saying, "We're going to stand up against racism."

Several of us pled guilty, because they said, "Either you plead guilty and pay a $25 fine or you will be expelled from UT." About four or five volunteered to go ahead and test the case and plead not guilty and take it to trial. The rest of us pled guilty and got out and stayed in school. Sure enough, David Richards, who was an attorney and Ann Richards's husband, and

Sam Houston Clinton, I think he was one of those attorneys, and they got all those charges [dropped].

You know what the charge was? A class C misdemeanor, which is like a speeding ticket. It was [in violation of] a Travis County ordinance: interfering with a man's rights in pursuit of his business. That was what I was charged with. Now, it was supposed to have been [dropped] after two months of going to AA lectures, the charges be taken off your record and all that, but of course it was not done. But it never showed up—class C misdemeanors don't show up on your criminal record anyway. When I went to law school many years later, it popped up in an FBI file. I've never asked for my FBI file, but I'm sure they got my file on it.

Carlos Richardson / River Parade Riot

Interviewed by Steve Arionus and Vinicio Sinta
San Antonio, Texas, June 30, 2016
https://crbb.tcu.edu/clips/5130/carlos-richardson-discusses-river-parade-riot

Arionus: Could you tell us what happened at that River Parade?

Richardson: I will not call any names. We had made a pact with a group of Latinos to have a demonstration at the River Parade. We were going to march down—I think it was Houston Street. No signs or anything. It was going to be impromptu, because we did not like the way that the city allowed you to have a demonstration. They were determined to really make it into something. It was a clandestine operation. It was just going to pop up. Well, they were not able to pull off their part of it. Because, you know, the Latino community was large enough that they did not figure that they had to do anything like that, and they were not going to get all excited about this, especially with a bunch of Black people out there. So when they came up from the river, the police had run them off. There were some—the Latinos had long hair, you could tell that they were ready to go. But they were not able to inspire the people down on the river to come up onto Houston Street.

Well, I had already hyped up all these people, so when they said, "No go," I said, "Well, there is going to be a go," and we went. We started up from—I cannot remember, the bridge from where you can come up from the river. We started from that point, and we started with a chant: "Beep beep! Bang bang! Ungawa! Black Power!" As we went down the street, more and more people joined in until I don't know how many hundreds of people were coming down Houston Street. And at the tail end of the thing, they were breaking windows and stuff. Then when we got to Houston and Alamo, everybody congregated and we started making speeches, and they had busted one of my people there, too. So we had determined that we were going to stay there. Later on, Mario [Salas] and the other fellows came up. They missed all of that part, but Mario made up for it by leaping up on one of the police cars and stomping on the roof.

They finally let my activist go, and we were halfway ready to leave when I noticed that they were starting to create a line on one side of the street. They were one person in front, one person in back. [Motions with hands] First the front, back, front, then they'd close it up. They were starting to build like a dam across the street. I saw what was going on. If they completed it, all the rest of the police are going to be behind them, and they were going to force us out of town, which is what happened. The rest of them, not being in shape, they were sitting on the corner [breathing heavily]. They said, "Get up! We're building a line!" [Laughs] They could not do it. By the time they got up, the line was built, and they started to move. They had sticks four or five feet long. I did not know they had a riot department here then. I found out.

That's when all hell broke loose. The windows started breaking. They started forcing us to the outskirts of downtown San Antonio, right from in front of the Alamo. It was pretty nasty. A lot of people got hurt. A lot of people got injured and stuff. A lot of innocent people got arrested. But there were several instances where we participated with the Latino community whenever we could, where we could be helpful in any way, and they did the same with us.

Robert Medrano / Police Brutality and Triethnic Coalition

Interview by Moisés Acuña Gurrola and Katherine Bynum
Dallas, Texas, June 10, 2015
https://crbb.tcu.edu/clips/254/police-brutality-and-tri-ethnic-coalition

Gurrola: There's still a lot about the Dallas Brown Berets that—even if you look through, like, in history books, I'm kind of confused on time lines, and I am sure other people are too. So there was—on July 20, 1973, there was a riot downtown. Do you remember that?

Medrano: Yes, I was there. The Santos thing? Well, we were already involved and already knew about police brutality, so it's not the first time. And prior to that, the officer that actually murdered Santos Rodríguez, Darrell Cain, he had killed an African American right here in the Black area less than a mile [away]: Michael Morehead, running away from a grocery store. Shot him in the back, similar to—nothing's changed! Look at TV and you see those things. Is this new? You've seen it on TV. This was done back there in the back, and nothing's changed!

So we saw this is what happened to Michael Morehead. Again, you know what the justification was: "He had a weapon, he was going to reach for something, feared for my life, and he ended up having nothing, but I feared for my life because I thought he was going to pull a gun." And you're trained that way. "So my right is to kill you and ask questions later." As long as he says, "I feared for my life, and I thought he was reaching for something"—but this [man] was shot in the back.

Anyway, we knew already about Michael Morehead. So that the Black activists, including Albert Lipscomb, was involved in that issue. So we [the Brown Berets] need to coalesce with the Blacks. And with the Bois d'Arc Patriots, Charlie Young. So Charlie Young says, "Let's all three of us get together, because it's all happening. We're all having the same issues." Poor housing. Dallas Housing Authority doesn't do nothing but collect the federal grants and let the people live there and don't do nothing to do maintenance, to do repairs. They kept the money. At that time we were involved with Dallas Legal Services and the political [people like] Ed Polk and then the War on Poverty. I'm getting together with the Brown Berets. And then finally he says, "Let's make a coalition with the Black Panthers, the Brown Berets, and the Bois d'Arc Patriots." Ledbetter and the Brown Berets said they don't want nothing to do with coalition: "There's no whites living here in West Dallas, there's no Blacks living here, over here in this section, so our issue is concentrate on our geographical area." But how come you don't look at the big picture, at the whole city of Dallas instead of the little one-mile radius you live in?

Trini Gamez/ Getting Involved in Politics and
Race Relations with African Americans

Interviewed by Joel Zapata and Karen Wisely
Hereford, Texas, June 4, 2016
https://crbb.tcu.edu/clips/2313/getting-involved-in-politics-2
https://crbb.tcu.edu/clips/2315/race-relations-with-african-americans

Gamez: I started to get involved in politics because I wanted the people—I didn't know how to make the people understand how important it was to get out and run for office. If you wanted to get something done, I used to tell them, "Look, we need to get together. We need to get more of our people in office. Let's everybody do it! What's wrong with you?!" I remember the men—I would get onto the men especially because the women had more courage, but their husbands didn't. They let them, you know, pull them back.

I organized [for] Mexican American Democrats, the GI Forum, sometimes voter registration—I don't remember how many organizations. And if I couldn't get the men involved, their wives couldn't do anything. So I wanted them to see what I was doing. Finally, at the end, I got a lot of them involved. But the first five men who registered to run for office, I had to shame them. I said, "Look, I'm a woman, and I'm not afraid to go and register," or "I'm going to go to sign up and register to run for judge." "Oh, you're not." "Oh, yes I am. And if I go and register to run for judge tomorrow, I want to see you all as city commissioners, county commissioners." "Oh we will! If you run for judge we will." Well, I did, and they hadn't gone. I said, "What happened? What happened? I thought you were men." [Laughs] "Oh, no, no, we will!" So they did the next day. And to their surprise, they both won. One was city commissioner and the other made it for county commissioner. So that's where they started to begin to believe me and to start campaigning.

And we did have good campaigns at the end, but the people still didn't get out to vote. I think because we didn't have the time. I didn't have the time. I was working, you know, eighteen hours a day. I had all my kids that I had to go feed at night because they were still elementary and junior high. The oldest of the three older boys were in the service. They joined the navy, so I just had the other kids, but I still had to have—besides my kids, I always had a house full of kids. And because I had a lot of kids at home all the time, the welfare, every time there was a child with problems at school, or who'd run away from home, or something, she would call me, "I'm sending you somebody because this child needs help." All the kid needed was attention, because I never had problems with all the kids that came to my house. You go to Hereford, there's grown men, older than these kids that I have here, that still call me "Mom" because they were raised in my home.

Zapata: I was wondering, when you were in Hereford, were there any African Americans in town, and if there were, what were the relations between African Americans and the Mexican Americans?

Gamez: That's another thing. When we came to Hereford, up until 1954, I think, Blacks could not come into town. They could drive by and get gas, but they could not stay. They had to leave. But I remember one doctor brought a couple to work for him, and that was the first Black couple that came to Hereford. And then, later on, all of a sudden, I remember seeing a school for the Blacks across the tracks, by the golf course, all of a sudden. It was a barrack that they put there, but for the Black people. I think there were two families.

Before I started getting really involved into politics, I remember, something happened in Hereford. I can't remember what was happening. I think that the police were coming to the packing sheds and stopping the people for—you know, working people are happy people. They're tired, but they loved to drink and dance and have parties, or eat, you know. So the owners of the packing shed let them have their picnics or something, on Saturday nights, and let them cook and eat there. Well, the police would come in there and arrest them for drunks, because they were drinking. Sometimes I guess they would get a little rough on them or something, because I remember getting involved with the Blacks in NAACP because of Sylvia Hyde. Something happened, someone was killed, and I don't remember that story, how it happened, but I remember she organized the NAACP. I went and I joined because I knew what they were talking about. And we joined them, me and my kids. I took my kids. My kids have been involved in everything I was.

Acknowledgments

All books represent the labor of many; this one reflects the contributions of very many. First and foremost, we thank everyone involved with the CRBB fieldwork, starting with the over 530 interviewees, the graduate student interviewers—Steve Arionus, Eladio Bobadilla, Katherine Bynum, Sandra Enríquez, Danielle Grevious, Moisés Acuña Gurrola, Jasmin Howard, Meredith May, David Robles, Samantha Rodriguez, Vinicio Sinta, James Wall, Karen Wisely, and Joel Zapata—and the community partners throughout the state who made this entire project possible. As the editors and lead authors of this volume, we also thank our CRBB faculty collaborators: José Ángel Gutiérrez supported an early phase of the project, and Marvin Dulaney and Maggie Rivas-Rodriguez saw it through to completion. We could not be prouder to have them as colleagues.

The team worked hard on this project for five years, and we completed the last substantial edits on the manuscript in the summer of 2020 during the Black Lives Matter protests responding to the death of Houston native George Floyd. We are grateful to the organizers in our adopted hometown of Fort Worth who worked hard to expand our collective sense of what is possible and to move our community forward, and we are gratified by the large numbers of white and Brown marchers who are joining the BLM protests. We hope that the "Tu Lucha Es Mi Lucha" signs that have been prevalent at these marches point toward a new era of Black-Brown coalition building.

Along with the contributors to this volume, we thank our community partners, including the Prairie View Special Collections and Archives Department; the Brazos Valley African American Museum; Southwest Texas Junior College, especially Raul Reyes Jr. and Ismael "Gizmo" Martinez; Café Mayapán and the La Fe Clinic of El Paso; the Museum of the Gulf Coast, in Port Arthur; the Orange African American Museum; Lamar University; the Sam Houston Regional Library, in Liberty; the Dallas Mexican American Historical League; the Tarrant County Black Historical and Genealogical Society, in Fort Worth; the East Texas Research Center, in Nacogdoches; the Kurth Memorial Library, in Lufkin; the Montgomery County Memorial Library; the Nacogdoches NAACP; the Lubbock NAACP; and the Diboll History Center.

The contributors offer special thanks to the Richard, Delma, and Feliz Abalos family, Helena Abdullah, Olga Agüero, Fred Aguilar, Narciso Aleman, Lorena

Andrade, Salvador Balcorta, Betell Benham, the late Warzell Booty, Anita Carmona-Harrison, Rosie Castro, Marilyn Clark, John "Bunchy" Crear, Nephtalí De León, Pete Duarte, Johnella Franklin, Homero Galicia, Manuel Díaz Garza, Guillermo Glenn, Vickie Gomez, Sheila Patterson Harris, the late I. D. Henderson Jr., Nick Hernandez, Gilbert Herrera, Jon Holmes, the late A. C. and Dora Jaime, María Jiménez, Matthew Johnson, Alpha Omega Jones, Maria Banos Jordan, Iris Lawrence, Miguel A. Levario, James Leveston, Agustin Loredo, Omowali Luthuli-Allen, Lydia Madrigal, Antonio Marin, Ana Martinez-Catsam, Ernest McMillan, Rogelio Nuñez, Richard Orton, Floyd Price, Dorothy Reece, Wayne Sadberry, Mario Salas, Mary Tolbert, Rafael Torres, Carl and Gloria White, and Rose Wilson.

We also thank the many advisers and mentors of our graduate student team members, all of whom supported our project by allowing us to benefit secondhand from their expertise, sharing their students' summers with us, and providing emotional and intellectual support for our team. These include Curtis Austin, Roberto Calderón, Gregg Cantrell, John R. Chávez, María Cotera, Matthew Countryman, Pero Dagbovie, Arnoldo De León, Sarah Deutsch, Delia Fernandez, Lilia Fernandez, Neil Foley, Cindy Hahamovitch, Hasan Kwame Jeffries, Matthew Lassiter, Yolanda Chávez Leyva, Treva Lindsey, Nancy MacLean, Monica Perales (several times over!), Clark Pomerleau, Raúl Ramos, Rebecca Sharpless, Jeff Shepherd, and Sherry L. Smith.

The CRBB project would not have been possible without the contributions of innumerable colleagues, friends, and supporters. Our many debts begin with June Koelker, the former dean of the Mary Couts Burnett Library at TCU, whom we approached without an appointment to float a harebrained idea about a new digital-humanities website. June's response could not have been more enthusiastic: "What can I do to help?" She quickly committed significant staff time to the CRBB project, and she remained a dedicated cheerleader throughout. She connected us with Jacob Brown, a rare digital library specialist with extraordinary technical expertise and advanced degrees in both library science and the humanities. Max gave Jacob a wish list for a site that he hoped could be built, and Jacob found a way to build it and has remained a close partner ever since. Mary Saffell, a senior archivist at TCU, oversaw quality control for the metadata on our website and coordinated the preservation of our interviews and the scattered archival documents that we collected. Thanks also to Allison Kirchner, who assisted Mary in this massive undertaking, and to social sciences librarian Robyn Reid, for her unending and enthusiastic support. Thanks to Jacob Mangum, Mark Phillips, and the entire staff at the Portal to Texas History, the permanent digital archive of our complete interviews. Thanks also to Andrew Torget, the digital humanities guru in the University of North Texas Department of History, for taking time to help us conceptualize the project in its infancy.

The CRBB project was supported by a competitive three-year Collaborative Research Grant from the National Endowment for the Humanities, along with private support from foundations and in-kind contributions from several universities. At the NEH, we thank Dan Sack, who read our first drafts and provided critical feedback on our first, unsuccessful application, and Lydia Medici, who has been a strong supporter and champion throughout the extended grant period. Thanks also to Peter Scott, who accepted our always-late reports. This book is the product of the NEH's insistence that we not only collect interviews but also interpret them for a wide scholarly and public audience. Thanks for the nudges! We also thank the staff of TCU's Office of Sponsored Research, especially its former director, Linda Freed. Thanks also to Teresa Hendrix, Laurie Heidemann, and Bonnie Melhart. Dennis Alexander, in TCU's Office of University Advancement, also saw the project's promise early on, and he pitched it to the private foundations that provided much-needed matching funds. Thanks very much to the Brown Family Fund of the Brown Foundation, Inc., of Houston, and the Summerlee Foundation of Dallas, both of which took a chance on this project and helped us prove to the NEH that we had a viable plan. Thanks especially to John Crain, the longtime president of Summerlee, who offered friendship and advice and a deep enthusiasm for Texas history—and thanks to Andy Graybill of the Clements Center for Southwest Studies at Southern Methodist University for introducing us.

Also at TCU, Max thanks Dean Andy Schoolmaster of the AddRan College of Liberal Arts for his unwavering support of the project and for some early startup grants from what is now the Center for Urban Studies. Thanks also to Rosangela Boyd of the Office of Community Engagement, which provided another early grant for service learning. Thanks to the chairs of the Department of History, Peter Worthing, Jodi Campbell, and Bill Meier, all of whom provided both in-kind and moral support. Thanks also to dear colleague Becca Sharpless, a leading oral historian, for her friendship and for believing in me always, and to the late great Tom Charlton, the godfather of oral history in Texas. Thanks to Katherine Polenz and her colleagues in TCU's Office of Marketing and Communications, who promoted the project in print and over the airwaves. And thanks especially to Stacey Theisen and Heather Confessore for helping us keep track of our finances and providing endless administrative and logistical help.

A small army of student assistants did the behind-the-scenes work on the CRBB project, including the processing and coding of interview clips for our website. We thank them profusely. Katherine Bynum served as our first graduate assistant and then became more critical to the project with each passing year, eventually serving as the project manager, supervisor of other student workers, coordinator of marketing, booker of logistics, and a million other duties that we are surely forgetting. Moisés Acuña Gurrola began working on the CRBB project as a master's student at UNT, spent two summers doing fieldwork, and has led the way on our digital projects since beginning doctoral work at TCU. Thanks also to Michael Green, Leah LaGrone Ochoa, Caleb Rouse, and Brady Winslow, each of whom spent months transcribing or processing interviews, and to Briana Salas, who is carrying us forward into the future. Thanks also to Sara Birdsong, a semester-long intern from the excellent public-history graduate program at Texas State University.

Numerous undergraduate students worked on the project as well. Most critically, Samantha Koehler processed more interviews than anyone, even after she graduated, and Adam Powell burned and mailed out hundreds of DVDs while working in Special Collections. Thanks also to our many work-study students: Isela Castro, Ernest Dominick, Madeline Dow, Andy Gonzalez, Shakeitha Gray, Destinee Jackson, Tammie Rhinehart, Tashell Simon-Hayward, Tauriah Stubblefield, Tyler Traylor, and Selina Vargas. Max also thanks Caleigh Prewitt Nava, Miles Davison, and all the students in his first TCU seminar on oral history methods, who conducted pilot projects that included some of the first CRBB interviews.

The CRBB project has benefited from dialogue with diverse communities of scholars, including innumerable audiences at the conferences where we presented early versions of this work. Thanks to attendees at the Oral History Association, Organization of American Historians, Labor and Working-Class History Association, Texas Oral History Association, Tarrant County College, the Texas Library Association, and the many local libraries and museums who invited members of the CRBB team to give talks. Thanks especially to Mario T. García and the comrades at the Sal Castro Memorial Conference on the Emerging Historiography of the Chicano Movement, and to David Montejano and Jimmy Patiño, both of whom offered support throughout and provided invaluable last-minute comments on the San Antonio case study. Thanks also to the mix of activists and scholars who attended the Latinos, the Voting Rights Act, and Political Engagement Conference, hosted by the Voces Oral History Project (now Center) at the University of Texas at Austin. *Mil gracias* to Maggie Rivas-Rodriguez for always pushing us with her tireless work and incredible example, and for hosting our midsummer retreat in 2016. Thanks again to Marvin Dulaney for sharing his much-sought-after time and energy with the CRBB project, for treating our grad students to "fancy" dinners in the field, and for writing the excellent foreword to this volume.

We also thank the many scholars who came before us in uncovering the histories of civil rights and liberation in Texas. Thanks especially to Brian Behnken, who donated his interviews and shared other sources and offered unflinching support for the project, and to the authors of the many excellent local studies on which our researchers depended as we entered the field each summer. Thanks in particular to John David Márquez, Arnoldo De León, and Guadalupe San Miguel Jr.

At UT Press, we thank Robert Devens for acquiring this book and for his years of checking in, nudging us along, and helping us figure out how to assemble such a sprawling manuscript. Thanks also to Sarah McGavick, who has helped throughout, and to Dawn Durante, our editor for the final phases. Thanks also to our two blind peer reviewers, both of whom provided great feedback and have since shared their identities: John Morán González and Merline Pitre. Thanks also to Erin Greb, who created our map, and to Pamela Gray, who assembled the index.

Max Krochmal wishes to acknowledge a long list of personal debts. These include mentors and friends at Duke's Center for Documentary Studies, including Bill Chafe, Bob Korstad, Wesley Hogan, and (by courtesy) the late Larry Goodwyn; Jacqueline Dowd Hall and all the folks at the Southern Oral History Program at the University of North Carolina; Paul Ortiz of the Samuel Proctor Oral History Program at the University of Florida; and Jim Gregory of the Seattle Civil Rights and Labor History Project.

I also thank the many educators and public history advocates who have welcomed me to Fort Worth with open arms. Collaborators in Leadership ISD and the Fort Worth ISD put me to work and asked me to give countless talks to teachers and education advocates that ended up undergirding the introduction to this book. Thanks especially to Erika Beltrán, Cinto Ramos, Q Phillips, Sherry Breed, and Shawn Lassiter for the endless workshop. Thanks also to Veronica Villegas with the City of Fort

Worth, along with our many partners on the Latino Americans project and the hard-working archivists at the Fort Worth Library. I appreciate and thank my collaborators in the Tarrant County Black Historical and Genealogical Society, Historians of Latino Americans (HOLA) Tarrant County, and Jodi Valenciano Perry and others in the Hispanic Heritage History Project.

Thanks also to all of my friends, colleagues, and students who helped found the Department of Comparative Race and Ethnic Studies (CRES) at TCU, and to colleagues in the Department of History who helped me sustain my work across campus. And a special shout-out to Cecilia Sánchez Hill, who has joined me in many of these endeavors and constantly reminds me why we do this work.

Many of the insights in this book stem from my engagement with present-day grassroots justice struggles, and with the many incredible activists who have taught me what matters and how to apply my scholarship in the present moment. It has been my honor to have been a part of United Fort Worth since its inception, in 2017. Thanks especially to Daniel García Rodríguez, Jessica Ramírez, Pamela Young, Norma García-López, Mindia Whittier, and the rest of the UFW Steering Squad. Thanks also to the many amazing organizers in Community Frontline, ICE Out of Tarrant, and others who are in the trenches every day.

Thanks, of course, to my family—Elijah, Rayna, and their many aunties and uncles and grandparents, and especially Courtney—and to my close friends and coparents in Fairmount and beyond. And thanks to Todd Moye for nudging the project and book along at every phase, for his inexhaustible patience with my many distractions and crises unrelated to our work, and for showing me what it looks like to be incredibly good at what you do while remaining humble, generous, and extraordinarily compassionate.

In addition to those named above, Todd Moye thanks Max for coming up with the idea for the CRBB project in the first place, for providing great leadership and friendship throughout the process, and for modeling a rock-solid commitment to justice at the center of his scholarship and his civic life. Thanks also to codirectors José Ángel Gutiérrez, Marvin Dulaney, and Maggie Rivas-Rodriguez for teaching me a great deal. Marvin hired me for my first job out of grad school, making my career possible. The CRBB project is the second commitment that Dr. Maggie has agreed to after I promised it wouldn't take up too much of her time but instead ate up years of her life. I wonder what she will fall for next? The University of North Texas Department of History and the College of Liberal Arts and Social Sciences provided research time and support without which I could not have done my share to complete this book. Thank you especially to department chairs Harold Tanner and Jennifer Jensen Wallach, Executive Dean Tamara Brown, Andrew Torget, and our colleagues in the UNT Libraries, especially in the Special Collections and Digital Libraries sections.

One of my great professional joys has been watching students with whom I have worked blossom into top-notch original scholars. I have been extremely lucky to have several former students develop into peers on this project. Katherine, Mo, James, and Karen, thanks for that. Chelsea Stallings and Briana Salas, who provided invaluable research assistance on the book, are on a similar path. Current graduate assistant extraordinaire Joshua Lopez saved my bacon with last-minute transcribing. Over the years, dozens of undergraduate students in my "Civil Rights and Black Power Movements", "Civil Rights Movements in Texas," and "African Americans in North Texas" courses; graduate students in my oral history theory and methods course at UNT; "students" in the Voces Summer Oral History Research Institute; and audience members at conferences who asked piercing questions and offered constructive feedback on aspects of the CRBB project, which helped improve it. Thank you! A special shout-out to my colleague at Collin College, Betsy Brody, who attended the 2019 Voces Institute, heard about the CRBB project, worked it into her award-winning teaching, and then shared those methods with me so that I could incorporate them into my own teaching. The circle of life, or at least academia at its most collegial.

I am thankful that my dissertation advisor, David Montejano, long ago sparked an interest in Texas civil rights history. Colleagues at UNT, in the Oral History Association, in my circle of civil rights historians, and elsewhere are too numerous to mention by name, but I hope they will recognize their own influences in much of what I have written here. I appreciate all y'all; *gracias a todos*. Thanks first, last, and always to Rachel, Luke, and Henry, and to my wider Moye, Davis, and Feit families.

I am donating proceeds from the book to the Texas Civil Rights Project, which fights for the civil and voting rights of Texas citizens, for immigrants and refugees, for criminal justice reform, and for racial and economic justice. Please learn more about the important work they do and lend whatever support you can at https://txcivilrights.org.

Notes

Foreword

1. United States Commission on Civil Rights, Texas Advisory Committee, *Civil Rights in Texas: Report of Texas Advisory Committee to U.S. Commission on Civil Rights* (Washington, DC: Government Printing Office, 1970); Tom Johnson, "Lingering School Segregation in Texas Condemned in Civil Rights Report," *Dallas Morning News*, March 10, 1970, 1.

2. For some of the early scholarship on the civil rights movement in Texas, see Conrey Bryson, *Dr. Lawrence A. Nixon and the White Primary*, Southwestern Studies Monograph 42, (El Paso: Texas Western Press, 1974); Darlene Clark Hine, "The Elusive Ballot: The Black Struggle against the Texas Democratic White Primary, 1932–1945," *Southwestern Historical Quarterly* 81 (April 1978): 371–392; Darlene Clark Hine, *Black Victory: The Rise and Fall of the White Primary* (Columbia: University of Missouri Press, 1979); Michael Gillette, "The Rise of the NAACP in Texas," *Southwestern Historical Quarterly* 81 (April 1978): 393–416; Alwyn Barr, *Black Texans: A History of Negroes in Texas, 1528–1971* (Austin: Jenkins, 1973), chs. 6 and 7. For one of the first profiles of Heman Marion Sweatt, the plaintiff in the US Supreme Court case that desegregated the University of Texas Law School, see Michael L. Gillette, "Heman Marion Sweatt: Civil Rights Plaintiff," in *Black Leaders: Texans for Their Times*, ed. Alwyn Barr and Robert A. Calvert (Austin: Texas State Historical Association, 1981), 157–190. For Texas as part of the "Rim South," see Chandler Davison, "Negro Politics and the Rise of the Civil Rights Movement in Houston, Texas" (Ph.D. diss., Princeton University, 1969), and Davison, *Biracial Politics: Conflict and Coalition in the Metropolitan South* (Baton Rouge: Louisiana State University Press, 1972).

3. W. Marvin Dulaney, "Whatever Happened to the Civil Rights Movement in Dallas, Texas?," *Essays on the American Civil Rights Movement*, ed. W. Marvin Dulaney and Kathleen Underwood (College Station: Texas A&M University Press, 1993), 66–98; Jim Schutze, *The Accommodation: The Politics of Race in an American City* (Secaucus, NJ: Citadel, 1986).

4. See Martin Kuhlman, "Direct Action at the University of Texas during the Civil Rights Movement, 1960–1965," *Southwestern Historical Quarterly* 98 (1995): 550–566; Merline Pitre, "Black Houstonians and the 'Separate But Equal Doctrine': Carter W. Wesley versus Lulu B. White," *Houston Review* 12 (1990): 23–36; Neil G. Sapper, "The Fall of the NAACP in Texas," *Houston Review* 7 (Summer 1985): 53–68; Richard B. McCaslin, "Steadfast in His Intent: John W. Hargis and the Integration of the University of Texas at Austin," *Southwestern Historical Quarterly* 95 (July 1991): 25–36; Ronald E. Marcello, "The Integration of Intercollegiate Athletics in Texas: North Texas State College as a Test Case," *Journal of Sport History* 14 (Winter 1987): 286–316. See also the six essays collected under the title "Segregation, Violence, and Civil Rights: Race Relations in Twentieth Century Houston," in *Black Dixie: Afro-Texas History and Culture in Houston*, ed. Cary D. Wintz and Howard Beeth, (College Station: Texas A&M University Press, 1992), 157–277.

5. Perhaps the best attempt to examine the movement in the state is Brian D. Behnken, *Fight-*

ing Their Own Battles: Mexican Americans, African Americans, and the Struggle for Civil Rights in Texas (Chapel Hill: University of North Carolina Press, 2011).

Introduction: Lone Star Civil Rights: Histories, Memories, and Legacies

1. See the chapter by Jasmin C. Howard in this volume. A note on terminology: throughout this book, we use "Black" and "African American" interchangeably to indicate all Black people of the African diaspora living in the United States. Of course, "Black" and "Blackness" could also include others from the African continent and elsewhere in the diaspora, but few such people appear in this story. Any Black or African immigrants that do appear in the text will be noted as such. We use lowercase "black" only when it appears in that form in quotations from written primary sources.

2. See the chapter by Joel Zapata in this volume. A note on terminology: throughout this book, "Mexicanos," "Mexicanas," and their combined constructions (Mexicano/a and Mexicanos/as) are used to describe all Mexican-origin people, regardless of national origin, citizenship, or current residency. "Mexican nationals" indicates those with clear citizenship in Mexico; "Mexican Americans" is used as an umbrella term to describe people of Mexican origin with US citizenship or long-standing residency and activism in *el norte*. "Chicano/a" is used to describe those Mexican Americans that self-identified as such or otherwise made clear that they subscribed to the political and ideological worldview of *Chicanismo*—this includes most of the Mexican-origin activists whom we interviewed, so it will be paired with "Black" or "African American" in most generalizations about the project. The more inclusive neologism "Chicanx" is used to describe the group in its most expansive form, with the term including Mexican Americans, Chicanos (men), Chicanas (women), and nonbinary gendered people of Mexican descent. "Hispanic" and "Latino/a/x" are used only in quotations and in references to pan-ethnic communities comprised partly of migrants from Latin American countries other than Mexico. Last, we capitalize "Brown" in all cases, both for literary symmetry when paired with "Black" in various phrases and also to acknowledge the construction of Chicanx/Latinx peoples in the US as non-Black people of color. (Lowercase "brown" is retained when it appears that way in quotations from written sources.) We do not capitalize "white" in any usage.

3. For more on the project's methodology, see my chapter in Part IV.

4. On Texas as a failed slaveholders' republic, see Andrew J. Torget, *Seeds of Empire: Cotton, Slavery, and the Transformation of the Texas Borderlands, 1800–1850* (Chapel Hill: University of North Carolina Press, 2015). Other sources consulted include Randolph B. Campbell, *An Empire for Slavery: The Peculiar Institution in Texas, 1821–1865* (Baton Rouge: Louisiana State University Press, 1989); Randolph B. Campbell, *Grass-Roots Reconstruction in Texas, 1865–1880* (Baton Rouge: Louisiana State University Press, 1997); Carl H. Moneyhon, *Texas after the Civil War: The Struggle of Reconstruction* (College Station: Texas A&M University Press, 2004); Lawrence Goodwyn, *The Populist Moment: A Short History of the Agrarian Revolt in America* (New York: Oxford University Press, 1978); David Montejano, *Anglos and Mexicans in the Making of Texas, 1836–1986* (Austin: University of Texas Press, 1987). On Texas's early Indigenous history and the conquest, see, for example, Juliana Barr, *Peace Came in the Form of a Woman: Indians and Spaniards in the Texas Borderlands* (Chapel Hill: University of North Carolina Press, 2007); Pekka Hamalainen, *The Comanche Empire* (New Haven, CT: Yale University Press, 2008); Brian DeLay, *War of a Thousand Deserts: Indian Raids and the US-Mexican War* (New Haven, CT: Yale University Press, 2008); F. Todd Smith, *From Dominance to Disappearance: The Indians of Texas and the Near Southwest, 1786–1859* (Lincoln: University of Nebraska Press, 2005); Gary Clayton Anderson, *The Conquest of Texas: Ethnic Cleansing in the Promised Land, 1820–1875* (Norman: University of Oklahoma Press, 2005).

5. On the Terrell Laws in context, see O. Douglas Weeks, "Election Laws," *Handbook of Texas Online*, June 12, 2010, tshaonline.org/handbook/online/articles/wde01. On the making of Jim Crow generally, see Grace Elizabeth Hale, *Making Whiteness: The Culture of Segregation in the South, 1890–1940* (New York: Pantheon, 1998). On Mexican Americans and boss voting, see

Evan Anders, *Boss Rule in South Texas: The Progressive Era* (Austin: University of Texas Press, 1982); Anthony R. Carrozza, *Dukes of Duval County: The Parr Family and Texas Politics* (Norman: University of Oklahoma Press, 2017).

6. This synthesis is my own, especially the argument that Juan Crow constituted a de jure racial caste system. For more on Juan Crow and its ties to the state, see Montejano, *Anglos and Mexicans in the Making of Texas*; David Montejano, *Quixote's Soldiers: A Local History of the Chicano Movement, 1966–1981* (Austin: University of Texas Press, 2010); Cristina Salinas, *Managed Migrations: Growers, Farmworkers, and Border Enforcement in the Twentieth Century* (Austin: University of Texas Press, 2018); Emilio Zamora, *Claiming Rights and Righting Wrongs in Texas: Mexican Workers and Job Politics during World War II* (College Station: Texas A&M University Press, 2009). An image of one such sign from El Paso circulates widely on the internet and has been listed on numerous auction websites. A Reddit forum warns that buyers should be careful, since there are many fake replicas available. See, for example, "CAST IRON NO DOGS, NEGROS, OR MEXICANS TEXAS SIGN," iCollector.com Online Auctions, accessed October 14, 2019, icollector.com/CAST -IRON-NO-DOGS-NEGROS-OR-MEXICANS-TEXAS-SIGN_i13937629.

7. William D. Carrigan and Clive Webb, *Forgotten Dead: Mob Violence against Mexicans in the United States, 1848–1928* (New York: Oxford University Press, 2013); Nicholas Villanueva Jr., *The Lynching of Mexicans in the Texas Borderlands* (Albuquerque: University of New Mexico Press, 2017). The scholarly literature on the lynch culture targeting African Americans is vast. See, for example, Crystal N. Feimster, *Southern Horrors: Women and the Politics of Rape and Lynching* (Cambridge, MA: Harvard University Press, 2009); Amy Louise Wood, *Lynching and Spectacle: Witnessing Racial Violence in America, 1890–1940* (Chapel Hill: University of North Carolina Press, 2009).

8. This draws on the award-winning collaborative project Refusing to Forget, refusing-toforget.org. See also Monica Muñoz Martinez, *The Injustice Never Leaves You: Anti-Mexican Violence in Texas* (Cambridge, MA: Harvard University Press, 2018); John Morán González, "Refusing to Forget Any of Texas' History," *Austin American-Statesman*, September 4, 2016, statesman.com/news/20160904/gonzlez-refusing-to-forget-any-of-texas -history; John Morán González, "Personal Reflections on *Life and Death on the Border 1910–1920*," Bullock Texas State History Museum: The Texas Story Project, January 29, 2016, thestoryoftexas .com/discover/texas-story-project/life-death-border-john-moran-gonzalez; Benjamin Heber Johnson, *Revolution in Texas: How a Forgotten Rebellion and Its Bloody Suppression Turned Mexicans into Americans*, Yale Western Americana (New Haven, CT: Yale University Press, 2003).

9. This argument draws on David R. Roediger's classic account, *The Wages of Whiteness: Race and the Making of the American Working Class* (New York: Verso, 1991). The southern context draws on the following scholarship: Glenda Elizabeth Gilmore, *Gender and Jim Crow: Women and the Politics of White Supremacy in North Carolina, 1896–1920* (Chapel Hill: University of North Carolina Press, 1996); David S. Cecelski and Timothy B. Tyson, eds., *Democracy Betrayed: The Wilmington Race Riot of 1898 and Its Legacy* (Chapel Hill: University of North Carolina Press, 1998); Jane Elizabeth Dailey, Glenda Elizabeth Gilmore, and Bryant Simon, eds., *Jumpin' Jim Crow: Southern Politics from Civil War to Civil Rights* (Princeton, NJ: Princeton University Press, 2000); Stephen Kantrowitz, *Ben Tillman and the Reconstruction of White Supremacy* (Chapel Hill: University of North Carolina Press, 2000). On Texas, see William D. Carrigan, *The Making of a Lynching Culture: Violence and Vigilantism in Central Texas, 1836–1916* (Urbana: University of Illinois Press, 2004); Cynthia Skove Nevels, *Lynching to Belong: Claiming Whiteness through Racial Violence* (College Station: Texas A&M University Press, 2007). I borrow the memorable title phrase from Alexander Saxton, *The Indispensable Enemy: Labor and the Anti-Chinese Movement in California* (Berkeley: University of California Press, 1971).

10. On modernization and urbanization (and their critics), see Walter L. Buenger, *The Path to a Modern South: Northeast Texas between Reconstruction and the Great Depression* (Austin: University of Texas Press, 2001); Kyle G. Wilkison, *Yeomen, Sharecroppers, and Socialists: Plain Folk Protest in Texas, 1870–1914* (College Station: Texas A&M University Press, 2008); Rebecca Sharpless, *Fertile Ground, Narrow Choices: Women on Texas Cotton Farms, 1900–1940* (Chapel Hill: University of North Carolina Press, 1999). For the Black experience of urbanization and

early Jim Crow, see Bernadette Pruitt, *The Other Great Migration: The Movement of Rural African Americans to Houston, Texas, 1900–1941* (College Station: Texas A&M University Press, 2013); Merline Pitre, *In Struggle against Jim Crow: Lulu B. White and the NAACP, 1900–1957* (College Station: Texas A&M University Press, 1999). On Mexicanos, see Arnoldo De León, *They Called Them Greasers: Anglo Attitudes toward Mexicans in Texas, 1821–1900* (Austin: University of Texas Press, 1983); Cynthia Orozco, *No Mexicans, Women, or Dogs Allowed: The Rise of the Mexican American Civil Rights Movement* (Austin: University of Texas Press, 2009); Gabriela González, *Redeeming La Raza: Transborder Modernity, Race, Respectability, and Rights* (New York: Oxford University Press, 2018).

11. Steven Fenberg, *Unprecedented Power: Jesse Jones, Capitalism, and the Common Good* (College Station: Texas A&M University Press, 2011); Joseph A. Abel, "Sunbelt Civil Rights: Race, Labor, and Politics in the Fort Worth Aircraft Industry, 1940–1980" (PhD diss., Rice University, 2011), 14, 42–43; Joseph Abel, "African Americans, Labor Unions, and the Struggle for Fair Employment in the Aircraft Manufacturing Industry of Texas, 1941–1945," *Journal of Southern History* 77, no. 3 (August 2011): 595–638. Abel estimates that there were "upwards of 60,000 men and women employed" in the "contract-dependent" aircraft industry in Fort Worth at the peak of World War II (30,500 at General Dynamics alone), plus 39,000 additional workers at North American Aviation in Grand Prairie, the largest but not sole defense employer in Dallas County.

12. See, among others, Ira Katznelson, *When Affirmative Action Was White: An Untold History of Racial Inequality in Twentieth-Century America* (New York: Norton, 2005); Thomas J. Sugrue, *The Origins of the Urban Crisis: Race and Inequality in Postwar Detroit* (Princeton, NJ: Princeton University Press, 1996); Bruce J. Schulman, *From Cotton Belt to Sunbelt: Federal Policy, Economic Development, and the Transformation of the South, 1938–1980* (Durham, NC: Duke University Press, 1994); Nancy MacLean, *Freedom Is Not Enough: The Opening of the American Workplace* (New York: Sage, 2006); Nelson Lichtenstein, *State of the Union: A Century of American Labor* (Princeton, NJ: Princeton University Press, 2002). For examples of employment discrimination in Texas, see Ernest Obadele-Starks, *Black Unionism in the Industrial South* (College Station: Texas A&M University Press, 2000); Zamora, *Claiming Rights and Righting Wrongs*.

13. For a beautifully succinct version of this history, see Ta-Nehisi Coates, "The Case for Reparations," *Atlantic*, June 2014, theatlantic.com/magazine/archive/2014/06/the-case-for-reparations/361631. For scholarly histories, see Sugrue, *Origins of the Urban Crisis*; Katznelson, *When Affirmative Action Was White*; Richard Rothstein, *The Color of Law: A Forgotten History of How Our Government Segregated America* (New York: Liveright, 2017); Keeanga-Yamahtta Taylor, *Race for Profit: How Banks and the Real Estate Industry Undermined Black Homeownership* (Chapel Hill: University of North Carolina Press, 2019); David M. P. Freund, *Colored Property: State Policy and White Racial Politics in Suburban America* (Chicago: University of Chicago Press, 2007); Jeffrey D. Gonda, *Unjust Deeds: The Restrictive Covenant Cases and the Making of the Civil Rights Movement* (Chapel Hill: University of North Carolina Press, 2015).

14. Jacquelyn Dowd Hall, "The Long Civil Rights Movement and the Political Uses of the Past," *Journal of American History* 91, no. 4 (March 2005): 1233–1263; Mark Brilliant, *The Color of America Has Changed: How Racial Diversity Shaped Civil Rights Reform in California, 1941–1978* (New York: Oxford University Press, 2010); Yohuru Williams, *Rethinking the Black Freedom Movement* (New York: Routledge, 2016); Marc Simon Rodriguez, *Rethinking the Chicano Movement* (New York: Routledge, 2015).

15. Will Guzman, *Civil Rights in the Texas Borderlands: Dr. Lawrence A. Nixon and Black Activism* (Urbana: University of Illinois Press, 2015); Michael Lowery Gillette, "The NAACP in Texas, 1937–1957" (PhD diss., University of Texas at Austin, 1984).

16. W. Marvin Dulaney, "Democratic Progressive Voters League," *Handbook of Texas Online*, June 12, 2010, tshaonline.org/handbook/online/articles/wed01; W. Marvin Dulaney, "A Research Challenge: The African American Experience in Dallas, Texas," *Legacies* 16, no. 1 (Spring 2004): 52–58; Dulaney, "Whatever Happened to the Civil Rights Movement in Dallas, Texas?," in *Essays on the American Civil Rights Movement*, ed. W. Marvin Dulaney and Kathleen Underwood (College Station: Texas A&M University Press, 1993), 66–95.

17. Max Krochmal, *Blue Texas: The Making of a Multiracial Democratic Coalition in the Civil*

Rights Era (Chapel Hill: University of North Carolina Press, 2016); Pitre, *In Struggle against Jim Crow*; Obadele-Starks, *Black Unionism in the Industrial South*; Darlene Hine, *Black Victory: The Rise and Fall of the White Primary in Texas* (Millwood, NY: KTO Press, 1979). The concept and periodization here depends on Robert Rodgers Korstad, *Civil Rights Unionism: Tobacco Workers and the Struggle for Democracy in the Mid-Twentieth-Century South* (Chapel Hill: University of North Carolina Press, 2003); Hall, "Long Civil Rights Movement."

18. Krochmal, *Blue Texas*; Gary M. Lavergne, *Before Brown: Heman Marion Sweatt, Thurgood Marshall, and the Long Road to Justice* (Austin: University of Texas Press, 2010); Amilcar Shabazz, *Advancing Democracy: African Americans and the Struggle for Access and Equity in Higher Education in Texas* (Chapel Hill: University of North Carolina Press, 2004).

19. On *Brown*, see Richard Kluger, *Simple Justice: The History of "Brown v. Board of Education" and Black America's Struggle for Equality* (New York: Vintage, 2004); James T. Patterson, *Brown v. Board of Education: A Civil Rights Milestone and Its Troubled Legacy* (New York: Oxford University Press, 2001). The best history of the critical years of the mid-1950s, when delay emboldened massive resistance, can be found in William Henry Chafe, *Civilities and Civil Rights: Greensboro, North Carolina, and the Black Struggle for Freedom* (New York: Oxford University Press, 1980). Also see George Lewis, *Massive Resistance: The White Response to the Civil Rights Movement* (London: Bloomsbury Academic, 2006); Clive Webb, ed., *Massive Resistance: Southern Opposition to the Second Reconstruction* (New York: Oxford University Press, 2005).

20. See Todd Moye's chapter on Tarrant County in this volume. See also Todd Moye and Andrew Torget, "The Crisis at Mansfield," accessed October 15, 2019, mansfieldcrisis.omeka .net; Robyn Duff Ladino, *Desegregating Texas Schools: Eisenhower, Shivers, and the Crisis at Mansfield High* (Austin: University of Texas Press, 1996).

21. On Little Rock, see Karen Anderson, *Little Rock: Race and Resistance at Central High School* (Princeton, NJ: Princeton University Press, 2010), chap. 4; Sondra Gordy, *Finding the Lost Year: What Happened When Little Rock Closed Its Public Schools?* (Fayetteville: University of Arkansas Press, 2008). On pairing and other devious methods of delay, see Chafe, *Civilities and Civil Rights*. On Christian academies and privatization in another context, see Emilye Crosby, "White Privilege, Black Burden: Lost Opportunities and Deceptive Narratives in School Desegregation in Claiborne County, Mississippi," *Oral History Review* 39, no. 2 (Summer/Fall 2012): 258–285, doi.org/10.1093/ohr/ohs088. The longest-lasting example of closing schools in order to resist integration can be found in Jill Ogline Titus, *Brown's Battleground: Students, Segregationists, and the Struggle for Justice in Prince Edward County, Virginia* (Chapel Hill: University of North Carolina Press, 2011).

22. See, for example, Timothy Paul Bowman, *Blood Oranges: Colonialism and Agriculture in the South Texas Borderlands* (College Station: Texas A&M University Press, 2016); Gilbert G. Gonzalez, *Chicano Education in the Era of Segregation* (1990; reprint, Denton: University of North Texas Press, 2013); David G. García, *Strategies of Segregation: Race, Residence, and the Struggle for Educational Equality* (Oakland: University of California Press, 2018); Montejano, *Quixote's Soldiers*; Arnoldo De León, *Ethnicity in the Sunbelt: Mexican Americans in Houston* (College Station: Texas A&M University Press, 2001); Sol Villasana, *Dallas's Little Mexico* (Charleston, SC: Arcadia, 2011).

23. Philippa Strum, *"Mendez v. Westminster": School Desegregation and Mexican-American Rights* (Lawrence: University Press of Kansas, 2010); V. Carl Allsup, "Delgado v. Bastrop ISD," *Handbook of Texas Online*, June 12, 2010, tshaonline.org/handbook/online/articles /jrd01; Benjamin Márquez, *LULAC: The Evolution of a Mexican American Political Organization* (Austin: University of Texas Press, 1993); Henry Ramos, *The American GI Forum: In Pursuit of the Dream, 1948–1983* (Houston: Arte Público, 1998).

24. See Michael A. Olivas, ed., *Colored Men And Hombres Aquí: Hernandez V. Texas and the Emergence of Mexican American Lawyering* (Houston: Arte Público, 2006); Carlos Sandoval, *A Class Apart*, American Experience (PBS, 2009); Thomas A. Guglielmo, "Fighting for Caucasian Rights: Mexicans, Mexican Americans, and the Transnational Struggle for Civil Rights in World War II Texas," *Journal of American History* 92, no. 4 (March 2006): 1212–1237; Neil Foley, "Straddling the Color Line: The Legal Construction of Hispanic Identity in Texas," in *Not Just*

Black and White: Historical and Contemporary Perspectives on Immigration, Race, and Ethnicity in the United States, ed. Nancy Foner and George M. Fredrickson (New York: Sage, 2004); Neil Foley, Quest for Equality: The Failed Promise of Black-Brown Solidarity (Cambridge, MA: Harvard University Press, 2010); Carlos K. Blanton, "The Citizenship Sacrifice: Mexican Americans, the Saunders-Leonard Report, and the Politics of Immigration, 1951–1952," Western Historical Quarterly 40, no. 3 (Autumn 2009): 299–320; Carlos K. Blanton, "George I. Sánchez, Ideology, and Whiteness in the Making of the Mexican American Civil Rights Movement, 1930–1960," Journal of Southern History 72, no. 3 (August 2006): 569–604; Mario T. García, Mexican Americans: Leadership, Ideology, and Identity, 1930–1960 (New Haven, CT: Yale University Press, 1989).

25. Guadalupe San Miguel, Brown, Not White: School Integration and the Chicano Movement in Houston (College Station: Texas A&M University Press, 2001); Brittany R. White, "Jose Cisneros v. Corpus Christi Independent School District: Mexican Americans, African Americans, and the Failed Promise of the Desegregation of Schools" (MA thesis, Texas Christian University, 2017).

26. Matthew F. Delmont, Why Busing Failed: Race, Media, and the National Resistance to School Desegregation (Oakland: University of California Press, 2016); Ansley T. Erickson, Making the Unequal Metropolis: School Desegregation and Its Limits (Chicago: University of Chicago Press, 2016); Chafe, Civilities and Civil Rights; Joyce A. Baugh, The Detroit School Busing Case: Milliken v. Bradley and the Controversy over Desegregation (Lawrence: University Press of Kansas, 2011); Rothstein, Color of Law; Cynthia E. Orozco, "Rodriguez v. San Antonio ISD," Handbook of Texas Online, June 15, 2010, tshaonline.org/handbook/online/articles/jrrht; Teresa Palomo Acosta, "Edgewood ISD v. Kirby," Handbook of Texas Online, June 12, 2010, tshaonline.org/handbook/online/articles/jre02.

27. Krochmal, Blue Texas; Thomas R. Cole, No Color Is My Kind: The Life of Eldrewey Stearns and the Integration of Houston (Austin: University of Texas Press, 1997); Chafe, Civilities and Civil Rights.

28. Krochmal, Blue Texas.

29. For introductions to both movements, see Williams, Rethinking the Black Freedom Movement; Rodriguez, Rethinking the Chicano Movement. Also see Peniel E. Joseph, ed., The Black Power Movement: Rethinking the Civil Rights–Black Power Era (New York: Routledge, 2006); Carlos Muñoz, Youth, Identity, Power: The Chicano Movement (London: Verso, 1989); Ignacio M. García, Chicanismo: The Forging of a Militant Ethos among Mexican Americans (Tucson: University of Arizona Press, 1997); George Mariscal, Brown-Eyed Children of the Sun: Lessons from the Chicano Movement, 1965–1975 (Albuquerque: University of New Mexico Press, 2005).

30. Albert Peña Jr., "Needed: A Marshall Plan for Mexican-Americans," Texas Observer, April 15, 1966, 1; National Advisory Commission on Civil Disorders, The Kerner Report, ed. Julian Zelizer (Princeton, NJ: Princeton University Press, 2016). Many others have made the argument about the movement hitting a wall as it began pushing for power and resources in the mid-1960s. See, for example, Stephen Tuck, We Ain't What We Ought to Be: The Black Freedom Struggle from Emancipation to Obama (Cambridge, MA: Belknap, 2011); Thomas J. Sugrue, Sweet Land of Liberty: The Forgotten Struggle for Civil Rights in the North (New York: Random House, 2008); Kevin Michael Kruse, White Flight: Atlanta and the Making of Modern Conservatism (Princeton, NJ: Princeton University Press, 2005).

31. See the case studies by Katherine Bynum and by me in this collection. On Houston, see Alex LaRotta, "The TSU Riot, 50 Years Later," Houston Chronicle, May 16, 2017, houstonchronicle.com/local/gray-matters/article/The-TSU-Riot-50-years-later-11149852.php; Brian D. Behnken, Fighting Their Own Battles: Mexican Americans, African Americans, and the Struggle for Civil Rights in Texas (Chapel Hill: University of North Carolina Press, 2011), chap. 6; Merline Pitre, Born to Serve: A History of Texas Southern University (Norman: University of Oklahoma Press, 2018), chap. 4; Charles E. Jones, "Arm Yourself or Harm Yourself: People's Party II and the Black Panther Party in Houston, Texas," in On the Ground: The Black Panther Party in Communities across America, ed. Judson L. Jeffries (Oxford: University Press of Mississippi, 2011).

32. Armando Navarro, La Raza Unida Party: A Chicano Challenge to the U.S. Two-Party Dictatorship (Philadelphia: Temple University Press, 2000); Navarro, Mexican American Youth Orga-

nization: Avant-Garde of the Chicano Movement in Texas (Austin: University of Texas Press, 1995); Ignacio M. García, *United We Win: The Rise and Fall of La Raza Unida Party* (Tucson: University of Arizona Press, 1989).

33. I borrow "counterinsurgency" from Jordan T. Camp, *Incarcerating the Crisis: Freedom Struggles and the Rise of the Neoliberal State* (Oakland: University of California Press, 2016). Also see Elizabeth Hinton, *From the War on Poverty to the War on Crime: The Making of Mass Incarceration in America* (Cambridge, MA: Harvard University Press, 2016); Kelly Lytle Hernández, *City of Inmates: Conquest, Rebellion, and the Rise of Human Caging in Los Angeles, 1771–1965* (Chapel Hill: University of North Carolina Press, 2017).

34. Paul J. Weber and Clarice Silber, "Sandra Bland's Own Video of 2015 Texas Traffic Stop Surfaces," Associated Press, May 7, 2017, accessed July 6, 2019, apnews.com/1a92859cc6d54b0 bb23dc1b6a6e30e36 (first quotation); Paul J. Weber, "Sister: Weakened 'Sandra Bland Act' in Texas 'Gut-Wrenching,'" Associated Press, May 13, 2017, accessed July 6, 2019, apnews.com/6a 2e63e81f2f4af983d2c0027cdfca24 (second quotation).

35. Among many other articulations of life under Jim Crow, see William H. Chafe, Raymond Gavins, and Robert Korstad, eds., *Remembering Jim Crow: African Americans Tell About Life in the Segregated South* (New York: New Press, 2001); Leslie Brown and Anne Valk, *Living with Jim Crow: African American Women and Memories of the Segregated South* (New York: Palgrave Macmillan, 2010). The scholarship on the interior life of Mexicanos in the age of Juan Crow in Texas is less established and still in development. Among others, see De León, *They Called Them Greasers*. Life in urban barrios is better documented. See, for example, Albert Camarillo, *Chicanos in a Changing Society: From Mexican Pueblos to American Barrios in Santa Barbara and Southern California, 1848–1930* (Cambridge, MA: Harvard University Press, 1979); Ricardo Romo, *East Los Angeles: History of a Barrio* (Austin: University of Texas Press, 1983); Jose M. Alamillo, *Making Lemonade out of Lemons: Mexican American Labor and Leisure in a California Town, 1880–1960* (Urbana: University of Illinois Press, 2006); González, *Redeeming La Raza*.

36. My thanks to Mónica Muñoz Martínez for her clarity in helping see the role of the state in sanctioning or sponsoring violence across ethnic groups in Texas. See her project in development, "Mapping Violence," mappingviolence.com. Also see her excellent book, *The Injustice Never Leaves You*. I also acknowledge the influence of Yohuru Williams's concept of "six degrees of segregation" against African Americans, as well as his argument that Black Power fundamentally addressed concerns parallel to those of the earlier civil rights movement; see Williams, *Rethinking the Black Freedom Movement*.

37. Among other works that have influenced my thinking about the role of ethnic studies, see Mariscal, *Brown-Eyed Children of the Sun*; Ibram X. Kendi, *The Black Campus Movement: Black Students and the Racial Reconstitution of Higher Education, 1965–1972* (New York: Palgrave Macmillan, 2012); Martha Biondi, *The Black Revolution on Campus* (Berkeley: University of California Press, 2012).

38. For similar stories, see Annelise Orleck and Lisa Hazirjian, eds., *War on Poverty: A New Grassroots History, 1964–1980* (Athens: University of Georgia Press, 2011); William S. Clayson, *Freedom Is Not Enough: The War on Poverty and the Civil Rights Movement in Texas* (Austin: University of Texas Press, 2010); Wesley G. Phelps, *A People's War on Poverty: Urban Politics and Grassroots Activists in Houston* (Athens: University of Georgia Press, 2014).

39. Robin D. G. Kelley, "'We Are Not What We Seem': Rethinking Black Working-Class Opposition in the Jim Crow South," *Journal of American History* 80, no. 1 (June 1993): 75–112, doi.org/10.2307/2079698; James C. Scott, *Domination and the Arts of Resistance: Hidden Transcripts* (New Haven, CT: Yale University Press, 1990).

40. My thanks to the historian Brian Behnken for his years of friendship and his willingness to serve as a foil and interlocutor. He also generously donated his own oral history interviews to the CRBB. The geographic argument that residential patterns in the state limited the possibilities for interracial alliances belongs to Brian, and it is one with which I fully agree. I take exception, however, to his argument that Black Power and Chicano/a Power produced ethnic nationalisms that were anathema to coalition building; see Behnken, *Fighting Their Own Battles*; Behnken, ed., *The Struggle in Black and Brown: African American and Mexican American Relations*

during the Civil Rights Era (Lincoln: University of Nebraska Press, 2011). For a powerful case for taking a relational approach, see Natalia Molina, Daniel Martinez HoSang, and Ramón A. Gutiérrez, eds., *Relational Formations of Race: Theory, Method, and Practice* (Oakland: University of California Press, 2019).

Chapter 1: Ignored News and Forgotten History

1. "Waller County's History," from James E. Johnson, oral history interview by Moisés Acuña Gurrola and Katherine Bynum, July 21, 2015, Prairie View, Texas, Civil Rights in Black and Brown Interview Database [hereafter cited as CRBB Interview Database], crbb .tcu.edu/clips/721/waller-county.

2. For two examples of Texas officials downplaying the history of racism in their localities, see Brian D. Behnken, "The 'Dallas Way': Protest, Response, and the Civil Rights Experience in Big D and Beyond," *Southwestern Historical Quarterly* 111 (2207): 1–29, and Michael Phillips, "Why Is Big Tex Still a White Cowboy? Race, Gender, and the 'Other Texas,'" in *Beyond Texas through Time: Breaking Away from Past Interpretations*, ed. Walter L. Buenger and Arnoldo De León (College Station: Texas A&M University Press, 2011).

3. W. Marvin Dulaney, "Whatever Happened to the Civil Rights Movement in Dallas, Texas?," in *Essays on the American Civil Rights Movement*, ed. W. Marvin Dulaney and Kathleen Underwood (College Station: Texas A&M University Press, 1993).

4. Jaeh Lee cited the Texas-based journalist Leah Binkovitz's tweet of a screenshot from the Equal Justice Initiative's "Lynching in America" project; the tweet falsely indicated that fifteen lynchings occurred in Waller County in the years 1877 to 1950. The Equal Justice Initiative, the source of Binkovitz's tweet, actually reported eight such killings in Waller County, a figure that could vary with the ways in which public lynchings are counted. For example, the EJI's count of eight includes one lynching that involved the simultaneous hanging of four Black men. Since the four murders were committed at once, EJI counted that instance as one lynching. Despite such methodological considerations, no estimate suggests that Waller County witnessed fifteen lynchings. Jaeah Lee, "The Texas County Where Sandra Bland Died Is Fraught with Racial Tensions," *Mother Jones*, July 17, 2015, motherjones.com/politics/2015/07/ texas-waller-county-sandra-bland-racial-tensions.

5. See also Tom Dart, "The Texas County Where Sandra Bland Died: 'There's Racism from Cradle to Grave,'" *Guardian*, July 17, 2015; Tom Rowley, "Sandra Bland's Death Divides Texas County with Ugly History of Racism," *Washington Post*, July 27, 2015; Julia Craven, "6 Things You Should Know about the County Where Sandra Bland Died," *Huffington Post*, July 23, 2015.

6. David A. Graham, "Sandra Bland and the Long History of Racism in Waller County, Texas," *Atlantic*, July 21, 2015, theatlantic.com/politics/archive/2015/07/sandra-bland -waller-county-racism/398975. For more on the political strategy and ascendancy of white su-premacy in response to Reconstruction, see Glenda Elizabeth Gilmore, *Gender and Jim Crow: Women and the Politics of White Supremacy in North Carolina, 1896–1920* (Chapel Hill: University of North Carolina Press, 1996).

7. Borrowing from W. E. B. Du Bois, the historian Leslie Brown defines "upbuilding" as "the literal and figurative construction of the structures African Americans used to climb out of slavery." She notes the extensiveness of upbuilding: "[Black] folk upbuilt families, homes, orga-nizations, institutions, and enterprises and erected atop a foundation laid in the past the physical and psychic spaces of black freedom." For more on the concept of generational upbuilding, see Leslie Brown, *Upbuilding Black Durham: Gender, Class, and Black Community Development in the Jim Crow South* (Chapel Hill: University of North Carolina Press, 2008), 10.

8. Charles W. Ramsdell, "Texas from the Fall of the Confederacy to the Beginning of Recon-struction," *Quarterly of the Texas State Historical Association* 11 (July 1907–April 1908): 216–218.

9. Editorial, *Texas Countryman* (Hempstead), May 6, 1868.

10. Editorial, *Texas Countryman* (Hempstead), May 20, 1868.

11. George Ruble Woolfolk, *Prairie View: A Study in Public Conscience, 1878–1946* (New York: Pageant, 1962), 29–30; Carole E. Christian, "Hempstead, TX," *Handbook of Texas Online,* tsha online.org/handbook/entries/hempstead-tx; Carole E. Christian and John Leffler, "Waller County," *Handbook of Texas Online,* tshaonline.org/handbook/entries/waller-county; Diane E. Spencer, "Waller, TX," *Handbook of Texas Online,* tshaonline.org/handbook/entries/waller-tx.

12. Ramsdell, "Texas from the Fall of the Confederacy," 216–218; Woolfolk, *Prairie View,* 339.

13. Woolfolk, *Prairie View,* 337.

14. Sanford N. Greenberg, "White Primary," *Handbook of Texas Online,* tshaonline.org/handbook /entries/white-primary; O. Douglas Weeks, "Election Laws," *Handbook of Texas Online,* tshaonline .org/handbook/entries/election-laws.

15. "Prairie View and Surrounding Towns," from Frank D. Jackson, oral history interview by Moisés Acuña Gurrola, Prairie View, Texas, July 16, 2015, CRBB Interview Database, crbb.tcu .edu/clips/327/prairie-view-and-surrounding-towns; "Living in Prairie View," from Al Bow- dre and Larneatha Bowdre, oral history interview by Katherine Bynum, July 14, 2015, Prairie View, Texas, CRBB Interview Database, crbb.tcu.edu/clips/1647/living-in-prairie-view.

16. Woolfolk, *Prairie View,* 338; "Living in Prairie View," Bowdre and Bowdre interview.

17. David L. Chapman, "Lynching in Texas" (master's thesis, Texas Tech University, 1973), 97–114.

18. Ibid., 1, 15.

19. Adam Rothman, "Slavery, the Civil War, and Reconstruction," in *American History Now,* ed. Eric Foner and Lisa McGirr (Philadelphia: Temple University Press, 2011), 87; Meg Jacobs, "The Uncertain Future of American Politics, 1940 to 1973," in ibid., 165.

20. Laura Smalley, interview by John Henry Faulk, Hempstead, Texas, 1941, "Voices Remem- bering Slavery," Library of Congress, loc.gov/item/afc1941016_afs05496a.

21. For more on the theory of the spectacle of public and mob violence, see Michel Foucault, *Discipline and Punish: The Birth of the Prison,* trans. Alan Sheridan (New York: Vintage, 1995).

22. David Roediger, *The Wages of Whiteness: Race and the Making of the American Working Class,* 3rd ed. (New York: Verso, 2007), 57.

23. Harriet Smith, interview by John Henry Faulk, Hempstead, Texas, 1941, "Voices Remem- bering Slavery," Library of Congress, loc.gov/item/afc1941016_afs05499a.

24. Ibid.; Virginia Neal Hinze, "Norris Wright Cuney" (master's thesis, Rice University, 1965); editorial, *Galveston Daily News,* April 19, 1896; editorial, *Bryan (TX) Daily Eagle,* March 28, 1896; Ernest William Winkler, ed., *Platforms of Political Parties in Texas,* Bulletin of the Uni- versity of Texas 53, (September 20, 1916); Robert Miller Worth and Stacy G. Ulbig, "Building a Populist Coalition in Texas, 1892–1896," *Journal of Southern History* 74, no. 2 (May 2008): 255–296.

25. Smith interview.

26. "Half-Day Schools," from Halcyon O. Watkins, oral history interview by Moisés Acuña Gurrola, Hempstead, Texas, July 23, 2015, CRBB Interview Database, crbb.tcu.edu/clips/279 /half-day-shcools; "Schools of Waller County: Sam Swartz School, 1928," Waller County His- torical Commission/Society, wallercountyhistory.org/apps/photos/photo?photoid=206251741.

27. "Interactions with Whites," from Amy Boykin, oral history interview by Katherine Bynum, July 9, 2015, Prairie View, Texas, CRBB Interview Database, crbb.tcu.edu/clips/386/interactions -with-whites.

28. Before its renaming as Prairie View A&M University in 1946, the university underwent several name changes. For the purposes of this chapter, I refer to pre-1946 iterations of Prairie View A&M University as the university at Prairie View.

29. "Prairie View and Surrounding Towns," from Jackson interview.

30. Dr. James E. Johnson, interview by Michael Phillips and Betsy Friauf, October 26, 2013, Prairie View, Texas, Baylor University Institute for Oral History, digitalcollections-baylor .quartexcollections.com/special-libraries-collections/oral-history.

31. Ibid., 46.

32. Ibid., 30.

33. Woolfolk, *Prairie View*, 331.

34. "Attending Prairie View A&M University," from Herbert Cross, oral history interview by Meredith May, June 20, 2016, Lufkin, Texas, CRBB Interview Database, crbb.tcu.edu/clips /2396/life-after-the-military.

35. "Immediately after Grad School," from Charles Urdy, oral history interview by Steve Arionus, June 17, 2016, Austin, CRBB Interview Database, crbb.tcu.edu/clips/5210/immediately -after-grad-school.

36. Johnson interview by Phillips and Friauf, 44; Associated Negro Press, "Strike Threat Gets P.V. Faculty Aid in Rights Fight: Boycott Pushed Against Jim Crow Hempstead Businesses," *San Antonio Register*, November 8, 1963; "Uncles Tom's, PVAMU, and The State Fair," from Maurice Portis, oral history interview by James Wall, June 14, 2016, Corpus Christi, Texas, CRBB Interview Database, crbb.tcu.edu/clips/4064/uncles-tom-s-pvamu-and-the-state -fair; "Principals and Presidents," Prairie View A&M University, pvamu.edu/about_pvamu /college-history/principals-and-presidents.

37. "Activism at Prairie View A&M—Turbulent Times," from Urdy interview, crbb.tcu.edu /clips/5212/activism-at-prairie-view-a-m-turbulent-times.

38. "Springtime Protest at Prairie View," *Bryan (TX) Daily Eagle*, March 16, 1960.

39. Johnson interview by Phillips and Friauf, 44.

40. "Riots at Prairie View University" and "Integration Marches in Hempstead, TX," from Boykin interview, crbb.tcu.edu/clips/1215/riots-at-prairie-view-university, crbb.tcu.edu/clips /1213/integration-marches-in-hempstead-tx.

41. Gary Younge, "1963: The Defining Year of the Civil Rights Movement," *Guardian*, May 7, 2013.

42. "Uncles Tom's, PVAMU, and The State Fair," from Portis interview.

43. "PV Meets the Inevitable," *Dallas Express*, November 9, 1963.

44. "Strike Threat Gets P.V. Faculty Aid in Rights Fight," *San Antonio Register*, November 8, 1963.

45. "Activism at Prairie View A&M—Turbulent Times" and "Immediately after Grad School," from Urdy interview.

46. "PV Students Ask Ouster of Solomn [*sic*]" *Dallas Express*, November 9, 1963.

47. *Sulphur Springs (TX) Daily News Telegram*, November 3, 1963.

48. "Activism at Prairie View A&M—Turbulent Times," from Urdy interview; "Strike Theater Gets P.V. Faculty," *San Antonio Register*, November 8, 1963.

49. "Students Shun P.V. Homecoming in Fight Against Racial Bias," *San Antonio Register*, November 15, 1963.

50. "Integration in Texas," *Texas Observer*, March 6, 1964; Robert Christopher Fink, "Black College Football in Texas" (PhD diss., Texas Tech University, 2003), 355–357; "Prairie View Students Boycott Game," *Dallas Express*, November 16, 1963.

51. S. T. McKibben, "Unbeaten PV Takes Bishop 53–14," *Dallas Express*, November 16, 1963.

52. "Students Shun P.V. Homecoming."

53. "Waller County's History," from Johnson interview by Gurrola and Bynum, crbb.tcu .edu/clips/721/waller-county.

54. "Integration Marches in Hempstead, TX," from Boykin interview.

55. "Voting and Voter Registration," from Boykin interview, crbb.tcu.edu/clips/1214/voting -and-voter-registration; "Children and School Desegregation," from Johnson interview by Gurrola and Bynum, crbb.tcu.edu/clips/720/children-and-school-desegregation; "Geographic Inequalities Associated with Prairie View," "Racial Issues in Their Children's Education," and "Racial Set Backs and Progress," from Bowdre and Bowdre interview, crbb.tcu.edu/clips/1757 /geographic-inequalities-associated-with-prairie-view, crbb.tcu.edu/clips/1648/racial-issues-in -their-children-s-education, crbb.tcu.edu/clips/1649/racial-set-backs-and-progress; "Half-Day Schools," from Watkins interview; "Incorporation of Prairie View," from Jackson interview, crbb .tcu.edu/clips/326/incorporation-of-prairie-view.

The chapter epigraph is from "Resistance to School Integration," from Herbert Cross, oral history interview by Meredith May, June 20, 2016, Lufkin, Texas, Civil Rights in Black and Brown Interview Database [hereafter cited as CRBB Interview Database], crbb.tcu .edu/clips/facing-a-crowd-carrying-guns.

1. Denise Hoephfner, "LISD Integration Order Lifted in 2000," *Lufkin (TX) Daily News*, February 22, 2007, lufkindailynews.com/news/article_b252803f-86e6-50ff-ba2f-c1976c777061 .html.

2. James Jennings, "7th Grade School Windows Broken," *Lufkin (TX) Daily News*, September 1, 1970, 1, 8.

3. James Rhone, interview by Marie Davis and L. D. Smith, April 24, 1986, Diboll, Texas, transcript, Diboll History Center, available online at thehistorycenteronline.com/oral-history /entry/rhone-james.

4. It was renamed Stephen F. Austin State University in 1969.

5. Megan Biesele, "Angelina County," *Handbook of Texas Online*, accessed July 28, 2017, tsha online.org/handbook/online/articles/hca03.

6. Christopher Long, "Nacogdoches County," *Handbook of Texas Online*, tshaonline.org /handbook/online/articles/hcn01.

7. Bob Bowman, "Lufkin, TX," *Handbook of Texas Online*, tshaonline.org/handbook/online /articles/hdl05.

8. Megan Biesele, *The Cornbread Whistle: Oral History of a Texas Timber Company Town* (Lufkin, TX: Lufkin Printing Company, 1986), 6–7.

9. George Creel, "The Feudal Towns of Texas," *Harper's Weekly* 60 (1915): 76–78.

10. Stephen D. Delear, *March! The Fight for Civil Rights in a Land of Fear* (College Station, TX: Travis Lake Publishing, 2011), ch. 2, Kindle.

11. Mary Jane Christian, interview by Elvia Esteves, September 29, 1987, Diboll, TX, transcript, Diboll History Center, available online at thehistorycenteronline.com/oral-history /entry/christian-mary-jane.

12. Delear, *March!*, ch. 1.

13. "Black Business Community," from Margaret Chumbley, Anita Farr, Thelma Sexton, and Elizabeth Simpson, oral history interview by Meredith May, June 21, 2016, Nacogdoches, Texas, CRBB Interview Database, crbb.tcu.edu/clips/black-business-community.

14. "Businesses in Nacogdoches," from Helena Abdullah, oral history interview by Jasmin Howard, June 30, 2016, Nacogdoches, Texas, CRBB Interview Database, crbb.tcu.edu/clips /neighborhood.

15. Delear, *March!*, ch. 1.

16. "Teaching in Lufkin," from Cross interview, crbb.tcu.edu/clips/getting-a-job-in-lufkin-tx.

17. "First Year of Integration at Lufkin," from Gloria Toran, oral history interview by Jasmin Howard, June 20, 2016, Lufkin, Texas, CRBB Interview Database, crbb.tcu.edu/clips/first -year-of-integration-at-lufkin.

18. "Family History and Background," from Larry Kegler, oral history interview by Meredith May, June 24, 2016, Lufkin, Texas, CRBB Interview Database, crbb.tcu.edu/clips/family -history-and-background-2.

19. "Growing Up in Lufkin, Part One," from Betell Benham, oral history interview by Jasmin Howard, June 27, 2016, Lufkin, Texas, CRBB Interview Database, crbb.tcu.edu/clips /growing-up-in-lufkin.

20. "Education in Lufkin," from S'ydney Benemon, oral history interview by Jasmin Howard, June 23, 2016, Lufkin, Texas, CRBB Interview Database, crbb.tcu.edu/clips/education-in-lufkin.

21. "Racism in Lufkin, TX," from Benham interview, crbb.tcu.edu/clips/racism-in-lufkin-tx.

22. Bettie Kennedy, interview by R. L. Kuykendall, September 12, 2001, Lufkin, Texas, transcript, Diboll History Center, available online at thehistorycenteronline.com/oral-history/entry /kennedy-bettie.

23. "Childhood Experiences during the Jim Crow Era," from Kegler interview, crbb.tcu.edu/clips/childhood-experiences-during-the-jim-crow-era; "Growing Up in Lufkin, Part 2," from Benham interview, crbb.tcu.edu/clips/growing-up-in-lufkin-part-2, Lufkin, Texas, CRBB interview; Lela Simmons, oral history interview by Jasmin Howard and Meredith May, June 30, 2016, Portal to Texas History, University of North Texas Libraries, texashistory.unt.edu/ark:/67531/metapth984134/m1.

24. Simmons interview.

25. "Medical Care, First Experiences with Jim Crow," from Chumbley, Farr, Sexton, and Simpson interview, crbb.tcu.edu/clips/medical-care-first-experiences-with-jim-crow.

26. Odis Rhodes, interview by R. L. Kuykendall, January 10, 2001, Lufkin, Texas, transcript, Diboll History Center, available online at thehistorycenteronline.com/oral-history/entry/rhodes-odis.

27. "Segregation and Discrimination in Nacogdoches, Part Two," from Chumbley, Farr, Sexton, and Simpson interview, crbb.tcu.edu/clips/segregation-and-discrimination-in-nacogdoches-part-two.

28. Ibid.

29. "Biographical Information," from Benemon interview, crbb.tcu.edu/clips/biographical-information-78.

30. "Lufkin High School after Integration, Part Two," from Kegler interview, crbb.tcu.edu/clips/lufkin-high-school-after-integration-pt-2.

31. Simmons interview.

32. Ibid.

33. "Lufkin High School after Integration, Part Two," from Kegler interview.

34. Delear, *March!*, ch. 3.

35. "How People Felt after Integration," from Kegler interview, crbb.tcu.edu/clips/how-people-felt-after-integration.

36. Simmons interview.

37. "Racism in Lufkin, TX," from Benham interview.

38. Ibid.

39. Josephine Rutland Frederick, Marion Franklin, and Jim Fuller, interview by Becky Bailey, October 13, 1984, Diboll, Texas, transcript, Diboll History Center, available online at thehistorycenteronline.com/oral-history/entry/frederick-josephine-rutland.

40. Howard Coleman, interview by R. L. Kuykendall, September 19, 1999, Lufkin, Texas, transcript, Diboll History Center, available online at thehistorycenteronline.com/oral-history/entry/coleman-howard.

41. Bob Bowman, "Murders Made Plenty of Good Copy for Lufkin Daily News Readers," *Lufkin (TX) Daily News*, February 22, 2007, lufkindailynews.com/news/article_cae6ce3a-5086-59fc-95a0-8861eeddc664.html.

42. "Man Slain in Courtroom was Innocent, Belief," *Pittsburgh Courier*, December 20, 1941.

43. Coleman interview.

44. Emma Jean and Lemon Ligon, interview by Jonathan Gerland, September 28, 1999, Diboll, Texas, transcript, Diboll History Center, available online at thehistorycenteronline.com/oral-history/entry/ligon-emma-jean-pat-allen.

45. Cleveland Mark, interview by Jonathan Gerland, September 4, 2014, Lufkin, Texas, transcript, Diboll History Center, available online at thehistorycenteronline.com/oral-history/entry/mark-cleveland.

46. Jim Ligon, interview by Jonathan Gerland, November 6, 2009, Diboll, Texas, transcript, Diboll History Center, available online at thehistorycenteronline.com/oral-history/entry/ligon-jim.

47. Mark interview.

48. Arthur Temple Jr., interview by Jonathan Gerland, June 2, 2000, Lufkin, Texas, transcript, Diboll History Center, available online at thehistorycenteronline.com/oral-history/entry/temple-arthur-56d.

49. Simmons interview.

50. Rhodes interview.

51. Ibid.

52. "African American Community and Law Enforcement," from Chumbley, Farr, Sexton, and Simpson interview, crbb.tcu.edu/clips/african-american-community-and-law-enforcement.

53. Georgi A. Vogel Rosen, "The Murder of Ellis Hutson: A Legal Legacy," (Civil Rights and Restorative Justice Clinic, Northeastern University School of Law, 2014), 4–8, repository .library.northeastern.edu/files/neu:cj82r688r.

54. Ibid., 9.

55. Ibid., 10–12.

56. Ibid., 12–14.

57. Ibid., 23.

58. Rhodes interview.

59. "African American Community and Law Enforcement," from Chumbley, Farr, Sexton, and Simpson interview.

60. Rhodes interview.

61. Delear, *March!*, ch. 3.

62. "African American Student Association at Stephen F. Austin University," from Abdullah interview, crbb.tcu.edu/clips/civil-rights-and-sfa-part-1.

63. Ibid. Abdullah states that the marches happened in 1969, but according to the lawsuit that McGuire brought against Roebuck, they happened in 1970.

64. *McGuire v. Roebuck*, 347 F. Supp. 1111 (E.D. Tex. 1972), available from Justia, law.justia .com/cases/federal/district-courts/FSupp/347/1111/1404750.

65. "African American Student Association at Stephen F. Austin University," from Abdullah interview.

66. "Protests and Marching, Part Two," from Abdullah interview, crbb.tcu.edu/clips/protests -and-marching-part-2; *McGuire v. Roebuck*.

67. Frank Kemerer, *William Wayne Justice: A Judicial Biography* (Austin: University of Texas Press, 1991), 187.

68. Delear, *March!*, ch. 4.

69. Ibid.

70. *McGuire v. Roebuck*.

71. Ibid. at 1125.

72. "Segregation, Police Brutality, the Civil Rights Movements," from Abdullah interview, crbb.tcu.edu/clips/segregation-police-brutality-civil-rights-movements.

73. "Integration in Lufkin—Experiences in and out of School," from Benemon interview, crbb.tcu.edu/clips/integration-in-lufkin-experiences-in-and-out-of-school.

74. "Resistance to School Integration," from Cross interview.

75. "School Walkout and Integration," from Benemon interview, crbb.tcu.edu/clips/school -walkout-and-integration.

76. "Role Models and Education," from Chumbley, Farr, Sexton, and Simpson interview, crbb.tcu.edu/clips/role-models-and-education; "Early Childhood, School Education," from Kegler interview, crbb.tcu.edu/clips/childhood-discipline.

77. "Teaching in Lufkin," from Cross interview.

78. "Parents Hope for a Better Education," from Kegler interview, crbb.tcu.edu/clips/parents -hope-for-a-better-education.

79. Emma Jones Callager, interview by Bettie Kennedy, June 1, 2002, Lufkin, Texas, transcript, Diboll History Center, available online at thehistorycenteronline.com/oral-history/entry /callager-emma-jones.

80. Rhodes interview.

81. "Working as a Bus Driver, Unequal Resources," from Cross interview, crbb.tcu.edu /clips/new-typewriters.

82. Queen Esther King, interview by Patsy Colbert, August 11, 2010, Diboll, Texas, transcript, Diboll History Center, available online at thehistorycenteronline.com/oral-history/entry /king-queen-esther-taylor.

83. Laverne Joshua, interview by Patsy Colbert, August 4, 2011, Diboll, Texas, transcript, Diboll History Center, available online at thehistorycenteronline.com/oral-history/entry/joshua-laverne; Clay Joshua, James Joshua, and Thomas Joshua, interview by Patsy Colbert, February 22, 2011, Diboll, Texas, transcript, Diboll History Center, available online at thehistorycenter online.com/oral-history/entry/joshua-thomas.

84. Billie Jean Capps, interview by Patsy Colbert, May 10, 2010, Diboll, Texas, transcript, Diboll History Center, available online at thehistorycenteronline.com/oral-history/entry/capps-billie-jean; Stacy Cooke, interview by Jonathan Gerland, February 1, 2010, Diboll, Texas, transcript, Diboll History Center, available online at thehistorycenteronline.com/oral-history/entry/cooke-stacy; Robert Ramsey, interview by Becky Bailey, March 12, 1985, Diboll, Texas, transcript, Diboll History Center, available online at thehistorycenteronline.com/oral-history/entry/ramsey-robert-sr.

85. Delear, *March!*, ch. 5; "Alumni Association's Purchase of Old School Building," from Chumbley, Farr, Sexton, and Simpson interview, crbb.tcu.edu/clips/alumni-association-s-purchase-of-old-school-building.

86. "College," from Chumbley, Farr, Sexton, and Simpson interview, crbb.tcu.edu/clips/college-5.

87. Cooke interview.

88. "Family Healthcare and Freedom of Choice," from Kegler interview, crbb.tcu.edu/clips/family-healthcare-freedom-of-choice.

89. "Lufkin High School before Integration," from Kegler interview, crbb.tcu.edu/clips/lufkin-high-school-befor-integration.

90. Ibid.

91. "Race Relations and Education," from Benham interview, crbb.tcu.edu/clips/a-lonely-time-in-my-life.

92. "Segregated Education," from Benham interview, crbb.tcu.edu/clips/not-friends-associates-segreation-in-education.

93. "New Integration Plan Submitted," *Lufkin (TX) Daily News*, August 17, 1970, 1.

94. "White Resistance to Integration," from Toran interview, crbb.tcu.edu/clips/white-resistance-to-integration.

95. "Resistance to School Integration," from Cross interview.

96. Ibid.

97. "Integration in Lufkin, TX," from Benham interview, crbb.tcu.edu/clips/intergration-in-lufkin.

98. "Struggles with Integration," from Cross interview, crbb.tcu.edu/clips/struggles-with-integration.

99. "Problems after Integration," from Cross interview, crbb.tcu.edu/clips/problems-after-integration.

100. Ibid.

101. "Lufkin High School after Integration," from Kegler interview.

102. "After Integration at the High School," from Cross interview, crbb.tcu.edu/clips/after-integration-at-the-high-school.

103. "First Year of Integration at Lufkin," from Toran interview.

104. "Integration Process in Lufkin, Part Two," from Toran interview, crbb.tcu.edu/clips/integration-process-in-lufkin-part-two.

105. "School Walkout and Integration," from Benemon interview.

106. "Being on the School Board," from Kegler interview, crbb.tcu.edu/clips/being-on-the-school-board.

107. Ibid.

108. "No Picture in the Paper—Brookhollow Elementary 25th Anniversary," from Cross interview, crbb.tcu.edu/clips/no-picture-in-the-paper-brook-hollow-elementary-25th-anniversary.

109. "Problems at Brookhollow Elementary," from Cross interview, crbb.tcu.edu/clips/problems-at-brook-hollow-elementary.

Chapter 3: "Something Was Lost"

The chapter epigraph comes from "Final Remarks," from Wanda Thompson, oral history interview by Eladio Bobadilla and Danielle Grevious, June 9, 2016, Port Arthur, Texas, Civil Rights in Black and Brown Interview Database [hereafter cited as CRBB Interview Database], crbb.tcu.edu/clips/final-remarks-30. All interviews cited here were conducted by the author, then a doctoral candidate at Duke University and now an assistant professor at the University of Kentucky, and Danielle Grevious, a doctoral student at Ohio State University.

1. See, for perhaps the most eloquent and popular historiographical treatment of the long civil rights movement, Jacquelyn Dowd Hall, "The Long Civil Rights Movement and the Political Uses of the Past," *Journal of American History* 91 (2005): 1233–1263, doi.org/10.2307/3660172.

2. See, for example, Barbara Ransby, *Ella Baker and the Black Freedom Movement: A Radical Democratic Vision*, new ed. (Chapel Hill: University of North Carolina Press, 2005); Katherine Mellen Charron, *Freedom's Teacher: The Life of Septima Clark* (Chapel Hill: University of North Carolina Press, 2009); Annelise Orleck, *Storming Caesar's Palace: How Black Mothers Fought Their Own War on Poverty* (Boston: Beacon, 2005).

3. Frances Fox Piven and Richard Cloward, *Poor People's Movements: Why They Succeed, How They Fail* (New York: Pantheon, 1977); Gordon K. Mantler, *Power to the Poor: Black-Brown Coalition and the Fight for Economic Justice, 1960–1974* (Chapel Hill: University of North Carolina Press, 2013); Robert R. Korstad and James L. Leloudis, *To Right These Wrongs: The North Carolina Fund and the Battle to End Poverty and Inequality in 1960s America* (Chapel Hill: University of North Carolina Press, 2010); Landon R. Y. Storrs, *The Second Red Scare and the Unmaking of the New Deal* (Princeton, NJ: Princeton University Press, 2012); William P. Jones, *The March on Washington: Jobs, Freedom, and the Forgotten History of Civil Rights* (New York: Norton, 2013).

4. See, for example, Charles Cobb, *This Nonviolent Stuff'll Get You Killed: How Guns Made the Civil Rights Movement Possible* (New York: Basic Books, 2014); Robert Williams, *Negroes with Guns* (Mansfield Centre, CT: Martino, 2013); Akinyele O. Umoja, *We Will Shoot Back: Armed Resistance in the Mississippi Freedom Movement* (New York: New York University Press, 2013); Nicolas Johnson, *Negroes and the Gun: The Tradition of Black Arms* (Amherst, NY: Prometheus, 2014); Lance Hill, *The Deacons for Defense: Armed Resistance and the Civil Rights Movement* (Chapel Hill: University of North Carolina Press, 2004).

5. I focus primarily on Beaumont and Port Arthur, where the project that this chapter resulted from primarily took me. My limited commentary on Orange is not a deliberate effort to ignore the voices of those who lived through segregation and integration there, but a result of a simpler obstacle: a limited source base.

6. Donald A. Ritchie, ed., *The Oxford Handbook of Oral History* (New York: Oxford University Press, 2010); Samuel Schrager, "What Is Social in Oral History?," *International Journal of Oral History* 4, no. 2 (1983): 76–98; Katherine Borland, "'That's Not What I Said': Interpretive Conflict in Oral Narrative Research," in *The Oral History Reader*, ed. Robert Perks and Alistair Thomson (New York: Routledge, 1998), 320–332; Natalie M. Fousekis, "Experiencing History: A Journey from Oral History to Performance," in *Remembering: Oral History Performance*, ed. Della Pollock (New York: Palgrave Macmillan, 2005); Alexander Stille, "Prospecting for Truth in the Ore Of Memory," *New York Times*, March 10, 2001, nytimes.com/2001/03/10/arts/prospecting-for-truth-in-the-ore-of-memory.html; Alessandro Portelli, *The Death of Luigi Trastulli, and Other Stories: Form and Meaning in Oral History* (Albany: State University of New York Press, 1990).

7. Several interviewees remember that the Golden Triangle, and especially Port Arthur, with its party atmosphere and glitzy game rooms, was often referred to as "Little New York." Some publications referred to East Texas more generally, and often to Houston specifically, as "Little New York." See, for example, Stephen Fox, *The Country Houses of John F. Staub* (Hong Kong: Everbest, 2007), 6.

8. Quoted in *Antone's: Home of the Blues*, dir. Dan Karlok (New York: Koch Vision, 2006).

9. Alan B. Govenar, *Texas Blues: The Rise of a Contemporary Sound* (College Station: Texas A&M University Press, 2008), 405.

10. Alice Echols, *Scars of Sweet Paradise: The Life and Times of Janis Joplin* (New York: Metropolitan, 1999), 1.

11. *Annual Report of the Chief of Engineers, US Army, 1953*, H.R. Doc. 253-83 at 794 (1954).

12. "Martial Law Declared as Texas Riots Kill Two," *Rocky Mountain News* (Denver, CO), June 17, 1943, 3. For secondary accounts, see James A. Burran, "Violence in an 'Arsenal of Democracy': The Beaumont Race Riot, 1943," *East Texas Historical Journal* 14, no. 1 (1976), 39–52; James S. Olson and Sharon Phair, "Anatomy of a Race Riot: Beaumont, Texas, 1943," *Texana*, no. 11 (1973).

13. Brian Piper, "Beaumont Race Riot," in *The Jim Crow Encyclopedia*, ed. Nikki L. M. Brown and Barry M. Stentiford (Westport, CT: Greenwood, 2008), 68.

14. Burran, "Violence in an 'Arsenal of Democracy,'" 39.

15. Quoted in Sam Savage, "Black History Month: Segregation in Southeast Texas Hospitals," *Red Orbit*, February 14, 2007, redorbit.com/news/health/841323/black_history_month_segregation_in_southeast_texas_hospitals.

16. Burran, "Violence in an 'Arsenal of Democracy,'" 40.

17. Rape accusations against Black men have featured prominently in the history of Black-white relations and served as typical justifications for lynching throughout the nineteenth century and well into the twentieth. See, for example, Jacquelyn Dowd Hall, *Revolt against Chivalry: Jessie Daniel Ames and the Women's Campaign against Lynching* (New York: Columbia University Press, 1979); Joel Williamson, *The Crucible of Race: Black-White Relations in the American South since Emancipation* (New York: Oxford University Press, 1984); Philip Dray, *At the Hands of Persons Unknown: The Lynching of Black America* (New York: Modern Library, 2007); James Goodman, *Stories of Scottsboro* (New York: Vintage, 1994); Amy Karen Phillips, "The Southern Rape and Lynching Complex: The Subordination of Southern Women through a Mechanism of White Supremacy," paper presented at the Gender and the Law in American History Seminar, Georgetown University, January 29, 1996 (copy in author's possession).

18. Marilynn S. Johnson, "Gender, Race, and Rumors: Re-Examining the 1943 Race Riots," *Gender and History* 10, no. 2 (August 1998): 259.

19. "Transition from Catholic to Public School," from Mabel Briggs, oral history interview by Eladio Bobadilla and Danielle Grevious, June 24, 2016, Beaumont, Texas, CRBB Interview Database, crbb.tcu.edu/clips/transition-from-catholic-to-public-school.

20. "First Time Recognizing Race Differences," from Richard Price, oral history interview by Eladio Bobadilla and Danielle Grevious, June 24, 2016, Beaumont, Texas, CRBB Interview Database, crbb.tcu.edu/clips/first-time-realizing-race-differences.

21. Ibid.

22. Robert D. Bullard, "Dismantling Toxic Racism," *Crisis*, July–August 2007, 24.

23. "Discrimination in Port Arthur," from Harvey Johnson, oral history interview by Eladio Bobadilla and Danielle Grevious, June 14, 2016, Houston, Texas, Civil Rights in Black and Brown Interview Database, crbb.tcu.edu/clips/discrimination-in-port-arthur.

24. "Race Relations, Part One," from Hilton Kelley, oral history interview by Eladio Bobadilla and Danielle Grevious, June 20, 2016, Port Arthur, Texas, CRBB Interview Database, crbb.tcu.edu/clips/discrimination-in-port-arthur.

25. Ibid.

26. Robert J. Robertson, *Fair Ways: How Six Black Golfers Won Civil Rights in Beaumont, Texas* (College Station: Texas A&M University Press, 2005), 27.

27. Ibid.

28. "The Environment in the Hospital Cont.," from Briggs interview, crbb.tcu.edu/clips/2795/the-racist-environment-in-the-hospital-cont.

29. "First Time Realizing Race Differences," from Price interview.

30. Ibid.

31. *Brown v. Board of Education of Topeka*, 347 U.S. 483 at 494 (1954).

32. "Leaving Port Arthur, Part Two," from Harvey Johnson interview.

33. Ashley Nkadi, "Domestic Workers: The Women Who Raised America," *Root*, March 27, 2018, accessed April 26, 2018, theroot.com/domestic-workers-the-women-who-raised -america-1823983133?utm_medium=sharefromsite&utm_source=The_Root_twitter.

34. For a sociohistorical overview of Black women's domestic labor in white homes, including their role in raising white American children, see Patricia Hill Collins, *Black Feminist Thought: Knowledge, Consciousness, and the Politics of Empowerment* (New York: Routledge, 2008), 56.

35. "Spivey's Mom and Her Domestic Work," from Brenda Spivey, oral history interview by Eladio Bobadilla and Danielle Grevious, June 27, 2016, Beaumont, Texas, CRBB Interview Database, crbb.tcu.edu/clips/spivey-s-mom-and-her-domestic-work.

36. Robin D. G. Kelley, "Resistance, Survival, and the Black Poor in Birmingham, Alabama, 1929–1970," Discussion Paper 950-91 (Madison: Institute for Research on Poverty, University of Wisconsin, 1991), 25.

37. "Childhood and Neighborhood," from Vernon Durden, oral history interview with by Eladio Bobadilla and Danielle Grevious, June 24, 2016, CRBB Interview Database, crbb .tcu.edu/clips/2523/childhood-and-neighborhood.

38. See the sources cited in footnote 4 above.

39. Jim Atkinson, "Bad Air Days," *Texas Monthly*, August 2003, texasmonthly.com/articles /bad-air-days-2.

40. "Violence in Port Arthur, Part One," from Kelley interview.

41. "Beaumont Will Study Integration," *Bryan (TX) Eagle*, August 28, 1955, 18.

42. "Beaumont Newest Integration Spot," *Brownsville Herald*, September 25, 1956, 1.

43. "Negroes Are Turned Away at Beaumont," *Bryan (TX) Eagle*, October 3, 1956, 1.

44. "Arrest White Beaumont Ministers," *Clovis (NM) News-Journal*, April 20, 1960, 1.

45. "Paul Jones Discusses Civil Rights Movement, NAACP," from Paul Jones, oral history interview by Eladio Bobadilla and Danielle Grevious, June 7, 2016, Beaumont, Texas, CRBB Interview Database, crbb.tcu.edu/clips/paul-jones-discusses-civil-rights-movement-naacp.

46. "Beaumont Integration Study Finds Respect for Order," *Corpus Christi Caller-Times*, January 11, 1957.

47. "Unions Aid Integration Move in Deep South, Survey Says," *Montgomery (AL) Advertiser*, September 22, 1958, 2; Bruce Nelson, "Organized Labor and the Struggle for Black Equality in Mobile during World War II," *Journal of American History* 80, no. 3 (December 1993): 954, 976.

48. "Union at Beaumont Opposes Integration," *Bryan (TX) Eagle*, December 24, 1956, 12.

49. *Brown v. Board of Education of Topeka*, 349 U.S. 294 (1955), syllabus, note 2.

50. "Education and Integration," from Durden interview, crbb.tcu.edu/clips/education-and -integration.

51. "Law Slows Texas School Desegregation," *Chicago Defender*, August 24, 1957, 22.

52. "Bills Offered to Bar Integration of Texas Schools," *Corsicana (TX) Daily Sun*, January 25, 1957, 3.

53. James Marlow, "Segregation Is Being Smashed in Triple Squeeze," *Delaware County (PA) Daily Times*, May 28, 1963, 31.

54. "Beaumont Integration Set," *Odessa (TX) American*, July 22, 1964, 1.

55. Ronnie Dugger, "Integration in Texas," *Texas Observer*, March 6, 1964, 9.

56. "Beaumont, Texas, School Charged with Segregation," *Atlanta Daily World*, November 29, 1973, 5.

57. See, for example, Greta De Jong, *You Can't Eat Freedom: Southerners and Social Justice after the Civil Rights Movement* (Chapel Hill: University of North Carolina Press, 2016); Nancy Mac-Lean, *Freedom Is Not Enough: The Opening of the American Workplace* (Cambridge, MA: Harvard University Press, 2008); Thomas F. Jackson, *Martin Luther King, Jr. and the Struggle for Economic Justice* (Philadelphia: University of Pennsylvania Press, 2007); Storrs, *Second Red Scare*; Jefferson Cowie, *The Great Exception: The New Deal and the Limits of American Politics* (Princeton, NJ: Princeton University Press, 2016).

58. "60 Leaders Joined Texas Rights Talks," *Chicago Defender*, December 18, 1965, 14.

59. Dugger, "Integration in Texas," 10.

60. See Adolph Reed Jr., "Marx, Race, and Neoliberalism," *New Labor Forum* 22, no. 1 (2013): 49–57; Adolph Reed Jr., *Class Notes: Posing as Politics, and Other Thoughts on the American Scene* (New York: New Press, 2001); Touré Reed, *Not Alms but Opportunity: The Urban League and the Politics of Racial Uplift* (Chapel Hill: University of North Carolina Press, 2008); Cedric Johnson, *Revolutionaries to Race Leaders: Black Power and the Making of African American Politics* (Philadelphia: University of Pennsylvania Press, 2007); Walter B. Michaels, *The Trouble with Diversity: How We Learned to Love Identity and Ignore Inequality* (New York: Metropolitan, 2006).

61. "Education and Integration," from Durden interview.

62. "Segregation vs. Integration," from Jerry High, oral history interview by Eladio Bobadilla and Danielle Grevious, June 8, 2016, Beaumont, Texas, CRBB Interview Database, crbb .tcu.edu/clips/segregation-vs-integration.

63. "Education and Integration," from Durden interview.

64. "Experiences with Racial Profiling and NAACP Involvement," from Spivey interview, crbb.tcu.edu/clips/experiences-with-racial-profiling-and-naacp-involvement.

65. "Integration's Consequences and Social Concerns," from High interview, crbb.tcu .edu/clips/integration-s-consequences-and-social-concerns.

66. "Education and Integration," from Durden interview.

67. Amilcar Shabazz, *Advancing Democracy: African Americans and the Struggle for Access and Equity in Higher Education in Texas* (Chapel Hill: University of North Carolina Press, 2004), 170.

68. Dick J. Reavis, emails to the author, February 18, 2018. All comments from Reavis come from this exchange.

69. "Race Relations, Politics, and Integration," from Margaret Toal, oral history interview by Eladio Bobadilla and Danielle Grevious, June 29, 2016, Orange, Texas, CRBB Interview Database, crbb.tcu.edu/clips/race-relations-politics-and-integration-in-east-texas.

70. "Vernice Moore and Hosea Gabriel Discuss Integration in Port Arthur," from Vernice Moore and Hosea Gabriel, oral history interview by Eladio Bobadilla and Danielle Grevious, June 1, 2016, Port Arthur, Texas, CRBB Interview Database, crbb.tcu.edu/clips/vernice -moore-and-hosea-gabriel-discuss-integration-in-port-arthur.

71. Robert J. Robertson, *Fair Ways: How Six Black Golfers Won Civil Rights in Beaumont, Texas* (College Station: Texas A&M University Press, 2005).

72. David Harrison, "Desegregation Brings Its Ills to the System," *Chicago Daily Defender*, December 5, 1970, 8.

73. "Overcoming Anger," from High interview, crbb.tcu.edu/clips/overcoming-anger.

74. "Education, Integration, and Interracial Contact," from Gethrel Williams, oral history interview by Eladio Bobadilla and Danielle Grevious, June 29, 2016, Beaumont, Texas, CRBB Interview Database, crbb.tcu.edu/clips/education-integration-and-interracial-contact.

75. Hilton Kelly, *Race, Remembering, and Jim Crow's Teachers* (New York: Routledge, 2010), 10.

76. "Leaving Port Arthur, Part Two," from Johnson interview.

77. For official statistics on hate crimes, see the Federal Bureau of Investigation's annual reports of its Uniform Crime Reporting Program, available through 2015: ucr.fbi.gov/hate -crime. For a detailed report on police killings of Black men and women, see "From Ferguson to Baton Rouge: Deaths of Black Men and Women at the Hands of Police," *Los Angeles Times*, July 12, 2016, latimes.com/nation/la-na-police-deaths-20160707-snap-htmlstory.html.

78. "Leaving Port Arthur, Part Two," from Johnson interview.

79. Harrison, "Desegregation Brings Its Ills."

80. "Segregation vs. Integration," from High interview.

81. Nicole Puglise, "Black Americans Incarcerated Five Times More than White People: Report," *Guardian* (US ed.), June 18, 2016, theguardian.com/us-news/2016/jun/18/mass -incarceration-black-americans-higher-rates-disparities-report.

82. Geoff Winningham, "Football, Game of Life," *Texas Monthly*, October 1983, 159.

83. Jesse J. Holland, "Segregation Is Making a Comeback in Texas, Other US Schools," *Beaumont Enterprise*, May 15, 2014.

84. Marilyn Tennissen, "PAISD Officially Desegregated after 37 Years in Court," *Southeast Texas*

Record, August 30, 2007, setexasrecord.com/stories/510608351-paisd-officially-desegregated
-after-37-years-in-court.

85. Tina M. Kibbe, "School Desegregation in Port Arthur: The Battle between the Community, the Board, and the Justice Department," *East Texas Historical Journal* 44, no. 2 (October 2006): 3–16.

86. Quoted in Patrick Michaels, "Race to the Bottom," *Texas Observer,* November 14, 2014, texasobserver.org/beaumont-isd-race-to-the-bottom.

87. "Education and Integration," from Durden interview.

88. Sam H. Verhovek, "Blacks Moved to Texas Housing Project," *New York Times,* January 14, 1994, nytimes.com/1994/01/14/us/blacks-moved-to-texas-housing-project.html.

89. Richard Rothstein, *The Color of Law: A Forgotten History of How Our Government Segregated America* (New York: Liveright, 2017).

90. Alana Semuels, "Has America Given Up on the Dream of Racial Integration?," *Atlantic,* June 19, 2015, theatlantic.com/business/archive/2015/06/segregatino-2015/396167.

91. "Civil Rights and the Union," from William "Bill" Sam, oral history interview by Eladio Bobadilla and Danielle Grevious, June 15, 2016, Port Arthur, Texas, CRBB Interview Database, crbb.tcu.edu/clips/civil-rights-and-the-union.

92. Jefferson Cowie, *Stayin' Alive: The 1970s and the Last Days of the Working Class* (New York: New Press, 2010); Daniel T. Rodgers, *Age of Fracture* (Cambridge, MA: Belknap, 2011); Robert O. Self, *All in the Family: The Realignment of American Democracy since the 1960s* (New York: Hill and Wang, 2012); Lizabeth Cohen, *A Consumers' Republic: The Politics of Mass Consumption in Postwar America* (New York: Vintage, 2003).

93. For background on integration efforts, especially through the courts, see *Bernard v. Gulf Oil Corp.,* 643 F. Supp. 1494 (E.D. Tex. 1986).

94. Michael Goldfield, *The Decline of Organized Labor in the United States* (Chicago: University of Chicago Press, 1989), 215.

95. Chad Montrie, *The Myth of Silent Spring: Rethinking the Origins of American Environmentalism* (Oakland: University of California Press, 2018), 157.

96. "Beaumont, TX," *Los Angeles Times,* September 29, 1991, D10; Diane Jennings, "Texas Slowly Emerges from Wreckage of Bust," *McAllen (TX) Monitor,* August 15, 1993, 23G.

97. Sharon Lerner, "A Legacy of Environmental Racism," *Intercept,* August 13, 2017, the intercept.com/2017/08/13/exxon-mobil-is-still-pumping-toxins-into-black-community-in
-texas-17-years-after-civil-rights-complaint.

98. Thomas J. Sugrue, *The Origins of the Urban Crisis: Race and Inequality in Postwar Detroit* (Princeton, NJ: Princeton University Press, 1996); Kevin Kruse, *White Flight: Atlanta and the Making of Modern Conservatism* (Princeton, NJ: Princeton University Press, 2005); Ira Katznelson, *When Affirmative Action Was White: An Untold History of Racial Inequality in Twentieth Century America* (New York: Norton, 2005); Douglas S. Massey and Nancy A. Denton, *American Apartheid: Segregation and the Making of the Underclass* (Cambridge, MA: Harvard University Press, 1993).

99. Atkinson, "Bad Air Days." See also "Texas Partners for Environmental Justice," *National Outlook,* Winter 1998; and for a more recent assessment, John D. Prochaska, Alexandra B. Nolen, Hilton Kelley, Ken Sexton, Stephen H. Linder, and John Sullivan, "Social Determinants of Health in Environmental Justice Communities: Examining Cumulative Risk in Terms of Environmental Exposures and Social Determinants of Health," *Human and Ecological Risk Assessment* 204, no. 4 (2014): 980–994.

100. Sam H. Verhovek, "One Man's Arrival in Town Exposes a Racial Fault Line," *New York Times,* February 27, 1993, nytimes.com/1993/02/27/us/one-man-s-arrival-in-town-exposes
-a-racial-fault-line.html?pagewanted=all.

Chapter 4: Texas Time

1. The chapter epigraph is taken from "A History of Violence / Present-Day," from Jimmie Shaw, oral history interview by Jasmin Howard, July 22, 2016, Conroe, Texas, Civil Rights in Black and Brown Interview Database [hereafter cited as CRBB Interview Database], crbb.tcu.edu/clips/conroe-tx-a-history-of-violence-present-day.

2. US Census Bureau. In 1950, Conroe's population was 7,313 and Houston's was 594,321 (April 1, preliminary estimates, www2.census.gov/library/publications/decennial/1950/pc-02/pc-2-43.pdf). In 1990, Conroe's population was 27,610 and Houston's was 1,630,553. Montgomery County's population increased from 24,504 in 1950 to 182,201 in 1990 (www2.census.gov/library/publications/decennial/1990/cp-1/cp-1-45-1.pdf).

3. Lucille Clifton, "why some people be mad at me sometimes," in *Next: New Poems*, (Brockport, NY: BOA Editions, 1987), 20; Erika E. Durham, "Desegregation Came Quietly to Area," *Houston Chronicle*, January 18, 2003.

4. Bellville is the county seat of Austin County and has a population of just above four thousand; see US Census Bureau, data.census.gov/cedsci/all?q=bellville%20tx; "City of Bellville, Texas," cityofbellville.com.

5. Lynn Garner and Jim Carlton, "Schools at Conroe, Bellville Beef Up Security after Murder," *Houston Chronicle*, August 26, 1980.

6. "Conroe Police Hunting Killer of Teen," *Houston Post*, August 27, 1980.

7. "Custodian Held in Rape-Slaying of Bellville Girl," *Houston Chronicle*, August 30, 1980; Nick Davies, *White Lies: Rape, Murder, and Justice Texas Style* (New York: Pantheon, 1991), 5. *White Lies* examines in detail the Clarence Brandley case and the history of racialized violence in Montgomery County.

8. Garner and Carlton, "Schools at Conroe, Bellville Beef Up Security."

9. "Custodian Held in Rape-Slaying."

10. "Community Law Enforcement in Conroe," from Mary Tolbert, oral history interview by Jasmin Howard, July 22, 2016, Conroe, Texas, CRBB Interview Database, crbb.tcu.edu/clips/community-law-enforcement-in-conroe.

11. Stephen Johnson, "Coalition, Kin Ask for Brandley's Exoneration," *Houston Chronicle*, March 27, 1987.

12. Peter Applebome, "The Truth Is Also on Trial in a Texas Death Row Case," *New York Times*, October 4, 1987.

13. "A History of Violence / Present-Day," from Shaw interview.

14. Cathy Gordon, "Judge Declares Mistrial in Murder Trial of Janitor," *Houston Chronicle*, December 14, 1980.

15. "Helping to Free Clarence Brandley," from Jew Don Boney, oral history interview by Samantha Rodriguez and Sandra Enríquez, July 27, 2016, Houston, CRBB Interview Database, crbb.tcu.edu/clips/2716/helping-to-free-clarence-brandley; "Clarence Brandley Case," from Johnella Franklin, oral history interview by Jasmin Howard, July 18, 2016, Houston, CRBB Interview Database, crbb.tcu.edu/clips/6368/clarence-brandley-case; Peter Applebome, "7 Years Later, Hope for Texas Death Row Inmate, *New York Times*, March 22, 1987; Johnson, "Coalition, Kin Ask for Brandley's Exoneration"; Applebome, "Truth Is Also on Trial"; Peter Applebome, "New Trial Urged for Texas Man on Death Row," *New York Times*, October 10, 1987; Lisa Belkin, "Texas Court, 6–3, Overturns Murder Conviction of Black," *New York Times*, December 14, 1989; "Chronology of the Clarence Lee Brandley case," *Houston Chronicle*, December 14, 1989; Patti Muck, "Victim's Family Decries Brandley Decision," *Houston Chronicle*, October 2, 1990; Jo Ann Zuniga, "Boney Asks Indictment of 2 White Ex-Janitors," *Houston Chronicle*, October 3, 1990; "Brandley Case Closed, but Furor Rages—Few Minds Changed with Dismissal," *Houston Chronicle*, October 7, 1990; John Makeig, "Dismissal of Murder Charges Clears Brandley from Retrial," *Houston Chronicle*, October 9, 1990; Mandy Oaklander, "Clarence Brandley: Demanded, Denied Compensation for Decade on Death Row," *Houston Press*, May 19, 2011; Keri Blakinger, "Wrongfully Convicted Ex-Death Row Inmate Clarence Brandley Dies,

Months after DA Reopens Case," *Houston Chronicle*, September 12, 2018; Michael Hall, "'He Never Got an Apology': Death Row Exoneree Clarence Brandley Dies at 66," *Texas Monthly*, September 10, 2018.

16. Cathy Gordon, "March Seeks New Trial for Conroe Man," *Houston Chronicle*, February 7, 1987; Gordon, "Supporters Pledge They'll Face Jail in Order to Free Death Row Inmate," *Houston Chronicle*, March 14, 1987; Paul McKay, "Brandley's Supporters Give Teamwork Credit," *Houston Chronicle*, January 28, 1990.

17. Cathy Gordon, "Charges of Racism Echo as Black Man's Execution Date Nears," *Houston Chronicle*, March 8, 1987.

18. Gordon, "Supporters Pledge They'll Face Jail"; Benjamin F. Chavis Jr., "Capital Punishment—Texas Style," *Atlanta Daily World*, November 17, 1987.

19. "In Remembrance of King—Texans Wish King Happy Birthday—Leader's Dream Commemorated," *Houston Chronicle*, January 16, 1990.

20. "Rallying for Justice," *Houston Chronicle*, April 2, 1988; "What We Did to Help Free Clarence Brandley," from Boney interview, crbb.tcu.edu/clips/2717/what-we-did-to -help-free-clarence-brandley.

21. "Youth Shot by Detective," *Longview (TX) News-Journal*, December 25, 1973; "Youth Killed in Police Station," *Abilene (TX) Reporter-News*, December 26, 1973; "Officer Indicted in Shooting Death," *Brownwood (TX) Bulletin*, January 13, 1974.

22. "Community Law Enforcement in Conroe," from Tolbert interview; "Police Shooting of Gregory Allen Steele," from Franklin interview, crbb.tcu.edu/clips/police-shooting-of -gregory-allen-steele; "History of Discrimination, the KKK, and Black Representation in Conroe," from Carl White and Gloria White, oral history interview by Jasmin Howard, July 7, 2016, Conroe, Texas, CRBB Interview Database, crbb.tcu.edu/clips/history-of-discrimination -the-KKK-and-black-representation-in-conroe; "The Reputation of Conroe, TX," from Charles Lee and Toddrick Proctor, oral history interview by Meredith May, July 21, 2016, Tamina, Texas, CRBB Interview Database, crbb.tcu.edu/clips/the-reputation-of-conroe-tx.

23. "The Reputation of Conroe, TX," from Lee and Proctor interview.

24. "Conroe Policeman Acquitted," *San Jacinto (TX) News-Times*, August 1, 1974.

25. "Mother of Victim Files Suit," *Austin American-Statesman*, May 13, 1975; "Parents Collect $65,000," *Port Arthur (TX) News*, July 8, 1977.

26. Paul McKay, "Conroe Council Votes to Settle Ex-Chief's Suit against Firing," *Houston Chronicle*, September 12, 1989; David Cannella, "A Trail Hounded by Trouble," *Arizona Republic* (Phoenix), June 10, 1984.

27. "Police Shooting of Gregory Allen Steele," from Franklin interview.

28. Ibid.

29. "Clip Two," from Dorothy Reece, oral history interview by Jasmin Howard and Meredith May, July 18, 2016, Conroe, Texas, CRBB Interview, Portal to Texas History, University of North Texas Libraries, texashistory.unt.edu/ark:/67531/metapth984013.

30. "Police and Community Relationship," from Lee and Proctor interview, crbb.tcu.edu /clips/3141/police-and-community-relationship.

31. Jay R. Jordan, "Larry Evans Sr. Was a Stern, yet Caring Conroe Police Chief," *Courier of Montgomery County* (Conroe, TX), November 6, 2017; Sondra Hernandez, "Documentary Chronicles History of Conroe's Black Community," *Courier of Montgomery County*, January 8, 2021.

32. "Community Law Enforcement in Conroe, Part Two," from Tolbert interview, crbb .tcu.edu/clips/community-law-enforcement-in-conroe-part-2.

33. "Becoming a Police Officer," "Gender Discrimination in the Sheriffs Department," and "Facing Discrimination in the Sheriffs Department," from Tolbert interview, crbb.tcu.edu/clips /3974/becoming-a-police-officer, crbb.tcu.edu/clips/3977/gender-and-race-discrimination-in -the-sheriffs-department, crbb.tcu.edu/clips/3975/facing-discrimination-in-the-sheriffs-depart ment.

34. "Family Members' Experiences and Discrimination in Law Enforcement" and "Gender

Discrimination in the Sheriffs Department, Part Two," from Tolbert interview, crbb.tcu.edu
/clips/3979/family-members-experiences-and-discrimination-in-law-enforcement, crbb.tcu
.edu/clips/3978/gender-discrimination-in-the-sheriffs-department-part-2.

35. Cathy Gordon, "Some Say Conroe Is Racist, and Some Say It Isn't," *Houston Chronicle*, October 11, 1987.

36. "Clip Two," from Reece interview.

37. *Crisis* 25, no. 1 (1922): 37.

38. "Two Negroes Lynched for Attacks on Girls," *New York Times*, May 21, 1922.

39. "Clip Two," from Reece interview.

40. "Federal Probe Asked in Bob White Killing," *Crisis* 48, No. 7 (1941): 230.

41. "Conference Resolutions," *Crisis* 48, no. 9 (1941): 296.

42. Nick Davies, "The Town That Loved Lynching," *Scotsman* (Edinburgh), April 10, 1989.

43. Cindy Horswell, "Badge of Early Montgomery County Sheriff Joins Collection," *Houston Chronicle*, August 24, 2015.

44. Davies, "Town That Loved Lynching"; Michael Rinehart, "Lynchings in Conroe," bishopmike.com/2019/04/14/lynchings-in-conroe; National Memorial for Peace and Justice; "Lynching in Texas," Sam Houston State University, lynchingintexas.org.

45. "Civil Rights Movement, Protesting, and Racism, Part One" and "Civil Rights Movement, Protesting, and Racism, Part Two," from Henry Calyen, oral history interview by Jasmin Howard, July 6, 2016, Conroe, Texas, CRBB Interview Database, crbb.tcu.edu/clips/civil-rights-movement -protesting-and-racism, crbb.tcu.edu/clips/3501/civil-rights-movement-protesting-and-racism -part-two.

46. "Officers Report Efforts [to] Identify Mob Unsuccessful," *Corsicana (TX) Daily Sun*, February 3, 1927.

47. Davies, "Town That Loved Lynching." The following accounts of the killing of Jackson are available from the "Lynching in Texas" project, lynchingintexas.org: "Judge Lynch," *Fort Worth Daily Gazette*, December 19, 1885; "Jackson Lynched," *Galveston Daily News*, December 20, 1885; "Lynched in Broad Daylight," *New York Times*, December 21, 1885.

48. "The Reputation of Conroe, TX," from Lee and Proctor interview.

49. The following accounts of the killing of Lewis are available from the "Lynching in Texas" project: "An 18 Year Old Negro Boy Pays Penalty to Mob," *Marshall (TX) News Messenger*, June 24, 1922; "Negro, Admits Attack on White Girl, Hanged," *Evening Star* (Washington, DC), June 24, 1922; "New Dacus Quiet after Lynching of Young Negro," *Victoria (TX) Advocate*, June 25, 1922.

50. "Jackson Lynched."

51. "Importance of Booker T. Washington School, Conroe, TX and Race Relations Growing Up," from Franklin interview, crbb.tcu.edu/clips/importance-of-booker-t-washington-school -conroe-tx-and-race-relations-growing-up; "Segregation and Discrimination Experiences," from Lee and Proctor interview, crbb.tcu.edu/clips/segregation-and-discrimination-experiences; "Clip Two," from Reece interview.

52. Brad Meyer, "Montgomery County Courthouse a Centerpiece of Downtown Conroe," *Courier of Montgomery County* (Conroe, TX), April 26, 2017; Texas Historical Marker number 17660, "Montgomery County Courthouses," Historical Marker Database, hmdb.org/m .asp?m=117350.

53. "Early Memories of Segregation," from Tolbert interview, crbb.tcu.edu/clips/early-memo ries-of-segregation.

54. "Segregation and Discrimination Experiences," from Lee and Proctor interview.

55. "Community Relations between Blacks and Whites," from Tolbert interview, crbb.tcu .edu/clips/3984/community-relations-between-blacks-and-whites; "Clip Two," from Wanda Harris, oral history interview by Jasmin Howard and Meredith May, July 26, 2016, Conroe, Texas, CRBB Interview, Portal to Texas History, University of North Texas Libraries, texas history.unt.edu/ark:/67531/metapth983137.

56. "Conroe KKK Rally Draws about 200," *Galveston Daily News*, February 20, 1993; "The Klan and the Confederate Flag in Conroe," from Tolbert interview, crbb.tcu.edu/clips/3986 /the-klan-and-the-confederate-flag-in-conroe.

57. "Segregation and Discrimination Experiences," from Lee and Proctor interview.

58. Paul McKay, "Racial Tension Troubles School—Principal at Conroe High Takes Steps to Bolster Security," *Houston Chronicle*, January 27, 1993; McKay, "Anti-racist Zeal Criticized—Conroe High Students Fight Rules on Dress," *Houston Chronicle*, January 28, 1993; "Conroe High Beefs Up Security amid Growing Racial Tension," *Dallas Morning News*, January 28, 1993.

59. "The Klan and the Confederate Flag in Conroe," from Tolbert interview.

60. Craig Malisow, "Fueling the Ire," *Houston Press*, November 14, 2002; White Camelia Knights of the Ku Klux Klan, wcKKKk.org.

61. Joy Ann Williamson, "Black Colleges and Civil Rights: Organizing and Mobilizing in Jackson, Mississippi," in *Higher Education and the Civil Rights Movement: White Supremacy, Black Southerners, and College Campuses*, ed. Peter Wallenstein (Gainesville: University Press of Florida, 2008), 116.

62. Royal College, founded in 1927, was another historically Black educational institution in Conroe; see the following articles from the *Courier of Montgomery County* (Conroe, TX): Robin Montgomery, "Royal College: Conroe's Historic Treasure," October 31, 2013; Montgomery, "Conroe Normal & Industrial College: A Quest for Intelligence and Virtue," September 26, 2018; Brad Meyer, "Conroe Normal & Industrial College Advanced Education for African Americans," November 10, 2013; Sondra Hernandez, "Longtime Educator Lucille Bradley Took Pride in Conroe's Evolution," February 1, 2019. See also Gordon, "Charges of Racism Echo"; "March in Conroe in 1968," from Calvin Vinson, oral history interview by Meredith May, July 26, 2016, Conroe, Texas, CRBB Interview Database, crbb .tcu.edu/clips/5024/march-in-conroe-in-1968.

63. Maggie Galehouse, "Pulitzer-Winner Works to Open Race Dialogue," *Houston Chronicle*, October 18, 2009; Annette Gordon-Reed, "A Childhood Obsession Blossoms into a Life of Lives," "Origin Stories," Pulitzer Prizes, pulitzer.org/article/childhood-obsession-blossoms-life -lives; Colleen Walsh, "Annette Gordon-Reed's Personal History, from East Texas to Monticello," *Harvard Gazette*, May 2, 2017; "Clip Five," from Reece Interview.

64. Douglas Martin, "William Wayne Justice, Judge Who Remade Texas, Dies at 89," *New York Times*, October 15, 2009.

65. "Integration in Montgomery and Conroe" and "High School Experiences," from Tommy Wilkerson, oral history interview by Meredith May, July 19, 2016, Conroe, Texas, CRBB Interview Database, crbb.tcu.edu/clips/4997/integration-in-montgomery-and-conroe, crbb.tcu.edu/clips/4998/high-school-experiences-4; "Memories from High School and of Conroe," from August Lastrappe, oral history interview by Meredith May, July 21, 2016, Spring, Texas, CRBB Interview Database, crbb.tcu.edu/clips/6831/memories-from-high-school -and-of-conroe; "School Experience, Integration, Football" and "Segregation and Integration," from Vinson interview, crbb.tcu.edu/clips/5050/school-experience-integration-football, crbb.tcu.edu/clips/5021/segregation-and-integration-part-1; "Sports / Early Integration" and "Extracurricular Activities—Tokenism and Discrimination," from Jimmy Johnson, oral history interview with Meredith May, July 20, 2016, Conroe, CRBB, crbb.tcu.edu/clips /6777/sports-early-integration, crbb.tcu.edu/clips/6778/extracurricular-activities-tokenism -and-discrimination; "High School Riot," from White and White interview, crbb.tcu.edu /clips/3995/high-school-riot; "School Desegregation in Conroe Part One," "School Desegregation in Conroe Part Two," "School Desegregation in Conroe Part Three," and "School Desegregation in Conroe Part Four," from Franklin interview, crbb.tcu.edu/clips/6325 /school-desegregation-in-conroe-part-one, crbb.tcu.edu/clips/6342/school-desegregation-in -conroe-part-two, crbb.tcu.edu/clips/6344/school-desegregation-in-conroe-part-three, crbb.tcu .edu/clips/6352/school-desegregation-in-conroe-part-four.

66. "Clip Three," "Clip Four," and "Clip Six" from Reece interview.

67. "Clip Five" and "Clip Six" from Reece interview; Kimberly Sutton, "50 Years Later, Two Conroe Football Teams Recognized," *Houston Chronicle*, September 4, 2014; "High School Experiences," "Past Work and High School Sports, Part One," and "Past Work and High School Sports, Part Two," from Calyen interview, crbb.tcu.edu/clips/3401/high-school -experiences-2, crbb.tcu.edu/clips/3410/past-work-and-high-school-sports, crbb.tcu.edu/clips

/3502/past-work-and-high-school-sports-part-two; "Importance of Booker T. Washington School, Conroe, TX and Race Relations Growing Up," from Franklin interview.

68. "The Reputation of Conroe, TX," from Lee and Proctor interview; "March in Conroe in 1968," from Vinson interview; "Student Activism," from Calyen, interview, crbb.tcu.edu/clips/3412/student-activism-2.

69. "School Desegregation in Conroe, Part Four," from Franklin interview; "School Experience, Integration, Football," from Vinson interview.

70. David Barron, "Sports Highlight: High School Football—Controversy in Conroe," *Houston Chronicle*, August 18, 1991; Lee Hancock, "In Cheerleading, Rifts Become Routine," *Dallas Morning News*, September 15, 1991; McKay, "Racial Tension Troubles School"; Paul McKay, "Gridders Penalized for Boycott—6 Conroe High Blacks out for '91," *Houston Chronicle*, August 13, 1991; "The Reputation of Conroe, TX," from Lee and Proctor interview.

71. "Voting and Voter Registration / Preserving History in Montgomery County," from White and White interview, crbb.tcu.edu/clips/4006/voting-and-voter-registration-preserving-history-in-montgomery-county; "Sharing Black History," from Alpha Omega (Faye) Jones, oral history interview by Jasmin Howard, July 12, 2016, Conroe, Texas, CRBB Interview Database, crbb.tcu.edu/clips/6408/sharing-black-history; "Clip Six" and "Clip Seven," from Reece interview; Hernandez, "Documentary Chronicles History of Conroe's Black Community."

72. Montgomery, "Conroe Normal & Industrial College"; Meyer, "Conroe Normal & Industrial College"; "March in Conroe in 1968," from Vinson interview.

73. Kelly Schafler, "Conroe ISD Discusses Future Transition for Booker T. Washington Junior High School," *Community Impact Newspaper* (Conroe/Montgomery), September 20, 2018; "Renaming School after Booker T. Washington," from Vinson interview, crbb.tcu.edu/clips/5049/renaming-school-after-booker-t-washington; "Sharing Black History," from Jones interview, crbb.tcu.edu/clips/6408/sharing-black-history.

74. See the following articles from the *Courier of Montgomery County* (Conroe, TX): Kimberly Sutton, "Beloved Conroe Teacher, Leader Dies at 100," January 13, 2014; Nora Olabi, "Conroe ISD Honors Lucille Bradley with School Name," September 20, 2016; Sondra Hernandez, "Longtime Educator Lucille Bradley Took Pride in Conroe's Evolution," February 1, 2019.

75. Sondra Hernandez, "Educator Froncell Reece Remembered for His Determination, Personable Nature," *Courier of Montgomery County* (Conroe, TX), August 1, 2017; Hernandez, "Statue Unveiled for Pulitzer Prize Winner and Conroe High Graduate," *Courier of Montgomery County*, February 15, 2019.

76. Megan Ellsworth, "Conroe's Black History Month Parade to Change Name to Honor the Late Leon Tolbert, Jr.," *Courier of Montgomery County* (Conroe, TX), February 6, 2020.

77. Meagan Ellsworth, "Legendary Coach Charles Brown Honored as Grand Marshal of J-MAC Black History Month Parade in Conroe," *Courier of Montgomery County* (Conroe, TX), February 9, 2019; Gordon, "Charges of Racism Echo."

78. "Controversy over Naming a Conroe Street after MLK," from Vinson interview, crbb.tcu.edu/clips/5048/controversy-over-naming-a-conroe-street-after-mlk.

79. Kidada E. Williams, *They Left Great Marks on Me: African American Testimonies of Racial Violence from Emancipation to World War I* (New York: New York University Press, 2012), 3.

80. Marti Corn, *The Ground on Which I Stand: Tamina, a Freedmen's Town*, 2nd ed. (College Station: Texas A&M University Press, 2019); "Marti Corn," marticorn.com/marticorn.

81. "The History of Tamina," from Warzell Booty and James Leveston, oral history interview by Meredith May, July 7, 2016, Tamina, Texas, CRBB Interview Database, crbb.tcu.edu/clips/the-history-of-tamina.

82. Sondra Hernandez, "Freedmen's Town Tamina Rich in History, Family Tradition," *Courier of Montgomery County* (Conroe, TX), August 8, 2017.

83. Thad Sitton and James H. Conrad, *Freedom Colonies: Independent Black Texans in the Time of Jim Crow* (Austin: University of Texas Press, 2005), 1.

84. Ibid., 171–189.

85. "Growing Up in Tamina, TX," "Moving to Tamina," "The History of Tamina," "Ownership Worked in Tamina," and "Hopes for The Community," from Booty and Leveston inter-

view, crbb.tcu.edu/clips/2647/growing-up-in-tamina-tx, crbb.tcu.edu/clips/2648/moving -to-tamina, crbb.tcu.edu/clips/2651/ownership-worked-in-tamina, crbb.tcu.edu/clips/2668 /hopes-for-the-community.

86. Marie Leonard, "Tamina Community Faces Challenges as Area Expands," *Community Impact Newspaper* (Conroe/Montgomery), December 9, 2015; "The Water Problem" and "Getting Involved with the Water Corporation," from Booty and Leveston interview, crbb .tcu.edu/clips/the-water-problem, crbb.tcu.edu/clips/getting-involved-with-the-water-corpora tion.

87. "Getting Involved with the Water Corporation," from Booty and Leveston interview; Leonard, "Tamina Community Faces Challenges."

88. Leonard, "Tamina Community Faces Challenges."

89. Mike Snyder, "Tamina Fighting for Its Survival; Unable to Obtain Sewage Service, Freedmen's Town Faces a Slow Death," *Houston Chronicle*, December 23, 2018; Matthew Tresaugue, "Tamina—Town Can't Seem to Get Its Share of Progress," *Houston Chronicle*, November 19, 2015.

90. "Ownership Worked in Tamina," from Booty and Leveston interview.

91. Robin Montgomery, "Rita Wiltz Is Volunteer Extraordinaire with Literacy Efforts," *Courier of Montgomery County* (Conroe, TX), January 8, 2013; Hernandez, "Freedmen's Town Tamina Rich in History."

92. Cindy George, John D. Harden and Brooke A. Lewis, "Family 'Risked It All' to Save Kids Killed in Fire," *Houston Chronicle*, May 13, 2017.

93. Meagan Ellsworth, "Tamina Cemetery Project Gains Momentum," *Courier of Montgomery County* (Conroe, TX), May 19, 2018; Ellsworth, "BBQ, Fish Fry Fundraiser to Save Tamina Cemetery Set for June 30," *East Montgomery County Observer* (Conroe, TX), June 13, 2018.

94. "Tamina Is an Original Settlement of African Americans Settled Shortly after the Civil War," available from the Internet Archive, web.archive.org/web/20180809115406/http: //taminatexas.org.

95. Ian Menzies, "A Texas Oilman Takes on America's Urban Congestion," *Boston Globe*, November 16, 1975.

96. Roger Galatas, *The Woodlands: The Inside Story of Creating a Better Hometown*, with James Barlow (Washington, DC: Urban Land Institute, 2004), 115–119.

97. US Census Bureau, QuickFacts, "The Woodlands CDP, Texas," census.gov/quick facts/fact/table/thewoodlandscdptexas/INC110219; QuickFacts, "Houston city, Texas," census .gov/quickfacts/fact/table/houstoncitytexas/PST120219.

98. Robert Downen, "Parents Fear for Daughter's Safety due to Threatening Messages," *Houston Chronicle*, October 11, 2017.

99. John S. Marshall, "Woodlands' Head Clarifies Confederate Statue Remark," *Houston Chronicle*, September 22, 2017.

100. "Facing Discrimination in the Sheriffs Department, Part Two" and "Gender Discrimination in the Sheriffs Department," from Tolbert interview, crbb.tcu.edu/clips/3976/facing -discrimination-in-the-sheriffs-department-part-2, crbb.tcu.edu/clips/3977/gender-and-race -discrimination-in-the-sheriffs-department.

101. Associated Press, "The Fastest-Growing U.S. Cities Are in the South; Four of the Top Five Are in Texas," *Los Angeles Times*, May 15, 2017.

102. US Census Bureau, "ACS Demographic and Housing Estimates," "Conroe city, Texas," data.census.gov/cedsci/table?g=0400000US48_1600000US4816432&d=ACS%20 5-Year%20Estimates%20Data%20Profiles&tid=ACSDP5Y2017.DP05; "Montgomery County, Texas," data.census.gov/cedsci/table?g=0400000US48_0500000US48339&d=ACS%205 -Year%20Estimates%20Data%20Profiles&tid=ACSDP5Y2017.DP05.

103. Lindsay Peyton, "Woodlands Business Groups Focus on Latino Growth in Region," *Houston Chronicle*, May 6, 2015.

104. Kelly Schafler, "Racial Discrimination in The Woodlands Concerns Residents, Board," *Houston Chronicle*, March 30, 2017.

105. Bridget Balch, "Hispanic Population in The Woodlands Continues to Grow," *Houston Chronicle*, June 23, 2015.

106. Schafler, "Racial Discrimination in The Woodlands"; J. K. Nickell, "The New—and Rich—Immigrants from Mexico: How Their Money Is Changing Texas," *Houston Chronicle*, January 14, 2013.

107. Click2Houston.com Staff, Samantha Ptashkin, Jennifer Bauer, "2 People Arrested at Donald Trump's Rally in The Woodlands," Click2Houston/KPRC2, June 20, 2016, click2houston.com/news/2016/06/20/2-people-arrested-at-donald-trumps-rally-in-the-woodlands.

108. Christopher Hooks, "Trump's Bigotry Is a Drug to Texas Republicans," *Rolling Stone*, July 21, 2016.

109. Schafler, "Racial Discrimination in The Woodlands."

110. "Demographic Shifts and Addressing Change," "Latino Outreach in Montgomery," "Building Connections Between Communities," and "Factoring in History and White Flight," from Maria Banos Jordan, oral history interview by Jasmin Howard, July 31, 2016, Houston, CRBB Interview Database, crbb.tcu.edu/clips/3384/demographic-shifts-and-addressing-change, crbb.tcu.edu/clips/3383/latino-outreach-in-montgomery, crbb.tcu.edu/clips/3385/building-connections-between-communities, crbb.tcu.edu/clips/3387/factoring-in-history-and-white-flight.

111. "Mexican American Experience in Texas," from Jordan interview, crbb.tcu.edu/clips/3389/mexican-american-experience-in-texas.

112. "A History of Violence / Present-Day," from Shaw interview.

113. "Changes in Conroe: 'It's really hard for me to dream,'" from Franklin interview, crbb.tcu.edu/clips/6369/changes-in-conroe-it-s-really-hard-for-me-to-dream.

114. "Ownership Worked in Tamina," from Booty and Leveston interview.

115. "African American Political Representation," from Vinson interview, crbb.tcu.edu/clips/5042/african-american-political-representation; "Social and Political Change, Part Two," from Jordan interview, crbb.tcu.edu/clips/3382/social-and-political-change-part-2.

Chapter 5: The South-by-Southwest Borderlands' Chicana/o Uprising

1. Andrés Tijerina, *A History of the Mexican-Americans in Lubbock County, Texas*, Graduate Studies 18 (Lubbock: Texas Tech University Press, 1979), 17–28; "The Brown Berets," from Gilbert Herrera, oral history interview by Joel Zapata, July 1, 2016, Lubbock, Texas, Civil Rights in Black and Brown Interview Database [hereafter cited as CRBB Interview Database], crbb.tcu.edu/clips/7418/the-brown-berets-2; "Discrimination and Schooling in Lubbock" and "Teaching as a Profession," from Anita Carmona-Harrison, oral history interview by Joel Zapata, June 24, 2016, Lubbock, Texas, CRBB Interview Database, crbb.tcu.edu/ clips/6412/discrimination-and-schooling-in-lubbock, crbb.tcu.edu/clips/6418/teaching-as-a-profession; "Segregation in Lubbock," from Jon Holmes, oral history interview by Karen Wisely and Joel Zapata, June 13, 2016, Lubbock, Texas, CRBB Interview Database, crbb.tcu.edu/ clips/6916/segregation-in-lubbock; "Race Relations in Amarillo," from Iris Lawrence, oral history interview by Karen Wisely, June 22, 2016, Amarillo, Texas, CRBB Interview Database, crbb.tcu.edu/ clips/4274/race-relations-in-amarillo; Anita Carmona-Harrison, interview by Daniel U. Sánchez, October 8, 2009, Southwest Collection / Special Collections Library, Texas Tech University, Lubbock; Rosalie Gomez, interview by David Zepeda, October 19, 1976, Southwest Collection / Special Collections Library, Texas Tech University, Lubbock; Mario García, interview by David Zepeda, November 15, 1976, Southwest Collection / Special Collections Library, Texas Tech University, Lubbock. John Weber has documented how the segregation and social immobility that Mexicans faced in Texas and across the nation "was largely borrowed from the Jim Crow South"; see Weber, *From South Texas to the Nation: The Exploitation of Mexican Labor in the Twentieth Century* (Chapel Hill: University of North Carolina Press, 2015), 7–10.

2. Raymond Flores, interview by Daniel U. Sánchez, December 8, 2000, Southwest Collection / Special Collections Library, Texas Tech University, Lubbock.

3. Zanto Peabody, "Lubbock Families Sue City over Missing Graves," *Houston Chronicle*, July 11, 2004, accessed March 13, 2019, chron.com/news/houston-texas/article/Lubbock -families-sue-city-over-missing-graves-1489918.php; Emily Pyle, "Dateline Lubbock; Oh, Bury Me Not," *Texas Observer*, December 17, 2004, accessed March 1, 2019, texasobserver .org/1833-dateline-lubbock-oh-bury-me-not.

4. Neil Foley, *The White Scourge: Mexicans, Blacks, and Poor Whites in Texas Cotton Culture* (Berkeley: University of California Press, 1997), 2–3, 186–190; Jeff Roche, "Identity and Conservative Politics on the Southern Plains," in *The Future of the Southern Plains*, ed. Sherry L. Smith (Norman: University of Oklahoma Press, 2003), 183–189; Weber, *From South Texas to the Nation*, 7–10.

5. Carlos Muñoz, *Youth, Identity, Power: The Chicano Movement*, rev. ed (1989; New York: Verso, 2017), 87.

6. "Student Activism," from Nephtalí De León, oral history interview by Joel Zapata, December 15, 2016, CRBB Interview Database, crbb.tcu.edu/clips/7799/student-activism; Nephtalí De León, interview by José Ángel Gutiérrez, November 20, 1999, Tejano Voices, University of Texas at Arlington Libraries Special Collections, library.uta.edu/tejanovoices /interview.php?cmasno=068; Nephtalí De León, interview by Daniel Urbina Sánchez, October 18, 2013, San Antonio, Texas, Hispanic Interview Project, transcript, 8, Southwest Collection / Special Collections Library, Texas Tech University, Lubbock; Yolanda G. Romero, "The Mexican American Frontier Experience in Twentieth-Century Northwest Texas" (PhD diss., Texas Tech University, 1993), 144; "Boycott in Abilene Schools Continues," *Odessa (TX) American*, October 29, 1969; "Abilene School Boycott Grows," *Corsicana (TX) Daily Sun*, October 19, 1969; "Chicanos Still Boycott Abilene Schools, Plan Rump Classes," *Amarillo (TX) Globe-Times*, October 29, 1969; Jim Donovan, "Mexican-American Parents Vote to Continue Boycott," *Abilene (TX) Reporter-News*, October 31, 1969; Joel Zapata, "Taking Chicana/o Activist History to the Public: Chicana/o Activism in the Southern Plains through Time and Space," *Great Plains Quarterly* 38, no. 4 (2018): 407–424; "Interactive Map and Timeline," Chicano Activism in the Southern Plains through Time and Space, plainsmovement.com/neatline/show/interactive-map -and-timeline; Arnoldo De León, "Blowout 1910 Style: A Chicano School Boycott in West Texas," *Texana* 12 (1974): 131–132.

7. Romero, "Mexican American Frontier Experience," 144–145; "Pro-Rivera Faction Asks UTEP Strike," *El Paso Herald-Post*, November 27, 1972; "Protestors Rounded Up at UTEP," *El Paso Herald-Post*, December 7, 1972.

8. Arnoldo De León, *San Angeleños: Mexican Americans in San Angelo, Texas* (San Angelo: Fort Concho Museum Press, 1985), 98–110; Tijerina, *Mexican-Americans in Lubbock County*, 67; "Shooting Case: Group to Picket Police Station before Meeting," *Lubbock (TX) Avalanche-Journal*, August 17, 1971; "'Grievance' Group Airs Nerios Case," *Lubbock (TX) Avalanche-Journal*, August 18, 1971; "LULAC Criticizes Agency Chosen to Probe Shooting," *Abilene (TX) Reporter-News*, November 20, 1977; "Shooting Victim's Family Meets with Latin Group," *Abilene (TX) Reporter-News*, October 6, 1977; "Mexican-Americans Protest Killing," *Town Talk* (Alexandria, LA), July 16, 1978; "Defense Urged by Brown Berets," *Longview (TX) News-Journal*, July 15, 1978; "Deaths Unify Hispanics," *Longview (TX) News-Journal*, July 16, 1978.

9. "Result of Lozano Case," Nick Hernandez, oral history interview by Joel Zapata, July 8, 2016, Odessa, Texas, CRBB Interview Database, crbb.tcu.edu/clips/2998/result-of-lozano-case.

10. "Shooting Case: Group to Picket Police Station."

11. Ibid.; Nephtalí De León, *Chicanos: Our Background and Our Pride* (Lubbock, TX: Trucha, 1972), 67; Tijerina, *Mexican-Americans in Lubbock County*, 66; the following articles from the *Lubbock (TX) Avalanche-Journal*: Bill Morgan, "Companion Held: City Man Slain in Police Chase," August 15, 1971; "Robbery Attempt Leads to Charge against Suspect," August 16, 1971; "Homicide 'Justifiable,'" August 18, 1971; "'Grievance' Group Airs Nerios Case"; "Agenda Appearances Eyed: Council Alters Meet Rules after Incident Thursday," September 10, 1971.

12. "Shooting Case: Group to Picket Police Station."

13. Morgan, "Companion Held."

14. Ibid.; "Hale Center Man Arraigned Here," *Lubbock (TX) Avalanche-Journal*, August 17, 1971; Mercedes M. Nerios, "English Version of Mrs. Nerios' Letter," in N. De León, *Chicanos*, 85; N. De León, *Chicanos*, 79.

15. N. De León, *Chicanos*, 79–81.

16. "'Grievance' Group Airs Nerios Case."

17. Ibid.; the following articles from the *Lubbock (TX) Avalanche-Journal*: "Homicide 'Justifiable'"; "Robbery Attempt Leads to Charge"; "Hale Center Man Arraigned Here"; "Pair Indicted," September 15, 1971; "19 Guilty Pleas Made," October 29, 1971.

18. "Shooting Case: Group to Picket Police Station"; "Special Meet of Councilmen, Negroes Slated," *Lubbock (TX) Avalanche-Journal*, June 15, 1971; Virginia Marie Raymond, "Mexican Americans Write toward Justice in Texas, 1973–1982" (PhD diss., University of Texas at Austin, 2007), 186.

19. Julius Amin, "Black Lubbock: 1955 to Present," *West Texas Historical Association Yearbook* 65 (1989): 24; Robert L. Foster and Alwyn Barr, "Black Lubbock," *West Texas Historical Association Yearbook* 54 (1978): 27–30, 109.

20. Amin, "Black Lubbock," 25–26; Foster and Barr, "Black Lubbock," 27–31; "Community, Segregation, Integration," from Sheila Patterson Harris and Rose Wilson, oral history interview by Karen Wisely and Joel Zapata, July 1, 2016, Lubbock, Texas, CRBB Interview Database, crbb .tcu.edu/clips/2888/community-segregation-integration.

21. "Shooting Case: Group to Picket Police Station"; "Special Meet of Councilmen, Negroes."

22. Tijerina, *Mexican-Americans in Lubbock County*, 66; "May 11, 1970 Tornado in Lubbock, TX Part One," and "May 11, 1970 Tornado in Lubbock, TX Part Two," from Carmona-Harrison interview, crbb.tcu.edu/clips/6417/may-11-1970-tornado-in-lubbock-tx-part-one, crbb.tcu .edu/clips/6421/may-11-1970-tornado-in-lubbock-tx-part-two; "Marches and Demonstrations, Part One," from Sheila Patterson Harris and Rose Wilson, oral history interview by Karen Wisely, July 1, 2016, Lubbock, Texas, CRBB Interview Database, crbb.tcu.edu/clips/2891 /marches-and-demonstrations-part-1; N. De León interview by Gutiérrez; Jerry Odom, "Chicano Groups Stage Peaceful March Here," *Lubbock (TX) Avalanche-Journal*, November 8, 1971.

23. "Chicano Groups Stage Peaceful March Here."

24. Raymond, "Mexican Americans Write toward Justice," 186.

25. "Shooting Case: Group to Picket Police Station"; "Special Meet of Councilmen, Negroes."

26. "Council Alters Meet Rules."

27. "City Calm after Three Days of Disturbance-Unrest," *West Texas Times* (Lubbock, TX), September 16, 1971.

28. Amin, "Black Lubbock," 30.

29. "City Calm after Three Days"; "1971 High School Shooting," from Floyd Price, oral history interview by Karen Wisely and Joel Zapata, June 29, 2016, Lubbock, Texas, CRBB Interview Database, crbb.tcu.edu/clips/3134/1971-high-school-shooting.

30. Martin Waldron, "Curfew Lifted in Lubbock, Tex., after 2 Nights of Race Violence," *New York Times*, September 12, 1971; "Shooting Starts City Unrest: Violence Causes Tense Weekend," *University Daily* (Lubbock, TX), September 13, 1971.

31. "City Calm after Three Days."

32. Waldron, "Curfew Lifted in Lubbock"; "Shooting Starts City Unrest"; "City Calm after Three Days"; "1971 High School Shooting," from Price interview. These incidents have been remarkably understudied. I intend to conduct further research on both the protests and the police response.

33. "Ecumenical Council to Act on Issues," *West Texas Times* (Lubbock, TX), September 23, 1971.

34. "Council Alters Meet Rules"; "Homicide 'Justifiable'"; "Robbery Attempt Leads to Charge"; "Hale Center Man Arraigned Here"; "Pair Indicted"; "19 Guilty Pleas Made."

35. N. De León interview by Gutiérrez; "The Brown Berets," from Herrera interview.

36. "The Brown Berets," from Herrera interview.

37. Tijerina, *Mexican-Americans in Lubbock County*, 66; N. De León, *Chicanos*, 70; Zapata, "Taking Chicana/o Activist History," 415–416.

38. Zapata, "Taking Chicana/o Activist History," 415–416.

39. Romero, "Mexican American Frontier Experience," 147.

40. Ibid., 148.

41. N. De León, *Chicanos*, 70.

42. "Chicanos Stage 'Peace March' Here Last Sunday to Protest Grievances," *West Texas Times* (Lubbock, TX), November 11, 1971.

43. Romero, "Mexican American Frontier Experience," 149.

44. Ibid.

45. Ibid., 147–149; N. De León, *Chicanos*, 70; Tijerina, *Mexican-Americans in Lubbock County*, 66; Zapata, "Taking Chicana/o Activist History," 415–416; Raymond, "Mexican Americans Write toward Justice," 186–187; Odom, "Chicano Groups Stage Peaceful March."

46. Nerios, "English Version of Letter," 85.

47. N. De León, *Chicanos*, 70–72.

48. Ibid., 70–72.

49. Ibid.

50. Ibid., 75.

51. "The Brown Berets," from Herrera interview.

52. Odom, "Chicano Groups Stage Peaceful March."

53. Tijerina, *Mexican-Americans in Lubbock County*, 66.

54. N. De León, *Chicanos*, 75.

55. "Shooting Case: Group to Picket Police Station."

56. Tijerina, *Mexican-Americans in Lubbock County*, 66; Romero, "Mexican American Frontier Experience," 149–150; Raymond, "Mexican Americans Write toward Justice," 187; "Citizens Grievance Committee Presents Good Recommendations," *West Texas Times* (Lubbock, TX), September 23, 1971.

57. Tijerina, *Mexican-Americans in Lubbock County*, 66–67; Romero, "Mexican American Frontier Experience," 149–150; Raymond, "Mexican Americans Write toward Justice," 187–189.

58. "The Brown Berets," from Herrera interview.

59. "Citizens Grievance Committee."

60. Ibid.

61. "City Council Appoints 15 Member Human Relations Commission," *West Texas Times* (Lubbock, TX), June 1, 1972.

62. "Marches and Demonstrations, Part One," from Harris and Wilson interview.

63. Ibid.; "Marches and Memory," from Harris and Wilson interview, crbb.tcu.edu /clips/2919/marches-and-memory; "Lucky Twelve Not to March, Christ Temple Offers Choice," *West Texas Times* (Lubbock, TX), September 1978.

64. "Bidal Aguero, *El Editor* and Lubbock Politics, Part One" and "'No Mexicans Allowed' in Lubbock," from Olga Agüero, oral history interview by Karen Wisely and Joel Zapata, June 24, 2016, Lubbock, Texas, CRBB Interview Database, crbb.tcu.edu/clips/6444/bidal-aguero -el-editor-and-lubbock-politics-part-one, crbb.tcu.edu/clips/6452/no-mexicans-allowed-in -lubbock; "Art Book / Race Relations," from N. De León interview, crbb.tcu.edu/clips/7808 /art-book-race-relations.

65. June M. Steele, "Edward Struggs and Mae Simmons: The African American Educators and the Provisions for Black Schools in Lubbock, Texas, 1930–1970," *West Texas Historical Association Yearbook* 77 (2001): 87.

66. "Art Book / Race Relations," from N. De León interview; "Marches and Demonstrations, Part One," from Harris and Wilson interview. For further reading on multiracial civil rights activism, see Max Krochmal, *Blue Texas: The Making of a Multiracial Democratic Coalition in the Civil Rights Movement* (Chapel Hill: University of North Carolina Press, 2016); Maggie Rivas-Rodriguez, *Texas Mexican Americans and Postwar Civil Rights* (Austin: University of Texas Press, 2015), 65–118.

67. Stevie Poole, "Diversity in City Leadership Still a Concern 30 Years Later," *Lubbock (TX) Avalanche-Journal*, September 19, 2014; Amin, "Black Lubbock," 30.

68. "Facts in Prisoner's Shooting Death to Go to Grand Jury," *Abilene (TX) Reporter-News*,

November 8, 1977; "Mexican Prisoner Killed," *Longview (TX) News-Journal*, November 8, 1977; "Rangers Present Review of Shooting," *Abilene (TX) Reporter-News*, November 17, 1977; Raymond, "Mexican Americans Write toward Justice," 138.

69. "Facts in Prisoner's Shooting Death."

70. Ibid.; "Rangers Probe Prisoner Killing," *Burlington (VT) Free Press*, November 8, 1977; "Rangers to Investigate Shooting of Prisoner," *Amarillo (TX) Globe-Times*, November 8, 1977; "Rangers Probe Shooting Death," *Odessa (TX) American*, November 17, 1977.

71. "State Enters Shooting Death Investigation," *Pampa (TX) Daily News*, November 18, 1977; "State Investigating Mexican's Death," *Abilene (TX) Reporter-News*, November 18, 1977.

72. "Rangers Probe Shooting Death"; "Rangers Present Review of Shooting."

73. "Shooting Victim's Family Meets with Latin Group."

74. Ibid.; "LULAC Criticizes Agency."

75. "LULAC Criticizes Agency"; "Shooting Victim's Family Meets with Latin Group."

76. Some news reports later stated that Juan attempted to abduct the woman whose car he had stolen. But those stories appeared in 1978, had the date of the police shooting wrong, at times spelled Tiburcio's name incorrectly, and claimed that he was in his midtwenties. All this suggests such stories were attempts to exaggerate Tiburcio's actions and make him seem like a hardened criminal; see "Brown Berets Tired of Demonstrations," *Valley Morning Star* (Harlingen, TX), February 16, 1978; "Big Spring Officer Quits after Shooting," *Odessa (TX) American*, March 16, 1978; "Big Spring Officer Resigns," *Austin American-Statesman*, March 16, 1978; Raymond, "Mexican Americans Write toward Justice," 138.

77. "Big Spring Officer Resigns"; "UPI Newsbreak," *Galveston Daily News*, February 18, 1978; "Grand Jury Investigates Shooting Death," *Odessa (TX) American*, March 28, 1978; "'No-Bill' Returned in Shooting Case," *Bryan (TX) Eagle*, April 2, 1978; "Big Spring Officer Quits after Shooting."

78. "Shootings Stir Tensions in West Texas Town," *El Paso Times*, March 20, 1978.

79. Robert Montemayor, Allen Pusey, and Dave Montgomery, "Minor Accident Beginning of End for Odessa Inmate," *Dallas Times Herald*, February 12, 1978.

80. Ibid.

81. Ibid.; "Dical Center Hospital, Department of Radiology, Odessa, Texas," Larry Ortega Lozano Information Summary, Herman Baca Papers, Special Collections and Archives, University of California, San Diego [hereafter cited as Baca Papers]; "Pecos Man Faces Assault Charges," *Odessa (TX) American*, January 11, 1978.

82. "A letter from Lozano to a friend," Larry Ortega Lozano Information Summary, Baca Papers.

83. Montemayor, Pusey, and Montgomery, "Minor Accident Beginning of End."

84. Richard Orr, "Cellmate Claims Jail Mistreatment; Rocker Flannigan Says He Heard Lozano's Account of Alleged Beatings," *San Angelo (TX) Standard-Times*, July 1, 1978.

85. Montemayor, Pusey, and Montgomery, "Minor Accident Beginning of End."

86. Orr, "Cellmate Claims Jail Mistreatment."

87. Montemayor, Pusey, and Montgomery, "Minor Accident Beginning of End."

88. "Race Relations in Odessa" and "Brown Beret Presence in Odessa," from Nick Hernandez, oral history interview by Joel Zapata, July 8, 2016, Odessa, Texas, CRBB Interview Database, crbb.tcu.edu/clips/2969/race-relations-in-odessa, crbb.tcu.edu/clips/2975/brown-beret-presence-in-odessa.

89. "Run-Ins with the Police," from Hernandez interview, crbb.tcu.edu/clips/2981/run-ins-with-the-police.

90. "Larry Lozano and Police Brutality, Part One," from Lydia Madrigal, oral history interview by Karen Wisely and Joel Zapata, July 29, 2016, Midland, Texas, CRBB Interview Database, crbb.tcu.edu/clips/5739/larry-lozano-and-police-brutality-part-one.

91. Ibid.; "Run-Ins with the Police, Part Two," from Hernandez interview, crbb.tcu.edu/clips/2982/run-ins-with-the-police-part-two. "Meeting about Police Brutality," from Hernandez interview, crbb.tcu.edu/clips/2992/meeting-about-police-brutality.

92. "Run-Ins with the Police," from Hernandez interview.

93. "Run-Ins with the Police, Part Two," from Hernandez interview.

94. "Meeting about Police Brutality," from Hernandez interview; Matt Conklin, "Key Witness Recounts Event of Night Pecos Man Died in Jail," *Odessa (TX) American*, April 12, 1978.

95. Orr, "Cellmate Claims Jail Mistreatment."

96. Ibid.; Montemayor, Pusey, and Montgomery, "Minor Accident Beginning of End."

97. Montemayor, Pusey, and Montgomery, "Minor Accident Beginning of End."

98. Ibid.

99. "Orders, Medical Center Hospital, Odessa, Texas" and "Remarks," Larry Ortega Lozano Information Summary, Baca Papers.

100. Montemayor, Pusey, and Montgomery, "Minor Accident Beginning of End."

101. Ibid.; Conklin, "Key Witness Recounts Event."

102. "Homicide Seen in Ector Jail Death," *Austin American-Statesman*, February 9, 1978.

103. Conklin, "Key Witness Recounts Event"; Orr, "Cellmate Claims Jail Mistreatment"; "An Odd Death," *Austin American-Statesman*, February 4, 1978.

104. Conklin, "Key Witness Recounts Event."

105. Montemayor, Pusey, and Montgomery, "Minor Accident Beginning of End"; "DA in Texas Denies Testimony Influence," *Santa Fe New Mexican*, July 20, 1978; "Prisoner's Death Homicide," *Childress (TX) Index*, February 9, 1979.

106. "Larry Lozano and Police Brutality, Part One," from Madrigal interview.

107. "Medical Examiner's Autopsy # 36–78," Larry Ortega Lozano Information Summary, Baca Papers.

108. "Prisoner's Death Homicide," *Childress (TX) Index*, February 9, 1979; "KOSA-TV—La Raza Meeting for Larry Ortega Lozano (1978)," Texas Archive of the Moving Image, accessed December 28, 2018, texasarchive.org/2013_01463.

109. Matt Conklin, "Jury Rules Lozano Death Accidental; Houston Pathologist Says Death Came from Injuries to the Larynx," *Odessa (TX) American*, April 13, 1978.

110. Montemayor, Pusey, and Montgomery, "Minor Accident Beginning of End."

111. Ibid.; Conklin, "Jury Rules Lozano Death Accidental."

112. "Medical Examiner's Autopsy # 36–78," Larry Ortega Lozano Information Summary, Baca Papers.

113. "Meeting about Police Brutality," from Hernandez interview.

114. "Larry Lozano and Police Brutality, Part One," from Madrigal interview.

115. "Conference in Lubbock," from Hernandez interview, crbb.tcu.edu/clips/2993/conference-in-lubbock; "Family of Dead Prisoner Seeks Independent Probe," *Odessa (TX) American*, January 25, 1978; Nicholas C. Chriss, "Chicanos, Bitter over Killings, Beatings by Police in Southwest, Protest in Houston," *Los Angeles Times*, April 3, 1978.

116. See the following articles from the *Odessa (TX) American*: "Pecos Sends Full Team to Relays," March 13, 1968; "Loboes Grab Loop Victory over Pecos," January 13, 1968; "Marcello Lozano," November 10, 1974; "Family of Dead Prisoner"; see also Montemayor, Pusey, and Montgomery, "Minor Accident Beginning of End."

117. "Rare Jury Inquest Schedule in Death," *Odessa (TX) American*, January 25, 1978.

118. Montemayor, Pusey, and Montgomery, "Minor Accident Beginning of End"; "DA in Texas Denies Testimony Influence"; "Prisoner's Death Homicide."

119. Raymond, "Mexican Americans Write toward Justice," 246.

120. James P. Sterba, "Chicano's Death Stirs a Texas Region," *New York Times*, August 16, 1976; Cynthia Biggers, "Lozano Lawyer Says Death Not Accident," *Odessa (TX) American*, April 27, 1978; "Texas Civil Rights Lawyer Ruben Sandoval, 55," *Chicago Tribune*, June 23, 1996; Greg Watson, "Lozano Lawyer says FBI Moving on Case," *Odessa (TX) American*, February 20, 1978; Greg Watson, "Justice Dept. to Get More Lozano Findings," *Odessa (TX) American*, February 16, 1978.

121. Watson, "Justice Dept. to Get Findings"; "City Councilmen Agree to Civil Rights March," *Odessa (TX) American*, February 28, 1978; Greg Watson, "Non-Violent Display of Solidarity Shown During Saturday Motorcade," *Odessa (TX) American*, February 26, 1978; Zapata, "Taking Chicana/o Activist History," 113–114.

122. Zapata, "Taking Chicana/o Activist History," 113–115; "St. Joseph Catholic Church Civil Rights Workshop (1978)," "Interactive Map and Timeline," Chicana/o Activism in the Southern Plains through Time and Space, accessed January 25, 2019, plainsmovement.com /neatline/show/interactive-map-and-timeline#records/8; "Politics and Protests in Odessa," from Hernandez interview, crbb.tcu.edu/clips/2994/politics-and-protests-in-odessa; "Beret Leader Predicts Non-Violent March," *Odessa (TX) American*, February 24, 1978; Watson, "Non-Violent Display of Solidarity."

123. Watson, "Non-Violent Display of Solidarity."

124. Ibid.; "Big Spring Police Brutality Protest (1978)," "Interactive Map and Timeline," Chicano Activism in the Southern Plains through Time and Space, accessed January 25, 2019, plainsmovement.com/neatline/show/interactive-map-and-timeline#records/9; Zapata, "Taking Chicana/o Activist History," 113–114; "Politics and Protests in Odessa," from Hernandez interview.

125. Conklin, "Key Witness Recounts Event"; Biggers, "Lozano Lawyer Says Death Not Accident."

126. Shelley Barker, "Sheriff 'Relieved' at Jury's Verdict," *Odessa (TX) American*, April 13, 1978.

127. Cynthia Biggers, "Demonstrators Protest Lozano Inquest Ruling," *Odessa (TX) American*, April 13, 1978.

128. See the following articles from the *Odessa (TX) American*: Matt Conklin, "Federal Probe into Lozano Death Sought," April 13, 1978; "Hill Says Lozano Case Is 'Judgmental Matter,'" April 8, 1978; "Attorney General Wants Tougher Civil Rights Laws," February 17, 1978; Cynthia Biggers, "Mexican-Americans Want Federal Grand Jury Probe," April 15, 1978.

129. Biggers, "Mexican-Americans Want Federal Grand Jury."

130. "Judge Says Probe Needed for Death," *Odessa (TX) American*, May 26, 1978.

131. Frank Trombley, "U.S. Attorney Says Lozano Probe Is out of His Hands," *Odessa (TX) American*, May 27, 1978; Attorney General Griffin B. Bell, press release, Friday, June 22, 1979, copy in Larry Ortega Lozano Information Summary, Baca Papers.

132. "Defense Urged By Brown Berets"; "Mexican-Americans Protest Shooting by Deputy Sheriff," *Albuquerque Journal*, July 16, 1978; "Texas Lawmen Probing Shooting of Hispanic," *Santa Fe New Mexican*, June 28, 1978; "Tim Rosales Killing in Hale County, Texas," "Interactive Map and Timeline," Chicano Activism in the Southern Plains through Time and Space, accessed January 26, 2019, plainsmovement.com/neatline/show/interactive-map-and -timeline#records/17; "Paul Villanueva Martinez Killing," "Interactive Map and Timeline," Chicano Activism in the Southern Plains through Time and Space, accessed January 26, 2019, plainsmovement.com/neatline/show/interactive-map-and-timeline#records/18.

133. "Larry Lozano and Police Brutality, Part Two," from Madrigal interview, crbb.tcu .edu/clips/5742/larry-lozano-and-police-brutality-part-two.

134. "Letters to the Editor: Chicano Response," *Odessa (TX) American*, April 23, 1978.

135. "Deaths Unify Hispanics."

136. Ibid. A. De León, *San Angeleños*, 98–111; "Group to Picket Police Station"; "'Grievance' Group Airs Nerios Case"; "LULAC Criticizes Agency"; "Shooting Victim's Family Meets with Latin Group"; "Mexican-Americans Protest Killing"; "Defense Urged by Brown Berets."

Chapter 6: The Long Shadow of Héctor P. García in Corpus Christi

1. Cecilia Garcia Akers, *The Inspiring Life of Texan Héctor P. García* (Charleston, SC: Arcadia, 2016). Although, as Rebecca Saavedra notes in her introduction, "those twenty babies, twenty speeches and twenty thousand votes took twenty-hour days and meant great sacrifices on his family's part. His wife and children felt the brunt of his compassion for the greater good, and his absence from their day-to-day lives took its toll."

2. "Organizations in Corpus Christi," from Nick Jimenez, oral history interview by James Wall and Moisés Acuña Gurrola, June 7, 2016, Civil Rights in Black and Brown Interview

Database [hereafter cited as CRBB Interview Database], crbb.tcu.edu/clips/organizations-in-corpus-christi.

3. "What Is Civil Rights? Part Two," from Daniel Noyola, oral history interview by James Wall and Moisés Acuña Gurrola, June 15, 2016, CRBB Interview Database, crbb.tcu.edu/clips/what-is-civil-rights; Jacquelyn Dowd Hall, "The Long Civil Rights Movement and the Political Uses of the Past," *Journal of American History* 91, no. 4 (March 1, 2005): 1234, doi.org/10.2307/3660172.

4. Ignacio M. García, *Héctor P. García: In Relentless Pursuit of Justice* (Houston: Arte Público, 2002), 2–7; Akers, *Life of Héctor P. García*, 17–19.

5. *Justice For My People: The Dr. Héctor P. García Story* (South Texas Public Broadcasting System, 2002), video available at pbs.org/video/justice-for-my-people-the-dr-hector-p-garcia-story-yxbxkf.

6. García, *Héctor P. García*, 38–39; *Justice For My People*.

7. García, *Héctor P. García*, 44–51.

8. Ibid., 66–69.

9. Although the town eventually took off, Kinney struggled to bring in settlers during its early years. He constantly found himself in sticky situations and was often accused of sabotaging his rivals. After a neighboring merchant was captured by a Mexican raiding force, Kinney was accused of serving as an informant for the Mexicans and was indicted and tried for treason. (He was later acquitted.) By the 1850s, Kinney was still having a hard time luring settlers, and he began losing money. In a desperate attempt to save his town, he went to Washington, where he pitched a number of zany proposals to governmental officials, including the purchase of a caravan of camels to transport goods between Corpus Christi and San Francisco. None of his ideas came to fruition, so Kinney left for Nicaragua, where he tried to build a colony on thirty million acres of land along the Mosquito Coast. He ran into stiff opposition from the US government, and after his largest financial backer died, he gave up on the project. After he returned to Texas, his wife took the kids and left him, and Kinney returned to politics. He served in the Texas Legislature until March 1861, when the Civil War broke out and Kinney, who was opposed to secession, resigned his seat and moved to Matamoros, Mexico, where he was killed in a gunfight on March 3, 1862; see García, *Héctor P. García*, 106–110.

10. Carol A. Lipscomb, "Karankawa Indians," rev. Tim Seiter, *Handbook of Texas Online*, June 15, 2010, tshaonline.org/handbook/entries/karankawa-indians; Mary Jo O'Rear, *Storm over the Bay: The People of Corpus Christi and Their Port* (College Station: Texas A&M University Press, 2009), 1–2; Murphy Givens and Jim Moloney, *Corpus Christi: A History* (Corpus Christi, TX: Nueces, 2011).

11. O'Rear, *Storm over the Bay*, 125–38; Alan Lessoff, *Where Texas Meets the Sea: Corpus Christi and Its History* (Austin: University of Texas Press, 2015), 68–70; Givens and Moloney, *Corpus Christi*, 47; Scott Williams, *Corpus Christi* (Charleston, SC: Arcadia, 2009).

12. O'Rear, *Storm over the Bay*, 132; Williams, *Corpus Christi*; Givens and Moloney, *Corpus Christi*.

13. "Texas Almanac: City Population History from 1850–2000," texasalmanac.com/sites/default/files/images/CityPopHist%20web.pdf; García, *Héctor P. García*, 74–75.

14. Benjamin Márquez, *LULAC: The Evolution of a Mexican American Political Organization* (Austin: University of Texas Press, 1993) 23; David G. Gutiérrez, *Walls and Mirrors: Mexican Americans, Mexican Immigrants, and the Politics of Ethnicity* (Berkeley: University of California Press, 1995), 79–81.

15. García, *Héctor P. García*, 79–80.

16. Ibid., 80–81.

17. Akers, *Life of Héctor P. García*, 35–36; "Relationship with Héctor P. García," from Willie Loa, oral history interview by James Wall, Moisés Acuña Gurrola, and Todd Moye, June 6, 2016, CRBB Interview Database, crbb.tcu.educrbb.tcu.edu/clips/relationship-with-Héctor-p-garcia.

18. García, *Héctor P. García*, 106–10; Akers, *Life of Héctor P. García*, 36–39.

19. García, *Héctor P. García*, 106–13; Akers, *Life of Héctor P. García*, 39–41.

20. García, *Héctor P. García*, 118.

21. "The Hispanic Community in Calvert," from Mary Helen Berlanga, oral history interview by James Wall and Moisés Acuña Gurrola, July 12, 2016, CRBB Interview Database, crbb.tcu .edu/clips/the-hispanic-community-in-calvert; "Childhood and College," from Tony Bonilla, oral history interview by James Wall and Moisés Acuña Gurrola, July 8, 2016, CRBB Interview Database, crbb.tcu.edu/clips/childhood-and-college; Esther Bonilla Read, *From the Porch Steps: Little Stories to Warm Your Heart and Make You Smile* (Corpus Christi, TX: Cerca del Mar, 2016).

22. "Past Presidents: William David Bonilla," LULAC, accessed July 8, 2017, lulac.org /about/history/past_presidents/william_bonilla; "Past Presidents: Reuben Bonilla," LULAC, accessed July 8, 2017, lulac.org/about/history/past_presidents/ruben_bonilla/; "Past Presidents: Tony Bonilla," LULAC, accessed July 8, 2017, lulac.org/about/history/past_presidents /tony_bonilla.

23. García, *Héctor P. García*, 237–50; Ignacio M. Garcia, *Viva Kennedy: Mexican Americans in Search of Camelot* (College Station: Texas A&M University Press, 2000), 153–155; José Ángel Gutiérrez, *Albert A. Peña Jr.: Dean of Chicano Politics* (East Lansing: Michigan State University Press, 2017); Benjamin Márquez, *Democratizing Texas Politics: Race, Identity, and Mexican American Empowerment, 1945–2002* (Austin: University of Texas Press, 2014), 67–70; Brian D. Behnken, *Fighting Their Own Battles: Mexican Americans, African Americans, and the Struggle for Civil Rights in Texas* (Charlotte: University of North Carolina Press, 2011), 90–92.

24. Mark Odintz, "Crystal City, TX," *Handbook of Texas Online*, tshaonline.org/handbook /entries/crystal-city-tx.

25. García, *Héctor P. García*, 244–248; Garcia, *Viva Kennedy*, 148–159; Rodolfo Rosales, *The Illusion of Inclusion: The Untold Political Story of San Antonio* (Austin: University of Texas Press, 2000), 83–95; Márquez, *Democratizing Texas Politics*, 67–68; Gutiérrez, *Albert A. Peña Jr.*

26. García, *Héctor P. García*, 246–250.

27. Garcia, *Viva Kennedy*, 153–156; García, *Héctor P. García*, 246–248, quoted material on 247.

28. García, *Héctor P. García*, 248–250.

29. "Differences between Black and Brown Civil Rights Movements," from T. Bonilla interview, crbb.tcu.edu/clips/differences-between-black-and-brown-civil-rights-movements.

30. Márquez, *Democratizing Texas Politics*, 77–79.

31. Spencer Pearson, "Bonilla Calls Foe Puppet of Garcia," *Corpus Christi (TX) Times*, May 27, 1966.

32. See the following articles from the *Corpus Christi (TX) Times*: Spencer Pearson, "Héctor Garcia, Labor Men Accused of Unfair Tactics," May 13, 1966; "Héctor Garcia to Attend Meeting at White House," May 25, 1966; "Bonilla Calls Foe Puppet of Garcia"; "House Race Puts Spice in Runoff: Second Primary Has Only Five County Contests," May 29, 1966; "Gonzalez Calls Foe Man of 'Many Faces,'" June 3, 1966; "Absentee Voting in Nov. 8 Election Begins Wednesday," October 16, 1966; see also Márquez, *Democratizing Texas Politics*, 79–80; "Reelection Campaign in 1966," from T. Bonilla interview, crbb.tcu.edu/clips/reelection-campaign-in-1966.

33. Jim Wood, "Dr. Garcia Disavows Allegiance to Texas," *Corpus Christi (TX) Times*, April 16, 1966; "Bonilla / Reelection Campaign in 1966," from T. Bonilla interview.

34. As late as 1979, *Texas Monthly* was still publishing details of the ongoing feud between the Bonillas and García. One account read: "The Bonillas are liberal lawyers, the Garcías conservative doctors, and they head warring Chicano-rights organizations. Fight never seems to end. Meanwhile the Anglo minority stays in power in Corpus. Latest flareup was over Bob Kreuger's possible appointment as ambassador to Mexico; [Ruben] Bonilla approved, so of course García didn't" ("Ethnic Feuds," *Texas Monthly*, June 1979, 100).

35. "Differences between Black and Brown Civil Rights Movements," from T. Bonilla interview; "Immigration, Economics, and Politics," from Ruben Bonilla, oral history interview by James Wall and Moisés Acuña Gurrola, June 28, 2016, CRBB Interview Database, crbb.tcu.edu /clips/immigration-economics-and-politics.

36. "People in Politics and Community Progress, Part Three," from Vincente Molina, oral history interview by Sandra Enríquez, David Robles, and Max Krochmal, July 8, 2015, CRBB

Interview Database, crbb.tcu.edu/clips/people-in-politics-and-community-progress-part-3; Márquez, *Democratizing Texas Politics*, 103–106.

37. "Organizations in Corpus Christi," from Jimenez interview, crbb.tcu.edu/clips /organizations-in-corpus-christi; "Organizations in Corpus Christi, TX," from Joe Ortiz, oral history interview by James Wall and Moisés Acuña Gurrola, CRBB Interview Database, crbb .tcu.edu/clips/civil-rights-organizations-in-corpus-christi-tx.

38. Akers, *Life of Héctor P. García*, ch. 3.

39. Ibid.; Ruben Bonilla, interview by José Ángel Gutiérrez, September 26, 1996, Center for Mexican American Studies, University of Texas at Arlington, Tejano Voices Oral History Collection, library.uta.edu/tejanovoices/xml/CMAS_008.xml.

40. "Organizations in Corpus Christi," from Jimenez interview; Akers, *Life of Héctor P. García*, 47.

41. "Ortiz / Organizations in Corpus Christi," from Ortiz interview; "The Torres Case and Joining LULAC" and "Suing for Single Member Districts, Part Two," from Butch Escobedo, oral history interview by James Wall and Moisés Acuña Gurrola, June 15, 2016, CRBB Interview Database, crbb.tcu.edu/clips/the-torres-case-and-joining-lulac, crbb.tcu.edu/clips /suing-the-city-for-single-member-districts-part-two.

42. "Activism in Corpus Christi Today," from R. Bonilla interview, crbb.tcu.edu/clips/activism -in-corpus-christi-today.

43. Lessoff, *Where Texas Meets the Sea*, 128.

Chapter 7: "It Was Us against Us"

1. From this point forward, I refer to the Rio Grande Valley as "the Valley" or "el Valle."

2. The rise of boss politics in Texas started in the latter half of the nineteenth century after the US war of aggression against Mexico in 1848. In the Valley, James B. Wells, the main political boss, settled in Brownsville in 1878, and once he consolidated his power in Cameron County, he and the "Wells Machine" reigned in the region from the 1880s to the 1920s; see Evan Anders, *Boss Rule in South Texas: The Progressive Era* (Austin: University of Texas Press, 1982).

3. Ignacio M. García, *United We Win: The Rise and Fall of La Raza Unida Party* (Tucson: Mexican American Studies and Research Center, University of Arizona, 1989), xi.

4. Ibid.

5. Ibid., 1.

6. "Script for Video Tape—Honoring Pharr City Officials," Glover Collection, folder 89.32.01a, Margaret H. McAllen Memorial Archives, Museum of South Texas History, Edinburg.

7. "Dedication of Texas Historical Marker for the First Pharr School," Hidalgo County Historical Commission, September 29, 1985, Pharr Memorial Library Archives, Pharr, Texas.

8. Anglos and others of European descent traveling and moving to the Valley during this period saw themselves as "pioneers" who were going to tame the region.

9. Efraín Fernández, "Community Organizing in the City of Pharr" (1974), 5, personal paper, Pharr Memorial Library Archives, Pharr, Texas.

10. Ibid., 2.

11. "Inequality Between Mexicans and Anglos," from A. C. Jaime, oral history interview by Sandra Enríquez and David Robles, July 2, 2015, McAllen, Texas, Civil Rights in Black and Brown Interview Database [hereafter cited as CRBB Interview Database], crbb.tcu .edu/clips/inequality-between-mexicans-and-anglos.

12. Ibid.

13. Ibid.

14. Ibid.

15. Ned Wallace, "The 1971 Pharr Riot," in *Studies in Rio Grande Valley History*, ed. Milo Kearney, Anthony Knopp, Antonio Zavaleta, UTB/TSC Regional History 6 (Brownsville: University of Texas at Brownsville and Texas Southmost College, 2005), 17.

16. "Attending Needs of Mexicans," from Jaime interview by Enríquez and Robles, crbb .tcu.edu/clips/attending-needs-of-mexicans. Jaime did not explain why educated Anglos did not support Bowe.

17. "The Politics Before and After the Riot," from Ruben Rosales, oral history interview by Sandra Enríquez and David Robles, June 23, 2015, Pharr, Texas, CRBB Interview Database, crbb.tcu.edu/clips/the-politics-before-and-after-the-riot.

18. Ibid.

19. Fernández, "Community Organizing in Pharr," 2.

20. Maria H. Magallan, interview by David Robles, Pharr, Texas, June 8, 2016, in author's possession.

21. Fernández, "Community Organizing in Pharr," 3.

22. Ibid.

23. "Fernando Ramirez Discusses the Protests and Riots in Pharr, Part One," from Fernando Ramirez, oral history interview by Eladio Bobadilla and Danielle Grevious, June 23, 2016, Port Arthur, Texas, CRBB Interview Database, crbb.tcu.edu/clips/5600/fernando-ramirez -discusses-the-protests-and-riots-in-pharr-part-one.

24. Magallan interview.

25. Ibid.

26. Fernández, "Community Organizing in Pharr," 5.

27. "The Politics Before and After the Riot," from Rosales interview.

28. Wallace, "1971 Pharr Riot," 19.

29. Fernández, "Community Organizing in Pharr," 6.

30. Wallace, "1971 Pharr Riot," 20.

31. Ibid.

32. "Pharr Riot," from Jesus Ramirez, oral history interview by Sandra Enríquez and David Robles, June 29, 2015, Pharr, Texas, CRBB Interview Database, crbb.tcu.edu/clips.pharr-riot.

33. Fernández, "Community Organizing in the City of Pharr," 5.

34. Ibid.

35. "It Was Us Against Us," from Rosales interview, crbb.tcu.edu/clips/it-was-us-against-us.

36. Ibid.

37. "Fernando Ramirez Discusses Police Brutality in Pharr, TX," from F. Ramirez interview, crbb.tcu.edu/clips/5596/fernando-ramirez-discusses-police-brutality-in-pharr-tx.

38. Wallace, "1971 Pharr Riot," 20, 21.

39. "Fernando Ramirez Discusses the Protests and Riots in Pharr, Part One," from F. Ramirez interview, crbb.tcu.edu/clips/5600/fernando-ramirez-discusses-the-protests-and-riots -in-pharr-part-one.

40. "Mexican Discrimination with Politics and Police, Part One," from Jaime interview by Enríquez and Robles, crbb.tcu.edu/clips/1851/mexican-discrimination-with-politics-and-police -part-1.

41. "Fernando Ramirez Discusses the Protests and Riots in Pharr, Part One," from F. Ramirez interview.

42. "Pharr Riot," from J. Ramirez interview.

43. "Fernando Ramirez Discusses Police Brutality in Pharr, TX," from F. Ramirez interview.

44. "Pharr Riot," from J. Ramirez interview.

45. "Fernando Ramirez Discusses Police Brutality in Pharr, TX," from F. Ramirez interview.

46. "Pharr Riot, Part Two," from Jaime Garza, oral history interview by Sandra Enríquez and David Robles, July 2, 2015, Mercedes, Texas, CRBB Interview Database, crbb.tcu.edu/clips /pharr-riot-part-two.

47. "Pharr Riot," from J. Ramirez interview.

48. "Pharr Riot, Part Two," from Garza interview.

49. "Pharr Riot," from J. Ramirez interview.

50. "Fernando Ramirez Discusses the Protests and Riots in Pharr, TX, Part Two," from F. Ramirez interview, crbb.tcu.edu/clips/5601/fernando-ramirez-discusses-the-protests-and -riots-in-pharr-tx-part-two.

51. Ibid.

52. "Pharr Riot, Part Two," from Garza interview.

53. "Pharr Riot," from J. Ramirez interview.

54. Wallace, "1971 Pharr Riot," 21.

55. "Funeral Procession after Pharr Riot," from Rosales interview, crbb.tcu.edu/clips/1717 /funeral-procession-after-pharr-riot.

56. "After the Pharr Riot," from Garza interview, crbb.tcu.edu/clips/after-the-pharr-riot.

57. "Aftermath of the Riot," from Rosales interview, crbb.tcu.edu/clips/1564/aftermath-of -the-riot.

58. Ibid.

59. Dora Leticia González, "A Look at the City of Pharr—Before and after the Riot," 9 (unpublished paper, April 20, 1989, University of Texas Pan-American, Edinburg), Pharr Memorial Library Archive, Pharr, Texas.

60. Ibid.

61. Lloyd H. Glover, "Pharr 'Quiet' after Week of Tension," *Pharr Press*, February 18, 1971.

62. González, "City of Pharr," 9; Fernández, "Community Organizing in Pharr," 7.

63. "Mujeres Marchan: Policias Renuncian," *¡Ya Mero!* (McAllen) 2, no. 23 (April 10, 1971): 1, M-film E184.M5 P3, Sect.III: Roll.3:v.1–3:no.1–23 (1969-1972), University of Texas Rio Grande Valley library, Edinburg.

64. "Women to Picket Police," *Corpus Christi (TX) Caller*, April 14, 1971, F381, Pharr, Pharr Riot Copy 1, Library Archives and Special Collections, University of Texas Rio Grande Valley, Edinburg [hereafter cited as UTRGV Special Collections].

65. "Mujeres Protestan," *¡Ya Mero!* (McAllen) 2, no. 3 (April 24, 1971): 1, William F. White Jr. Library, Del Mar College, Corpus Christi.

66. Lloyd H. Glover "Grand Jury Indicts Ten over Pharr Violence," *Pharr (TX) Press*, March 18, 1971.

67. "From San Juan to Pharr: 1,000 Join Peaceful Protest," *McAllen (TX) Monitor*, March 8, 1971.

68. "Chicano March Is Quiet in a Tense Texas Town," *New York Times*, March 9, 1971, F381, Pharr, Pharr Riot, Copy 1, UTRGV Special Collections.

69. "PASSO Involvement, Part 2," from Abel Ochoa, oral history interview by Sandra Enríquez and David Robles, July 1, 2015, McAllen, Texas, CRBB Interview Database, crbb.tcu .edu/clips/p-a-s-s-o-involvement-part-2.

70. "Funeral Procession After Pharr Riot," from Rosales interview.

71. "Witness Says Lopez Did Not Throw Rocks," *McAllen (TX) Monitor*, June 16, 1971, F381, Pharr, Pharr Riot, Copy 1, UTRGV Special Collections.

72. Wallace, "1971 Pharr Riot," 30.

73. "After the Pharr Riot," from Garza interview.

74. Wallace, "1971 Pharr Riot," 34.

75. Jaime interview by Robles, file 1.

76. "Inequality Between Mexicans and Anglos," from Jaime interview by Enríquez and Robles.

77. "Deciding to Run for Mayor," from Jaime interview by Enríquez and Robles, crbb.tcu .edu/clips/1845/growing-up-and-my-family-part-2.

78. Ibid.

79. Ibid.

80. Ibid.

81. "Inequality Between Mexicans and Anglos," from Jaime interview by Enríquez and Robles.

82. Ibid.

83. Jaime interview by Robles, file 1.

84. Ibid., file 2.

85. "Rumors Fly in City Race; Stories Branded as 'Lies,'" *Pharr (TX) Press*, April 27, 1972, 1.

86. Jaime interview by Robles, file 1.

87. "Inequality Between Mexicans and Anglos," from Jaime interview by Enríquez and Robles.

88. "Fernando Ramirez Discusses Politics in Pharr, TX," from F. Ramirez interview, crbb.tcu.edu/clips/5602/fernando-ramirez-discusses-politics-in-pharr-tx.

89. "Mexicans' Reaction to Being Mayor," from Jaime interview by Enríquez and Robles, crbb.tcu.edu/clips/1858/mexicans-reaction-to-being-mayor.

90. Ibid.

91. "The Politics Before and After the Riot," from Rosales interview.

92. "Mexicans' Reaction to Being Mayor," from Jaime interview by Enríquez and Robles.

93. "Fernando Ramirez Discusses Politics in Pharr, TX," from F. Ramirez interview.

94. Ibid.

95. Ibid.

96. "The Politics Before and After the Riot," from Rosales interview.

97. "Were the Police Properly Trained," from Jaime interview by Enríquez and Robles, crbb.tcu.edu/clips/1854/was-the-police-properly-trained.

98. Ibid.

99. Ibid.

100. Douglas W. Perez and William Ker Muir, "Administrative Review of Alleged Police Brutality," in *Police Violence: Understanding and Controlling Police Abuse of Force*, ed. William A. Geller and Hans Toch (New Haven, CT: Yale University Press, 1996), 213.

101. Ibid.

102. "Were the Police Properly Trained," from Jaime interview by Enríquez and Robles.

103. "Changes after Mayor Jaime," from Rosales interview, crbb.tcu.edu/clips/1711/changes-after-mayor-jaime.

104. Ibid.

105. Linda Swartz, "A Quiet Revolution in Pharr," *Texas Observer*, August 9, 1974, 8.

106. "Were the Police Properly Trained," from Jaime interview by Enríquez and Robles.

107. "Attending Needs of Mexicans," from Jaime interview by Enríquez and Robles.

108. Ibid.

109. Ibid.

110. "Mexican Discrimination with Politics and Police, Part Two," from Jaime interview by Enríquez and Robles, crbb.tcu.edu/clips/1852/mexican-discrimination-with-politics-and-police-part-2.

111. "Mexican Discrimination with Politics and Police, Part One," from Jaime interview by Enríquez and Robles, crbb.tcu.edu/clips/1851/mexican-discrimination-with-politics-and-police-part-1.

112. Swartz, "Quiet Revolution in Pharr," 8.

113. "Mexican Discrimination with Politics and Police, Part Two," from Jaime interview by Enríquez and Robles.

114. During Jaime's second mayoral term, there was a meeting at the Pharr Civic Center on December 1, 1977, at which 350–400 citizens, plus organizers, met to discuss the "smut" being shown at some theaters, and to sign petitions against the showing of these "sexually-explicit" movies. The attorneys Emilio Vela and Bill Ellis, Mrs. Betty Bundy (the president of Mission Morality), and Mayor Jaime led the campaign. Jaime, the city commission, and Police Chief Don Jackson submitted the petitions to the federal district court on December 5 in hope of getting a permanent injunction against showing the films. Ellis recognized the free speech questions involved, but noted that obscenity "does not come under intent of the First Amendment." During this time, Ellis worked on an antipornography ordinance for Pharr; see "350 to 400 Pharr Citizens Show Up at Anti-Smut Meet," *McAllen (TX) Monitor*, December 2, 1977.

115. "Mexicans' Reaction to Being Mayor," from Jaime interview by Enríquez and Robles.

116. "Mexican Discrimination with Politics and Police, Part One," from Jaime interview by Enríquez and Robles.

117. Ibid.

118. "Mexican Discrimination with Politics and Police, Part Two," from Jaime interview by Enríquez and Robles.

119. Ibid.

120. "Police Harassment Claimed: Pharr Tavern Owners Protest Ordinances," *McAllen (TX) Monitor*, January 7, 1976, 1.

121. "Mexican Discrimination with Politics and Police, Part Two," from Jaime interview by Enríquez and Robles.

122. "Police Harassment Claimed," 1.

123. Ibid.

124. "Ending Police Harassment at the Tavern," from Rosales interview, crbb.tcu.edu/clips /1710/ending-police-harassment-at-the-tavern.

125. "Police Harassment Claimed," 1.

126. "Mexican Discrimination with Politics and Police, Part Two," from Jaime interview by Enríquez and Robles.

127. Ibid.

128. "The Politics Before and After the Riot," from Rosales interview.

129. "Mexicans' Reaction to Being Mayor," from Jaime interview by Enríquez and Robles.

Chapter 8: The 1970 Uvalde School Walkout

1. Elvia Perez, video interview by Reina Olivas, April 9, 2016, Uvalde, Texas, Voces Oral History Center, Nettie Lee Benson Latin American Collection, University of Texas at Austin [hereafter cited as Benson Collection].

2. Rachel Gonzales-Hanson, oral history interview by Vinicio Sinta and Steve Arionus, July 14, 2016, Uvalde, Texas, July 14, 2016, CRBB Interview, Portal to Texas History, University of North Texas Libraries, texashistory.unt.edu/ark:/67531/metapth987609.

3. Gary B. Starnes, "Ugalde, Juan de (1729–1816)," *Handbook of Texas Online*, tshaonline.org /handbook/entries/ugalde-juan-de. Starnes writes that de Ugalde, from southern Spain, was stationed in what is now northern Mexico and South Texas. In 1790, he led a successful campaign against Lipan, Lipiyan, and Mescalero Apaches. In honor of his victory, the battlefield was named for him. The city and county of Uvalde take their names from Juan de Ugalde.

4. Gonzales-Hanson interview.

5. Ibid.

6. Modesto Arriaga, video interview by Maggie Rivas-Rodriguez, March 23, 2014, Richmond, Texas, Voces Oral History Center, Benson Collection.

7. In 1963, the Mexican American community of Crystal City had its "first revolt" with the successful election of five candidates, "Los Cinco," to the town's city council. The effort was bolstered by the heavy support of the Political Association of Spanish Speaking Organizations (PASO) and of the International Brotherhood of Teamsters; see Ignacio M. Garcia, *Chicanismo: The Forging of a Militant Ethos among Mexican Americans* (Tucson: University of Arizona Press, 1997), 23–34. That election has also been called the "first uprising"; see David Montejano, *Anglos and Mexicans in the Making of Texas, 1836–1986* (Austin: University of Texas Press, 1988).

8. Abelardo Castillo, video interview by Maggie Rivas-Rodriguez, April 19, 2017, Austin, Texas, Voces Oral History Center, Benson Collection.

9. Ibid.

10. "Early Childhood," from José Uriegas, oral history interview by Steve Arionus and Vinicio Sinta, July 9, 2016, Austin, Texas, Civil Rights in Black and Brown Interview Database [hereafter cited as CRBB Interview Database], crbb.tcu.edu/clips/4329/early-childhood-2.

11. Elías Menendez, video teleconference interview by Maggie Rivas-Rodriguez, July 7, 2020, Voces Oral History Center, Benson Collection.

12. "Discrimination at School and Moving," from Uriegas interview by Arionus and Sinta, crbb.tcu.edu/clips/4330/discrimination-at-school-and-moving.

13. José Uriegas, video teleconference interview by Maggie Rivas-Rodriguez, June 30, 2020, Voces Oral History Center, Benson Collection.

14. Menendez interview.

15. "High School Football," from Uriegas interview by Arionus and Sinta, crbb.tcu.edu/clips/4331/high-school-football.

16. Uriegas interview by Rivas-Rodriguez.

17. Ibid.

18. Gilbert Torres, interview by José Ángel Gutiérrez, CMAS No. 106, January 14, 1998, Uvalde, Texas, Tejano Voices, University of Texas at Arlington Library.

19. Eleazar Lugo, videotaped interview by Jorge Haynes, April 9, 2016, Uvalde, Texas, Voces Oral History Center, Benson Collection.

20. Ibid.

21. José Aguilera, video interview by Raquel Garza, April 8, 2016, Uvalde, Texas, Voces Oral History Center, Benson Collection.

22. "U.S. Census Bureau, "QuickFacts: Uvalde city, Texas," accessed July 4, 2020, census.gov/quickfacts/uvaldecitytexas.

23. U.S. Congress, Senate, Select Committee on Equal Educational Opportunity, *Equal Educational Opportunity: Hearings before the Select Committee on Equal Educational Opportunity of the United States Senate, Ninety-First Congress, Second Session on Equal Educational Opportunity, Part 4—Mexican American Education* (Washington, DC: Government Printing Office, 1971), 2463, available from ERIC, ED052877.

24. Olga Charles, video interview by Anna Casey, April 8, 2016, Uvalde, Texas, Voces Oral History Center, Benson Collection. The Williamson-Dickie Manufacturing Co., maker of the Dickie's clothing line, operated a factory in Uvalde until 2019.

25. Ibid.

26. Sergio Porras, video interview by Brigit Benestante, April 8, 2016, Uvalde, Texas, Voces Oral History Center, Benson Collection.

27. Josué "George" Garza, video interview by Prakriti Bhardwaj, April 9, 2016, Uvalde, Texas, Voces Oral History Center, Benson Collection.

28. Ibid.

29. Garza interview by Bhardwaj. "*Mija*" is a shorted version of "*mi hija*," my daughter.

30. Ibid.

31. Now Texas State University.

32. Garza interview by Bhardwaj.

33. Josué "George" Garza, interview by José Ángel Gutiérrez, June 9, 1996, Uvalde, Texas, Tejano Voices, University of Texas at Arlington Library.

34. "School Walk Out in Uvalde," from Alfredo Santos, oral history interview by Vinicio Sinta and Steve Arionus, July 4, 2016, Austin, Texas, CRBB Interview Database, crbb.tcu.edu/clips/4176/school-walk-out-in-uvalde. Santos described Uriegas as Cisneros's local counterpart: "He was good-looking and his wife was better-looking." Uriegas had a college degree and ran a small grocery store on the Mexican side of town. Henry Cisneros served as San Antonio's mayor from 1981 to 1989 and later served in the cabinet of President Bill Clinton. Cisneros was widely regarded as a Hispanic leader nationally; see britannica.com/biography/Henry-Cisneros.

35. Uriegas interview by Rivas-Rodriguez.

36. Castillo interview.

37. José Ángel Gutiérrez, *A Gringo Manual on How to Handle Mexicans* (Houston: Arte Publico, 2003), 103.

38. Ibid.

39. James B. Barrera, "The 1968 Edcouch-Elsa High School Walkout: Chicano Student Activism in a South Texas Community," *Aztlán: A Journal of Chicano Studies* 29, no. 2 (2004): 93–122.

40. Ibid., 102–104. Here he quotes from the Edcouch-Elsa school board meeting minutes, November 4, 1968; the *McAllen (TX) Monitor*, November 7, 1968; and a letter sent to parents by the school board, November 5, 1968. Those requests included that students be allowed to speak Spanish on school grounds, that discrimination against Mexican American students cease, and that new classes include the contributions of Mexican Americans to Texas and to the area.

41. There were also demands for more Mexican Americans to be hired as teachers, and for more classes on Mexican American studies.

42. In Los Angeles, organizations included the Mexican American Student Association, the United Mexican-American Students, the Mexican-American Youth Association, the National Organization of Mexican-American Students, and the Student Initiative, formed before 1967, which became the Mexican-American Student Confederation; see Armando Navarro, *Mexican American Youth Organization: Avant-garde of the Chicano Movement in Texas* (Austin: University of Texas Press. 1995), 52–53, 80.

43. Alfredo Santos, video interview by Anna Casey, April 8, 2016, Uvalde, Texas, Voces Oral History Center, Benson Collection.

44. Ibid.

45. Gonzales-Hanson interview.

46. Santos interview by Casey.

47. Juan Alonzo, recorded telephone interview by Maggie Rivas-Rodriguez, October 2, 2017, Voces Oral History Center, Benson Collection.

48. Charles interview.

49. Ibid.

50. Uriegas interview by Rivas-Rodriguez.

51. Santos interview by Casey.

52. "School Walk Out in Uvalde," from Santos interview by Sinta and Arionus.

53. Gonzales-Hanson interview.

54. Ibid.

55. Garza interview by Bhardwaj.

56. Perez interview.

57. Roberto Morales, oral history interview by Vinicio Sinta and Steve Arionus, July 10, 2016, Uvalde, Texas, CRBB interview, Portal to Texas History, University of North Texas Libraries, texashistory.unt.edu/ark:/67531/metapth992328.

58. Gonzales-Hanson interview.

59. Uriegas interview by Rivas-Rodriguez.

60. Alonzo interview.

61. Ibid.

62. "Walkout Continues As School Year Ends," *Uvalde (TX) Leader-News*, May 21, 1970.

63. "Summer School," *Uvalde (TX) Leader-News*, June 11, 1970.

64. "Mexican American Group Makes Public Statement," *Uvalde (TX) Leader-News*, June 21, 1970; "Parents Turn Down Plan," *Uvalde (TX) Leader-News*, June 25, 1970.

65. Perez interview.

66. Lugo interview.

67. Castillo interview.

68. Gonzales-Hanson interview.

69. Ibid.

70. Aguilera interview.

71. Chris Reyes Mendeke, oral history interview by Vinicio Sinta and Steve Arionus, July 15, 2016, Uvalde, Texas, CRBB interview, Portal to Texas History, University of North Texas Libraries, texashistory.unt.edu/ark:/67531/metapth987646.

72. Olga Rodriquez, video interview by Alfredo Santos, April 9, 2016, Uvalde, Texas, Voces Oral History Center, Benson Collection.

73. "Parents Association of Mexican-Americans Explains Objectives," *Uvalde (TX) Leader-News*, May 10, 1970.

74. "HEW Probe Is Sought in Uvalde," *Abilene (TX) Reporter-News*, April 24, 1970.

75. "Walter F. Mondale: Spokesman for Reform and Justice in the U.S. Senate," University of Minnesota Law Library, moses.law.umn.edu/mondale/school_integration.php.

76. "Senator Blasts at City," *Uvalde (TX) Leader-News*, July 30, 1970. Note: This headline was handwritten on the news clipping, and there appears to be a word missing after "city."

77. Ibid.

78. "School Desegregation Talks Held," *Uvalde (TX) Leader-News*, July 30, 1970.

79. Statement of José V. Uriegas and Jesús J. Rubio Jr.

80. "Walk-Outs Draw News On Draft," *Uvalde (TX) Leader-News*, August 23, 1970.

81. "MAPA Decides on 'Firm' Policy," *Uvalde (TX) Leader-News*, July 30, 1970.

82. "Walk-Outs Back in Class as School Suits Are Filed," *Uvalde (TX) Leader-News*, August 27, 1970.

83. Barrera, "Edcouch-Elsa High School Walkout," 116; Miguel A. Guajardo and Francisco J. Guajardo, "The Impact of *Brown* on the Brown of South Texas: A Micropolitical Perspective on the Education of Mexican Americans in a South Texas Community," *American Educational Research Journal* 41, no. 3 (January 2004): 501–526. doi.org/10.3102/00028312041003501.

84. "Walk-Outs Back in Class."

85. "Dishman Resigns from School Board," *Uvalde (TX) Leader-News*, October 15, 1970.

86. "MAPA Sets Meeting Today," *Uvalde (TX) Leader-News*, October 18, 1970; "MAPA Names New Officers," *Uvalde (TX) Leader-News*, October 22, 1970.

87. "Letters to the Editor," *Uvalde (TX) Leader-News*, April 11, 1971.

88. "School Board Again Denies MAPA Request," *Uvalde (TX) Leader-News*, April 15, 1971.

89. "School Reports 77 Absent for Walkout," *Uvalde (TX) Leader-News*, April 15, 1971.

90. "Wood, John Howland, Jr.," Federal Judicial Center, accessed July 6, 2020, fjc.gov/node/1390051; Joseph C. Elliott, "In Memory of the Honorable John H. Wood, Jr. United States District Judge," *St. Mary's Law Journal* 11 (1979–1980): xi.

91. "Federal Judge Calls School Suit 'a Local Matter,'" *Uvalde (TX) Leader-News*, April 15, 1971.

92. Rodriquez interview.

93. "Uvalde School District Has Never Segregated Mexican-American Students," *Uvalde (TX) Leader-News*, June 3, 1971.

94. "MAPA President States School Suit Appeal Begun," *Uvalde (TX) Leader-News*, June 6, 1971.

95. Michael W. Giles and Thomas G. Walker, "Judicial Policy-Making and Southern School Segregation," *Journal of Politics* 37, no. 4 (November 1975): 917–936. doi.org/10.2307/2129183.

96. Wilson McKinney, "Uvalde Bias Suit in Limbo till High Court Rules," *San Antonio Express*, June 25, 1971.

97. "Garza Case in Court Yesterday," *Uvalde (TX) Leader-News*, July 21, 1971.

98. "Judge Remands Garza-Shannon Case to School Board Hearing," *Uvalde (TX) Leader-News*, August 1, 1971.

99. "School Board Votes Not to Rehire Garza," *Uvalde (TX) Leader-News*, September 12, 1971.

100. "MAPA Support for Garza Ahead of Hearing," *Uvalde (TX) Leader-News*, November 21, 1971.

101. "Dr. Edgar Sustains Board Action on Garza Hearing," *Uvalde (TX) Leader-News*, March 5, 1972.

102. "State Board Defeats Garza Appeal," *Uvalde (TX) Leader-News*, April 9, 1972.

103. "Federal Suits in San Antonio Start Monday," *Uvalde (TX) Leader-News*, November 12, 1972.

104. Garza interview by Bhardwaj.

105. John Lumpkin, "District Judge Wood Delays Action in Case Involving Uvalde Schools," *San Antonio Express*, February 14, 1973.

106. *Morales v. Shannon*, 366 F. Supp. 813 (W. D. Tex. 1973). In 1973, the Uvalde school district merged with that of neighboring Batesville, adding one elementary school to its area of coverage.

107. "Fifth Circuit to Hear Oral Arguments Today," *Uvalde (TX) Leader-News*, December 5, 1974. By this point, MALDEF had moved its headquarters to San Francisco.

108. *Morales v. Shannon*, 516 F.2d 411 (5th Cir. 1975).

109. "Appeals Court Reverses District Court Rulings," *Uvalde (TX) Leader-News*, July 27, 1975.

110. "UCISD Appeals Ruling," *Uvalde (TX) Leader-News*, August 31, 1975.

111. "Supreme Court Rejects Uvalde Schools Appeal," *Uvalde (TX) Leader-News*, December 18, 1975.

112. "Uvalde School Decision Appealed," *Uvalde (TX) Leader-News*, June 29, 1976.

113. *Morales v. Shannon*, Cause No. DR-70-CA-14 (W. D. Tex. Aug. 9, 2007); "Bilingual Suit Dropped against Uvalde Schools," *Uvalde (TX) Leader-News*, December 5, 1976.

114. "Judge Hears School Suit," *Uvalde (TX) Leader-News*, December 16, 1976.

115. "Judge Hears School Suit," *Uvalde (TX) Leader-News*, December 16, 1976; "Judge Awards $8,000," *Uvalde (TX) Leader-News*, January 30, 1977.

116. *Morales v. Shannon*, Cause No. DR-70-CA-14 (W. D. Tex. Aug. 9, 2007).

117. Charley Robinson, "Decades-Old UCISD Suit Resolved," *Uvalde (TX) Leader-News*, August 3, 2017, uvaldeleadernews.com/articles/decades-old-ucisd-suit-resolved.

118. Morales interview.

119. Lugo interview.

120. Torres interview.

121. Perez interview.

122. Gonzales-Hanson interview.

123. Morales interview.

124. Porras interview.

125. Josué "George" Garza, interview by José Ángel Gutiérrez and Alfredo Santos, in *Recuerdos de Uvalde, Texas*, vol. 1 (Austin: Nopalito, 2004), 34, orig. pub. in *La Voz de Uvalde*, January 2, 1997.

126. Aguilera interview.

Chapter 9: "A Totality of Our Well-Being"

The title of this chapter comes from La Fe Clinic's philosophy of comprehensive and holistic community health care; see "Welcome," Centro de Salud Familiar La Fe, accessed January 6, 2019, lafe-ep.org/welcome.

1. I use the terms "South El Paso," "Southside," and "El Segundo Barrio" interchangeably throughout the chapter. The name El Segundo Barrio stems from South El Paso comprising the city's second political ward in the earlier part of the twentieth century. I use the term "ethnic Mexican" in reference to the first wave of Mexican immigrants who settled in El Paso, and "Mexican American" when discussing later generations. "Chicana/o" is used only for people who identified themselves as such.

2. "Background information," from Salvador Balcorta, oral history interview by Sandra Enríquez and David Robles, July 23, 2015, El Paso, Civil Rights in Black and Brown Interview Database [hereafter cited as CRBB Interview Database], crbb.tcu.edu/clips/1721/background-information-2.

3. For historic discussions regarding Mexican American social inequalities in El Paso, see Sandra I. Enríquez, "'¡El Barrio Unido Jámas Será Vencido!': Neighborhood Grassroots Activism and Community Preservation in El Paso, Texas" (PhD diss., University of Houston, 2016); Mario T. García, *Desert Immigrants: The Mexicans of El Paso, 1880–1920*, (New Haven, CT: Yale University Press, 1981); Oscar J. Martínez, *The Chicanos of El Paso: An Assessment of Progress*, (El Paso: Texas Western Press, 1980); Monica Perales, *Smeltertown: Making and Remembering a Southwest Border Community*, (Chapel Hill: University of North Carolina Press, 2010).

4. "Home," Centro de Salud Familiar La Fe, accessed January 6, 2019, lafe-ep.org.

5. For works on Mexican American public health in the late nineteenth and early twentieth

centuries, see John McKiernan-González, *Fevered Measures: Public Health and Race at the Texas-Mexico Borderlands, 1848–1942*, (Durham, NC: Duke University Press, 2012); Natalia Molina, *Fit to Be Citizens? Public Health and Race in Los Angeles, 1879–1939*, (Berkeley: University of California Press, 2006).

6. Felipe Hinojosa, "¡Medicina Sí Muerte No!: Race, Public Health, and the 'Long War on Poverty' in Mathis, Texas, 1948–1971," *Western Historical Quarterly* 44 (Winter 2013): 439.

7. For more on grassroots health initiatives, clinics, and community institutions, see Robert Bauman, *Race and the War on Poverty: From Watts to East L.A.* (Norman: University of Oklahoma Press, 2008); John Chavez, *Eastside Landmark: A History of the East Los Angeles Community Union, 1968–1993* (Stanford, CA: Stanford University Press, 1998); Lilia Fernandez, *Brown in the Windy City: Mexicans and Puerto Ricans in Postwar Chicago* (Chicago: University of Chicago Press, 2012); Mario T. García, "Gloria Arellanes," in *The Chicano Generation: Testimonios of the Movement* (Berkeley: University of California Press, 2015), 113–210; Judson L. Jeffries, ed., *On the Ground: The Black Panther Party in Communities across America* (Oxford: University of Mississippi Press, 2010); Alondra Nelson, *Body and Soul: The Black Panther Party and the Fight against Medical Discrimination* (Minneapolis: University of Minnesota Press, 2011); Annelise Orleck, *Storming Caesars Palace: How Black Mothers Fought Their Own War on Poverty* (Boston: Beacon, 2005).

8. Some of the clinic's founders and early staff members have passed away. Nina Cordero, one of the clinic's most influential founders, died in 1984 at the age of fifty-one.

9. García, *Desert Immigrants*, 65.

10. For more on the early development of El Paso's border economy, see García, *Desert Immigrants*; Oscar J. Martínez, *Border Boomtown: Ciudad Juárez since 1848* (Austin: University of Texas Press, 1978); Perales, *Smeltertown*.

11. Martínez, *Chicanos of El Paso*, 6.

12. Ibid., 11–16.

13. Telles is also the first Mexican American mayor in a major city. For more on Telles and his political career, see Mario T. García, *The Making of a Mexican American Mayor: Raymond L. Telles of El Paso and the Origins of Latino Political Power*, (Tucson: University of Arizona Press, 2018).

14. García, *Desert Immigrants*, 158; García, *Mexican American Mayor*, 44–46.

15. "Challenge for Single-Member Districts," from Fermin Dorado, oral history interview by Sandra Enríquez and David Robles, July 24, 2015, El Paso, CRBB Interview Database, crbb.tcu.edu/clips/2102/challenge-for-single-member-districts.

16. "Politics in El Paso," from Antonio Marin, oral history interview by Sandra Enríquez and David Robles, July 15, 2015, El Paso, CRBB Interview Database, crbb.tcu.edu/clips/2378/politics-in-el-paso.

17. "We Were Born in Hell," from Balcorta interview, crbb.tcu.edu/clips/1850/we-were-born-in-hell.

18. "Problems of South El Paso Rate as a Big Challenge to the Whole City," *El Paso Times*, March 4, 1970; for more on activism on housing conditions, see Enríquez, "¡El Barrio Unido Jámas Será Vencido!"; Benjamin Márquez, *Power and Politics in a Chicano Barrio: A Study of Mobilization Efforts and Community Power in El Paso* (Lanham, MD: University of America Press, 1985).

19. "'El Segundo' Old, Neglected, Dying," *El Paso Times*, November 28, 1973; Martínez, *Chicanos of El Paso*, 17.

20. "Poor Can't Get Good Medical Aid," *El Paso Times*, November 29, 1973.

21. "Becoming a Part of VISTA," from Homero Galicia, oral history interview by Sandra Enríquez and David Robles, July 21, 2015, El Paso, CRBB Interview Database, crbb.tcu.edu/clips/1493/becoming-apart-of-vista; "Father Rahm Service Center Inc., Heath Proposal rough draft," c. 1971, MS637, box 8, Amelia Mendez Castillo Papers, C. L. Sonnichsen Special Collections, University of Texas at El Paso Library [hereafter cited as Castillo Papers]; "La Fe Clinic Brings a Better Way of Life for the People of South El Paso," *Mantenga La Fe*, January 1992.

22. "Starting a Clinic and Student Activism Arising," from Galicia interview, crbb.tcu.edu/clips/1494/starting-a-clinic-and-student-activism-arising.

23. Ibid.

24. For more on health care availability in South El Paso, see Vicki Ruiz, "Confronting America," in *From Out of the Shadows: Mexican Women in Twentieth-Century America* (New York: Oxford University Press, 1998), 33–50; Monica Perales, "'Who Has a Greater Job than a Mother?': Defining Mexican Motherhood on the U.S.-Mexico Border in the Early Twentieth Century," in *On the Borders of Love and Power: Families and Kinship in the Intercultural American Southwest*, ed. Crista DeLuzio and David Wallace Adams (Berkeley: University of California Press, 2012), 163–184; Ann Gabbert, "Defining the Boundaries of Care: Local Responses to Global Concerns in El Paso Public Health Policy" (PhD diss., University of Texas at El Paso, 2006); Eve Carr, "Missionaries and Motherhood: Sixty Years of Public Health Work in South El Paso" (PhD diss., Arizona State University, 2003).

25. Enríquez, "¡El Barrio Unido Jámas Será Vencido!," 128–134.

26. For more on the Farah strike, see Ruiz, *From Out of the Shadows*, 127–132; Emily Honig, "Women at Farah Revisited: Political Mobilization and Its Aftermath among Chicana Workers in El Paso, Texas, 1972–1992," *Feminist Studies* 22, no. 2 (Summer 1996): 425–452.

27. William S. Clayson, *Freedom Is Not Enough: The War on Poverty and the Civil Rights Movement in Texas* (Austin: University of Texas Press, 2010), 114.

28. "Vista Involvement," from Felipe Peralta, oral history interview by Sandra Enríquez and David Robles, July 22, 2015, El Paso, CRBB Interview Database, crbb.tcu.edu/clips /1771/vista-involvement.

29. "JD Group Trains Leaders, Sets Protests," *El Paso Herald-Post*, December 31, 1971.

30. Ibid.

31. Ibid.

32. "Barrio: Community Control Would End 'Poverty Pimps,'" *El Paso Times*, April 27, 1977.

33. "Residents Seek Community Control," *El Paso Times*, April 27, 1977.

34. The story was pieced together from the memories of Salvador Balcorta and Guillermo Glenn; see "Origins of La Fe Clinic," from Balcorta interview, crbb.tcu.edu/clips/902/origins -of-la-fe-clinic, and "Adjusting to El Paso," from Guillermo Glenn, oral history interview by Sandra Enríquez and David Robles, July 16, 2015, El Paso, CRBB Interview Database, crbb.tcu .edu/clips/2435/adjusting-to-el-paso. While the interviewees' memories of the accident differ, the two agree that the girl fell and cut herself with a glass bottle or bottles. This story is also high-lighted in a newspaper article praising Dr. Raymond Gardea's work: "Pioneer of Health Care for Needy Lauded," *El Paso Times*, October 17, 2005.

35. "Origins of La Fe Clinic," from Balcorta interview.

36. Ibid.; "Adjusting to El Paso," from Glenn interview; A. C. Westover, "La Fe Clinic Services South El Paso," *Borderlands* 15 (1997), accessed August 1, 2017, El Paso Community College Library Services, epcc.libguides.com/content.php?pid=309255&sid=2629661.

37. "Origins of La Fe Clinic," from Balcorta interview.

38. Mary Margaret Davis, "Dr. Raymond Gardea: Outstanding Ex," *Nova* 7, no. 1 (October 1971): 1–4.

39. "Starting a Clinic and Student Activism Arising," from Galicia interview.

40. For more on Father Rahm's role in South El Paso, see Elizabeth Zinn, "He Begged That Gang Violence End with His Death," *Federal Probation* 23 (September 1959).

41. "Origins of La Fe Clinic," from Balcorta interview.

42. There are conflicting opening dates for the clinic. Salvador Balcorta, the history found on La Fe's website, and some newspaper articles cite 1967 as the year when the clinic opened. Grant applications and newspaper articles note that the clinic opened its doors in 1968. Grant applications also mention that the initial discussions to open the clinic occurred in 1967. See Expansion Proposal I&R Outline, c. 1972, MS637, box 8, Castillo Papers.

43. "Starting a Clinic and Student Activism Arising," from Galicia interview.

44. "Father Rahm Clinic Gets $5,000 Check," *El Paso Herald-Post*, July 28, 1970.

45. "La Fe Clinic Brings a Better Way of Life."

46. "Fund Raising Dance Set," *El Paso Herald-Post*, October 22, 1969.

47. "Father Rahm Clinic Gets $5,000 Check."

48. "Father Rahm Clinic Gets Grant," *El Paso Herald-Post*, August 13, 1970.

49. Information and Referral Services formal plan of community outreach announcement, March 1971; Family Health Center Grant II—Information & Referral Center (I&R) brief report on resources utilized by (I&R) and Father Rahm Clinic, c. 1972; both in MS637, box 7, Castillo Papers.

50. "Renaming the Clinic," from Balcorta interview, crbb.tcu.edu/clips/1832/renaming-the -clinic.

51. Pete Duarte, oral history interview by Sandra Enríquez and David Robles, July 23, 2015, El Paso, CRBB Interview Portal to Texas History, University of North Texas Libraries, texas history.unt.edu.ask:/67531/metapth104086.

52. "Announce Grant," *El Paso Herald-Post*, December 10, 1970.

53. "Details Released on ACTION Grant," *El Paso Herald-Post*, March 5, 1973.

54. "Renaming the Clinic," from Balcorta interview.

55. "Father Rahm Moves to New Quarters," *El Paso Herald-Post*, April 29, 1971.

56. "Announcement on Groundbreaking Ceremony for New Clinic," *El Paso Herald-Post*, June 8, 1971.

57. "Mejorando la salud; mejora el Chicano," *Nosotros*, August–September 1971, 2, translated from the Spanish by the author. Original text: "No se va a cobrar un centavo a aquellos hermanos que no puedan pagar. La clinica del Father Rahm es la clinica de los pobres, para los pobres, por los pobres."

58. I&R Background for Proposal, 2, c. 1972, MS637, box 8, Castillo Papers.

59. Woodie W. White to Amelia Castillo, December 27, 1971, MS637, box 7, Castillo Papers.

60. "Move to Aid Barrio Began Six Years Ago," *El Paso Times*, November 27, 1973.

61. "Clinic Receives Grant," *El Editorial* 2, no. 4 (August 15, 1972).

62. "Adjusting to El Paso," from Glenn interview.

63. "Health Centers: A New Concept for Health Delivery," *Nosotros*, August–September 1973, 2.

64. "El Paso's Second Ward Not like Health Resort," *El Paso Times*, November 25, 1973.

65. "Grass Roots Clinic Gets a Grant," *San Antonio Express*, July 6, 1972.

66. "Adjusting to El Paso," from Glenn interview.

67. "Barrio Health Center Location Major Issue," *El Paso Times*, November 29, 1973.

68. Ibid.

69. "Health Centers: A New Concept," 2.

70. Lamar A. Byers to Amelia Castillo, May 20, 1971, MS637, box 7, Castillo Papers.

71. "South El Paso Poor Can't Get Good Medical Aid for Many Reasons," *El Paso Times*, November 26, 1973.

72. "La Fe Head Tells Concept of Care," *El Paso Herald-Post*, May 1, 1975.

73. "Adjusting to El Paso," from Glenn interview.

74. Ruíz, "Confronting America," 36.

75. "Adjusting to El Paso," from Glenn interview; "Renaming the Clinic," from Balcorta interview.

76. "Renaming the Clinic," from Balcorta interview.

77. For more on the history of contraception and Chicana reproductive justice on the US-Mexico border, see Lina-Maria Murillo, "Birth Control on the Border: Race, Gender, Religion, and Class in the Making of the Birth Control Movement, El Paso, Texas, 1936–1973" (PhD diss., University of Texas at El Paso, 2016).

78. Amendment to Agreement for Delegation of Activities, September 1971, MS637, box 7, Castillo Papers; "Family Planning Grant Approved for Hospital," *El Paso Times*, June 22, 1971; "Hospital Family Planning Clinic Has Many Services," *El Paso Times*, April 25, 1973.

79. "College Education & Community," from Peralta interview, crbb.tcu.edu/clips/1780 /college-education-community.

80. "Renaming the Clinic," from Balcorta interview.

81. Ibid.

82. "La Fe Center Averages 100 Patients Daily," *El Paso Herald-Post*, February 12, 1975.

83. "Renaming the Clinic," from Balcorta interview.

84. "La Fe Clinic Dedicates South Side Facilities," *El Paso Times*, January 8, 1975.

85. "Cookies Count More than Dollars to La Fe Staff," *El Paso Times*, February 13, 1975.

86. "La Fe Center Averages 100 Patients Daily."

87. Ibid.

88. "Departments at La Fe Clinic: Pre Natal and WIC," *Mantenga La Fe*, January 1992.

89. "La Fe Clinica," from Glenn interview, crbb.tcu.edu/clips/2436/le-fe-clinica.

90. "La Fe Head Tells Concept of Care," *El Paso Herald-Post*, May 1, 1975.

91. "Tech Medical School Asked to Staff Clinic," *El Paso Herald-Post*, March 24, 1977.

92. Ibid.; "Tangled Web of Intrigue Covers $750,000 HEW Grant, *El Paso Journal*, April 6, 1977.

93. "Clinic Suffers Chaos Overdose," *El Paso Times*, April 14, 1977; "Tangled Web of Intrigue."

94. "Southside Residents Air Gripes about La Fe Clinic before HEW," *El Paso Times*, June 10, 1977.

95. "Renaming the Clinic," from Balcorta interview; "Tangled Web of Intrigue."

96. "Thinking Out Loud: La Fe Problem," *El Paso Herald-Post*, April 11, 1977.

97. "Tech Medical School Asked to Staff Clinic."

98. "La Fe Clinica," from Glenn interview.

99. "La Fe Head Tells Concept of Care."

100. "Thinking Out Loud: La Fe Problem."

101. "A Takeover of the Clinic," from Balcorta interview, crbb.tcu.edu/clips/1833/a-takeover -of-the-clinic.

102. "La Fe Directors Defy HEW Order to Quit," *El Paso Times*, July 2, 1977.

103. "Tangled Web of Intrigue."

104. "A Takeover of the Clinic," from Balcorta interview.

105. "2° Toma Clinica 'La Fe,'" *El Mestizo* 4, no. 3 (June 1977).

106. "MAYA and Local Political Groups," from Salvador Avila, oral history interview by Sandra Enríquez and David Robles, July 24, 2015, El Paso, CRBB Interview Database, crbb.tcu .edu/clips/940/maya-and-local-political-groups.

107. "Leadership in College and MEChA," from Fernando Chacón, oral history interview by Sandra Enríquez and David Robles, July 20, 2015, El Paso, CRBB Interview Database, crbb .tcu.edu/clips/1078/leadership-in-college-and-mecha.

108. "La Fe Demands Reported," *El Paso Herald-Post*, April 18, 1977.

109. Ibid.

110. "Police Action Ends La Fe Takeover," *El Paso Herald-Post*, April 20, 1977.

111. "La Fe Demands Reported."

112. "Police Action Ends La Fe Takeover."

113. "Health Care," from Peralta interview, crbb.tcu.edu/clips/1781/health-care.

114. "La Fe Court Order Issued," *El Paso Herald-Post*, April 28, 1977; "Restraining Order Continued," *El Paso Herald-Post*, May 5, 1977; "Judge to Restrain La Fe Protesters," *El Paso Herald-Post*, June 1, 1977; "Judge to Impose New Restraints on La Fe Clinic Protest Group," *El Paso Times*, June 2, 1977.

115. "2° Toma Clinica 'La Fe,'" translated from the Spanish by the author. Original text: "la gente de este barrio ha sido arrestada, calumniada y amenazada por las cortes, la policia, la preasa [*sic*] vendida, y el grupo oportunista que no quiere dejar el gueso [*sic*] que tiene en dicha clinica."

116. "HEW Studies Clinic," *El Paso Herald-Post*, June 11, 1977.

117. "Southside Residents Air Gripes about La Fe Clinic."

118. "New La Fe Elections Ordered," *El Paso Times*, June 24, 1977; "La Fe Clinic Protesters Block Security Guard," *El Paso Times*, August 5, 1977.

119. "New La Fe Elections Ordered."

120. "Elections for La Fe Ordered," *El Paso Times*, June 24, 1977.

121. "La Clinica Triunfa," *El Mestizo* 4, no. 4 (September 1977); "Clinic Patients Vote to Elect 10 to Board," *El Paso Times*, August 8, 1977.

122. "La Fe Clinic—An Example of Struggle," *Insurgencia Estudiantil* 1, no. 1 (September 1977).

123. "We Were Born in Hell," from Balcorta interview.

124. Duarte interview.

125. Ibid.

126. "La Fe Clinic Brings a Better Way of Life."

127. "Pete Duarte Loves People, and the Segundo Barrio," *Mantenga La Fe*, January 1992.

128. "Health Restored, Clinic's Future Is Bright," *El Paso Times*, April 6, 1986; "Pete Duarte: Association of Unfortunate and the Forgotten," *El Paso Times*, May 14, 1989; "La Fe Clinic Meets Standard," *El Paso Times*, September 6, 1991.

129. "La Fe, Library Form Partnership," *El Paso Citizen*, March 1992.

130. "Chicano AIDS Coalition" and "Chicano AIDS Coalition, Part Two," from Balcorta interview, crbb.tcu.edu/clips/1864/chicano-aids-coalition, crbb.tcu.edu/clips/1865/chicano-aids -coalition-part-two.

131. Duarte interview.

132. "What the Press Had to Say: La Fe Excels," *Mantenga La Fe*, January 1992.

133. "Director Turns 'Culture Shock' to Success Story," *El Paso Times*, April 6, 1986.

134. "What the Press Had to Say: La Fe Clinic Succeeds Because of Hard Work and Dedication," *Mantenga La Fe*, January 1992; "Health Status & Needs of Minorities in the 1990s," C-SPAN, June 8, 1990, accessed August 1, 2017, c-span.org/video/?12625-1/health -status-needs-minorities-1990s.

135. "La Fe Clinic Brings a Better Way of Life."

136. Monica Ortiz Uribe, "Health Hero: Centro de Salud La Fe's Salvador Balcorta," Latino USA, accessed August 1, 2017, latinousa.org/2012/09/28/health-hero-centro-de-salud-la-fes -salvador-balcorta.

137. "Work in the Health Department," from Balcorta interview, crbb.tcu.edu/clips/1862 /work-in-the-health-department.

138. "Activist Heads Clinic He Helped Create," *El Paso Times*, August 5, 1992.

139. "Community Reaction to the Expansion of La Fe Clinic, Part Two," from Balcorta inter-view, crbb.tcu.edu/clips/1878/community-reaction-to-the-expansion-of-la-fe-clinic-part-two.

140. "Activist Heads Clinic He Helped Create."

141. "The Clinic Since 1992," from Balcorta interview, crbb.tcu.edu/clips/1853/the-clinic -since-1992.

142. "The Clinic Since 1992" and "We Were Born in Hell," from Balcorta interview.

143. "The Clinic Since 1992," from Balcorta interview.

144. "Fixing the Housing Issues in El Paso," from Balcorta interview, crbb.tcu.edu/clips/1855 /fixing-the-housing-issues-in-el-paso.

145. "Culture & Technology Center," Centro de Salud Familiar La Fe, accessed January 6, 2019, lafe-ep.org/culture-technology-center.

146. "Push-out rates" refers to systemic challenges such as the lack of bilingual education and the irrelevancy of a curriculum, which ultimately force underrepresented students to drop out of school; see "Problems with Education in El Paso," from Balcorta interview, crbb.tcu.edu /clips/1874/problems-with-education-in-el-paso.

147. "2017 La Fe Children's César Chávez Day March Set for Friday," *El Paso Herald-Post*, March 30, 2017.

148. "La Fe Preparatory School," Centro de Salud Familiar La Fe, accessed August 1, 2017, lafe-ep.org/affiliates/la-fe-preparatory-school.

149. "Community Reaction to the Expansion of La Fe Clinic," from Balcorta interview, crbb .tcu.edu/clips/1877/community-reaction-to-the-expansion-of-la-fe-clinic.

150. "Health Care," from Peralta interview; "Salvador Balcorta: CEO, Centro de Salud Familiar La Fe," *El Paso Inc.*, April 29, 2012, accessed August 1, 2017, elpasoinc.com/news /q_and_a/article_cb046410-9241-11e1-bda8-001a4bcf6878.html (subscription required).

151. "Community Reaction to the Expansion of La Fe Clinic, Part Two," from Balcorta interview.

152. "Community Reaction to the Expansion of La Fe Clinic," from Balcorta interview.

1. For a nuanced look at Amon Carter, the "Where the West Begins" slogan, and Fort Worth's competing regional identities, see Brian Cervantez, *Amon Carter: A Lone Star Life* (Norman: University of Oklahoma Press, 2019).

2. Diane Smith, "Confederate Battle Flag Disputes Were Settled Years Ago at UT Arlington, Richland High," *Fort Worth Star-Telegram*, June 27, 2015. I am grateful to Gregory Kosc for pointing out Arlington's origins to me.

3. Randolph B. Campbell, *An Empire for Slavery: The Peculiar Institution in Texas, 1821–1865* (Baton Rouge: Louisiana State University Press, 1989), 1.

4. "Personal Experiences with Segregation," from Bob Ray Sanders, oral history interview by Miles Davison, February 27, 2013, Fort Worth, Texas, CRBB Interview, crbb.tcu.edu/clips /personal-experiences-with-segregation.

5. See Peter C. Martinez, "Ready to Run: Fort Worth's Mexicans in Search of Representation, 1960–2000" (PhD diss., University of North Texas, 2017), ch. 4.

6. Gray quoted in "Fort Worth Must Address Race as It Tackles Demands on Police Reform, Councilwoman Says," *Fort Worth Star-Telegram*, June 23, 2020.

7. Katie Sherrod, "Who Runs Fort Worth?," *D Magazine*, November 1995, accessed June 19, 2017, dmagazine.com/publications/d-magazine/1995/november/power-who-runs-fort -worth. For more recent critiques of the Fort Worth Way, see "The 'Fort Worth Way' Needs Adjustment," *Fort Worth Star-Telegram*, June 5, 2017; Richard B. Gonzales, "If You Think Criticism of SB4 Is Just Perception, Maybe That's the Problem," *Fort Worth Star-Telegram*, August 7, 2017.

8. Bob Ray Sanders, *Calvin Littlejohn: Portrait of a Community in Black and White* (Fort Worth: TCU Press, 2009), 10.

9. Richard F. Selcer, *Fort Worth: A Texas Original!* (Austin: Texas State Historical Association, 2004), 45.

10. "Undermining Black-Brown Coalitioning, Part Two," from Estrus Tucker, oral history interview by Todd Moye and David Robles, June 12, 2015, Fort Worth, Texas, CRBB Interview Database, crbb.tcu.edu/clips/undermining-Black-brown-coalitioning-part-ii.

11. "Passive-Aggressive Discrimination in Fort Worth," from Marilyn Jean Johnson, oral history interview by Sarah Travis, March 24, 2014, Fort Worth, Texas, CRBB Interview Database, crbb.tcu.edu/clips/passive-aggressive-discrimination.

12. "Race Relations in Fort Worth," from Clifford Davis, oral history interview by Todd Moye, Sandra Enríquez, and David Robles, June 11, 2015, Fort Worth, Texas, CRBB Interview Database, crbb.tcu.edu/clips/race-relations-in-fort-worth.

13. "Klan Composed of Leaders in City, Camp Asserts," *Fort Worth Star-Telegram*, April 23, 1922; see also "Good Deeds by Day, Dark Deeds by Night," *Hometown by Handlebar* (blog), November 6, 2020, hometownbyhandlebar.com/?p=12678.

14. Cervantez, *Amon Carter*, 31; Bud Kennedy, "For Opal Lee, 89, Juneteenth Is More than a License Plate," *Fort Worth Star-Telegram*, October 17, 2015; Kennedy, "She Was 12 When Whites Burned Her House Down," *Fort Worth Star-Telegram*, June 12, 2020; Richard F. Selcer, *A History of Fort Worth in Black and White: 165 Years of African-American Life* (Denton: University of North Texas Press, 2015), 146, 434, 438–443.

15. Carlos E. Cuéllar, *Stories from the Barrio: A History of Mexican Fort Worth* (Fort Worth: TCU Press, 2003), 42–43.

16. Ibid., xiv, 3.

17. Selcer, *Fort Worth*, 47.

18. Cuéllar, *Stories from the Barrio*, 49; see also Moisés Acuña Gurrola, "Barrios," *Historians of Latino Americans Tarrant County*, holatarrantcounty.org/barrios.

19. Cuéllar, *Stories from the Barrio*, 23–24.

20. Sanders, *Calvin Littlejohn*, 11.

21. Zapata quoted in Selcer, *Fort Worth*, 49; "Discrimination at Movie Theater," from Raúl

Durán, oral history interview by Moisés Acuña Gurrola, January 1, 2014, Fort Worth, Texas, CRBB Interview Database, crbb.tcu.edu/clips/discrimination-at-movie-theater.

22. Mae Cora Peterson, oral history interview by Todd Moye, July 25, 2012, University of North Texas Oral History Program, Denton, Texas.

23. "Segregation in Fort Worth," from Durán interview, crbb.tcu.edu/clips/segregation.

24. "Hunger for Social Justice," from Eva Bonilla, oral history interview by unidentified interviewer, March 28, 2013, Fort Worth, CRBB Interview Database, crbb.tcu.edu/clips/9/hunger-for-social-justice.

25. "Personal Experiences with Segregation," from Sanders interview.

26. "Arriving at Fort Worth," from Marilyn Jean Johnson, oral history interview by Sarah Travis, March 24, 2014, Fort Worth, Texas, CRBB Interview Database, crbb.tcu.edu/clips/arriving-at-fort-worth.

27. "Growing Up in Fort Worth," from Eddie Griffin, oral history by Todd Moye, February 1, 2014, Fort Worth, Texas, CRBB Interview Database, crbb.tcu.edu/clips/growing-up-in-fort-worth.

28. Selcer, *Fort Worth*, 46; see also Bob Ray Sanders, "A Local Woman, a Different Bus, Same Bias," *Fort Worth Star-Telegram*, February 19, 2003, and Sanders, "Bus Case Settled the Fort Worth Way," *Fort Worth Star-Telegram*, February 21, 2003.

29. See, for instance, "Bethlehem Baptist Church Mural," The Crisis at Mansfield, accessed June 5, 2017, mansfieldcrisis.omeka.net/items/show/8.

30. John Howard Hicks, oral history interview by Moisés Acuña Gurrola and Judy Cortinas, April 28, 2015, University of North Texas Oral History Program, Denton, Texas; see also "John Howard Hicks on Saturdays in Mansfield," The Crisis at Mansfield, accessed June 5, 2017, mansfieldcrisis.omeka.net/items/show/240.

31. See "We Don't Serve Negroes," The Crisis at Mansfield, accessed June 5, 2017, mansfieldcrisis.omeka.net/exhibits/show/mansfield-before-1956/item/81.

32. Floyd Moody, oral history interview by Kimberly Moody, May 22, 2014, University of North Texas Oral History Program, Denton, Texas; see also "Floyd Moody Talks about What He Did for Leisure Growing Up in Mansfield," The Crisis at Mansfield, accessed June 5, 2017, mansfieldcrisis.omeka.net/items/show/300.

33. See "Mansfield Community Cemetery," The Crisis at Mansfield, accessed June 5, 2017, mansfieldcrisis.omeka.net/items/show/12.

34. Moody interview.

35. Ibid.; see also "Floyd Moody Discusses Utilities in West Mansfield," The Crisis at Mansfield, accessed June 5, 2017, mansfieldcrisis.omeka.net/items/show/301.

36. See "Jackson v. Rawdon," The Crisis at Mansfield, accessed June 5, 2017, mansfieldcrisis.omeka.net/exhibits/show/jackson-v-rawdon.

37. Bill Hanna, "60 Years Ago, 3 Black Teens Tried to Enroll in Mansfield High—'Never' Was the Reply," *Fort Worth Star-Telegram*, March 29, 2016, accessed June 19, 2017, star-telegram.com/news/local/community/arlington/article68837362.html; "Jackson v. Rawdon Overview," The Crisis at Mansfield, accessed June 19, 2017, mansfieldcrisis.omeka.net/exhibits/show/jackson-v-rawdon/jackson-v-rawdon-overview; see also Ramona Houston, "The NAACP State Conference in Texas: Intermediary and Catalyst for Change," *Journal of African American History* 94, no. 4 (Fall 2009): 509–528; Hicks interview.

38. See "Mansfield Local History, Before 1956," The Crisis at Mansfield, accessed June 5, 2017, mansfieldcrisis.omeka.net/exhibits/show/mansfield-before-1956/mansfield-local-history—befor; see also "Desegregation Case in Mansfield, Part One," from Davis interview, crbb.tcu.edu/clips/desegregation-case-in-mansfield-part-one; Neil R. McMillen, *The Citizens Council: Organized Resistance to the Second Reconstruction, 1954–1964* (Urbana: University of Illinois Press, 1971).

39. See "Mansfield Public Memory, Before 1956," The Crisis at Mansfield, accessed June 5, 2017, mansfieldcrisis.omeka.net/exhibits/show/mansfield-before-1956/mansfield-public-memory—befor.

40. "Separate But Equal or Full Integration?," From Davis interview, crbb.tcu.edu/clips /separate-but-equal-or-full-integration.

41. Houston, "NAACP State Conference in Texas," 518–519; see also "Jackson v. Rawdon Overview."

42. "Jackson v. Rawdon Overview"; *Jackson v. Rawdon*, 235 F.2d 93 (5th Cir. 1956), available on Justia, law.justia.com/cases/federal/appellate-courts/F2/235/93/334511.

43. Robyn Duff Ladino, *Desegregating Texas Schools: Eisenhower, Shivers, and the Crisis at Mansfield High* (Austin: University of Texas Press, 1996); and Ricky F. Dobbs, *Yellow Dogs and Republicans: Allan Shivers and Texas Two-Party Politics* (College Station: Texas A&M University Press, 2005), 136–141.

44. Ladino, *Desegregating Texas Schools*.

45. Moody interview; "Floyd Moody Discusses President Eisenhower's Lack of Involvement with 1956 Integration Attempts at Mansfield High School," The Crisis at Mansfield, accessed August 7, 2017, mansfieldcrisis.omeka.net/items/show/260.

46. "Mansfield, Part Two," from Davis interview, crbb.tcu.edu/clips/mansfield-part-two.

47. "Telegram Joe Pool to Allan Shivers 1956-08-31," The Crisis at Mansfield, accessed August 7, 2017, mansfieldcrisis.omeka.net/items/show/182.

48. "Mansfield, Part Two," from Davis interview.

49. Michael L. Gillette, "The Rise of the NAACP in Texas," *Southwestern Historical Quarterly* 81, no. 4 (April 1978): 393–416.

50. Ibid.

51. "Neighborhood Riot," from Lloyd Austin, oral history interview by Madison Scott, April 2, 2013, Fort Worth, Texas, CRBB Interview Database, crbb.tcu.edu/clips/housing-riots.

52. "News Script: New Racial Strife in Fort Worth," WBAP-TV, September 2, 1956, Portal to Texas History, University of North Texas Libraries, texashistory.unt.edu/ark:/67531 /metadc306385/m1/1/?q=%22lloyd%20austin%22; "News Clip: New Racial Strife in Fort Worth; Mansfield," WBAP-TV, September 2, 1956, Portal to Texas History, University of North Texas Libraries, texashistory.unt.edu/ark:/67531/metadc307692.

53. Selcer, *Fort Worth*, 440; "Neighborhood Riot," from Austin interview; WBAP coverage of the demonstration on North Judkins, Portal to Texas History.

54. "News Script: Mansfield," WBAP-TV, September 2, 1956, Portal to Texas History, University of North Texas Libraries, texashistory.unt.edu/ark:/67531/metadc306291.

55. Houston, "NAACP State Conference in Texas," 518, 520.

56. Sanders, *Calvin Littlejohn*, 15; see also "History of the Kirkpatrick School in Fort Worth," from Benny Sherman, oral history interview by Todd Moye and David Robles, June 12, 2015, Fort Worth, Texas, CRBB Interview Database, crbb.tcu.edu/clips/benny-sherman-birth-story.

57. See Tina Nicole Cannon, "Cowtown and the Color Line: Desegregating Fort Worth's Public Schools" (PhD diss., Texas Christian University, 2009), chs. 1, 3; "Single Member Districts in Fort Worth," from Davis interview, crbb.tcu.edu/clips/single-member-districts-in-fort-worth.

58. See Cannon, "Cowtown and the Color Line," ch. 4.

59. Sanders, *Calvin Littlejohn*, 15.

60. "Transplanted" and "Eighteen Years to Comply," from Tucker interview, crbb.tcu.edu /clips/transplanted, crbb.tcu.edu/clips/eighteen-years-to-comply.

61. "Eighteen Years to Comply," from Tucker interview.

62. See Cecelia Sanchez Hill, "¿Mi Tierra, También? Mexican American Civil Rights in Fort Worth, 1940–1990s" (MA thesis, University of Texas at Arlington, 2016), ch. 3.

63. Brenda Norwood, oral history interview by Megan Middleton, April 11, 2015, University of North Texas Oral History Program, Denton, Texas.

64. Ibid.

65. Cannon, "Cowtown and the Color Line," 71.

66. "Single Member Districts in Fort Worth," from Davis interview.

67. "Black Power and the United Front in Fort Worth," from Sanders interview, crbb.tcu.edu /clips/Black-power.

68. Roy Brooks quoted in "United Front," Uncovering the Movement: An Exploration of Civil Rights in Fort Worth, accessed August 7, 2017, fortworthcivilrights.wordpress.com/the-themes/united-front.

69. Marjorie Crenshaw quoted in ibid.

70. "Clifford Davis and Marion Brooks" and "Women in Civil Rights," from Vivian Wells, oral history interview by Max Krochmal and David Robles, June 13, 2015, Fort Worth, Texas, CRBB Interview Database, crbb.tcu.edu/clips/clifford-davis-and-marion-brooks, crbb.tcu.edu/clips/women-in-civil-rights.

71. Hill, "¿Mi Tierra, También?"; Selcer, *Fort Worth*, 50; Martinez, "Ready to Run"; Max Krochmal, *Blue Texas: The Making of a Multiracial Democratic Coalition in the Civil Rights Era* (Chapel Hill: University of North Carolina Press, 2016), 259–265.

72. "Direct Action Protests," from Pauline Gasca-Valenciano, oral history interview by Max Krochmal, Sandra Enríquez, and David Robles, Fort Worth June 10, 2015, CRBB Interview Database, crbb.tcu.edu/clips/2152/direct-action-protests.

73. Richard J. Gonzales, "Fort Worth's Chicana Queen Devoted Her Life to Social Justice," *Fort Worth Star-Telegram*, June 12, 2018, star-telegram.com/latest-news/article213055704.html.

74. "Growing Up in Fort Worth," from Gasca-Valenciano interview, crbb.tcu.edu/clips/2144/growing-up-in-fort-worth-2.

75. "Becoming an Activist," from Gasca-Valenciano interview, crbb.tcu.edu/clips/2148/becoming-an-activist.

76. Selcer, *Fort Worth*, 49.

77. US Census Bureau, "Quick Facts: Tarrant County, Texas," census.gov/quickfacts/fact/table/tarrantcountytexas/PST120219; all figures as of July 1, 2019.

78. "Black-Brown Relations," from Davis interview, crbb.tcu.edu/clips/single-member-districts-in-fort-worth.

79. "Fighting Gerrymandering," from Renny Rosas, oral history interview by Caleigh Prewitt, March 21, 2013, Fort Worth, Texas, CRBB Interview Database, crbb.tcu.edu/clips/fighting-gerrymandering.

80. Houston, "NAACP State Conference in Texas," 517.

81. "Working with the War on Poverty," from Gasca-Valenciano interview, crbb.tcu.edu/clips/2149/working-with-the-war-on-poverty.

82. "Working in the CAA," from Gasca-Valenciano interview, crbb.tcu.edu/clips/2157/working-in-the-caa.

83. Ibid.

84. "Black-Brown Coalition Building" and "New Black-Brown Coalitioning," from Tucker interview, crbb.tcu.edu/clips/Black-brown-coalition-building, crbb.tcu.edu/clips/new-Black-brown-coalitioning.

85. "Black-Brown Coalition Building," from Tucker interview.

86. "Hispanic Population Growth in Poly, Fort Worth," from Tucker interview, crbb.tcu.edu/clips/hispanic-population-growth-in-poly-fort-worth.

87. J'Nell Pate, *North of the River: A Brief History of North Fort Worth* (Fort Worth: TCU Press, 1994), ch. 4; Cuéllar, *Stories from the Barrio*; Selcer, *Fort Worth*, 104; see also "History of Shiloh Missionary Baptist Church," from Benny Sherman, oral history interview by Todd Moye and David Robles, June 12, 2015, Fort Worth, Texas, CRBB Interview Database, crbb.tcu.edu/clips/history-of-shiloh-missionary-baptist-church.

88. "Chambers of Commerce in Fort Worth," from Tucker interview, crbb.tcu.edu/clips/chambers-of-commerce-in-fort-worth.

89. US Census Bureau, "Quick Facts: Tarrant County, Texas."

Chapter 11: Civil Rights in the "City of Hate"

1. I use the term "Mexican Americans" to refer to American-born people of Mexican descent; "Mexican nationals" to refer to people born in Mexico but living in the United States; and

"Mexicans" and "Mexicanas/os" to refer to both Mexican Americans and Mexican nationals. "Chicanas/os," which refers to a specific political identity of the late 1960s and 1970s, is used only to identify those who referred to themselves as such.

2. Eduardo Celis, "The Ghost of Santos Rodríguez," *Dallas Observer*, July 16, 1992, 14–16, Vertical Files, Dallas Public Library; Osmín Hernández, "¡Justicia for Santos! Mexican American Civil Rights and the Santos Rodríguez Affair in Dallas, Texas, 1969–1978" (master's thesis, Texas Christian University, 2016), 1.

3. René Martínez, interview by the author, September 10, 2017, recording in author's possession.

4. "Santos Rodríguez Protest," from Robert Medrano, oral history interview by Moíses Acuña Gurrola, June 10, 2015, Dallas, Civil Rights in Black and Brown Interview Database [hereafter cited as CRBB Interview Database], Texas Christian University, crbb.tcu.edu /clips/santos-rodriguez-protest-2.

5. "Police Taunted by Crowd," *Dallas Morning News*, July 29, 1973; "Protest at First More like Picnic or School Rally," *Dallas Times Herald*, July 29, 1973.

6. "Cain Put Behind Bars," *Dallas Morning News*, July 27, 1973; "Jury Finds Cain Guilty of Murder," *Dallas Morning News*, November 16, 1973.

7. The Reverend Peter Johnson, interview by the author, September 29, 2017, recording in author's possession; "Burglary Suspect's Death Brings Citizens Protest," *Dallas Morning News*, May 22, 1970.

8. "Attorneys Seek Cain Probation," *Dallas Times Herald*, November 16, 1973.

9. "About That No. 3 ranking: Fatal Police Shootings Are Down in Dallas since 1980s," *Dallas Morning News*, August 14, 2015.

10. Max Krochmal, *Blue Texas: The Making of a Multiracial Democratic Coalition in the Civil Rights Era* (Chapel Hill: University of North Carolina Press, 2016), 64.

11. W. Marvin Dulaney, "Whatever Happened to the Civil Rights Movement in Dallas, Texas?," in *Essays on the American Civil Rights Movement*, ed. John Dittmer, W. Marvin Dulaney, and Kathleen Underwood (College Station: Texas A&M University Press, 1993), 69.

12. "Dallas Mob Hangs Negro from Pole at Elks' Arch," *Dallas Morning News*, March 4, 1910; Dulaney, "Whatever Happened to Civil Rights," 68.

13. For more on Texas and the Ku Klux Klan during the 1920s, see Norman Brown, *Hood, Bonnet, and the Little Brown Jug: Texas Politics, 1921–1928* (College Station: Texas A&M University Press, 1984).

14. Dulaney, "Whatever Happened to Civil Rights," 70–71.

15. W. Marvin Dulaney, "The Progressive Voters League: A Political Voice for African Americans in Dallas," *Legacies: A History Journal for Dallas and North Central Texas* 3, no. 1 (Spring 1991): 27–32; Dulaney, "Whatever Happened to Civil Rights," 72.

16. Michael Phillips, *White Metropolis: Race, Ethnicity, and Religion in Dallas, 1941–2001* (Austin: University of Texas Press, 2006), 96.

17. Dulaney, "Whatever Happened to Civil Rights," 74.

18. For more on the elimination of the white primary, see Darlene Clark Hine, *Black Victory: The Rise and Fall of the White Primary in Texas* (1979; Columbia: University of Missouri Press, 2003); for *Sweatt v. Painter*, see Michael L. Gillette, "Blacks Challenge the White University," *Southwestern Historical Quarterly* 86, no. 2 (October 1982): 321–344; Merline Pitre, *In Struggle against Jim Crow: Lulu B. White and the NAACP, 1900–1957* (College Station: Texas A&M University Press, 2009).

19. For more on the work of the NAACP in Texas, see Michael L. Gillette, "The Rise of the NAACP in Texas," *Southwestern Historical Quarterly* 81, no. 4 (April 1978); Dulaney, "Whatever Happened to Civil Rights," 73–74; Brian Behnken, "The 'Dallas Way': Protest, Response, and the Civil Rights Experience in Big D and Beyond," *Southwestern Historical Quarterly* 111, no. 1 (July 2007): 7–10.

20. See Harvey Graff, *The Dallas Myth: The Making and Unmaking of an American City* (Minneapolis: University of Minnesota Press, 2008).

21. For more, see Jim Schutze, *The Accommodation: The Politics of Race in an American City* (Secaucus, NJ: Citadel, 1987).

22. "Jim Crow Out on City Buses," *Dallas Express*, April 28, 1956; Behnken, "Dallas Way," 10.

23. Dulaney, "Whatever Happened to Civil Rights," 77. For more on the desegregation of Dallas's schools, see Glenn M. Linden, *Desegregating Schools in Dallas: Four Decades in the Federal Courts* (Dallas: Three Forks, 1995).

24. Ramona Houston, "The NAACP State Conference in Texas: Intermediary and Catalyst for Change, 1937 to 1957," *Journal of African American History* 94, no. 4 (Fall 2009): 522–523.

25. Judge Dunagan lifted the permanent injunction against the NAACP in Texas on May 8, 1957; see Dulaney, "Whatever Happened to Civil Rights," 77.

26. Dulaney, "Whatever Happened to Civil Rights," 79.

27. "Negro Clergyman Served at Downtown Lunch Counter," *Dallas Express*, May 2, 1960; "Negroes Are Served at Several Downtown Eating Places," *Dallas Post Tribune*, April 30, 1960.

28. The Reverend Earl Allen, interview by Stephen Fagin, June 23, 2006, The Sixth Floor Museum at Dealey Plaza Oral History Collection, Dallas, Texas.

29. Dulaney, "Whatever Happened to Civil Rights," 83; Behnken, "Dallas Way," 21–22.

30. For more on the post-1955 ideology of SNCC, see Clayborne Carson, *In Struggle: SNCC and the Black Awakening of the 1960s* (Cambridge, MA: Harvard University Press, 1981).

31. Ernest McMillan, interview by the author, July 20, 2017, recording in author's possession; Dulaney, "Whatever Happened to Civil Rights," 86–87.

32. "Tactics Against Police Harassment," from Fahim Minkah, oral history interview by Katherine Bynum, August 26, 2017, Dallas, Texas, CRBB Interview Database, crbb.tcu.edu /clips/7141/tactics-against-police-misconduct.

33. "Falsely Accusing SNCC Members," from Minkah, crbb.tcu.edu/clips/7142/falsely -accusing-sncc-members.

34. Ava Tiye Kinsey and Judson L. Jeffries, "From Civil Rights to Black Power in Texas: Dallas to Denton and Back to Dallas," in *The Black Panther Party in a City Near You*, ed. Judson L. Jeffries (Athens: University of Georgia Press, 2018), 154–155.

35. "Dallas Marchers Protest Slayings," *Dallas Morning News*, May 24, 1970; Johnson interview.

36. The Black Panther Party leader purged the entire chapter of the Dallas NCCF after suspecting Gaines of being a police informant; see "Dallas NCCF Disbanded," *Black Panther*, February 20, 1971, and Kinsey and Jeffries, "From Civil Rights to Black Power," 166–167.

37. Bianca Mercado, "With Their Hearts in Their Hands: Forging a Mexican Community in Dallas, 1900–1925 (master's thesis, University of North Texas, 2008), 28–29.

38. Gwendolyn Rice, "Little Mexico and the Barrios of Dallas," *Legacies: A History Journal for Dallas and North Central Texas* 4, no. 2 (Fall 1992): 21; Sol Villasana, *Dallas's Little Mexico* (Charleston, SC: Arcadia, 2011), 17; Mercado, "With Their Hearts in Their Hands," 45–46.

39. Rice, "Little Mexico and the Barrios," 23.

40. Arthur T. Tattman, "Colonia, Commerce, and Consuls: The Dallas Mexican American Chamber of Commerce, the Early Years, 1939–1948" (master's thesis, Southern Methodist University, 2005), 21; Rice, "Little Mexico and the Barrios," 23.

41. Francisco Medrano, interview by José Ángel Gutiérrez, July 16, 1997, Tejano Voices, Center for Mexican American Studies, interview 37, University of Texas at Arlington Libraries, library.uta.edu/tejanovoices/xml/CMAS_037.xml.

42. "Discrimination Experiences & Involvement with NAACP," from Ricardo Medrano, oral history interview by Katherine Bynum, June 13, 2015, Dallas, Texas, CRBB Interview Database, crbb.tcu.edu/clips/1630/discrimination-experinces-involvement-with-naacp.

43. "Little Mexico: El Barrio" (1997), posted on YouTube by KERA, August 1, 2013, accessed September 3, 2019, youtube.com/watch?v=DFXH9q_av4s.

44. Mario T. García, *Mexican Americans: Leadership, Ideology, and Identity, 1930–1960* (New Haven, CT: Yale University Press, 1989), 1–3.

45. George N. Green, "The Felix Longoria Affair," *Journal of Ethnic Studies* 19, no. 3 (Fall 1991): 23.

46. David Montejano, *Anglos and Mexicans in the Making of Texas, 1836–1986* (Austin: University of Texas Press, 1987), 278–279. For more on the range of issues in which LULAC assisted,

see Cynthia Orozco, *No Mexicans, Women, or Dogs Allowed: The Rise of the Mexican American Civil Rights Movement* (Austin: University of Texas Press, 2009), 5–9; Emilio Zamora, *Claiming Rights and Righting Wrongs: Mexican Workers and Job Politics during World War II* (College Station: Texas A&M University Press, 2008). For more on *Hernandez v. Texas*, see Michael A. Olivas, ed., *"Colored Men" and "Hombres Aqui": "Hernandez v. Texas" and the Emergence of Mexican-American Lawyering* (Houston: Arte Publico, 2006), 43–46.

47. García, *Mexican Americans*.

48. Villasana, *Dallas's Little Mexico*, 34.

49. F. Medrano interview.

50. Anita Martínez, interview by José Ángel Gutiérrez, June 10, 1999, Tejano Voices, Center for Mexican American Studies, interview 129, University of Texas at Arlington, library.uta.edu /tejanovoices/interview.php?cmasno=129.

51. Max Krochmal, "Chicano Labor and Multiracial Politics in Post–World War II Texas," in *Life and Labor in the New New South*, ed. Robert Zieger (Gainesville: University Press of Florida, 2012), 133–138; Krochmal, *Blue Texas*, 364–365.

52. F. Medrano interview.

53. "Mexican Americans for Progressive Action (MAPA)" and "First Political Campaign," from Frances Rizo, oral history interview by Katherine Bynum, June 10, 2015, Dallas, Texas, CRBB Interview Database, crbb.tcu.edu/clips/mexican-americans-for-progressive-action-mapa, crbb.tcu.edu/clips/first-political-campaign.

54. "Getting Involved with the PTA" and "Work in the PTA," from Rizo interview, crbb.tcu .edu/clips/getting-involved-with-the-pta, crbb.tcu.edu/clips/work-in-the-pta.

55. For more on the Brown Berets, see David Montejano, *Sancho's Journal: Exploring the Political Edge with the Brown Berets* (Austin: University of Texas Press, 2016); Ernesto Chávez, *Mi Raza Primero: Nationalism, Identity, Insurgency in the Chicano Movement in Los Angeles 1966–1978* (Berkeley: University of California Press, 2002).

56. "Kiko's Grocery Store," from Ricardo Medrano interview, crbb.tcu.edu/clips/my-grocery -store-kikos.

57. "Brown Berets," from Ricardo Medrano interview, crbb.tcu.edu/clips/the-start-with -brown-berets; Juan M. Pérez, *Through Brown Eyes: A Short History of the Dallas Brown Berets Organization and the Chicano Movement from My Point of View* (CreateSpace, 2014), Kindle ed.

58. "Brown Berets," from Ricardo Medrano interview.

59. Ibid.

60. Hernández, "Justicia for Santos," 64; "The Search for Common Recognition," from Ricardo Medrano interview, crbb.tcu.edu/clips/the-search-for-common-recognition.

61. "Local Issues," from Robert Medrano interview, crbb.tcu.edu/clips/local-issues.

62. United States Commission on Civil Rights, Texas State Advisory Committee, *Civil Rights in Texas: A Report* (1970).

63. "Annual Police Report, 1971," Dallas Police Department, box 3, folder 2, Dallas Police Department Historical Reports, Records, and Newsletters, 1930–Current, Dallas Municipal Archives, Dallas, Texas.

64. Dallas's two Black-owned newspapers, the *Dallas Express* and the *Dallas Post Tribune*, reported numerous instances of police brutality throughout the twentieth century. Similarly, *El Sol de Texas*, the only Spanish-language newspaper in Dallas, reported cases of police violence.

65. "Santos Rodríguez Case, Part One," from Rizo interview, crbb.tcu.edu/clips/santos -rodriguez-case-part-one; Hernández, "Justicia for Santos," 69–70.

66. "Suspects Arrested in Trinity Slayings," *Dallas Morning News*, February 16, 1971; "Racial Profiling," from Richard Menchaca, oral history interview by Moíses Acuña Gurrola, June 13, 2016, Dallas, Texas, CRBB Interview Database, crbb.tcu.edu/clips/racial-profiling-in-dallas.

67. "Santos Rodriguez Case, Part One," from Rizo interview.

68. Hernández, "Justicia for Santos," 71; "Authorities Nab Guzman: Apartment Search Also Nets 2nd Man," *Dallas Morning News*, February 18, 1971.

69. The district attorney eventually dropped the charges against Tomás due to a lack of evidence, see Hernández, "Justicia for Santos," 72.

70. "Poetic Justice," from Minkah interview, crbb.tcu.edu/clips/poetic-justice; "Black Party Leader Defies Mayor, Finishes Speech," *Dallas Morning News*, February 23, 1971.

71. "Bois d'arc" is pronounced "boh-dark." Charlie Young, telephone interview by the author, September 9, 2017, recording in author's possession; Susanne Starling, "Stopping the Bulldozers: The East Dallas Community Design Committee and Urban Renaissance in the 1970s," *Legacies: A History Journal for Dallas and North Central Texas* 25, no. 1 (Spring 2013): 42; "Bois d'Arc Patriots, Part One," from John Fullinwider, oral history interview by Katherine Bynum, July 7, 2017, Dallas, Texas, CRBB Interview Database, crbb.tcu.edu /clips/activism-part-one.

72. Young interview; "Man Killed by Police," *Dallas Morning News*, January 18, 1971.

73. "Santos Rodríguez and Michael Morehead," from Minkah interview, crbb.tcu.edu /clips/7293/santos-rodriguez-and-michael-morehead; "Tomas and Berta Rodriguez and Santos Rodríguez," from Ricardo Medrano interview, crbb.tcu.edu/clips/1640/thomas-v-berto -rodriques-case.

74. "Jobless Stage Downtown March to Demand Work," *Dallas Morning News*, April 27, 1975; Young interview.

75. Young interview; "40 Klansmen March in Dallas," *Dallas Morning News*, November 4, 1979. The five-year statute of limitations ran out, and Cain was never indicted on federal charges. He served only two and a half years in Huntsville State Penitentiary for the murder; see Hernández, "Justicia for Santos," 102.

76. "Santos Rodríguez Case, Part One," from Rizo interview; "Woman, 27, Held in Shooting Death," *Dallas Morning News*, May 8, 1971.

77. "Getting Involved in the PTA," from Rizo interview.

78. "Domestic Violence," from Rizo interview, crbb.tcu.edu/clips/domestic-violence.

79. "Racial Profiling in Dallas," from Menchaca interview.

80. For more on conservative politics in Dallas, see Edward H. Miller, *Nut Country: Right-Wing Dallas and the Birth of the Southern Strategy* (Chicago: University of Chicago Press, 2015).

81. "1st Negro Named to Dallas Council," *Dallas Morning News*, February 21, 1967.

82. "Jonsson Leads CCA to Another Victory," *Dallas Morning News*, April 2, 1969.

83. See Benjamin Márquez, *Democratizing Texas Politics: Race, Identity, and Mexican American Empowerment, 1945–2002* (Austin: University of Texas Press, 2014).

84. Al Lipscomb, interview by Bonnie A. Lovell, September 17, 2002, Dallas Public Library.

85. Ibid.; "Leaders Zero In on Racial Breach," *Dallas Morning News*, November 22, 1968.

86. "Negro, Latin May Run for Mayor," *Dallas Morning News*, January 21, 1971.

87. The CCA later expanded its descriptive representation campaign when, in 1973, it supported Allen for a third term. In addition, it backed Lucy Patterson, a Black social worker, and Pedro "Pete" Aguirre, a Mexican American architect, for places on the city council. For more, see Katherine E. Bynum, "Civil Rights in the 'City of Hate': Grassroots Organizing against Police Brutality in Dallas, Texas, 1935–1990," (PhD diss., Texas Christian University, 2020).

88. "City Races to Wire," *Dallas Morning News*, April 6, 1971; *Lipscomb v. Jonsson*, CA 71-1451 (1971); Roy Williams and Kevin Shay, *Time Change: An Alternative View of the History of Dallas* (Dallas: To Be, 1991), 103.

89. Williams and Shay, *Time Change*, 105; *Lipscomb v. Wise*, CA-3-4571-E (1975); "8-3 Ruling Reaction," *Dallas Morning News*, February 9, 1975.

90. "Court Upholds Dallas Districting," *Dallas Morning News*, June 23, 1978.

91. For more on politics in the gayborhood, see Karen Wisely, "When We Go to Deal with City Hall, We Put on a Shirt and Tie: Gay Rights Movement Done the Dallas Way, 1965–2003," (PhD diss., University of North Texas, 2018).

92. "Run for City Council," from Ricardo Medrano interview, crbb.tcu.edu/clips/my -run-for-city-council; "Running for City Council," from Diane Ragsdale, oral history interview by Marvin Dulaney, October 21, 2011, CRBB Interview Database, crbb.tcu.edu/clips /running-for-city-council-2.

93. "Rise in Police Shootings Sparks Investigation," *Dallas Times Herald*, April 28, 1980, Vertical Files, Dallas Public Library.

94. "Hispanics Expect Council to Reject Police Review Plan," *Dallas Times Herald*, May 24, 1980, Vertical Files, Dallas Public Library; "Hernandez Decides Not to Work with Police Review Board Group," *Dallas Times Herald*, June 3, 1980, Vertical Files, Dallas Public Library; "Police Review Board Fails," *Dallas Morning News*, June 26, 1980.

95. "Police Review Board, Part One," from Diane Ragsdale, oral history interview by Katherine Bynum, July 12, 2017, Dallas, Texas, CRBB Interview Database, crbb.tcu.edu /clips/police-review-board-part-one-2.

96. "Protesters Camp on Guinn's Lawn," *Denton (TX) Record-Chronicle*, March 10, 1972; Skip Shockley, *Mother's Son* (Xlibris, 2009), 255.

97. "Working with SCLC," from Ragsdale interview by Dulaney, crbb.tcu.edu/clips /working-with-sclc.

98. "Black Women's United Front," from Ragsdale interview by Bynum, crbb.tcu.edu /clips/black-women-s-united-front.

99. "Organizers Planning New Petition Drive for Police Board," *Dallas Times Herald*, September 20, 1980, Vertical Files, Dallas Public Library; "Police Panel Proponents Call for Vote," *Dallas Morning News*, June 27, 1980; "Review Board Petition Effort Falls Short," *Dallas Morning News*, September 23, 1980.

100. Dick Hickman was cleared in the 1972 shooting of Napoleon Vinson, an unarmed African American. According to reports, Hickman and another officer were patrolling in South Dallas in plainclothes when they were approached by Vinson with a gun; see "Dallas Man Killed in Police Confrontation," *Dallas Morning News*, October 12, 1972; "Police Ask Public to Oppose Board," *Dallas Morning News*, June 24, 1980.

101. "Passion Play," *Texas Monthly*, October 1980, 131.

102. "Hispanics Expect Council to Reject Police Review Plan."

103. "Racism and Police Brutality in Dallas," from Roy Williams, oral history interview by Marvin Dulaney, October 6, 2011, CRBB Interview Database, crbb.tcu.edu/clips /racism-and-police-brutality-in-dallas; "DPA Frowns on Police Panel," *Dallas Morning News*, June 30, 1980; Dallas City Council, Ordinance No. 17418, September 30, 1981, Dallas Municipal Archives.

104. "Pancho Medrano Says Ad for Taylor Tries to Fool Voters," *Dallas Morning News*, March 29, 1983.

105. "Running for City Council," from Ragsdale interview by Dulaney; Lipscomb interview.

106. "Wade to Review Shooting," *Dallas Morning News*, October 29, 1986.

107. "Police Brutality Congressional Hearing," from Williams interview, crbb.tcu.edu /clips/police-brutality-congressional-hearing.

108. Quotation from "Statement of Al Lipscomb," *Hearing Before the Subcommittee on Criminal Justice of the Committee on the Judiciary*, US House of Representatives, May 8, 1987, 338.

109. "Statement of Lori Palmer, Member, Dallas City Council, Dallas, TX," in ibid., 331–333.

110. "Statement of Captain John Chappelle, Dallas Police Department," in ibid., 377.

111. "Statement of Rick Stone, Captain, Dallas Police Department," in ibid., 377.

112. "Marlin R. Price, Supplemental Testimony," in ibid., 260.

113. "Police Killing of Man Angers Minority Leaders," *Dallas Morning News*, May 20, 1987.

114. "Police React to Concerns—Minority Affairs Division Established," *Dallas Morning News*, May 30, 1987.

115. Ibid.

116. "City Council Panel OKs New Police Review Board," *Dallas Morning News*, November 24, 1987; "Council OKs New Police Review Panel," *Dallas Morning News*, December 17, 1987.

Chapter 12: Self-Determined Educational Spaces

1. MAYO, a statewide organization that emerged in 1967, was most notable for bringing together students and barrio youth for the purpose of challenging the cultural, political, and economic power structure, which was dominated by Anglos. For an overview of MAYO, see

Armando Navarro, *Mexican American Youth Organization: Avant-Garde of the Chicano Movement in Texas* (Austin: University of Texas Press, 1995).

2. "Fight for Women's Studies," from María Jiménez, oral history interview by Samantha Rodriguez and Sandra Enríquez, June 13, 2016, Houston, Civil Rights in Black and Brown Interview Database [hereafter cited as CRBB Interview Database], crbb.tcu.edu/clips /4588/fight-for-women-s-studies.

3. In Houston, there were two MAYO chapters: one at the university level (UH MAYO) and one in the community (Barrio MAYO).

4. Carlos Muñoz's *Youth, Identity, Power: The Chicano Movement* (New York: Verso, 1989) is a pioneering text that locates Chicana/o student militancy within the larger political history of the 1960s. While this monograph was among the first in the field to assess Chicana/o youth movements, it set up a prevailing trend in Chicana/o Movement scholarship that centers on the Chicana/o experience in California and lacks a critical gender analysis. Muñoz posits that Chicanas challenged Chicano patriarchy by forming separate groups and thus does not address how women sought gender liberation within the *movimiento*. The California-centric trend continues to prevail in recent texts such as Rodolfo Acuña's *The Making of Chicana/o Studies: In the Trenches of Academe* (New Brunswick, NJ: Rutgers University Press, 2011), which principally surveys the trajectory of Chicana/o studies within the University of California system. Acuña does explore "the evolution of sexism and homophobia within Chicana/o studies that took too long to get right," but that investigation is relegated to one chapter, and thus, Chicana feminism is not at the center of the study.

5. Maylei Blackwell, *¡Chicana Power! Contested Histories of Feminism in the Chicano Movement* (Austin: University of Texas Press, 2011), 89–90. Recent scholarship has begun to delve more critically into Tejana fights for gender liberation during the Chicana/o movement; see David Montejano, *Quixote Soldiers: A Local History of the Chicano Movement, 1966–1981* (Austin: University of Texas Press, 2010), and Samantha Rodriguez and Stalina Emmanuelle Villarreal, "Maria Jiménez: Reflexiones on Traversing Multiple Fronteras in the South," in *Chicana Movidas: New Narratives of Activism and Feminism in the Movement Era*, ed. Dionne Espinoza, María Eugenia Cotera, and Maylei Blackwell (Austin: University of Texas Press, 2018).

6. Relational studies place multiple ethnic groups at the center of the narrative to uncover how such groups engage with one another and mutually develop a movement. For more information on relational studies, see Luis Alvarez, *The Power of the Zoot: Youth Culture and Resistance during World War II* (Berkeley: University of California Press, 2009), and Natalia Molina, *How Race Is Made in America: Immigration, Citizenship, and the Historical Power of Racial Scripts* (Berkeley: University of California Press, 2014). For more scholarship on how the Chicana/o movement was connected with other ethnic struggles, see George Mariscal, *Brown-Eyed Children of the Sun: Lessons from the Chicano Movement, 1965–1975* (Albuquerque: University of New Mexico Press, 2005), and Laura Pulido, *Black, Brown, Yellow, and Left: Radical Activism in Los Angeles* (Berkley: University of California Press, 2006).

7. Chicana/o scholars use the term "ethnic Mexican" to refer to "people of Mexican descent, whether they are native-born citizens, naturalized citizens, legal residents, or undocumented residents"; see Gabriela González, *Redeeming La Raza: Transborder Modernity, Race, Respectability, and Rights* (New York: Oxford University Press), xv.

8. Thomas H. Kreneck *Del Pueblo: A History of Houston's Hispanic Community* (College Station: Texas A&M University Press, 2012), loc. 327, Kindle.

9. Raúl Ramos, *Beyond the Alamo: Forging Mexican Ethnicity in San Antonio, 1821–1861* (Chapel Hill: University of North Carolina Press, 2008), 184.

10. William D. Carrington and Clive Webb, *Forgotten Dead: Mob Violence against Mexicans in the United States, 1848–1928* (New York: Oxford University Press, 2013), 6.

11. Arnoldo De León, *They Called Them Greasers: Anglo Attitudes toward Mexicans in Texas, 1821–1900* (Austin: University of Texas Press, 1983), loc. 1898, Kindle.

12. Miguel Antonio Levario, *Militarizing the Border: When Mexicans Became the Enemy* (College Station: Texas A&M Press, 2012), 34; see also "Refusing to Forget," refusingto forget.org; Carrington and Webb, *Forgotten Dead*; Benjamin Heber Johnson, *Revolution in Texas:*

How a Forgotten Rebellion and Its Bloody Suppression Turned Mexicans into Americans (New Haven, CT: Yale University Press, 2003); Monica Muñoz Martínez, *The Injustice Never Leaves You: Anti-Mexican Violence in Texas* (Cambridge, MA: Harvard University Press, 2018); Nicolas Villanueva Jr., *The Lynching of Mexicans in the Texas Borderlands* (Albuquerque: University of New Mexico Press, 2017).

13. Documenting ethnic Mexican fights for civil rights, the journalist Maggie Rivas-Rodriguez argues that Tejanas/os experienced a de facto segregation that placed ethnic Mexican students in separate and inferior schools and restricted their social and political power; see Maggie Rivas-Rodriguez, *Texas Mexican Americans and Postwar Civil Rights* (Austin: University of Texas Press, 2015). The historians Brian D. Behnken and Max Krochmal concur that ethnic Mexicans experienced their own brand of Jim Crow, which crippled access to citizenship rights; see Brian D. Behnken, *Fighting Their Own Battles: Mexican Americans, African Americans, and the Struggle for Civil Rights in Texas* (Chapel Hill: University of North Carolina Press, 2011); Max Krochmal, *Blue Texas: The Making of a Multiracial Democratic Coalition in the Civil Rights Era* (Chapel Hill: The University of North Carolina Press, 2016).

14. Arnoldo De León, *Ethnicity in the Sunbelt: Mexican Americans in Houston* (College Station: Texas A&M University Press, 2001), 126–127. For an understanding of Tejanas/os' appeals to whiteness, see Neil Foley, *The White Scourge: Mexicans, Blacks, and Poor Whites in Texas Cotton Culture* (Berkeley: University of California Press, 1999). For more information on LULAC, see Cynthia E. Orozco, *No Mexicans, Women, or Dogs Allowed: The Rise of the Mexican American Civil Rights Movement* (Austin: University of Texas Press, 2009).

15. Guadalupe San Miguel Jr., *Brown, Not White: School Integration and the Chicano Movement in Texas* (College Station: Texas A&M University Press, 2005), loc. 530, Kindle.

16. "Attending the Mexican School in Mathis," from Daniel Bustamante, oral history interview by Sandra I. Enríquez and Samantha Rodriguez, July 1, 2016, Houston, CRBB Interview Database, crbb.tcu.edu/clips/2577/attending-the-mexican-school-in-mathis.

17. Ibid.

18. Orozco, *No Mexicans, Women, or Dogs*, 55.

19. Navarro, *Mexican American Youth Organization*, 85–86.

20. "Migrating to America," from Jiménez interview, crbb.tcu.edu/clips/4581/migrating-to -america.

21. "Childhood in Houston," from Jiménez interview, crbb.tcu.edu/clips/4583/childhood -in-houston.

22. "Discrimination and White Flight," from Louise Villejo, oral history interview by Samantha Rodriguez and Sandra I. Enríquez, June 15, 2016, Houston, CRBB Interview Database, crbb.tcu.edu/clips/3455/discrimination-and-white-flight.

23. Muñoz, *Youth, Identity, Power*, 137.

24. Carlos L. Cantú asserts that Chicana/o educational self-determination has its roots in middle-class educational legal battles of the early twentieth century. Deploying confrontational tactics and a provocative rhetoric, MAYO advanced the battle for educational self-determination in the 1960s and 1970s by merging cultural nationalism and the desire to control institutions in barrios throughout Texas; see Cantú, "Self-Determined Education and Community Activism: A Comparative History of Navajo, Chicano, and Puerto Rican Institutions of Higher Education in the Era of Protest" (PhD diss., University of Houston, 2016).

25. Cynthia Pérez, videotaped interview by Maria Cotera, July 6, 2012, El Paso, Chicana Por Mi Raza Digital Memory Collective, El Paso, Texas.

26. "Involvement with UFW," from Bustamante interview, crbb.tcu.edu/clips/2600 /involvement-with-ufw.

27. Bill Bridges, "The Rangers and La Huelga," *Texas Observer*, June 9–23, 1967, 13.

28. Ibid., 14.

29. Navarro, *Mexican American Youth Organization*; Ignacio M. Garcia, *Chicanismo: The Forging of a Militant Ethos among Mexican Americans* (Tucson: University of Arizona Press, 1997). On UFW iconography, see Miriam Pawel, *The Union of Their Dreams: Power, Hope, and Struggle in Cesar Chavez's Farm Worker Movement* (New York: Bloomsbury, 2009).

30. "A History of Chicano Scholarship and Chicano Studies," José Limón, interview by Linda Fregoso, *Onda Latina: The Mexican American Experience*, aired October 2, 1980, laits.utexas.edu /onda_latina/program?sernum=MAE_80_43_mp3&term=a%20history%20of%20chicano%20 scholarship%20and%20chicano%20studies; María Jiménez, interview by Samantha M. Rodriguez, audio recording, July 25, 2013, Houston Oral History Project, University of Houston.

31. Martha Biondi, *The Black Revolution on Campus* (Berkley: University of California Press, 2012); Ibram X. Kendi, *The Black Campus Movement: Black Students and the Racial Reconstruction of Higher Education, 1965–1972* (New York: Palgrave Macmillan, 2012).

32. "Reproduction of the AABL Statement," box 44, folder 22, "Student Power, 1966–1968," President's Office Records, 1927–2015, Subject Files, Special Collections, University of Houston Libraries [hereafter cited as UH President's Office Records].

33. *In The Black Campus Movement*, Ibram X. Kendi asserts that the Black campus movement of the 1960s and 1970s represented a turn in the civil rights student struggle. For Kendi, the long Black student movement, 1919–1972, underscores the distinct but related battles towards university transformation. For more information on African American student activism during the Black Power movement, see Biondi, *Black Revolution on Campus*; Stefan M. Bradley, *Harlem vs. Columbia University: Black Student Power in the Late 1960s* (Urbana: University of Illinois Press, 2009); Fabio Rojas, *From Black Power to Black Studies: How a Radical Social Movement Became an Academic Discipline* (Baltimore: Johns Hopkins University Press, 2007); Jeffery A. Turner, *Sitting In and Speaking Out: Student Movements in the American South, 1960–1970* (Athens: University of Georgia Press, 2010); Joy Ann Williamson, *Black Power on Campus: The University of Illinois, 1965–1970* (Urbana: University of Illinois Press, 2003).

34. "African American Student Activism at the University of Houston, Part Two," from Michelle Barnes, oral history interview by Samantha M. Rodriguez and Sandra I. Enríquez, June 17, 2016, Houston, CRBB Interview Database, crbb.tcu.edu/clips/6064/african-american -student-activism-at-the-university-of-houston-part-two.

35. Henry Holcomb, "Panther Leader Urges Revolution," *Houston Post*, May 9, 1969; "Reproduction of the AABL Statement," introduction.

36. After months of student protests against the Texas Southern University administration and amid growing racial tensions in Houston, "a standoff between students and police escalated into an hours-long shootout, resulting in the death of one rookie patrolman and the arrest of nearly 500 students." This "TSU riot" emboldened student activism in Houston; see "Riots and Demonstrations (1967)," KPRC-TV, Houston, Texas Archive of the Moving Image, accessed June 15, 2020, texasarchive.org/2018_00038.

37. "Activism during College," from Omowali Luthuli-Allen, oral history interview by Sandra I. Enríquez and Samantha Rodriguez, June 17, 2016, Houston, CRBB Interview Database, crbb.tcu.edu/clips/3444/activism-during-college.

38. Ibid.

39. "Reproduction of the AABL Statement," introduction.

40. "A Tree Without Roots," from Luthuli-Allen interview, crbb.tcu.edu/clips/3437/a-tree -without-roots.

41. Robinson Block, "Afro-Americans for Black Liberation and the Fight for Civil Rights at the University of Houston," *Houston History Magazine* 8, no. 1 (2011): 25; Rick Campbell, "Queen Lynn, from Glory to Tragedy," *Houston Chronicle*, December 22, 2008.

42. "Reproduction of the AABL Statement," list of demands.

43. Tatcho Mindiola, videotaped interview by David Goldstein, June 4, 2008, Houston Oral History Project, Houston Public Library Digital Archives, digital.houstonlibrary.net /oral-history/tatcho-mindiola.php; LOMAS Statement, box 44, folder 30, "Student Organizations, 1969-1970," UH President's Office Records. The League of Mexican-American Students (LOMAS) sought civil rights for ethnic Mexicans at UH. Like the Committee on Better Race Relations, LOMAS became radicalized toward the late 1960s and became a chapter of the Mexican American Youth Organization.

44. "Organizing in Higher Education," from Luthuli-Allen interview, crbb.tcu.edu/clips /3436/organizing-in-higher-education.

45. Ibid.

46. Mindiola interview.

47. In Texas and throughout the nation, a handful of dedicated students made Mexican American studies possible; see Center for Mexican American Studies, "MAYO and the Mexican American Studies at UH in 1972," Fall Speaker Series, University of Houston, October 3, 2012; "MAYO meeting with President Hoffman," box 44, folder 21, "Student Organizations, 1969–1973," UH President's Office Records.

48. "Becoming Heavily Involved in MAYO," from Jiménez interview, crbb.tcu.edu/clips /4587/becoming-heavily-involvemed-in-mayo.

49. María Jiménez was able to become the first female SGA president in part because she had worked out a deal with white liberal student groups and Black student groups. She ran with Steve Umoff, who agreed to be student body president for six months and then resign, allowing Jiménez to be the president for the remaining six months.

50. Pedro Vasquez, "Maria Jimenez; Vice-President University of Houston Students," *Papel Chicano* 1, no. 8 (1971): 5.

51. "Cross-collaboration With Different Organizations," from Jiménez interview, crbb.tcu .edu/clips/4589/cross-collaboration-with-different-organizations.

52. Ibid.

53. Maria Jiménez, "Women Still Powerless," *Papel Chicano* 1, no. 4 (1971): 8.

54. "Cross-collaboration With Different Organizations," from Jiménez interview.

55. University of Houston Mexican American Studies Program, box 7, folder 11, "Chicano Studies, 1974–1980," José Ángel Gutiérrez Papers, LLILAS Benson Latin American Studies and Collections, University of Texas Libraries.

56. "Becoming Heavily Involved in MAYO," from Jiménez interview.

57. Julius Rivera (sociology) was the chairman of the Mexican American Studies Program Committee from 1971 to 1972. The committee also included Norris Lang (anthropology), Thomas DiGregori (economics), Harvey Johnson (Spanish and other languages), Edward Gonzalez (pharmacy), and Guadalupe Quintanilla (Spanish and other languages). UH-MAYO incorporated their views within this ethnic studies committee; see Mexican American Studies Program Committee, box 15, folder 19, Mexican American Studies, College of Arts and Sciences Records, 1937–1973, Special Collections, University of Houston Libraries.

58. Larry Johnson, "Meaningful Chicano Studies," *Daily Cougar*, March 10, 1972; Guadalupe Castillo, "Mexican-American Studies: Fall Program Appears Grey," *Daily Cougar*, August 17, 1972; "MAYO meeting with President Hoffman."

59. "Becoming Heavily Involved in MAYO," from Jiménez interview.

60. "UH MAYO Open Letter to President Hoffman," box 44, folder 31, "Student Organizations, 1969–1973," UH President's Office Records.

61. Ibid.

62. Inés Hernández Avila (Tovar), telephone interview by Samantha M. Rodriguez, audio recording, January 19, 2015, Houston, copy in author's possession.

63. "Estela Portillo Trambley," Women in Texas History, womenintexashistory.org/audio /trambley.

64. Hernández Avila (Tovar) interview.

65. "Teatro and the University of Houston," from Villejo interview, crbb.tcu.edu/clips/3458 /teatro-and-the-university-of-houston.

66. Tejana feminisms were cultivated and solidified at women's conferences, including the national 1971 Conferencia de Mujeres Por La Raza (Women for the People Conference), held at the Houston YWCA, and the 1975 Mujeres Unidas Chicana Identity Conference, held at the University of Houston. For more information, see Samantha M. Rodriguez, "Carving Spaces for Feminism and Nationalism: Tejana Activism in the Matrix of Social Unrest, 1967–1978" (PhD Diss., University of Houston, 2018).

67. "Chicana Course Tries to Cope with Stereotyping," *Ft. Worth Star-Telegram*, October 2, 1975.

68. Tatcho Mindiola Jr., "Finding a Way: Developing the Center for Mexican American

Studies at UH," *Houston History Magazine* 9, no .1 (2011): 39. The UH Chicana/o studies program was originally titled Mexican American studies, and did not become a center until 1974. At the time, Guadalupe Quintanilla was a doctoral student in the department of curriculum and instruction in the College of Education. She served as the director of CMAS until 1978. The funding for her directorship was largely due to UH-MAYO lobbying the state legislature.

69. "Director of the UH Center for Mexican American Studies and the First Classes," from Guadalupe Quintanilla, oral history interview by Sandra I. Enríquez and Samantha Rodriguez, June 30, 2016, Houston, CRBB Interview Database, crbb.tcu.edu/clips/5882 /director-of-the-uh-center-for-mexican-american-studies-and-the-first-classes.

70. Ibid.

71. "The First MAS director: Lupe Quintanilla, Ed.D.," Center for Mexican American Studies, *Noticias* 10, no. 1 (2012): 4.

72. Ibid., 3-4.

73. "Director of the UH Center for Mexican American Studies and the First Classes," from Quintanilla interview.

74. "Becoming Heavily Involved in MAYO," from Jiménez interview.

75. "Fight for Women's Studies," from Jiménez interview.

76. "Cougar Den Mural at the University of Houston," from Edward Castillo, oral history interview by Sandra I. Enríquez and Samantha M. Rodriguez, June 9, 2016, Houston, CRBB, crbb.tcu.edu/interviews/198/interview-with-edward-castillo.

77. Educational self-determination was not the only fight that Brown and Black Houstonians coalesced around in the 1960s and 1970s. Tejanas/os and African Americans worked together to tackle electoral politics, including the championing of candidates in La Raza Unida Party. Black and Brown coalitions were also forged around the antiwar movement, including the Chicana/o moratorium. The killing of Jose Campos Torres in 1977 and the subsequent Moody Park insurrection, in 1978, brought Tejanas/os and African Americans together in the struggle against police brutality. For more information, see Rodriguez, "Carving Spaces for Feminism and Nationalism."

78. "Chicana Feminism and Ideologies," from Villejo interview, crbb.tcu.edu/clips/3462 /chicana-feminism-and-ideologies.

Chapter 13: From Police Brutality to the "United Peoples Party"

The chapter epigraph comes from "Activism in San Antonio," from Claudis Minor, oral history interview by Steve Arionus and Vinicio Sinta, June 25, 2016, San Antonio, Civil Rights in Black and Brown Interview Database [hereafter cited as CRBB Interview Database], crbb .tcu.edu/clips/6579/activism-in-san-antonio. SNCC is the Student Nonviolent Coordinating Committee.

1. On the origins of MAYO, see Armando Navarro, *Mexican American Youth Organization: Avant-Garde of the Chicano Movement in Texas* (Austin: University of Texas Press, 1995); José Ángel Gutiérrez, *The Making of a Chicano Militant: Lessons from Cristal* (Madison: University of Wisconsin Press, 1998). On Cortés, see, for example, Mark R. Warren, *Dry Bones Rattling: Community Building to Revitalize American Democracy* (Princeton, NJ: Princeton University Press, 2001).

2. David Montejano, *Quixote's Soldiers: A Local History of the Chicano Movement, 1966–1981* (Austin: University of Texas Press, 2010).

3. On civil rights struggles in San Antonio through the early 1960s, see Max Krochmal, *Blue Texas: The Making of a Multiracial Democratic Coalition in the Civil Rights Era* (Chapel Hill: University of North Carolina Press, 2016); see also Brian D. Behnken, *Fighting Their Own Battles: Mexican Americans, African Americans, and the Struggle for Civil Rights in Texas* (Chapel Hill: University of North Carolina Press, 2011).

4. A scholarly example of this tendency can be found in Robert A. Goldberg, "Racial Change on the Southern Periphery: The Case of San Antonio, Texas, 1960–1965," *Journal of Southern History* 49, no. 3 (August 1983): 349–374.

5. On the GGL, see Rodolfo Rosales, *The Illusion of Inclusion: The Untold Political Story of San Antonio* (Austin: University of Texas Press, 2000).

6. "Police 'Cool' Big Houston St. Melee," *San Antonio Light*, April 23, 1968, 19; "Well Done!" (editorial), *San Antonio Light*, April 23, 1968, 10; "City Apologizes to 'Innocents' Caught in Fracas," *San Antonio Express*, April 26, 1968, 19-D. For diverging takes on the Fiesta tradition and Hemisfair, see Laura Hernández-Ehrisman, *Inventing the Fiesta City: Heritage and Carnival in San Antonio* (Albuquerque: University of New Mexico Press, 2008); Sterlin Holmesly, *Hemisfair '68 and the Transformation of San Antonio* (San Antonio: Maverick, 2003).

7. "Local SNCC and Police Brutality," from Carlos Richardson, oral history interview by Steve Arionus and Vinicio Sinta, June 30, 2016, San Antonio, CRBB Interview Database, crbb .tcu.edu/clips/5126/carlos-richardson-discusses-formation-of-local-sncc-police-brutality.

8. Ken Bunting, "Black San Antonio III: They Call It 'Police Brutality,'" *San Antonio Express*, February 15, 1972, 1.

9. "Local SNCC and Police Brutality," from Richardson interview. For more on the killing of Phillips and its aftermath, see "Knife Wielder Killed Defying S.A. Police," *San Antonio Light*, May 8, 1968, 1; "S.A. Negroes Protest Man's Death," *San Antonio Light*, May 13, 1968, 11; "Report Says No Unnecessary Force Used," *San Antonio Express*, June 5, 1968, 6-D; "Bexar Grand Jury Agrees to Halt of Phillips Case," *San Antonio Express*, September 11, 1968, 6-B; "Statement of Mrs. Nancy Phillips," Regular Meeting of the City Council of the City of San Antonio, May 16, 1968, 11, available via Municipal Archives & Records, City of San Antonio, accessed April 25, 2020, sanantonio.gov/Municipal-Archives-Records /Search-Collections; see also the council minutes for June 6, 1968.

10. "Military Family," from Richardson interview, crbb.tcu.edu/clips/5107/carlos-richard son-discusses-military-family; see also the complete "Interview with Carlos Richardson," crbb .tcu.edu/interviews/277/interview-with-carlos-richardson.

11. "Discrimination in School and the Vietnam War" and "Civil Rights Organization," from Richardson interview, crbb.tcu.edu/clips/5115/carlos-richardson-discusses-discrimination-in -school-vietnam-war, crbb.tcu.edu/clips/5122/carlos-richardson-discusses-civil-rights-organi zation.

12. "Civil Rights Organization," "Political and Local Activism," and "Local Activism and Discrimination, Part Two," from Richardson interview, crbb.tcu.edu/clips/5122/carlos -richardson-discusses-civil-rights-organization, crbb.tcu.edu/clips/5123/carlos-richardson -discusses-activism, crbb.tcu.edu/clips/5127/carlos-richardson-discusses-local-activism-and -discrimination-part-2. On Larry Jackson, also see "'You Either Support Democracy or You Don't,'" by Todd Moye, in this volume.

13. The scholarly literature on SNCC is voluminous; see, for example, Clayborne Carson, *In Struggle: SNCC and the Black Awakening of the 1960s* (Cambridge, MA: Harvard University Press, 1987); Wesley C. Hogan, *Many Minds, One Heart: SNCC's Dream for a New America* (Chapel Hill: University of North Carolina Press, 2007). For the transition to Black Power, see, among others, Yohuru Williams, *Rethinking the Black Freedom Movement* (New York: Routledge, 2016). For an early example of a historian locating the origins of Black Power in the earlier integrationist movement, see William Henry Chafe, *Civilities and Civil Rights: Greensboro, North Carolina, and the Black Struggle for Freedom* (New York: Oxford University Press, 1980). For counterpoints, see Charles M. Payne, *I've Got the Light of Freedom: The Organizing Tradition and the Mississippi Freedom Struggle*, rev. ed. (Berkeley: University of California Press, 2007); Peniel E. Joseph, ed., *The Black Power Movement: Rethinking the Civil Rights–Black Power Era* (New York: Routledge, 2006).

14. On Dallas, see "Civil Rights in the 'City of Hate,'" by Katherine Bynum in this volume; see also Bynum, "Civil Rights in the 'City of Hate': Grassroots Organizing against Police Brutality in Dallas, Texas, 1935-1990" (PhD diss., Texas Christian University, 2020). On Houston, see Merline Pitre, *Born to Serve: A History of Texas Southern University* (Norman: University of Oklahoma Press, 2018); Dwight D. Watson, *Race and the Houston Police Department, 1930–1990: A Change Did Come* (College Station: Texas A&M University Press, 2005); see also Special SNCC Report, "Will They Die!—Five Black Students Charged with Murder in Houston," box

15, folder "SNCC National 1967–1973, n.d.," MS 142, Mario Marcel Salas Papers, University of Texas at San Antonio Libraries Special Collections [hereafter cited as Salas Papers, UTSA]; also available in the online Civil Rights Movement Archive (Bay Area Veterans), accessed July 27, 2020, crmvet.org/docs/670507_sncc_tsu.pdf.

15. "History of San Antonio and Direct Action," from Mario Salas, oral history interview by Steve Arionus, June 23, 2016, San Antonio, CRBB Interview Database, crbb.tcu.edu/clips/7044 /history-of-san-antonio-and-direct-action.

16. "Leaving the Military / Joining SNCC," from Minor interview, crbb.tcu.edu/clips/6572 /leaving-the-military-joining-sncc.

17. "What Protest Looked Like in the 70s—San Antonio," from Salas interview, crbb .tcu.edu/clips/7045/what-protest-looked-like-in-the-70s-san-antonio.

18. "College Years," from Salas interview, crbb.tcu.edu/clips/7066/college-years-2; invitation from Jerald Fernandezz to "Dear Student," n.d. [c. November 23, 1970], box 15, folder "SNCC S.A., 1967–1975, n.d., (1–2)," Salas Papers, UTSA. The Black Student Coalition persisted into the late 1970s; see, for example, "Voting Set January 15," *Community Unifier* 1, no. 1 (January 15, 1977): 3 (photograph caption), clipping in box 15, folder 5, Salas Papers, UTSA.

19. "SNCC in San Antonio—The Late 60's" and "SNCC in San Antonio," from Salas interview, crbb.tcu.edu/clips/7062/sncc-in-san-antonio-the-late-60-s, crbb.tcu.edu/clips /7046/sncc-in-san-antonio; Carlos Richardson, "Black Community News: Student National Coordinating Committee," n.d. [1969], box 15, folder "SNCC S.A., 1967–1975, n.d., (1–2)," Salas Papers, UTSA; *San Antonio S.N.C.C. News*, n.d. [1969–1970], in ibid.; "Black Panthers and the Federal Government," from Salas interview, crbb.tcu.edu/clips/7054/black-panthers-and -the-federal-government; see also Mario Salas, "SNCC Black Panthers in San Antonio," *African American News & Issues*, July 26–August 1, 2006, 4.

20. See the following articles from the *San Antonio Light*: "SNCC 'Coming to S.A.,'" January 21, 1969, 8-B (quotation); "SNCC Office Shooting Scene," September 9, 1968, 6-D; "Jury Convicts SNCC Officials," August 24, 1968, 2; "Negro Leaders to Testify," December 7, 1968, 2.

21. "Regular Meeting of the City Council of the City of San Antonio," January 23, 1969, 18, available via Municipal Archives & Records, City of San Antonio, sanantonio.gov/Municipal -Archives-Records/Search-Collections (quotations); "Suspect Shot While Fleeing," *San Antonio Light*, December 30, 1968, 4. The Reverend Claude W. Black Jr., an African American leader, joined the Mexican American activists in calling for action, and he spoke out in support of Councilman Torres.

22. "Regular Meeting of the City Council of the City of San Antonio," February 20, 1969, 18–18-A, available via Municipal Archives & Records, City of San Antonio, accessed April 25, 2020, sanantonio.gov/Municipal-Archives-Records/Search-Collections ("wild dogs" quotation); "S.A. Police Called 'Mad Dog' Killers," *San Antonio Light*, February 20, 1969, 1 (other council meeting quotations); "Police Brutality and Segregation," from Richardson interview, crbb.tcu.edu/clips/5125/carlos-richardson-discusses-police-brutality-and-segregation ("later recalled").

23. "Police Brutality and Segregation," from Richardson interview.

24. On Velásquez, see Juan Sepúlveda, *The Life and Times of Willie Velásquez: Su Voto Es Su Voz* (Houston: Arte Publico, 2003); Hector Galán, *Willie Velasquez: Your Vote Is Your Voice*, Voces (Latino Public Broadcasting, 2016), pbs.org/video/voces-willie-velasquez-your-vote-your -voice-full-episode; Navarro, *Mexican American Youth Organization*.

25. Montejano, *Quixote's Soldiers*, chs. 4–5.

26. Ibid., quotations on 102–103. On the election, see also James McCrory, "Pete Torres Re-Elected," *San Antonio Express*, April 2, 1969, 1; "Anti-Hate Drive Backed," *San Antonio Express*, April 10, 1969, 6-E; "Gonzalez Reveals Threats," *San Antonio Express*, April 12, 1969, 10-G; Paul Thompson, "Top of News," *San Antonio Express-News*, April 12, 1969, 1-A.

27. "History of San Antonio and Direct Action," from Salas interview. My account of this protest also draws on "Rampage in Downtown S.A.," *San Antonio Light*, April 22, 1969, 1, 6.

28. "Community Organizations—Relationships," from Minor interview, crbb.tcu.edu/clips /6575/community-organizations-relationships; "Rampage in Downtown S.A." ("white hippies").

29. "River Parade Riot," from Richardson interview, crbb.tcu.edu/clips/5130/carlos-rich ardson-discusses-river-parade-riot.

30. Ibid.; Mario Marcel Salas, "The Persistence of Paternal Continuity, Its Anti-Thesis, and the Colonial Mindset in the African American Community of San Antonio: 1937–2001" (draft of MA thesis, UTSA, 2004; copy in author's possession), 31; "Rampage in Downtown S.A." Due to a closure caused by COVID-19, the published version of Salas's thesis was unavailable from UTSA at the time of writing; see Mario Marcel Salas, "Patterns of Persistence: Paternal Colonialist Structures and the Radical Opposition in the African American Community of San Antonio, Texas, 1937–2001" (M.A. thesis, University of Texas, San Antonio, 2004).

31. See the following articles from the *San Antonio Light*: "City Dads, Negroes Air Issues," April 23, 1969, 1 (quotation listing the police weapons); Ron White, "Danger," April 23, 1969, 14 (first quotation on "truce"); "Henckel Promises Report on 'Charges,'" April 24, 1969, 10 (final quotations describing attack); Ron White, "Meeting to Nip Violence Set," April 24, 1969, 10; "5 Charged in Disturbance," April 23, 1969, 31.

32. "Henckel Promises Report on 'Charges'" (all quotations).

33. White, "Meeting to Nip Violence Set" (all quotations); see also "Fuss Erupts over East Side Beating Charges," *San Antonio Light*, April 25, 1969, 4; "Regular Meeting of the City Council of the City of San Antonio," April 24, 1969, available via Municipal Archives & Records, City of San Antonio, sanantonio.gov/Municipal-Archives-Records/Search-Collections.

34. Salas, "Persistence of Paternal Continuity," 33.

35. "Student Activism and Organizations—College," from T. C. Calvert, oral history interview by Steve Arionus, July 1, 2016, San Antonio, CRBB Interview Database, crbb.tcu.edu /clips/6375/student-activism-and-organizations-college.

36. "SNCC Action," from Richardson interview, crbb.tcu.edu/clips/5129/carlos-richardson -discusses-sncc-action.

37. "SNCC Chief on Probation," newspaper clipping, unknown publication, October 24, 1969, box 15, folder "SNCC S.A., 1967–1975, n.d., (1–2)," Salas Papers, UTSA.

38. "Community Organizations—Relationships," from Minor interview.

39. Pam Smisek, "Class Hears Militants from SNCC Speak on 400 Year Negro Suffering," *College Star*, August 12, 1969, clipping in box 15, folder "SNCC S.A., 1967–1975, n.d., (1–2)," Salas Papers, UTSA; Larry H. Jackson to "Dear Brothers & Sisters," box 15, folder "SNCC Austin, 1969, n.d.," Salas Papers, UTSA.

40. "Synopsis of Bexar County Jail Conditions," February 6, 1970; untitled summary of Hawthorne Junior High School incident, 1969; "Four Defendants Freed," *SNCC News*, February 13, 1970—all in box 15, folder "SNCC S.A., 1967–1975, n.d., (1–2)," Salas Papers, UTSA.

41. "Mexican-Americans / Discrimination," *NBC Evening News*, July 6, 1970, Vanderbilt Television News Archive, clip #452457, tvnews.vanderbilt.edu/broadcasts/452457 (all quotations; transcribed by author); "Motion to Censure McAllister For Television Statements Fails," *San Antonio Express*, July 10, 1970, 7-A. McAllister appeared again in the second part of the series on July 7, doubling-down on his anticommunist strategy; see "Mexican-Americans / Agnew / Texas," *NBC Evening News*, July 6, 1970, Vanderbilt Television News Archive, clip #452482, tvnews.vanderbilt.edu/broadcasts/452482.

42. "Regular Meeting of the City Council of the City of San Antonio," July 9, 1970, 1, 8–19, available via Municipal Archives & Records, City of San Antonio, sanantonio .gov/Municipal-Archives-Records/Search-Collections; "Motion to Censure McAllister for Television Statements Fails"; Nell Fenner Grover, "Lulac National President Disputes Ambition Quote," *San Antonio Express-News*, July 11, 1970, 12-B (third quotation); Miguel Berry, "TV Remarks Bring 'La Raza' Together," *San Antonio Express/News*, July 12, 1970, 12-A; "Group Asks Boycott of S.A. Firm," *San Antonio Express*, July 16, 1970, 10-E (first quotation); "Picketing Begins at McAllister's SASA," *San Antonio Light*, July 27, 1970, 2; "Raza Group Pickets

SASA," *San Antonio Express*, July 28, 1970, 6-D; "Boycott of SASA Called For," *San Antonio Light*, July 28, 1970, 13 (last quotation); "Regular Meeting of the City Council of the City of San Antonio," July 30, 1970, 33, available via Municipal Archives & Records, City of San Antonio, sanantonio.gov/Municipal-Archives-Records/Search-Collections; "Pena Endorses SASA Boycott," *San Antonio Light*, August 2, 1970, 29; "Pena Backs SASA Picket," *San Antonio Express*, August 4, 1970, 6-A.

43. "Mayor, Boycotters Meet to No Avail" and "The Council Session," *San Antonio Express*, August 21, 1970, 10-F; "Mayor's TV Remarks Tape Asked," *San Antonio Express*, September 4, 1970, 7-B; "Regular Meeting of the City Council of the City of San Antonio," August 20, 1970, 2–3, and "Regular Meeting of the City Council of the City of San Antonio," September 10, 1970, 11–14, both available via Municipal Archives & Records, City of San Antonio, sanantonio.gov /Municipal-Archives-Records/Search-Collections (the reference to activists traveling to LA is on 13). The scholar and former Chicano movement activist David Montejano contends that the McAllister controversy began only after the Chicano Moratorium march on August 29, but the video and documentary archive reveals an earlier backstory. I conclude instead that the events in Los Angeles reinvigorated the SASA boycott and made it more militant (and memorable) by bringing to the fore a new cadre of youthful leaders, chiefly women. (Montejano also highlights the leadership of Chicanas.) See Montejano, *Quixote's Soldiers*, 156–160; David Montejano, emails to the author, December 2, 2020, in author's possession.

44. Alice Murphy, "Pena, Sutton Vow Return after Arrest," *San Antonio Express*, September 10, 1970, 1-A, 20-A; "Mayor Assailed in Chamber Again as NBC Interview Controversy Goes On," *San Antonio Express*, September 11, 1970, 6-E; Leo Cardenas and R. B. Fields, "10 Arrested after Melee at Frost National Bank," *San Antonio Express*, September 11, 1970, 14-A; Jesse Clements, "On the Scene: 'Get Him, Get Him,' Cried the Crowd," *San Antonio Express*, September 11, 1970, 12-F; James McCrory, "SASA Boycotters, Mayor Talk Asked," *San Antonio Express/News*, September 12, 1970, 1, 18-A; Tom Bach, "Mayor-Boycotters Talk Plans Fail," *San Antonio Express*, September 14, 1970, 1, 12-A; James McCrory, "Mayor Issues Statement," *San Antonio Express*, September 15, 1970, 1 (second quotation); "Picketing at SASA," *San Antonio Light*, October 4, 1970, 3-B; Montejano, *Quixote's Soldiers*, 159 (first quotation, citing an interview with Rosie Castro). Also see the city council meeting minutes for September 17, 24, and 28, 1970, all available via Municipal Archives & Records, City of San Antonio, sanantonio.gov /Municipal-Archives-Records/Search-Collections.

45. "Local Activism and Discrimination, Part Two," from Richardson interview.

46. "Police Brutality and Segregation," from Richardson interview.

47. "Local Activism and Discrimination," from Richardson interview, crbb.tcu.edu/clips /5124/carlos-richardson-discusses-local-activism-and-discrimination.

48. For examples of conflict, see Behnken, *Fighting Their Own Battles*. For examples of Black-Brown coalitions before the Chicano movement, see Krochmal, *Blue Texas*, 124–170, 203–213. For an introduction to this debate, see Neil Foley, "Becoming Hispanic: Mexican Americans and the Faustian Pact with Whiteness," *Reflexiones*, 1997, 53–70; Foley, "Straddling the Color Line: The Legal Construction of Hispanic Identity in Texas," in *Not Just Black and White: Historical and Contemporary Perspectives on Immigration, Race, and Ethnicity in the United States*, ed. Nancy Foner and George M. Fredrickson (New York: Sage, 2004); Thomas A. Guglielmo, "Fighting for Caucasian Rights: Mexicans, Mexican Americans, and the Transnational Struggle for Civil Rights in World War II Texas," *Journal of American History* 92, no. 4 (March 2006): 1212–1237; Ariela J. Gross, "'The Caucasian Cloak': Mexican Americans and the Politics of Whiteness in the Twentieth Century Southwest," *Georgetown Law Journal* 95 (2007): 337–392; Carlos K. Blanton, "George I. Sánchez, Ideology, and Whiteness in the Making of the Mexican American Civil Rights Movement, 1930–1960," *Journal of Southern History* 72, no. 3 (August 2006): 569–604; Carlos K. Blanton, "The Citizenship Sacrifice: Mexican Americans, the Saunders-Leonard Report, and the Politics of Immigration, 1951–1952," *Western Historical Quarterly* 40, no. 3 (Autumn 2009): 299–320.

49. For background, see Dwayne Mack, "Angela Davis (1944–)," *BlackPast* (blog), February 10, 2011, blackpast.org/african-american-history/davis-angela-1944; "Inventory of the Angela

Davis Legal Defense Collection, 1970–1972: Biography," New York Public Library, Digital Library Collections, digilib.nypl.org/dynaweb/ead/scm/scmdavisa; Bettina Aptheker, *The Morning Breaks: The Trial of Angela Davis*, 2nd ed. (Ithaca, NY: Cornell University Press, 1999).

50. "Newsletter of the San Antonio Committee to Free Angela Davis," no. 1, n.d. [1971], box 15, folder 20, Salas Papers, UTSA.

51. San Antonio Committee to Free Angela Davis, "Freedom for Angela Davis" [petition to Free Angela Davis], 1970 [probably 1971], Portal to Texas History, University of North Texas Libraries, texashistory.unt.edu/ark:/67531/metapth1261114; Mario Salas to Franklin Alexander, n.d. [probably 1971], box 15, folder 20, Salas Papers, UTSA; see also Mario Salas, "San Antonio Played a Part in the 'Free Angela Davis' Movement," *African-American News & Issues*, June 20–26, 2007, 1, 3, clipping in box 15, folder 2, Salas Papers, UTSA.

52. "Newsletter of the San Antonio Committee to Free Angela Davis," 1970 [actually 1971; probably no. 2 or no. 3], Portal to Texas History, University of North Texas Libraries, texashistory.unt.edu/ark:/67531/metapth1261683/m1/1/?q=metapth1261683.

53. SACTFAD, newsletter no. 4, box 15, folder 2, Salas Papers, UTSA (first two quotations); SACTFAD, newsletter no. 7, box 15, folder 2, Salas Papers, UTSA (remaining quotations); Jim Price, "Shouting Match Erupts over Use of Sheriff's Deputies," *San Antonio Light*, May 21, 1971, 6-A; "Reeves, Sutton Fuss over Davis Dance," *San Antonio Express-News*, May 22, 1971, 18-C.

54. SACTFAD, newsletter no. 7, 1 (all quotations); "750 Attend 'Angela Rally," *San Antonio Light*, May 24, 1971, 5-C; Robert Denman, "Free Angela Petition Campaign Pushed in S.A.," *San Antonio Express*, May 24, 1971, 7-D.

55. SACTFAD, newsletter no. 7, 2; Salas, "San Antonio Played a Part"; Paul Thompson, "The Boys" and "Puzzle," *San Antonio Express-News*, July 3, 1971; Carlos Richardson, "San Quentin Questions," *San Antonio Express*, September 6, 1971; box 8, folder "Southern Conference Educational Fund, 1971–1972," Salas Papers, UTSA.

56. The Spanish word "*Raza*" can translate as either "people" or "race." Generally, the title of the party is thought to refer to "*la raza cósmica*" (the cosmic race), a blending of Spanish and indigenous roots that produced the mixed-race people that predominate in Mexico. Many Chicano movement activists embraced cultural nationalism, leading both adherents and detractors to assume that the "Raza" in the party's name referred only to people of Mexican descent. But in San Antonio, the party's tight alliance with SNCC led activists to use an alternate, broader, plural translation, "Peoples."

57. Ken Bunting, "Black San Antonio V: Political Inroads," *San Antonio Express*, February 17, 1972, 18-A (all quotations). On the earlier history, see Krochmal, *Blue Texas*.

58. Bunting, "Black San Antonio V: Political Inroads"; Navarro, *Mexican American Youth Organization*; Armando Navarro, *La Raza Unida Party: A Chicano Challenge to the U.S. Two-Party Dictatorship* (Philadelphia: Temple University Press, 2000), chs. 1–2; Rosales, *Illusion of Inclusion*, 143; Joe Carroll Rust, "Raza Unida Offers Political Slate," *San Antonio Light*, February 10, 1972, 8-A. The analysis of the impact of single-member districts is my own.

59. Rust, "Raza Unida Offers Political Slate"; "Eleven State Legislative Positions Are Contested," *San Antonio Express-News*, November 5, 1972, 4-III.

60. "United Peoples Party (Raza Unida)," letter, box 7, folder "La Raza 1970–1978, n.d.," Salas Papers, UTSA.

61. Ibid.

62. Ibid.

63. Flores Amaya and Mario Salas to Le Duc Tho, May 4, 1972, box 7, folder "La Raza 1970–1978, n.d.," Salas Papers, UTSA; "Raza Candidates Write to Hanoi," *San Antonio Express*, May 11, 1972, 2-A; "S.N.C.C. Show & Dance," flyer, n.d. [1972?], box 7, folder "La Raza 1970–1978, n.d.," Salas Papers, UTSA; Tony Castro, "La Raza Unida Given Surprise SCLC Support," *Dallas Morning News*, August 18, 1972, clipping in box 7, folder "La Raza 1970–1978, n.d.," Salas Papers, UTSA.

64. Peter D. Franklin, "GOP Legislative Upset," *San Antonio Light*, November 8, 1972, 1 (quotations); "Sage Leading Floyd by 60 Votes," *San Antonio Express*, November 9, 1972, 2-A; "November Election Vote Canvassed," *San Antonio Express-News*, November 25, 1972, 5-A. Ini-

tial reports gave Salas 674 votes, and the margin between the victor and runner-up was just 60. In the final canvass, however, Salas won 732 votes, but the margin between the top two grew to 1,003. Still, his campaign likely had a negative impact on the Democratic incumbent.

65. "SNCC in San Antonio," from Salas interview; "Methodists Okay Controversial Legal Assistance Fund," *San Antonio Express*, May 31, 1972, 16-A; "Eleven State Legislative Positions Are Contested"; "Benefit Concert to Aid 'Anemia,'" *San Antonio Express*, June 15, 1972, 2-A; Mario Salas to United Nations, March 29, 1973, box 15, folder "SNCC S.A., 1967–1975, n.d., (1–2)," Salas Papers, UTSA; Salas, "Persistence of Paternal Continuity," 35.

66. For introductions to this transition, see Joseph, *Black Power Movement; Jeffrey Ogbonna Green Ogbar, Black Power: Radical Politics and African American Identity* (Baltimore: Johns Hopkins University Press, 2004); Charles E. Jones, ed., *The Black Panther Party (Reconsidered)* (Baltimore: Black Classic Press, 1998). Newer works on gender and Black Power include Robyn C. Spencer, *The Revolution Has Come: Black Power, Gender, and the Black Panther Party in Oakland* (Durham, NC: Duke University Press, 2016); Ashley D. Farmer, *Remaking Black Power: How Black Women Transformed an Era* (Chapel Hill: University of North Carolina Press, 2017); Ula Yvette Taylor, *The Promise of Patriarchy: Women and the Nation of Islam* (Chapel Hill: University of North Carolina Press, 2017); Keisha N. Blain, *Set the World on Fire: Black Nationalist Women and the Global Struggle for Freedom* (Philadelphia: University of Pennsylvania Press, 2018). For the decline of the Chicano movement, including discussions of intersectionality, see Montejano, *Quixote's Soldiers*, parts 2–3. On the War on Crime and counterinsurgency, see Elizabeth Hinton, *From the War on Poverty to the War on Crime: The Making of Mass Incarceration in America* (Cambridge, MA: Harvard University Press, 2016); Jordan T. Camp, *Incarcerating the Crisis: Freedom Struggles and the Rise of the Neoliberal State* (Oakland: University of California Press, 2016); Naomi Murakawa, *The First Civil Right: How Liberals Built Prison America* (Oxford: Oxford University Press, 2014).

67. "SNCC Chapt 3," unpublished manuscript, box 4, folder "SNCC in Texas, undated," Salas Papers, UTSA (first and second quotations); "Rough Draft Reflections on the 60s, the Black Liberation Struggle, SNCC, and Texas," box 15, folder 3, Salas Papers, UTSA (third quotation on "lumpen"). On both the emotional toll of the movement and the role of self-reflection, see Faith S. Holsaert et al., eds., *Hands on the Freedom Plow: Personal Accounts by Women in SNCC* (Urbana: University of Illinois Press, 2010).

68. "East Side Protest Murder Trial," *SNAP*, May 19, 1979, 1, copy in box 15, folder 5, Salas Papers, UTSA; Mario Marcel Salas, "Salas' Point: The Killing of Webb Boyd," *African-American News & Issues*, January 31–February 6, 2007, clipping in box 15, folder 1, Salas Papers, UTSA; Salas, "Persistence of Paternal Continuity," 29; see also box 15, folder "SNCC S.A., 1967–1975, n.d., (1–2)," Salas Papers, UTSA.

69. "Coalitions and Activism," from Calvert interview, crbb.tcu.edu/clips/6376/coalitions -and-activism.

70. "What Are You Most Proud Of," from Salas interview, crbb.tcu.edu/clips/7069/what-are -you-most-proud-of.

71. "Local SNCC Success," from Richardson interview, crbb.tcu.edu/clips/5131/carlos -richardson-discusses-local-sncc-success.

72. "Elected Officials of San Antonio: CURRENT–2000," City of San Antonio Municipal Archives & Records, sanantonio.gov/Municipal-Archives-Records/About-Archives-Records /Officials.

Chapter 14: "You Either Support Democracy or You Don't"

1. "Problems in Austin," from Larry Jackson, oral history interview by Vinicio Sinta and Steve Arionus, June 10, 2016, Austin, Civil Rights in Black and Brown Interview Database [hereafter cited as CRBB Interview Database], crbb.tcu.edu/clips/6517/problems-in -austin. Special thanks to Chelsea Stallings for her research assistance on this chapter, and to Vinicio Sinta and Lourdes Cueva Chacón for sharing their research on single-member districts.

2. "Austin's Progressives and At-Large Districts," from David Van Os, oral history interview

by Steve Arionus and Vinicio Sinta, June 24, 2016, San Antonio, CRBB Interview Database, crbb.tcu.edu/clips/6296/austin-s-progressives-and-at-large-districts.

3. Robert J. Mundt and Peggy Heilig, "District Representation: Demands and Effects in the Urban South," *Journal of Politics* 44, no. 4 (1982): 1035, 1046. See also Chandler Davidson and George Korbel, "At-Large Elections and Minority-Group Representation: A Re-Examination of Historical and Contemporary Evidence," *Journal of Politics* 43, no. 4 (1981): 982–1005.

4. Emily Badger, "Study: Austin Is Most Economically Segregated Metro Area," *Texas Tribune*, February 23, 2015, texastribune.org/2015/02/23/austin-most-economically-segre gated-metro-area.

5. J. Morgan Kousser, "The Strange, Ironic Career of Section Five of the Voting Rights Act," *Texas Law Review* 86, no. 4 (2008): 667–775 (quoted material on 679); see also Kousser, "Voting Districts and Minority Representation," available from CalTechAUTHORS, authors.library.caltech.edu/41179/1/voting%20districts%20and%20minority%20represen tation.pdf.

6. Anthony M. Orum, *Power, Money, and the People: The Making of Modern Austin* (Austin: Texas Monthly Press, 1987), 175–176; David C. Humphrey, *Austin: A History of the Capital City* (Austin: Texas State Historical Association, 1997), 35.

7. Humphrey, *Austin*, 42.

8. Orum, *Power, Money, and the People*, 174–177.

9. Andrew Busch, "Building 'A City of Upper-Middle-Class Citizens': Labor Markets, Seg-regation, and Growth in Austin, Texas, 1950–1973," *Journal of Urban History* 39, no. 5 (Septem-ber 2013): 982.

10. "Segregation and Racial Discrimination in Austin, Part One," from Susana Almanza, oral history interview by Steve Arionus and Vinicio Sinta, June 8, 2016, Austin, CRBB Interview Database, crbb.tcu.edu/clips/6254/segregation-and-racial-discrimination-in-austin.

11. Orum, *Power, Money, and the People*, 171; Andrew Busch, *City in a Garden: Environmental Transformations and Racial Justice in Twentieth-Century Austin, Texas* (Chapel Hill: University of North Carolina Press, 2017), 157.

12. Wells Dunbar, "The Single-Member Situation," *Austin Chronicle*, February 25, 2011.

13. "Single Member Districts in Austin" and "Working for Dr. Charles Urdy's Campaign for Austin City Council," from Van Os interview, crbb.tcu.edu/clips/6291/single-member -districts-in-austin, crbb.tcu.edu/clips/6293/working-for-dr-charles-urdy-s-campaign-for -austin-city-council.

14. "Electoral Politics in Austin—Then and Now," from Charles Urdy, oral history interview by Steve Arionus and Vinicio Sinta, June 17, 2016, Austin, CRBB Interview Database, crbb.tcu .edu/clips/5221/electoral-politics-in-austin-then-and-now.

15. "Austin's Progressives and At-Large Districts," from Van Os interview.

16. Busch, *City in a Garden*, 144.

17. Ibid., 156; Busch, "City of Upper-Middle-Class Citizens," 977.

18. Busch, *City in a Garden*, 133.

19. Ibid., 133–134.

20. "Activism and Organization in Austin," from T. L. Wyatt, oral history interview by Steve Arionus, June 9, 2016, Austin, CRBB Interview Database, crbb.tcu.edu/clips/7781/activism -and-organization-in-austin.

21. Mike Kanin, "What's Left? For Nearly Four Decades, White Liberals Have Dominated Austin Politics," *Texas Observer*, December 21, 2013, texasobserver.org/whats-left.

22. Busch, *City in a Garden*, 153.

23. Ibid., 130.

24. Busch, "City of Upper-Middle-Class Citizens," 978.

25. "White Progressive Groups," from Gilbert Rivera, oral history interview by Steve Arionus, June 15, 2016, Austin, CRBB Interview Database, crbb.tcu.edu/clips/5118/gilbert -rivera-discusses-white-progressive-groups.

26. "Politicization and Childhood Experience," from Rivera interview, crbb.tcu.edu/clips /5119/gilbert-rivera-discusses-politicization-and-childhood-experience.

27. "Police Brutality and Militancy," from Rivera interview, crbb.tcu.edu/clips/5116/gilbert-rivera-discusses-police-brutality-and-militancy.

28. "Cooperation Between Black Panthers and Brown Berets in Austin," from Rivera interview, crbb.tcu.edu/clips/5117/gilbert-rivera-discusses-cooperation-between-Black-panthers-and-brown-berets-in-austin.

29. Ibid.

30. Douglas C. Rossinow, *The Politics of Authenticity: Liberalism, Christianity, and the New Left in America* (New York: Columbia University Press, 1999), 200; "Black Power / Community Relationships," from Jackson interview, crbb.tcu.edu/clips/6515/Black-power-community-relationships.

31. "Biographical Information," from Roen Salinas, oral history interview by Steve Arionus and Vinicio Sinta, June 16, 2016, Austin, CRBB Interview Database, crbb.tcu.edu/clips/7361/biographical-information-102.

32. "Gentrification," from Salinas interview, crbb.tcu.edu/clips/7369/gentrification.

33. "Saltillo Collaborative and the Chicano Economic Development Corporation," from Rivera interview, crbb.tcu.edu/clips/5143/gilbert-rivera-discusses-the-saltillo-collaborative-and-the-chicano-economic-development-corporation.

34. "Gentrification, Pricing People Out with Property Taxes," from Rivera interview, crbb.tcu.edu/clips/5141/gilbert-rivera-discusses-gentrification-pricing-people-out-with-property-taxes.

35. "Gentrification," from Salinas interview.

36. Ibid.; "Final Remarks," from Salinas interview, crbb.tcu.edu/clips/7370/final-remarks-66.

37. Busch, *City in a Garden*, 147.

38. Sylvia Herrera, oral history interview by Steve Arionus and Vinicio Sinta, June 10, 2016, Austin, CRBB Interview, Portal to Texas History, University of North Texas Libraries, texashistory.unt.edu/ark:/67531/metapth987629; see also "People Organized for Defense of Earth and her Resources (PODER)," Resist, July 6, 2015, resist.org/grantees/people-organized-defense-earth-and-her-resources-poder; "Best East Austin Watchdog: PODER," *Austin Chronicle*, 1997, accessed August 14, 2019, austinchronicle.com/best-of-austin/year:1997/poll:critics/category:politics-and-personalities/poder-people-organized-in-defense-of-earth-and-her-resources-best-east-austin-watchdog.

39. Herrera interview; Susana Almanza, oral history interview by Steve Arionus and Vinicio Sinta, June 8, 2016, Austin, CRBB Interview, Portal to Texas History, University of North Texas Libraries, texashistory.unt.edu/ark:/67531/metapth987614.

40. Herrera interview; Almanza, Portal to Texas History interview.

41. Herrera interview; Almanza, Portal to Texas History interview.

42. Herrera interview.

43. Ibid.

44. Humphrey, *Austin*, 45–46.

45. Sarah Coppola, "Council Districts: 7th Time a Charm?," *Austin American-Statesman*, September 16, 2012.

46. "Austin's Progressives and At-Large Districts," from Van Os interview.

47. "Single Member Districts in Austin," from Van Os interview.

48. "Legal Work on Single-Member Districts and School Desegregation," from Van Os interview, crbb.tcu.edu/clips/6297/legal-work-on-single-member-districts-and-school-desegregation.

49. "Challenging At-Large, Majority Districts in Austin," from Van Os interview, crbb.tcu.edu/clips/6299/challenging-at-large-majority-districts-in-austin.

50. "Arthur Dewitty and the 1951 Austin City Council Election," from Van Os interview, crbb.tcu.edu/clips/6295/arthur-de-witty-and-the-1951-austin-city-council-election.

51. Kanin, "What's Left?"

52. Sarah Coppola, "Austin Voters Rejected City Council Districts Six Times in the Past. Will This Year Be Different?" *Austin American-Statesman*, July 16, 2014 (Young comment); Kanin, "What's Left?"; Carrie Powell and Laura Rice, "With 10-1 Map in the Books, Austin Concludes Redistricting (Update)," November 26, 2013, KUT, kut.org/post/map-10-1-map-books-austin-concludes-redistricting-update; Coppola, "Council Districts: 7th Time a Charm?"; Coppola,

"Observers: Door-to-Door Effort Fueled Prop. 3 Win," *Austin American-Statesman*, November 8, 2012.

53. US Census Bureau, "Quick Facts: Austin, Texas," census.gov/quickfacts/fact/table/austin citytexas/LND110210; Kanin, "What's Left?"

54. "Problems in Austin," from Jackson interview.

55. Susan Nold and Christopher Kennedy, "It's Up to the People of Austin to Make Meaningful Change Out of the '10-1' System," *UT News*, November 17, 2015, accessed August 6, 2019, news.utexas.edu/2015/11/17/making-meaningful-change-out-of-the-10-1-system.

56. "City of Austin Cumulative Results," Travis County Clerk's Elections Division. See countyclerk.traviscountytx.gov/results-for-november-4-2014.html, countyclerk.traviscountytx .gov/results-for-november-6-2018.html, and countyclerk.traviscountytx.gov/results-for-de cember-11-2018.html, accessed February 9, 2021.

57. "Austin's Progressives and At-Large Districts," from Van Os interview.

Chapter 15: Recovering, Interpreting, and Disseminating the Hidden Histories of Civil Rights in Texas

1. For an introduction to the growing body of community studies on the movement, see Emilye Crosby, ed., *Civil Rights History from the Ground Up: Local Struggles, a National Movement* (Athens: University of Georgia Press, 2011). Examples include William Henry Chafe, *Civilities and Civil Rights: Greensboro, North Carolina, and the Black Struggle for Freedom* (New York: Oxford University Press, 1980); J. Todd Moye, *Let the People Decide: Black Freedom and White Resistance Movements in Sunflower County, Mississippi, 1945–1986* (Chapel Hill: University of North Carolina Press, 2004); Hasan Kwame Jeffries, *Bloody Lowndes: Civil Rights and Black Power in Alabama's Black Belt* (New York: NYU Press, 2009); Matthew Countryman, *Up South: Civil Rights and Black Power in Philadelphia* (Philadelphia: University of Pennsylvania Press, 2006).

2. Examples of community studies include David Montejano, *Quixote's Soldiers: A Local History of the Chicano Movement, 1966–1981* (Austin: University of Texas Press, 2010); Guadalupe San Miguel, *Brown, Not White: School Integration and the Chicano Movement in Houston* (College Station: Texas A&M University Press, 2001); Ernesto Chávez, *"¡Mi Raza Primero!" (My People First!): Nationalism, Identity, and Insurgency in the Chicano Movement in Los Angeles, 1966–1978* (Berkeley: University of California Press, 2002); George J. Sanchez, *Becoming Mexican American: Ethnicity, Culture, and Identity in Chicano Los Angeles, 1900–1945* (New York: Oxford University Press, 1993). The generational terms hail from Mario T. García, *Mexican Americans: Leadership, Ideology, and Identity, 1930–1960* (New Haven, CT: Yale University Press, 1989).

3. Jacquelyn Dowd Hall, "The Long Civil Rights Movement and the Political Uses of the Past," *Journal of American History* 91, no. 4 (March 2005): 1233–1263; Robert Korstad and Nelson Lichtenstein, "Opportunities Found and Lost: Labor, Radicals, and the Early Civil Rights Movement," *Journal of American History* 75, no. 3 (December 1988): 786–811. Likewise, the "labor feminism" that flourished in the 1950s often disappears in accounts of both the labor and civil rights movements in the following decades. On the earlier period, see Dorothy Sue Cobble, *The Other Women's Movement: Workplace Justice and Social Rights in Modern America* (Princeton, NJ: Princeton University Press, 2004).

4. For an introduction to the new bottom-up history of the Great Society, see Annelise Orleck and Lisa Hazirjian, eds., *War on Poverty: A New Grassroots History, 1964–1980* (Athens: University of Georgia Press, 2011). For Texas cases, see William S. Clayson, *Freedom Is Not Enough: The War on Poverty and the Civil Rights Movement in Texas* (Austin: University of Texas Press, 2010); Wesley G. Phelps, *A People's War on Poverty: Urban Politics and Grassroots Activists in Houston* (Athens: University of Georgia Press, 2014). On the connections between federal programs, reformist politics, and Chicano/a Power, see, among others, Marc Simon Rodriguez, *Rethinking the Chicano Movement* (New York: Routledge, 2015); Montejano, *Quixote's Soldiers*; Armando Navarro, *Mexican American Youth Organization: Avant-Garde of the Chicano Movement in Texas* (Austin: University of Texas Press, 1995). On Black Power, start with Peniel E. Joseph, ed.,

The Black Power Movement: Rethinking the Civil Rights–Black Power Era (New York: Routledge, 2006); Peniel E. Joseph, "The Black Power Movement: A State of the Field," *Journal of American History* 96, no. 3 (December 2009): 751–776; Rhonda Y. Williams, *Concrete Demands: The Search for Black Power in the 20th Century* (New York: Routledge, 2015); Yohuru Williams, *Rethinking the Black Freedom Movement* (New York: Routledge, 2016). For women in the Black freedom struggle, see Bettye Collier-Thomas and V. P. Franklin, eds., *Sisters in the Struggle: African-American Women in the Civil Rights–Black Power Movement* (New York: NYU Press, 2001); Dayo F. Gore, Jeanne Theoharis, and Komozi Woodard, eds., *Want to Start a Revolution? Radical Women in the Black Freedom Struggle* (New York: NYU Press, 2009); Christina Greene, *Our Separate Ways: Women and the Black Freedom Movement in Durham, North Carolina* (Chapel Hill: University of North Carolina Press, 2005); Danielle L. McGuire, *At the Dark End of the Street: Black Women, Rape, and Resistance; A New History of the Civil Rights Movement from Rosa Parks to the Rise of Black Power* (New York: Knopf, 2010); Ashley D. Farmer, *Remaking Black Power: How Black Women Transformed an Era* (Chapel Hill: University of North Carolina Press, 2017). On Chicanas in the long struggle against Juan Crow, see Maylei Blackwell, *¡Chicana Power! Contested Histories of Feminism in the Chicano Movement* (Austin: University of Texas Press, 2011); Dionne Espinoza, María Eugenia Cotera, and Maylei Blackwell, eds., *Chicana Movidas: New Narratives of Activism and Feminism in the Movement Era* (Austin: University of Texas Press, 2018); Gabriela González, *Redeeming La Raza: Transborder Modernity, Race, Respectability, and Rights* (New York: Oxford University Press, 2018); Cynthia Orozco, *No Mexicans, Women, or Dogs Allowed: The Rise of the Mexican American Civil Rights Movement* (Austin: University of Texas Press, 2009); Vicki Ruíz, *From Out of the Shadows: Mexican Women in Twentieth-Century America* (New York: Oxford University Press, 1998).

5. On memory, see, for example, Marvin Dulaney, "Whatever Happened to the Civil Rights Movement in Dallas, Texas?," in *Essays on the American Civil Rights Movement*, ed. W. Marvin Dulaney and Kathleen Underwood (College Station: Texas A&M University Press, 1993), 66–95; W. Marvin Dulaney, "A Research Challenge: The African American Experience in Dallas, Texas," *Legacies* 16, no. 1 (Spring 2004): 52–58; Yvonne Davis Frear, "Generation versus Generation: African Americans in Texas Remember the Civil Rights Movement," in *Lone Star Pasts: Memory and History in Texas*, ed. Gregg Cantrell and Elizabeth Hayes Turner (College Station: Texas A&M University Press, 2007), 203–219.

6. This point on the state's racial geography also appears in Brian D. Behnken, *Fighting Their Own Battles: Mexican Americans, African Americans, and the Struggle for Civil Rights in Texas* (Chapel Hill: University of North Carolina Press, 2011); Brian D. Behnken, ed., *The Struggle in Black and Brown: African American and Mexican American Relations during the Civil Rights Era* (Lincoln: University of Nebraska Press, 2011).

7. Alessandro Portelli, "What Makes Oral History Different," in *The Death of Luigi Trastulli, and Other Stories: Form and Meaning in Oral History* (Albany: State University of New York Press, 1991), 45–58. For a sampling of oral history theory, see Robert Perks and Alistair Thomson, eds., *The Oral History Reader*, 2nd ed. (New York: Routledge, 2006); Donald A. Ritchie, ed., *The Oxford Handbook of Oral History* (New York: Oxford University Press, 2011).

8. Neil Foley, "Becoming Hispanic: Mexican Americans and the Faustian Pact with Whiteness," *Reflexiones*, 1997, 53–70; Ariela J. Gross, "'The Caucasian Cloak': Mexican Americans and the Politics of Whiteness in the Twentieth Century Southwest," *Georgetown Law Journal* 95 (2007): 337–392; Thomas A. Guglielmo, "Fighting for Caucasian Rights: Mexicans, Mexican Americans, and the Transnational Struggle for Civil Rights in World War II Texas," *Journal of American History* 92, no. 4 (March 2006): 1212–1237; Carlos K. Blanton, "George I. Sánchez, Ideology, and Whiteness in the Making of the Mexican American Civil Rights Movement, 1930-1960," *Journal of Southern History* 72, no. 3 (August 2006): 569–604; Blanton, "The Citizenship Sacrifice: Mexican Americans, the Saunders-Leonard Report, and the Politics of Immigration, 1951-1952," *Western Historical Quarterly* 40, no. 3 (Autumn 2009): 299–320.

9. Shana Bernstein, *Bridges of Reform: Interracial Civil Rights Activism in Twentieth-Century Los Angeles* (New York: Oxford University Press, 2011); Laura Pulido, *Black, Brown, Yellow, and Left: Radical Activism in Los Angeles* (Berkeley: University of California Press, 2006).

10. Lauren Araiza, *To March for Others: The Black Freedom Struggle and the United Farm Workers* (Philadelphia: University of Pennsylvania Press, 2013); John D. Márquez, *Black-Brown Solidarity: Racial Politics in the New Gulf South* (Austin: University of Texas Press, 2013).

11. Gaye Theresa Johnson, *Spaces of Conflict, Sounds of Solidarity: Music, Race, and Spatial Entitlement in Los Angeles* (Berkeley: University of California Press, 2013); Luis Alvarez and Daniel Widener, "A History of Black and Brown: Chicana/o–African American Cultural and Political Relations," *Aztlán: A Journal of Chicano Studies* 33, no. 1 (Spring 2008): 143–154; Luis Alvarez, *The Power of the Zoot: Youth Culture and Resistance during World War II* (Berkeley: University of California Press, 2008); Daniel Widener, *Black Arts West: Culture and Struggle in Postwar Los Angeles* (Durham, NC: Duke University Press, 2010).

12. Nicolás C. Vaca, *The Presumed Alliance: The Unspoken Conflict between Latinos and Blacks and What It Means for America* (New York: Rayo, 2004).

13. Behnken, *Fighting Their Own Battles*; Behnken, *Struggle in Black and Brown*; Michael Phillips, *White Metropolis: Race, Ethnicity, and Religion in Dallas, 1841–2001* (Austin: University of Texas Press, 2006); Robert Bauman, *Race and the War on Poverty: From Watts to East L.A.* (Norman: University of Oklahoma Press, 2008); Clayson, *Freedom Is Not Enough*.

14. Mark Brilliant, *The Color of America Has Changed: How Racial Diversity Shaped Civil Rights Reform in California, 1941–1978* (New York: Oxford University Press, 2010). On Black–Japanese American relations, also see the foundational work by Scott Kurashige, *The Shifting Grounds of Race: Black and Japanese Americans in the Making of Multiethnic Los Angeles* (Princeton, NJ: Princeton University Press, 2008). Also on California, see Daniel Martinez HoSang, *Racial Propositions: Ballot Initiatives and the Making of Postwar California* (Berkeley: University of California Press, 2010).

15. Gordon K. Mantler, *Power to the Poor* (Chapel Hill: University of North Carolina Press, 2013).

16. Max Krochmal, *Blue Texas: The Making of a Multiracial Democratic Coalition in the Civil Rights Era* (Chapel Hill: University of North Carolina Press, 2016).

17. Sonia Song-Ha Lee, *Building a Latino Civil Rights Movement: Puerto Ricans, African Americans, and the Pursuit of Racial Justice in New York City* (Chapel Hill: University of North Carolina Press, 2014); Frederick Douglass Opie, *Upsetting the Apple Cart: Black-Latino Coalitions in New York City from Protest to Public Office* (New York: Columbia University Press, 2015).

18. Danielle R. Olden, "Becoming Minority: Mexican Americans, Race, and the Legal Struggle for Educational Equity in Denver, Colorado," *Western Historical Quarterly* 48, no. 1 (January 2017): 43–66, doi.org/10.1093/whq/whw197; Laurie Lahey, "'The Grassy Battleground': Race, Religion, and Activism in Camden's 'Wide' Civil Rights Movement" (PhD diss., George Washington University, 2013); Alyssa M. Ribeiro, "'The Battle for Harmony': Intergroup Relations between Blacks and Latinos in Philadelphia, 1950s to 1980s" (PhD diss., University of Pittsburgh, 2013). Also on Denver, and with wider implications, see the foundational work by Tom Romero, "¿La Raza Latino? Multiracial Ambivalence, Color Denial, and the Emergence of a Tri-Ethnic Jurisprudence at the End of the Twentieth Century," *New Mexico Law Review* 37, no. 2 (Spring 2007): 245–306.

19. Allyson Brantley, *Brewing a Boycott: How a Grassroots Coalition Fought Coors and Remade American Consumer Activism* (Chapel Hill: University of North Carolina Press, 2021).

20. Rodriguez, *Rethinking the Chicano Movement*; Williams, *Rethinking the Black Freedom Movement*.

21. Jeffrey Ogbonna Green Ogbar, *Black Power: Radical Politics and African American Identity* (Baltimore: Johns Hopkins University Press, 2004).

22. Jama Lazerow and Yohuru Williams, eds., *In Search of the Black Panther Party: New Perspectives on a Revolutionary Movement* (Durham, NC: Duke University Press, 2006); Jakobi Williams, *From the Bullet to the Ballot: The Illinois Chapter of the Black Panther Party and Racial Coalition Politics in Chicago* (Chapel Hill: University of North Carolina Press, 2013).

23. George Mariscal, *Brown-Eyed Children of the Sun: Lessons from the Chicano Movement, 1965–1975* (Albuquerque: University of New Mexico Press, 2005).

24. Pulido, *Black, Brown, Yellow, and Left*.

25. Jason Michael Ferreira, "All Power to the People: A Comparative History of Third World Radicalism in San Francisco, 1968–1974" (PhD diss., University of California, Berkeley, 2003); Aaron Byungjoo Bae, "The Ideological Impetus and Struggle in Praxis for Multiracial Radical Alliances in the San Francisco Bay Area, 1967–1980" (PhD diss., Arizona State University, 2016).

26. Jason M. Ferreira, "'With the Soul of a Human Rainbow': Los Siete, Black Panthers, and Third Worldism in San Francisco," in *Ten Years That Shook the City: San Francisco, 1968–1978*, ed. Chris Carlsson (San Francisco: City Lights Books, 2011), 31; emphasis in the original.

27. For other excellent studies that take up these questions of region, see Julie M. Weise, *Corazon de Dixie: Mexicanos in the U.S. South since 1910* (Chapel Hill: The University of North Carolina Press, 2015); Cecilia Márquez, "The Strange Career of Juan Crow: Latino/as and the Making of the US South, 1940–2000" (PhD diss., University of Virginia, 2016); Sarah McNamara, "From Picket Lines to Picket Fences: Latinas and the Remaking of the Jim Crow South, 1930–1964" (PhD diss., University of North Carolina, Chapel Hill, 2016).

28. Note my careful reference to "civil rights activism in the postwar period," which does *not* encompass the centuries of struggles for sovereignty among Native Americans, or Asian immigrants' fights for survival and legal incorporation at the turn of the twentieth century, or the exciting transitions among Asian Americans taking place in twenty-first-century Texas. Useful starting points for research on both groups in the long civil rights era might include Sherry L. Smith, *Hippies, Indians, and the Fight for Red Power* (New York: Oxford University Press, 2012); Douglas K. Miller, *Indians on the Move: Native American Mobility and Urbanization in the Twentieth Century* (Chapel Hill: University of North Carolina Press, 2019); Uzma Quraishi, *Redefining the Immigrant South: Indian and Pakistani Immigration to Houston during the Cold War* (Chapel Hill: University of North Carolina Press, 2020); Stephanie Hinnershitz, *A Different Shade of Justice: Asian American Civil Rights in the South* (Chapel Hill: University of North Carolina Press, 2017); Perla M. Guerrero, *Nuevo South: Latinas/os, Asians, and the Remaking of Place* (Austin: University of Texas Press, 2017). On Asian Americans in the turn-of-the-century Texas borderlands, see, for example, Julian Lim, *Porous Borders: Multiracial Migrations and the Law in the U.S.-Mexico Borderlands* (Chapel Hill: University of North Carolina Press, 2017).

29. See Daniel R. Kerr, "Allan Nevins Is Not My Grandfather: The Roots of Radical Oral History Practice in the United States," *Oral History Review* 43, no. 2 (2016): 367–391. For an influential, paradigmatic example of this approach, see Lawrence C. Goodwyn, "Populist Dreams and Negro Rights: East Texas as a Case Study," *American Historical Review* 76, no. 5 (December 1971): 1435–1456. For a more recent articulation, see Leslie Brown and Anne Valk, *Living with Jim Crow: African American Women and Memories of the Segregated South* (New York: Palgrave Macmillan, 2010).

30. For example, see Devra Weber, "Raiz Fuerte: Oral History and Mexicana Farmworkers," *Oral History Review* 17, no. 2 (Fall 1989): 47–62; Mario T. García, *Memories of Chicano History: The Life and Narrative of Bert Corona* (Berkeley: University of California, 1994); F. Arturo Rosales, ed., *Testimonio: A Documentary History of the Mexican American Struggle for Civil Rights* (Houston: Arte Publico, 2000).

31. See, for example, Alice Lynd and Staughton Lynd, eds., *Rank and File: Personal Histories by Working-Class Organizers* (Princeton, NJ: Princeton University Press, 1973); see also Kerr, "Allan Nevins Is Not My Grandfather."

32. See, for example, Michael Frisch, "Oral History and the Digital Revolution: Toward a Post-Documentary Sensibility," in Perks and Thomson, *Oral History Reader*, 102–114; Charles Hardy III, "Authoring in Sound: Aural History, Radio, and the Digital Revolution," in Perks and Thomson, *Oral History Reader*, 393–405; Douglas A. Boyd and Mary A. Larson, eds., *Oral History and Digital Humanities: Voice, Access, and Engagement* (New York: Palgrave Macmillan, 2014), pt. 1.

33. Alessandro Portelli, *They Say in Harlan County: An Oral History* (New York: Oxford University Press, 2011), 7.

34. "OHMS: Oral History Metadata Synchronizer," *Louie* (blog), Louie B. Nunn Center for Oral History, University of Kentucky Libraries, accessed November 15, 2018, nunncenter.org

/ohms-info; see also Doug Boyd, "OHMS: Enhancing Access to Oral History for Free," *Oral History Review* 40, no. 1 (2013): 95–106.

35. For a full list of subject terms in our controlled vocabulary, visit "Subjects," Civil Rights in Black and Brown, crbb.tcu.edu/subjects. I am grateful to the audiences at the Oral History Association meeting in Long Beach (2016) and the Organization of American Historians in New Orleans (2017) for raising these issues and giving us the opportunity to grapple with them. Thanks especially to Natalie Fousekis, Anne Valk, and Wesley Hogan.

Appendix: Selected Interview Transcripts

1. These excerpts highlight themes from the CRBB interviews, some of which are covered in previous chapters. Todd Moye has edited the transcripts lightly—removing, for instance, *uh*s, *um*s, and false starts, and in some cases condensing or adding words in brackets for clarity. Rich and detailed as these interview transcripts are, they only scratch the surface of the themes and topics that our narrators and interviewers discussed. This set of excerpts is not necessarily representative of the entire collection, and it certainly is not definitive. We encourage others to consult the online CRBB archives in two places: for clipped and tagged excerpts, see the Civil Rights in Black and Brown Oral History Project online archive, crbb .tcu.edu, and for full interviews, see the Portal to Texas History, texashistory.unt.edu.

The Houston riot, also known as the Camp Logan mutiny, of August 1917 resulted in the deaths of 16 white men, 5 of them policemen, and 4 African American soldiers. Courts-martial found 110 African American soldiers guilty of participating in the mutiny. Nineteen were hanged, and 63 were sentenced to life in federal prison. See Robert V. Haynes, "Houston Riot of 1917," *Handbook of Texas Online*, tshaonline.org/handbook/online/articles/jch04.

2. The 1964 Civil Rights Act did not include protections against racial discrimination in the area of housing, though it did prohibit racial segregation in public accommodations and public education. The 1968 Civil Rights Act, also known as the Fair Housing Act, added protections against racial discrimination in housing.

3. M. Elayne Hunt, *Dreams Fulfilled: One Family's Triumph Over Adversity* (Mustang, OK: Tate, 2014).

4. Daryl Hunt was a football prodigy, and he wanted to play for Odessa's Permian High School, a traditional powerhouse. After his family moved into the Permian school zone, he became the first African American to do so, and the first African American added to the school's Athletic Wall of Fame. Hunt went on to play at the University of Oklahoma, where he still holds the record for most tackles in a career, and in the National Football League.

5. Gene Green, an Anglo politician, represented part of the Houston area in the US House of Representatives for twenty-six years, 1993–2019. He was succeeded by Sylvia Rodriguez Garcia.

6. The collective that published *Space City!* from 1969 to 1972 included members of Students for a Democratic Society who had previously worked for the influential underground newspaper the *Rag*, published in Austin.

Contributors

Eladio Bobadilla is assistant professor of history at the University of Kentucky, where he teaches courses in modern US and Latinx history. He earned his PhD at Duke University and his bachelor of integrated studies from Weber State University, where he was recognized as the College of Social and Behavioral Sciences' Outstanding Graduate. He was given the university's highest academic honor for students when he was named Crystal Crest Scholar of the Year. Bobadilla received several prestigious fellowships and grants as a graduate student, including the Mellon Fellowship for Dissertation Research in Original Sources, the Ottis Green Fellowship, a Bass Instructional Fellowship, the John Higham Research Fellowship, and the George Pozzetta Dissertation Award. His dissertation, "'One People without Borders'": The Lost Roots of the Immigrants' Rights Movement, 1954–2006," won the Labor and Working-Class History Association's 2020 Herbert G. Gutman Prize for Outstanding Dissertation and will soon be published by the University of Illinois Press.

Katherine Bynum is assistant professor of history at Arizona State University. Bynum earned her PhD from Texas Christian University and her bachelor's and master's degrees from the University of North Texas, where she worked for the UNT Oral History Program. Bynum was a summer 2015 research assistant for the Civil Rights in Black and Brown Oral History Project, stationed in East Texas (Tyler, Marshall, Bryan–College Station, Huntsville, and Prairie View), and conducted more than thirty interviews with social justice activists. She continued to assist in managing the project, including interview processing, website maintenance, and designing promotional materials, until 2020. Bynum's dissertation, "Civil Rights in the 'City of Hate': Grassroots Organizing against Police Brutality in Dallas, Texas, 1935–1990," was supported by the 2019 Sara Jackson Graduate Student Award from the Western History Association.

Marvin Dulaney is deputy director of the African American Museum of Dallas and associate professor of history emeritus, former interim director of the Center for African American Studies, and the former chair of the Department of History at the University of Texas at Arlington. In between stints at UT-Arlington, he served as director of the Avery Research Center for African American History and chair of the History Department at the College of Charleston. He is a graduate of Central State

University in Wilberforce, Ohio, where he earned his bachelor of arts degree in history, magna cum laude. He earned his master of arts and doctor of philosophy degrees in American and African American history at Ohio State University. Dulaney is the author of *Black Police in America* (Indiana University Press, 1996) and the influential article "What Ever Happened to the Civil Rights Movement in Dallas, Texas?" He founded the Dallas–Fort Worth branch of the Association for the Study of African American Life and History, which has since been named in his honor.

Sandra I. Enríquez is assistant professor of history and director of the Public History Emphasis at the University of Missouri–Kansas City. Her research and teaching interests include Chicanx and Latinx history, urban history, borderlands, social movements, and public history. She received her bachelor's degree in history and a master's in US-Mexico border history from the University of Texas at El Paso and earned her PhD in history from the University of Houston. Her first book project examines Mexican American grassroots approaches to preserving the neighborhoods of South El Paso in the 1960s and 1970s, and how these fights served as stages for political and social empowerment. Enríquez served as a research assistant for the Civil Rights in Black and Brown Oral History Project in 2015 and 2016. She has also participated in several public history initiatives, including the Gulf Coast Food Project, Museo Urbano, in El Paso, and the Guadalupe Centers Centennial projects in Kansas City.

Moisés Acuña Gurrola is a PhD candidate in Texas Christian University's history department. He earned his bachelor's degree in history from Texas A&M University–Corpus Christi in 2012 and his master's in history from the University of North Texas in 2015. Acuña Gurrola's dissertation deals with the history of juvenile detention and incarceration in Texas from the 1880s to the 1970s. He has collaborated on several public-facing digital history projects, including Latino Fort Worth, The Crisis at Mansfield, and The Texas Runaway Ads Project. Acuña Gurrola has worked with the Civil Rights in Black and Brown Oral History Project since 2015.

Jasmin C. Howard is a doctoral student in the Department of History at Michigan State University. She earned a master's degree from Ohio State University and a bachelor's from the University of North Carolina at Chapel Hill. Her research interests include Black women's history, student activism, Black women's sexuality, queerness, resistance, the South, oral history, commemoration, and media representation. Her current research focuses on the activism and resistance of Black college students in North Carolina.

Max Krochmal is associate professor of history at Texas Christian University, where he was the founding chair of the Department of Comparative Race and Ethnic Studies. He is the author of *Blue Texas: The Making of a Multiracial Democratic Coalition in the Civil Rights Era* (University of North Carolina Press, 2016), winner of the Frederick Jackson Turner Award of the Organization of American Historians, the National Association of Chicana and Chicano Studies Tejas Foco Non-Fiction Book Award, and prizes from the Texas State Historical Association and the Texas Institute of

Letters. In 2020, he won a Fulbright–García Robles Fellowship and was named chair of US studies at the Universidad de las Américas, Puebla, México. Krochmal also served as cochair of the Fort Worth Independent School District's Racial Equity Committee and on the steering committee of United Fort Worth, a multicultural grassroots racial justice organization. A native of Reno, Nevada, he majored in community studies at the University of California, Santa Cruz, before earning his graduate degrees in history at Duke University.

Meredith May is instructor in history at Kilgore College. Hailing from Huntington, Texas, she received her bachelor's degree from Stephen F. Austin State University. She earned her master's and PhD at Texas Christian University and wrote her dissertation on the development of woman-owned small businesses in Houston after 1945. She has focused her scholarly work on the intersections of gender, race, class, and entrepreneurship in the post–World War II United States.

J. Todd Moye is Robnett Professor of US History at the University of North Texas, where he teaches twentieth-century US history and oral history and serves as the director of the UNT Oral History Program. He was a founding series editor of the Oxford Oral History Series published by Oxford University Press and the 2017–2018 president of the Oral History Association. Moye is the author of *Let the People Decide: Black Freedom and White Resistance Movements in Sunflower County, Mississippi, 1945–1986* (University of North Carolina Press, 2004); *Freedom Flyers: The Tuskegee Airmen of World War II* (Oxford University Press, 2010); and, most recently, *Ella Baker: Community Organizer of the Civil Rights Movement* (Rowman and Littlefield, 2013). Moye earned his bachelor's degree at the University of North Carolina–Chapel Hill and his master's and PhD at the University of Texas at Austin. He was a postdoctoral fellow at the Avery Research Center during Dulaney's tenure and then directed the National Park Service's Tuskegee Airmen Oral History Project from 2000 to 2005.

David Robles is an instructor at Kansas State University in the American Ethnic Studies Department. He received his bachelor's degree in Mexican American history in 2008 and his master's in history in 2012 from the University of Texas Pan-American (now University of Texas Rio Grande Valley), and his doctorate from the University of Texas at El Paso in May 2018. His research and teaching interests include Chicana/o history, US-Mexico borderlands history, Texas history, oral histories, and social movement history. His current manuscript project focuses on the dynamic political and social change in Pharr, Texas, after a riot that occurred during a Chicano protest in 1971. Robles served as a research assistant for the Civil Rights in Black and Brown Oral History Project in the summer of 2015, and as an organizer for the Borderlands History Conference at UTEP from January 2017 to February 2018.

Maggie Rivas-Rodriguez is a professor of journalism and new media at the University of Texas at Austin, where her research interests include the intersection of oral history and journalism, and US Latinos and the news media, both as producers of news and as consumers. Rivas-Rodriguez founded the Voces Oral History Center (formerly the US Latino and Latina World War II Oral History Project) in 1999, which has videotaped interviews with over 1,400 men and women throughout the country. She has worked as a newspaper, television, and radio reporter and bureau chief, and has long worked to bring greater diversity to the news media. She received her PhD as a Freedom Forum doctoral fellow from the University of North Carolina at Chapel Hill, her master's degree from Columbia University's Graduate School of Journalism, and her bachelor of journalism degree from the University of Texas at Austin.

Samantha M. Rodriguez is a history professor at Houston Community College. Her dissertation investigated the ways that Tejanas in Austin, Houston, and San Antonio straddled a commitment to gender equality and ethnic self-determination within the broader nexus of the Chicana/o movement, the Black Power movement, and the mainstream, Anglo feminist movement. Rodriguez served as a researcher, oral historian, and interview processor for the Civil Rights in Black and Brown Oral History Project. Her research has been published in the *Journal of South Texas* and the University of Texas Press anthology *¡Chicana Movidas! New Narratives of Activism and Feminism in the Movimiento Era* (2018).

Vinicio Sinta is an assistant professor in the department of communication at the University of Texas at Arlington. He was formerly a lecturer in communication at Texas A&M–San Antonio and manager of the Univision Media Lab, a joint initiative of A&M-SA and Univision KWEX-41 that provides students the opportunity to complete a capstone project and immersive practicum internship in radio and television at the station's studios in northwest San Antonio. Sinta earned his PhD in journalism from the University of Texas at Austin. His dissertation is a historical study of the formation of the National Association of Hispanic Journalists, its antecedents and context. His broader research interests revolve around Latinxs in US media and oral history. In addition to his work with the CRBB project, Sinta has worked with the Voces Oral History Project at the University of Texas at Austin in a variety of capacities, including acting as the founding managing editor of the *US Latina & Latino Oral History Journal*, published by the University of Texas Press.

James B. Wall is a visiting professor of history at Angelo State University, where he teaches and researches in the fields of US history, African American history, oral history theory and methods, labor history, and rural and agrarian history. He earned his bachelor's degree at the University of North Texas, his master's at the University of Houston, and his PhD at the University of Georgia. He is currently at work on a book project (under contract with the University of North Carolina Press) about the Black Freedom Movement in Albany, Georgia. Wall worked as a research associate with the CRBB project in 2016, recording oral history interviews throughout Southeast Texas.

Joel Zapata is an assistant professor of history at Oregon State University. Zapata earned a PhD in history from Southern Methodist University, and his dissertation, "The Mexican Southern Plains: Creating an Ethnic Mexican Homeland on the Llano," won the 2020 National Association for Chicana and Chicano Studies

Tejas Foco Dissertation Award. His "Taking Chicana/o Activist History to the Public" received the Frederick C. Luebka Award for the best article published in the *Great Plains Quarterly* in 2018. He has also published in the *Journal of the West*, the *Panhandle-Plains Historical Review*, the *Journal of South Texas*, and *Rio Bravo: A Journal of the Borderlands*.

Index

Some lesser known Texas place-names will have "Tex." after them but otherwise assume any place-names without a state signifier are in Texas.

Bonilla, Eva Sandoval, 203–4, 218
Bonilla, María, 121
Bonilla, Ruben (father), 121
Bonilla, Ruben (son), 114, 121, 124–25, 126, 127, 128–29
Bonilla, Tony, 121, 123–24, 125
Bonilla, William, 121, 123
Bonilla clan, 121–22, 123–25, 128–29, 396n34
Booker T. Washington High School, Dallas, 236
Booker T. Washington School, Conroe, 81, 82, 83, 84, 89
Booty, Warzell, 84, 85, 89
Border Patrol, 148
Border Workers Association, 337, 338
Boren, Jay, 40
Borgelt, Roger, 301
Bornstein, Frederick, 109, 110, 112
Bowdre, Al, 31
Bowdre, Larneatha, 31
Bowe, R. S., 134, 135, 136, 140, 141, 142, 143, 145, 398n16
Boyd, Jamie C., 113
Boyd, Webb Eugene, 284
Boykin, Amy, 30
Bradley, Lucille J., 83
Brandley, Clarence Lee, 1, 73–75, 77, 78–79, 80, 81, 82, 83
Brandley, Minnie, 83
Brandley, Ozell, 74, 75
Brantley, Allyson, 309
Briggs, Mabel, 59, 60
Brilliant, Mark, 308
Briones, Francisco, 330
Briscoe, Dolph, 153, 160
Briscoe, Leonard, 215
Broadnax, Clarence, 227
Brooks, Allen, 225
Brooks, Marion J. "Doc," 216, 219
Brooks, Roy C., 216
Brown, E. G., 210, 211
Brown, Jacob, 320, 321
Brown, Leonard, 235
Brown Berets, 14, 178, 216; Austin and, 287, 294, 295, 299; Black-Brown alliances and, 18, 94, 102, 234, 260, 269, 272, 284, 285, 294, 295, 299, 355; Dallas and, 224, 231, 232, 234, 238, 355; Lubbock and, 95, 99, 100, 101, 102, 110; Odessa and, 2, 94, 106, 107, 110, 111, 112; San Antonio and, 260, 269, 272, 284, 285, 333–35; West Texas and, 2, 94, 112, 113, 330–31; women activists and, 330–31, 333–35. *See also* Mexican

American Chicano movement; Mexican American civil rights activism
Brown Foundation, Inc., 311
Brown II, 8, 62, 207, 208
Brownsville, 118
Brown v. Board of Education, 8, 9, 10, 16, 60–61, 63, 64, 65, 129, 205, 206, 213, 214, 226
Bryan, Tex., 326
Bryant, Darwin, 76
Bunch, Gordy, 86–87
Bunting, Ken, 279–80
Burley, Willie Mae, 33
Burnett, Warren, 142
Burran, James, 56
Burrell, Sandra, 325–26
Busch, Andrew, 290, 292–93, 294, 297
Bush, George H. W., 178
Bustamante, Daniel, 247–48, 249
Byers, Lamar A., 186
Bynum, Katherine, 316, 326, 336, 349, 355
Byrom, R. E., 171

Cain, Darrell, 221, 222, 223, 235, 355, 418n75
California, 176, 266; Angela Davis and, 276, 278, 279; Black-Brown alliances and, 308, 310; Mexican American Chicano movement and, 9, 17, 125, 160, 178, 249, 274, 295, 403n42, 420n4
Callager, Emma Jones, 46
Callapalli, Kris, 109, 110
Calvert, T. C., 272, 280, 281, 284
Calvert, Tex., 121
Campbell, Randolph B., 199
Canales, Tony, 128
Cano, Anita, 167
Cantú, Mario, 274
Cardenas, José, 173
Cardona, Amaro, 160
Carmichael, Stokely, 250, 268
Carr, Waggoner, 123
Carswell Air Force Base, 213
Carter, Amon, Sr., 199
Carter, Jimmy, 104
Carter, Robert, 207
Carver, Jeff Carl, 97
Casar, Gregorio, 301
Cásares, Gilbert, 119
Casburn, Ed, 33
Cassiano Resident Association, 267
Castillo, Abelardo, 153, 160, 166
Castillo, Amelia "Amy," 178, 181, 184, 186, 188, 196
Castillo, Edward, 256

school integration and, 81–82; segregation and racism and, 77, 80–81, 82. *See also* Montgomery County; Tamina; Woodlands, The

Conroe College, 81, 83

Conroe High School, 73, 74, 80–81, 82

Conroe Independent School District, 83, 84

Conroe Police Department, 1, 75–77

Conyers, John, 75, 241

Cooke, Stacy, 47

Cooper, Barbara, 326

Cordero, Enedina "Nina," 178, 181, 182, 183, 185, 188, 191, 194, 196, 406n8

Corn, Marti, 84

Corpus Christi, 17, 117–18, 122, 128–29, 207, 395n9; League of United Latin American Citizens (LULAC) and, 9, 229; Mexican American civil rights activism and, 10, 18, 115–16, 119–21, 128–29, 164, 173, 229, 230, 249, 314; Mexican American political activism and, 123–25, 126; segregation and racism and, 119–20. *See also* García, Héctor P.

Corpus Christi Caller-Times, 120, 126, 143

Corpus Christi State University. *See* Texas A&M—Corpus Christi

Corral, Eddie, 332

Cortés, Ernesto, 259

Cotera, Martha, 336

cotton, 3, 117, 118, 205

Cotulla, 121

Countryman, 25

Courier of Montgomery County, 76, 80, 84

Craft, Juanita, 210, 225, 226, 227, 231, 237, 238, 239

Crear, John, 326–27

Creel, George, 34

Creighton University, 117

Crenshaw, Marjorie, 216

Crenshaw, Marvin, 239, 241

Crisis magazine, 77

Cross, Herbert, 28, 33, 35–36, 45, 46, 49–50, 51

Cruz, Mario, 327–29

Crystal City, 176; Mexican American civil rights activism and, 152, 156–57, 161, 333, 342–43; Mexican American political activism and, 18, 122–23, 159, 280, 281, 401n7

Culture and Technology Center (CTC), El Paso, 195

Cut and Shoot, Tex., 80

Cypert, Charles, 113

Daily Sentinel, Nacogdoches, 35

Dallas, 5, 28, 199, 207, 267, 289, 311, 313, 366n11; African American political activism and, 7, 225–26, 236–43, 282, 418n87; Black-Brown alliances and, 17, 19, 221–24, 230–32, 236–43, 282, 355; Black civil rights activism and, xi–xii, 11, 14, 65, 201, 210, 221–24, 226–28, 231–32, 264, 270, 336–37, 416n36; desegregation and, xi, 226–28; Mexican American civil rights activism and, 221–24, 229–32; Mexican American political activism and, 230, 236–43, 349–51, 418n87; Mexican Americans and, 9, 228–32, 335; NAACP and, 225–26, 227, 230, 231, 237, 239; police brutality and, 23, 221–24, 233–35, 236–43, 355, 417nn64, 69, 418n75, 419n100; poor whites and, 234, 235, 243, 355; racial violence and, 224–25, 226. *See also* Fort Worth

Dallas Brown Berets, 224, 231, 232, 234, 238, 355

Dallas Citizens Council (DCC), 225, 226, 227, 236, 238

Dallas Citizens / Police Relations Board, 240

Dallas City Council, 236, 238–39, 240, 242

Dallas Independent School District, 226, 227, 231

Dallas Morning News, 239, 240

Dallas Police Association (DPA), 239–40, 241, 243

Dallas Police Department (DPD), 221, 226, 233, 239; police killings and, 222, 224, 234, 235, 238–39, 240–42, 243

Dallas Times Herald, 109, 225, 239

"Dallas way, the," 226

Daniel, Price, 122

Davies, Nick, 78–79

Davis, Angela, 260, 276, 277, 278–79

Davis, Clifford, 207, 208, 209–10, 213, 215, 216, 218

Davis, Darry, 105

Davis, Tommy Lee, 102

Day, Vickie June, 109

death penalty, 74, 75, 80

Decker, Bill, 336

De Colores, 99

defense industry, 5–6, 366n11

De La Isla, Jaime, 245

de la Luz Zubia, Maria, 194

De La Rosa, Manuel, 184, 186

Delco, Wilhelmina, 287, 299

De Leon, Arnoldo, 246–47

El Paso Community Action Agency, 181
El Paso Community College, 185
El Paso County, 109, 112
El Paso County Medical Society, 186
El Paso Herald-Post, 181, 183, 189, 190
El Paso Journal, 189
El Paso Police Department, 191
El Paso Public Library, 193
El Paso Times, 105, 179, 181, 183, 186, 188, 193, 194, 407n34
El Paso Urban Coalition, 183–84
El Plan de Santa Bárbara: A Chicano Plan for Higher Education, 249
Elsa, Tex., 135, 138, 160
El Segundo Barrio. *See* El Paso
El Uvalde Times, 169
Encinia, Brian, 23
Engram, Will, 36
Enríquez, Sandra I., 312, 316, 326, 329, 332, 335, 337, 338–40, 342, 343, 344, 348–49, 351, 352
Escalante, Alicia, 256
Escobedo, Butch, 128
Escobedo, Maria de Jesus, 188
Espinoza, Gilberto, 140
Estes, Joe E., 207, 208
Estes, Nolan, 231
ethnic Mexicans, 202, 422n43; citizenship rights and, 131, 247, 421n13; Dallas and, 229, 230; El Paso and, 178–79, 405n1; farmworkers and, 122, 249–50, 278; healthcare and, 180, 193; living conditions and, 119, 133–34, 229; racial violence against and, 246–47, 278; segregation and racism and, 247, 421n13; South Texas and, 116, 119, 122, 131, 132, 133–34, 136, 139, 144, 148–49; terminology and, 364n2, 405n1, 414–15n1, 420n7. *See also* Mexican Americans
ethnic studies movement, 16, 245–46, 249, 250, 251, 256, 420n6, 421n24; Black-Brown alliances and, 251–52, 255. *See also* African American civil rights activism; Mexican American Chicano movement
Euless, 206
Eureste, Arturo, 248–49, 348–49
Evans, Edward B., 27, 28, 29–30
Evans, John, 241
Evans, Larry, Sr., 76–77

Family Place, Dallas, 235
family planning services, 187
Farah Manufacturing Company, 180, 337, 339, 340

Farr, Anita, 35, 37, 41
Father Rahm Clinic, 183, 184–88, 192, 196. *See also* La Fe Clinic
Faught, Elton, 105, 108, 109, 111, 112
Faulk, John Henry, 26
Federal Bureau of Investigation (FBI), 40, 43, 49, 104, 110, 111, 222, 272, 276, 333, 354
Felix, Carmen, 181
Fergeson, Cheryl Dee, 73, 74
Fernández, Efraín, 135–36, 139, 141, 142, 150
Ferreira, Jason, 309–10
Fielding, Paul, 240
Fifteenth Amendment, 7
Fifth Circuit Court of Appeals, 172, 173–74, 208
Flannigan, Rocke, 106, 107
Flax, Weirless, Sr., 213
Flax v. Potts, 213, 214
Flemmings, George D., 215
Flores, Alfonso Loredo, 139, 140, 141, 142, 150
Flores, Manuela, 167, 168–69
Flores, Raymond, 93
Florida, 23
Flournoy, Mott, 39, 41
Flowers, Tom, 277
Foley, Neil, 307, 308
Fort Worth, 5, 8, 264, 311, 313, 366n11; African American political activism and, 215–16, 218; Black-Brown alliances and, 17, 19, 200, 217, 218–20; Black civil rights activism and, 11, 199, 200, 201, 205, 206–8, 210–11, 212–13, 216; desegregation of housing and, 210–12, 215, 219; "Fort Worth Way, The" and, 200–202, 205, 215; immigrant population and, 217, 219–20; Jim Crow and, 199, 200–201, 204–5, 220; Juan Crow and, 199, 202–3, 220; Mexican American civil rights activism and, 199, 200, 214, 216–17; Mexican American political activism and, 203, 215–20; Mexican American population and, 200, 202–3, 217, 219, 220; school integration and, 205, 206–10, 212–15, 219; segregation and racism and, 199, 201–6. *See also* Dallas; Mansfield; Tarrant County
Fort Worth Board of Education, 200
Fort Worth City Council, 200, 210, 215
Fort Worth Independent School District, 200, 213, 214
Fort Worth Star-Telegram, 200, 203, 209, 211, 216, 218, 223
"Fort Worth Way, The," 200–202, 205, 215
Foster, Sam Houston, 153

Incorporated Mexican-American Government Employees union, 217
Independent Citizens Redistricting Commission, Austin, 301
Indigenous peoples. *See* American Indians
Inés de la Cruz, Sor Juana, 256
Inman, John, 276
integration. *See* desegregation; school integration
Interstate 27, 96
Interstate 35, 289, 292–93, 294, 300

Jachimczyk, Joseph, 110
Jackson, Bennett (Andy), 78, 79–80
Jackson, George, 279
Jackson, Larry, 263, 287, 295, 301–2
Jackson, Nathaniel, 207
Jackson v. Rawdon, 207–8, 210
Jaime, A. C., 131–32, 134, 137, 142–50, 398n16, 400n114
James, H. Rhett, 227
Japanese Americans, 9, 308
Jefferson, Ruth, 336–37
Jefferson County, 18, 64, 68
Jewish Americans, 308
Jim Crow, 2, 7, 11, 84, 246; Austin and, 289, 290, 292; Black resistance to and, 17, 205; Dallas and, 225, 228; East Texas and, 4, 5, 60, 66; Fort Worth and, 203, 204–5, 211, 213, 220; oral history interviews and, 15–16, 306, 307, 325–26; San Antonio and, 261, 262–63; Tarrant County and, 199–206, 211, 213, 220. *See also* African Americans, segregation and racism; lynchings; racial violence against African Americans; racism; racism against African Americans; segregation; white supremacy
Jiménez, María, 245, 248, 249, 252–53, 256, 423n49
Jimenez, Nick, 116, 126, 128
J-MAC Black History Month Parade, 83
John Birch Society, 236
John Brown Revolutionary League, 352
John Nance Garner House, 151
John Peter Smith Hospital, Tarrant County, 204
Johns, Dee, 105
Johnson, Alexander, 225
Johnson, Cedric, 64
Johnson, Gaye Theresa, 308
Johnson, Harvey, 59, 61, 62, 66, 67
Johnson, James E., 23, 30
Johnson, Lady Bird, 236
Johnson, Lee Otis, 264, 272

Johnson, Lyndon B., 2, 11, 120–21, 122, 123, 125, 180, 214, 263, 345, 346
Johnson, Marilyn Jean, 201, 204
Johnson, Marilynn S., 58
Johnson, Matthew, 227–28
Johnson, Peter, 228, 237
Johnson, Tyrone, 345
Johnson, Virgil, 96
Joint Commission on Accreditation of Healthcare Organizations (JCAHO), 193
Jones, Alpha Omega, 83
Jones, Jesse H., 5
Jones, Paul, 318
Jonsson, Erik, 236
Joplin, Janis, 55
Jordan, Barbara, 12
Jordan, Maria Banos, 88
Joshua, Clay, 47
Joshua, Laverne, 47
Juan Crow, 2, 7, 11, 17, 203–4, 246, 292, 365n6, 369n35; Dallas and, 228–32; Fort Worth and, 202–3, 220; oral history interviews and, 15–16, 151, 306, 307, 328–29; San Antonio and, 260–63; South Texas and, 4, 5, 9, 10, 115, 116, 328–29; Tarrant County and, 199–200, 202, 220; West Texas and, 4, 9, 10, 93, 116, 247, 388n1. *See also* Mexican Americans, segregation and racism; racial violence against Mexican Americans; racism; racism against Mexican Americans; segregation; white supremacy
Juarez, Gloria Gomez, 112
jury service, 10
Justice, William Wayne, 44, 81
Juvenile Delinquency Project, El Paso, 181

Karam, Dorothy, 332
Karankawa tribes, 117–18
Kegler, Larry, 33, 36, 37, 38, 46, 47–48, 50, 51
Kelley, Hilton, 59, 62
Kelley, John Connally, 133
Kelley, Robin D. G., 62
Kellogg Foundation, 193
Kelly, Hilton, 66
Kendi, Ibram X., 250, 422n33
Kennedy, Bettie, 36
Kennedy, John F., 11, 122, 217, 236, 241
Kennedy, Robert F., 123
Kennedy, Tom, 120
Kent State University, 43
Kerner Commission, 13

Fe" (March of Faith) and, 98, 99–101,
102; police brutality and, 94–100, 101–2,
105–7, 390n32; segregation and racism
and, 93, 96, 101–2, 388n1
Lubbock Avalanche-Journal, 95, 101, 102
Lubbock Brown Berets, 95, 99, 100, 101, 102,
110
Lubbock City Council, 96, 97, 101
Lubbock Police Department, 97, 100, 102
Lucille J. Bradley Elementary, Conroe, 83, 89
Lufkin, 42; police brutality and, 40, 45; racial
violence and, 39, 41, 49, 341–42; school
integration and, 18, 33–34, 45, 48–51,
341–42; segregation and racism and,
35–40, 45–46, 47–49, 51. *See also* Diboll;
East Texas; Nacogdoches
Lufkin Daily News, 33, 48
Lufkin High School, 33, 45, 46, 47–51,
341–42
Lufkin Independent School District Board
of Trustees, 33
Lugo, Eleazar, 154, 163, 166, 175
lumber industry, 34
Lumpee, Virgil, 105, 109, 111, 112
Luthuli-Allen, Omowali, 250–51
Lydia Patterson Institute, 185
lynchings: African Americans and, 1, 5,
25–26, 27, 71, 77, 78–80, 88, 201, 225,
370n4, 378n17; Mexican Americans and,
5, 246; Montgomery County and, 1, 71,
77, 78–80, 88; Waller County and, 25–26,
27, 370n4. *See also* racial violence against
African Americans; racial violence against
Mexican Americans

Madrigal, Lydia, 106, 109, 113
Maeso, Dan, 104
Magallan, Maria, 135, 136, 138, 141, 144
Magallan, Oralia, 135
Makemson, W. K., 27
Malcolm X, 216, 263, 333
Maloney, Pat, 160, 171, 173
Manriquez, Raúl, 203
Mansfield, 8, 19, 205–6, 207, 210, 213
Mansfield Colored School, 206
Mansfield High School, 206, 208–10, 212,
214–15
Mansfield Independent School District, 215
Mantler, Gordon, 308
March for Human Dignity, Dallas, 242
Marin, Antonio, 179
Mariscal, George, 309
Mark, Cleveland, 40
Márquez, Benjamin, 236

Márquez, John D., 308
Marshall, 11
Marshall, Thurgood, 8, 12, 205, 207
Martin, Joy, 184
Martin, Phil, 108
Martin, Trayvon, 23
Martin County, 103
Martínez, Anita, 230, 236, 237
Martínez, Faustina, 230
Martinez, Francisco, 105
Martinez, Joel, 187
Martinez, Marty, 277
Martínez, Miguel "Mike," 230–31
Martínez, Oscar J., 179
Martínez, René, 221
Martinez, Vilma, 173
Martin Luther King Day, 284
Mathis, Tex., 247–48
Mathis Independent School District
(MISD), 247–48
May, Meredith, 316, 325–26, 331, 341
Maynard, John, 78
Mays, Avery, 237
McAllen, 19, 137, 142, 147, 149, 335, 344
McAllen Monitor, 139, 143, 335
McAllister, Walter, 261, 268, 269, 273–74,
275, 276, 284, 285, 334–35, 427n41,
428n43
McCalebb, Rene, 267, 269
McCurley, A. D., 233
McDaniel, C. A., 166
McGehee, Frank (Andrew), 78, 80
McGuire, Mickey, 43, 44, 45, 375n63
McKenzie, Russell, 97
McKinney v. Blankenship, 207
McLaine, W. C. "Cleo," 78
McMillan, Ernest, 227–28, 231–32
Medrano, Esperanza, 232
Medrano, Francisco "Pancho," 229, 230–31,
232, 234, 237
Medrano, Ricardo, 231, 232, 237, 238, 240
Medrano, Robert, 231–32, 237, 355
Menchaca, Luis M., 113–14
Menchaca, Richard, 233
Mendeke, Chris Reyes, 168
Mendez, Lupe, 329
Mendez v. Westminster, 9
Mendoza, Rufino, Sr., 214, 216
Menendez, Elías, 153–54
Mercedes, Tex., 116, 121, 127, 129, 135
Mercer, H. T., 62
Mergerson, Willie Lee, 41
Mexican American Chicano movement,
217, 306, 414–15n1; Austin and, 287,

297; Black-Brown alliances and, 17–18, 228, 273, 278, 279, 283, 285, 297, 309, 369–70n40; California and, 9, 17, 125, 160, 178, 249, 274, 295, 403n42, 420n4; Chicano/a Power and, 13–14, 17–18, 19, 309, 369–70n40; Chicano studies at universities and, 16, 94, 135, 245–46, 250, 251–52, 253–57, 339, 423nn47, 57, 423–24n68; Dallas and, 231–32; El Paso and, 19, 180, 181, 339–41; healthcare and, 178, 190–91, 192, 194, 196; Houston and, 247, 248–49; police brutality and, 113–14, 133; San Antonio and, 259–60, 268, 269–70, 275–76, 281–82, 333–36, 428n43, 429n56; South Texas and, 125–26, 131, 132, 135–42, 160–61, 330–31; West Texas and, 2, 93–94, 99–101, 110, 113–14. *See also* Brown Berets; La Raza Unida Party; Mexican American civil rights activism; Mexican American women activists; Mexican American Youth Organization (MAYO)

Mexican American civil rights activism, xii, 13–14, 307, 368n30, 403nn40–41, 422n43; Austin and, 160, 273, 294–95, 296, 297–99, 344–45, 353–54; Black-Brown alliances and, 17, 19, 96–100, 102–3, 112, 114, 260–61, 308; Corpus Christi and, 10, 18, 115–16, 119–21, 128–29, 164, 173, 229, 230, 249, 314; Crystal City and, 152, 156–57, 161, 333, 342–43; Dallas and, 19, 221–24, 229–32; El Paso and, 180, 181, 182–86; Fort Worth and, 199, 200, 214, 216–17; Houston and, 88, 245, 248–49, 252–56, 332, 349, 420n3, 423nn49, 66; Odessa and, 1–2, 110–14; San Antonio and, 10, 11, 14, 248, 260–61, 264–85, 333–36, 354, 402n34, 428n43; South Texas and, 115–16, 119–21, 141, 160, 161, 162–76; West Texas and, 1–2, 93–94, 96–103, 104–5, 110–14. *See also* American GI Forum; League of United Latin American Citizens (LULAC); Mexican American Chicano movement; Mexican American women activists; Mexican American Youth Organization (MAYO); police brutality against Mexican Americans; schools

Mexican American Committee on Honor and Service (MACHOS), 181, 182, 183

Mexican American Development Group, 170

Mexican American Educational Advisory Council (MAEAC), 214

Mexican American gender equality. *See* Mexican American women activists

"Mexican American Generation," 229–30

Mexican American Legal Defense and Educational Fund (MALDEF), 94, 171, 173, 174, 284, 287, 300, 344

Mexican American living conditions, 203; Austin and, 294, 295, 296, 297–98; Dallas and, 229, 231; El Paso and, 179–80, 181, 182–83; Houston and, 247, 252; San Antonio and, 261, 267; South Texas and, 119, 127, 131, 133–34, 145, 150, 151–52, 160–61

Mexican American Parents Association (MAPA), 166, 168, 170, 171, 172, 173

Mexican American political activism, 12–14, 16–17, 88, 103, 329, 355–56, 397n2; Austin and, 299–300, 301; Corpus Christi and, 123–25, 126; Crystal City and, 18, 122–23, 159, 280, 281, 401n7; Dallas and, 230, 236–43, 349–51, 418n87; El Paso and, 179, 406n13; Fort Worth and, 203, 215–20; Pharr and, 131–32, 135, 142–50; San Antonio and, 11, 12, 259–60, 261, 269, 277, 279–85, 402n34, 429n56, 429–30n64; Tarrant County and, 200, 215–20, 350; Uvalde and, 151, 154, 159–60, 175, 176; Viva Kennedy campaign and, 11, 121–22, 129, 217, 230. *See also* American GI Forum; La Raza Unida Party; League of United Latin American Citizens (LULAC)

Mexican American Political Association (MAPA), 231, 234

Mexican Americans: African Americans and, 217–18, 307–10, 356; cantinas and, 139, 140, 148–50, 329; communities of and, 9, 72, 86, 87–88, 89, 118, 200, 202–3, 217, 219, 220, 301; diseases and, 119, 180, 193, 229; equal employment opportunities and, 12, 100, 101–2, 156, 170; farmworkers and, 119, 125–26, 135, 154, 193, 335; healthcare and, 177–78, 180, 182–86, 187–88, 192, 193, 194–96, 203, 407n34; as police officers and, 99, 101–2, 136, 233, 241; public health and, 119–20, 178, 193; Spanish language and, 94, 119, 155, 158, 160, 167, 173–74, 231, 247, 248, 329–30, 338, 341, 403n40, 410n146; as teachers and, 156, 157–59, 161–62, 171, 174, 175, 403n41; terminology and, 364n2, 405n1, 414–15n1, 420n7; whiteness and, 10, 203, 230, 247, 248, 275, 307–8. *See also* Black-Brown alliances; ethnic Mexicans; Juan Crow; Mexican American Chicano movement; Mexican American civil rights activism; Mexican American political activism; Mexican Americans, segregation and racism; Mexican American voting rights; police brutality against Mexican Americans; police killings of Mexican Americans; racial violence against Mexican Americans; racism against Mexican Americans; schools

Mexican Americans, segregation and racism, 16; Austin and, 289–90, 292–93, 296; cemeteries and, 120–21, 152, 230; Dallas and, 228–32; El Paso and, 4, 177, 179; housing and, 6–7, 9, 18, 143, 151, 177, 179, 181, 194–95, 203; Houston and, 10, 245, 246, 247, 248; Lubbock and, 93, 96, 101–2, 388n1; San Antonio and, 260–63; South Texas and, 4, 9, 115, 116, 119–20, 131, 132–36, 151, 247, 248; Tarrant County and, 199–200, 202–4; Uvalde and, 151–52, 153–54, 155–56, 158–59, 167–68, 171, 172, 173–74, 327–29. *See also* schools

Mexican American voting rights, 4, 5, 16, 289, 348–49; Austin and, 19, 287–89, 291–92, 300–301; Dallas and, 230, 232, 237; San Antonio and, 259, 268, 281; South Texas and, 12, 122, 128, 134–35, 144, 160; voter registration and, 122, 135, 217, 232, 268, 355–56; West Texas and, 93, 103, 179. *See also* African American voting rights; voting rights

Mexican American women activists, 306, 355–56; Dallas and, 231, 235; domestic violence and, 235; El Paso and, 178, 181, 182, 183–85, 190, 191, 192, 193, 194, 196; Fort Worth and, 217, 219; gender equality and, 245, 246, 248–49, 252–55, 256, 257, 334, 335, 336, 338–39, 420nn4–5, 423n66; Houston and, 88, 245, 248–49, 252–56, 332, 423nn49, 66; San Antonio and, 274, 277, 285, 333–36, 428n43; South Texas and, 141, 167, 168–69, 170, 171, 174–75; women workers and, 180, 231, 337–38, 339–41

Mexican American Youth Organization (MAYO), 94, 216, 294, 403n42; Chicano studies at universities and, 249, 421n24; El Paso and, 177, 180; formation and, 14, 126, 248, 259, 268, 281, 419–20n1; Houston and, 252, 352; political activism and, 269, 280; San Antonio and, 14, 248, 259, 268, 269, 280, 281, 333; South Texas and, 135, 142, 160–61, 163, 344; University of Houston and, 245, 247, 248–49, 251, 252, 253–54, 255–57, 420n3, 423–24n68

Mexican immigrants. *See* ethnic Mexicans

Mexican Revolution of 1910–1920, 116, 122, 178, 202, 229, 230, 247

Mexico, 4, 116, 155, 180

Michaels, Walter Benn, 64

Midland, Tex., 1, 103, 104, 111, 112

Miller, Roy, 118, 119

Miller, Stephen, 88

Milliken v. Bradley, 10

Milton L. Kirkpatrick High School, Fort Worth, 213, 214, 220

Mindiola, Tatcho, 255

Mineral Wells, 35–36

Minkah, Fahim, 228, 234, 239

Minor, Claudis, Jr., 259, 260, 264, 269, 271, 272, 284

Mississippi Freedom Democratic Party, 263

Mitchell, George P., 86

Mitchell, Jack, 95

Mitchell, Kaila, 85

Mitchell, Kyle, 85

Mitchell, Terrence "TJ," 85

Molina, Vincente, 126

Mondale, Walter, 169–70

Montejano, David, 261, 332–35, 428n43

Montemayor, Aurelio "Hershey," 163–64

Montgomery, Eddie, 109

Montgomery County, 382n2; African American communities and, 71–72, 83–86, 88–89; Black civil rights activism and, 1, 72, 73–75, 78, 81–82; law enforcement and, 75–76, 77; lynchings and, 1, 71, 78–80; Mexican Americans and, 72, 86, 87–88, 89; racial diversity and, 87, 88; racial violence and, 18, 77–80, 89; racism and, 77, 79, 86–88; segregation and racism and, 71, 77, 80–81, 82. *See also* Conroe; Tamina; Woodlands, The

Montoya, Greg, 329, 330

Moody, Charles, 207

Moody, Floyd, 206, 207, 208–9

Moody, T. M., 205, 206, 207, 208

Moore, Ed, 68

Moore, Joe P., 212–13

Moore, Vernice, 66

Morales, Genoveva, 164, 167, 170, 171, 172, 173, 174–75

Morales, Richard, 111

Morales, Roberto, 164, 174–75

Morales v. Shannon, 171, 172, 173

Morehead, Michael, 222, 223, 228, 243, 355

Morehouse, Lucille, 39

Morehouse, Roy, 39

Morgan, Ted, 76

tuberculosis, 119, 180, 229
Tucker, Estrus, 201, 214, 219, 220
Tyler, 227

United Auto Workers union, 230
United Black Coalition, 97
United Brotherhood of Carpenters and Joiners of America, 231
United Community Front, 295
United Farm Workers (UFW), 147, 180, 217, 246, 249–50, 279, 287, 308, 335, 345
United Fort Worth, 220
United Front, 216
US Army, 117
US Commission on Civil Rights, xi, 124, 169, 170, 233, 267, 344
US Congress, 12, 75, 156, 169–70, 193, 241, 243, 349, 350, 437n5
US Court of Appeals, 9
US Department of Agriculture, 85
US Department of Health, Education and Welfare (HEW), 47, 48, 168–69, 170, 173, 184, 185, 186, 187–88, 189, 190, 191, 192
US Department of Housing and Urban Development (HUD), 85, 86, 143
US Department of Justice (DOJ), 49, 112, 235, 288; Civil Rights Division and, 111, 113, 242
US Department of Labor, 337, 338
US District Court for the Western District of Texas, 171–72
US-Mexico Chamber of Commerce, 87
US Public Health Service, 193
US Senate Subcommittee on Equal Educational Opportunity, 156, 169–70
US Supreme Court, 10, 74, 78; school integration and, 8, 47, 172, 173, 174, 205, 207, 208, 213, 214, 226, 230, 289; voting rights and, 8, 226, 289. *See also Brown v. Board of Education*
U.S. v. Texas Education Association and Austin Independent School District, 173
US war of aggression against Mexico, 132, 397n2
United Steel Workers of America, 68
University of Houston, 245–46, 250–52; Black-Brown alliances and, 251–52, 255, 256–57, 423n49; Center for Mexican Studies (UH CMAS), 245, 246, 253–54, 255–56, 423n57, 423–24n68; Chicano studies at universities and, 250, 251–52, 253–54, 255–57, 423n57, 423–24n68;

Mexican American Youth Organization (UH MAYO), 245, 247, 248–49, 251, 252, 253–54, 255–57, 420n3, 423–24n68; Student Government Association president and, 252, 423n49
University of Minnesota, 338
University of North Texas (UNT), xii, xiii, 311
University of Texas at Arlington (UTA), xi, xii, 199, 215, 231–32, 264, 311
University of Texas at Austin, xii, 117, 157, 165, 254–55, 263, 287, 294, 315, 352–54
University of Texas at El Paso (UTEP), 180, 190, 192
University of Texas at San Antonio (UTSA), 427n30
University of Texas Law School, 8, 226
University of Texas Medical Branch, 117
University of Virginia, 87
University Year for Action (UYA), 185
Urdy, Charles, 292
Uriegas, José "Joe" V., 153–54, 156, 159–60, 162–63, 164, 165–66, 170, 175, 181, 402n34
Uvalde, 19, 160–61, 181, 342, 343, 401n3; Mexican American civil rights activism and, 162–76; Mexican American political activism and, 151, 154, 159–60, 175, 176; Mexican Americans, segregation and racism and, 151–52, 153–54, 155–56, 158–59, 167–68, 171, 172, 173–74, 327–29. *See also* South Texas
Uvalde Consolidated Independent School District (UCISD), 173, 174, 404n106
Uvalde County Commission, 154, 175
Uvalde County Jail, 161
Uvalde High School, 154, 155–57, 160, 162–65, 168, 171
Uvalde Independent School District, 170–71, 172, 173
Uvalde Leader-News, 168, 171, 172

Vaca, Nicolás, 308
Valdez, Dennis, 339
Van Os, David, 287, 292, 300, 301, 302
Vega, Cecilia, 190
Velásquez, George, 281, 333, 335
Velásquez, Willie, 248, 259, 268, 281, 349
Vidal, Eloy, 267
Vidor, 68, 69
Vietnam War, 152, 263, 274, 282, 351–52
Villejo, Louise, 248, 254, 257
Vinson, Calvin, 83